INTRODUCTION TO AMERICAN HISTORY

SEVENTH EDITION

VOLUME II — SINCE 1865

INTRODUCTION TO AMERICAN HISTORY

SEVENTH EDITION

VOLUME II — SINCE 1865

CARL N. DEGLER
STANFORD UNIVERSITY

VINCENT P. DE SANTIS
UNIVERSITY OF NOTRE DAME

CLARENCE L. VER STEEG
NORTHWESTERN UNIVERSITY

BVT
Publishing

Managing Editor: Traci Burton

Manager of Art and Design: Suzanne Morse

Text Layout: Rhonda Minnema

Cover Design: Suzanne Morse and Jason James

Text and Cover Printing: Quebecor World, Dubuque

Photo Editor: Brae Buhnerkemper

Textbook Editor: Brian Farmer

Copyeditor: Joyce Bianchini

Marketing Manager: Robert Rappeport

Printed in the United States of America

ISBN: 978-1-60229-993-1

BRIEF CONTENTS

CONTENTS

The opportunity to take a fresh look at the nation's history is always an exciting one. This text represents a solid interpretation of traditional economic and political history, while also including many original insights into social and cultural changes that have influenced and been influenced by economic and political events. Special attention has also been paid to the role of technology. What emerges, in fact, is a vivid picture of the interrelationship of a nation's technology with its culture and its political and economic life. It is hoped that students will gain insights into the ideas and events that inspired this nation's founding and continue to influence its development.

Of special importance are the biographies. The fascinating people profiled range from Phillis Wheatley to W. E. B. DuBois, from Parson Weems to Belva Lockwood, from Dorothea Dix to J. Robert Oppenheimer.

The book that results is an engrossing story of a young nation engaged in what Thomas Paine described as a "bold and sublime experiment" in government. We hope you enjoy the story of the continuing effort to realize the high ideals of this nation's founding.

SPECIAL ACKNOWLEDGEMENTS

In *Introduction to American History's* earlier iteration the textbook had been a collaboration among Carl N. Degler, Thomas C. Cochran, Vincent P.de Santis, Holman Hamilton, William H. Harbaugh, James M. McPherson, Russel B. Nye, and Clarence L. Ver Steeg. These prestigious authors had brought to it many strengths which resulted in a well received and respected textbook for nearly two decades.

We must also extend our appreciation to the many other historians and scholars whose work is reflected in this edition, including Dr. Brian R. Farmer, who provided extensive editing. Special gratitude goes to those teachers and historians who read the manuscript for the previous editions and gave their comments: Frank W. Abbott, University of Houston, Downtown College; Thomas J. Archdeacon, University of Wisconsin at Madison; Morris H. Holman, Eastfield College; Arthur McClure, Central Missouri State University; and Thomas R. Tefft, Citrus College.

Finally, we want to acknowledge the contributions of Dee Andrews of California State University, East Bay, who consulted on early American history, and John Snetsinger of California State Polytechnic University, San Luis Obispo, who consulted about twentieth-century diplomatic history.

The Publisher

LIST OF MAPS & CHARTS

EMANCIPATION AND RECONSTRUCTION, 1865–1877

(Library of Congress)

LINCOLN'S PLAN OF RECONSTRUCTION

The process of readmission of Southern states to the Union had begun as early as 1862 when Union troops began reclaiming Southern territory. Lincoln appointed provisional governors for those parts of the Union controlled and occupied by federal troops. Although he had always opposed slavery on moral as well as political grounds, Lincoln was skeptical about the prospects for racial equality in the United States. The legacy of slavery and race prejudice, he believed, would prevent blacks from rising to the level of whites or prevent whites from allowing blacks to rise to their level. This was why Lincoln had supported the colonization abroad of freed slaves as a possible solution of the race problem.

By 1864, however, the President was convinced of the impracticality if not the injustice of this policy. The contribution of blacks to the Union war effort and the growing strength of Northern antislavery convictions also made him more hopeful about the chances for eventual black advancement and racial adjustment. On this question, though, Lincoln remained a moderate and a gradualist to the end of his life.

Lincoln and the Northern moderates also believed that victory in war could not really restore the Union. It could only prevent secession. The Union would be restored only if the Southern people again accepted the Union and gave their loyalty to it. To bring the South to that point, Lincoln wanted a conciliatory policy. In 1864 when Congress adopted a measure known as the Wade-Davis Bill that imposed stringent terms for the restoration of the former Confederates, including a requirement that Southerners could only establish state governments after the majority in a state had sworn a loyalty oath. Lincoln quickly disposed of the bill with the Pocket Veto (the President did not sign the bill during the last 10 days of a Congressional session, thus killing the bill through his inaction).

When people raised technical questions about the legal status of the Confederate states (Were they still states, or were they conquered territories? Had they committed "state suicide"?), Lincoln was impatient about such "pernicious abstractions." All that mattered was whether the states could be brought back into their proper relationship with the Union.

By 1864, the Union had regained enough control in Louisiana, Tennessee, and Arkansas to start a process of restoring these states to the Union, and Lincoln laid down generous terms on which this could be done. He would grant amnesty to former Confederates who took an oath of allegiance; and when as many as one tenth of the number who had been citizens in 1860 did so, he would permit them to form a new state government. When Southern government accepted the abolition of slavery and repudiated the principle of secession, Lincoln would receive it back into the Union. States did not have to recognize the rights of blacks or give a single black person the right to vote.

Louisiana was the first state reorganized on this basis; despite its denial of black suffrage, Lincoln accepted it, though he did ask the governor, "whether some of the colored people may not be let in, as for instance the very intelligent, and especially those who have fought gallantly in our ranks." In Virginia, Tennessee, and Arkansas, also, Lincoln recognized state governments that did not enfranchise the black Americans.

It was clear, however, that Republicans in Congress were suspicious of these states—more because of their leniency toward the former Confederates than because of their treatment of the blacks. Secondly, the Radical Republicans favored a reconstruction policy that would punish the South; and they, therefore, opposed Lincoln's plan because it was not punitive. Radical Republicans in Congress also disliked Lincoln's conciliatory "10 percent plan" because it allowed the President to establish reconstruction policy rather than Congress. It was also clear that Congress might deny the re-established states recognition by refusing to seat their newly elected senators and representatives.

In 1864, when the time came for a new presidential election, the Democrats nominated General McClellan to run against Lincoln. Some of the so-called Radical Republicans, who were dissatisfied with Lincoln's leniency, tried to block his renomination and put up the Secretary of the Treasury, Salmon P. Chase, in his stead. This effort failed, however, and Lincoln was renominated. In an effort to put the ticket on a broad, bipartisan basis, the party dropped the name Republican, called itself the Union party, and nominated for the vice-presidency a Southern Democrat who had stood firmly for the Union, Andrew Johnson of Tennessee.

In November 1864 Lincoln and Johnson were elected, carrying all but three Union states (New Jersey, Delaware, and Kentucky). In the following March, the new term began. Lincoln delivered his Second Inaugural Address, calling for "malice toward none and charity for all," in order "to bind up the nation's wounds." On April 9, Lee surrendered the Army of Northern Virginia. It was clear that the work of Reconstruction must now begin in earnest.

John Wilkes Booth (*Teaching Politics*)

On April 14, however, as celebrations still continued in the North in the wake of the Confederate surrender, Lincoln attended a performance at Ford's Theater where an assassin, John Wilkes Booth, shot him. Booth broke into Lincoln's theater box and shot the President in the back of the head with a small pistol at point blank range. Then Booth jumped to the stage with a dagger in one hand, breaking an ankle in the process, and escaped through the back door of the theater. As he left the theater, Booth shouted the Virginia state motto, "Sic simper tyrannis" (thus always to tyrants). Lincoln died the next morning, without ever recovering consciousness; and Andrew Johnson, who was also stabbed in his bed by an attempted assassin while Lincoln was being shot across town, survived the attack and became President of the United States.

Unknown to Booth, a Southern sympathizer who evidently killed Lincoln in a spirit of Southern revenge, he had probably just killed the South's best friend. It does not appear that Lincoln favored any sort of punitive reconstruction, but he was in favor of allowing the South to manage their own affairs as much as would be possible. With Lincoln out of the way, the path was much more open for those in the North who favored a more punitive peace.

JOHNSON'S POLICY OF RECONSTRUCTION

Although a Southerner and the only Senator from a Southern state to remain loyal to the Union, Andrew Johnson was expected to be more severe in his Reconstruction policy than Lincoln. Johnson was the son of poor, illiterate parents in Raleigh, North Carolina, who could not afford to send their son to school. Instead, Johnson's mother apprenticed him to a tailor after his father died, and Johnson later worked as a tailor in Tennessee. The ambitious Johnson, who had been illiterate until his wife taught him to write, became not only a successful tailor but, also, accumulated a fortune in land and at one time even owned five slaves. He was a man of strong emotions; and as a Southerner with the roots of a common man, Johnson hated both aristocrats, whom he blamed for secession, and secessionists—in general. When his policy developed, it turned out that Johnson disliked abolitionists and radicals even more. In the end, Johnson proved even more lenient toward former Confederates than Lincoln had been. Johnson was a strong states' rights advocate, who as a Senator voted against everything that smacked of increased federal power. He even once voted against a bill to pave the streets of Washington, D.C.

Johnson was also a defender of slavery and accepted emancipation only grudgingly. Johnson's eventual opposition to slavery developed more out of his dislike for the planter class than out of any moral outrage against slavery or sympathy for blacks. Johnson believed blacks to be intellectually inferior and, naturally, more suited to manual labor.

On May 29, 1865, Johnson issued a broad amnesty to all who would take an oath of allegiance, including ex-Confederate government officials and military officers, although men with property valued at more than $20,000 (in other words, planters) were required to ask special pardon, which was freely given. In the six weeks after May 29 he appointed provisional governors in each of the remaining Southern states to reorganize governments for these states. Only men who had been voters in 1860 and who had taken the oath of allegiance could participate in these reorganizations. This meant, of course, that blacks were excluded. When the new governments disavowed secession, accepted the abolition of slavery, and repudiated the Confederate debt, Johnson would accept them. As to what policy should be followed toward the freedmen— that was to be determined by the states themselves.

Andrew Johnson (*Teaching Politics*)

The Southern states moved swiftly under this easy formula. Before the end of the year, every state except Texas, which followed soon after, had set up a new government that met the President's terms. Two conspicuous features of these governments, however, were deeply disturbing to many Republicans.

First, these Southern states had adopted a series of laws known as "Black Codes," that denied to blacks many of the rights of citizenship—including the right to vote and to serve on juries. Blacks could not testify against whites, and laws were passed against interracial marriage. Of course, blacks were also denied the right to bear arms. Other laws were passed that excluded them from certain types of property ownership and certain occupations. In some cases, black employment was limited to agriculture and domestic servitude. Unemployed Negroes might be arrested as vagrants and bound out to labor in a new form of involuntary servitude. Black workers truant from jobs were forced to do public service until they returned to their former employer to whom they were contractually bound.

Secondly, the former Confederates were in complete control. Between them, the newly organized states elected to Congress no fewer than nine Confederate congressmen, seven Confederate state officials, four generals, four colonels, and Confederate Vice-President Alexander Stephens.

CONGRESSIONAL RADICALS

When Congress met at the end of 1865, it was confronted by presidential Reconstruction as a *fait accompli*. At this point, the Republicans were far from ready for the kind of all-out fight against Johnson that later developed, but they were not willing to accept the reorganized states. They were especially resentful because these states could now claim a larger representation in Congress with the free black population (only three fifths of the blacks had been counted when they were slaves), without actually allowing the blacks any voice in the government. It would be ironical indeed if the overthrow of slavery should increase the representation of the South in Congress and if the Rebels should come back into the Union stronger politically than when they left.

For some months, the Republicans in Congress moved slowly, unwilling to face a break with a President of their own party, and far from ready to make a vigorous stand for the rights of blacks. They would not seat the Southern congressmen-elect, however, and they set up a Joint Committee of the Senate and the House to assert their claim to a voice in the formulation of Reconstruction policy. They also passed a bill to extend the life and increase the activities of the Freedmen's Bureau—an agency created to aid blacks in their transition from slavery to freedom. The new duties Congress wanted to grant to the Freedmen's Bureau were to expand its responsibilities to include federal protection of blacks against white oppression in the South.

Johnson vetoed this measure as an unnecessary and unconstitutional use of the military during peacetime. In addition, he vetoed a Civil Rights bill that declared blacks to be United States citizens and denied Southern states the ability to withhold property rights on the basis of race. Tensions increased; and in April 1866, Congress re-passed the Civil Rights Act of 1866 over Johnson's veto, the first Congressional over-ride of a Presidential Veto in American history. The over-ride of the President's veto shifted the political upper hand to Congress, which would, henceforth, assume the lead in Reconstruction policy.

In June 1866, Congress voted a proposed Fourteenth Amendment, which clearly asserted the citizenship of blacks stating, "All persons born or naturalized in the United States are citizens," and thus effectively overturned the Dred Scott decision that held that blacks were not citizens and did not have standing to sue. It also asserted that they were entitled to the "privileges and immunities of citizens," to the "equal protection of the laws," and to protection against being deprived of "life, liberty, and property without due process of law." In effect, the Amendment was designed to overturn the Black Codes.

Lawyers have been kept busy for more than a century determining exactly what these terms meant, but one thing was clear. The amendment did not specify a right of black suffrage. It did, however, provide that states that disfranchised a part of their adult male population would have their representation in Congress proportionately reduced. It almost seemed that Congress was offering the Southerners a choice. They might disfranchise the blacks if they were willing to pay the price of reduced representation, or they might have increased representation if they were willing to pay the price of black suffrage. This might not help the blacks, but it was certain to help the Republicans. It would either reduce the strength of Southern white Democrats or give the Republicans black political allies in the South.

The Fourteenth Amendment also provisionally excluded from federal office any person who had held any important public office before the Civil War and had then gone over to the Confederacy. This sweeping move to disqualify almost the entire leadership of the South led the Southern states to make the serious mistake of following President Johnson's advice to reject the amendment. During the latter half of 1866 and the first months of 1867, 10 Southern states voted not to ratify the Fourteenth Amendment. By March 1867, Tennessee was the only Southern State that had ratified the Fourteenth Amendment.

RADICAL RECONSTRUCTION

Southern rejection of the Fourteenth Amendment precipitated the bitter fight that had been brewing for almost two years. Congressional elections of 1866, however, gave Radical Republicans a two thirds majority in Congress, thus solidifying their power to over-ride Presidential vetoes and take the lead in Reconstruction. Congress now moved to replace the Johnson governments in the South with new governments of its own creation. Between March and July 1867, it adopted a series of Reconstruction Acts that divided 10 Southern states into five military districts under five military governors. The governors were vested with "all powers necessary" to protect the civil rights of all persons, maintain order, and supervise the administration of justice. These governors were to hold elections for conventions to frame new state constitutions. In these elections adult males, including blacks, were to vote, but many whites, disqualified by their support of the Confederacy, were not to vote. The constitutions these conventions adopted must establish black suffrage, and the governments they established must ratify the Fourteenth Amendment. Then and only then might they be readmitted to the Union. Congress followed with a second Reconstruction Act that required military authorities in the South to register voters and supervise the election of the delegates to state constitutional conventions. Furthermore, new constitutions had to be ratified by a majority of voters. Thus, two years after the war was over, when the South supposed that the postwar adjustment had been completed, the process of Reconstruction actually began.

The period that followed has been the subject of more bitter feeling and more controversy than perhaps any other period in American history, and the intensity of the bitterness has made it hard to get at the realities. During 1867 the military governors conducted elections, and in late 1867 and early 1868, the new constitutional conventions met in the Southern states. They complied with the terms

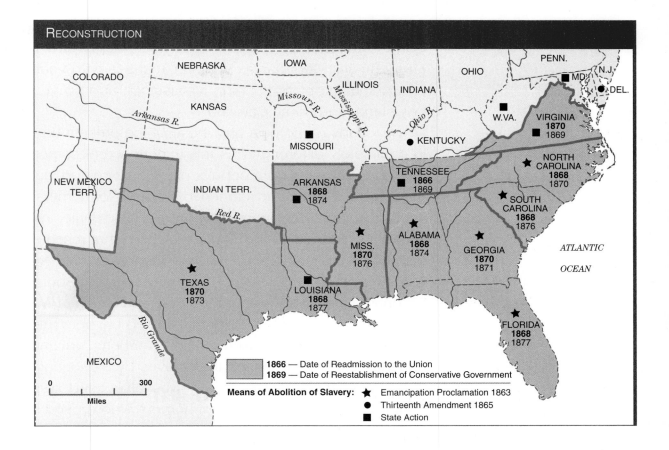

RECONSTRUCTION

1866 — Date of Readmission to the Union
1869 — Date of Reestablishment of Conservative Government

Means of Abolition of Slavery:
★ Emancipation Proclamation 1863
● Thirteenth Amendment 1865
■ State Action

Congress had laid down, including enfranchisement of the black men; however, many Southerners resisted. Military authorities in many places found that they could not get together a majority of voters at the polls, as Congress had required. In essence, the former Confederates protested their new constitutions, which they viewed as externally imposed, by staying home and not voting. In March 1868, Congress altered the rules to allow state constitutions to be ratified by the majority of those who voted in an election. Three months later, Arkansas fulfilled the requirements necessary for readmission to the Union. Within a year after the third Reconstruction Act (of July 1867), seven states had adopted new constitutions, organized new governments, ratified the Fourteenth Amendment, and been readmitted to the Union. In Virginia, Mississippi, Georgia, and Texas, however, the process was for one reason or another not completed until 1870. In July 1870, Georgia became the last Southern state to be readmitted to the Union.

All of these new governments, except the one in Virginia, began under Republican control, with more or less black representation in the legislatures. In one state after another, however, the Democrats, supporting a policy of white supremacy, soon gained the ascendancy. Military and "Radical" rule lasted for three years in North Carolina; four years in Tennessee (never under military government) and Georgia; six years in Texas; seven years in Alabama and Arkansas; eight years in Mississippi; and 10 years in Florida, Louisiana, and South Carolina.

Historians of the past and those of the present have interpreted, in completely different terms this experience of carpet bag rule—so named in reference to a popular nineteenth-century suitcase literally made from carpet and carried by many Northerners who moved south in search of economic opportunity. The earlier interpretation reflected the feelings of the Southern whites that resented this regime bitterly, seeing it as one of "military despotism" and "Negro rule." According to this version, later elaborated by a pro-Southern school of historians, the South was at the outset the victim of military occupation in which a brutal soldiery maintained bayonet rule. Then came the "carpetbaggers"—unscrupulous Northern adventurers whose only purpose was to enrich themselves by plundering the prostrate South. The term "carpetbagger" was also used disparagingly by Southerners in reference to Northerners who moved south and became involved in Southern politics.

In the view of Southerners, the carpetbaggers—in order to maintain their ascendancy—incited the blacks, who were essentially well disposed, to assert themselves in swaggering insolence. Thereupon, majorities made up of illiterate blacks swarmed into the legislatures where the carpetbaggers manipulated them. A carnival of riotous corruption and looting followed until at last the outraged whites, excluded from all voice in public affairs, could endure these conditions no longer and arose to drive the vandals away and to redeem their dishonored states.

This picture of Reconstruction has a very real importance, for it has undoubtedly influenced subsequent Southern attitudes; but it is an extreme distortion of the realities. Historical treatments since 1950 have presented quite a different version, stressing the brief nature of the military rule and the constructive measures of the "carpetbag" governments. As for bayonet rule, the number of troops in the "Army of Occupation" was absurdly small. In November 1869 there were 1,000 federal soldiers scattered over the state of Virginia and 716 over Mississippi with hardly more than a corporal's guard in any one place.

For certain, Southern politics during Reconstruction was fraught with factionalism and corruption, and some of the blame must be placed at the feet of the "carpetbaggers." For example, Illinois native Henry Clay Warmoth was elected Governor of Louisiana in 1868 with

African Americans moved from the plantations to the state legislatures during the Reconstruction of the South. (*Library of Congress*)

an annual salary of $8,000. Four years later, Warmoth had a net worth of over $1 million. A full 50 percent of the state budget in Louisiana during Warmoth's tenure went to state representatives and their staff members for salaries and "mileage." This, however, was not the only incident of overpaid public officials. One year, South Carolina's legislature voted an additional $1,000 in salary for one member who had recently lost the same amount on a horse race. Inflated and corrupt government contracts were also rampant. For example, the state of Arkansas constructed a bridge one year at a cost of $500

Mark Twain (*Library of Congress*)

and then repaired the bridge the next year at a cost of $9,000. To be sure, not all of the corruption was due to "carpetbaggers" in government, but for Southerners, the transplanted Northerners made easy targets. Among the American writers who familiarized the country with the looters and scoundrels was Mark Twain, whose fictional writings presented unscrupulous characters with which Southerners became all too familiar.

Among the carpetbaggers, though there were indeed looters and scoundrels, there were also idealists that did all they could to improve conditions in the South. Many Northern women came to teach the freed slaves. Many men came to develop needed industry, which even if it enriched the Northern carpetbagger in the process, was also good for the South as a whole. Many others worked with integrity and self-sacrifice to find a constructive solution for the problems of a society devastated by war and left with a huge population of former slaves to absorb and support. Many native Southerners, who joined with the "carpetbaggers" in their programs and who were denounced as "scalawags," were equally public-spirited and high-minded.

As for "Negro rule," the fact is that the blacks were in a majority only in the convention and the first three legislatures of South Carolina. Elsewhere they were a minority, even in Mississippi and Louisiana, where they constituted a majority of the population. In view of their illiteracy and their political inexperience, the blacks handled their new responsibilities well and they tended to choose educated men for public office. Thus many of the black legislators, congressmen, and state officials they chose were well qualified. They were, on the whole, moderate and self-restrained in their demands; and they gave major support to certain policies of long-range value, including notably the establishment of public school systems, which the South had not had in any broad sense before the Civil War.

As for the "carnival of corruption," the post-Civil War era was marked by corruption throughout the country. All the Southern states combined did not manage to steal as much money from the public treasury as did the Tweed Ring in New York City, led by William Marcy Tweed, commonly known as "Boss Tweed." New York was also famous for fraudulent elections, and the corruption in government spearheaded by Tweed would become a major issue in national politics in the 1870s. It was true, however, that the impoverished South could ill afford dishonesty in government. Nevertheless, much that was charged to "corruption" really stemmed from increased costs necessary to provide new social services such as public schools and to rebuild the Southern economy laid waste by war.

Finally, it should be noted that the Southern whites were never reduced to abject helplessness as is sometimes imagined. From the outset they were present in all of the Reconstruction conventions and legislatures—always vocal, frequently aggressive, and sometimes dominating the proceedings.

THE FALL OF RADICAL RECONSTRUCTION

For an average of six years, then, the regimes of Radical Republican Reconstruction continued. After that they gave way to the Democratic Redeemers—those who wanted to "redeem" the South to white rule—delaying until the twentieth century further progress toward equal rights for blacks.

When one considers that the South had just been badly defeated in war, that Radical Reconstruction was the policy of the dominant party in Washington, and that black and white Republicans constituted a majority of the voters in a half-dozen Southern states, it is difficult to understand why the Radical regimes were so promptly—almost easily—overthrown. Several contributing factors must be recognized.

First, the former slaves lacked experience in political participation and leadership. Largely illiterate and conditioned for many decades to defer to white people, they grasped the new opportunities with uncertain hands. Very often they seemed to wish, quite realistically, for security of land tenure and for education more than for political rights. At the same time, however, a number of articulate and able blacks, some of them former slaves, came to the fore and might have provided effective leadership for their race if Reconstruction had not been abandoned so soon.

Second, and more importantly, one must recognize the importance of the grim resistance offered by the Southern whites. With their deep belief in the superiority of their own race, these Southerners were convinced that civilization itself was at stake. They fought with proportionate desperation, not hesitating to resort to violence and terror.

THE KU KLUX KLAN

On Christmas Eve 1865, a half-whimsical secret society—known as the Ku Klux Klan (KKK)—was formed in Tennessee by six Confederate army veterans who were simply bored and restless after the war and sought something for their own amusement. The name "Ku Klux Klan" was derived from the Greek word "Kuklos," the root of the English word "circle." Since the six founding members were of Scotch-Irish ancestry, they added the word "Klan" and then added the made-up word "Klux" to add "mystery and baffle" as well as something "secret-sounding" and "nonsensically inscrutable." With nothing sinister in mind, Jon C. Lester reportedly said to his other listless five founding members, "Boys, let's start something to break the monotony and cheer up our mothers and girls. Let's start a club of some kind." The original purpose of the young men, evidently, was merely to play practical jokes and serenade women and had nothing to do with racism or terror.

In furtherance of their playful goals, however, the men donned white regalia and rode through the Tennessee countryside in search of adventure. Accidentally, the men discovered that their midnight marauding frightened the black refugees who were aimlessly wandering the Tennessee countryside in large numbers. This accident began to take on a more purposeful character, and the Klansmen began a campaign of scare tactics against the wandering black refugees. An unforeseen consequence was that blacks tended to avoid the roadways in the area where Klansmen were playing their games. Word of the KKK fun and games spread across the South. People in surrounding areas contacted the Klan wanting to know how they, too, could set up KKK Dens of their own for the express purpose of scaring vagrant blacks away from the roadways. Soon every Southern state had its organization of masked and robed riders, either as part of the Klan or under some other name. Klan tactics quickly escalated from jokes and scare tactics to naked violence, contrary to the original intensions of the Klan's founders. By use of threat, horsewhip, and even rope, gun, and fire, they spread fear not only among blacks but also, perhaps even more among the Republican leaders. By 1868, the Klan claimed to have 500,000 members, and their expressed purpose had grown from playful mischief to overt resistance to the Congressional Reconstruction Act of 1867.

Ku Klux Klan members burn a cross. (A/P World Wide)

Klan members were sworn to secrecy and had to swear that they were opposed to negro equality and in favor of a white man's government, including the "restoration of the civil rights to Southern White men." In its bylaws, the Klan stated a reverence for the "majesty and supremacy of the Divine Being" and recognized the supremacy of the United States Constitution. The Klan claimed that it was an institution of chivalry, humanity, mercy, and patriotism that existed to protect the weak, defend the Constitution, and execute all Constitutional laws.

In 1870, KKK violence had grown so steadily that it drew the attention of the Radical Republicans in Congress, who passed "An Act to Enforce the Provisions of the Fourteenth Amendment to the Constitution of the United States, and for Other Purposes"—more generally known as the First Ku Klux Klan Act. The Act imposed heavy penalties for violations of the Fourteenth and Fifteenth Amendments and gave the state governments the authority to take whatever action they deemed necessary against the Klan. In furtherance of the execution of the Act, Union troops and state militiamen arrested Klansmen and tried them for their crimes, sending many to prison. By the end of 1872, under this pressure from the federal and state governments, the KKK was no longer a force.

The dramatic quality of the Klan has given it a prominent place in the public's mental picture of Reconstruction. Though violence played a prominent role, the white South had other, less spectacular weapons that were no less powerful. Southern whites owned almost all of the land. Whites controlled virtually all employment, and they dominated the small supply of money and credit that was to be found in the South. They, also, dominated the legal system. In unspectacular ways they could make life very hard for individuals who did not comply with the system. These factors, perhaps more than the acts of night-riders and violent men, made the pressure against Radical rule almost irresistible.

Another important reason for the downfall of "Radical" Reconstruction was that it was not really very radical. It did not confiscate the land of plantation owners and distribute that land among the freed slaves, as radicals and abolitionists such as Thaddeus Stevens and Wendell Phillips had urged. It, also, did not reduce the former Confederate states to the status of territories for a probationary period as many Radicals also advocated. Furthermore, it did not permanently disfranchise the South's former ruling class, nor did it permanently disqualify more than a handful of ex-Confederate leaders from holding office. It did not enact Charles Sumner's bill to require universal public education in the South and to provide federal aid for schools there; hence, the former slaves were to remain largely uneducated. These would have been genuinely radical measures; but they went beyond what a majority of Northern voters were willing to support and perhaps they would have even risked the renewal of revolt in the South.

Indeed, even the limited radicalism of the Fourteenth Amendment and the Reconstruction Acts strained the convictions of most Northerners to the utmost. The North was not a racially equalitarian society. Black men did not have the right to vote in most Northern states at the time the Reconstruction Acts of 1867 enfranchised them in the South. The enactment of Negro suffrage in the South was accomplished by the Radical Republicans—not because of a widespread conviction that it was right in principle but because it seemed to be the only alternative to Confederate rule.

Later, Republicans found that many Northern voters cared little about black suffrage in the South. They also found that the white South would not consent to a real reunion on this basis and that the restoration of former Confederates to political power did not threaten Northern or national interests. As a result, the Republicans let the existing forces in the South find their own resolution, which was one of white supremacy.

Yet Reconstruction was far from a total failure. It established public schools in the South that gradually brought literacy to the children of freed slaves. By 1900, illiteracy among blacks had dropped from 90 percent after the Civil War to an estimated 48 percent by 1900. It brought abolitionists and missionaries from the North to found such colleges as Howard, Fisk, Morehouse, Talladega, and many others. These colleges trained future generations of black leaders who in turn led the black protest movements of the twentieth century. Furthermore, though Reconstruction did not confiscate and redistribute land, many freed slaves became landowners through their own hard work and savings. In 1865 scarcely any black farmers owned their farms, but by 1880, one fifth of them did.

BLACK SHARECROPPERS

A full 80 percent of black farmers were not landowners, even of small plots, but became sharecroppers, often working for the same landowner that had once owned them on the same plantation. Sharecropping was a wage-labor system where blacks worked the land for the white owners and paid the white owners a percentage of their harvest (normally 25 percent of the cotton crop and a third of other crops) for the privilege of working on the owner's land. Planters generally divided their plantations into small 25–30 acre plots and signed contracts with individual black sharecroppers to work each plot. Landowners supplied the sharecroppers with the necessary mules, seed, plows, and tools, while the sharecroppers were responsible for their own food and necessities. A

Sharecroppers, such as the man in this photo, worked the land for its white owners and paid the owners a percentage of the harvest. (*Library of Congress*)

system of credit developed where local merchants would advance goods to black sharecroppers with payment due at the time of harvest.

Sharecropping allowed blacks the beginnings of economic freedom and, also, the freedom to decide which family members would work the land, how long they would work each day, and how the labor would be divided. Blacks, typically, moved out of the slave cottages and into their own dwellings. On some plantations, however, blacks worked for wages in gangs, as they had under slavery, complete with white overseers and even whippings in some instances.

Still, change did come with emancipation in that a full third of the black women that had worked in the fields abandoned fieldwork either to tend to the home and child rearing or for paid domestic servitude. Indoor work, even if it consisted of cleaning and laundry, was much preferable to working in the field in the hot southern sun.

FREEDMEN'S BUREAU

Reconstruction also created the Freedmen's Bureau, which was perhaps charged with more responsibility than any federal agency in history. The Freedmen's Bureau was created for the purpose of aiding the former slaves in their transition to freedom. Though woefully undermanned and inadequately funded, the Freedmen's Bureau provided food, clothing, medical care, and shelter for former slaves. In the first two years after the War, the Freedmen's Bureau issued over $20 million to needy black Americans and treated 450,000 illnesses. The Bureau also constructed 40 hospitals across the South to help meet the medical needs of the former slave population.

After the Civil War, the Southern roadways were literally clogged with refugees as Southern plantation owners, who had no money with which to hire their labor, released thousands of free blacks. With nowhere to go, thousands of blacks wandered aimlessly across the South. These refugees, without shelter on the roadways, made easy targets for terrorizing by the night rides of the KKK. The Freedmen's Bureau helped transport the dislocated refugees to shelter, helped blacks find family members from whom they had become separated either before or after the War, and performed formal marriage ceremonies for many blacks that wanted legal sanction for the de facto marriages within which they had lived under slavery. In the first two years after the war, the Freedmen's Bureau helped resettled 30,000 displaced black Americans.

The Freedmen's Bureau also attempted to ensure fair trials for blacks in the South, to provide for black education, and to serve as an employment agency for the thousands of unemployed black refugees. In total, the Freedmen's Bureau constructed over 4,300 schools in the first two years following the Civil War.

Finally, Reconstruction also left as a permanent legacy the Fourteenth and Fifteenth Amendments, which formed the constitutional basis for the civil-rights movements of the post-World War II generation.

JOHNSON VERSUS THE RADICALS

The Republicans did not abandon their program all at once; rather, it faded out gradually although the Radicals remained militant while Johnson remained President. Johnson had used his administrative powers to evade or modify the enforcement of some Republican Reconstruction measures. This convinced most Republicans that his removal was necessary if their policy was to be carried out in the South; and in 1868, they tried to remove him by impeachment. The immediate pretext for impeachment was Johnson's dismissal of Secretary of War Stanton in February 1868.

A year earlier Congress had passed a series of acts designed to strengthen the legislative branch at the expense of the executive. Among these laws was the Tenure of Office Act, which forbade removals of public officials who had been confirmed by the Senate without first obtaining Senate approval. The Tenure of Office Act was subsequently found to be unconstitutional by the Supreme Court; but at the time that Johnson removed Stanton, who was reporting to the Radicals what went on in administration councils, there had been no judicial ruling. Therefore, the House of Representatives voted to impeach Johnson, which meant that the Senate must try him on the articles of impeachment.

The trial was conducted in a tense atmosphere and scarcely in a judicial way. Immense pressure was put on all Republican senators to

A Congressional document showing the impeachment of President Andrew Johnson
(*Teaching Politics*)

vote for conviction. When a vote was finally taken on May 16, 1868, conviction failed by one vote of the two thirds required. Seven Republicans had stood out against the party. Johnson was permitted to serve out his term, and the balance between executive and legislative power in the American political system, which had almost been destroyed, was preserved. Johnson, however, would fail to win the Democratic Party's nomination for President at their national convention two months later.

The determination of Republicans to achieve congressional domination of the Reconstruction process also manifested itself in restrictions on the judiciary. When a Mississippi editor named McCardle appealed to the Supreme Court to rule on the constitutionality of one of the Reconstruction acts, under which he had been arrested by the military, Congress—in March 1868—passed an act changing the appellate jurisdiction of the Court so that it could not pass judgment on McCardle's case.

THE GRANT ADMINISTRATION

In 1868 the country faced another election, and the Republicans turned to General Grant as their nominee. He was elected over the Democratic candidate, Governor Horatio Seymour of New York, by a popular majority of only 310,000—a surprisingly close vote. Without the votes of the newly enfranchised blacks in the seven reconstructed Southern states, Grant might have had no edge in popular votes at all. The Radical Republicans were alarmed at their narrow margin of victory and, therefore, sought to find ways to add more black voters to the ranks. Although the Fourteenth Amendment theoretically forced black suffrage in the South, the issue of suffrage for blacks had been generally ignored in a number of Northern states. Between 1865 and 1869, a number of Northern states had held referendums on black suffrage; voters in Kansas, Ohio, Michigan, Missouri, Wisconsin, New York, and the District of Columbia all voted down black suffrage. The vote in the District of Columbia was an overwhelming 6,521 to 35 against black suffrage. Of the Northern states that held elections on the issue, only Iowa and Minnesota passed laws granting the franchise to blacks. To implant Negro suffrage permanently in the Constitution—for the North as well as the South—Congress in 1869 passed the Fifteenth Amendment, forbidding the states to deny any citizen his right to vote "on account of race, color, or previous condition of servitude." The Amendment was ratified in 1870; and it had almost immediate impact as black men, just five years removed from slavery, were elected to public office. Though blacks were still severely under-represented in the 1870s, 17 black men served in Congress, one served in the United States Senate, and one black man served as Chief Justice of the South Carolina Supreme Court. For a brief interlude, blacks even held a majority of the seats in the South Carolina legislature.

President Grant supported the measures of the Radicals and in some ways gave his backing to their policies. Like the good military man he was, he believed that where violence broke out, it should be put down uncompromisingly. Accordingly, he favored the adoption of Enforcement Acts for the use of federal troops to break up the activities of the Ku Klux Klan. When these laws were passed, he did not hesitate to invoke them; troops were sent in on a number of occasions.

Fundamentally, however, Grant was not a radical. He wanted to see tranquility restored, and this meant reuniting North and South on any basis both would be willing to accept. Accordingly, he urged a broader extension of amnesty to all former Confederates, and he

President Ulysses S. Grant delivering his inaugural address at the U.S. Capitol on March 4, 1873. (*Library of Congress*)

grew to resent the frequent appeals of Republican governments in the South for troops to uphold their authority. Though he realized that the tactics of the Redeemers were very bad—"bloodthirsty butchery" and "scarcely a credit to savages"—he became convinced that constant federal military intervention was worse in the long run.

During the eight years of Grant's presidency, Republican governments were overthrown in eight of the Southern states. As Grant's second term neared its end, only three states—Louisiana, Florida, and South Carolina—remained in the Republican ranks. The program of Radical Reconstruction still remained official policy in the Republican Party, but it had lost its steam. The country was concerned about other things.

In foreign affairs, Secretary of State Hamilton Fish was busy putting through an important settlement by which Great Britain and the United States adopted the principle of international arbitration. This was a means of settling American claims that had grown out of the raiding activities of the *Alabama* and other ships, which British shipyards had built for the Confederacy.

In financial circles there was a controversy over what to do about the greenback dollars issued during the war. Since greenbacks were not backed by gold, people had saved the more valuable gold dollars and spent the less valuable greenback dollars, thus driving gold out of circulation. The government was willing to give gold for greenbacks even though such a policy would tend to increase the value of the dollar. Debtor interests (such as farmers), who wanted a cheap dollar, fought hard against the policy of redemption; but the policy was adopted in 1875.

In politics, public confidence in the government was shaken by a series of disclosures concerning government corruption. In 1869, investors Jay Gould and Jim Fisk began purchasing gold futures for the purpose of driving up the price of gold, which skyrocketed from $4.00 per ounce to $25.00 per ounce. It was expected that at a certain point the United States Treasury Department would place U.S. gold reserves on the market in an effort to stabilize the gold market. Grant's brother-in-law in the Treasury Department struck a deal, unknown to Grant, with Gould to inform him in advance about when the Treasury Department would release its gold reserves so that Gould could sell before the prices dropped. Grant's brother-in-law dutifully sent Gould a telegraph the morning that the Treasury Department released its gold to the open market, but Gould was out of the office and did not get the message. Prices quickly fell back to the pre-panic price of $4.00 per ounce, and Gould's losses were $16 million.

In 1872 it was revealed that several congressmen had accepted gifts of stock in a construction company, the Crédit Mobilier, which was found to be diverting the funds of the Union Pacific Railroad—including the funds the government had granted to it—with the knowledge of the officers of the road. In 1875 Grant's private secretary was implicated in the operations of the "Whiskey Ring," which, by evading taxes, had systematically defrauded the government of mil-

Jay Gould (*Teaching Politics*)

lions of dollars. The following year, the Secretary of War was caught selling appointments to Native American posts. Meanwhile, in the New York City government, the Tweed Ring, headed by Tammany boss William Marcy Tweed, was exposed as guilty of graft and thefts that have seldom been equaled in size and have never been surpassed in effrontery.

The epidemic of corruption inspired a revolt by reform Republicans, who bolted the party in 1872, organized the Liberal Republican party, and nominated Horace Greeley, editor of the *New York Tribune*, for President. Although the Democrats also nominated Greeley and formed a coalition with the Liberal Republicans, Grant easily won reelection because most Northern voters were not yet prepared to trust the Democrats.

In the economic orbit, the country was trying to weather the financial depression that began with the panic of 1873. All in all, the problems posed by the South and the blacks seemed more and more distant, less and less important, to the people of the North.

THE HAYES-TILDEN ELECTION OF 1876

The election of 1876 brought to an end the program of Reconstruction, which probably would have ended soon in any case. In this election the Republicans, who were badly divided, turned to a Civil

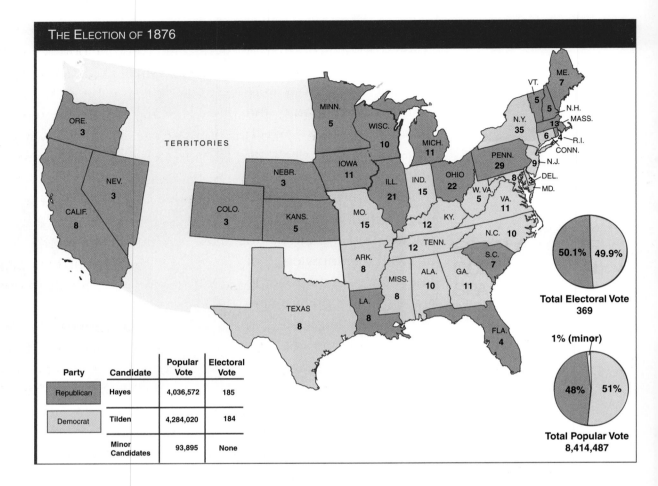

THE ELECTION OF 1876

Party	Candidate	Popular Vote	Electoral Vote
Republican	Hayes	4,036,572	185
Democrat	Tilden	4,284,020	184
	Minor Candidates	93,895	None

War veteran and governor of Ohio, Rutherford B. Hayes, as their nominee. Hayes was a conspicuously honest man, and so was his Democratic opponent, Samuel J. Tilden of New York, who owed his reputation to his part in breaking up the Tweed Ring.

When the votes were counted, Tilden had a popular majority (obtained partly by the suppression of black votes in some Southern states) and was within one vote of an electoral majority. However, there were three states—Florida, Louisiana, and South Carolina—in which the result was contested; and rival officials filed two sets of returns—though Tilden had clearly won the popular vote in all three states. To count the votes in such a case, the Constitution calls for a joint session of the Congress, but the House of Representatives, with a Democratic majority, was in a position to prevent an election by refusing to go into joint session with the Senate. Congress agreed to appoint an Electoral Commission to provide an impartial judgment, but the commission divided along party lines with eight Republicans and eight Democrats, voting eight to seven for Hayes. As late as two days before the inauguration it was doubtful whether the Democrats in the House would accept the decision.

Many Northern Democrats were prepared to fight to a finish against what they regarded as a stolen election, but the Southern Democrats had found that one civil war was enough. Moreover, various negotiations had been in progress behind the scenes. Important groups of Southern Democrats who had been left out when the government largesse of the Union Pacific-Central Pacific was distributed now hoped for a Texas and Pacific Railroad that would provide bountiful federal grants for Southern interests. They received assurances from friends of Governor Hayes that he would look with favor upon such programs of internal improvement. Moreover, they were assured that he would withdraw the last remaining federal troops from Louisiana and South Carolina, which meant that their Republican governments would collapse and the score of states would be: redeemed, 11—reconstructed, none.

With these understandings, Southern congressmen voted to let the count proceed so that Hayes would be elected. Later, when they were explaining their conduct to their constituents, they thought it best to say quite a great deal about how they had ransomed South Carolina and Louisiana and very little about their hopes for the Texas and Pacific Railroad and other such enterprises. Thus a legend grew up that there had been a "compromise" by which Reconstruction was ended.

What had really happened was that Southern Democrats and Northern Republicans had discovered that there were many features of economic policy on which they were in close harmony. The slaves were emancipated, the Union was restored, and bygones were bygones. The harmony of their views made reconciliation natural and Reconstruction unnecessary. There was still the question of the blacks, but only a few whites had ever supported black suffrage or racial equality for

Rutherford B. Hayes (*Teaching Politics*)

its own sake. It had been an expedient; and now that the expedient was no longer needed, it could be laid aside. Such was the spirit of reconciliation.

Thus, the country ended a period of intense friction and entered upon a long era of sectional harmony and rapid economic growth. This was done, however, at the expense of leaving the question of racial relations still unattended to—even though slavery itself had, at immense cost, been removed.

2

INDUSTRIALISM AND AMERICAN LIFE

(Library of Congress)

Capt. IRWIN and MAUL, Phila

SMOKE KALAMAZOO BATS

LIFE IN THE GILDED AGE

After the Civil War and Reconstruction, Americans largely turned their attention from the immense social issues of the day, such as equal rights for African Americans, toward securing economic advancement. After the failures of active government during Reconstruction, Americans, in general, came to favor a laissez faire approach to governing, assuming that the free market and capitalism was, essentially, self-regulating. James Bryce wrote of the situation in the 1880s that politicians were "clinging too long to outworn issues" and "neglecting to discover and work out new principles capable of solving the problems which now perplex the country."

Nevertheless, the era following Reconstruction was one of great invention and economic growth. All, however, did not share that prosperity equally; and the politics of the era was fraught with corruption. The existence of this situation is what led Mark Twain to label the era as the Gilded Age. In terms of definition, "gilded" is a description of something that has been altered to appear more attractive or valuable than it actually is. In reference to the Gilded Age, Twain described it as "dazzling on the surface, but base metal beneath." The "dazzling" part to which Twain made reference was the robust economic growth and the explosion of invention, along with 75 percent voter turnout, much higher than that in the early twenty-first century. The "base metal beneath," however was gross income inequality, segregation and legal inequalities for blacks, gender inequality, xenophobia, political corruption, monopolies, worker exploitation, and the lack of empathy that accompanied Social Darwinism. Social Darwinism, the application of the "survival of the fittest" approach to the human existence, will be discussed in greater detail later in this chapter.

THE GROWTH OF INDUSTRY

The years following the Civil War were a period of rapid and vast economic expansion known as the American Industrial Revolution. No factor fueled this Industrial Revolution more than the construction of the railroads. Between 1860 and 1900 the total railroad mileage increased from 30 thousand to 193 thousand while the capital invested in manufacturing jumped from $1 billion to almost $10 billion, the number of workers from 1.3 million to 5.3 million, and the value of the annual product from under $2 million to over $13 billion. The economy absorbed 2.5 million new workers from Europe in the 1870s and another 5 million in the 1880s. Industry had come of age, and the United States had become the greatest industrial nation in the world.

This enormous economic growth not only made the United States potentially the most powerful country in the world but also transformed it from a rural and agrarian nation into an urban and industrial one. By 1890 the value of this country's manufactured goods exceeded that of its agricultural products. Ten years later manufactured products were worth twice as much. This was in spite of the fact that agricultural production also increased in the Gilded Age due to a seemingly endless stream of new machines for cultivating and harvesting and the construction of railroads to get agricultural products to the markets. The advances in agricultural production combined with the industrial revolution to create a boom in commercial packaging of food, including packaged cereals and canning factories.

Big business came to dominate economic life. Antebellum factories and plants—where the relationship between owners and employees was close, where the workshop was small and the market was local, where the ownership comprised an individual or a partnership—gave way to large, impersonal corporations. The demand for immense sums of capital to build railroads and factories led to the rise of the stock market as a way to finance the industrial revolution. The hitherto scattered banking institutions now became concentrated in four or five financial centers, with New York becoming the most important. East of the Mississippi River, factory and foundry workers and their families helped change towns into cities and create sprawling industrial centers. Into these centers came millions of immigrants, who were to alter the racial and ethnic composition of the nation.

Although the Civil War is generally regarded as marking the beginning of the triumph of industrial capitalism, it did not produce the Industrial Revolution. The forces responsible for the rapid postwar expansion of American industry had been developing for more than half a century. In the 1850s railroads had revolutionized transportation, and many inventions had transformed both industry and agriculture.

Then, in the post-Civil War years, major advances in every field of science, especially in chemistry and physics, provided the principles for new technology. Inventions that spurred industrial growth were made in transportation, communications, electrical power, the production of steel, and the use of oil.

As we shall see in Chapter 3, railroad development played a key role in the expansion of industry, the economy, and the nation. By 1900 the American railroad system extended into every region. Moreover, through the use of standard-gauge track, the rolling stock of railroads could travel over each other's lines all over the country, greatly facilitating the shipment of goods. Equipment improved when steel replaced heavier and more brittle iron in the construction of tracks, locomotives, and freight and passenger cars. Service also improved. The Westinghouse airbrake, the automatic coupler, and the block and signal system increased safety while the Pullman sleeping car, the dining car, and improved lighting offered both comfort and safety.

The telegraph had been widely used before the Civil War, and in the following decades came the submarine cable, the telephone, the stock ticker, the typewriter, and wireless telegraphy. Cyrus W. Field succeeded first in laying a cable across the Atlantic Ocean in 1866, and Alexander Graham Bell and his assistant Thomas A. Watson invented the telephone in 1876. Even more significant was the development of wireless telegraphy by Italian electrical engineer Guglielmo Marconi in 1901, from which came the radio, television, and radar.

Also vital to industrial growth was the typewriter, the first practicable one invented by Charles L. Scholes in 1867. By the mid-eighties the typewriter was used by most large business concerns. It assisted business by making communication more legible, preserving records, and providing carbon copies of correspondence and other papers. (Parenthetically, it can be noted, it opened up a whole new avenue of employment for women, called, at first, "typewriter girls"). These advances were as essential as those in transportation to the development of business.

The use of electricity also contributed to industrial growth. In 1879, after much trial and error, Thomas Edison invented a practical incandescent light bulb that enabled entire towns and even large cities to be illuminated. Another major accomplishment was his development of a system of central power stations for generating the electric current necessary for any extensive lighting system. The opening of the Pearl Street Central Station in New York in 1882 was considered to be the beginning of the electrical age. Early customers were *The New York Times* and the banking firm of J. P. Morgan and Company. Out of these developments in the 1880s came a workable electric railway, a practical dynamo, and electric motor. The use of electric light and power brought a revolution—in the home, in transportation, and in the factory—where electric motors would replace the steam engine.

Of major importance, too, was the development of ways to mass-produce steel. In the 1850s William Kelly of Kentucky and Henry Bessemer, an Englishman, independently invented the open-hearth process of making steel, which came to be known as the Bessemer

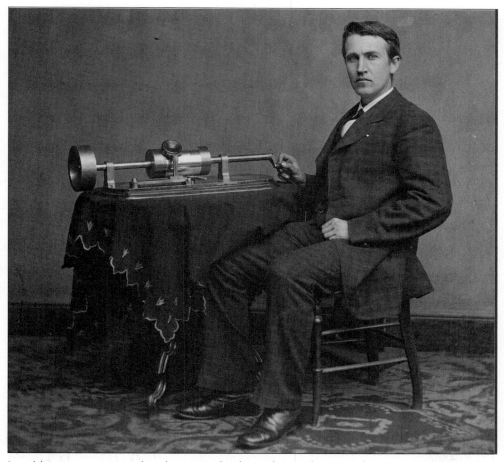

In addition to inventing the phonograph, shown here, Thomas Edison invented both an incandescent light bulb and a system of central electric power stations that enabled the illumination of cities. (*Library of Congress*)

process. The air burned most of the carbon and other impurities in the iron; and when certain amounts of carbon, silicon, and manganese were added, the product was steel. What had previously been a rare metal could now be mass-produced, and the country's vast supplies of iron ore and coal could be more fully utilized.

In 1870 only 77,000 tons of steel were manufactured, but by 1880 1.39 million tons were produced yearly and by 1900 nearly 11.4 million tons. Historians regard this rapid expansion of the steel industry as one of the most important reasons for the Industrial Revolution of the late nineteenth century. At the same time the petroleum industry expanded from a state of nonexistence before the Civil War to that of about 50 million barrels annually by the early 1890s. Similarly, George B. Eastman created a new industry with his development of mass-produced roll photographic film and the Kodak camera. The Bonsack cigarette-rolling machine essentially created a new industry that ended up changing the habits of millions, eventually "hooking" Americans on cigarettes.

All these inventions increased productivity. They also offered opportunities for vast wealth to entrepreneurs with drive, initiative, and the courage to compete in a free-enterprise system that accepted graft, corruption, and the worship of material goods. Many took the chance, and many acquired immense fortunes.

At the same time, the new inventions and the vast economic growth created a new social geography of gender. With so many more employment options, women were much less confined to the home than they had been formerly. The burgeoning department stores in cities all over the country now attracted women shoppers "downtown." Dance halls and amusement parks in the growing cities gave young working-class people a place to go where even the women were unsupervised. Finally, for the first time in American history, a small number of single women began to live alone or with other single women.

POPULAR CULTURE

Since they shared neither the cultivated tastes of the intellectuals nor the bankrolls of the industrialists and financiers, most Americans sought their own cultural pleasures. In time, catering to this mass audience would create whole new industries.

Most Americans knew no more about the lives of the very rich than what they read in their newspapers and magazines, and these media were developing as never before. The Gilded Age was the age of the warring newspaper barons, Joseph Pulitzer and William Randolph Hearst, of the first major newspaper chains and press services. Magazines were being aimed at particular segments of the public—lowbrow, middlebrow, and highbrow. As circulations mounted, advertising, another whole new industry, began to surge.

Since readers of the time did not know that Mark Twain was a major figure in American literature, they simply enjoyed his books. They also enjoyed the hacks that turned out dime novels and books for boys—the writers of historical romances, sentimental stories, exposés, inspirational works, love stories. A few are remembered: Horatio Alger, Jr. and his successful "rags to riches" young heroes; Lew Wallace and his sensational success, *Ben Hur.* There were, also, the popular poets: James Whitcomb Riley, Eugene Field, and Mrs. Ella Wheeler Wilcox. In at least one way the writers for mass audiences had a kinship with the captains of industry. They believed in production—poets turned out a daily poem, novelists a hundred novels. With few exceptions what they wrote ignored the real world and offered escape.

Family fun was largely do-it-yourself. The middle-class family would leave its home—often a wooden "Gothic" structure surrounded by a lawn and shade trees—to have a picnic. After consuming quantities of food, the men and boys might pitch horseshoes. Later on, the women and girls might join them for a game of croquet. In the 1890s every American seemed to want a bicycle.

There were no movies in the Gilded Age, but many towns had theaters where plays, vaudeville, and minstrel shows were performed. One of the great thrills of the late nineteenth century was the circus. When the circuses of Barnum and Bailey or the Ringling Brothers or "Buffalo Bill's Wild West Show" came to town, hundreds of patrons bought tickets to get into the big tents. Another attraction was the county fair with its horse racing, sideshows, fireworks, livestock exhibitions, and possibly even a baseball game. Here families had picnics and reunions with relatives and friends from other towns.

There was growing interest in outdoor sports in the Gilded Age, but it was not until the end of the century that athletic contests began to draw large crowds. In 1869, a professional baseball club, the Cincinnati Red Stockings, was organized. In 1871, the National Association of Professional Baseball Players was created in an effort to deal with abuses then afflicting the game, such as foul language by the players, gambling, and bribing the players. Then in 1876, the National Association of Professional Baseball Clubs came into being. Though professional baseball became more respectable, not everyone thought it was proper to attend games, especially those played on Sunday. In some cities—Philadelphia, Cleveland, and Boston—Sunday baseball was prohibited. Baseball in the Gilded Age was a simpler, far less expensive game than it is today. There were no huge salaries for players or imposing grandstands and playing fields, nor did the games receive much space in the newspapers.

Football was played almost entirely at universities and colleges with Harvard, Yale, and Princeton leading the way. The first intercollegiate football game was played in 1869. Virtually all the players who made Walter Camp's All American team were from Eastern schools. Little money was budgeted for football, and there were no large, high-salaried coaching staffs, huge stadiums, or intersectional games. Even though the railroads had made transcontinental travel possible, it would not be efficient enough for collegiate or professional sports to become intersectional in character until the development of jet travel in the 1950s.

THE NEW RICH

John D. Rockefeller walking with John D. Rockefeller, Jr. *(Library of Congress)*

At the top of the social and economic structure in the United States in the Gilded Age were the Captains of Industry, as many contemporaries called them and as they considered themselves to be. They were the new rich—Standard Oil king John D. Rockefeller leading the way with his nearly $900 million. The economic inequality in the country became acute during the Gilded Age. By 1900, it was estimated that one tenth of the population owned nine tenths of the wealth in the country, and the few millionaires at the time of the Civil War had increased to 3,800. Meanwhile, though there was no government-set poverty line, average wages for American workers hovered around $600 per year, a figure that many economic historians argue would have been approximately equal to the "poverty line" if any such government-set standard had existed.

One of the symbols of the great capitalists' position in society was their style of living, which included palatial mansions and gold-trimmed carriages. Their big houses had libraries, billiard rooms, art galleries, several dining rooms, small theaters, and chapels. They lived in brownstone houses in the large cities and in manor houses in the suburbs or in the country. Built in virtually every known style and copied from those of the Europeans and Persians, these residences often showed bad and even vulgar taste. It was a time when the jig-saw, the cupola, the mansard roof with its dormer windows, and an orgy of decoration were in vogue. Historian and socio-literary critic Vernon L. Parrington described it as "flamboyant lines and meaningless detail" with "tawdry decorations" and "a stuffy and fussy riot of fancy."

"The Gilded Age" was a fitting label for the tawdriness characteristic of this period. This term captured the cynical spirit and crudeness of the new age. The United States, wrote E. L. Godkin in *The Nation* in 1866, is a "gaudy stream of bespangled, belaced, and beruffled barbarians. ... Who knows how to be rich in America? Plenty of people know how to get money; but ... to be rich properly is, indeed, a fine art." The new rich were unsure of themselves and used gaudy display to impress others. The conspicuous waste of money was the measure of social status. This prompted the craze whereby wealthy Americans went on shopping sprees for European antiques and art collections, launching perhaps the greatest plunder of the continent since the sacking of Rome.

Though perceptive social critics assailed the new rich for their coarse taste and lack of business ethics, the typical American saw the rich as respected members of society, pillars of the churches, and philanthropists who occupied positions of prestige and power both at home and abroad. Vernon L. Parrington, though sharply critical of the period, was also fascinated. He interpreted the Gilded Age as one in which the energies damned up by the limitations of frontier life and the inhibitions of backwoods religion had been suddenly released.

Economist Thorstein Veblen considered this extravagant and ostentatious living intentionally conspicuous waste and a clear sign of the increasing inequality of wealth. He maintained that ornamentation, too, was a form of conspicuous waste and that buildings, household interiors, and even spoons should be designed simply for use. The young Gifford Pinchot—later to be a leading progressive in the country, a governor of Pennsylvania, and eventually head of the federal Forest Service under Theodore Roosevelt—worked as a forester on Vanderbilt's Biltmore estate (located near Asheville, North Carolina, and the largest house in America). Pinchot observed about the chateau: "As a feudal castle, it would have been beyond criticism, and perhaps beyond praise. But in the United States of the nineteenth century and among the one-room cabins of the Appalachian mountaineers it did not belong. The contrast was a devastating commentary on the injustice of concentrated wealth."

THE MIDDLE CLASS

More representative of the American lifestyle of these years was that enjoyed by the middle class—the clerks, professionals, shopkeepers, and lower-level executives and their families. For these people, home was a simple house or an apartment (something rather new then) with heavy furniture and draperies, marble-topped tables, and considerable bric-a-brac. Their standard of living was usually better than that of their parents. They could educate their children, and they

A newspaper illustration of the great fire of Chicago in 1871 *(Library of Congress)*

could hope and work for a better status. The middle-class enjoyed the increased comforts resulting from the inventions of the day: the telephone in the 70s, the electric light in the 80s, and the gas burner after 1890. If they lived in a city, they might enjoy the benefits of electric trolley cars, elevated railways, better sewage disposal, improved water distribution plants and street paving, and more efficient fire departments. They would also suffer, however, the dreadful noise of the "el," the congested traffic of wagons and hacks, and the constant danger of large-scale fires, such as the great Chicago fire of 1871, laying waste to large sections of cities.

Walking city streets could be dangerous, especially at night, and wise citizens stayed at home after darkness came. In the *Centennial Guide to New York City and Its Environs*, published in 1876, travelers were advised to "reach the city in the day-time," to "avoid being too free with strangers," to "avoid all crowds, particularly at night," and, if they were obliged to make inquiries on the street, to "apply to a policeman or go into a respectable place of business." Present-day Americans may find small comfort in the knowledge that the dangers of urban living are nothing new.

In the country, travel was still by horseback, wagons, or buggies over muddy trails and roads filled with bumps and holes. A trip to the village or to the county seat, accomplished now in a matter of minutes or, at most, an hour or so, was then generally an all-day event. Mail reached post offices only several times a week, and rural free delivery did not come to some areas until the 90s. With no radios and only weekly newspapers in rural areas, the general store was the center for news and gossip, much of it inaccurate.

THE WORKER

In contrast with the visible wealth and comfort of the new entrepreneurs were the wretched living conditions of the workers, brought in great numbers to the cities by the lure of jobs. Many of them lived in tenements that were cheerless, cold, frequently without running water, and cut off from the sun and air. Tenements were built to crowd as many people as possible into the smallest possible space. For block upon block in the slum areas, these ugly structures were to be found covering every inch of building space. Jacob Riis, the reformer, estimated in 1890 that about 330,000 persons were living in one square mile on the lower East Side of New York City. Even the stables of the rich cost more and were more comfortable than the tenements of the poor.

Despite these miserable living conditions, the industrial growth of the Gilded Age did bring material benefits for American workers. The technological advances expanded production and thus made higher wages possible. Between 1870 and 1890 both money and real wages increased, the former by more than 10 percent, the latter from 10 to 25 percent. In the same decades the cost of living fell, with the price index (taking 1860 as 100) going down from 141 to 98.

Whether or not the worker received a fair share of the great economic growth of the last quarter of the nineteenth century or not is a debatable matter. With half of the period being a depression or recession, it is uncertain how many workers shared the benefits, and the benefits were unequal even among those receiving them. Skilled and white-collar workers received the highest wages with adult males receiving about 75 percent more for similar work than women, and two to three times as much as children—whose gainful employment was then taken for granted if they had been born to a poor family.

As for the length of the working day and week, there were many variations. By 1890, the typical worker labored 10 hours a day, six days a week; but bakers averaged more than 65 hours a week, steelworkers over 66, and canners about 77. In the construction industry the average workweek was slightly more than 55 hours.

Although it was commonly believed that workers had unlimited opportunities to advance and thus had much upward economic mobility, studies do not support this assumption. The evidence shows that few unskilled workers went beyond the ranks of the semiskilled and virtually none achieved middle-class status. The myth, however, popularized by the stories of Horatio Alger and others, persisted; and a number of Americans continued to believe that anyone who worked hard and was thrifty and virtuous could, with some luck, become a millionaire.

THE NEW IMMIGRATION

Europeans came to the United States in unprecedented numbers during this period, as did a smaller number of Asians. By the 1890s New York City had as many Italians as Naples, as many Germans as Hamburg, and twice as many Irish as Dublin. By 1900, three fourths of the people of Chicago were foreign born. In San Francisco, Chinese immigrants flocked to Chinatown—to which they were largely confined by virulent prejudice. By 1900 immigrants were also coming from Japan, Korea, and the Philippines.

The most important thing about this huge movement of peoples was not its size but the immigrants' origins. Previously, nearly all im-

A group of Eastern European immigrants sits on the deck of the S.S. *Amsterdam*. In the late 1800s, immigration to the U.S. shifted from northern and western Europe to southern and eastern Europe. (*Library of Congress*)

migrants had come from northern and western Europe—Germany, Ireland, England, and Scandinavia. Now the tide flowed from southern and eastern Europe—particularly from Italy, Austria-Hungary, Poland, and Russia—along with those from Asia who arrived on the West Coast. In the 1860s southern and eastern Europeans had constituted only 1.4 percent of all immigrants. Their percentage rose to 7.2 in the 70s, to 18.3 in the 80s, to 51 percent in the 90s, and to 70 percent in the first decade or so of the twentieth century. This heavy influx, the "new immigration," brought a variety of ethnic groups who had never been here before in appreciable numbers.

Most of the "old" immigrants had been able to read and write, most (except for the Irish) were Protestants, and most settled on farms. In contrast, the immigrants from southern and eastern Europe came from "backward" countries, and most were illiterate. Most were Roman Catholic, Greek Orthodox, or Jewish, and most of them turned to industry and settled in the cities. As for the Asian immigrants, their religious and cultural practices struck most Americans as even more exotic.

Promoters of American industry recruiting cheap labor and agents of steamship companies seeking passengers spread the

Immigrants landing at the Battery in New York (*Library of Congress*)

news that America was the land of opportunity and the haven of the oppressed. Their claims were amply substantiated in letters from immigrants already here and in stories told by those who returned to their native lands. Transportation was cheap and wages, by European standards, were high. Also, there was religious freedom, no compulsory military service, and best of all, the overpowering lure of freedom.

Strangers in a new world and ignorant of its language and customs, immigrants of the same nationality flocked together in the same areas, spoke the same languages, and clung to their own customs and beliefs. Crowding into the large cities, they formed their own communities with newspapers and even theatrical productions in their own languages.

Because the newcomers were so different, older Americans wondered whether these immigrants could ever be assimilated into the mainstream of American life. They also feared that the waves of "racially inferior" immigrants would annihilate the original American stock and resented the fact that so many immigrants were Catholics and Jews. Columnist Finley Peter Dunne's "Mr. Dooley" expressed a popular position when he said,

> As a pilgrim father that missed the' first boats, I must raise me claryon voice again' th' invasion in this fair land by th' paupers an' anychists in effete Europe. Ye bet I must—because I'm here first.

Labor leaders contended that the new workers from abroad were degrading American labor standards by accepting lower wages, working longer hours, and allowing themselves to be used as strike breakers. Labor leaders also found it hard to unionize people who spoke so many strange and different languages.

These hostilities and fears led to anti-immigrant movements that bore various names—the United Order of Deputies, the American League, the Red, White, and Blue, and so on. In San Francisco during the depression of the 1870s, white workingmen organized against the Chinese, and for a brief time mobs ruled the streets. The political pressure exerted then convinced Congress to pass the Chinese Exclusion Act in 1882, by which Chinese workingmen were denied entry to the country along with idiots, lunatics, and criminals. Perhaps the most powerful anti-immigrant group was the American Protective Association, organized in 1887 to rally Americans for a fight against Catholicism. It grew with startling rapidity after the onset of the Panic of 1893 and stirred hostilities that would affect American society for decades to come.

This influx created acute problems in the cities. Too many people moved in too rapidly, and wretchedness resulted. There were too many to be housed, too many for water or sewage or transportation facilities to accommodate, too many for the police and fire departments to look after. For employers seeking cheap labor, the situation was splendid, and so it was for the middle-class family looking for servants. An amazing number of ordinary American households had live-in maids and cooks. For others, however, urban living was a horror. In 1890 the immigrant journalist Jacob Riis published his shocking report on New York's slums, *How the Other Half Lives*. It was in part upon this "other half" that the vast fortunes of the Gilded Age were built.

"Survival of the Fittest"

THE SHOCK OF DARWINISM

A very strong influence on Americans in the Gilded Age was the theory of evolution set forth by Charles Darwin in his *Origin of Species*,

Charles Darwin (*Library of Congress*)

published in 1859 and soon applied to social and economic life by English philosopher Herbert Spencer. According to Darwin's theory, all complex forms of plant and animal life, including human beings, had evolved over a long period of time from lower organisms. In the process there had been a natural selection of those individual organisms best adapted to survive in their environment. Thus there was "survival of the fittest," with the strong and hardy surviving and the weak falling by the wayside.

Darwin's theory of evolution directly challenged the Biblical story of creation and, according to Sigmund Freud, severely wounded the self-love of human beings when they learned that the presumed gulf between themselves and lower forms of life did not really exist. The new biology of the nineteenth century, wrote Jacques Barzun, a leading cultural historian, "seemingly made final the separation between man and his soul." Naturally such a theory and such a trauma provoked considerable debate among Gilded Age Americans, especially scientists, theologians, and clergymen.

SOCIAL DARWINISM

Spencer's theory, applying Darwin's biological theory to economic and social life, was invaluable to the new industrial order because it seemed to justify the acquisition of wealth and power and gave an explanation of why some became wealthy while others stayed poor. Spencer maintained that evolution was leading inevitably to a society in which people would enjoy "the greatest perfection and the most complete happiness," and that competitive struggle was the natural means whereby this would come about. The weak would fall by the wayside, while the strong and able would push forward.

The new doctrine thus opposed poor relief, housing regulations, and public education and justified poverty and slums. Any governmental attempt to alter the situation would be interfering with natural law and impeding progress. The poor were poor because they were the "less fit," and any attempt to help them was fighting nature and a waste of time. The Christian equivalent was "casting pearls before swine." Thus, any government efforts to help the poor, in general, or blacks (the poorest), in particular, were doomed to failure because those on the societal "bottom" were there due to natural forces that could not be resisted.

Spencer's ideas were especially attractive to American businessmen, who could thus feel that they themselves were the finest flower of evolution. Of his first reading of Spencer, Andrew Carnegie exclaimed, "I remembered that light came in as a flood and all was clear. Not only had I got rid of theology and the supernatural, but I had found the truth of evolution."

Spencer enjoyed a great vogue in the United States from 1870 to 1890. Numbered among his many devoted American followers were Edward Livingston Youmans and John Fiske, who spread the gospel of Social Darwinism all over the country through magazine articles, popular books, and lectures. Such leading universities as Harvard, Johns Hopkins, and Yale included the Spencerian philosophy in courses on religion, biology, and social science.

Spencer's most influential American disciple was William Graham Sumner, who taught sociology and political economy at Yale from 1872 until his death in 1910. Sumner vigorously supported economic individualism and hailed the millionaires as products of natural selection. He scornfully derided reformers and their programs to protect the weak. He ridiculed democracy as the "pet superstition of the age" and repudiated the idea of human equality.

LAISSEZ-FAIRE

Much of the reasoning of Social Darwinism was found in the other dominant theory of the times, laissez-faire, which included ideas of the classical economists going back as far as Adam Smith's *Wealth of Nations* (1776). Beyond what was necessary to maintain law and order and to protect life and property, the government was not to interfere in the conduct of business or in personal matters. According to this view, those pursuing their business interests free of government meddling would achieve the best possible use of resources, would promote steady economic progress, and would be rewarded, all according to their desserts. Acquisition of wealth was considered evidence of merit, for did not wealth come as a result of frugality, industriousness, and sagacity? Poverty carried the stigma

In the Ladder of Fortune, 1875, by Currier and Ives individual choice is seen as key. *(Library of Congress)*

of worthlessness, for did it not result from idleness and wastefulness? During most of the late nineteenth century these attitudes prevailed in America and were upheld by prominent educators, editors, clergymen, and economists.

Somewhat paradoxically, philanthropy also was expected to play a part in the behavior of those who were successful in business. They were expected to be humanitarian and to relieve distress but were forbidden by the dictates of Social Darwinism from offering any aid that might undermine self-reliance, initiative, and ambition. Andrew Carnegie's *The Gospel of Wealth* (1889) offered the solution to this dilemma. While asserting that wealth must necessarily be concentrated in the hands of the few, Carnegie also set forth the maxim that the man who dies rich dies disgraced. The duty of the man of wealth, he maintained, was to administer his surplus funds as a trust to yield the greatest value to the community. Funds should be given, for example, to help found public libraries, improve education, and promote world peace. To support a needy individual, on the other hand, was wrong. Carnegie argued that every person maintained by charity was a source of moral infection to the community. He asserted that of every 1,000 dollars spent for poor relief 950 would better be thrown into the sea.

INDUSTRIALISM AND RELIGION

PROTESTANTISM AND DARWINISM

The churches had to adapt themselves to industrialism and the challenge of Darwinism. This proved to be difficult for the Protestant churches. Most Protestants considered the Bible to be the supreme authority and had closely identified their ethics with the economic individualism of the middle class. The Darwinian theory of evolution, however, undermined confidence in the authority of the Bible, and the concentration of power and the wealth of a few weakened the belief in the virtues of economic individualism.

In the 80s and 90s, however, an increasing number of Protestant clergymen accepted the theory of evolution and reconciled it with their religious beliefs. Henry Ward Beecher, for instance, one of the most celebrated preachers of the time, declared in his *Evolution and Religion* (1885) that evolution was merely "the deciphering of God's thought as revealed in the structure of the world." A few clergymen went beyond this to deny some of the supernatural events in Christianity. This alarmed the Protestant "fundamentalists," who reasserted their literal belief in the supreme authority of the Bible as the only solid foundation for religious faith. A struggle ensued between the fundamentalists and the liberals.

Throughout the Gilded Age most Protestant clergymen believed that the existing economic order was just. For instance, Beecher condemned the eight-hour day (as not enough work), insisted that poverty was a sign of sin, and advocated the use of force, if necessary, to put down strikes. Beecher, the younger brother of Harriet

Beecher Stowe, argued that poverty was the result of the "improvidence of laborers who squandered their wages on tobacco." Beecher further argued, "No man in this country suffers from poverty unless it be more than his fault—unless it be his sin." Commenting in 1877 on the sharp wage cuts suffered by railway workers, Beecher concluded:

> It is said that a dollar a day is not enough for a wife and five or six children. NO, not if the man smokes or drinks beer. ... But is not a dollar a day enough to buy bread with? Water costs nothing; and a man who cannot live on bread is not fit to live.

Beecher and other clergymen like him were unconcerned with the social causes of poverty, certain that poverty was an act of God and the result of sin. Perhaps Beecher and other clergymen like him were conservative because wealthy businessmen in their congregations made heavy contributions to church funds. In any case, the conservative sentiments of many of the clergy and their lack of sympathy for the workers' demands caused a drop in working-class attendance in the churches.

THE SOCIAL GOSPEL

In the 1880s a few socially conscious Protestant clergymen took issue with Beecher' five teachings on current economic questions and began to preach the Social Gospel, which focused on improving living conditions and feeding "God's children" rather than upon saving souls. The basic idea was that tending to the physical needs of the poor was God's work, and sin and decadence in the urban areas could be reduced through meeting the physical needs of the poor. Social Gospel preachers advocated civil service reform and the end of corruption in politics, child labor regulation, regulation of big corporations and monopolies, and graduated income taxes, especially taxes on large inheritances. They insisted that the problems created by industrialism could be solved only by a universal application of the teachings of Christ, and in particular his admonitions to help the poor. Among the chief exponents of the Social Gospel were Josiah Strong, Washington Gladden, Dwight L. Moody, Charles M. Sheldon, and Walter Rauschenbusch. In his writings and sermons Gladden upheld the right of labor to organize and strike, and he recommended that industrial disputes be eliminated by an "industrial partnership" that would allow workers to receive "a fixed share" of industry's profits. Gladden espoused the idea of government ownership of public utilities and factory inspection laws although he rejected socialism as a system. Other Social Gospel preachers, however, such as William D. P. Bliss of Boston, believed in welfare state capitalism or socialism and government relief programs designed to aid the urban poor. Walter Rauschenbusch, for example, severely censured industrial capitalism as a "mammonistic organization with which Christianity can never be content." Moody evangelized in the urban slums and urged people to cast aside sin in the inner cities. Moody founded schools in the urban slums and provided recreational facilities for the poor in hopes that people would abandon their sinful ways and adopt the ways of Jesus. Charles M. Sheldon, in his novel *In His Steps,* asked the simple question, "What would Jesus do?" before deciding on any course of action. The inference of Sheldon's work, however, was that Jesus would be engaged in helping the less fortunate.

THE CATHOLIC VIEW

The position of the Catholic Church on evolution was that the hypothesis had to stop short of human beings. The attitude of the Church toward social reform was more negative than positive, more tolerating than approving. Only in part was the hierarchy moved by considerations of justice and charity. James Cardinal Gibbons, Archbishop of Baltimore, insisted that Catholics cultivate a patriotic citizenship in keeping with the nation's civil institutions and customs. Gibbons asserted, "The accusation of being un-American—that is to say, alien to our national spirit—is the most powerful weapon which the enemies of the Church can employ against her." Only in this sense—as an aspect of Americanization—did the Catholic Church display any marked interest in social reform before the second decade of the twentieth century.

Archbishop John Ireland of St. Paul minimized the economic problems of the time and advocated only temperance and conservative trade unionism. In 1903 he said publicly, "I have no fear of greater fortunes in the hands of individuals, nor of vast aggregations of capital in the hands of corporations." Ireland's friendship with President McKinley and with James J. Hill, the railroad builder, brought him under the criticism of reformers. Yet he often expressed strong sympathy for organized labor, saying on one occasion, "Until their material condition is improved it is futile to speak to them of spiritual life and duties."

Through its indifference to social reform, the Church jeopardized its hold on the loyalty of its communicants. Catholics in large numbers lost interest in a church that seemed indifferent, if not hostile, to

Pope Leo XIII (*Library of Congress*)

movements promoting their economic welfare. As the Church began to lose members to Protestantism and socialism, it developed a greater interest in social problems. Also helping to change the Church's attitude was Pope Leo XIII's famous encyclical *De Rerum Novarum* (1891), which condemned the exploitation of labor and asserted that it was the duty of the state to bring social justice. The Pope condemned the excesses of capitalism, including what he termed as the "greed of unchecked competition," and defended the right of workers to form unions and stressed the obligation of governments to care for the poor. According to Pope Leo, workers were entitled to wages that would guarantee their families a reasonable, frugal comfort; workers did not sin by seeking government assistance in obtaining a living wage.

IDEALISM

Perhaps in response to the horrifying bloodshed of the Civil War or perhaps to the stresses and strains of the new urban industrial order—or both—there was an outpouring of creativity among American philosophers in the Gilded Age. From the 1870s on probably the most important new influence on philosophy was German idealism, particularly as expressed by Georg Wilhelm Friedrich Hegel (1770–1831). Hegel viewed the whole course of history as the working out of divine purpose by certain general laws of nature, culminating in the achievement of perfect freedom. But Hegelianism, however, rationalized existing conditions, and what Hegel meant by freedom was very different from the traditional American conception. Hegel's philosophy glorified the state and taught that individuals could be free only by subordinating themselves to their national government and to their social institutions.

The idealist movement was strongest in New England, where its leaders were Josiah Royce of Harvard and C. E. Garman of Amherst but the idealist awakening was evident also at such universities as California, Columbia, Cornell, Johns Hopkins, Michigan, and Princeton. The idealists believed in the priority of the mind over matter and in the fundamental unity of the universe, but they modified these concepts to support American individualism.

AMERICAN PRAGMATISM

Meanwhile a school of philosophy more distinctively American and opposed to idealism was growing in popularity. Pragmatism, unlike most earlier philosophies, did not offer theories about God and the universe. It presented instead a way of evaluating acts and ideas in terms of their consequences in concrete experience. Pragmatism says that we cannot reject any hypothesis if consequences useful to life flow from it. The pragmatist's decision regarding the truth or falsity of an idea, then, is based on experiential test: One decides whether an idea is true or false by seeing whether it works. This concept was closely associated with two ideas that had gained wide currency in American thought—the idea of progress through evolution, and the idea of truth obtained through scientific investigation. The forerunners of pragmatism were Chauncey Wright and Charles S. Peirce, but two other men, William James and, later, John Dewey, developed it.

William James, philosopher and psychologist at Harvard, rejected Spencerian determinism, which afforded no place for chance or human will. He upheld the independence of the mind and "the right to believe at our own risk any hypothesis that is live enough to tempt our will." At times he was inclined to suggest that if someone felt happier or behaved better as a result of believing some idea, that idea should be regarded as true. While James repudiated absolutes, however, he also spoke out against a skepticism that would inhibit impulsively generous commitment. He distrusted all general laws and abstractions that denied the human capacity for free action. James contended that a person's decisions would influence the course of events and that, in spite of the existence of God, good or evil would result from human device and intelligence.

In his *Principles of Psychology* (1890), James made the first important American contribution to the scientific study of the mind. In later books he expounded his views on pragmatism. Theories to him were "instruments, not answers to enigmas." Pragmatism "has no dogmas, and no doctrines save its method," and that was a method for reaching the truth.

"The true is the name of whatever proves to be good in the way of belief," James said, "and good, too, for definite, assignable reasons."

Oliver Wendell Holmes (*Library of Congress*)

Such views were a sharp departure from nearly all the philosophies and religions of the past, and they captivated many Americans; yet they also laid James open to the charge that pragmatism was simply another name for expedience: Anything is good that works.

THE NEW LEGAL THEORY

There was also a revolt against formalism in law. The preceding generation had regarded the law as fixed and unchanging and as a standard measure that the judge simply applied to the question at hand like a yardstick. However, a new school of legal theorists arose following the reasoning of Oliver Wendell Holmes, son of the poet of the same name and friend of William James, that law should be based on changing social needs or political policies rather than simply upon logic or precedent. "It is revolting," said Holmes, "to have no better reason for a rule of law than that it was laid down in the time of Henry I. It is still more revolting if the grounds upon which it was laid down have vanished long since, and the rule simply persists from blind imitation of the past." The new school of theorists went on to contend that the meaning of any general legal principle must always be judged by its practical effects.

CHALLENGES TO DARWINISM AND LAISSEZ-FAIRE

REFORM DARWINISM

In the 1880s a number of sociologists and economists revolted against the fatalism and lack of social responsibility of Social Darwinism. These "reform Darwinists" accepted evolution but maintained that societies could command their own destinies and that human intelligence applied to social problems could improve the existing system.

A leader among the dissenters was Lester Ward, a largely self-educated sociologist. He came from a poor family in Illinois, endured privations in his early life, worked in factories, fought in the Civil War, and for many years was a government official. When he was 65, Ward became Professor of Sociology at Brown University, where he taught "A Survey of All Knowledge." His ideas were first presented in his *Dynamic Sociology* (1883) but were more readable in *The Psychic Factors of Civilization* (1893). Ward believed that a laissez-faire economic system did not necessarily advance human progress, and he advocated state management and social planning.

Younger professors of sociology—such as Albion Small of Illinois, Charles Horton Cooley of Michigan, and Edward Allsworth of Wisconsin—seconded Ward's assault on Social Darwinism. Contrary to Spencer's notion that society was composed of separate individuals operating independently of one another, they asserted that social institutions, which were amenable to social control, shaped each individual personality. In *Sin and Society* (1907) Ross argued that in the new industrial society morality required the impersonal corporation to accept full responsibility for its antisocial acts. Followers of Spencer and Sumner declined in numbers and influence in the universities. In 1906 the American Sociological Society was founded and Ward was its first president. His ideas on government social planning eventually came to be very influential in American social thinking.

THE NEW ECONOMISTS

Similarly, the viewpoint of economists changed. In the mid-1880s, a new group of scholars, many of whom had been trained in German universities, began to challenge laissez-faire sentiments. In 1885 they founded the American Economic Association, which boldly declared that the state was "an agency whose positive assistance is one of the indispensable conditions of human progress" and that "the doctrine of laissez-faire is unsafe in politics and unsound in morals." Among the leaders of this revolt were Richard T. Ely of Johns Hopkins University and the University of Wisconsin, Simon Nelsen Patten of the University of Pennsylvania, John R. Commons of the University of Wisconsin, and Wesley C. Mitchell of Columbia University. Although they differed in their economic and political programs, they all dissented from the classical belief in absolute economic laws valid for all societies. They insisted that society, constantly changing, had to be examined in terms of process and growth. Using the historical approach to study economic realities, they discovered that there were great differences between what actually had happened and what, according to classical economics, was supposed to have happened. In recent years, it should be noted, there have been challenges to these theorists from conservative economists and social thinkers.

THORSTEIN VEBLEN

The leading academic rebel was Thorstein Veblen. Born in Wisconsin of Norwegian immigrants and educated at Yale and Johns Hopkins, he taught at Chicago, Stanford, and Missouri. Veblen bitterly assailed what he called the "kept classes" and their "pecuniary" society. He derided the idea that the wealthy leisure class was the most biologically fit and millionaires were a product of natural selection. Veblen argued that the millionaire was not responsible for the creation of the industrial technology but rather had taken possession of the wealth produced by the skill and labor of other people. In his most widely read book, *The Theory of the Leisure Class* (1899), and a number of other volumes Veblen analyzed the role of the upper class in American society. Although he had little popular appeal, he wielded a great deal of influence among subsequent intellectuals, particularly after the Great Depression of 1929.

REFORMERS

Outside of academic circles, increasing numbers of radical reformers began to attack the existing social and economic system and to propose new plans for economic organization. They, too, rejected Spencer's fatalism and the idea that progress resulted from the struggle for existence and the consequent removal of the unfit.

The most important of these reformers was Henry George. Born in Philadelphia, he moved to San Francisco as a young man and for 20 years watched a frontier society become transformed into a wealthy and class-stratified society. What was the cause of the imbalance that deepened the poverty of the masses and increased the wealth of a few? George believed the explanation lay in the inequities of private land ownership that allowed landowners to enrich themselves solely through the rise of real-estate values. Land took on value not because of anything the owner did but because people lived on it. George maintained that the unearned increment, instead of going to private individuals, ought to be taken by the government in the form of a "single tax" on land values. This would make other taxes and other forms of government intervention unnecessary, leave individual enterprise otherwise free, and promote "the Golden Age of which poets have sung and high-raised seers have told us in metaphor!"

George set forth his theories in *Progress and Poverty* (1879) and found a wide audience both in the United States and abroad. He spent the rest of his life working for the single tax program and continued to develop his theme in subsequent books. In addition, he edited a newspaper, gave many speeches, and came close to being elected mayor of New York City in 1886. George's ideas influenced virtually every reformer for years to come, and they still have appeal as a practical way to change the social system.

Somewhat more radical than George's program was that of his contemporary Edward Bellamy. Rejecting both classical economics and the fatalism of the Social Darwinists, Bellamy concentrated his attack on the free-enterprise system itself. He attacked excessive individualism, private monopoly, and competition, characterizing the latter as "sheer madness, a scene from bedlam" and the price system as "an education in self-seeking at the expense of others." He assailed the "imbecility of the system of private enterprise" and the callousness of industrialists, who "maim and slaughter [their] workers by thousands."

In his utopian novel *Looking Backward* (1888), Bellamy portrayed an ideal community in the year 2000 whose beauty and tranquility contrasted sharply with the ugly industrial towns of his day. In this utopia the government owned all the means of production, and material rewards were shared equally by everyone. At least 500,000 copies of the book were sold. Bellamy called his system "Nationalism," and "Nationalist" clubs sprang up to spread the new faith. "Nationalist" magazines advocated public ownership of railroads and utilities, civil service reform, and government aid to education. This served to renew interest in socialism and caused Americans to consider socialist ideas and programs. Both George and Bellamy, however, rejected Marxian socialism.

George regarded Karl Marx as "the prince of muddleheads," and Bellamy maintained that American Marxists were really in the pay of the "great monopolists,"

Karl Marx *(Library of Congress)*

employed by them "to wave the red flag and talk about burning, sacking, and blowing people up, in order, by alarming the timid, to head off any real reforms."

Young social reformers seeking a way to refute Social Darwinism were influenced by the ideas of the reform Darwinists and of reformers like George and Bellamy. They were also influenced by the social-justice movement that had its roots in European, especially English, reform movements. Nearly every leading English reformer had visited the country, and many young American progressives and reformers came under their influence. Implicit in all these new ideas and ferment was the vision of a life of service, thus conducing toward the ideal of social work as a way young reformers could serve society. Jane Addams of Chicago's Hull House became a leading symbol in this country of these social reformers and their work. She had visited Toynbee Hall in the slums of London, and when she returned to the United States in 1889, she established Hull House, a slum-relief center in Chicago. Her experiences at Hull House showed her that people could become stronger and learn to deal with adversity. Thus she began to reject Social Darwinism. Hull House served its immediate neighborhood, but it also became a center of creative thinking about social issues because many of the most brilliant men and women of the day spent brief periods of time in residence there.

Also involved in the social justice movement was the Salvation Army, which had come from England at the end of the nineteenth century. The Salvation Army offered assistance as well as religion, as did the clergy of various faiths now working in the slums. Joining in the movement, too, were middle-class and upper-class women, who had begun to join a variety of socially-oriented organizations and were pushing not only for the ballot and legal equality for themselves (the suffrage movement will be discussed in detail in Chapter 4) but also for reforms on behalf of children, working women, and Indians. (See "*Helen Hunt Jackson: Crusader for the Indian*".)

SOCIALISM

Bellamy and other reformers avoided the word socialism not only because they found it distasteful but also because they realized that in the United States it was often identified with anarchism and communism, labels that frightened most Americans. The first socialist political parties in this country appeared in New York, Philadelphia, Chicago, St. Louis, Milwaukee, and other large cities in the years immediately following the Civil War. In the beginning, most American socialists, like their European counterparts, were followers of Karl

Marx. Seeking to develop a revolutionary spirit among American workers, these socialists urged workers to "offer an armed resistance to the invasions by the capitalist class and capitalist legislatures" and exhorted them to overthrow American capitalism by "energetic, relentless, revolutionary and international action."

A National Labor Reform party was organized in 1868 with a platform declaring that "our government is wholly perverted from its true design. ... [The] mass of the people have no supply beyond their daily wants and are compelled ... to become paupers and vagrants." These appeals were too radical for the masses of wage earners and found only a small receptive audience among them. The National Labor Reform party's presidential candidate in 1868 polled fewer than 30,000 votes.

In 1877, a Socialist Labor party was formed. Marxian doctrines were the basis of its program, and recent European immigrants provided most of its members. The party's purpose was not to reform but to revolutionize the industrial order. It blamed the plight of the masses on the concentration of economic power in private hands, and it advocated having all the basic means of production run by the government in democratic association with the workers. For some years the Socialist Labor party avoided regular political activities and instead attempted to bore its way into control of the labor federations. The leaders of post–Civil War unionism, however, successfully opposed the efforts of socialists to control labor and rejected their radical solutions to economic and social problems.

Eventually, in the 1890s, the splintered factions of the Socialist Labor party united under the leadership of Daniel De Leon, who became known as "the socialist pope." Born on the island of Curacao and educated in Germany, De Leon had come to the United States, where he studied law and taught for a short time at Columbia College. A brilliant orator and pamphleteer, he became a champion of Marxism and took a militant stand against traditional trade unionism. He derided the American Federation of Labor as "a cross between a windbag and a rope of sand" and called its founder, Samuel Gompers, "a labor faker" and "a greasy tool of Wall Street."

De Leon urged all workers to join an independent political movement that would win control of the government and establish "a socialist or co-operative commonwealth, whereby the instruments of production shall be made the property of the whole people." In 1892, however, the Socialist Labor presidential ticket polled only 22,000 votes and in the next election only 34,000. The party was too foreign in its makeup and too radical in its program to attract wide support. To offset some of this deficiency, a rival organization,

PEOPLE THAT MADE A DIFFERENCE

Helen Hunt Jackson: Crusader for the Indian

One of the most influential champions of the Indian during the late nineteenth century was the writer Helen Hunt Jackson Her biting criticism of federal Indian policy in A Century of Dishonor (1881) and her sentimental novel Ramona (1884) presented the classic statement of American injustice toward the Indian and aroused the national conscience. Described by some of her contemporaries as "the most brilliant, impetuous, and thoroughly individual woman of her time," she is, ironically, almost forgotten today.

Helen Hunt Jackson *(Library of Congress)*

She was born Helen Maria Fiske on October 13, 1830 in Amherst, Massachusetts, the daughter of Nathan Welby and Deborah (Vinal) Fiske. A professor of Latin, Greek, and philosophy at Amherst College, her father was also a Congregational minister and author. Her mother, a Bostonian, also wrote. Helen had two brothers, who died in infancy, and a sister, Anne. Her mother died when she was 14 and her father three years later, leaving Helen in the care of an aunt. But her father had given her a good education at the well-known Ipswich (Massachusetts) Female Seminary and the private school of Reverend J. S. C. Abbott in New York City. She was a neighbor and schoolmate of Emily Dickinson, who would become one of America's great poets, and they remained lifelong friends.

In 1852, Helen married Army Captain Edward Bissell Hunt, brother of a former governor of New York. Helen's husband was an accomplished engineer officer and thus held high army rank. For the next 11 years she and her husband led the usual wandering life of a military family.

Then there were tragedies in store for her. Her first child, Murray, died of a brain disease in 1854, when he was only 11 months old. In 1863 her husband suffocated while experimenting with an underwater naval vessel he had designed. Two years later her other son, "Rennie," died of diphtheria. With her parents, husband, and sons dead, she was now alone.

Up to this time, Helen Hunt had shown no signs of literary ability. In 1866, she returned to Newport, Rhode Island, where she and her husband had once been stationed. For a while, she was interested in spiritualism and clairvoyance. After spending some time with Emily Dickinson and coming to know Thomas Wentworth Higginson, well-known author, soldier, and reformer, she decided to turn to a writing career.

She began to write travel sketches, children's stories, novels, poems, and essays under the pseudonyms "H. H." and "Saxe Holm," eventually writing over 30 books and hundreds of articles. The pseudonyms kept her from becoming more prominent. It was still the convention for women writers to conceal their authorship because respectable women were not supposed to play any public role. Only after she began to write her books about Indians did she use her full name. By that time she was perhaps the most productive woman writer in the country. In 1874 Ralph Waldo Emerson rated her "the greatest American woman poet" and placed her poetry above that of almost all American men.

In May 1872, Helen Hunt took a trip to California, and then, because of bronchial trouble, spent the winter of 1873–1874 at Colorado Springs, Colorado. There she met Pennsylvania Quaker William Sharpless Jackson, a wealthy banker and railroad manager, whom she married on October 22, 1875. Relieved of her financial concerns, she moved to Colorado. From that time on, the West and its Indians took up more and more of her attention.

During an 1879 visit to Boston, Helen Hunt Jackson heard a lecture by the Ponca chief, Standing Bear, about the sufferings of the dispossessed Plains Indians. This was a turning point in her life, and she began to champion the cause of Indians almost at once. Not only did she expose the government's mistreatment of Indians in her writings, but also she sent out petitions, wrote letters to newspapers, and endeavored to awaken public opinion on behalf of the Indians. Soon she was a reformer at war with government officials over their Indian policy.

Her book, A Century of Dishonor, published in 1881, is a powerful story of dispossession, broken treaties, crooked dealings, unfulfilled promises, and the federal government's inhumane treatment of the Indian tribes who were its powerless wards. The book caused a national sensation. An emotional and partisan book, it is not a balanced history but an impassioned plea on behalf of the Indian. At her own expense, she sent a copy to every member of Congress with the following words printed in red on the cover: "Look upon your hands! They are stained with the blood of your relations."

The impact of this book was so great that it has been called the Uncle Tom's Cabin of the Indian cause. Helen Hunt Jackson regarded herself as an "Indian Harriet Beecher Stowe," saying "If I can do one-hundredth for the Indians as Mrs. Stowe did for the Negro, I will be thankful." Within a year of her book's publication, the strong Indian Rights Association was created. In 1883 President Chester Arthur appointed Mrs. Jackson a Commissioner of Indian Affairs, and in 1887 the first comprehensive reform legislation for Indians was enacted in the Dawes Act, (Subsequent opinion has been very critical of this legislation, to be discussed more fully later).

Helen Hunt Jackson continued her fight for the Indian and also continued to be a prolific writer of poetry, novels, and essays until her death. Probably her best known fictional work is Ramona (1884), an idyllic account of the Indian past, which is set in California. In 1886, the North American Review called this book "unquestionably the best novel yet produced by an American woman," ranking it with Uncle Tom's Cabin as one of the two famous ethical novels of the century. Since then it has gone through hundreds of printings and countless stage and screen showings. Written as an act of conscience, it proved a boon to tourism in the Golden State since hordes of people wanted to see Ramona's supposed home.

Jackson also continued to have personal tragedy in her life. In June 1884, she suffered a severe fracture of her leg. Then she was transferred to a place in California that proved to be malarial. While confined there, a cancer developed. During all this period, "her sunny elasticity never failed," wrote one of her closest friends, "and within a fortnight of her death she wrote long letters, in clear and vigorous hand, expressing only cheerful hopes for the future." On August 12, 1885, she died and was interred temporarily in San Francisco. Later she was buried near the summit of Mount Jackson, Colorado, one of the Cheyenne peaks named in her honor, about four miles from Colorado Springs. Still later, to escape commercialism and the possible vandalism of the spot, her body was taken to Evergreen Cemetery at Colorado Springs, where it remains.

the Social Democratic party, was organized in 1896 by Eugene V. Debs, president of the American Railway Union. In 1901 the anti-De Leon group in the Socialist Labor party joined Debs to form the Socialist Party of America. In its heyday it won allegiance from hundreds of thousands of Americans, including those in the rural heartland as well as in the cities.

ACHIEVEMENTS OF THE GILDED AGE

Despite the obvious cultural excesses and the long list of social problems, intellectual and artistic developments of the Gilded Age were impressive. The original and creative thinkers of the 80s and the 90s made these two decades one of the most intellectually fertile periods in the whole of American history. In scholarship, the age saw the birth of two new social sciences: Lewis Henry Morgan founded anthropology and Lester Ward fathered American sociology. The period also witnessed a revolution in higher education. Until this time colleges and universities had concentrated on training ministers and lawyers, but now learning began to shake off its fetters and to range freely in the physical, natural, and social sciences, the arts, and the humanities.

The most famous of the daring new university presidents were Charles W. Eliot of Harvard and Daniel Coit Gilman of Johns Hopkins. At Harvard, Eliot greatly expanded the curriculum and sponsored the elective system, which had originated at the University of Virginia at the time of its founding. He also drastically reformed Harvard's medical and law schools and gave them true professional status. At Johns Hopkins, Gilman built the first great graduate school in America. The graduate school and the seminar method were introduced from Germany in the 1870s, and some graduate work was done at Harvard and Yale in that decade; but Johns Hopkins, designed primarily as a center for gradu-

Eugene V. Debs (*Library of Congress*)

ate work at its founding in 1876, took the lead in this field and held it for the next quarter of a century. At that time also, professional schools got under way—the Columbia School of Mines (1864), the Massachusetts Institute of Technology (1865), Stevens Institute (1871), and the Johns Hopkins Medical School (1893).

ARTS AND LETTERS

During the two or three decades following the Civil War, there developed a new realism in American literature, stimulated by Darwinism, the influence of European writers, and a reaction against the sentimentality—and the women writers—that had come to dominate the sales of fiction. An early manifestation of the trend was the regional short story. Bret Harte in the West, Hamlin Garland in the Midwest, George Washington Cable and Joel Chandler Harris in the South, and Sarah Orne Jewett in New England gave readers a fresh and exciting view of regional America.

In his own day Mark Twain (Samuel L. Clemens) was considered a regional author, but his novels, essays, and sketches have made a lasting reputation for him as a major figure in American literature. The materials for Twain's best narratives—*The Adventures of Tom Sawyer* (1876), *Life on the Mississippi* (1883), and *The Adventures of Huckleberry Finn* (1884)—were his boyhood home, Hannibal, Missouri, and the great Mississippi River that rolled before it. Along with many other writers of the period, he deplored the evils of crass materialism and ridiculed the get-rich-quick schemes of his money-mad countrymen. In *The Gilded Age,* for example, Twain and Charles Dudley Warner pointed out that sober industry and contentment with a modest income honestly earned are infinitely

Mark Twain (Samuel Langhorne Clemens)
(Library of Congress)

An 1885 lithograph by Joseph Keppler titled, *Mark Twain Lecturing* (Library of Congress)

preferable to frantic moneymaking schemes. Twain himself, however, tirelessly sought ways to increase his own wealth.

The growing social ills of the Gilded Age called forth specific indictments that became increasingly prominent in the realistic literature of the late nineteenth and early twentieth centuries. William Dean Howells, who by 1900 was considered by many young writers to be the dean of American letters, exhibited the grime and squalor of New York City in *A Hazard of New Fortunes* (1890). Stephen Crane's *Maggie: A Girl of the Streets* (1893) exposed the ugly life of New York's Bowery. Hamlin Garland in *Main-Travelled Roads* (1891) described the hardships and injustices suffered by farmers in Iowa and Wisconsin. While they emphasized the abuses of the new industrial order, however, writers were comparatively gentle in their treatment of the captains of industry. In Howells' *The Rise of Silas Lapham* (1884), for example, the author implied that the great majority of American financiers were honest—that "robber barons" were the exception, not the rule.

Even the much more subtle and sensitive novelist and literary critic Henry James (brother of psychologist William James), who lived abroad most of his life, presented American financiers as men of integrity and charm in several of his books. James' particular interest was the interaction of men and women—American and European—in sophisticated international society. *The American* (1877), *The Portrait of a Lady* (1881), and *The Ambassadors* (1903) present Americans that are morally superior to their more cultured European counterparts.

Because many poets—Bryant, Longfellow, Holmes, Lowell, Emerson, and Whittier—whose careers had begun in an earlier period continued to satisfy tastes after the war, much of American poetry showed remarkably few effects of the changing intellectual climate. By the end of the century American poets and prose writers were feeling its impact. For example, much of Stephen Crane's poetry inferred from the biological struggle for survival and the astronomical immensity of the universe that the individual is unimportant, a grim attitude congruent with European naturalism:

> A man said to the universe
>
> "Sir, I exist!"
>
> "However," replied the universe,
>
> "The fact has not created in me
>
> A sense of obligation."

The Gilded Age knew nothing of Emily Dickinson because only seven of her poems were published during her lifetime (1830–1886), but she is today considered one of the leading poets of the post–Civil War period. She began to write poetry in the mid-50s and continued until her death, but she spent the last half of her life as a recluse in Amherst, Massachusetts. Spare and unsentimental, her

Walt Whitman *(Library of Congress)*

poems constituted a new voice in American literature.

In striking contrast was Walt Whitman, whose revolutionary volume of poetry, *Leaves of Grass*, had been published in three editions before the Civil War and who continued to be an important figure in American poetry of the postwar period. Although many critics objected to his departures from the conventions of versification and to his frankness about sex, he became for many others the very voice of America—enthusiastic, optimistic, energetic, and free. His Quaker inheritance contributed to the independence, love and peace, and sense of brotherhood celebrated in so many of his works—among them *Drum Taps* (1866), a volume of poems recounting the experiences and suffering shared by both North and South, and the richest account of the Civil War to be found in our poetry.

Increasing wealth and leisure time after the Civil War contributed to a new awareness of art among Americans. The work of the artists George Inness, Thomas Eakins, Winslow Homer, and Albert Pinkham Ryder was of such high caliber that some might call the Gilded Age the most important era in American painting. Inness pioneered a new landscape school. Homer and Eakins were the leading American representatives of the naturalistic movement in painting. Homer grounded his art in direct observation of nature, while Eakins depicted ordinary middle-class city life of the United States in the late nineteenth century. Ryder, haunted throughout his life by the sea, was the most original Romantic of his time. Two American expatriates, James McNeill Whistler and John Singer Sargent, both of whom lived most of their lives in London, enjoyed international reputations—Whistler for his muted, poetic compositions, Sargent as the most sought-after portraitist of the Anglo-Saxon world. A third expatriate artist, Mary Cassatt, the sister of a railroad executive, settled in Paris and exhibited with the great French Impressionists.

Although in architecture the Gilded Age has been said to mark the low point in taste, fine and outstanding architects did exist. Henry Hobson Richardson and Louis H. Sullivan were the first major architects to meet the demands of industrialism upon their art. To these men, buildings had a sociological function as well as an artistic one. In his *Autobiography of an Idea,* Sullivan wrote, "masonry construction was a thing of the past ... (and) the old ideas of superimposition must give way before a sense of vertical continuity." For a number of architects it was a golden age. The rich commissioned them to design giant urban residences, baronial country homes, and great stone "cottages" on the shore. The imitation French chateaus and Italian palaces were sometimes ugly and often absurd, but gifted and imaginative architects like Richard Morris Hunt put the limitless funds of their patrons to good use.

THE CHAUTAUQUA MOVEMENT

There was a mass desire for knowledge in the Gilded Age, and various efforts were made to meet the demand. Most successful of these ventures was the Chautauqua movement, founded in 1874 by Lewis Miller, an Ohio businessman, and John H. Vincent, a Methodist minister. The two-week summer course they organized for a few Sunday-school teachers at Lake Chautauqua in New York proved to be such an enjoyable experience for those who attended that the word spread and within a few years thousands from all parts of the country were coming to Lake Chautauqua. The Chautauqua movement, like the earlier Lyceum Movement, expanded its activities. The founders broadened their range of instruction to include such subjects as economics, government, science, and literature. During the years of Chautauqua's greatest popularity, eminent authorities, including some of the Presidents of the period, gave talks to open-air audiences on every subject conceivable. In addition, the Chautauqua Literary and Scientific Reading Circle was organized and became a national society. This organization provided correspondence courses leading to a diploma. Textbooks were written for the program, and a monthly magazine, the *Chautauquan,* was published. According to the Reverend Vincent, the program was formulated to give "the college outlook" to those who did not have a higher education.

Because the Chautauqua movement was so successful, various imitators appeared. By 1900 there were about 200 Chautauqua-type organizations. Most were of a more commercial character but were designed to satisfy the same craving for self-culture. They furnished a varied fare of music, humor, and inspirational lectures and probably provided more entertainment than enlightenment for those who attended.

The Chautauqua movement and its imitators helped popularize information that earlier had been the property of experts only. Too, thousands of Americans who sought cultural and intellectual improvement probably felt rewarded by many of the programs, and perhaps their interests were broadened.

From all contemporary accounts, Americans of the Gilded Age pursued diverse cultural interests. They listened to lectures, went to museums, plays, and circuses, sought more education at Chautauqua institutes, sat through religious revival meetings, and began to watch new phenomena such as baseball and football. In all this they had a sense of assurance and optimism that would begin to decline as the Gilded Age neared its close. We now turn to an account, in more depth, of the era's big business.

THE AGE OF BIG BUSINESS, 1865–1900

(Library of Congress)

THE AMERICAN INDUSTRIAL REVOLUTION

THE EFFECT OF THE CIVIL WAR

It has been customary to credit the Civil War with a major role in bringing about the Industrial Revolution through the great impetus that it supposedly gave to the growth of manufacturing in the North. In fact, the Civil War was fought amidst a long-term trend of industrial and technological growth and may have retarded American industrial development, because growth rates slowed during the conflict. Between 1839 and 1899 total output for commodities, including agricultural products, increased 11 fold, or at an average rate per decade of slightly less than 50 percent. Growth rates, however, varied widely from decade to decade. The 1840s and 1880s were periods of considerably more rapid advance than the 1850s, 1860s, and 1870s, and the lowest level of industrial growth occurred during the decade of the Civil War.

Nevertheless, the government gave strong encouragement to entrepreneurs during the Civil War. The Republican Party, seeking the votes of businessmen in the 1860 campaign, promised them favorable legislation, and once in power, the Republicans carried out their pledges and through tariff, railway, banking, and immigration legislation that created conditions suitable for industrial capitalism.

THE POST–CIVIL WAR BOOM

A number of factors were responsible for the post–Civil War industrial boom. The United States possessed bountiful raw materials, and the government was willing to turn them over to industry for little or no money. Coupled with the abundance of natural resources and continuing technological progress was a home market steadily expanding through immigration and a high birthrate. Both capital and labor were plentiful. The increase in trade and manufacturing in the Northeast in the years before the war produced an accumulation of savings while additional millions of dollars came from European investors. Furthermore, from 1860 to 1900, unbroken waves of millions of European immigrants provided American industry with workers as well as with customers.

THE ROLE OF GOVERNMENT IN BUSINESS

One factor in the growth of industrialism was the continuation of the government's friendly attitude toward big business. The protective tariff—beginning with the Morrill Tariff of 1861 and expanded by the McKinley bill of 1890, the Wilson-Gorman law of 1894, and the Dingley Tariff of 1897—allowed American manufacturers to charge high prices without fear of foreign competition. The national banking system, adherence to the gold standard, and the financial policies pursued by the Treasury Department resulted in a currency deflation that benefited creditors over debtors. Businesses also received grants of land and of natural resources. While these measures can be considered a sign of governmental favoritism toward business at the expense of farmers and labor unions, they can also be seen as a way to encourage economic growth, a traditional policy of American government since the days of the Federalists. For example, over the years, the railroads were granted over 180 million acres of federal land (in other words, an area of acreage larger than the state of Texas). The railroads then reaped huge profits by selling the land to settlers who purchased land in the West along the rail lines.

Equally friendly to the development of business was the lax public control of it. There were few investigations of business practices, no legislation to protect consumers, and few effective regulatory commissions or laws. Businessmen knew that almost any action could be justified by the doctrines of Social Darwinism and laissez-faire, and most Americans in the Gilded Age considered governmental regulation of business to be unnecessary, unjust, and even immoral. Even reformers felt that governmental regulation of business should be confined to those cases where it was clearly necessary and where a careful study had been made. With cheerful inconsistency, the business leaders who championed laissez-faire welcomed governmental intervention in the economy in the form of tariffs, grants, and subsidies—measures that clearly violated laissez-faire doctrine. The down sides of laissez faire, however, were corporate corruption, worker exploitation, unsafe consumer products, and rampant degradation of the environment. For example, after the discovery of the Comstock silver mine at Virginia City, Nevada, the mining companies cut down every tree at Lake Tahoe for the timber needed to build mine shafts. Laissez faire also meant that the inevitable economic recessions were especially harsh since there were no social safety nets such as unemployment insurance or worker's compensation insurance; and the Social Darwinist outlook dictated that efforts to help the poor were doomed to

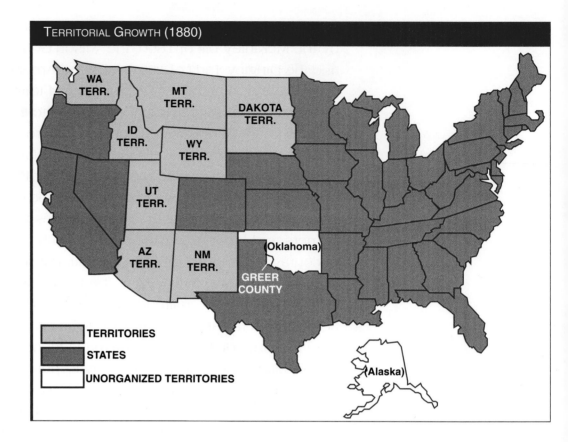

TERRITORIAL GROWTH (1880)

WA TERR.

MT TERR.

DAKOTA TERR.

ID TERR.

WY TERR.

UT TERR.

AZ TERR.

NM TERR.

(Oklahoma)

GREER COUNTY

(Alaska)

TERRITORIES

STATES

UNORGANIZED TERRITORIES

failure because the poverty itself proved that the poor and unemployed were naturally inferior. Any effort to help them was, therefore, akin to "casting pearls before swine."

John D. Rockefeller perhaps best summed up the prevailing Social Darwinist attitude when he told a YMCA group in Cleveland that "the growth of a large business is merely a survival of the fittest," and that like the growth of a beautiful rose, "the early buds which grow up around it" must be sacrificed. This situation, according to Rockefeller, was not anything to be corrected, but "merely the working out of a law of nature and a law of God."

THE ROLE OF THE COURTS

Also beneficial to the growth of business was the protection given by the Supreme Court in its interpretation of the Fourteenth Amendment. This amendment, added to the Constitution in 1868, was presumably designed to safeguard the newly emancipated blacks. The original intent of the amendment, however, somehow disappeared, and it became instead a refuge for private enterprise.

In its first section the Fourteenth Amendment declares: "No state shall make or enforce any law which shall abridge the privileges or immunities of citizens of the United States; nor shall any state deprive any person of life, liberty, or property, without due process of law." The purpose, of course, was to overturn the last vestiges of the Dred Scott Decision and grant equal citizenship rights to the former slaves. In the first postwar cases involving the question of governmental regulation of business, however, the Court interpreted this "due process" clause in favor of the state governments. In the Slaughterhouse Cases of 1873, involving a Louisiana law that granted a monopoly of the slaughterhouse business in New Orleans to one corporation, the Court declared the law to be a legitimate exercise of the police powers of a state to protect its citizens. The Court also significantly weakened the federal government's ability to protect black Americans under the Fourteenth Amendment by making a distinction between national and state citizenship. The Court ruled that the Fourteenth Amendment protected only those rights that stemmed from the federal government under the United States Constitution, such as the right to vote in federal elections. Most rights, however, remained the jurisdiction of the states, thus severely limiting federal protections of the rights of all Americans, but especially those of former slaves.

Even when the Supreme Court ruled against big business, as in *Munn v. Illinois* (1877) where the Court approved an Illinois law that fixed maximum storage rates for grain elevators on the grounds that a state could regulate "a business that is public in nature though privately owned and managed," the power of big business ensured that the ruling would not last long.

The *Munn v. Illinois* decision so alarmed American businessmen that some predicted the end of private property. Others believed that the only remedy lay in a constitutional amendment to protect business against state regulation. Then a change occurred in the make-up of the Court with the appointment of more conservative justices. The *Munn v. Illinois* decision was reversed by the Court in 1886 in *Wabash v. Illinois*, where the Court ruled that since railroads crossed state boundaries, they fell outside the realm of state jurisdiction and into the federal realm because Congress was granted the exclusive powers to regulate interstate commerce.

The end of the depression years of the mid-80s quieted demands from farmers, who had pushed for federal regulation of railroads and grain elevators; and a series of decisions beginning in the Santa Clara case of 1886 and culminating in *Smyth v. Ames* in 1898 made the Fourteenth Amendment into something quite new. In these cases the Court greatly broadened the interpretation of the amendment by holding that the word *person* in its first section meant corporations as well as individuals. Thus, corporations became "persons" under the law endowed with standing to sue while labor unions did not, thus giving corporations an edge in their legal battles with organized labor. The Court also widened the application of the "due process" clause (which had originally been intended only to prohibit confiscation of property or other arbitrary violations of individual rights) to invalidate any regulation that would prohibit a corporation from making a "reasonable" profit on its investment. Finally, the Court held that the courts and not the states should decide how much profit was reasonable. Thus it became corporations, rather than the former slaves, whose rights were protected by the Fourteenth Amendment.

With these last cases the Fourteenth Amendment had practically been rewritten. Businessmen who denounced the rule laid down in *Munn v. Illinois* found protection in the later decisions. Lower courts handed down injunctions that tied the hands of regulatory commissions, and the Supreme Court became the stronghold of laissez-faire.

THE RAILROAD AGE

The new industrialism could never have been possible without the tremendous expansion of the railroad systems in America. In fact, they played such a dominant role that the period could well be called

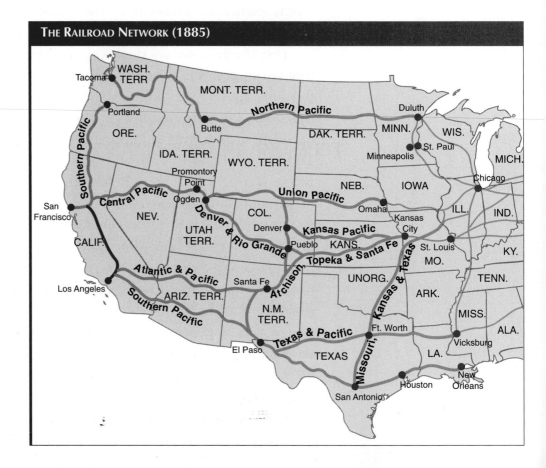

THE RAILROAD NETWORK (1885)

Pennsylvania Railroad in West Philadelphia *(Library of Congress)*

the railroad age. Between 1831 and 1861, 30,000 miles of railroad created a network connecting the Atlantic seaboard and the Mississippi valley. The war slowed down construction, but between 1867 and 1873 about 30,000 miles of railroad were added and during the 1880s a record-breaking 73,000 miles were constructed. In 1900 the American railroad system, extending into every section of the country, measured 193,000 miles. This represented 40 percent of the world's railroad mileage and was more than the mileage of all Europe combined. Railroad building increased more rapidly than the population. In 1865 there was one mile of track in operation for every 1,150 Americans. Twenty years later there was one mile for every 450. Capital invested in railroads jumped in this period from $2 billion to nearly $10 billion.

After the war most of the short lines were consolidated into a few large systems. Cornelius Vanderbilt, who had already made a fortune in steamboats, led the way. Before his death in 1877 he had extended the New York Central System to Chicago, offering improved service at reduced rates.

The New York Central's chief competitor for the traffic between the East and the Middle West was the Pennsylvania Railroad, which became the most important railroad and one of the foremost business enterprises in the country. At the end of the nineteenth century the Pennsylvania had lines tapping the most important Middle Atlantic and North Central industrial centers.

The Erie Railroad was a competitor for much of this traffic, but in the 1860s and 1870s it suffered from being in the hands of three of the most disreputable railroad manipulators of the era: Daniel Drew, Jay Gould, and Jim Fisk. Through bribery, chicanery, and fraud they made the Erie synonymous with all the vices of the Industrial Revolution. Consolidation enabled the Baltimore and Ohio to push into the Middle West, and the New York, New Haven, and Hartford to fan out into New England. By 1900 railroad consolidation had reached such vast proportions that groups led by Cornelius Vanderbilt, James J. Hill, E. H. Harriman, Jay Gould, John D. Rockefeller, and John Pierpont Morgan controlled more than two thirds of the railroad mileage of the country.

Gould was primarily a speculator who invested money in everything from gold, to stocks, to railroads. Gould purchased his first railroad at age 24 and then sold it two years later at a profit of $130,000. Bolstered by this success, Gould purchased stock in other railroads, normally buying enough to take control of railroad operations, then dropping his prices to a point at which his competitors could not make a profit. Gould would then sell his stock to competitors who desired to rid themselves of their cheap competitor. Though Gould's primary purpose was simply to purchase railroads and sell them at a profit, his methods caused consolidation in the industry and forced his competitors to expand their operations in order to keep pace with Gould's purchases. The result was exponential expansion, not only in miles of railroad track but also in the size of corporations. For example, in 1860, the largest textile mill in New England (the center of the American textile industry) employed only 800 people. In the 1870s, the Pennsylvania Railroad alone employed over 55,000 workers and had a stock value of over $400 million, making it the largest corporation in the world at the time.

Gould's practices may have made him the "richest man in America" by the time of his death in 1892. Upon his death,

Jay Gould (Library of Congress)

newspapers proclaimed that the country had lost the "world's richest man," and his net worth was estimated at over $100 million at a time of no income taxes and an average wage in America of approximately $600 per year. Competitor Cornelius Vanderbilt, who built both the largest house in America, the "Biltmore" near Asheville, North Carolina, and the New York Central Railroad proclaimed Gould to be the "smartest man in America." Gould himself, however, perhaps put it more accurately when he described himself shortly before he died as "the most hated man in America."

Gould's competitive practices induced other railroads to engage in collusion and set up what were known as "pool" agreements whereby they essentially divided the map into separate areas for each and promised not to compete in each other's area so that each could set prices high. Pool agreements normally did not hold, however, as competing railroads seeking an edge tended to violate their own agreements and undercut their competition.

THE TRANSCONTINENTALS

More spectacular and more important than railroad building in the older sections of the country was the construction of the transcontinentals. In 1862 Congress had chartered the Union Pacific and the Central Pacific railroads. Upon their completion of the transcontinental line in 1869—with Chinese immigrant labor having done much of the heaviest work, it should be noted—the two railroads had received 54 million acres of government land and government loans amounting to about $60 million. In addition, the Union Pacific had issued one million shares of stock at $100 a share.

Much of the profiteering that accompanied the building of both roads can be ascribed to the separation of ownership and control in modern corporate enterprise. Managers systematically bled their companies for their own profit. The public first became aware of the large scale of this practice in the Crédit Mobilier scandal of 1872. Officers of the Union Pacific Railroad had used a dummy construction company (the Crédit Mobilier), which they owned, to build the road and had turned over most of the assets of the road, including loans from the government and investments by shareholders, to themselves as constructors, paying themselves, by a conservative estimate, $73 million for a $50 million job. Their bribery of congressmen in connection with this deal was only incidental. Although the concept of "conflict of interest" present in intimate relationships between government officials and business did not yet exist, more fundamental to an understanding of this evil is the fact that executives were placed in a position that

The completion of the transcontinental railroad in 1869 *(Library of Congress)*

gave them constant opportunity to enrich themselves at the expense of the investors and of the enterprise itself.

The Crocker Company, which built the Central Pacific, amassed a profit of about $63 million on an investment of $121 million. Most of this went to the four leading officials of the Central Pacific—Leland Stanford, Collis P. Huntington, Charles Crocker, and Mark Hopkins— who left a fortune of $40 million or more at each death. Critics of the railroad magnates in California referred to their railroad as an "octopus," with tentacles that controlled San Francisco's financial district, California agriculture, lumber interests, shipping, stage lines, and mining. Frank Norris expanded this theme in 1901 in his best-selling novel, *The Octopus.*

GOVERNMENTAL AID TO RAILROADS

While individual initiative and enterprise played a large part in the building of America's great railroad empire, it is doubtful if American railroads would have become so highly developed had it not been for the generosity of the federal, state, and local governments. Between 1850 and 1871 the railroads received from the federal government alone more than 130 million acres of land—an area as large as the New England states, Pennsylvania, and New York combined—and from the states about 49 million acres of land. It is nearly impossible to assess the value of this land, but a conservative estimate (based on $2.00 an acre) would place the value at $360 million. Some estimates have been as high as $2.5 billion.

Because they failed to meet all the conditions under which this land was granted, the railroads were able to retain only about 116 million acres. Even so, at the end of the land-grant era it was discovered that railroads had been granted one fourth of the entire area of Minnesota and Washington; one fifth of Wisconsin, Iowa, Kansas, North Dakota, and Montana; one seventh of Nebraska; one eighth of California; and one ninth of Louisiana. At one point (1882) Texas discovered that its donations of land to railroads exceeded by 8 million acres the amount remaining in the public domain.

To such grants of land were added loans and subsidies. Towns, cities, and counties gave the railroads about $300 million, and the states, at a conservative estimate, furnished an additional $228 million. The federal government made loans of approximately $65 million, most of which went to the Union and Central Pacific. A town was at the mercy of a railroad, which could bypass it and, thereby, cause it to dry up. By this threat the railroads were able to secure cash grants, loans, exemption from taxation, and subscription to their stocks.

Many loans were made voluntarily and enthusiastically to get local railroad advantages. For, as the governor of Maine asked in 1867, "Why should private individuals be called upon to make a useless sacrifice of their means when railroads can be constructed by the unity of public with private interests, and made profitable to all?" By 1870, according to one estimate, public subsidies plus land grants contributed 60 percent of the costs of all railroad construction.

PUBLIC BENEFITS

The national railroad system no doubt brought great benefits to the economy. In addition to facilitating the movement of goods, the railroads used enormous amounts of iron and steel, coal, lumber, and other products and provided employment for hundreds of thousands of workers. In the decade of the 1880s the railroad companies bought nearly 15 million tons of rails, purchasing in some years over 90 percent of the rolled steel manufactured in the United States.

The railroads were also one of the most active colonizers of the last West. They possessed vast tracts of land grants to sell, and they stood to gain in increased passenger and freight business as settlement expanded. They offered rail tickets at reduced prices to prospective settlers and sometimes even provided free transportation for a settler's furniture. In addition, railroads employed agents at eastern seaports to welcome immigrants and to arrange for their transportation to the West. They even had immigration agencies in Europe to persuade Europeans to come to America.

THE INDUSTRIALISTS

"ROBBER BARONS" OR "CAPTAINS OF INDUSTRY"?

It is important to recognize that the foregoing factors were not wholly responsible for the American Industrial Revolution. It required the superb talent found among those Americans who mobilized the nation's productive energies to build the railroads and factories. The new industrialists were ambitious, resourceful, and extremely able. At times they were ruthless and dishonest but probably no more so than many other Americans of their day. They displayed the vigor, cleverness, and strength of will that have characterized the great entrepreneurs of all epochs of capitalistic expansion. They lived at a time when the highest goal was to acquire wealth and when one's position in society was determined by the amount amassed. In their day they were known as Captains of Industry and praised for the economic growth of modern America. In time, however, they came to be described in many quarters as Robber Barons, who exploited the working class and exacted tribute from the public.

Few of the industrialists were guided by the morality and ethics that had prevailed in business before the Civil War. To eliminate competitors and get around legal and political obstacles, they did not hesitate to use trickery, bribery, and corruption. Their attitude toward complaints about their methods was summed up in William Vanderbilt's famous reply to a reporter's questions about the motives for his management of the railroads: "The public be damned."

If we indict or criticize these industrialists for what they did to attain economic and industrial power, we must remember that they were the products of their time, an era of lax regulation when many of their activities, now judged as unscrupulous, were perfectly legal. Probably even the worst and coarsest of their activities reflected the dominant Social Darwinist mores of American society in the Gilded Age. While they used wasteful and ruthless methods to promote economic development, they also faced such risks as overexpansion

A nineteenth century steel mill *(Library of Congress)*

and unfair competition. Some now regard these businessmen more as creative agents in economic change whose long-run material contributions to society outweighed their short-run self-serving activities. Of course, historians making such arguments also have been spared the punishment of working 72-hour weeks in nineteenth-century steel mills. Whether "Captains of Industry" or "Robber Barons," they were launching the beginnings of a great economic expansion and economical mass production, but they also did it very much on the backs of exploited American workers.

As already noted, in the Gilded Age there was great faith in the rags-to-riches story. Andrew Carnegie's success in climbing from the lowly position of immigrant bobbin-boy in a cotton textile mill at the wage of $1.20 a week to that of multimillionaire of the American steel industry is the classic American story of the poor boy making good. Carnegie's autobiography and the work of historians helped to keep alive for many years the "rags-to-riches" dream and the belief that the Captains of Industry came from poor, immigrant, rural, uneducated families, without social advantages—that, in fact, they became rich and powerful by pulling themselves up not only by their own bootstraps but also by a strict adherence to the Calvinist ethic of hard work, thrift, chastity, and abstinence. New research, however, has shown that the bulk of the business leaders came from white Anglo-Saxon Protestant, urban, northeastern, educated professional and business families. It seems that the doors of business success were not generally opened to immigrants, farm boys, or youths of poor education and background. Carnegie was the exception rather than the rule.

While these tycoons accumulated large fortunes, many insisted they were not materialistic. "I know of nothing more despicable and pathetic than a man who devotes all the waking hours of the day to making money for money's sake," wrote John D. Rockefeller in his *Reminiscences*. He maintained it was "the association with interesting and quick-minded men," not money alone, that prompted him to follow his course to success. Critics point out, however, that Rockefeller was less disinterested in profit when the federal government moved to break up his Standard Oil monopoly. Andrew Carnegie expressed a similar view when he said that many of his "clever partners" in the steel business had been his friends from boyhood. He emphasized the joy he found in "manufacturing something and giving employment to many men." While Carnegie may have been speaking the truth, critics argue that he was less caring and sympathetic to his steel mill workers during labor disputes such as the famous Homestead Steel Mill strike.

A number of the new industrialists were of military age during the Civil War, but most of them took advantage of a law that allowed them to hire a substitute or to pay a certain amount of money in lieu of military service. Writing from Pittsburgh in 1863, Thomas Mellon, the founder of an aluminum fortune, declared "such opportunities for making money had never existed before in all my former experience." When his son James asked permission to enlist, the elder Mellon wrote, "Don't do it. It is only greenhorns who enlist. Those who are able to pay for substitutes do so, and no discredit attaches." Then he added, "It is not so much the danger as disease and idleness and vicious habits. ... I had hoped my boy was going to make a smart, intelligent businessman and was not such a goose as to be seduced from his duty by the declamations of buncombed speeches."

Simon Cameron, as Secretary of War during the Civil War, handed out war contracts left and right and asked only for production in return. As a result, gigantic frauds and great fortunes resulted from shoddy contracts and shady deals. For example, Cornelius Vanderbilt supplied the government with leaky ships, and J. P. Morgan, 24 years old in 1861, purchased 5,000 discarded carbines and sold them back to the army for $112,000. These deals of both Morgan and Vanderbilt were exposed, but neither man was punished. Similarly, Jim Fisk went south to smuggle out cotton and sell it in the North for large profits. Jay Gould's inside information enabled him to cash in on railroad deals and speculation in gold. Hence, the term "Robber Barons" is, in many cases, at least as accurate as "Captains of Industry."

THE TRUST

Before the Civil War, American business was highly competitive and consisted of small units—mostly individual enterprises or partnerships. After the war, businessmen sought ways to check increasing competition, which they had come to regard as inefficient, wasteful, and threatening to their profits. They established trade agreements, associations, and pools to limit competition. Because, however, these devices depended upon voluntary cooperation and were not enforceable in the courts, none proved sufficiently reliable. The answer seemed to lie in the formation of industrial trusts, which provided businessmen with more efficient control over the policies of all members within a single industry.

Under the trust system the stock of several competing companies was placed under the control of a group of trustees in exchange for trustee certificates. Ownership remained with the original companies, but management was consolidated in a single board of directors. John D. Rockefeller was by far the most important figure in the trust movement, and the formation of his Standard Oil Trust in 1882 established the trust pattern in the United States. Standard Oil's chief attorney, T. C. Dodd, established a board of nine trustees empowered to "hold, control, and manage" all of Standard Oil's assets. Stockholders in Standard Oil exchanged their Standard Oil stock for Trust Certificates, essentially stock in the trust, on which dividends were paid. Rockefeller's trustees held stock in numerous oil refinery companies "in trust" for Standard Oil Company stockholders. Rockefeller's trustees then coordinated policy among all the refineries, ensuring that they would all follow the same policies and essentially giving Rockefeller controlling interest in virtually all of the oil refineries in America.

Other companies copied the Standard Oil Trust structure, and soon trusts existed in the railroad, whiskey, lead, sugar, and other industries. The word "trust" became synonymous with the word "monopoly"; but it must be remembered that Rockefeller had essentially established a monopoly in oil refining in America prior to the reorganization of Standard Oil as a trust.

JOHN D. ROCKEFELLER AND THE STANDARD OIL TRUST

At age 14, John D. Rockefeller received his pay from his first pay period on his first job and gave 10 percent to God, kept 50 percent for himself, and saved 40 percent, a practice he would continue essentially for the rest of his life. By age 19, Rockefeller had enough saved that he was able to purchase a produce business in Cleveland, Ohio. Finding success in the produce business at age 23, he decided to enter the oil industry during the Civil War by purchasing an oil refinery in Cleveland. Here he found violence, lawlessness, and waste; and, being no exponent of such free enterprise, he took steps to end this competitive strife. Rockefeller considered competition itself to be wasteful and small-scale enterprises to be inefficient. In his view, the wave of the future would be consolidation of small businesses into large corporations. Rockefeller adopted the most efficient methods of production, regularly saved a part of his profits, and surrounded himself with some of the ablest men in the industry. It was said that Rockefeller himself "could see farther ahead than any of them, and then see around the corner." Rockefeller's mantras were "nothing in haste, nothing ill-done," and "your future hangs on every day that passes." Rockefeller paid attention to minute details, counting rivets in oilcans and stoppers in barrels. In one famous case of efficiency, Rockefeller experimented with exactly how many drops of solder were required on kerosene cans to prevent them from leaking, and he reduced the number of welds through trial and error from 40 to 39. In another instance, Rockefeller found that he could shorten barrel hoops to save metal. Meanwhile, he employed a chemist, Herman Frasch, who made numerous advancements in increasing the efficiency of refining oil. Rockefeller would triumph over his competition by providing better products at lower costs, a sound path to business success even in the twenty-first century if one can accomplish it.

By 1867 Rockefeller was the largest refiner of oil in Cleveland, and in 1870 he organized the Standard Oil Company of Ohio with a capitalization of $1 million. This was the original *trust*, and the term came to be applied to any large combination with monopolistic powers.

With his trust, Rockefeller soon eliminated his Ohio competitors. He then proceeded to take on refiners in New York, Pittsburgh, and Philadelphia. Those who accepted Rockefeller's terms shared in the large profits. Those who continued to resist him were attacked with every weapon in cutthroat competitive warfare. He usually crushed his competitors with ruthless price-cutting, but he also had an immense competitive advantage in the rebates[1] and drawbacks[2] he re-

---

[1] Powerful industrial shippers, in a strong bargaining position with railroads, often demanded—and received—secret "rebates," or discounts, from publicly posted shipping rates. Rebates sometimes were given in return for a specified volume of business or in return for the shipper's distributing his traffic in accordance with a pooling agreement made among competing lines.

[2] In exchange for the privilege of transporting the freight of a large shipper (e.g., Standard Oil), railroads agreed to pay the shipper "drawbacks," or subsidies drawn from a percentage of all receipts of its competitors.

ceived from the railroads. By 1879 Rockefeller controlled about 90 percent of America's refining industry.

Of all the trusts that appeared in the 80s and 90s, none aroused more alarms or pointed up more moral issues than the Standard Oil Trust. Even the means Rockefeller used to gain a monopoly in the oil industry produced conflicting opinions. "I ascribe the success of the Standard Oil Company to its consistent policy of making the volume of its business large through the merit and cheapness of its products," declared Rockefeller. Senator James K. Jones of Arkansas, however, offered another explanation on the floor of the United States Senate in 1889:

> "The iniquities of the Standard Oil Company have been enumerated and recounted until some of them are familiar to everyone," said Jones, "and the colossal fortunes which have grown from it, which in all their vastness do not represent one dollar of honest toil or one trace of benefit to mankind, nor any addition to the product of human labor, are known everywhere."

Indeed, Rockefeller threatened his competitors and bribed politicians when necessary. He also employed spies to harass the customers of competing refiners. Hence, some writers see in the rise of Standard Oil a dark record of unfair trade practices, railroad favors, bribery and blackmail, and an alliance between the corporation and politics by which legislators, officials, and judges closed their eyes to practices that violated the law. Others have argued that Standard Oil straightened out a disorderly industry and, by introducing efficiency and competency, lowered prices and created a great industry. Both sides, however, agree that Standard's methods frequently were ruthless.

Rockefeller had a way of being ahead of the law most of the time. William Vanderbilt, testifying about the leaders of Standard Oil before a congressional committee in 1879, expressed an opinion prevalent in those years: "Yes, they are very shrewd men. I don't believe that by any legislative enactment or anything else, through any of the States or all of the States, you can keep such men down. You can't do it! They will be on top all the time. You see if they are not."

Rockefeller not only had his oil monopoly integrated horizontally, i.e., he took over competing refineries until he completely dominated the oil refining industry, but he also integrated vertically, owning every phase of the oil exploration, production, manufacturing, transportation, and marketing industries. Standard Oil, therefore, not only owned drilling rigs, but also timberlands, barrel and chemical plants, refineries, warehouses, pipelines, rail cars, and eventually ocean-going oil tankers. Standard also exported oil across the oceans to

Asia, Africa, and South America. Rockefeller retired in 1897 with a fortune approaching $1 billion. Eventually, it is estimated that Rockefeller would control two percent of the gross domestic product of the United States.

Be that as it may, in 1892 the Supreme Court of Ohio ordered the dissolution of the Standard Oil Trust on the grounds that it was designed to "establish a virtual monopoly" and was "contrary to the policy of our state." This decision, however, did not produce the desired results; for the Standard trustees, although they returned the stock to the stockholders, continued to manage the member concerns as "liquidating trustees" until 1897, when the court forced them to abandon this stratagem.

Prior to this, in 1889, New Jersey had changed its corporation laws in such a way as to make legal the formation of a holding company—a company that owned a majority of the stock in a number of subsidiary corporations and was established to unify their control. Put simply, a holding company was a corporation that owned controlling interest in other companies. In 1899 the various subsidiaries of Standard were legally combined through the creation of a giant holding company, the Standard Oil Company of New Jersey, capitalized at $110 million. Standard's control over the refining business continued as complete as ever. In 1911 the United States Supreme Court, after it adopted the "rule of reason" whereby any combination that placed a "reasonable" restraint on trade could be in violation, held that Standard had violated the 1890 Sherman Antitrust Act. This decision, like earlier ones in the state courts, had little effect upon the management of Standard's affairs.

CARNEGIE AND STEEL

Andrew Carnegie came to America as a Scottish immigrant in 1848 at the age of 12 and quickly went to work in a Pennsylvania cotton mill for $1.20 per week. From there, Carnegie took a job in a telegraph office where he worked until 1852 when he was offered a job by Thomas A. Scott of the Pennsylvania Railroad as Scott's personal telegrapher. Seven years later, Carnegie had risen to become a well-paid divisional superintendent for the railroad at age 24, and by 1868, Carnegie's income was upwards of $50,000 per year. Over the decade, of the 1860s, Carnegie amassed a fortune of over $1 million from shrewd investments and had enough to build a steel mill.

Just as Rockefeller captured the refining market from his competitors, so Andrew Carnegie captured much of the steel market although he never achieved a monopoly. Like Rockefeller, however,

Carnegie gained an edge over his competitors by finding a more efficient way to make his product. Upon purchasing his first steel mill, Carnegie was surprised to discover that there was no hard and fast recipe for steel. Consequently, he hired chemists to determine the exact ingredients that would produce the best mix. Carnegie also instituted the Bessemer process, a method of eliminating the impurities in steel developed by Henry Bessemer in 1859. Bessemer discovered that blowing a stream of air into a mass of molten iron caused carbon and other

Andrew Carnegie *(Library of Congress)*

impurities to combine with oxygen and burn off. When measured amounts of carbon, silicon, and manganese were then added to the purified iron, higher quality steel resulted. Soon, Carnegie was producing top quality steel from waste discarded by his competitors. When Carnegie first introduced the Bessemer process into his steel mill in the 1870s, the price of steel dropped 50 percent. As more technological innovations were introduced, the price of steel eventually declined from $100 per ton in the 1870s to $12 per ton by 1890.

As his steel enterprise grew, Carnegie found that he could get ahead of the competition by expanding his business during slow times when purchasing a competing steel mill was less expensive. Given that the steel industry in the late nineteenth century was very prone to boom-bust cycles, Carnegie was able to expand quickly and greatly during the bust cycles when others were selling off their assets.

By 1890, steel had become a cheaper, stronger, and more durable material than iron, and its greater malleability lent the metal to new uses. Railroads converted their rails from iron to steel, and bridges were soon designed with steel cables. Eventually, steel would be used as the frames for high-rise buildings in American cities as well as for all forms of wire, nails, bolts, nuts, and screws.

Like Rockefeller, Carnegie secured rebates from the railroads. He also was materially aided by the depression of the 70s, for as he said about it afterward, "so many of my friends needed money, that they begged me to repay them (for their investments in early Carnegie enterprises). I did so and bought out five or six of them. That was what gave me my leading interest in this steel business."

From this time on, Carnegie led the field in the steel industry. He bought out and took into his business Henry Clay Frick, who in the 70s had gained control of most of the coke ovens around Pittsburgh. Together they created a great vertical combine of coalfields, coke ovens, limestone deposits, iron mines, ore ships, and railroads. In 1892 the Carnegie Steel Company was formed at a capitalization of $25 million. It controlled all its sources of supply and was soon making one fourth of all unfinished steel in the United States. At the turn of the century it became a New Jersey corporation with a capitalization of $160 million.

Carnegie was essentially an *industrial capitalist* in that his money came from industry and not from bankers. He put a large part of his profits back into his business, and he did not allow his corporation's stock to be sold to persons outside his organization. He was successful because of his efficient business methods and driving energy and because he skillfully chose partners of almost equal ability, such as Frick and Charles Schwab. However, his labor policy, like that of most of the corporation leaders of this era, was one of long hours, low wages, and hostility to trade unions. Carnegie was willing to make innovations in methods and machinery and ready to discard equipment whenever better came along. He made his improvements in times of depression; and when prosperity returned, he was ready to produce.

Carnegie believed that it was a disgrace to die rich, so he desired to retire and engage in philanthropic work. In 1901, Carnegie essen-

Ohio Works of the Carnegie Steel Co. in Youngstown, Ohio *(Library of Congress)*

tially sold out to J. P. Morgan. Morgan had reportedly asked Carnegie's associate, Charles M. Schwab, to "go and find his price." Schwab then discussed the matter with Carnegie on the golf course, and the next day Carnegie handed Schwab a note hand-written in pencil asking for almost a half billion dollars. Upon viewing the note, Morgan exclaimed, "I accept this price." The owners of Carnegie Steel received $492 million, of which $250 million went to Carnegie alone. According to legend, Carnegie later teased Morgan, stating that he should have asked for $100 million more, to which Morgan replied, "You would have got it if you had."

THE GROWTH OF TRUSTS

Soon after Standard Oil Company had set the trust pattern, other business enterprises of this type appeared. The McCormick Harvester Company of Chicago secured almost a monopoly of mechanical farm equipment. James B. Duke's American Tobacco Company, established in 1890, and Henry O. Havemeyer's American Sugar Refining Company, founded in 1891, gained almost complete monopolies, while Philip D. Armour and Gustavus Swift won domination of the meat packing business. The E. C. Knight Company controlled 98 percent of the sugar manufacturing in the United States. Other consumer goods controlled by trusts were salt, whisky, matches, crackers, wire, and nails.

Eventually, prosecution by states or state legislation declaring trusts illegal ended these organizations. Though the original form of trust disappeared, the term trust continued in use, applied to any type of monopoly. Many of the former trusts reorganized themselves into holding companies under the friendly corporate laws of New Jersey. Others became corporate combines created by mergers of separate firms. Fewer combinations occurred during the depression of 1893–1897, but after this they increased at an extraordinary rate.

OPPOSITION TO THE TRUSTS

As the American people watched the proliferation of trusts and millionaires, they became convinced that something must be done to restore competition. There arose a popular outcry against monopolies, and by the 80s public speakers and writers began to condemn them. In 1881 Henry D. Lloyd attacked the Standard Oil Trust in "The Story of a Great Monopoly" in the *Atlantic Monthly*. Similar articles against other examples of big business followed. Edward Bellamy in his *Looking Backward* (1887) assailed economic conditions of the time and pictured a future socialist utopian state where life's necessities and luxuries would be produced by a cooperative society for the benefit of all. Henry George in his *Progress and Poverty* (1879) maintained that the problems of the times were largely the result of a monopoly of land. "All who do not possess land," he argued, "are toiling for those who do, and this is the reason why progress and poverty go hand in hand." George proposed that the unearned increments in land values be confiscated by the government in the form of a single tax on land. This would benefit the whole of society and adjust those economic disparities from which American society was suffering. (The ideas of Bellamy and George were discussed more fully in Chapter 4.)

During the 80s a number of states passed laws prohibiting trusts, but these failed to check the increasing concentration of industry. Some trusts appeared more powerful than the states that attempted to regulate them; and when one device for creating monopoly ran afoul of the law, another was substituted. State legislation also proved ineffective so long as such states as New Jersey, Delaware, and West Virginia placed few restrictions on the chartering corporations and permitted the creation of holding companies.

THE INTERSTATE COMMERCE ACT

These frustrations aroused the opponents of monopoly to demand federal action. Between 1873 and 1885 more than 30 measures were introduced in the House of Representatives providing for the regulation of interstate railroads, an economic sector in which there were frequent abuses. Railroads discriminated significantly between the rates they charged on routes where they had competition as opposed to those where they did not. In general, railroads would charge very low rates where they had competition; but on routes where they had none, the prices they set were exorbitant, placing extreme burdens on farmers and shippers from remote areas. For instance, the dome for the Texas State Capitol in Austin was made in Belgium, but it cost more to ship the dome via rail from Houston to Austin than it did to transport it from Belgium to Texas via cargo ship. Farmers and shippers in remote areas, along with railroads who faced competition from other railroads that charged low prices in one area to force out competitors while making up for it with the high rates charged elsewhere, pressured Congress to intervene.

The House of Representatives passed some of the measures favored by those who supported federal railroad regulation, only to have those measures fail in the Senate. Under the pressures of Easterners as well as Westerners, however, the Senate yielded at last and appointed the Cullom Committee to investigate. In 1886 the committee made its report, concluding: "It is the deliberate judgment of the Committee that upon no public question are the people so nearly unanimous as upon the proposition that Congress should undertake in some way the regulation of interstate commerce." This recommendation together with the Supreme Court's Wabash decision in 1886, forbidding the states to continue their regulation of *interstate* railroad traffic, led to the Interstate Commerce Act of 1887.

This law provided that all railway rates "shall be reasonable and just." It prohibited such discriminatory practices as rebates and drawbacks and made illegal some of the long and short haul abuses.[3] It forbade pooling agreements[4] and required that all rates and fares be printed and publicly posted. The act established a five-man Interstate Commerce Commission, the first federal regulatory agency, with power to investigate the railroads and to require reports from them. The Commission could hear complaints of violations of the law but could not impose fines, cease and desist orders, or other penalties by itself. Instead, it had to depend upon the courts to enforce its rulings, and the five-member Interstate Commerce Commission was overwhelmed with thousands of petitions. Thus the commission did not receive the powers necessary to regulate the transportation system. Also, the commissioners were virtually required by the act to be inexperienced in railroad practices, so they had difficulties fully understanding and acting on the complaints of the shippers.

The chief weakness of the law, however, was its vagueness in not defining "reasonable and just" rates. Such grave defects in the act were recognized even by such a staunch opponent of federal regulation as Senator Nelson W. Aldrich of Rhode Island, who described the new law as a "delusion and a sham, an empty menace to great interests, made to answer the clamor of the ignorant and unreasoning."

The Commission soon discovered that it could not compel witnesses to testify and that appeals to the courts produced endless delays. Even in those cases that reached the Supreme Court, the decisions generally favored the railroads over the Commission.

---

[3] The "long and short haul" abuse pointed out the fact that railroads charged rates based not on operating costs but on what the public could be forced to pay. Over "long hauls"—e.g., from Chicago to New York—competition between railroads was keen and freight charges were low (sometimes lower than operating costs); but over "short hauls"—i.e., between local points serviced by only one line—a railroad, in a noncompetitive situation, could charge rates as high as the public could bear, thereby recouping whatever losses it might have suffered on long hauls.

[4] By means of "pooling agreements" competing railroads sometimes agreed to maintain uniformly high rates in a particular locality by apportioning traffic among themselves or dividing accumulated earnings. Pooling was intended to avoid competitive rate wars.

Between 1887 and 1905 the Court heard 16 cases appealed by the I.C.C., and in 15 of those cases, it upheld the railroads.

THE SHERMAN ANTITRUST ACT

Senator John Sherman of Ohio outlined the need for stronger federal control of the trusts when he said in 1890:

> Congress alone can deal with the trusts, and if we are unwilling or unable there will soon be a trust for every production and a master to fix the price for every necessity of life.

In 1890 Congress passed the Sherman Antitrust Act, another departure from laissez-faire policies, by an almost unanimous vote. Although Sherman introduced it, Senators George F. Edmunds of Vermont and George F. Hoar of Massachusetts, mainly, wrote the act. The act declared that "every contract, combination in the form of trust or otherwise, or conspiracy in restraint of trade or commerce" was illegal. It was left to the courts, however, to determine the meaning of the terms and phrases in the law, and it could not be enforced without the cooperation of the Attorney General. Senator Orville Platt of Connecticut in commenting on the act stated, "The conduct of the Senate ... has not been in the line of honest preparation of a bill to prohibit and punish trusts. It has been in the line of getting some bill with that title that we might go to the country with." Senator Shelby Cullom of Illinois thought that if the act "were strictly and literally enforced the business of the country would come to a standstill."

Whether or not Cullom was correct is unknown, however, because the act was not enforced. From 1890 to 1901 the Justice Department instituted only 18 antitrust suits, and the Supreme Court—in *United States v. E. C. Knight Co.* (1895)—undermined the law by holding that manufactur-

Senator John Sherman *(Library of Congress)*

ing, being wholly intrastate in character even though ultimately affecting interstate commerce, was not subject to federal regulation. This limited definition of the "commerce clause" in the Constitution put trusts beyond federal control. Hence, the E. C. Knight Company, which at the time controlled 98 percent of sugar manufacturing in the United States, could not be broken up as a monopoly by the federal government because "manufacturing" was not "interstate commerce" under the definition of the Supreme Court.

EDISON, ELECTRICITY, AND INVENTIONS

Perhaps the greatest inventor in American history who had an almost unparalleled impact on American life with his inventions was Thomas Edison of Menlo Park, New Jersey. Edison was a tireless worker who slept only three to four hours per night, spending the rest of his time in his laboratory and vowing to produce a "minor invention every 10 days and a big thing every six months or so." At the height of his inventing career, Edison employed as many as 200 chemists, machinists, engineers, and experimenters, averaging a patent every 11 days. He provided the world with the "big" inventions that included not only the electric light bulb, but also the phonograph and the motion picture camera, all three of which would eventually change America and the world indelibly. In his lifetime, Edison would own over 1,000 patents, including the mimeography and the electric storage battery. Furthermore, although it was Ben Franklin who discovered that lightning was electricity in the eighteenth century, it was Edison, who along with competitor George Westinghouse, harnessed electricity as a power source to fuel not only electric lights, but factory machinery, urban trolleys, and a host of other items common in urban America at the turn of the century. Edison built his first electric power station in New York in 1882, supplying electric power to 85 customers. By 1898, there were over 3,000 electric power stations supplying electricity to homes and industry all over the country. Electricity would transform American industry from one that was fueled primarily by water power in 1900, to one that was driven primarily by electricity by 1930.

Edison did not, however, amass the type of fortune that one might imagine from his inventions. Patent laws in the late nineteenth century provided Edison with far less protection than Edison had expected, and he spent the next four decades after the invention of his incandescent bulb in patent lawsuits. In the words of Edison, "My electric light inventions have brought me no profits, only 40 years of litigation." Later Edison lamented that "a patent, is simply an invitation to a lawsuit." Nevertheless, in 1892 Edison and his competi[tor] Thomson-Houston Electric merged to form General Electric, a cor[po]ration with an estimated net worth of $35 million. Thereafter, Gene[ral] Electric and Westinghouse would dominate the manufacture of li[ght] bulbs and other electrical equipment along with the distribution [of] electric power to run the new electric inventions.

ALEXANDER GRAHAM BELL AND THE TELEPHONE

Alexander Graham Bell, like Andrew Carnegie, was a Scottish im[mi]grant who came to America as a young man (age 24 in Bell's case) [to] seek his fortune. Both Bell's wife and his mother were deaf mut[es], which gave him a passion for developing a way for the deaf [to] speak. Instead, what he developed was a way to transmit the hum[an] voice over a wire, and his invention became known as the te[le]phone. Bell first demonstrated his invention to the world at [the] Philadelphia Centennial Exposition in 1876, and communications [in] America has never been the same since. Bell formed his compa[ny,] American Bell, in 1880. He worked with Theodore N. Vail, who [pio]neered long telephone lines, and created American Telephone a[nd] Telegraph as a subsidiary of Bell. In 1900, the corporation was re[or]ganized with AT&T as the parent company, controlling Bell and We[stern]

Alexander Graham Bell's first telephone (*Library of Congress*)

ern Electric, which manufactured and installed Bell's telephone equipment. By 1900, there were almost 800,000 telephones in America with people communicating from coast to coast.

Other inventions in the Gilded Age that changed the nature of America included the typewriter (1867), barbed wire (1867), cash register (1879), adding machine (1885), Kodak camera (1888), zipper (1891), safety razor (1895), and tape recorder (1899).

THE GROWTH OF FINANCE CAPITALISM

During the 1890s industrial capitalism began to give way to *finance capitalism* as investment bankers became more influential in the development of American industry. The industrial capitalists like Rockefeller and Carnegie were producers who had grown rich with their own industries. Finance capitalists like J. P. Morgan and August Belmont, in contrast, came to power not because they were skilled industrial organizers but because they had enormous sums of money with which they could invest in and purchase control of an industry. A corporation in need of capital could ask a banking house to sell the corporation's securities. In return the investment banker demanded a share in the management of the corporations in which his customers had invested. Hard-pressed industrialists could not refuse, and gradually the bankers assumed supervision of corporate policies. By the turn of the century control of a number of corporations had passed from industrialists to bankers.

The leading American finance capitalist was J. P. Morgan, who was also a dominant figure in the national economy. The New York banking houses—August Belmont and Company and Kuhn, and Loeb and Company—and the Boston banking houses—Lee, Higginson and Company and Kidder Peabody and Company—were also important. Morgan worked to bring about order and stability in one industry after another, for he wanted to make sure that dividends would be paid regularly to stockholders. He disliked competition because he felt it would lead to cutthroat price-cutting, which would be bad for business. Instead, he wanted corporations to collude in order to control prices and markets. Morgan's disdain for competitors induced rivals to refer to him as "Jupiter," after the ruler of the Roman gods. Morgan's policies meant more protection to stockholders but higher prices to consumers. Eventually, his domination of American finance was so thorough that critics complained that he controlled a "money trust."

Morgan's finance capital brought a reorganization of American industry as he took over struggling railroads and other businesses and then consolidated them into a larger entity. Eventually, Morgan had nominal control over two thirds of America's rail lines. Morgan increased his profits from the railroads by issuing more shares of stock than the assets of the companies were worth. Morgan's practices not only set up the stock market for an eventual fall but, also, saddled the railroads with debt problems that hindered continued investment in research and development. Morgan did not stop with railroads, however; he used the same approach in creating massive corporations in other industries such as General Electric and United States Steel.

Probably the biggest of Morgan's ventures was his launching of the United States Steel Corporation in 1901. He bought out the Carnegie Steel Corporation and combined it with 10 other steel companies into one vast corporation capitalized at the unprecedented figure of slightly over $1 billion plus a bonded debt of over $303 million. This made United States Steel America's first billion-dollar company (though the Bureau of Corporations later estimated that the total value of the combined assets of all the merged companies was actually only $676 million). United States Steel controlled 60 percent of America's steel business and employed almost 170,000 people.

With Carnegie's sale to Morgan the era of industrial capitalism came to a close. Finance capitalism brought even greater economic consolidation. In 1893 there were 12 great companies with an aggregate capital of about $1 billion. By 1904 there were 318 industrial combinations—one of them Morgan's United States Steel Corporation—with a combined capital in excess of $7.25 billion. Together these 318 companies controlled more than 5,000 separate plants. Corporations had become larger and larger, and fewer and fewer companies owned an ever-increasing share of American gross domestic product. In 1870, over 800 iron and steel firms competed in the American marketplace, but by 1900, fewer than 10 percent remained. This pattern repeated itself in industry after industry so that by 1900, one percent of American corporations overall controlled over one third of America's manufacturing.

At the time of Morgan's death in 1913, his estate was estimated at $118 million, including $50 million in art treasures. Though his fortune was much less than that of Carnegie or Rockefeller, he indirectly controlled billions of dollars worth of assets. Morgan's power in the American economy may have been unparalleled.

LABOR

Labor had a difficult time in the new industrial age. While businessmen solicited governmental assistance in the form of tariff protection and did not regard this as governmental intervention, they bitterly opposed any attempt to improve the conditions of labor by legislation on the ground that this would be unwarranted interference with the economic system. Most businessmen regarded as absurd the notion that employees had the same right to government protection and aid as had already been afforded business. Instead businessmen believed that they alone had the right to determine the terms and conditions of employment, and they dismissed the idea of collective bargaining.

As business formed ever-larger combinations, however, so did labor. The rise of labor organizations was further boosted by the age of invention itself as more and more skilled workers found themselves replaced by machinery and unskilled workers who merely tended the machines. Labor discontent was also fueled by the fact that an absence of labor protections, such as worker's compensation insurance, left thousands impoverished after family breadwinners were disabled on the job. The rate of on-the-job injury in the United States during the Gilded Age was the highest in the world.

Among the earliest of the significant labor organizations was the National Labor Union, (NLU) that organized in 1866 and was mainly a reform organization that summed up various grievances labor had had since the 1840s. The NLU argued for an eight-hour day, the abolition of slums, and the establishment of cooperatives. It favored arbitration over strikes in labor disputes, and it frowned, at first, upon independent political action by labor groups. Its most important leader was William Sylvis, who died in 1869 after heading the organization for only a year. Had he lived longer, the union might have played a greater role in the history of labor. After his death, however, it turned more and more to political activity, and in 1873 its trade-union aspect disappeared when it became the National Labor Reform party. The NLU withered and died amidst an economic recession at the same time. Even so, the National Labor Union prepared the way for more effective labor organizations, such as the Knights of Labor.

THE KNIGHTS OF LABOR

The Knights of Labor were organized in 1869 under the leadership of Uriah Stephens. Believing in the solidarity of labor, the Knights admitted almost everyone to membership, excluding only lawyers, bankers, stockbrokers, liquor dealers, and professional gamblers. This meant that for the first time there was a substantially male labor organization that accepted women members—albeit grudgingly at first—and a substantially white labor organization that was not invariably opposed to

Cardinal James Gibbons *(Library of Congress)*

black members. The Knights' announced primary purpose was "to secure to toilers a proper share of the wealth they create." They hoped to achieve their goals through secrecy, the organization of cooperatives, and education and propaganda.

Secrecy was of prime importance to the members, for their jobs were at stake: Industries locked out workers who belonged to unions. Even the name of the organization was not made public until 1881. Their secrecy, however, caused the Knights trouble with the churches, especially the Catholic Church, which feared the members might be taking a secret oath that was in conflict with their religion. Only the intercession of Cardinal Gibbons of Baltimore kept the Pope from excommunicating the Catholics in the federation.

The Knights were of national importance from 1879 to 1893, while *Terence v. Powderly,* who replaced Uriah Stephens, was their Grand Master Workman. Powderly was denounced by some as a revolutionary and by others as a faker who sold out labor. He seldom gave full attention to the union, considering it only a part-time position, and engaged himself in other activities such as being Mayor of Scranton, Pennsylvania, from 1878 to 1884 and a leader of the Irish Land League. His great strength with the workers, however, was his oratorical power. Powderly supported land reform, temperance, and public education. More importantly, Powderly also abandoned Stephens' strategy of secrecy, and the Knights of Labor would recruit members and make their grievances known openly.

The Knights hoped to organize all workers, skilled and unskilled, black and white, into one big union for mutual protection against "the aggression of employers." They worked for the eight-hour day, abolition of child labor, settlement of labor disputes by arbitration rather than by strikes, and encouragement of cooperative stores and factories.

The Knights' official opposition to the use of strikes—like that of unions generally in the 70s—was because most strikes up to this point had been unsuccessful. The depression of the 70s had dealt unions some severe blows. They lost strength, and workers saw wages drop as much as 40 percent in textiles and on the railroads where the strikes led to much turbulence. Moreover, workers faced increasing unemployment, prosecution of strikers, and use of police and private detective agencies as strike breakers. In addition to lock-outs (restricting employment to nonunion labor) employers resorted to blacklisting (circulating names of union leaders and members) and to "yellow dog" contracts (pacts whereby employees agreed not to join unions). So the 70s and the depression of that decade were a very difficult time for unions. Only a handful of the national ones pulled through these years.

Although Powderly himself was opposed to use of the strike as a weapon and was willing to come to terms with employers at almost any price, the hard times of the mid-80s led to boycotts and strikes, notably on the Union Pacific in 1884 and Jay Gould's Wabash in 1885. Spontaneous strikes by shop men and trainmen caught the companies off guard and compelled Powderly's support of his followers. These were labor's first major victories, and they forced Gould to negotiate with the Knights. An illusion of easy success arose, and suddenly the Knights were flooded with members. In 1886, their peak year, membership shot up to 700,000.

Fast on the heels of these successes, however, came the Great Southwestern Strike of 1886 and failure. Powderly had agreed in the Wabash settlement to have no more strikes without notifying the railroads in advance. It was an agreement he could not enforce. The strikes that had occurred were not of his making but were strikes of local origin that had drawn him in only after they had begun. In the Southwestern strike Gould refused to negotiate with the union because the Knights had given no advance notice to the railroad, and the workers were unable to hold out.

Of all the labor upheavals of the period, none was more frightening to men of property and order or did more damage to the prestige of labor than the bombing at Haymarket Square in Chicago in 1886. On May 1, a number of independent trade unions struck for recognition of the eight-hour day at the McCormick Harvester plant in Chicago. Two days later the police shot and clubbed some of the strikers who were beating up strikebreakers, and four persons were killed. The violence of the police prompted growls of resentment and threats of retaliation in the labor press. The next day, May 4, a group of anarchists called a protest meeting in Haymarket Square. As the speeches were coming to a close, almost 200 policemen arrived on the scene and ordered the crowd to go home. Before anyone could move, however, a bomb exploded, killing one policeman outright and fatally wounding several others. Almost immediately the police opened fire on the workers, and soon a riot was in full swing. Ten people were killed, six who were policemen, dozens wounded, and in the confusion and excitement several of the policemen shot each other.

The reaction in Chicago and throughout the nation was one of horror. In the resulting hysteria, hundreds of labor union leaders were arrested, including eight who were anarchists that were indicted for "inciting the person who threw the bomb into doing it." They were tried and convicted on what later has come to be seen as flimsy, inconclusive evidence. In fact, witnesses in the trial even testified that none of the eight men on trial actually threw the bomb. In spite of this, the state's prosecutor, Julius S. Grinnell sought to make examples of the men as a deterrent to others to refrain from violence and union activities, in general. Grinnell argued that the state must "make examples of them, hang them, and save our institutions." Seven of the eight men were sentenced to death—one committed suicide, four were executed and the others sentenced to imprisonment for life—in spite of the fact that the state could not link any of the defendants to the Haymarket bomb. Clearly, the men had been arrested and convicted primarily for their political views rather than for the evidence against them. The next year, Illinois governor John Peter Altgeld recognized it as such when he pardoned the three remaining Haymarket convicts at the cost of his own political career. Labor leaders reacted by designating May 1 as an international celebration of labor in memory of the Haymarket martyrs.

The rest of the nation was not so sympathetic, however. The Haymarket Riot had a disastrous impact on labor unions as it convinced Americans, in general, that labor unions were dangerous and full of "bomb throwing radicals." Although the Knights of Labor had nothing to do with the Haymarket Riot, they were identified in the public mind with the anarchists, and skilled workers began to desert the Knights in large numbers. From this time on, the Knights declined in influence, and by 1890 the membership had fallen to 100,000. The failure of their cooperatives also contributed to their downfall.

In addition, they were weakened by the same conflict that had earlier rent the National Labor Union. It was the division between a national leadership dedicated to general economic and political reform and the trade unions that preferred to concentrate on the immediate economic betterment of workers. This controversy came to a head, ironically, during 1886, when the Knights had their most spectacular growth, largely as a result of the success of strikes and when Powderly and other union leaders refused to support new strikes. These and other dissensions over immediate strategy and long-range goals led to a loss in the numbers and influence of the Knights.

THE RISE OF THE AFL

While the power and influence of the Knights waned, a new labor organization, the American Federation of Labor (AFL), was created in 1886 under the leadership of Samuel Gompers. The AFL was essentially a federation of autonomous craft unions representing skilled workers. Gompers abandoned the Knights' idea of labor solidarity and, with it, the outreach to women and people of color, except in a few limited cases. Trade unionism was his aim, and his plan was to group workers according to crafts. Thus, the AFL was for "skilled" workers only and closed to the "unskilled." Gompers believed that female and black workers drove down wages for everyone and were more easily manipulated by big business. Nevertheless, the AFL did seek equal pay for women that did work under the premise that by raising female wages, the AFL could make women less attractive to employers; in effect, women would be driven from the workforce.

The AFL pursued three practical objectives: higher wages, shorter hours, and better working conditions. Gompers opposed direct affiliation of labor unions with political parties. He also, favored cooperation with employers and mediation of labor disputes on the premise that what government gave, it could also take away. Therefore, the best route for laborers was to negotiate directly with the employers. Gompers did, however, advocate strikes when necessary to secure better working conditions, including the eight-hour day.

The Knights and the AFL competed for supremacy in American labor unions at the end of the nineteenth century. In 1896, the AFL had only 138,000 members to the Knights' 730,000, but by the end of the nineteenth century the AFL had won. The Knights of Labor would dissipate into existence only in history books.

LABOR CONFLICT

Most labor organizations rejected violence as a weapon in their struggle to improve the conditions of labor, but there were some exceptions. One was the Molly Maguires, an organization active among Pennsylvania coal miners from the mid-60s to the late 70s, that resorted to violence, intimidation, and to the destruction of property. Making them more ominous to the public, the Molly Maguires was a predominantly Irish organization that operated within the Ancient Order of Hibernians, an Irish fraternal society about which Americans had little knowledge, but much fear. The Molly Maguires threatened mine owners and managers with death and, occasionally, made good on their threats. Mine owners, however, often hired persons to perform dastardly acts for the purpose of blaming the violent acts on the Mollies, thus justifying ruthless suppression of the labor union with public support. Another exception to the nonviolent labor unions was the Anarchists, a small group that supported acts of terror directed at ending capitalism.

THE GREAT RAILROAD STRIKE OF 1877

There was, however, violence in some of the strikes, often, if not invariably, owing to decisions made by employers. The first truly national strike occurred among railroad workers in 1877. An economic recession, which hit in 1873, led to severe declines in wages. For example, brakemen in West Virginia had experienced a drop in pay from $70 per month to $30. In the words of one railroad worker, "We eat our hard bread and tainted meat two days old on the sooty cars up the road, and when we come home, find our children gnawing on bones and our wives complaining that they cannot even buy hominy and molasses." Beginning on the Baltimore & Ohio in response to wage cuts (the Baltimore and Ohio had announced a 10 percent wage cut while simultaneously declaring a 10 percent dividend to stockholders), the Great Railroad Strike of 1877 spread to several other rail lines from coast to coast. An estimated 100,000 railroad workers walked off the job, and another half million workers, most notably steel workers and longshoremen, staged sympathetic strikes. In Pittsburgh and Philadelphia workers fought militia and also committed property damage, but the Pennsylvania militia made the situation even worse by firing into a crowd of workers and killing 20 people in Pittsburgh. Workers retaliated with even more violence and burned two miles of property along the railroad tracks. The militia responded by shooting another 20 workers before the day was over. Property damage in Pittsburgh was estimated at over $2 million. In Reading, Pennsylvania, the situation was the opposite as militiamen refused to fire on strikers, stating that "we may be militiamen, but we are workers first."

Within a little more than a week, governors of nine states declared a state of insurrection and called for federal troops to put down the strike. President Rutherford B. Hayes sent the United States army to the hot spots; but by the time the troops arrived, the violence had subsided and the United States army did not shoot a single striking worker. The army did, however, protect "scab" workers and get the railroads moving again. In a matter of three weeks, the strike was over, but the bloody violence and slanted journalism against the strikers caused many more Americans to view labor unions as dangerous. *The New York Times* warned Americans about the "dangerous classes" and the *Independent* magazine urged the use of force to put down strikers. In the words of one *Independent* editorialist, "If the club of a policeman, knocking out the brains of the rioter, will answer, then well and good, ... but if it does not ... then bullets and bayonets, canister and grape (shot) ... constitutes the one remedy."

President Rutherford B. Hayes *(Library of Congress)*

THE HOMESTEAD STEEL MILL STRIKE

Another bloody episode occurred in a strike of steelworkers against Carnegie's Homestead plant near Pittsburgh in 1892. Ironically, labor unrest at the Homestead Steel Mill during the 1870s had been one of the factors that had helped Carnegie purchase the mill from his competitors at a low cost. Furthermore, Carnegie fancied himself as a friend of the workers, writing in 1886 "the right of the workingmen to combine and to form trades unions is no less sacred than the right of the manufacturer to enter into associations and conferences with his fellows."

In 1892, however, Carnegie attempted to rid the Homestead Mill of union contracts since most of its workers were non-union employees. Carnegie's manager, Henry Clay Frick erected a 15 foot fence around the mill and hired over 300 Pinkerton detectives to defend scab workers against an expected onslaught from striking employees. On June 28, 1992, Frick locked the regular employees out of the Mill. On July 6 at 4:00 a.m., the Pinkertons attempted to sneak into the mill undetected via two river barges on the Monongahela River. Union men spotted the Pinkertons and put out a call to all workers. A 12-hour gun battle ensued between the Pinkertons and the union men, and 30 union men were wounded and three killed. In the end, however, the Pinkertons were forced to surrender and one Pinkerton agent was killed. Another Pinkerton agent had his eye gouged out by an angry woman with an umbrella.

The union workers temporarily took over the Homestead Steel Mill and elected a council to govern the Homestead community. Four days later, however, Pennsylvania's governor ordered the entire Pennsylvania National Guard, some 8,000 troops, to Homestead to reclaim Carnegie's property. The National Guard troops occupied the mill for three months and ushered scab workers into the mill to take the jobs of the union men. One union man attempted to retaliate by assassinating Frick, whom he shot twice and stabbed with a knife; but Frick had a doctor remove the bullets and tend to his wounds while remaining seated at his desk. Unfortunately for the union men, the assassination attempt turned public opinion against the union. The assassin, Alexander Berkman, a Russian immigrant and anarchist, was arrested and sentenced to prison, but his ethnicity and political leanings convinced many that unions were violent and filled with dangerous men with foreign ideas.

In the end, the Homestead strike was a major defeat for the unions as the workers gave in after four and a half months and returned to work. Union leaders were blacklisted and could not find work; the mill cut wages, reinstated the 12-hour day, and cut some 500 jobs. The Amalgamated Labor Union, which had a membership of 24,000 in 1891, saw its membership decline to less than 7,000 within a decade; and virtually every steel mill in the Northeastern United States broke its relationship with the union.

With the onset of depression in the summer of 1893, however, unrest and dissatisfaction among the working class deepened. Among the most violent of the labor upheavals, which aroused national apprehension, was the Pullman strike called by the American Railway Union in sympathy for the distress of Pullman workers. The Pullman Palace Car Company made railroad sleeper cars at a factory near Chicago. Pullman constructed a "company town" where employees lived in 1,800 company houses, children played in company parks; there was a company library, and company stores, but no saloon. The Pullman houses were better than those most workers lived in near Chicago; but rent on Pullman houses was 10–20 percent more, and Pullman workers could not own the homes in the company town. Between May and December 1893 as the economic panic hit hard at the Pullman Company, wages at Pullman were cut 28 percent, but rents in the Pullman housing remained the same. Furthermore, the Pullman Company garnished the rent from the employee's wages. Meanwhile, Pullman paid stockholders an 8 percent dividend, and the company showed a $25 million profit. During the spring of 1894, the desperate Pullman workers went on strike, and the American Railway Union (ARU), led by Eugene V. Debs, staged a sympathetic strike and refused to work trains that pulled Pullman cars. By the end of June 1894 some 20,000 railroad men were on strike in and around Chicago, tying up every Midwestern railroad. Debs urged his union men to avoid violence, but the nation's newspapers printed slanted anti-union stories claiming that there were "Wild Riots" in Chicago.

In retaliation the railroad companies fired all of the protesting switchmen who refused to work trains that carried Pullman cars. United States Attorney General Richard Olney, who was sympathetic to the railroads, appealed to a federal court for an injunction against the strikers on the basis of the Sherman Antitrust Act, arguing that the unions were combinations in a restraint on trade such as the act forbade and interfering with the mail. The court issued the injunction, and Olney argued to President Grover Cleveland that federal troops had to intervene to prevent interruption of the mail, which was hauled by rail. Meanwhile, two Chicago judges issued an injunction that prevented ARU leader Debs from speaking in public. Debs defied the injunction and reminded his followers, "troops cannot move trains."

The Railroads made sure that Pullman cars were put on every mail train so that the Union would interrupt the mail.

At the same time, violence broke out in Chicago, and President Cleveland (over the protest of Governor Altgeld of Illinois) sent in 8,000 federal soldiers to "protect the mails." Before order was restored, some 20 people were reported killed, 60 more wounded, and 2,000 railway cars destroyed, causing over $340,000 in damage. Eugene V. Debs, president of the American Railway Union, and other labor leaders were arrested, convicted of contempt of court for violating the injunction and sentenced to six months to a year in jail. The conviction of the A.R.U. leaders was upheld by the Supreme Court of the United States, which declared the injunction issued against the union to be a legitimate device for the protection of interstate commerce and the mails. Pullman reopened his factory with scab workers, and 1,600 union employees of Pullman suddenly found themselves unemployed.

For 30 years after the Debs case, a federal court injunction was a potent weapon in the hands of employers threatened with a strike. Although the Clayton Act of 1914 appeared to limit the court's authority to interfere in labor disputes on behalf of employers, many anti-labor injunctions continued to be granted by the federal courts; and it was not until the Norris-La Guardia Anti-Injunction Act was passed in 1932 that labor gained the protection it had long sought against injunctions.

It is noteworthy that in the Homestead and Pullman strikes the companies were run by two of the leading industrialists in the country who themselves believed that they were among the most enlightened and concerned of American employers—and were so regarded in many quarters. Carnegie had written magazine articles supporting the rights of labor, and George Pullman had built what he considered a "model town" where his employees could live.

We have talked about the labor strife, but a large number of American workers in these years accepted existing working conditions as inevitable and made the best of it. Although they might be discontented, they did not protest. In fact, many industrial workers were influenced by rural values. Many were unskilled, poorly educated, and socially underprivileged. They were also awed by the enormous achievements of the new industry and were proud of being a part of it; and those who were upwardly mobile generally identified with their employers and accepted the values of American capitalism.

UNIONS AND THE BLACK WORKER

Unlike the politicians of the day, who managed to evade the race issue, the national labor organizations of the post–Civil War decades had to deal with it. Should they organize black workers? If they did, should they allow black workers to join the same unions as white workers, or should they put them in segregated unions? This was a difficult problem for labor leaders, most of whom shared the prejudicial attitudes of the day, because they also recognized that black workers were potential competitors. The National Labor Union, owing to the wide diversity of opinion among its members, never took any specific action on this matter; however, the Knights of Labor, whose goal was to organize all workers, skilled and unskilled, sought to bring blacks into the labor movement. Thus it organized black as well as mixed locals, not only in the North, but also in the South, where vigilantes and lynch mobs attacked Knights organizers. It is not possible to tell from the available records how many blacks became members of the Knights; but at the 1886 convention of the union, the general secretary reported that "the colored people of the South are flocking to us, being eager for organization and education ..." That same year, the peak year for the Knights, it has been estimated that there were no fewer than 60,000 blacks in the Knights of Labor.

Since the American Federation of Labor was comprised of national craft unions (skilled workers only), it had few black members for few black workers qualified as "skilled workers" and had been admitted to craft unions. Gompers' position on the black worker was made clear in his annual report of 1890 when he emphasized the "necessity of avoiding as far as possible all controversial questions."

It would be many years before blacks became "a regular element in the labor force of every basic industry."

WOMEN AND "THE INCORPORATION OF AMERICA"

Women responded to the vast economic transformation, to what has been called "the incorporation of America," in multiple ways. During times of labor conflict, such as the railroad strikes of 1877, they comprised a part of the mobs that destroyed property. Because increasing numbers of them were gainfully employed, they sought entrance to unions—successfully during the heyday of the Knights of Labor, less successfully once the AFL became dominant. A few of them did become organizers for the AFL. Many joined the Socialist Party, including middle-class clubwomen and even farm wives. Historian Mari-jo Buhle has written an authoritative account of women and socialism, in which she documents the presence of such seemingly unlikely adherents. Finally, two of the best-known women in the country gained their fame owing to their activism in response to labor conflict: Mother Jones and Emma Goldman.

Mary Harris "Mother" Jones was born in Ireland in 1837, came to the United States, married, and had four children. In 1867 yellow fever took the lives of her entire family. She then made the workers of the whole country into her family, traveling incessantly to places where a strike was in progress and organizing the wives and children of the striking men so as to strengthen support for the strike. Active in the Socialist Party, she was one of the founders of the Industrial Workers of the World in 1905. By the time of her death in 1930, Mother Jones was a living legend, and 50,000 miners attended a memorial service in her honor.

Emma Goldman, another immigrant like Mother Jones, was born in what is now Lithuania in 1869 and came to this country in 1885, just in time for the Haymarket bombing the next year. When four anarchists were hanged after a trial that seemed a travesty of justice,

Mary Harris "Mother" Jones (Library of Congress)

Goldman became an anarchist herself and spent the rest of her life speaking, writing, and agitating on behalf of various radical causes, including birth control—at the time a very avant-garde position. In 1919 the director of the Radical Division of the Justice Department, J. Edgar Hoover, deported Goldman from the United States after speaking out against military conscription during World War I. Goldman died in Canada in 1940.

THE LAST FRONTIER

THE WEST

While industrial expansion was transforming post-Civil War America, there took place another movement of momentous consequence— the settlement of the western half of the country. It was a migration probably unparalleled in the history of the world, as in one generation Americans established more than a million farms in this last West and occupied more new land than earlier Americans had settled in two and a half centuries. From 1607 to 1870 Americans had occupied 407 million acres and had placed 189 million of them under cultivation. In the last three decades of the nineteenth century they took up 430 million acres and brought 225 million of them under cultivation.

THE MINING FRONTIER

Miners were the first to reveal to the nation the resources and potentialities of the territory between the Missouri River and the Pacific. The discovery of gold in 1848 had lured many miners to California, and later, throughout the 1860s, miners hurried to "strikes" in Colorado, Arizona, Idaho, Montana, and Wyoming. In each case gold attracted the first settlers, the miners. When the pay dirt was exhausted, ranchers and farmers, aided by the government and the railroads, laid the foundations of the territory.

The discovery of gold in the foothills of the Rocky Mountains close to Pike's Peak, near Lake Tahoe on the eastern slopes of the Sierra Nevada, on the reservation of the Nez Perce Indians in the eastern part of Washington territory, in Last Chance Gulch in Montana, and in the Black Hills region of South Dakota on the reservation of the Sioux Indians, brought thousands upon thousands of persons to these areas. Into them crowded all the elements of a rough and active civilization. A large number of the miners, such as those in Idaho, "were like quicksilver," said H. H. Bancroft, the historian: "A mass of them dropped in any locality, broke up into individual globules, and ran off after any atom of gold in their vicinity. They stayed nowhere longer than the gold attracted them." Others, as in Colorado, stayed on, once the mining boom had spent itself, to farm and to help their area become a territory.

The story of the mining towns is a familiar one in fiction and motion pictures, and their lawlessness has attracted much attention. To be sure, it existed; but it would be a mistake to represent the mining communities as mere nests of lawlessness, or to argue, as most Easterners did, that mining camps had abandoned the institutions of civilized society. Mining camps had few churches, schools, newspapers, theaters, and so forth, but they quickly established them. For example, in the town of Deadwood, South Dakota, known as the most lawless place in the country and consisting mainly of two long rows of saloons, a stage company played Gilbert and Sullivan's *Mikado* for a record run of 130 nights.

Each mining camp was a separate administrative and judicial district having its own governing officials who passed and enforced its own laws. The legal codes and practices of these mining camps were eventually recognized in American courts, and a number of them were incorporated into constitutions and laws of the Western states.

The miners' frontier came to an end in the 1880s. No more important discoveries were made, and the individual prospector was gradually replaced by big corporations, usually run by Eastern financiers. Between 1860 and 1890, $1,242,000,000 in gold and $901,000,000 in silver were taken out of the mines in the West. These amounts enabled the federal government to resume specie payment and helped precipitate the money question, a major political issue during the last quarter of the nineteenth century (see the next chapter).

COMSTOCK LODE

In 1859, silver ore was discovered near Virginia City, Nevada, and it quickly became known as the "Comstock Lode," named after prospector Henry Comstock. In the two decades that followed, over $300 million in silver was hauled out of the earth in Nevada. Virginia City became a short-lived industrial center with over 3,000 laborers working in the mines and another 2,000 working in stamping mills and other silver manufacturing industries. The mines spawned an investment boom in California, which unfortunately led to fraud as unscrupulous businessmen sold more stock in the mines than the silver was worth. The mines spawned new technology as pumps sucked water from mine shafts and new ventilators circulated the underground shafts with air. Due to the labor demands, Comstock miners earned $4 per day, well above the average wage for miners in the West. By 1875, Virginia City had a population of 25,000 people, making it the largest city in Nevada at the time and one of the largest cities between St. Louis and San Francisco.

THE SETTLERS

The opportunities for obtaining cheap or free land induced many settlers to go west. They could buy a farm outright from the national government under the terms of the Preemption Act of 1841, which allowed them to obtain a quarter section (160 acres) at the price of $1.25 an acre. They could, also, purchase their quarter section from one of the land-grant railroads or from one of the states, whose holdings of public domain were greatly increased by the passage of the Morrill Act of 1862. (The Morrill Act had given every state that established a public, agricultural college 30,000 acres for each senator and representative then in Congress.) Finally, western settlers could secure their quarter section free of charge under the Homestead Act of 1862. This law made it possible for any American citizen, or any alien who had declared the intention of becoming a citizen, to acquire 160 acres of unoccupied government land by living on it or by cultivating it for five years. A homesteader who wished to gain ownership sooner could, after six months of residence, buy the quarter

The availability of cheap or free land induced many settlers to go west. *(Library of Congress)*

section at the prevailing minimum price, usually $1.25 an acre. The residence requirement went up to 14 months in 1891.

The Homestead Act has been called "the greatest democratic measure of all history," but it had a number of faults. The best farming lands east of the 100th meridian (the line approximately bisecting the Dakotas and Nebraska east and west) were largely taken by 1862, and in the region from the Great Plains to the Pacific, to which the law chiefly applied, small homesteads were inadequate. because the climate was too arid and rainfall too unpredictable. Moreover, the Homestead Act did not end land speculation. Individuals made larger purchases than ever. For example, William S. Chapman bought a million acres in California and Nevada, and Francis Palms and Frederick E. Driggs together procured 486,000 acres of timberland in Michigan and Wisconsin. There was also fraudulent administration of the law. False claims were made, and claims were turned over to speculators and to land, mining, and timber companies. In addition, perjury and bribery of land officials were common, so—in practice—the act was a perversion of the land reformers' ideas.

During this period a generous Congress passed other measures to dispose of the public domain. The Timber Culture Act of 1873 provided free grants of 160 acres in certain regions on condition that the settler plant 40 acres (later reduced to 10 acres) in trees and keep them growing for 10 years. Under the terms of the Desert Act of 1877 the government offered semiarid lands in 640-acre tracts to those who would irrigate them; but since irrigation projects usually required more capital than most settlers had, the law benefited primarily the large-scale grazing companies. The Timber and Stone Act of 1878 permitted the sale of quarter sections of land not suited for agriculture but valuable for timber. Large corporations and speculators managed to get possession of more than 13 million acres of such government lands.

THE RANCHING FRONTIER

Flourishing on the Great Plains for about two decades after the Civil War was an open-range cattle industry, originating with the Long Drive of cattle from Texas northward to railroads on the Great Plains for shipment eastward to the large cities. After the Civil War, some five million unclaimed head of cattle roamed the plains of Texas. The cattle were worth only $1.00 per head in Texas, but worth $60.00–$70.00 in Chicago. Hence, to reap profits, one had only to round up the cattle in Texas and drive them to rail connections, none of which had yet made it to Texas in 1866. One of the most accessible meeting places for ranchers and packers was at Abilene, Kansas, on the Kansas Pacific railroad line. Here Joseph G. McCoy, an enterprising meat dealer from Illinois, built a hotel and erected barns, stables, pens, and loading chutes. In 1868 Abilene received 75,000 head of cattle and in 1871, a record year, 700,000 head. Over the next dozen years a total of four million cattle were driven over the Chisholm Trail from Texas to Abilene and other Kansas cow towns. The cattle were moved slowly across the plains from Texas to Kansas in herds of 2,000–3,000 head. This procedure required the services of 16 or 18 cowboys, a cook with a chuck wagon, and a wrangler with extra cow ponies.

It was on the Long Drive that the cowboy came into his own as a unique character of the frontier. He was a picturesque figure, usually clothed in a flannel shirt, with a brightly colored handkerchief loosely knotted around his neck, high-heeled boots into which his trousers were tucked, a pair of leather chaps—or heavy riding overalls—and a broad-brimmed felt hat. Heavy spurs and a revolver completed his costume. The cowboy's work, however, was hazardous. With only a cow pony, a lasso, and a six-shooter, he and his companions tried to keep under safe control several thousand head of cattle during two months of continuous travel.

There were many risks along the trail—the danger of stampedes (which could be set off by a sudden noise or lightning flash), thefts by rustlers, and raids by Indians. One of the veterans of the Long Drive wrote, "It was tiresome grimy business for the attendant punchers who traveled ever in a cloud of dust and heard little but the constant chorus from the crackling of hoofs and of ankle joints, from the bellows, lows, and bleats of the trudging animals."[5] The cowboy's life was also a lonely one. He sang sentimental words to soothe the restless cattle and to cheer himself as he whiled away the lonely hours on the Chisholm Trail. Although fans of Western stories and movies might never suspect the fact, blacks were numerous among the cowboys who drove the herds to market.

That year, rail lines had reached Abilene, Kansas, and cattlemen shifted to the Chisholm Trail, going from South Texas to Abilene, Kansas. Only 35,000 head of cattle would make it to Abilene in 1867, but over 1.5 million head would make it across the Chisholm Trail over the next two decades.

The cattle drive reached its peak in the early 1880s, when profits of 40 to 50 percent were common and profits of 10,000 percent were achieved on occasion. Such returns, however, quickly at-

---

[5] Philip Ashton Rollins, *The Cowboy* (New York: Charles Scribner's Sons, 1922), p. 253.

tracted so many prospective ranchers that they overstocked the range. The unfenced plains of the public domain in the 1870s were bountiful and free, and the ranchers made use of this public land. Between 1882 and 1884, they sent as many young steers north to the ranges as they shipped east to the markets. Unfortunately, the two disastrous winters of 1885–1886 and 1886–1887 and the blistering summer of 1886, however, destroyed most of the feed and the cattle. The steers that eventually did reach market were so inferior in quality that the bottom fell out of beef prices despite the great shortage. Ninety percent of the cattle died, and 90 percent of the cattle ranchers went broke.

At this time, too, large numbers of sheepherders began to cross the plains. The sheep stripped the range of grass, so when the sheep men came to stay, the cattlemen had to fight or leave. Farmers were also homesteading the plains and fencing the open range after the invention of barbed wire made fencing affordable. Many of them, also, turned to raising cattle. Soon they were able to produce beef of higher quality than that found on the open range. With the increase of railroad facilities, including the extension of the railroads to Fort Worth, Texas, the Long Drive became unnecessary. Gradually this stage of the colorful cattle industry was ending, and with it came an end to the last frontier.

THE INDIAN

An essential step in the conquest of the last West was a solution of the Indian "problem." The Indians of the Great Plains and the Rocky Mountains, about 250,000 in number, actively opposed white settlement in their areas. The land had been theirs for centuries, and they were determined to fight, if necessary, to keep it. The strongest and most warlike were the Sioux, Blackfoot, Crow, Cheyenne, Comanche, and Apache tribes. These nomadic buffalo-hunting tribes clung tenaciously to their land and fought valiantly for it. Mounted on swift horses and armed with bows and arrows, the Indians of the Great Plains were more than a match for the whites until the repeater rifle was perfected.

Until the time of the Civil War, the Plains Indians had been relatively peaceful, but this was largely because whites had avoided the Great Plains as an uninhabitable "Great American Desert." Then the miners invaded the mountains, cattlemen moved into the grasslands, and white settlers followed the railroads across the prairies. The invention of the windmill allowed whites to settle in remote locations far from natural sources of surface water. Wanton destruction of the buffalo by the intruding whites threatened the Indians' very existence because the Indians depended on the animal for food, fuel, clothing, robes, bowstrings, tools, and other essentials. Faced with all these pressures, the tribes became dissatisfied with their treaties with the federal government.

During the quarter-century Indian war that followed the Civil War, whites clashed with the Comanche, Apache and Navaho in the Southwest and with the Sioux, Arapaho and Cheyenne on the Great Plains. For the next 25 years Indian warfare constantly recurred. In the mountain areas most of the tribes were eventually persuaded to give up their lands and move to reservations, but the tribes on the plains were not willing to abandon their hunting grounds to the encroaching whites.

In 1867, Congress enacted legislation providing for the removal of all Indians to reservations, thereby breaking the promises given to the Plains Indians in the 1820s and 1830s that they could keep their lands forever. The federal government decided to create two reservations for the Plains Indians—one in the Black Hills of Dakota, the other in present-day Oklahoma. Of course, however, difficulties would quickly arise. While the tribal chieftains signed the treaties, individual Indians often refused to be bound by them. General W. T. Sherman wrote, "We have … provided reservations for all, off the great roads. All who cling to their old hunting grounds are hostile and will remain so till killed off. We will have a sort of a predatory war for years—every now and then be shocked by the indiscriminate murder of travelers and settlers, but the country is so large, and the advantage of the Indians so great, that we cannot make a single war to end it." Sherman added that because of the Indians' swiftness and guerrilla tactics, "Fifty Indians could checkmate 3,000 United States soldiers." Indeed, the Indians won 90 percent of their encounters with the United States Army during this time period, but due to the sheer numbers of white men, they would ultimately lose any war of attrition against a larger population with superior resources and technology.

Sherman's predictions and estimations proved accurate. Between 1869 and 1875 more than 200 battles between the United States army and the Indians took place. What went on in these conflicts can be derived from a statement of General Francis A. Walker, Commissioner of Indian Affairs, in 1871: "When dealing with savage men, as with savage beasts, no question of national honor can arise. Whether to fight, to run away, or to employ a ruse, is solely a question of expediency." A few years earlier General S. R. Curtis, United States Army commander in the West, had told his subordinate officers: "I want no peace till the Indians suffer more."

A Native American war party *(Library of Congress)*

The Indians, of course, did suffer. A white trader reported that Cheyenne "were scalped, their brains knocked out; the men used their knives, ripped open women, clubbed little children, knocked them in the head with their guns, beat their brains out, mutilated their bodies in every sense of the word." This barbarity surely raised the question: Who were the savages, the Indians or the whites?

The Indian wars after 1865 cost the federal government millions of dollars and hundreds of lives, yet a solution to the problem seemed to be nowhere in sight. Much of the failure rested with the national government whose officials regarded each tribe as a separate nation. Indians frequently misunderstood the terms of the tribal treaties, and many individual Indians did not feel obligated by them. Moreover, authority over Indian affairs was divided between the Department of the Interior and the War Department, and each pursued different policies and objectives. Finally, frontiersmen, in general, believed that the only good Indian was a dead one, and most soldiers agreed.

Easterners, far removed from the scene of strife, had a different attitude. Here churchmen and reformers united to urge a policy of humanitarianism toward the Indians. As the War Department followed its policy of fighting the Indians, new ideas about the problem began to have influence at Washington. A new civilian Board of Indian Commissioners, created in 1869, attempted to convert the nomadic Plains Indians to agriculture on the reservations and sought to persuade the government to break down tribal autonomy.

In 1871 Congress abolished the policy of dealing with tribes as though they were separate nations. In the 70s, too, the government began to establish Indian boarding schools removed from the reservations. To give Indians greater incentive, the Indian Commissioners recommended individual land holdings and the gradual elimination of the system of reservations. Books on behalf of the Indian began to appear, among them Helen Hunt Jackson's *Century of Dishonor* (1881), which had the greatest influence in stirring up public opinion behind efforts to improve the Indians' lot.

Finally, in 1887, the Dawes Act initiated a new Indian policy that reversed the old military policy of extermination. The Act provided for the dissolution of tribal autonomy and the division of tribal lands, with each family head receiving 160 acres. To protect the Indian in his property, the right of disposal was withheld for 25 years. At the end of this probationary period the Indian received full rights of ownership and full United States citizenship.

The new policy did not work well, however. In dividing up the reservations, the best tracts were usually sold to white settlers and the worst given to the Indians. Often the Indian owners were disheartened and failed to cultivate adequately the land they kept. Furthermore, when individual Indians, without experience as property owners, acquired good land, they were too easily persuaded to sell it. (The Burke Act of 1906 gave the Secretary of the Interior

Helen Hunt Jackson *(Library of Congress)*

discretionary authority to reduce the probationary period preceding legal sale.) Nor was the policy universally applied. Some tribes, especially in Arizona and New Mexico, retained their tribal organizations and continued to hold their land in tribal fashion. To make matters worse, the Dawes Act actually reduced the total volume of land held by the Indians since the number of Indian "heads of household" times 160 acres did not equal the total amount of land that had been held by the Indians when it was granted to tribes instead of individuals. Furthermore, many whites married Indian widows to get their 160 acres and then divorced them. Then all-white juries and judges awarded the land to the white men who had married the Indian women for the sole purpose of getting their land.

Gradually the feeling developed that it had been a mistake to have the Indians abandon their traditional way of life. An effort was made to reverse the policy laid down by the Dawes Act and to allow the tribes to hold their land as communal property. This was to be realized in the Indian Reorganization Act of 1934, but clearly it was too little, too late.

LAST STANDS AND MASSACRES

The battles between the Indians and the white men were simply too numerous to detail in this limited space, but there are several incidents that stand out as worthy of further attention. Among those was the Sand Creek Massacre in Colorado in 1864. The discovery of gold near Pike's Peak in 1858 had led to a rush of white fortune-seekers to Colorado. Cheyenne and Arapaho Indians were then further concentrated onto reservations in southeastern Colorado. Renegade Indians, resisting further concentration, raided white settlements and stagecoach lines in retaliation. The governor of Colorado responded by urging all friendly Indians to gather at army forts for protection before the government launched a campaign to stop Indian raiders. One group of Cheyenne and Arapaho Indians under the leadership of Black Kettle camped near Fort Lyon on Sand Creek, apparently in response to the governor's urging. On November 29, 1864, Colonel John Chivington (a Methodist elder) and the Colorado militia (made up of unemployed miners—many of whom were drunk) massacred a village of 133 Indians, 105 of which were unarmed women and children. A Congressional inquiry into the incident resulted in a court martial for Chivington, but this was of little consolation for the slaughtered Indians. Black Kettle escaped, only to be killed four years later near the Texas border in a skirmish with United States troops under General George Armstrong Custer.

LITTLE BIG HORN

In 1874 gold was discovered in the Black Hills, leading hordes of whites to encroach on land reserved for the Indians. By 1875, over 1,000 whites had arrived in Dakota Territory and the Northern Pacific Railroad planned to build railroad connections. The federal government offered to purchase the Black Hills, but the Indians refused to sell, regarding the area as sacred Indian lands. The United States responded by ordering the Indians to further concentration on the Pine Ridge Reservation southeast of the Black Hills. Many of the Dakota Indians resisted and, instead, fled to southeastern Montana in the area of the Big Horn River where the Sioux under Chief Red Cloud had waged a guerrilla war against whites encroaching on their land several years before. In June 1876, General George A. Custer led a scouting party of 265 men to find the Indians' camp. Led by Chiefs Crazy Horse and Sitting Bull, an Indian army of some 2,000 Sioux warriors surprised Custer and his men, overwhelming the scouting party with superior numbers. Custer and all 265 of his men were killed, and their bodies mutilated. The Indian victory would be short-lived, however, as within six years Sitting Bull surrendered and Crazy Horse had been killed.

COCHISE, GERONIMO, AND THE APACHES

During the late 1860s, the Apaches under Chief Cochise waged a war of raids and resistance against the United States Army in New Mexico and Arizona. In 1872, Cochise accepted a peace treaty that included some of the Apaches' tribal lands. Cochise, however, also agreed that the Apaches would follow assimilation policies favored by whites. Cochise died in 1874, and his successor, Chief Geronimo, an Apache shaman or medicine man, rejected white assimilation policies and renewed raids on white settlements and outposts. Geronimo raided isolated ranches and stole food, horses, and ammunition while killing the white ranchers and burning their homesteads. Riding with Geronimo's raiders was Lozen, a female warrior armed with a rifle, who rode and raided with the men. In 1885, Lozen and Geronimo launched a series of raids over 10 months on both sides of the United States/Mexico border. At one time, over 2,000 United States troops under General Nelson Miles were involved in searching for Geronimo, but the Indians seemed to always stay one step ahead of the United States Army. Finally, in 1886, Geronimo met with General Miles to negotiate a peace. By the time Geronimo surrendered, his band of raiders numbered only 33 and the group included a good number of women and children. Upon his surrender, Geronimo explained that "we have not slept for six months" and "we are worn out."

Geronimo's career as a raider may have been over, but his legend grew over the years to the point that when he appeared at the St. Louis Exposition in 1904, he sold photographs of himself for a quarter each. Geronimo also rode with President Theodore Roosevelt in his inaugural parade in 1905. Geronimo and the Apaches were not allowed, however, to return to their homeland in Arizona, and Geronimo was buried in Oklahoma in 1909.

WOUNDED KNEE

In 1889 an Indian religious man known as Wovoka combined elements of Christianity with traditional Indian religious practices into a new religion known as the "Ghost Dance." Wovoka claimed that God spoke through him and promised that all whites would soon be destroyed in an apocalypse, that all Indians slain by whites would be resurrected from the dead, and that the buffalo, which whites had essentially wiped out by 1890, would return in great numbers to roam the plains. Central to the ceremony of Wovoka's new religion was a "ghost dance" where Indians danced in a circle in traditional style, often until some collapsed of exhaustion. As the religion spread, it grew and mutated. Wovoka's Sioux disciples taught that wearing white ghost shirts made them impervious to bullets.

Whites feared the dance as a prelude to an Indian uprising, and the Bureau of Indian Affairs agent at Pine Ridge Indian Reservation in South Dakota asked Republican President Benjamin Harrison for federal troop reinforcements in anticipation of an Indian uprising. In December 1890, Chief Sitting Bull was arrested and then shot and killed by Indian police when he joined the ghost dancers. Sitting Bull's followers fled the scene of his death, but the United States Army met them at Wounded Knee Creek. The soldiers of the United States Army opened fire and massacred some 200 defenseless Indians, many of them women and children, in the snow. An eye-witness to the scene, an Indian named American Horse, described the event thusly:

> They turned their guns, Hotchkiss guns (cannons that fired an explosive shell) upon the women who were in the lodges standing there under a flag of truce, and of course as soon as they were fired upon they fled. ... There was a woman with an infant in her arms who was killed as she almost touched the flag of truce, and the women and children of course were strewn all along the

circular village until they were dispatched. Right near the flag of truce a mother was shot down with her infant; the child not knowing that its mother was dead was still nursing, and that especially was a very sad sight. The women as they were fleeing with their babes were killed together, shot right through, and the women who were very heavy with child were also killed. ... After most all of them had been killed a cry was made that all those who were not killed or wounded should come forth and they would be safe. Little boys who were not wounded came out of their places of refuge, and as soon as they came in sight a number of soldiers surrounded them and butchered them right there."

In addition to the obvious tragedy, the Wounded Knee massacre represents an end to the Indian way of life. In the words of the Indian leader Black Elk, "The nation's hoop is broken and scattered. There is no center any longer and the sacred tree is now dead." Similarly, Chief Joseph of the Nez Perce in the Pacific Northwest uttered the following speech after being captured by federal troops 40 miles south of his goal of the Canadian border,

"I am tired of fighting. Our chiefs are killed. ... It is cold and we have no blankets. The little children are freezing to death. My people, some of them, have run away to the hills, and have no blankets, no food; no one knows where they are—perhaps freezing to death. I want to have time to look for my children and see how many I can find. Maybe I shall find them among the dead. Hear me, my Chiefs, I am tired; my heart is sick and sad. From where the sun now stands, I will fight no more forever."

THE WHITE VICTORY AND THE DESTRUCTION OF THE BUFFALO

The white victory over the Native Americans can be attributed to numerous factors, including the European diseases that had wiped out over 90 percent of the Indians since the landing of Columbus and the superior technology of the Europeans, as well as the European mastery of the horse that was not present in North America until the arrival of the Spanish. The destruction of the plains Indians and the final victory, however, should be attributed to the destruction of the buffalo, which must be listed as another in a long list of American tragedies. At the close of the Civil War, an estimated 15 million buffalo roamed the Great Plains. By 1900, however, the American Bison was in danger of extinction, and only an estimated 300 remained.

Several factors worked to bring about this waste of life. First, the United States Army well understood that the buffalo were the source of food, shelter, and clothing for the Plains Indians. Without the buffalo the Plains Indians would not survive. Therefore, some of the buffalo were methodically shot by the United States Army in an effort to vanquish their foe. Second, given that one buffalo would feed 100 people, the railroads slaughtered the buffalo to feed their workers as they built the railroad lines across the Great Plains. Third, buffalo rugs became a fashionable item, not only on the east coast of the United States but also in Europe, so thousands of buffalos were killed to provide rugs for the wealthy—both in the United States and in Europe. Fourth, a popular societal myth was that the buffalo tongue was an aphrodisiac; therefore, millions of buffaloes were slaughtered just for the tongue. Dodge City, Kansas alone shipped some seven million pounds of buffalo tongue. Finally, the railroads sold buffalo hunting expeditions for sport, in spite of the fact that since it had few natural enemies, the buffalo tended not to run when hearing a shot. Although mountain lions could and did kill young buffaloes, any animal predators were simply no match for the adult buffaloes due to their size and strength—until Europeans arrived with lead and gunpowder.

A NEW ETHNIC MIX

In the first two centuries of American history, the nation's ethnic mix was more or less tripartite: Native American, European, and African American. After the Mexican War and the acquisition of the Southwest, the mix began to include Latinos, among them were mestizos of mixed Spanish and Indian ancestry. After the California gold rush, immigrants began to arrive on the West Coast from China and then from other Asian countries. Sadly, the record of the treatment of the people of color in the American West is a story of virulent prejudice, discriminatory legislation, and ghettoization—patterns that would not really change until World War II. In California, for example, the state legislature enacted the Foreign Miners' Tax in 1850, a measure whereby "foreigners" had to pay an additional $20 in order to mine. What was especially unfortunate was the fact that Latinos, many of whom had been born in Mexican California, were often defined as "foreign," despite the guarantees of protection for the Californios in the Treaty of Guadalupe Hidalgo, ending the Mexican War. Furthermore, we have already discussed the violent reaction to Chinese immigration in San Francisco, followed by Congress's passage of the

Chinese Exclusion Act of 1882, which barred entrance of Asian immigrants to the United States.

The new ethnic mix, the voluminous immigration to the East Coast from southern and eastern Europe, the labor turmoil and the exploitation of the vulnerable, the overcrowded cities, the problems for farm families, struggling to market their crops profitably—all these constituted challenges to the nation's political system. In the next chapter, we shall see how well the system responded.

THE POLITICS OF CONSERVATISM AND DISSENT, 1877–1900

(Library of Congress)

POLITICAL DOLDRUMS

CRITICS OF THE GILDED AGE

In contrast to the dramatic industrial and economic progress in the post-Reconstruction years—to say nothing of the vibrant intellectual life we have explored—the political activity of the United States in the Gilded Age seemed to lack the vitality and productivity of earlier periods. The Presidents had executive ability and high principles, but they, like most of the important men in Congress, proved to be mediocre and uninspiring leaders. "No period so thoroughly ordinary has been known in American politics since Christopher Columbus first disturbed the balance of power in American society," wrote Henry Adams, that biting commentator of the Gilded Age. "One might search the whole list of Congress, Judiciary, and Executive during the 25 years 1870 to 1895 and find little but damaged reputation. The period was poor in purpose and barren in results."

This era in American politics has been kicked and scuffed by historians until little remains of its reputation. Most critics believe that at no other time in American history was the moral and intellectual tone of political life so uniformly low and political contests so preoccupied with political gain and patronage. "Even among the most powerful men of that generation," said Henry Adams, speaking of the politicians, there were "none who had a good word for it." It has become a historical convention to censure the politicians of these years for degenerating into a group of spoilsmen who served the business community as they were themselves served by it.

The most serious charge leveled against the major parties was that they failed to meet the problems generated by the Industrial Revolution and the anguish being endured by African Americans in the post-Reconstruction South. Far-reaching economic changes necessitated extensive social readjustments; and problems arising from recurrent industrial crises and depressions demanded vigorous governmental action, as did the intransigence of the white South. A variety of factors, however, dissipated the political energies that might have been directed at these social problems.

TWO EMPTY BOTTLES

The common explanation for this failure is that there were no important differences on major issues between Democrats and Republicans. "Neither party has any principles, any distinctive tenets," wrote

James Bryce, a contemporary English observer of the American party system. "The two major parties in this period," concluded Bryce, "were like two bottles. Each bore a label denoting the kind of liquor it contained, but each was empty." Historians have called the period the "age of negation" and its politics "the politics of dead center."

The Republican Party was a loose combination of Northeastern business groups and upper Midwestern farming groups—an alliance that had been formed in 1860 and had fought and won the Civil War. In much of the North and West, Republicans were the party of wealth and respectability.

Two other large groups attached to the Republican Party were blacks and Union army veterans. The blacks, loyal to the party of emancipation, had been able to elect a few congressmen from the South; but after the Republicans abandoned them in 1877, they became more openly critical of the party and rapidly lost what little political power they had previously enjoyed. War veterans, on the other hand, increased their political importance by organizing the Grand Army of the Republic in 1866 and pressuring Congress into voting for generous pension laws.

Sharply divergent views between Northeastern businessmen and Western farmers occasionally threatened party unity, but Republican orators tried to sidestep their differences by "waving the bloody shirt"—equating party loyalty with national patriotism and charging the Democrats with having fought under the Confederate flag.

The bloody shirt itself was a reference by Northerners to the continued Southern defiance and rebellion. Radical Republican leader Charles Sumner had once waved a bloody shirt on the floor of Congress that had been worn by a Northern resident who moved South seeking his fortune and was flogged in Mississippi. To Northerners, the bloody shirt was a negative symbol, but to Southerners, the bloody shirt was a positive symbol

Charles Sumner *(Library of Congress)*

of the Southern spirit. Though the South had been crushed militarily in the Civil War, the spirit of the South had risen again; and no northerner in his right mind would entertain the notion of moving south with a carpetbag lest he be flogged as well.

The Democratic Party, known in the South as the "Southern White Man's Party," was a more regional coalition than the Republicans. Its support came chiefly from the "solid South" and the city machines of the Northeast, but it also had some support from the industrial workers of the big cities and from those Northeastern bankers and merchants—"sound money" men—who opposed protective tariffs and government subsidies to special interests and who favored contraction of the currency. The Democrats also made inroads in the Gilded Age among Western farmers that were experiencing falling agricultural prices combined with arbitrary high shipping charges from railroads and high interest rates charged by banks due to the shortage of currency.

In the South the Democrats were the party of white supremacy. Southern Democratic leaders, often of Whig background, called themselves "Conservatives" and were frequently labeled "Bourbons" (after the discredited French monarchs) by their opponents. They had much in common with Democratic leaders in the Midwest, who shared their conservative economic views and were also known as "Bourbons." In large Northern cities the Democratic Party had the allegiance of most immigrants, who were attracted by the name of the party and their sympathy toward labor unions, and whose leaders had sometimes risen to places of influence in it. The rank-and-file Democrats—farmers, industrial workers, and small businessmen—were often restive under the conservative leaders, but those leaders prevailed until the mid-1890s.

In the early twenty-first century, the big cities of the country will usually vote Democratic, but in the Gilded Age, most of the large urban centers outside the South were more likely to be Republican than Democratic. New York and Boston ordinarily went Democratic due to large Catholic populations, but in the three presidential elections of the 1880s, for example, a majority of the cities of over 50,000 outside the South went Republican. The Republican Party in these years was able to appeal successfully to urban voters and many immigrants as the party of prosperity and economic growth. In contrast, the Democrats appeared as the more conservative and frugality-minded party of the South and did not have the same appeal.

To account for the seeming impotence of political parties during the era, it must be remembered that a generally held opinion in America, in line with laissez-faire, was that government should "let well enough alone." Consequently, government rarely concerned itself with economic and social problems.

There were, however, other deterrents to governmental action. Probably most important of these was the sharp contest between the parties and the failure of either to control the national government for any appreciable length of time. Contrary to popular belief, the years of the Gilded Age were not years of Republican supremacy. Rather, they were a period of party stalemate and equilibrium.

In the six presidential elections from 1876 to 1896, the Republicans, while winning four, gained a majority of the popular vote in only one (1896) and a plurality in only one (1880)—and even that plurality was less than one tenth of one percent. In three of these elections the difference between the popular vote for the two major party candidates was less than one percent although electoral vote majorities ranged from one in 1876 to 132 in 1892. The Democrats—while electing a President twice, in both 1884 and 1892 when they elected Grover Cleveland—won a majority of the popular vote in 1876 and a plurality in 1884, 1888, and 1892. Each party managed to control the presidency and Congress at the same time for only two years—Republicans from 1889 to 1891 and the Democrats from 1893 to 1895.

In recent years, the two major parties in the Gilded Age have received much attention from historians. One might have expected the parties to show increasing centralization and bureaucracy, paralleling the centralization then going on in American business, with the national committees rising to a position of power over the state organizations. Instead there was decentralization—a lack of continuity between campaigns, weak national administrations, and even weaker national party committees.

In place of increasing professionalism, political adventurers—businessmen without firm state party bases—almost invariably beat the pros in presidential politics. Political coalitions were formed to serve during approaching elections and

Grover Cleveland *(Library of Congress)*

then fell apart soon afterwards, only to be rebuilt, many times, in different forms. In general, the increased bureaucratization and centralization of American life were largely thwarted in political life.

The two major parties had few if any national leaders. Of course, there were Democratic and Republican officeholders, and some of these people were well known to voters beyond their immediate constituencies; but public office and a degree of popularity seldom transferred themselves into effective power. Leaders of both parties worked to keep abreast of the changes in the public mood but did not often try to change that mood. The greatest strength of the party system was its ability to reflect the diversity and diffuseness of the American electorate. Finding an issue to appeal to a broad cross-section of the party's voters or office-holders in a country so large and diverse was a formidable task in the late nineteenth century and one rarely undertaken successfully. Politicians acted less to address the national problems arising from industrialism and more to satisfy newly created sectional interests.

THE PULL OF SECTIONALISM

Sectional interests resulting from the growth of industry and the expansion of the West served to dissipate and disrupt legislative activity during the 70s and 80s. The leading issues of the country, as indicated by party platforms and congressional action, were currency and banking, tariffs, public lands, internal improvements, railroad and trust regulation, immigration, issues involving blacks in the South, and the "bloody shirt" or continued Southern defiance and rebellion. While all of these produced strong sectional feeling, they generally had one common feature—opposition in the agricultural regions to politics of the industrial centers of the nation. One result was that political personalities seemed to play a subordinate role in determining the outcome of votes on national policies while efforts to find adjustments between sectional interests and party allegiances took priority.

Because the Industrial Revolution had made them the new ruling class in the country, businessmen could obtain political favors, supplanting the Southern planters and Northeastern merchants in the seats of power. The usual explanation for this alliance between business and politics is that the politicians were the hirelings of the business community. "Business ran politics, and politics was a branch of business," writes one historian.

Despite its favored position, business did not control American politics without opposition. Businessmen had to pay heavily for political favors, and often they were blackmailed by threats of regulation or of withdrawal of government assistance. Businessmen complained that politicians treated them simply as customers, compelling them to pay for protection, selling political benefits to the highest bidders, and refusing to do "the proper thing" (in the eyes of the businessmen) without pay. As we shall see, farmers and workers, too, were able to win political favors once they became organized and began to put pressure on politicians. Democracy, it seemed, was open to the highest bidder.

Voters, for their part, did more sectional voting during depressions and showed more party loyalty in times of prosperity. Those sections hardest hit in a depression broke party ranks and combined with other distressed areas to attempt to do something about their grievances. The vagueness of party platforms until 1888 also stimulated sectional divisions since it allowed representatives from discontented sections to interpret the planks to suit their own interests. In Congress sectional voting was more pronounced when the control of the houses was divided between the two parties than in those instances when one party was in control. This was equally true for depression and prosperity years in the 70s and 80s. Thus Presidents had to deal not only with divided Congresses, but also with Congresses in which their own party members did more sectional than party voting.

THE DISABLED PRESIDENCY

The President might have been expected to mediate sectional interests, but the office of the presidency was at low ebb in power and prestige during this period. National political power was vested chiefly in Congress. Congressional leaders almost overthrew Andrew Johnson, gained nearly complete control of Grant, and had tried to put subsequent Presidents in the Gilded Age at their mercy. Senator John Sherman, Republican leader of Ohio and a perpetual aspirant to the office, wrote: "The executive department of a republic like ours should be subordinate to the legislative department. The President should (merely) obey and enforce the laws." Presidents in the Gilded Age, such as Grover Cleveland and Benjamin Harrison, tended to agree.

Congressional leaders acted accordingly. "The most eminent Senators," observed George F. Hoar, Republican of Massachusetts, about his colleagues in the Senate, "would have received as a personal affront a private message from the White House expressing a desire that they should adopt any course in the discharge of their legislative duties that they did not approve. If they visited the White

Benjamin Harrison *(Library of Congress)*

House, it was to give, not to receive advice."

THE PARTY BOSSES

The political rulers of the day were not the titular leaders but the party bosses, many of them United States senators, who headed powerful state machines and rewarded their followers with public offices. Among the important bosses were Senators James G. Blaine of Maine, Roscoe Conkling of New York, Zachariah Chandler of Michigan, and John A. Logan of Illinois—all Republicans—and Arthur P. Gorman of Maryland, a Democrat. Before 1883, these party bosses had at their disposal an enormous amount of spoils in the form of federal, state, and local offices, as well as government contracts. They controlled a hierarchy of workers down to the ward heelers, to whom they gave offices in return for faithful service. The assessment of officeholders and the sale of nominations and offices tightened the bosses' grip on local machines.

When the Civil Service Reform Act of 1883 (to be discussed later in this chapter) began to remove these powers by eliminating the federal spoils that produced them, politicians turned increasingly to businessmen for money and support. A new type of political boss appeared—a business type who resembled and worked closely with corporation executives, made few speeches, and conducted his activities in anterooms, caucuses, and committees. Matthew S. Quay of Pennsylvania, Leland Stanford of California, Philetus Sawyer of Wisconsin, Thomas Platt of New York, and Nelson W. Aldrich of Rhode Island were bosses of the new type. Some had been prosperous bankers and businessmen and had entered the Senate to protect their interests. In 1889 journalist William Allen White could say: "a United States Senator ... represented something more than a state, more even than a region. He represented principalities and powers in business." According to White, one senator "represented the Union Pacific Railway System, another the New York Central. ... Coal and iron owned a coterie from the Middle and Eastern seaport states. Cotton had half a dozen senators. And so it went." Many labeled this imposing body the "Millionaires' Club." Senator George Hearst of California, one of the group, echoed Darwinian theory when he said: "I do not know much about books; ... but I have traveled a good deal and have observed men and things and I have made up my mind after my experiences that the members of the Senate are the survivors of the fittest."

Besides these prominent Establishment bosses, there were the backroom bosses, who often ruled without ever holding elective office. The principal effect of the spoils system was to transfer party control from publicly elected leaders to "inside" rulers. The most flagrant examples of "invisible government" occurred in the cities, many of which were run by corrupt political machines. Whether Democratic, like Tammany Hall in New York led by William Marcy "Boss" Tweed, or Republican, like the Gas Ring in Philadelphia, their methods were the same. James Bryce expressed the opinion that municipal government was "the one conspicuous failure of the United States." Similarly, Andrew D. White in an article in *Forum* in 1890 stated that "with very few exceptions, the city governments of the United States are the worst in Christendom—the most expensive, the most inefficient, and the most corrupt."

New York City furnished the country its most notorious example of a municipal machine. Tammany Hall, an organization dating back to the eighteenth century, controlled the Democratic Party and the local government. William Marcy Tweed and his followers—A. Oakey Hall, the mayor, Peter B. Sweeney, county and city treasurer, and Richard B. Connally, the city controller—ran Tammany Hall and plundered the city. By every type of embezzlement this repulsive crew robbed the city treasury year after year until, at the height of their power, they were splitting among themselves 85 percent of the total expenditures made by the city and county.

Their technique was simple. Everyone who had a bill against the city was instructed to pad it—at first by 10 percent, later 66 percent, finally 85 percent. Tweed's gang received the padding. For example, the courthouse, originally estimated at $3 million cost the taxpayers $11 million. The plastering bill alone amounted to $2.87 million and the carpeting to $350,000, "enough to cover the whole City Park three times." The loot taken by the Tweed Ring has been variously estimated at from $45 million to $100 million.

Although respectable citizens protested, they were powerless for several years to move against Tweed because he controlled every arm of the government. Finally, courageous editorials in *The New*

York Times and the cartoons of Thomas Nast in *Harper's Weekly* exposed the corruption of the Tweed Ring and aroused the general public. His own followers, Tweed said, could not read, but they could "look at the damn pictures." Tweed offered George Jones, owner of *The New York Times*, $1 million to quiet his paper and Nast $500,000 to study art in Europe, but they refused. A citizens' committee headed by Samuel J. Tilden and Charles O'Conor launched an investigation that was able by the end of 1872 to drive every member of the Tweed Ring out of office, and Tweed himself died in jail.

Yet the traditional view of the boss as nothing but a corrupting force in American politics needs to be modified. Studies of Boss Tweed and of the Cox machine in Cincinnati show that these political organizations furnished some element of order and stability in a rapidly expanding and disordered society. They point out that the boss provided a valuable service in giving services to many people—especially immigrants—who had no other institutional or social order to which to appeal. The political party machines essentially ran informal welfare systems, providing food and necessities, housing, and employment to immigrants and the working classes in the nation's urban centers in exchange for political support. The result was very high (75 percent) voter turnout since more people had a vested interest in whether their preferred party remained in office.

Moreover not all bosses used politics to advance their material interest. Common as the various forms of graft and corruption were in the Gilded Age, not all bosses sought material profit. Boies Penrose, Republican boss of Pennsylvania, apparently never made a dollar out of politics; and according to Theodore Roosevelt, "Senator Platt [Republican boss of New York state] did not use his political position to advance his private fortunes—therein differing from many other political bosses. He lived in hotels and had few extravagant tastes."

UPPER-CLASS REFORMERS

In this age of corruption, voices such as those of the "single-tax" advocate Henry George and the socialist Edward Bellamy, about whom we have already learned, were calling for reform; and Jane Addams and her colleagues in the settlement house movement were reaching out to new immigrants, as we have seen. Into this mix, there were also reformers with an upper-class orientation. Probably the most respectable of all the reformers were the "Mugwumps," as their opponents called them. The term was first used politically in 1884 to describe the independent Republicans who refused to support presidential candidate James G. Blaine due to his reputation for political corruption. Mugwumps generally were newspapermen, scholars, and intellectuals—earnest men of high ideals and prominent social position, of conservative economic views, and usually of Republican background. Foremost among them were George William Curtis, editor of *Harper's Weekly*; E. L. Godkin, editor of *The Nation*; Carl Schurz; William Cullen Bryant; Whitelaw Reid; and Samuel Bowles. They lashed out against the spoils system and worked to purify politics through civil service reform. Since they believed in laissez-faire, however, they restricted their economic program to tariff reform and sound money.

The Mugwumps spoke in moralistic terms rather than in economic ones. They appealed primarily to the educated upper classes and seldom identified themselves with the interests of the masses, whom they viewed with an aristocratic disdain. They regarded the reform movements of labor and farmers as radical and dangerous and had little use for other reform movements of the period; but this was characteristic of most contemporary reform movements which had little in common and had great difficulty in understanding one another. Divided and mutually suspicious, the reformers thus exerted little influence.

Historians have long praised the Mugwumps, whose censure of the Gilded Age they generally have accepted; but recent studies of these reformers challenge both the indictment of that period and Mugwump beliefs. It will be difficult for future writers to extol these "independents," who condemned corruption, without recognizing that they too were elitists who opposed the democratizing direction of their time. The Mugwumps "seemed to dislike thinking about the workingman as such," writes Geoffrey Blodgett. "They had no solution for the poor," doubting in fact that there *was* a solution because poverty "resulted from the poor people spending too much money." Furthermore, unlike the Progressives of the succeeding generation, they "made no real effort to break the control of the elective process enjoyed by party professionals."

These liberal reformers of the Gilded Age believed that political independence helped to purify politics, but they also had a price for their reforms. They wanted a small, efficient government run by themselves or by men like themselves—reducing property taxes, encouraging individual effort, and cutting back public services. "Unable to come to terms with his age, the liberal reformer exaggerated its defects and overrated the past," observes John G. Sproat. "Everything considered—this campaign to reform postwar society was a pathetic failure." Liberal reformers of the Gilded Age are now found wanting almost as much as the Gilded Age was found wanting by them.

THE VOTERS

There were limits to what could be done about relieving social and economic discontent, and mainly the voters themselves imposed these limits. For one thing, those interested in reform did not give consistent support to either party. Victory in national elections depended on heavily populated "doubtful" states, which had enough shifting voters to swing the results either way. These were Connecticut, New York, and New Jersey in the East, and Ohio, Indiana, and Illinois in the Midwest. These states, especially New York and the three Midwestern ones, enjoyed strong bargaining power with which they secured favorable posts for their politicians and obtained most of the funds from the campaign treasuries at election time. The doubtful states were wedded to neither party but courted by both. The parties chose presidential and vice-presidential candidates from these areas and awarded their congressmen important committee assignments.

"Not the Republican politician but the voting public failed reform in the early years of the Gilded Age," writes La Wanda Cox about New York. "Civic improvement did not win the anticipated votes from New York City's Democratic faithful, and Republican support for equal suffrage (for African Americans) brought political disaster. The hopeful union of idealism and practical politics within the state Republican party could not be consummated in the face of public repudiation at the polls."

In the Northeast, and in Massachusetts in particular, according to Blodgett, the political leaders were all acting in an essentially conservative manner because of these restraints. They realized that the country was changing, and they were willing to make adjustments. But their constituents—native born Americans and immigrants alike—opposed basic change, because to them perpetuating their community was more important than improving it. As a result, the Democratic Party in Massachusetts did not rise to the occasion and by the end of the nineteenth century could no longer be considered an effective instrument of social and economic change.

It is important to remember that some pieces of major legislation were passed during this period, despite the limitations imposed by voters and the politicians' reluctance to address the issues. The abiding belief that this was a period in which issues were steadfastly ignored is testimony to the lasting quality of the progressive-liberal historians' interpretation of the Gilded Age, which is echoed even by modern historians. The assumptions of the early historians also overlooked the fact that there was proportionately a heavier turnout of voters in the Gilded Age than in the twentieth century, evidence of their concern with politics and partisanship.

Both voter behavior and party alignment revolved primarily around ethno-cultural issues and responses, mostly religious and sectarian in nature. The expansion in the Catholic population in the country in the last third of the nineteenth century by the flood of immigrants from Europe

A parochial school. The flood of Catholic immigrants in the late nineteenth century greatly strengthened the Democratic Party. *(Library of Congress)*

greatly strengthened the Democratic Party, which has traditionally been identified with Catholic voters. Then in the 1880s there was a revival of anti-immigrant activism that was supported by many Republican Protestants. The very moralistic Protestants sharply assailed the drinking habits and the easy Sunday recreational activities of the immigrants, especially the Germans and the Irish Catholics. These Republicans wanted prohibition and Sunday laws, demands that angered many Americans who believed their personal liberties were in danger. German Lutherans and Irish and Polish Catholics were alarmed that the Republicans would also attempt to eliminate their parochial schools, which they considered essential for maintaining their religion and their culture; thus, they gave their support to the Democratic Party.

THE FIGHT FOR RIGHTS

THE ABANDONMENT OF THE BLACKS

The failure of Americans in the Gilded Age to deal adequately with the pressing issues of the day can be clearly seen in the way they handled their greatest and most tragic problem—the plight of American blacks, who comprised one tenth of the population. Though the Civil War had settled the question of human slavery, it did not settle the problem of securing for all Americans the inalienable rights set forth in the Declaration of Independence. Nor did it alter the fact that white supremacy was generally taken for granted. During Reconstruction significant constitutional and legislative steps—the Thirteenth, Fourteenth, and Fifteenth Amendments and the passage of civil rights legislation in 1866 and 1875—were taken to insure the freedpeople's political and civil rights but developments during the last quarter of the nineteenth century virtually destroyed these political gains.

When President Hayes removed the last of the federal troops and federal control from the South in April 1877, he left Southern blacks in the custody of Southern whites. Governor Wade Hampton of South Carolina had promised, "We ... will secure to every citizen, the lowest as well as the highest, black as well as white, full and equal protection in the enjoyment of all his rights under the Constitution." Because of such promises Hayes believed that a new "era of good feeling" was developing in the South between the two races. Even before 1877 was over, he learned differently. "By state legislation, by frauds, by intimidation, and by violence of the most atrocious character, colored citizens have been deprived of the right of suffrage," he wrote in his diary. He did practically nothing, however, to correct the situation as he had earlier said he would, partially because he believed that Congress—rather than the President—should assume policy leadership, and partially because Hayes was never viewed as a legitimate ruler in the South due to the fraudulent election of 1876. Hayes successor, James Garfield, was no more proactive, stating only, "Time is the only cure."

The Republican Party had emerged from the Civil War as the champion and protector of the Southern blacks. It had emancipated and enfranchised them and had provided them with the same political and civil rights as whites. In their platforms from 1876 to 1896, the Republicans solemnly pledged themselves to enforce the Fourteenth and Fifteenth Amendments, to secure to "every American citizen of whatever race and color complete liberty and exact equality in the exercise of all civil, political, and public rights," protect "honest voters" against terrorism, violence and fraud, and never to relax their efforts "until the integrity of the ballot and purity of elections ... be fully guaranteed in every state." In Congress they sponsored investigations of fraud and violence in elections in the South, accused Southern Democrats of holding their seats illegally and of exercising a disproportionate voting influence, and focused attention upon indiscreet statements by Southern leaders and the press. Unfortunately, while Republicans talked much, they took few steps to remedy the desperate situation of African Americans or to meet their obligations to the freedmen.

Actually, throughout most of the last quarter of the nineteenth century, the Republicans were in no position in Congress to enforce the Fourteenth and Fifteenth Amendments, but their abandonment of blacks was also part of a well-planned policy. Their new plans called for a shift in Republican appeals in the South from blacks to whites. They wanted to maintain and even increase their black support, but that was subsidiary to their main aim: swelling their ranks with southern whites.

Thus, Hayes abandoned the Southern blacks when he removed the Union troops from the South in the hope of reconciling North and South, conciliating Southern whites and ingratiating the Republican Party with them. President Chester Arthur deserted the blacks when he chose to work with Independents in the South in the belief that it was necessary to subordinate the freedmen to exploit the Democratic cleavages in the South, which he had concluded was the only path to Republican success there. Furthermore, in 1890, when Republicans had control of the presidency and the Congress at the same time for the only period in these years, they again forsook blacks when they failed to pass the Federal Elections or "Force" Bill, providing for national supervision of federal elections as a way of protecting the rights of Southern blacks to vote. They did so because they had a greater interest in the tariff and silver measures, but also because there was considerable opposition to the elections legislation in party ranks.

The Republican abandonment of the blacks was also a part of a general abandonment by all Northerners. By the end of Reconstruction most Northerners probably agreed with Southern whites that the blacks were not prepared for equality and that the South should be allowed to deal with them in its own way. Northerners had also come to believe that the elimination of the issue of blacks from politics was necessary for a return to national solidarity and a development of trade relations between the North and South.

To make matters worse, the courts also abandoned the blacks. After 1877 practically every Supreme Court decision affecting blacks nullified their rights or curtailed them somehow. The Court

President Chester Arthur *(Library of Congress)*

drastically limited the powers of the federal government to intervene in the states to protect the rights of blacks. To all intents and purposes, it invalidated the Fourteenth and Fifteenth Amendments as effective safeguards for black people. When in 1883 the Court set aside the Civil Rights Act of 1875 on the ground that the Fourteenth Amendment was binding on states but not individuals, it ended federal attempts to protect blacks against discrimination by private persons. There would be no federal civil rights legislation thereafter until 1957. In the 1870s, when the Court held in *United States v. Reese* and *United States v. Cruickshank* that the Fifteenth Amendment did not confer the right to vote upon anyone and that Congress did not have the authority to protect the right to vote generally, sections of the Enforcement Act of 1870 were declared unconstitutional because they provided penalties for hindering a person in voting. In 1894, Congress repealed the entire law. Again, there was no further legislation on the subject until 1957.

Finally, in two decisions in the 1890s, the Court paved the way for additional curtailment of the rights of blacks. In *Plessy v. Ferguson* (1896), the Court laid down the "separate but equal" rule in defense of segregation. Reflecting adherence to Social Darwinism, the Court ruled that "if one race be inferior to another," it was not the role of the court to place them "on the same plane." The "separate but equal doctrine" became the law of the land until 1954. Then, in *William v. Mississippi* (1898), the Court opened the road to legal disfranchisement by approving Southern plans for depriving blacks of the vote.

Blacks had continued to vote, though in reduced numbers, after the return of white supremacy in the South. In some parts of the South they were prevented from voting by threats or intimidation, and in other parts their vote was nullified by artful means such as the use of tissue ballots and a complicated system of ballot boxes. In the 1890s, however, the Southern states proceeded to disfranchise them with laws. Within two decades practically all black voters had been disfranchised by means of poll taxes, white primaries, tests of "moral character," and literacy or property qualifications that were enforced against blacks but not against whites. Illiterate whites were generally exempt from literacy tests by so-called "Grandfather Clauses" that stated that persons were exempt from the tests if their grandfather voted. For African Americans, none could be exempt under the Grandfather Clauses because none of the grandfathers were allowed to vote during the days before emancipation. "White Primaries" disfranchised blacks by preventing them from voting in party primaries. Since in the South the only real question in any election was who would win the Democratic nomination for any particular position in the primary—because voting Republican was considered "unsouthern" and "dishonored the confederate dead"—blacks were allowed to vote in the general election in some counties after the Democratic Party nominee had already been chosen by whites only. The Democratic nominee would then defeat the Republican in the general election in a landslide, thus cutting blacks out of the "real decision" that had been made at the primary level.

In the same years the Southern states also passed numerous "Jim Crow" laws, segregating blacks in virtually every aspect of public life. State and municipal laws were passed against such crimes as "night walking," "leering," "lurking," and "misspending one's income." Blacks were denied the right to bear arms, limited by zoning to certain sections of town (normally the east side of town so that they would be downwind from whites rather than vice versa), and even banned from residence in some towns by "sundown laws" that required that no blacks could remain in town after sundown. Economically, laws were passed limiting blacks to employment only in agriculture or domestic servitude.

Most Northerners shared the segregationists' attitudes toward blacks. They deplored agitation on behalf of blacks and were willing to accept the South's racial policies. Even educated, intelligent Northerners believed that black people were racially inferior because most scientists at the time also believed this. Furthermore, most of the Northern press supported the discriminatory decisions in the civil rights cases. As historian Rayford W. Logan has shown, Northern newspapers usually described blacks in a derogatory manner, regardless of the actual circumstances, strengthening a stereotype of the "criminal Negro." The leading literary magazines of the North such as *Harper's, Scribner's* and the *Atlantic Monthly*, mirroring the refined tastes of the upper classes, regularly used derisive terms when they referred to blacks.

Most Americans did not especially wish blacks ill, writes John A. Garraty, a leading historian of the Gilded Age. "... They simply refused to consider them quite human and consigned them complacently to oblivion, along with the Indians."

The position of black leader Booker T. Washington among his race may have also contributed to the assault upon the rights of blacks. Washington, founder and principal of Tuskeegee Institute in Alabama was, according to Louis R. Harlan, a biographer, a "white man's black man" and a "safe, sane Negro" to Southern whites. In the Northern white world, Washington was "deferential but dignified," drawing philanthropy from such men as Carnegie. Among Southern whites, says Harlan, Washington made a point of not crossing the

Booker T. Washington *(Library of Congress)*

color line and sought to reduce social friction. He believed that for the time being blacks should forgo agitation for the vote and social equality and devote their efforts to achieving economic security and independence. "In all things that are purely social," he said in 1895, "we can be as separate as the fingers, yet one as the hand in all things for mutual progress."

"Washington unmistakably accepted a subordinate position for Southern Negroes," writes Rayford Logan. "This position was far different from the unequivocal standard for equal citizenship advanced by (Frederick) Douglass in 1889. He definitely renounced social equality. ... In return he asked for a chance to gain a decent livelihood. Washington was convinced, and rightly so," continues Logan, "that it would have been folly to ask in 1895 for equal rights for Negroes." Washington's position won the enthusiastic support of the white community and had much to do with fixing the pattern of race relations in the country for most of the remainder of his lifetime. Most blacks of that time probably accepted Washington's view. Supporters of Washington, however, argue that the attitudes of whites were so racist and that blacks were so outnumbered, impoverished, and without political power that Washington was simply a realist who adopted the only practical approach. Washington was famous for the statement "Cast down your bucket where you are," which was a janitorial reference imploring blacks to work for economic success within the segregated system imposed by whites. If all whites would allow blacks to do was be janitors, Washington was essentially saying that blacks should do their very best at being janitors and their hard work would eventually pay off. Washington is also known for what is termed as the "Atlanta Compromise," whereby Washington urged blacks to accept segregation in return for white support of black educational and economic success.

As for black people in "the New South" (the way that many of its white businessmen advocates chose to bill it), their plight was desperate in the years after Reconstruction ended. They faced not only disfranchisement and discrimination but also physical intimidation and the ultimate penalty, lynching. In the 1890s the numbers of lynching in the South rose precipitously, with 161 black people being lynched in the peak year of 1892—and these are only the victims who show up in the public record—and they do not include hundreds of other beatings, castrations, and other forms of nonlethal intimidation. Black men, in particular, might be lynched on the merest suspicion of a sexual assault on a white woman. Moreover, the vast majority of African Americans lived in a state of peonage, owing to their being sharecroppers with little ability to get ahead. They were the poorest of the poor in a poor region—despite the trumpeting of change by New South boosters.

Even in this dark time, with Booker T. Washington preaching accommodation, there was one African American who fought lynching publicly, Ida B. Wells-Barnett. Born to slave parents in the waning days of the Confederacy, Wells-Barnett became a newspaper editor in Memphis. In March 1892, a mob lynched three black men whom she knew and admired; and she wrote an editorial denouncing this event. She had to leave the South to continue her crusade against lynching, eventually settling in Chicago. In 1895 she published *The Red Record*, her account of lynching in the South over a three-year period. Similarly, other black leaders, such as Harvard and Berlin University-educated William E. B. DuBois and T. Thomas Fortune, argued that blacks should accept nothing short of full citizenship rights.

Many scholars have explored the way that the black churches offered both leadership and comfort, as the clergy and the laity struggled to deal with an impossible situation. Prior to the Civil War, blacks in the South had attended white-dominated churches where they were taught that God sanctioned slavery and the slaves were to submit to their masters. After the Civil War, blacks in the South generally abandoned the white-dominated churches and established their own. These black churches became the center of the black community in the South, providing not only community leadership, but also often meeting the basic needs of food and shelter for the most impoverished. It should also be noted that these tragic years were the seedtime for cultural developments within the African American community—above all, jazz—that would be of enormous consequence in the twentieth century, both at home and abroad. The segregated society also spawned a limited level of black entrepreneurship as blacks, who were denied service at whites-only businesses, were forced to establish their own in order to meet the black community's needs.

NEW ACHIEVEMENTS FOR WOMEN

While blacks were slowly losing their rights, women in the Gilded Age were struggling for more rights, opportunities, and privileges and for a more equal place with men in the participation in and conduct of American affairs. Much of this activity centered on the effort to win the vote.

The battle for women's suffrage had been renewed with fresh vigor after the end of the Civil War. This was because the discussion over broadening the franchise to include African Americans gave suffragists hope that women might be included in any new legislation or Constitutional amendments. This did not prove to be the case, and the result was a schism within the ranks of suffragists. One group, led by Lucy Stone, accepted the Reconstruction amendments, even though they did not include women; another, led by Elizabeth Cady Stanton and Susan B. Anthony, opposed them.

Indeed, there was considerable opposition to women's claim of equal political rights with men in this period. Gilded Age politicians insisted that the political arena was a male preserve, that politics itself was masculine, and that any effort to change that situation was contrary to human nature. Politicians, however, were not alone in holding this view. Francis Parkman, one of the era's most prominent historians, thought women's suffrage would leap over "Nature's limitations," disrupt the home and give women excitement and cares "too much for their strength." Publicly he wrote that especially in the "crowded cities" women's suffrage would be "madness" and would certainly make bad governments worse. Similarly, many Protestant fundamentalists argued that women's suffrage violated the natural place in society designed for women by God. Some even argued that women's suffrage would lead to "divorce and destruction of the family" since many suffragettes, such as Emma Goldman, argued for less restrictive divorce laws.

A number of supporters of women's rights, including Wendell Phillips, a leading social reformer of the day, vigorously disagreed. "One of two things is true," declared Phillips, "either woman is like man—and if she is, then a ballot based on brains belongs to her as well as to him; or she is different, and then man does not know how to vote for her as well as she herself does."

Although they still struggled to gain the right to vote, women in the late 1800s were increasingly working outside the home. (*Library of Congress*)

The major political parties, however, generally either ignored or opposed the demand for women's suffrage, and many women—although probably not a majority—decided to take action themselves. Under the leadership of Susan B. Anthony and Elizabeth Cady Stanton there was agitation for women's suffrage from the 1870s until women finally secured the right to vote in 1920. Then some women's groups, such as the Equal Rights Party, took direct political action by nominating women for President of the United States—Victoria Claflin Woodhull in 1872 and Belva Ann Bennett Lockwood in 1884 and 1888.

Other women worked to unite the two disputing groups. By 1890, the two principal competing groups fighting for women's suffrage had merged into the National American Women's Suffrage Association, which sought to win support for the cause from Congress and the state legislatures.

In the last third of the nineteenth century there was a great battle for women's suffrage in the nation's magazines, public meetings, legislative assemblies, and state constitutional conventions. As Thomas Wentworth Higginson, a Civil War commander of a black regiment and a well-known reformer and feminist of these years pointed out, "Mrs. (Harriet Beecher) Stowe helps to free Uncle Tom in his cabin, and then strikes for the freedom of women in her own 'Hearth and Home.' Mrs. (Julia Ward) Howe writes the 'Battle Hymn of the Republic,' and keeps on writing more battle hymns in behalf of her own sex. Miss [Louisa May] Alcott not only delineates 'Little Women,' but wishes to emancipate them." Other prominent persons such as George William Curtis, civil service reformer, and John Greenleaf Whittier, poet and abolitionist, as well as the two most important labor organizations of the day, the Knights of Labor and the American Federation of Labor, supported the movement for women's suffrage.

Women tried unsuccessfully to win the vote through the Fifteenth Amendment, which the denial of voting rights based on race, but not gender. At first, the suffragettes failed in efforts in the states as seven states turned down women's suffrage proposals between 1867 and 1877. They also suffered a serious legal setback when the Supreme Court in *Minor v. Happersett* (1875) refused to accept the argument that women could vote because they were citizens and unanimously ruled that the Fourteenth Amendment had not conferred the vote upon women. When some state laws barred women from the legal profession, the Supreme Court upheld such laws, with one justice saying, "The natural and proper timidity and delicacy which belongs to the female sex, unfits it for many ... occupations." Women, he said, should stay with "the noble and benign offices of wife and mother."

In 1878, Senator Aaron Augustus Sargent of California introduced into Congress an equal suffrage amendment. During the remaining years of the century, Senate committees reported five times and House committees twice in favor of the amendment, but Congress never took action on it. Despite considerable effort by the suffragists, the increasing militancy of the women's suffrage movement, and a growing sympathy and backing for it generally, only four states at the close of the nineteenth century had given the vote to women—Wyoming (1869), Colorado (1893), Utah (1896), and Idaho (1896).

Women made more progress in some other aspects of American life than they did politically. More women were working outside their homes and going to college than had been the case in earlier periods of American history, for example. The old prejudice against self-support for women was beginning to weaken, and at the same time colleges and universities were preparing increasing numbers of women for positions previously held mainly by men. "We have reached a new era," asserted *Harper's Bazaar*, a leading woman's magazine, in 1883. "Slowly as woman has come to her inheritance, it stretches before her now into illimitable distance, and the question of the hour is rather whether she is ready for her trust than whether that trust is hampered by conditions."

As Arthur M. Schlesinger, Sr., one of America's most distinguished historians, pointed out two generations ago, "Women who would have

A Thanksgiving issue of *Harper's Bazaar*. In 1875 the Supreme Court denied women the right to vote, with one justice saying women should keep to domestic duties. *(Library of Congress)*

shrunk from factory work and domestic service or even from teaching trooped forth with a sense of adventure to become typists, telephone girls, typesetters, bookkeepers, nurses, librarians, journalists, lecturers, social workers, doctors, lawyers, artists. Even in the realm of mechanical invention, a time-honored monopoly of men," added Schlesinger, "they were displaying surprising capacity in a variety of fields." According to Emily Faithfull, an English social worker and observer of American life in the late nineteenth century, there were in 1882, in Massachusetts alone, almost 300 branches of industry and business where women could earn from $100 to $3,000 a year.

Though there had long been a large number of women who worked for a living outside the home, the great economic expansion of the late nineteenth century brought increasing numbers into the work force. From 1880 to 1890, the number of women workers went up from 2.5 million to more than 4 million, about one sixth of the total work force, and by 1900, to 5.3 million. Unfortunately, this was counterbalanced by the fact that women usually filled the lowest-paid jobs and received unequal pay in virtually every position they held for work equal to that performed by men.

Since unions did not pay much attention to working conditions for women, not much was done to correct the injustice of the unequal wage scale. One gain was made when Congress in 1872 enacted the Arnell Bill, giving female government employees equal pay with men for equal work. Belva Ann Bennett Lockwood had much to do with the passage of this act. She drafted the measure, and a petition she circulated at the meetings of the National and American Women's Suffrage Associations in New York in 1870 hastened its passage. (See *"Belva Ann Bennett Lockwood: A Campaigning Woman."*) Another gain was that legislatures in the industrial states began in the 1880s to consider legislation regulating working conditions of women in factories.

Women also made progress in education in these years despite the fact that they were up against a generally held view, expressed by a minister in 1880, that women's emotional nature "painfully disqualifies" them from the effort to be educated. By this time women had been accepted in colleges for about 20 years. In fact, by 1870 one third of American colleges were coeducational.

Probably the greatest educational opportunities for women occurred in the Middle West and in the South where the new state universities began to admit women as well as men. President James B. Angell of the University of Michigan told a visitor to the campus in 1883 that while coeducation was still an experiment in the East it was definitely settled in the West, adding "none of the ladies had found the curriculum too heavy for their physical endurance."

Angell's concern about women's physical stamina for the rigors of study was shared by a number of Americans, both women and men. M. Carey Thomas, a graduate of Cornell in 1877 and the first president of Bryn Mawr, expressed this concern when she said, "The passionate desire of the women of my generation for higher education was accompanied ... by the awful doubt, felt by women themselves as well as by men, as to whether women as a sex were physically and mentally fit for it."

Women clearly demonstrated their fitness for college, and coeducation grew rapidly in these years. Between 1880 and 1898, the proportion of coeducational colleges increased from 51 percent to 70 percent and the number of female students from 2,750 to more than 25,000. At the same time some women's colleges on a level with the top ones for men were established—Vassar (1861), Wellesley (1870), Smith (1871), and Bryn Mawr (1885). Mount Holyoke, a girl's seminary begun in 1836, became a college in 1893. Also, two of the country's leading universities, Harvard and Columbia, added women's colleges—Radcliffe in 1879 and Barnard in 1889. By the end of the nineteenth century four out of every five colleges, universities, and professional schools in the country admitted women.

Women, especially of the upper middle class, also turned their attention to club activities and joined in large numbers the women's organizations springing up all over the country. "We have art clubs, book clubs, dramatic clubs, pottery clubs," wrote one woman in 1880 in the *Atlantic Monthy*. "We have sewing circles, philanthropic associations, scientific, literary, religious, athletic, musical, and decorative art societies." These various associations provided a good way for women to find out about the world in which they were now playing a larger role. They also furnished good training for many women who became active civic and humanitarian leaders in their communities. In one decade, 1888–1897, four important groups were formed that placed more women in public affairs: the National Council of Women, the General Federation of Women's Clubs, the National Association of Colored Women's Clubs, and the National Congress of Parents and Teachers. By the close of the nineteenth century, the General Federation of Women's Clubs (which did not then admit black women) claimed a membership of 150,000 and was supporting such reforms as child welfare, education, and sanitation.

Of course, as we have seen, the participation of women in reforms was not new to the Gilded Age. Women had taken an active role in reform movements before the Civil War, and this momentum continued. Probably the strongest women's reform group of this era was the Woman's Christian Temperance Union (W.C.T.U.), formed in Cleveland in 1874 to fight the saloon and to promote prohibition of alcohol. The movement for prohibition had begun in the first half of the nineteenth century. By the time of the Gilded Age four states—Maine, New Hampshire, Vermont, and Kansas—had prohibition laws. The United States Supreme Court upheld such laws in 1847 but reversed itself in 1888 on the grounds that the interstate control of liquor belonged to Congress.

Frances E. Willard became the head of the W.C.T.U. in 1879 and began to campaign for legislation for the outright banning of strong drink. She also worked through schools and churches to arouse public opinion against liquor. Under her vigorous leadership the W.C.T.U. became the leading force in the prohibition movement. A generation of scholarship in women's history has demonstrated how inclusive Willard was in her political imagination. She convinced her organization to endorse women's suffrage, worked with other Gilded Age reformers on a broad array of issues, became a Socialist (though not of the Marxist variety), and galvanized grass-roots female political energy as did no other nineteenth-century woman leader.

In 1893, the Anti-Saloon League, comprised of both women and men, joined the anti-liquor crusade. With pressure from the W.C.T.U. all states but two added the requirement of "scientific temperance instruction" to the school curriculum between 1882 and 1898.

PEOPLE THAT MADE A DIFFERENCE

Belva Ann Bennett Lockwood: A Campaigning Woman

Belva Ann Bennett Lockwood, lawyer
(*Library of Congress*)

Few American have achieved as much prominence and subsequently been so forgotten as Belva Ann Bennett Lockwood, who was twice nominated for President. Until she died at the age of 87, she spent more than 50 years of tireless work expanding the opportunities, privileges, and human rights of her sex. She never doubted that women would eventually have an equal place with men in the conduct of American affairs.

Belva Ann Bennett was born October 24, 1830, on her parents' farm in Royalton, New York. She attended country schools and in later years recalled the hard benches of the one-room schools and the white line painted on the floor where she had to "toe the mark" when reciting. "I always wanted an education, even when a girl," she said, "and when I was 14 I had enough money to attend the Royalton Academy a year." Belva gave great credit to her mother for both moral and financial support. However, at 15, a lack of funds and her father's opposition compelled her to give up her education and teach in various area country schools. Her pay was 10 shillings a week and "boarding around." Even in those early years, Belva was vexed that men teachers were paid more for the same work.

Belva was first married on November 8, 1848, shortly after she became 18, to a young neighbor farmer, Uriah H. McNall. They had a daughter Lura in 1849 before her husband died of a foot injury in 1853. The young widow sold the farm, sent Lura to her grandparents, and went back to school: first a year at the nearby Gasport (N.Y.) Academy and then to Genesee Wesleyan Seminary and Genesee College (later Syracuse University). In her last year at school, Belva heard and met Susan B. Anthony, who also resented the inferior position of women in American life. This meeting increased Belva's determination to work for women's rights.

After graduating from Genesee in 1857 with honors and a B.S., Belva was elected preceptress (principal) of the Lockport (N.Y.) Union School. For the next four years she supervised the small staff, taught, and, despite some disapproval, promoted gymnastics, public speaking, nature walks, and skating. The school code allowed her assistant men teachers to receive nearly twice the salary she was paid. When she protested this injustice, she was told by the minister's wife, "You can't help yourself; it is the way of the world." So she resigned. As she reported later, "Those words opened my eyes and raised my dander."

In 1866 Belva moved to Washington, D.C., opened a successful private school, and in 1868 married Dr. Ezekiel Lockwood, a former Baptist minister and dentist 27 years her senior. He ran the school until it was closed because of his ill health. He died in 1877, again leaving Belva a widow. Their only child, Jesse, had died in infancy.

With her husband's encouragement, Belva had begun reading law. Her application to the law school of Columbia College was turned down on the traditional ground that her presence would distract the young men. After being rejected at Georgetown and Howard Universities as well, Belva, along with 14 other women, gained admission to the newly established National University Law School in 1871. Only she and one other woman finished the course.

Even then, because of prejudice against women in the professions, the Law School finally refused to grant them diplomas. But after Belva wrote a spirited letter to President Grant, who was ex-*officio* President of the Law School, she received her diploma, signed by Grant himself. In September 1873 she was admitted to the District of Columbia bar, after overcoming the objection that she was a woman—and, in addition, a married woman.

In her law training, Lockwood had specialized in claims cases against the government. But because she was a woman, both the Court of Claims (1874) and the United States Supreme Court (1876) refused her admission. Undaunted, Lockwood pushed for the passage of legislation that would remove this restriction. In 1879, after her persistent lobbying, Congress enacted the "Lockwood Act" allowing women lawyers to practice before both the Supreme Court and the Court of Claims.

Some of the highlights of Lockwood's career include her successful efforts to obtain equal pay for women government workers (1872) and to secure equal property rights and equal guardianship of children for women in Washington, D.C. (1896). She also worked unsuccessfully (1903) to include women's suffrage clauses in the statehood bills for Oklahoma, Arizona, and New Mexico. And in 1906, she represented the Eastern Cherokee Indians, who were awarded $5 million in land claims against the government.

By the 1880s Lockwood was widely known for her work in the women's rights movement. She decided it was time for women to take political action and be nominated for public office. She contended that, while women could not vote, they could legally receive votes and, if elected, hold office. In 1884 the National Equal Rights Party nominated Belva Lockwood for President and Mrs. Marietta L. B. Stow for Vice-President.

Lockwood's nomination was a daring act, designed to revive interest in women's rights. Her platform embraced all her interests—equal rights for all, including blacks, Indians, and immigrants; uniform marriage and divorce laws; reduction of the liquor traffic; and universal peace. Her campaign, ridiculed by many, was opposed by the two most important leaders of women's suffrage, Susan B. Anthony and Elizabeth Cady Stanton, who supported James G. Blaine, the Republican nominee. Nevertheless, Lockwood ran a strong campaign, received 4,149 votes in six states, and claimed she was defrauded of more. She ran again in 1888 with less impressive results.

Disappointed with politics and estranged from the major women's suffrage groups, Lockwood worked for international peace, attending nearly every major peace conference from 1890 to 1914 and serving on the nominating committee for the Nobel Peace Prize. She also lectured and was prominent both nationally and internationally in promoting women's rights, temperance, peace, and arbitration.

Lockwood lived her last years in severe financial difficulty. Her lucrative law practice faded, and irregularity in the Cherokee claims case forced her to return half of her legal fee. Most of her remaining money was lost when she entrusted it to an unscrupulous male admirer. Evicted from her large Washington home at the age of 84, she lived on a pension provided by Andrew Carnegie. After a period of declining health, she died in Washington on May 19, 1917, and was buried in the Congressional Cemetery. Belva Lockwood had several lives and careers—teacher, lawyer, public speaker, wife, and mother—and her contribution to the cause of women's rights did not end with her death. She deserves to be remembered.

Many women who saw the saloon as an implacable foe were also aware of a number of other social problems—such as child labor, unsanitary housing, lack of public-health measures, penal conditions that needed their support for reform—with prompting from Willard herself. Not all women, however, agreed that the increased activities of women meant progress. "What is this curious product of today, the American girl or woman?" asked a woman writer in 1880 in the *Atlantic Monthly*. "… Is it possible for any novel, within the next fifty years, truly to depict her as a finality, when she is still emerging from new conditions …, when she does not yet understand herself …?" She added, "The face of today is stamped with restlessness, wandering purpose, and self-consciousness."

Thus, by the end of the nineteenth century, increasing economic independence and more educational opportunities for women had enlarged their social freedom and widened their range of activity. They had gone far, but they had much farther to go.

FROM HAYES TO HARRISON

HAYES AND THE PRESIDENCY

An Electoral Commission chose Rutherford B. Hayes for President, and historians have portrayed him as a respectable mediocrity with an average capacity and an impeccable public and private life. True, there was no dramatic flair in his personality, and he lacked brilliance; but he was a man of integrity and honest intentions, and his determination and steadfastness of purpose eventually frustrated even his bitterest foes. Hayes' presidency is an excellent illustration of how party stalemate and equilibrium can hamper effective executive leadership. Hayes worked under severe handicaps that have not been fully appreciated.

His right to the office had been disputed, and Republicans and Democrats alike referred to him as "the *de facto* President" and "His Fraudulency." His programs for the South and for civil service reform, plus his show of independence, caused such a deep split within his own Republican Party that he was nearly read out of it. At one time Hayes had but three supporters in the Senate, one of them a lifelong friend and relative. Moreover, the Democrats controlled the House of Representatives throughout his administration and the Senate the last two years of his term. Under these circumstances, it is amazing that he could accomplish anything.

Hayes endeavored to reestablish presidential power and prestige and to redress the balance between the executive and legislative branches. He first challenged congressional dominance in the make-up of his cabinet when he picked men who were most unwelcome to the bosses, particularly the liberal Republican Carl Schurz for Secretary of the Interior and the Southern Democrat and former Confederate David M. Key for the important patronage-dispensing position of Postmaster General. At first the Senate balked and refused to confirm the entire cabinet list, but under much public pressure it finally gave in to the President.

Hayes gained another victory over congressional encroachment by refusing to yield the right given him by the Force Acts of 1870–1871 to intervene in federal elections in the states. Democratic majorities in Congress sought to nullify these Reconstruction laws by attaching to army appropriation bills riders aimed at removing federal supervision of elections. Hayes fought these attempts because they would have placed him under the "coercive dictation" of a "bare" majority in Congress and because he wanted to make the executive "an equal and independent branch of the government." He vetoed eight such bills, and Congress lacked enough votes to override him.

Hayes also struck a daring and spectacular blow for reform against the spoils system and its greatest champion, Senator Roscoe Conkling of New York. Hayes had already vexed the bosses with his inaugural statement: "He serves his party best who serves his country best," and he further angered them with his comment, "Party leaders should have no more influence in appointments than other equally respectable citizens." He appointed a commission headed by John Jay of New York, grandson of the first Chief Justice, to investigate the largest patronage office in the federal service, the New York Custom House—long an example of the spoils system at its worst. The commission found that most of the employees had been appointed in the interest of the Conkling machine, that 20 percent of them were superfluous, and that the place was ridden with "ignorance, inefficiency, and corruption." When Conkling's lieutenants, Collector of the Port Chester A. Arthur and Naval Officer Alonzo B. Cornell, refused to clean up the corruption or to resign, Hayes boldly removed them and named two others to the posts. On Conkling's insistence the Senate refused to confirm the nominations, but Hayes persisted and within a year his choices were approved. He had won a battle, but he had not routed the spoilsmen.

THE END OF RESCONSTRUCTION

Hayes removed the last of the federal troops from the South and ended military Reconstruction, acting to restore harmony between

North and South and between whites and blacks. In doing so, he responded to a general demand for a change in policy in the South. Hayes considered that Reconstruction governments had lost so much support that they had become completely unable to sustain themselves even with the use of force; and he dreamed of building in the South a strong Republican party that would no longer depend upon the blacks for its main strength and that could command the esteem and support of Southern whites.

Hayes became the first Republican President to experiment with the plan of appointing regular Democrats to important posts in the South in the hope of gaining Republican success there. He seldom was credited with any honest motives, however, for the public in 1877—and many years later—believed this was part of the bargain that had made him President. In any case, his experiment was a sharp departure from the strategy of the Radicals during Reconstruction. Had it worked, the "solid South" as a Democratic stronghold might not have come to be. As it was, however, the strategy did not work; and black people were left even more vulnerable than they had been previously, as Hayes' Democrat appointees in the South generally remained committed to segregation.

DEPRESSION AND THE SILVER QUESTION

When Hayes entered the presidency, the country was experiencing the worst years of a depression that had begun in 1873. Almost immediately he was confronted with the first great industrial conflict in our history—a railroad strike that began on the Baltimore and Ohio and spread through 14 states, affecting two thirds of the railroad mileage in the country outside New England and the South. At the request of four state governors, Hayes sent federal troops to intervene in the strike and restore order.

Hayes ran further afoul of labor, especially on the West Coast, when he vetoed a bill passed in 1879 to restrict Chinese immigration. He felt the bill violated the Burlingame Treaty of 1868, which had given the Chinese the right of unlimited immigration to the United States. (However, Hayes sent a mission to China to negotiate a new treaty, and the resultant Treaty of 1880 gave the United States the right to regulate or suspend Chinese immigration. The Exclusion Act, passed by Congress in 1882, suspended such immigration for 10 years.)

The President also took an unpopular stand on the currency question. Discontented agrarians, suffering from falling agricultural prices, wanted "cheap money" and inflationary monetary policies so as to bring about increases in the prices of agricultural products.

Consequently, farmers favored the repeal or modification of the Resumption Act of 1875, which obligated the Treasury to redeem greenbacks in specie at full face value on January 1, 1879. Many predicted that such redemption would wreck the monetary system, for everyone would want gold rather than paper notes. Hayes, however, resisted the pressure and aided Secretary of the Treasury John Sherman in accumulating a gold reserve to redeem the currency. Greenback dollars, which were worth only 67 cents in 1865, rose to 100 cents before the deadline of resumption; and people, realizing this, preferred the notes that were easier to handle. Thus no run on the gold reserve developed.

Inflationists now pushed demands for free coinage of silver, meaning that the federal government would purchase all the silver that could be mined and press it into coins, thus devaluing the currency and leading to a rise in agricultural prices. Once again, however, Hayes took the unpopular side. The old ratio between gold and silver had been 16 to 1: there was 16 times as much silver in a silver dollar as there was gold in a gold dollar. When the Gold Rush of 1849 lowered the price of gold, however, an ounce of silver became worth more than one sixteenth of an ounce of gold; and Americans sold their silver on the open market rather than have it coined at a loss. Silver dollars nearly disappeared from circulation, and in 1873 Congress abolished their coinage. The government discontinued the purchase of silver because no one was willing to sell silver to the government at the government-set price that was well below the market price. Farmers and miners, however, believed that the discontinuation of silver purchase by the government was some sort of plot against them and thus referred to the government action as the "Crime of 73." Subsequently, silver mines in Nevada, Arizona, and Colorado produced such large quantities of silver that the market price of silver fell below the government-set price, and miners and agrarians called for a return to the coinage of silver at the old ratio.

Hayes and the Republicans, however, were advocates of the gold standard and Hayes opposed the resumption of silver coinage. Congress responded by passing over Hayes' veto in 1878 the Bland-Allison Act, authorizing the Treasury to purchase not less than $2 million and not more than $4 million worth of silver each month and coin it into dollars at the former gold/silver price ratio of 16 to 1. The act, however, did not fully meet the demands of the silverites that wanted the "free and unlimited coinage of silver." Moreover, the Treasury, dominated by gold-advocate Republicans, consistently purchased only the minimum amount of silver required by the act.

THE ELECTION OF 1880

With virtually no support among Democrats and some opposition from within his own party over Hayes' failure to fully support the spoils system, Hayes did not seek reelection; and the Republican convention of 1880 was divided in its support. The "Stalwart" faction, which favored continuation of the spoils system, was led by party boss Roscoe Conkling and sought a third term for Ulysses S. Grant. James G. Blaine of Maine and John Sherman of Ohio, however, also had Republican supporters. Blaine was a leader of the opposing Republican faction in Congress known as the "Half-Breeds" that, at least in rhetoric, favored eliminating the spoils system, though Blaine's own political career appeared just as spoils-oriented as Conkling's when placed under the microscope. When it became clear that none of the three could secure a majority, the delegates nominated Congressman James A. Garfield of Ohio, a "Half-Breed," on the thirty-sixth ballot.

To appease the Stalwarts, second place on the Republican ticket went to one of Conkling's closest associates, Chester A. Arthur, whom Hayes in 1878 had dismissed as head of the New York Customs House in reaction to a scandal involving Customs House corruption. When Samuel J. Tilden, who had won the popular vote for the Democrats in 1876, declined to run, the Democrats picked General Winfield Scott Hancock, a Pennsylvanian and a Union hero in the Battle of Gettysburg. His running mate was William H. English of Indiana.

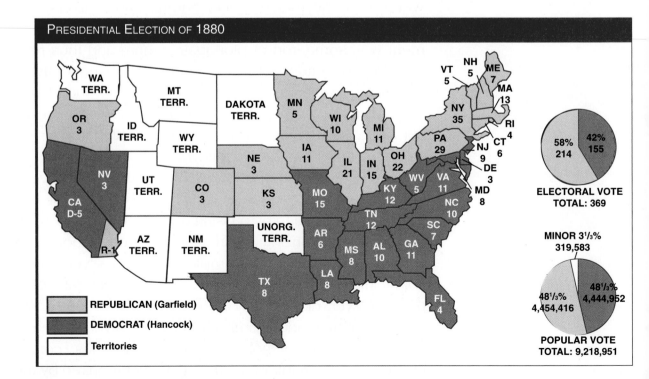

PRESIDENTIAL ELECTION OF 1880

ELECTORAL VOTE TOTAL: 369 — 58% 214, 42% 155

MINOR 3⅓% 319,583

POPULAR VOTE TOTAL: 9,218,951 — 48⅓% 4,454,416, 48⅓% 4,444,952

REPUBLICAN (Garfield)
DEMOCRAT (Hancock)
Territories

President James Garfield, his mother (left), and his wife (right) *(Library of Congress)*

The platforms of the two parties revealed few basic differences on policy and no real understanding of the country's problems. Despite the failure of the major parties to discuss the vital issues of the day, less than four percent of the electorate voted for a protest party candidate—General James B. Weaver of Iowa of the Greenback Labor Party, which advocated inflationary policies and stricter federal regulation of interstate commerce.

The campaign, which turned largely on personalities and irrelevant issues, produced a great deal of sound and fury but nothing of importance. Five sixths of the voters turned out, and Garfield won by fewer than 40,000 popular votes, although his electoral vote was 214 as compared to 155 for Hancock. The Republicans had retained the White House, but their margin in the popular vote was razor-thin, reflecting the close balance between the two major parties that had been reflected in 1876 and would continue throughout the Gilded Age. The Republican victory also reflected the sectional nature of the parties that had developed in 1860 with the Republicans carrying the northern states, but the Democrats dominating the South. The Republicans, however, won slim majorities in both Houses of Congress, setting them up for what they believed would be a productive four years.

GARFIELD AND ARTHUR

The new President James Garfield had been an effective speaker and an able party leader in the House; and many historians argue that if there were a President during the Gilded Age that might have achieved greatness, it was Garfield. Garfield draws many comparisons to Abraham Lincoln in that he, like Lincoln, was born in a log cabin and worked as a laborer on the Ohio canal as a youth. Garfield put himself first through college and then law school. Garfield displayed other interesting talents in that he was both ambidextrous and multilingual and could write in Greek with one hand while writing Latin with the other. During the Civil War, Garfield organized a volunteer regiment of the Union Army and rose from lieutenant colonel to major general in just two years. In 1863, Garfield was elected to the House of Representatives where he quickly became a leader among the Republican Half-Breeds.

As great as Garfield's potential might have been, however, many of his contemporaries found him timid and vacillating. Overwhelmed with the demands of office seekers, he once exclaimed, "My God! What is there in this place that a man should ever want to get into it?" After accepting the aid of the Stalwarts during the campaign and apparently reaching some understanding with them on patronage matters, Garfield antagonized Roscoe Conkling by making Conkling's great rival, James G. Blaine, Secretary of State and by appointing a Conkling opponent in New York Collector of the Port.

In the ensuing fight between the President and the Stalwarts, Conkling and his colleague from New York, Thomas "Me Too" Platt, resigned their seats in the Senate and were not reelected by the New York legislature. At the height of the conflict, on July 2, 1881, Charles J. Guiteau, a disappointed office seeker who was mentally unbalanced, shot Garfield at a Washington railroad station and shouted, "I am a Stalwart and Arthur is President now." Attending physicians assured Garfield that he would survive, to which Garfield famously replied, "I'm a dead man." Doctors were unable to find the bullet in Garfield's abdomen, and Alexander Graham Bell was even invited in to search for the bullet with his newly invented metal detector. Garfield died of infection from the wound on September 19, and Chester Arthur became President.

The certifiably insane Guiteau was tried for murder and executed, but not before he revealed his deranged nature at his trial. Guiteau evidently suffered from illusions of grandeur and believed that God had planned for him some special destiny. Guiteau credited himself with Garfield's election and then, when Garfield refused to appoint him to

The assassination of President Garfield at a Washington train station *(Library of Congress)*

the position he desired, he viewed Garfield as "blocking his destiny." Guiteau pleaded, "insanity by Divine power, " stating that "It was God's act, not mine," and claiming, "God told me to kill." Guiteau's final words at the gallows were reportedly, "I am going to the Lordy."

To many Americans the succession of Arthur was a calamity, for he had the reputation of a New York machine politician. Reformers shuddered at the thought of a spoilsman in the presidency, and there was a widespread feeling that the Stalwarts would take over. In spite of his unsavory reputation and political career as a defender of the spoils system, Arthur was personally honest and did have ability. The responsibilities and dignity of the high office caused him to rise to the occasion and to give the country a good administration. He did not turn over the patronage to Conkling, as many thought he would. He supported civil service reform, thus abandoning his previous position on the issue and alienating the Stalwarts in his own party that had supported his nomination for Vice President. Arthur prosecuted frauds in the Post Office, cleared the way for the construction of a modern navy, and had the Chinese immigration question settled, though in a way that modern Americans find unacceptable. He also tried to bring about a reduction in the tariff and to check federal spending on unnecessary public works by vetoing an $18 million rivers-and-harbors bill, but Congress defeated both efforts.

THE CIVIL SERVICE ACT

The most important legislation during Arthur's presidency was the Pendleton Civil Service Act of 1883. Since the end of the Civil War, reformers had been denouncing the spoils system and advocating the establishment of a permanent civil service where government jobs would be awarded based on merit rather than party affiliation. Garfield's murder dramatically advanced their cause by shocking the public into believing there was something dreadfully wrong with the patronage system if crazed office seekers were shooting the President. The Pendleton Act authorized the President to appoint a Civil Service Commission of three members to provide "open competitive examinations for testing the fitness of applicants for the public service now classified or to be classified." In addition, the act forbade the levying of political campaign assessments on federal officeholders and protected them against ouster for failure to make such contributions.

At first the act affected only the lowest offices—about 14,000, or 12 percent of the total number of federal employees, leaving the remainder under the spoils system, but the President was given authority to extend the classified list at his discretion. Arthur demonstrated good faith by making excellent appointments to the Commission. Every subsequent President extended the classified list to protect the jobs of those whom he had appointed to office, and at the end of the century it included 40 percent of all federal positions. By the end of World War II, approximately 90 percent of federal jobs would be Civil Service jobs with political appointees typically occupying only the upper echelon of the federal bureaucracy.

THE ELECTION OF 1884

In 1884 the Republicans turned their backs on Arthur, who was also ill with a disease (probably cancer) that would take his life two years later, and nominated Half-Breed leader James G. Blaine of Maine for President. The Democrats named Grover Cleveland, a former mayor of Buffalo and governor of New York. Cleveland was most famous at the time for vetoing a bill that would have reduced fares charged by the New York City elevated railway. According to Cleveland, the bill was unconstitutional government interference into private business. Cleveland was also viewed as honest, and his popularity soared among conservative Democrats.

Though a Half-Breed and theoretically against the spoils system, Blaine had been connected with the granting of favors to the Little Rock and Fort Smith Railroad, perhaps in exchange for "gifts." View-

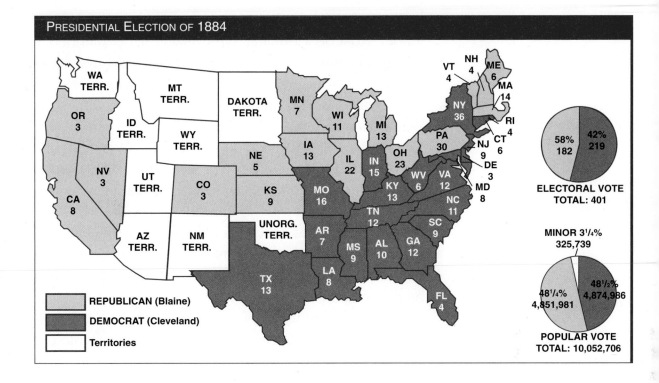

PRESIDENTIAL ELECTION OF 1884

REPUBLICAN (Blaine)
DEMOCRAT (Cleveland)
Territories

ELECTORAL VOTE
TOTAL: 401

POPULAR VOTE
TOTAL: 10,052,706

ing Blaine as an old guard politician inimical to good government, William Curtis, Carl Schurz, and other reformist Mugwumps bolted the Republican Party and supported Cleveland. As in 1880, few real issues were discussed, and the campaign degenerated into one of personal abuse and vilification. "The public is angry and abusive," observed Henry Adams. "Everyone takes part. We are all doing our best, and swearing like demons. But the amusing thing is that no one talks about real issues." The Democrats publicized the "Mulligan letters" to prove that Blaine, as Speaker of the House, had been guilty of unethical conduct in connection with land-grant railroads; and the Republicans retaliated with the charge that Cleveland was the father of an illegitimate child. At Cleveland's rallies, Republican hecklers chanted, "Ma, Ma, where's my pa?" Cleveland, however, turned the accusation to his favor by showing that he had supported the child over the years and taken responsibility for his mistakes. In retaliation, Democrats pointed out that Blaine's wife had been pregnant when the two married and that Cleveland had not required a shotgun to stir his conscience. To the chant of "Ma, Ma, where's my pa?", the Democrats added, "Gone to the White House, ha, ha, ha!" Cleveland had also twice played the role of hangman as sheriff of Erie County, New York in the 1870s. Cleveland himself had affixed the noose around the neck of the condemned and pulled the lever. The idea of a "hangman President" was unsettling to a few. Blaine, however, had even greater problems within his own party where many Stalwarts refused to support his candidacy. When Stalwart leader Roscoe Conkling was asked if he planned to support his party's nominee, he replied that he would not support Blaine because "I do not engage in criminal activities." Democrats heckled Blaine rallies with chants of "Blaine, Blaine, James G. Blaine, Continental Liar from the state of Maine."

Overall, the decision in 1884 was even closer than in 1880. Cleveland's plurality in popular votes was only 29,000 and his electoral vote was 219 to Blaine's 182. So narrow was the margin of victory for Cleveland that he carried the pivotal state of New York by a mere 1,149 votes. Two weeks prior to the election, a Protestant Blaine campaign worker in New York City referred to the Democrats as the party of "Rum, Romanism, and Rebellion." Many viewed this as a slur against the Catholic Church, and New York City, in particular, had a large Catholic population. Whether or not that slur cost Blaine the votes needed in New York City to win the state of New York cannot be known, but less than 600 votes cast the other direction in New York would have given Blaine the victory. It is at least possible that without that speech, James G. Blaine would have been President of the United States. It was said that no candidate could slur the Catholic Church and expect to win New York.

CLEVELAND AND THE PRESIDENCY

Cleveland, a strapping figure of well over 200 pounds, came to the White House in 1885 with a reputation as a reformer and a man of courage, integrity, and prodigious work habits. Actually he was unimaginative, stolid, obdurate, and brutally candid, and he lacked a sense of timing. He was also a thoroughgoing conservative, a believer in sound money, and a defender of property rights. In his inaugural he promised to adhere to "business principles," and his cabinet included conservatives and business-minded Democrats of the East and South. His administration signified no break with his Republican predecessors on fundamental issues. Cleveland's proclamation that he made when vetoing $10,000 in federal drought relief for farmers, in which he stated, "People should support the Government. The Government should not support the people," perhaps best sums up his philosophy of government.

Cleveland faced the task of pleasing both the Mugwumps and the hungry spoilsmen of his own party, who had been cut off from federal patronage for 24 years. At first he refused to yield to the bosses on appointments and, thereby, won the acclaim of reformers; but faced with a revolt within his party, Cleveland gave in to the spoilsmen and replaced Republicans with "honest Democrats." Carl Schurz wrote, "Your attempt to please both reformers and spoilsmen has failed," and Cleveland broke with the Mugwumps. At the end of his presidency he had removed about two thirds of the 120,000 federal officeholders. On the credit side, he increased the civil service classified list to 27,380 positions—almost double the number when he took office.

Cleveland had more success as a watchdog of the Treasury. Cleveland opposed silver purchase as a drain on the treasury; and he halted the scandalous pension racket by vetoing hundreds of private military pension bills that congressmen pushed through for constituents whose claims had been rejected by the Pension Office. Cleveland signed more of these bills than had all his predecessors since Johnson put together, but he was the first President to veto any. The Grand Army of the Republic (G.A.R.) screamed at the vetoes; and in January 1887 Congress responded by passing a Dependent Pension Bill, which provided a pension for all honorably discharged disabled veterans who had served as little as three months in the Union army, irrespective of how they had become disabled. Cleveland vetoed it and angered the G.A.R.

Aside from the Interstate Commerce Act, for which Cleveland deserves no credit and which he signed with reluctance and "with reservations," little significant legislation was enacted during his

The Grand Army of the Republic (*Library of Congress*)

term. He did not compel railroad, lumber, and cattle companies to give up 81 million acres of public land that they had fraudulently occupied. In Cleveland's view, Congress was the legislative branch and, therefore, should lead in policy while the President's job, as chief executive, was to carry out policy made elsewhere. In 1886 Congress passed a Presidential Succession Law, which provided that after the Vice-President, the succession should pass to the members of the cabinet, beginning with the Secretary of State, in the order of the creation of their departments. In 1887 the Dawes Act was passed, initiating a new Indian policy.

THE TARIFF ISSUE

Cleveland devoted his entire annual message of December 1887 to the tariff question, advocating a drastic reduction in duties. The federal government at the time enjoyed a surplus, and Cleveland viewed the government surplus largely as an invitation for Congress to waste money. The Democratic-controlled House responded with a low tariff measure; but the Republican-dominated Senate turned it down and passed a highly protective bill that the House would not accept. This led to a deadlock and the injection of the tariff question into the 1888 election. For the first time in this era both major parties were forced to take a position on the tariff issue. Northern Republicans, typically, supported high tariffs as a measure to support Northern manufacturing against foreign competition while Southerners tended to favor lower tariffs in an effort to induce Europeans to lower tariffs as well and, thus, boost Southern agricultural exports to Europe.

THE ELECTION OF 1888

The Democrats renominated President Cleveland and chose the elderly ex-Senator Allen G. Thurman of Ohio as his running mate. The Republicans nominated Senator Benjamin Harrison of Indiana, the grandson of former President and hero of Tippecanoe, William Henry Harrison, for President, and Levi P. Morton, a wealthy New York banker, for Vice-President. Harrison had run unsuccessfully for the Governorship of Indiana in 1876, but was elected to the United States Senate in 1880. Harrison had fought for the Union under General Sherman and gained a reputation as a stern military disciplinarian. Two labor parties, voicing the industrial unrest of the period, entered the campaign. Union Labor and United Labor condemned the major parties for being under the control of monopolies and for being indifferent to the welfare of workers.

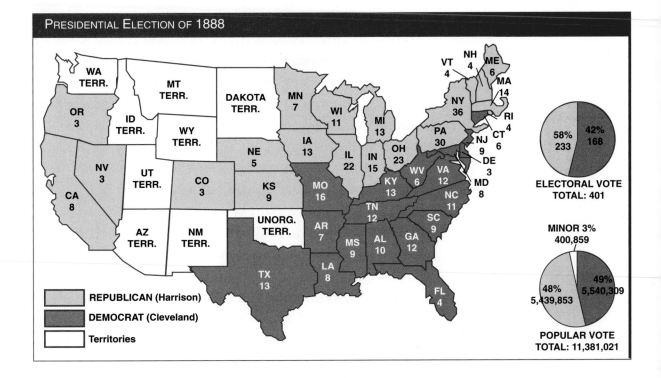

PRESIDENTIAL ELECTION OF 1888

REPUBLICAN (Harrison)

DEMOCRAT (Cleveland)

Territories

ELECTORAL VOTE TOTAL: 401

58% 233 — 42% 168

POPULAR VOTE TOTAL: 11,381,021

MINOR 3% 400,859

48% 5,439,853 — 49% 5,540,309

The campaign was waged largely on the tariff issue, with Republicans defending protection and Democrats advocating a reduction of duties. The Republicans appealed to the manufacturing interests, who would profit from a high tariff, and to veterans, who were promised generous pension legislation. The Republican candidate, Harrison, announced that he was opposed to reducing the tariffs because he was opposed to "cheaper costs" and that "cheaper costs" necessarily led to a "cheaper man and woman under the coat." Both parties used money freely as throughout the country voters were bribed in one of the most corrupt presidential elections in our history. Although Cleveland had a plurality of more than 90,000 popular votes, Harrison carried the crucial states of Indiana, New York, and Ohio and gained 233 electoral votes to Cleveland's 168. The decisive factors were probably the efficiency of the Republican organization and the purchase of the floating vote in the doubtful states.

HARRISON AND THE REPUBLICANS

Harrison possessed intellectual and oratorical gifts, but he was very cold in his personal relationships. "Harrison sweats ice water" became a popular phrase; and one of his close associates remarked, "Harrison can make a speech to 10,000 men and every man of them will go away his friend. Let him meet the same 10,000 in private, and every one will go away his enemy." Harrison's unflattering nickname on Capitol Hill became, "the human iceberg." Theodore Roosevelt, whom Harrison appointed to the Civil Service Commission, referred to Harrison as a "cold-blooded, narrow-minded, prejudiced, obstinate, timid old psalm-singing Indianapolis politician."

Although Harrison had ability, he lacked forcefulness; the leadership passed largely to the Republican leaders in Congress, especially to Senator Nelson W. Aldrich of Rhode Island and Speaker of the House Thomas B. Reed of Maine. Reed pushed through the House a revision of the rules that gave him almost dictatorial powers over proceedings and earned him the title of "czar."

For the first time since 1875 the Republicans had the presidency and a majority in both houses of Congress, and they began to pay off their political debts. The McKinley Tariff of 1890 raised rates to a higher level and protected more products than any previous tariff in American history. In the same year the Dependent Pension Act, substantially the same measure vetoed by Cleveland, granted pensions to all G.A.R. veterans suffering from any disability, acquired in war service or not, and to their widows and children. In the same year, to meet the demands of the silverites, the Sherman Silver Purchase Act increased the amount of silver to be purchased by the Treasury to 4.5 million ounces a month. To appease the popular clamor against monopolies, the Sherman Antitrust Act was also passed in 1890.

This same Congress earned itself the label "the Billion Dollar Congress." By distributing subsidies to steamship lines, passing extravagant rivers-and-harbors bills, offering large premiums to government bondholders, and returning federal taxes paid by Northern states during the Civil War, it handed out so much money that by 1894 the Treasury surplus was gone. The United States has never had a surplus since.

Instead of the widespread support that such policies were expected to bring, the public reaction was one of hostility; and in the congressional elections of 1890 the Republicans were severely rebuked. They retained only 88 of the 332 seats in the House and had their majority in the Senate reduced from 14 to 6. The appearance of nine new congressmen representing farm interests and not associated with either of the major parties indicated that a third-party revolt was shaping up and that a new phase in American politics was under way.

THE AGRARIAN REVOLT

THE PLIGHT OF THE FARMER

The third-party revolt took the form of an agrarian insurgency in the West and South, that had been coming on since the Civil War and which reached its culmination in the 1890s. There were a number of causes for agrarian discontent. The conversion of American agriculture to a commercial basis made the farmer a specialist whose role was to produce a surplus by which the United States could adjust an unfavorable balance of trade. Unlike the manufacturer, however, the farmer had no control over his market or his prices. He worked alone and competed with other farmers, American and foreign. Instead of benefiting from the new order of things, he was one of its victims.

Prices for agricultural products had declined. Between 1870 and 1897 wheat prices dropped from $1.06 to 63.6 cents a bushel, corn from 43.1 to 29.7 cents a bushel, and cotton from 15.1 to 5.8 cents a pound. These were market prices, after warehouse and transportation charges were added. The net prices paid to the farmer were even lower. Farmers of the Old Northwest received only 42 cents a bushel for wheat that government economists estimated cost 45.1 cents a

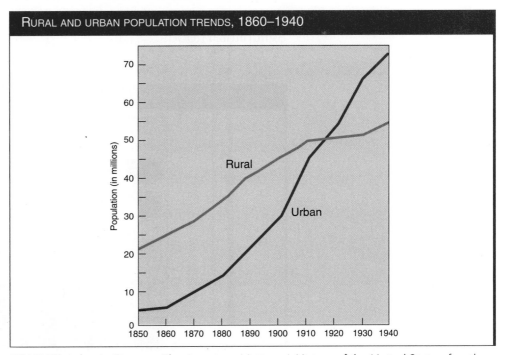

RURAL AND URBAN POPULATION TRENDS, 1860–1940

SOURCE: John A. Garraty, *The American Nation: A History of the United States,* fourth edition, p. 476. Copyright © 1966, 1971, 1975, 1976 by Harper & Row, Publishers, Inc. Reprinted by permission of the publisher.

bushel to produce. In Kansas in 1889, corn sold for 10 cents a bushel and was commonly used for fuel, and in 1890 a farmer in Nebraska shot his hogs because he could neither sell nor give them away.

Farmers increasingly were shackled with debts and loss of proprietorship over their land. In 1900 nearly one third of the country's farms were mortgaged. In the Middle West the percentages were highest—45 percent in Wisconsin, 48 percent in Michigan, and 53 percent in Iowa. Mortgages were few in the South because of the crop-lien system, by which local merchants advanced seed, equipment, and personal necessities to planters in return for a first lien on the planter's future cotton crop. Throughout the country the number of tenant farmers increased from 25.9 percent of all the farms in 1880 to 29.4 percent in 1890 and to 35.3 percent in 1900. In Kansas in the 1880's wagons were seen moving east with the signs, "In God we trusted, but in Kansas we busted."

The basic cause of the farmer's misfortune was an overexpansion in agricultural production. In addition to the continuing increase in agricultural production, the number of farmers also kept going up. Between 1860 and 1890 the number of farms increased from 2 million to 4.5 million, the wheat crop from 173 million bushels to 449 million, and the cotton from 5.3 million bales to 8.5 million. Supply was outrunning demand, and the farmers were falling behind in the economic race. To make matters worse, total economic growth in the United States exceeded the growth of the money supply, thus inflating the value of the American dollar but causing price deflation in agricultural goods.

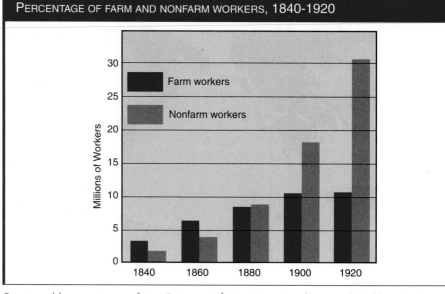

PERCENTAGE OF FARM AND NONFARM WORKERS, 1840-1920

Reprinted by permission from *Promise of America: Breaking and Building* by Larry Cuban and Philip Roden; Copyright © 1971, 1975 Scott, Foresman, and Company.

The farmers blamed, most particularly, the railroads, the middlemen, and the banks. They resented railroad rate differentials and discriminations against them. On through routes and long hauls, rates were low, because the railroads competed with one another; however, on local or short hauls where there was little or no competition, rates were high. Sometimes the Western local rate was four times that charged for the same distance and commodity in the East where rail lines were more numerous. Farmers paid more to ship their grain from Minnesota towns to St. Paul or Minneapolis than a shipper in Minneapolis had to pay for a haul to New York. In addition, farmers resented the way railroads favored shippers and dominated state politics.

The farmers also believed themselves to be at the mercy of the middlemen—local merchants, grain dealers, brokers, and speculators. The national banks' rules precluded loans on real estate and farm property, and the banks did not respond to the farmers' seasonal needs for money. Due to the currency shortage that plagued the Gilded Age, interest rates soared to as high as 36 percent due to the demand for money that exceeded supply. Farmers, however, ignorant of the market forces around them, viewed the high interest rates as a plot by bankers to take their farms.

The farmers also complained that they bore the brunt of the tax burden. The merchants could underestimate the value of their stock, householders might exclude some of their property, the owners of securities could conceal them; but the farmers could not hide their land. Finally, the protective tariff hurt the farmers because they purchased manufactured goods in a highly protected market and sold their crops in an unprotected one. They shared none of the benefits of protection and withstood all of the liabilities. Instead, in their view, they contributed heavily to the subsidization of business. This injustice was all the more difficult to bear in view of their belief that the tariff was "the mother of trusts."

THE GRANGER MOVEMENT

Feeling they were being left behind and believing that politicians were indifferent and even hostile to their interests, farmers decided to organize and protest against their condition. In 1867 Oliver Hudson Kelley, a government clerk, founded National Grange of the Patrons of Husbandry, which became better known as the Grange. Kelley began the organization as a social organization that farmers could use to share information about new technology and common problems; however, the farmers quickly saw in the Grange a weapon with which to fight their foes. By 1874, its peak year, the Grange had an estimated membership of 1.5 million. The Grangers established a number of cooperatives in an effort to eliminate the profits of the middleman, but mismanagement and business opposition doomed most of them.

Although the Grange officially declared itself "nonpolitical," individual members joined various agrarian third parties organized in the Midwest. In coalition with either the Democrats or the Republicans, these third parties gained control of several state legislatures and enacted Granger laws to regulate the rates charged by grain elevators and railroads. The new regulations favored by the Grangers were challenged in the courts, but in *Munn v. Illinois* in 1877, the most important of these cases, the Supreme Court upheld the "police power" of the state regulation.

After 1875 Grange membership decreased rapidly. Out of the 20,000 local granges extant in 1874, only 4,000 remained in 1880. Many farmers had been attracted by the novelty and vogue of the Grange, and others had believed it would provide a panacea for all their ills. They left when they found there was not immediate and universal success.

THE GREENBACK MOVEMENT

Farmers next were attracted to the Greenback movement. From 1867 to 1872, Eastern labor dominated the movement, and its primary objectives then were to lower the interest rate on money and to reduce taxation. After 1873, farmers favored an expansion of the currency in the hope that it would bring higher prices for their products. When the panic of 1873 intensified the agricultural depression and the Granger movement failed to relieve the situation, farmers took over the Greenback movement. Its high-water mark was the election of 15 congressmen in 1878; but with the resumption of specie payment in 1879 and with the rise of the price of corn in 1880, farmers lost interest in Greenbackism, and its support rapidly declined. In the presidential election of 1880 the Greenback candidate, James B. Weaver of Iowa, received only 300,000 votes, about three percent of the total; and by 1888 the party was dead.

THE FARMERS' ALLIANCE

With the decline of the Grange and the disappearance of Greenbackism, a new set of farm groups appeared. Most important were the Farmers' Alliances, two distinct organizations of different origins. Milton George in Chicago organized the Northwestern Alliance in 1880, while the Southern Alliance was formed in 1875 in a frontier county of Texas for protection against horse thieves and land sharks. It remained small until 1886, when it expanded throughout the South under the vigorous leadership of C. W. Macune and absorbed rival farmers' organizations. For blacks, there was a Farmers' National Alliance and Cooperative Union.

The Alliances experimented with cooperatives more than the Grange had, but with no greater success. A merger of the Northwestern and the Southern Alliance was unsuccessfully attempted in a meeting at St. Louis in 1889. The Southern Alliance insisted upon the retention of its secret rituals and the exclusion of blacks, at least from the national body. The Northwestern Alliance wanted a federation in which each organization would keep its identity.

Then, the Southern Alliance changed its name to the National Farmers' Alliance and Industrial Union and induced the three strongest state alliances of the Northwestern Alliance, those of Kansas and North and South Dakota, to join. Due to its support for urban workers, the National Farmers' Alliance then gained the endorsement of the Knights of Labor.

THE EMERGENCE OF POPULISM

Though the Alliances proclaimed themselves nonpolitical organizations, they issued demands each year that could be realized only by political means. For example, the Ocala, Florida, platform of 1890 called for the abolition of national banks, establishment of subtreasuries, a graduated income tax, direct election of United States senators, lower tariffs, federal grain warehouses, and government control of communication and transportation facilities.

By 1890 the Northwestern Alliance concluded that nonpartisan activities were a failure and, therefore, decided to enter electoral politics. Kansas led the way by organizing a People's (Populist) party in June 1890, and Alliancemen in other Western states set up independent parties under other names. Suddenly, the West was in the throes of a mighty political party upheaval. A later commentator called it "a pentecost of politics in which a tongue of flame sat upon every man and each spoke as the spirit gave him utterance."

"Sockless" Jerry Simpson, Ignatius Donnelly, Mary Elizabeth Lease, Annie L. Diggs, and General James B. Weaver were among the leaders of Western Populism. The party, though hastily constructed, was successful in three states. In Kansas it elected five congressmen and one senator in the 1890 elections. In Nebraska it

"Sockless" Jerry Simpson *(Library of Congress)*

gained control of both houses of the legislature and elected two congressmen. In South Dakota it elected a senator.

In the South, the Alliance feared that the establishment of a third party might split the white vote and bring the Republicans and their black supporters into power again. At first the Alliance tried to gain control of the Democratic Party machinery. It attacked the industrial and urban leadership of the Democrats and endorsed candidates who pledged themselves to the Ocala platform. The Alliance appeared to have captured the Democratic Party in the elections of 1890 when four governors, eight state legislatures, 44 congressmen, and three senators promised to support Alliance demands; but after the election nearly all these elected officials reverted to Democratic orthodoxy once in office. This disillusioning experience, plus the prospects of Cleveland's renomination by the Democratic Party, stimulated Southern Alliancemen to become Populists. In July 1892 the national People's Party was formally organized in Omaha.

Populist ideology of the nineteenth century was a combination of anti-elitism, plot mentality, paranoia, and elements of rational reform. Populists viewed American society as corrupt and in decay and believed in the myth of a better, vanished time from a bygone era to which they desired to return. The populists believed that they could redirect society to the just and stable course that would benefit the common people, whom they viewed as the moral backbone of America. The populists harbored animosity toward intellectuals—in the form of scientists, economists, and the media—and hysterically denounced their political enemies, the railroads, bankers, grain elevators, intellectuals, scientists, and middlemen of all forms as plotting against them. The populists viewed themselves as putting the power back in the hands of the common people; and their means of doing so was through the implementation of direct primaries, ballot initiatives and referendums, and direct election of United States Senators, whom they viewed as elites out of touch with the common

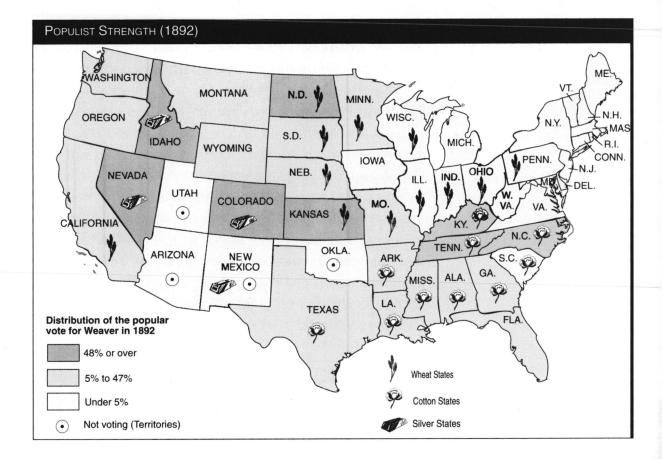

POPULIST STRENGTH (1892)

Distribution of the popular vote for Weaver in 1892

- 48% or over
- 5% to 47%
- Under 5%
- ⊙ Not voting (Territories)

- Wheat States
- Cotton States
- Silver States

man. The populists also favored free silver, the inclusion of blacks in the political process, the eight-hour day, and the elimination of the Pinkertons detective agency, which they viewed as a tool of elites to oppress the common man. The populist goal was to build a coalition of farmers, miners, urban workers, and blacks who would overthrow the rule of elites in favor of rule by the common man.

THE ELECTION OF 1892

The Populist platform of 1892 restated earlier Alliance demands, including the free and unlimited coinage of silver at the ratio of 16 to 1; government ownership and operation of railroads and the telephone, telegraph, and postal systems; prohibition of alien ownership of land; restriction of immigration; and a graduated income tax. The death of L. L. Polk of North Carolina, just before the convention met in Omaha on July 4, probably deprived the Populists of their strongest candidate. They nominated General James B. Weaver of Iowa for President and General James G. Field of Virginia for Vice-President. Both Cleveland and Harrison were renominated by the major parties. Their running mates were Adlai E. Stevenson of Illinois and Whitelaw Reid, editor of the New York *Tribune*.

The free silver plank was the only exciting issue in the campaign, and Weaver polled 1,040,000 popular votes and 22 electoral votes. Populists became the first third party since the Civil War to break into the Electoral College—winning the states of Kansas, Colorado, Idaho, and Nevada. Furthermore, Populist governors were elected in Kansas and North Dakota. They also elected 10 representatives, five senators, three governors, and 1,500 members of state legislatures. Populists were unsuccessful, however, in their attempt to lure urban workers who feared job competition from black workers. In the end, it is evident that the appeal of the Populists was strongest among miners who favored free silver. In terms of the major parties. Cleveland defeated Harrison with 277 to 145 electoral votes and 5,555,426 to 5,182,690 popular votes. Cleveland won his second term in office as President, but he had won the popular vote for the Presidency for the third straight time.

CLEVELAND AND THE DEPRESSION OF 1893

Shortly after Cleveland assumed the presidency in 1893, the country began to experience the worst financial panic in years. Following the failure of a number of prominent firms, most notably the Philadelphia and Reading Railroad and the National Cordage Company, the stock market suddenly collapsed. Banks, which had invested heavily in the stock market, called in their loans; and credit just about dried up. Businesses failed daily, runs on banks followed, and before the year was out, 500 banks, including Baring Brothers of London, and nearly 16,000 businesses had gone into bankruptcy. This included over 150 railroads. An estimated one million workers became unemployed, approximately 20 percent of the workforce. The bank collapses produced a capital shortage in the economy, and corporations could not find the loans necessary to operate. According to the *Commercial and Financial Chronicle*, never before had there been such a sudden and striking cessation of industrial activity, and no part of the nation escaped it. Everywhere mills, factories, furnaces, and mines closed down in large numbers, and hundreds of thousands of workers lost their jobs. By the fall of 1893, the *Banker's Magazine* of London reported the American people to be "in the throes of a fiasco unprecedented even in their broad experience" and declared "ruin and disaster run riot over the land."

The panic developed into a major depression, but there was no agreement as to its causes. Conservative business leaders attributed it to the Sherman Silver Purchase Act and to radical attacks on property. Labor leaders and agrarians blamed it on the capitalists. The Democrats blamed the Republicans, and the Republicans accused the Democrats.

There had been periodic panics followed by depressions ever since the end of the Civil War, and in each instance, reckless speculation overinflated stock market values. The over-inflated market was then followed by a collapse in confidence, with attendant business failures and unemployment. The primary cause for the debacle of 1893 was the overexpansion of transportation facilities and industrial production, accompanied by stock manipulation and reckless speculation. Following the pattern of previous recessions, it had been preceded by a similar depression abroad.

Like his predecessors in office, Cleveland believed it was not the duty of the federal government to alleviate suffering in a depression. As he complacently stated in his second inaugural, "... while the people should patriotically and cheerfully support their Government, its functions do not include the support of the people." In his view, the Sherman Silver Purchase Act had caused the depression by depleting the Treasury, and his proposed remedy was to repeal the act and maintain the gold standard. The silverites, however, disagreed. They contended that the cure lay in the free and unlimited coinage of silver at a ratio of 16 to 1 of gold and that the Sherman Act had provided inadequate relief; and many debtor agrarians agreed.

Cleveland, however, was convinced that the silver certificates issued under the Sherman Act and redeemed in gold were responsible for the drain on the gold reserve that was being lowered to the established minimum of $100 million. This was an oversimplification, for there were several causes for the drain on gold, most certainly including a decline in revenues from import tariffs due to the severe economic recession. Cleveland, however, summoned Congress into special session in 1893 and, through a combination of Gold Democrats and Republicans, had the Sherman Silver Purchase Act repealed. Most Western and Southern Democrats voted against the Democratic administration, widening the split within the party on the currency issue.

Repeal of the Sherman Silver Purchase Act, of course, failed to restore prosperity, and the Treasury's gold reserve continued to fall. To keep the country on the gold standard, Cleveland had the Treasury sell government bonds for gold. A group of bankers headed by J. P. Morgan absorbed three bond issues in 1894 and 1895; but it was not until 1897, when the depression had finally run its course, that the Treasury crisis ended. Although the gold purchases enabled the Treasury to meet its obligations, the bond sales intensified the silverites' hatred of the President. Meanwhile, many

Americans became alarmed over the government's dependence upon a syndicate of New York bankers. As the economy improved in the late 1890s, gold standard advocates felt vindicated; but the fact of the matter was that new gold finds in Alaska and the Yukon territory had flooded the cash-short economy with new currency and thus remedied the currency shortage that had been endemic in the Panic of 1893. Good fortune in gold prospecting, rather than monetary responsibility in adherence to the gold standard, had ended the panic and the price deflation that had plagued the Gilded Age since the 1870s.

Cleveland himself, however, failed to bring about any substantial reduction of the tariff. In the House the Democrats, fulfilling their campaign promises, had passed a tariff bill drawn up by William L. Wilson of West Virginia that provided for a modest reduction in rates. In the Senate, though, a group of protectionists from both parties led by Senator Arthur Gorman, an influential Democrat from Maryland, attacked the bill with more than 600 amendments, restoring some old rates and raising others. The resultant Wilson-Gorman Tariff of 1894, which Cleveland denounced as "party perfidy and party dishonor" and which became law without his signature, was a far cry from reform. It did provide for a small income tax of two percent on incomes over $4,000, but the Supreme Court, as unpopular as Cleveland, held the tax to be unconstitutional.

For the remainder of his presidency, Cleveland confined his role to that of protector of the status quo. He vetoed the Seigniorage bill, which would have increased the supply of the currency. Through subordinates he rudely rejected the petitions of "armies" of unemployed workers who, under the nominal leadership of men like Populist Jacob S. Coxey, marched on Washington in 1894 to plead for public works relief programs. "Coxey's Army," as it was called, was a group of some 500 men who marched from Ohio to Washington to demand free coinage of silver and the establishment of a $500 million federal public works program to provide jobs for the unemployed. Cleveland, however, did not view a public works program as within the proper role of government and did not view Coxey's protest as legal. Consequently, when Coxey's army arrived at the Capitol, they found themselves barred from entry by armed police. Coxey and two others were arrested and convicted of trespassing (for walking on the grass), and police dispersed the rest of Coxey's followers. In the same year, Cleveland sent federal troops to crush the Pullman strike. The combination of the two, along with Cleveland's unwillingness to introduce a major program to combat the recession, convinced Americans that Cleveland neither understood nor cared about their plight. On a personal note, Cleveland suffered from serious health problems and had a secret operation aboard an offshore yacht to remove a cancerous upper jaw. Things could hardly be worse for Cleveland in his second term.

Three Supreme Court decisions in 1895 added to the general discontent in the country. The Court in a 5–4 decision in *Pollock v. Farmers' Loan and Trust Company* invalidated the income tax clause of the Wilson-Gorman Tariff on the ground that it was a direct tax. Therefore, according to the Constitution, it had to be apportioned among the states on the basis of population. Moreover, Justice Stephen J. Field had earlier called the income tax "an assault upon capital" and a "stepping stone to others, larger and more sweeping, till our political contests ... become a war of the poor against the rich."

Shortly after this, the Court, in the case of *in re Debs*, unanimously upheld the injunction sending Debs to prison at the time of the Pullman strike. At the same time, the Court in an 8–1 decision in *United States v. E. C. Knight Company*, in the first United States Supreme Court case involving the Sherman Antitrust Act of 1890, distinguished manufacturing from commerce and held that the Sherman Act did not apply to manufacturing combinations within states. This decision seriously weakened the enforcement of the antitrust laws, and for some time, placed most monopolies beyond the reach of federal regulation. Partially due to these elitist Supreme Court decisions, there was a widespread feeling in the country during the mid-90s that there was a war on between the rich and the poor and that the President, the Supreme Court, and Congress were on the side of the rich.

THE ELECTION OF 1896

The Republicans met in St. Louis in June 1896 and nominated William McKinley of Ohio for President and Garret A. Hobart, a corporation lawyer of New Jersey, for Vice-President. Marcus Alonzo Hanna, a wealthy Ohio industrialist, was largely responsible for McKinley's nomination. Hanna was a good example of the new kind of political boss then emerging—the businessman holding office and actually running the party instead of remaining in the background and paying out political favors. As a leader of the Republican Party in Ohio and soon to become Republican national chairman, Hanna gathered the necessary delegate votes for McKinley's nomination and financed and managed his preconvention campaign.

On the preeminent question of the day, the monetary question, however, McKinley's record was not consistent. He had voted for both the Bland-Allison Act and the Sherman Silver Purchase Act, yet

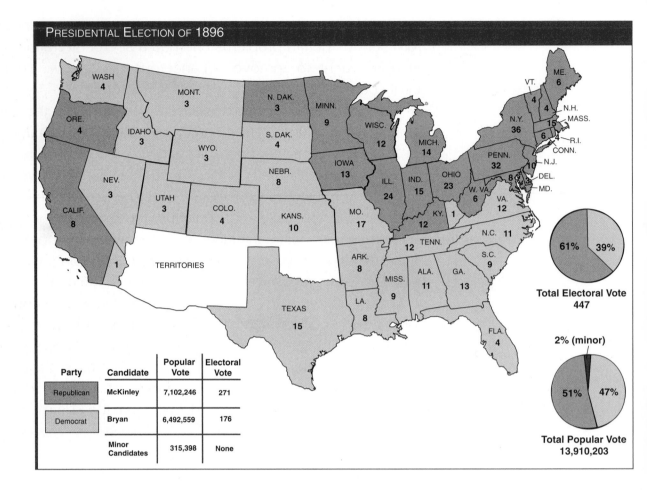

PRESIDENTIAL ELECTION OF 1896

Party	Candidate	Popular Vote	Electoral Vote
Republican	McKinley	7,102,246	271
Democrat	Bryan	6,492,559	176
	Minor Candidates	315,398	None

Total Electoral Vote 447: 61% / 39%

Total Popular Vote 13,910,203: 51% / 47% / 2% (minor)

in 1891, in running for governor, he had condemned the free coinage of silver and advocated international bimetallism. Hanna had already decided upon a gold standard plank, but at the convention he gave the impression he had to be "persuaded" by the Eastern delegates that "the existing gold standard must be maintained." After a gold plank was adopted at the Republican Convention, a small group of silver advocates led by Senator Henry M. Teller of Colorado left the hall and organized the Silver Republican Party.

Similarly, the Democrats were torn by bitter strife when they met in Chicago in July. The agrarians looked upon their own President, Grover Cleveland, as an enemy. He personified the Northeastern conservatism against which they were in revolt. Consequently, within the Democratic Party, insurgency was rampant. In the elections of 1894, the Democrats had barely retained control of the Senate and had lost the House.

Insurgent Democrats prepared to outdo the silverites in denouncing Cleveland and in advocating free silver. In short, they hoped to win back the Populists and take over the Democratic Party. Their work was so effective that by the summer of 1896 they had gained

William Jennings Bryan (left) and William McKinley (right), opponents in the fiercely fought election of 1896
(Library of Congress)

control of every state Democratic organization south of the Potomac and west of the Alleghenies—except South Dakota, Minnesota, and Wisconsin.

The silverites dominated the convention, and Cleveland was denounced in Democratic Party resolutions and speeches. The Democratic Platform of 1896 repudiated the Cleveland program and attacked the protective tariff, national banks, trusts, and the Supreme Court. It, also, called for an income tax and the free coinage of silver at the ratio of 16 to 1. The leading contender for the nomination was Congressman Richard P. ("Silver Dick") Bland of Missouri, who had fought for free silver since the 70s; but the convention passed him by and on the fifth ballot nominated William Jennings Bryan, "the silver-tongued orator from Nebraska," who had captivated the silver delegates with a speech that rose to a stirring peroration. "You shall not press down upon the brow of labor this crown of thorns, you shall not crucify mankind upon a cross of gold," at which point the demonstrative Bryan spread out his arms and mimicked a crucifixion. The delegates roared in approval, but some viewed Bryan's antics as more bluster than substance. For example, Congressman Joseph

Foraker once commented, "Boy Orator of the Platte" was an apt name for Bryan since like the Platte, Bryan was about "Six inches deep and a mile wide at the mouth."

Bryan, only 36 at the time, seemed to have been nominated by the accident of a spontaneous speech. He had, however, been rounding up support for several years and had presented his ideas many times to other audiences; his convention speech was simply the last step. As a recent biography by Michael Kazin demonstrates, Bryan had an exceptional ability to connect with audiences with his use of rhetoric, speaking in political terms in the style of a Protestant evangelist. Bryan's running mate was Arthur Sewall of Maine, a wealthy shipbuilder, banker, and protectionist, but an advocate of free silver.

The Populists faced a dilemma when their convention met in St. Louis in July. If they nominated their own candidate, they feared they would split the reform vote and permit the Republican William McKinley to win. If they endorsed Bryan, they would surrender their identity to the Democrats and sacrifice their broad program of reform for one that placed a disproportionate emphasis on the silver question. Western Populists were eager to nominate Bryan, but Southern Populists wanted a separate party ticket.

The Populists finally were induced to nominate Bryan through trickery. Senator William V. Allen of Nebraska, chairman of the convention, told the Southerners that the Democrats had promised to withdraw Sewall and accept Thomas E. Watson, Populist leader of Georgia, as their vice presidential candidate—if the Populists would nominate Bryan. Watson's decision to accept this compromise persuaded Southern opponents of "fusion," whereby Populists would "fuse" with the Democrats, to vote for Bryan's nomination. This would have created a true Democratic-Populist partnership, but the Democrats refused to withdraw Sewall. Henry Demarest Lloyd watched the convention with great disgust and finally concluded, "The People's party has been betrayed ... but after all it is its own fault." Similarly, Populist candidate for Vice President Tom Watson proclaimed, "Fusion means that we play Jonah while they play whale," fully understanding that "fusion between the Populists and the Democrats" would mean the end of the Populist Party and their absorption by the Democrats.

The campaign of 1896 was a highly emotional and dramatic one. In spite of the fact that Bryan was a very large man who weighed over 300 pounds, he possessed tremendous energy and spoke in 21 states, traveled 18,000 miles on his "whistle-stop" railroad tour, and addressed some 5 million people in more than 600 speeches— an unprecedented achievement.

William McKinley, in contrast, was a rather poor speaker and Hanna's strategy was, therefore, to shield him from the public. Hanna's strategy called for a "front porch" campaign where McKinley remained at his home in Canton and read well-prepared speeches from his front porch to carefully coached delegations that visited him. Ostensibly, the candidate had to remain at home because his mother's health was failing, his wife suffered from seizures, and both needed his care. Exactly how McKinley planned to carry out the affairs of state while playing nursemaid to the invalid women in his life was not explained. Furthermore, there is some evidence that McKinley's wife and mother could hardly have suffered through worse care. William Howard Taft later told a story of attending a dinner function with the President McKinley and his wife where Mrs. McKinley suffered an epileptic seizure. McKinley's response was simply to place a white dinner napkin over his wife's face to shield others from having to watch her convulsions and then continue with his dinner discussion virtually uninterrupted.

Whether the reasons McKinley stayed home were a farce or not, Hanna's strategy worked. The railroads brought staunch Republican partisans from all over the country to McKinley's home in Canton to witness the charade. The speeches were carefully choreographed by Hanna, complete with places where the crowd would drown out the candidate with seemingly spontaneous applause. Pro-Republican newspapers then reported the daily speeches with high praise for McKinley and details of the crowd's enthusiasm.

The powerful response to Bryan's appeal frightened Eastern conservatives, and Hanna took advantage of their panic to collect campaign funds. From trusts, banks, railroads, and tycoons he raised a sum estimated at between $3.5 million and $15 million as against a bare $300,000 for Bryan. John D. Rockefeller, alone, contributed $300,000 to the Republican cause, a sum equal to what Bryan and the Democrats were able to garner in total.

Hanna used the money lavishly but wisely. The Republicans printed 250 million pieces of campaign literature, in 12 languages so as not to miss new immigrants. Some 1,500 professional speakers were paid to go into closely contested districts and stump for McKinley. The Republicans also received great assistance from the press, which heaped all kinds of abuse upon Bryan with slanted journalism. *The Louisville Courier Journal* called him "a dishonest dodger ... a daring adventurer ... a political faker," and the New York *Tribune* referred to him as a "wretched, rattle-prated boy." The Philadelphia *Press* described the "Jacobins" of the Democratic convention as "hideous and repulsive vipers," and Theodore Roosevelt was reported as saying that

William McKinley giving a speech *(Library of Congress)*

the silver men might well "be stood up against the wall and shot." John Hay, writing to Henry Adams in London, said of Bryan, "The Boy Orator makes only one speech—but he makes it twice a day. There is no fun in it. He simply reiterates the unquestionable truths that every man who has a clean shirt is a thief and should be hanged, and there is no goodness or wisdom except among the illiterates and criminal classes." Bryan's Protestant fundamentalist-style speeches also tended to alienate Catholics, a group whose vote would be critical to winning a number of states in the North and East. In addition, there were dire warnings that Bryan's victory would bring disaster. Farmers were told that mortgages would not be renewed, and workers were informed that factories would be closed or wages cut.

Out of almost 14 million popular votes cast, McKinley won with a margin of over a half million and with 271 electoral votes to 176 for Bryan. Bryan failed to carry a single industrial and urban state and did not win a single state north of the Potomac and east of the Mississippi. Despite the widespread unrest among labor, he failed to elicit its support, and this failure was one of the principal reasons for his defeat; but, also, he had nowhere near the material resources backing McKinley, and he represented the party blamed for the depression. The election was a sound defeat for the Democrats overall as the Republicans also gained a majority in both houses of Congress.

McKinley lost all the mining states and the wheat-growing states of South Dakota, Nebraska, and Kansas where Republicans had always been strong; but he held onto the corn-producing states of the Middle West, where the farmers were better off than those on the Plains. He also gained an ascendancy in the Northeast such as no previous Republican President had had. From Maine south to Virginia and from the Great Lakes to Tennessee he carried every state. While the margin by which he carried some was narrow, McKinley had a majority of the popular vote in the nation. The Republicans continued to hold the bulk of the Northern farmers and had gained new strength among the commercial and industrial interests of the North and the Upper South. For the first time since 1872, New England and the Middle Atlantic, Central, and North Central states were solidly Republican, and these sections were strong enough, if united, to control the electoral college and, thereby, the presidency itself.

Historians are generally agreed that the election of 1896 was the most important one since 1860, and they have regarded it as a turning point in American history. For one thing, it gave the Republicans a clear majority of the popular vote in the country as a whole for the first time since Reconstruction. For another, it ushered in a series of Republican triumphs and a period of Republican supremacy in the national government that was to last until 1932, interrupted only by Woodrow Wilson's two terms. McKinley's victory also marked a triumph for conservatism and industrialism, and the backbone of agrarian resurgence was broken in 1896.

In the mourning for Bryan, the fate of Populism was largely forgotten. Its passing seemed to be the concern of few, yet it was one of the most significant results of the election of 1896. Fusion with the Democrats and the abandonment of a broad program of reform for the sake of silver had all but destroyed the Populist Party on the national level. It was Populism, not Bryanism, that furnished the backbone of agrarian resurgence; and when that backbone was broken in 1896, it meant that agrarian radicalism had made its last aggressive political stand.

THE POPULISTS IN PERSPECTIVE

Despite their defeat in 1896 and their disappearance from the political scene, the Populists have an important, albeit a controversial, place in American history. For quite a number of years historians portrayed the Populists as the champions of the common man and as the makers of modern reform in the country. John D. Hicks in *The Populist Revolt* put the favorable and traditional point of view about the Populists forth in 1931, and this remained the standard general account for many years. According to Hicks, Populism represented "the last phase of a long and perhaps a losing struggle—the struggle to save agricultural America from the devouring jaws of industrial America." Hicks wrote in the tradition of the Progressive historians, who were very critical of American industrial society and who regarded the older agrarian America as having many virtues.

This favorable view of the Populists came under attack in the 1950s when critics like Richard Hofstadter and Victor C. Ferkiss charged them with all kinds of mischief—including racism, anti-Semitism, jingoism, nativism, anti-intellectualism, xenophobia, and even being the forerunners of American fascism. Though the critics agreed that Populism was the first modern political movement of practical importance in the United States to insist that the federal government had some responsibility for the common weal, they also believed that the Populist leaders were haunted by nonexistent conspiracies and frequently were given to scapegoating rather than to rational analysis.

The 1960s witnessed another turnabout. A more favorable view of Populism reappeared. C. Vann Woodward and William P. Tucker, while conceding some of the points scored by the critics of Populism, found that the negative and unlovely characteristics of the Populists were not peculiar to them and that the irrational and illiberal side of Populism was no reason to repudiate its heritage.

Thereafter, some of the new writers saw the Populists as hoping to transform the American social system by putting forth a logical and reasonable analysis of industrial America, including the rejection of laissez-faire capitalism, Social Darwinism, and the success ethic. Others showed that Populism, at least in Kansas—the most Populist of the western states, was not hostile "to things non-American" but instead was a rational, legitimate political response to economic distress. Still others reported that the Populists in Alabama, at least, were neither revolutionaries nor reformers but repeatedly even voted against reforms to which they were pledged.

Then in 1976 Lawrence Goodwyn published the first scholarly, general study of the Populist movement on a national scale since that of Hicks. In *Democratic Promise: The Populist Moment in America*, Goodwyn contended that Hicks had missed the essential dynamics of Populism, thereby opening the way for the later distortions and misinterpretations. He accused Hicks of mistaking "the shadow movement" accompanying Populism for the real thing. The real thing, argued Goodwyn, was the political revolt growing out of the cooperative movement of the Alliance and the elaborate program of structural economic and political reforms developed in that struggle getting under way in the 1880s. The shadow movement was the effort to substitute for that entire program and the reform spirit behind it the single demand for the free coinage of silver. Even more recently Michael Kazin has written a book, *The Populist Persuasion*, in which he not only evaluates the Populists of the Gilded Age (mostly favorably), but also looks at their heirs, in some cases evaluating these not so favorably.

Despite the extensive literature on Populism, it remains difficult to assess its place in American history although, in general, scholars are far more positive than they were a few decades ago. In any case, it is generally acknowledged that the Populists pioneered many measures that would eventually be enacted in the twentieth century, during either the Progressive period or the New Deal.

MCKINLEY AND THE END OF AN ERA

The McKinley administration was ushered in under highly favorable circumstances. Businessmen knew that their interests would be safeguarded for four years. There was a return to prosperity, that was to continue for several years although many long-term structural problems remained, especially where workers were concerned. Farmers largely dropped politics—though in some parts of the country they continued to be unhappy with the status quo and even voted for the Socialist Party. Politicians were happy and looked forward to a long period of abundance. McKinley, well aware of the economic distress that had affected Americans, promised in his first inaugural that this would be his chief concern. To maintain recovery he advocated two principal measures—a higher tariff and a gold standard act, the latter having been the panacea of Cleveland. Congress responded with the Dingley Tariff of 1897, which raised duties to an average of 52 percent, the highest in our history, and the Gold Standard Act of 1900, which declared the gold dollar from that time on would be the sole standard of currency.

With these two laws, the McKinley administration made good its campaign promises. Beyond this, neither the President nor Congress intended to interfere with the economy. They planned to let it alone and to allow business to create prosperity in good laissez-faire fashion. The attitude was perhaps best summed up by Marcus Hanna, who stated "a man had a right to do what he pleased with his own." McKinley's inauguration marked the beginning of the greatest consolidation movement in American industry (1897–1904). This, coupled with the Spanish–American War, produced golden years of prosperity for business. The McKinley years would be less "golden," however, for African Americans. On the subject of black rights, McKinley essentially chose the same path that had been chosen by all his predecessors throughout the Gilded Age and did nothing, in spite of an upsurge in racial violence in the 1890s. When a riot in Wilmington, North Carolina, resulted in the death of 11 blacks, McKinley had little to say about the matter and did even less. T. Thomas Fortune spoke for many blacks when he described McKinley as "a man of jelly, who would turn us loose to the mob and not say a word."

Nevertheless, McKinley's presidency marked the beginning of a new era not only in national politics but also in the running of the national government. According to historian Lewis Gould, William McKinley was the first modern president, for reasons such as his appointing a de facto chief of staff, creating a war room, and, in general, skillfully employing bureaucratic means to advance his agenda. McKinley would also be the last of the Union Civil War officers to become President. We now turn to the new century, over which he would preside, if only briefly.

SOCIETY AND CULTURE IN THE PROGRESSIVE ERA

(Library of Congress)

Known as "the Progressive Era," the period lasting roughly from 1900 until American entry into World War I, was replete with changes in public policy, innovative reforms on many fronts, breakthroughs in technology, and exciting cultural developments. There were also changes in American foreign policy that foreshadowed the subsequent course of the twentieth century. The progressives, drawn from both Republican and Democratic ranks, had in common a belief both in the power of human intelligence and in the power of government to deal with social problems. We turn first to culture and to the intense speed-up in urbanization that underlay much of the Progressive Era cultural transformation.

PROGRESSIVISM

Progressivism was essentially the popular response to the excesses of the industrial age from the late nineteenth century through World War I. Progressivism was based on a number of basic assumptions, one of which was that society was capable of improvement—morally, socially, and politically, as well as economically and technologically. The progressives believed that order is essential to progress. Hence, growth should not be allowed to occur recklessly as it had in the laissez faire nineteenth century; but, rather, it should be controlled through societal institutions, including government, which they viewed as a legitimate tool for improving society. Progressives argued that the natural laws of the marketplace, laissez faire, and Social Darwinism were insufficient means to promote progress, justice, and the greater good; hence, direct, purposeful intervention into human affairs was essential to creating a better society. The progressive vision, essentially, rested on the idea of the good of the whole; and progressives argued that individuals had a responsibility to the whole, and the whole had a responsibility to the individual. As such, laissez faire economics that allowed unsafe workplaces, child labor, low wages, and monopolies were rejected as bad both for individuals and the whole. The breakup of corporate monopolies, even if they had done nothing wrong or illegal, but had just played the free market game better than competitors, was justified in the interest of the good of the whole.

THE GROWTH OF CITIES

THE FLIGHT FROM THE FARM

The population of the cities increased sevenfold between 1860 and 1910. About 30 percent of this increase reflected a movement of native whites, and to a much lesser extent blacks, out of rural areas. Although farm prices rose so high during the Progressive Era that the years 1909–1914 are known as "The Golden Age of Agriculture," the exodus continued through World War I. (It should be noted, however, that these high prices were an average, and that many pockets of desperate poverty remained). By 1920 well under a third of all Americans still lived on farms and less than half in rural areas.

Three interrelated factors caused this migration to the cities. Rural births exceeded deaths, output per farmer increased, and the quality of rural life suffered a relative decline. Just before the Civil War, it took 39 man-hours to produce 40 bushels of corn. By 1894 improved farm machinery had reduced that number to 15. The increase in the efficiency of wheat production was even more dramatic. In 1896, with full mechanization, a wheat farmer could harvest 18 times more crop than in 1830. This increase in output per farmer, together with a relatively high rural birthrate and a shortage of good new land, created a surplus of agricultural workers. The rise in output and increase in farm prices also drove up land values disproportionately. These same factors further contributed to a growth in tenancy from 25 percent of all farmers in 1880 to 37 percent in 1910. Partly because of the extraordinarily high incidence of black tenants, South Carolina, Georgia, Alabama, and Mississippi led the nation at between 60 and 70 percent, but even in Illinois the rate stood at 44 percent.

For the more substantial farmers, rural life remained moderately rewarding, but for those on the margins of existence, it became more depressing. Tens of thousands of farm families lived without church, school, or society. Thousands of mothers died in childbirth, and more thousands of children died from privation and inadequate medical care.

Southern farmers fared the worst. Both blacks and whites accepted the recurring fevers and chills of malaria as facts of life, and at least a half million whites were infected, through ignorance of elementary sanitation, with the debilitating hookworm disease. As a distraught southern physician wrote to Theodore Roosevelt, "I would prefer to see my own daughter, 9 years old, at work in a cotton mill than have her live as a tenant on the average southern tenant one-horse farm."

In 1909 the privately financed Rockefeller Sanitary Commission opened a campaign that eventually wiped out the hookworm disease, and in 1912 the United States Public Health Service began a prolonged assault on malaria; but by then a generation or more of afflicted Southerners had lost all opportunity for normal development.

THE NEW IMMIGRANTS: PROBLEMS AND ACHIEVEMENTS

The wave of "new immigrants," discussed in a previous chapter, continued to rise until the outbreak of World War I. Between 1901 and 1914 some 3 million Italians, 1.5 million Jews, and 4 million Slavs poured into the United States. The relatively high literacy rate of male Jews and the skills they had learned in eastern European villages enabled them to adapt quite readily to urban economic and social life. Most other new immigrants, however, came from peasant backgrounds and were ill-prepared for city life. A small number of Poles, Bohemians, and Italians settled on run-down farms, which their superior diligence and use of women and children in the fields made into productive units; however, the lack of transferable skills forced most to take menial jobs in overcrowded cities or grime-ridden industrial and mining towns. On the other hand, the Italians who found their way to the West, especially to California, fared considerably better than this dismal picture would suggest because they were able to establish a toe-hold in the burgeoning fruit industry.

No society could have absorbed so many disparate people without social tension, nor could any society have been expected to adequately housed such vast numbers upon arrival. One result—and the one most often emphasized—was a pronounced increase in social and economic discrimination. Among the new arrivals, perhaps those from Asia suffered most; but all immigrants—including the Germans, Scandinavians, and Irish, who still came in large (though sharply reduced) numbers, suffered in degree. This was in spite of the counter-ideal personified by the inscription plaque placed on the Statue of Liberty in 1903, which stated, "Give us your tired, your poor, your huddled masses yearning to breathe free."

Much of the social tension was rooted in class and economic rivalries. Old-stock employers, for example, often used the most recent immigrants as strikebreakers. They also kept certain ethnic groups from management positions in many industries. Conversely, members of a particular ethnic group would establish themselves in a certain occupation and close out other ethnic strains. In fact, virtually every ethnic group discriminated to some degree against others: German Jews against east European Jews; Germans against Slavs; Norwegians against Swedes; Irish against Italians, Slavs, Jews, and even French-Canadians.

Much of the tension was also religious, and as such, it long antedated the American experience. Anti-Catholicism was particularly acute. For example, in 1910, former Populist candidate Tom Watson denounced the Catholic hierarchy as "the deadliest menace to our liberties and our civilization." Watson also wrote a book entitled *Maria Monk and Her Revelation of Convent Crimes* where he argued that there were murders of infants in Catholic convents. Watson even argued that the Pope had secretly organized and armed the Knights of Columbus for a takeover of the United States.

Conflict between Catholics and Protestants went back to the Reformation—that between Christians and Jews, to the Roman Empire. Thus most of the Jews who came to the United States during this period were fleeing systematic discrimination and even outright persecution—both official and unofficial—by Rumanians, Russians, Ukrainians, and Poles, just as many Irish had earlier fled Ireland because of their long economic repression by the English. It is a tribute to the openness of American society and its institutions, including the absence of a state church, that discrimination proved mild on balance, at least by the standards of most of the rest of the world. This does not, however, mean that the United States was void of anti-Semitism as the Leo Frank case in 1914 demonstrated.

THE LEO FRANK CASE

Leo Frank was a Jewish manager of a pencil factory in Georgia who was accused of murdering a 14 year-old girl, Mary Phagan. Phagan's body had been found in the cellar of the factory. She had been raped and strangled, but before dying she had managed to scribble a note accusing an unnamed black man of the crime. In spite of the note, Frank was charged with the crime and convicted based on the testimony of a black man who had been in the factory at the time of the murder. Prominent lawyers throughout the country pointed out the obvious—that it was most likely the black man that testified against Frank who was the real culprit. Frank was sentenced to death, but his sentence was later commuted, causing outrage

Leo Frank *(Library of Congress)*

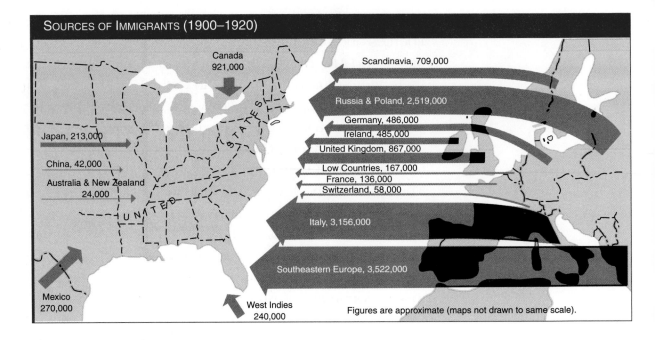

SOURCES OF IMMIGRANTS (1900–1920)

Canada 921,000
Scandinavia, 709,000
Russia & Poland, 2,519,000
Germany, 486,000
Ireland, 485,000
United Kingdom, 867,000
Low Countries, 167,000
France, 136,000
Switzerland, 58,000
Italy, 3,156,000
Southeastern Europe, 3,522,000
Japan, 213,000
China, 42,000
Australia & New Zealand 24,000
Mexico 270,000
West Indies 240,000
Figures are approximate (maps not drawn to same scale).

among Georgian nativists. Frank was eventually lynched in 1915 by a Georgia mob, an action that Tom Watson defended as just and argued that it would be prudent to reorganize the Ku Klux Klan. Watson also published his own magazine where he continually railed against Catholics and Jews and accused them of working together to undermine American society. Watson would ride his anti-Semitism and anti-Catholicism to a seat in the United States Senate in 1920.

Meanwhile the rise of racist theory in Europe, much of it popularized in the United States, gave a pseudo-intellectual cast to the notion that the old immigrants from northwestern Europe were inherently superior and that the new immigrants should be refused entry. Nativists in America argued that the new immigrants were somehow diluting the pure American race. Madison Grant, in *The Passing of the Great Race,* argued that immigration would lead to a "mongrelization" of America and that in cases of intermarriage between persons of different races, the children of the union tended to go to the "lower case."

Even John R. Commons—progressive economist, Christian layman, and zealous friend of labor—favored immigration restriction on genetic grounds. Markedly higher scores by northern Europeans on the crude intelligence tests then coming into use gave a further veneer of scientific truth to these views. Not until after the new immigration had ended did more sophisticated research indicate that cultural and environmental factors such as urban or rural origin, family occupational and educational background, and quality of schooling figured crucially in intelligence test scores.

Actually, the heavy environmental emphasis of reform Darwinism led many progressives to remain skeptical of the more sweeping racist theories. Unlike conservatives, they equated race more with culture than genetics, though they also believed that excessive immigration enabled employers to hold down wages and feared that immigrants from non-democratic countries would not readily be assimilated, partly because many constituted a kind of migrant work force. In 1908, more Italians and Hungarians returned to their homelands than entered the United States.

Progressives strove, nevertheless, to "Americanize" those who were here and to give them a measure of political representation. "I grow extremely indignant at the attitude of coarse hostility to the immigrant," President Theodore Roosevelt wrote privately in 1906:

> I have one Catholic in my Cabinet ... and I now have a Jew ... and part of my object in each appointment was to implant in the minds of our fellow Americans of Catholic or Jewish faith, or of foreign ancestry or birth, the knowledge that they have in this country just the same rights and opportunities as every one else.

Yet probably a majority of progressives joined conservatives and the American Federation of Labor in supporting a literacy test designed to curtail the new immigration drastically. Passed four times and vetoed four times—by Cleveland in 1896, Taft in 1913, and Wilson in 1915 and 1917—it was finally enacted over Wilson's second veto in 1917.

Most new immigrants tended to enter lower-class occupations, obscuring another development of great importance. They, or at least their children, moved from unskilled to skilled jobs with the same or higher frequency as old-stock whites of the same economic class. Many also became homeowners with somewhat greater frequency, though Jews invested much more heavily in education than housing. Regardless, whether as owners or renters, most immigrants gravitated toward the familiar. Virtually every American city developed neighborhood pieces of Europe—"Little Italy," "Little Polonia," and so forth. Through foods, music, customs, and ways of looking at life, these distinctive settlements enriched American culture as a whole and helped transform the United States into a pluralistic society.

EDUCATION AND SOCIAL MOBILITY

Public education served as the broadest avenue of upward mobility in American society. For cultural and economic reasons, not all ethnic groups took that route in the same proportions. For the same reasons, most old-stock whites in the South and many in rural areas

Immigrants at Ellis Island in New York *(Library of Congress)*

elsewhere did not take it either. For those who did, however, including numerous sons and daughters of substantial Midwestern farmers and rural and small-town clergymen, it opened new social and economic opportunities.

Urban Jews made the most notable advances. Despite the impoverishment of many of their immigrant parents, Jewish youngsters—especially males—graduated from high school in much higher proportions than the offspring of most other ethnic groups. One result was a lower delinquency rate and another, adequate preparation for college. In 1908, at a time when Jews made up about 2 percent of the population, male Jews of the first and second generations comprised 8.5 percent of the male student bodies at 77 major colleges and universities. By the next generation they constituted a disproportionately high percentage of physicians and lawyers in the larger cities. This led to the institution of quotas at many private colleges—though not public ones—and a drive by the American Bar Association to eliminate night law schools, where Jewish males were able to gain ready access.

The teaching profession itself became an agency of upward mobility for rural whites and blacks, for small-town Americans of older stock, and for urban Jews and Irish, especially in New York and New England. Teaching in grammar and secondary schools was one of the few careers open to women, and the proportion of female teachers rose from 70 percent in 1900 to 85 percent in 1920—though males maintained a firm hold on higher-paying administrative positions. In the colleges and universities, it should be said, women who were not enrolled in a "female" course of study—such as teaching, nursing, or librarianship—were probably subjected to even greater discrimination than were Jews.

THE MODERN CITY

If one word were to characterize the new urban society, it would be *mass*—mass transit, mass entertainment, mass circulation of written matter, mass education, mass production, and mass distribution.

In transit, the electric streetcar and the commuter train hastened the breakup of mixed residential sections in or near the city's core. The upper classes moved out first, but in time even clerks and factory workers bought or rented bungalows and flats in three-story frame houses far removed from offices and plants. Most new neighborhoods and suburbs had discrete ethnic and religious identities, but they tended to be more socially stratified than the old ones. No longer, for example, did workers, managers, and professionals reside on the same block though all might live, say, in the new Irish or Jewish neighborhood. Meanwhile the vacated residences were replaced by new stores and plants or occupied by the latest immigrants and newly arrived rural families, both white and black.

Not until after World War I would the outlines of the modern city's central problem—loss of industry, tax base, and gainfully employed residents—become perceptible. During the Progressive Era many cities retained administrative cohesiveness by annexing suburbs, while the growth of small businesses, great department stores, and white-collar industries like insurance and banking actually increased city tax bases. New civic leaders emerged among the offspring of the immigrants and the rural old stock and, especially, from the ranks of professional men, usually lawyers. Through much of the period America enjoyed an urban renaissance, characterized by beautifying movements, administrative reforms, a new level of public responsibility for health, improved schools, and new or expanded parks, playgrounds, libraries, museums, and zoos.

THE RISE OF MASS CULTURE

THE GROWTH OF SPECTATOR SPORTS

The city further stimulated interest in mass spectator sports—football, boxing, and baseball. By the turn of the century the Yale-Princeton

Yale-Princeton football game on November 13, 1915, at New Haven, Connecticut *(Library of Congress)*

football game was drawing between 30,000 and 40,000 fans, the Army-Navy game had become a national event, and Walter Camp's "All-America" selections were an annual feature of the sports pages. The winning of the heavyweight boxing championship in 1909 by a black man, Jack Johnson, induced race riots. His defeat in 1915 by a white, Jess Willard, brought a kind of national celebration. Six years later a new champion, Jack Dempsey, drew 80,000 fans and the first million-dollar gate in a bout in Jersey City. But in the early twentieth century it was baseball, not boxing, that came closest to being the national pastime.

Major league attendance climbed from 4.75 million in 1903 to 9 million in 1920. Through most of the period it was, in fact, the game of both the classes and the masses. Participation in the major leagues, though hardly the minor ones because they did not pay enough, also enabled many old-stock, small-town boys and Irish and German urban youths to escape dreary lives in the mills or factories. Significantly, throughout these years blacks were barred from organized baseball, as the white leagues were known.

The greatest "stars" of the era included Ty Cobb, a fiery Georgian whose lifetime .367 career batting average is still unequaled; Honus Wagner, probably the finest all-round player ever; Walter Johnson, whose 413 pitching victories, 110 shutouts, and 3,499 strike-outs set impressive records; and gentlemanly Christy Mathewson, who won more than 30 games in three separate seasons and pitched three shutouts in the World Series of 1905. So attached to the game was the American male that the revelation that the Chicago White Sox had "thrown" the 1919 World Series drove the Red Scare (see Chapter 9) off the front pages. A year later, "Babe" Ruth, formerly a superb pitcher for the Boston Red Sox, transformed the game by hitting 54 home runs for the New York Yankees.

MOTION PICTURES

Movies were one of the rare popular amusements to come up from the masses rather than down from the classes. They began in the

1890s as extra attractions in cheap variety houses, and in 1905 found their own home in nickelodeons. The working class—both native-born and immigrant—embraced the new medium. When subtitles flashed on the screen, those in the audience who could read English often read them aloud to their neighbors. For many of the foreign-born, the movies offered a course in Americanization.

By 1910 motion pictures were playing to a weekly audience of 10 million in 10,000 theaters across the nation. With few exceptions, American movie-makers fixed their sights firmly on the mass market, turning out films that delivered a good laugh or a good cry, some hair-raising excitement, or steamy passion (then seen as an un-American phenomenon portrayed by exotics like Theda Bara and Rudolph Valentino). American directors displayed an early awareness of the medium's technical potential, and beginning with D. W. Griffith's *The Birth of a Nation* in 1915—as brilliant in technique as it is obnoxious in content, owing to its virulent racism—they created some great spectacles.

America's silent movies celebrated traditional moral values in sentimental and melodramatic cliches, but they also revealed a good-humored, street-smart cynicism. Besides seeing virtue triumph, movie fans could see the police portrayed as bumbling idiots (the Keystone Kops) and the high and mighty brought low by the plucky urchin (Mary Pickford) or the cheeky rogue (Douglas Fairbanks). Master of this subversive theme was the comic genius, Charlie Chaplin, one of the few silent stars who appealed to both sophisticated and unsophisticated tastes, as did another comic genius, Buster Keaton.

POPULAR READING

Taste in reading matter was much like that in movies, though popular literature lacked the movies' cynical strain. Russel Nye writes of the pulp magazines, which replaced the dime novel by 1910: "Pulp stories were frankly mass-produced items, written to a rather rigid formula, never realistic, never disturbing, never disappointing. War could never be

Charlie Chaplin *(Library of Congress)*

grim, a hero must never show fear, airplanes could never have accidents … courtship must end in marriage." By 1915 pulp magazines, led by *Argosy*, were enjoying monthly sales in the millions.

On a somewhat higher plane stood the better Western novels. Foremost among their authors was the dentist from Zanesville, Ohio, Zane Grey. In 1912 he published his first success, *Riders of the Purple Sage*, in 1912, and then went on to write 70 more. Among mystery writers, Mary Roberts Rinehart was queen. Influenced by the domestic novel and the Gothic tale, as well as by both the stories of Edgar Allen Poe and Sir Arthur Conan Doyle, she added a parallel love story (always with a happy ending) to the crime story. The most successful popular novelists of the time were Gene Stratton-Porter, whose sentimental stories sold millions of copies, and Harold Bell Wright, who offered action and inspiration as well as sentiment. The most widely read poet of the era, the unassuming Detroit newspaperman Edgar A. Guest, was really a versifier whose talent lay in the expression of commonplace emotions and experiences in colloquial rhymes.

Today even more than the movie fare of that period, the most popular reading matter seems singularly innocent and unsophisticated. Ordinary Americans were beginning to have some leisure time, and their quest for diversion in reading led them to romance, moral uplift, and happy endings. Their tastes were not unremittingly mediocre, however. They also read with enthusiasm the books of Jack London and other authors of whom the critics approved.

MUSIC

Technology, mass distribution, and increases in per capita income also affected America's musical patterns. As early as the 1890s mass-production techniques made pianos available to people of moderate means, and the sale of sheet music consequently soared. In 1909, 5 million copies of "Meet Me Tonight in Dreamland" were sold and the following year 8 million of "Let Me Call You Sweetheart." Yet even as more and more Americans gathered around the piano in the parlor, Thomas Edison's recently developed phonograph was sounding the comparative decline of this homemade music making. When given the choice, most people chose to listen rather than play or sing, and by the outbreak of World War I sales of phonograph records had skyrocketed while those of pianos and sheet music had plummeted. The decline in participation in music making, however, was partly, perhaps largely, offset by the dance craze sparked by the glamorous husband-and-wife team, Vernon and Irene Castle, who came to New York in 1912. Soon almost every good restaurant had an orchestra and a dance floor and every middle-class party a phonograph and dance records.

Some of the new music was indigenous, and much of it was of high quality. The first important development was highly syncopated ragtime, which crossed the color line late in the 1890s. Shelton Brooks wrote ragtime's most famous song, "The Darktown Strutter's Ball," and Scott Joplin, a Texas-born African American, emerged as its finest composer. Hardly had ragtime captured the popular imagination when the blues, which evolved from black Southern folk music and became popular in white circles following the issuance of W. C. Handy's "Memphis Blues" in 1913, challenged it.

Vernon and Irene Castle *(Library of Congress)*

A black minister's son from Alabama, Handy composed several other classics, including "Beale Street Blues" and that perennial favorite, "St. Louis Blues." By the 1920s jazz, having been born in the red-light district of New Orleans and then having traveled up the river to Chicago and other points north, was in full flower.

JOURNALISM

Another aspect of the new urban culture was Yellow, or "People's," Journalism. It began with the purchase of the *New York World* in 1883 by Joseph Pulitzer. Sports coverage was greatly expanded, comic pages were introduced, murders and sex crimes were reported in gruesome detail, and scandals of all sorts were given featured treatment. In 15 years the *World's* circulation increased from 15,000 to 1.5 million. During the Progressive Era, Pulitzer and the *World* turned responsible, though the paper continued to be lively and popularly written. Meanwhile, Pulitzer's archrival, young William Randolph

Hearst, perfected the new sensationalism in a nationwide chain of newspapers and magazines. The most demagogic of the mass-circulation publishers, Hearst forced his editors to promote his political ambitions and to propagandize his shifting political views. He was especially adept at catering to the passions and prejudices—religious, political, and even ethnic—of his largely lower-middle-class urban readers.

Concurrently, Adolph Ochs, scion of a Southern German-Jewish family, was transforming The *New York Times* from a partisan editorial sheet to "a newspaper of record." Under Ochs' aegis, The *Times* focused on non-sensational news in commerce, education, the arts, government, and foreign events. Its circulation remained small, for its stodgy make-up appealed only to the better educated. Nonetheless, editors and publishers the nation over subscribed to the *Times*, and its broad coverage and high reportorial standards had a pronounced effect upon the more highly principled of them.

MUCKRAKING

Of more direct relevance to the emerging progressive movement was the rise of investigative reporting. In 1902 a group of journalists, later dubbed "muckrakers" by Theodore Roosevelt, because in his view all they did was "rake up the muck," began to publish articles about social, economic, and political problems that appeared in such middle-class magazines as *McClure's, Collier's, Everybody's*, and *Cosmopolitan*. The muckrakers' subject matter ranged from the traffic in prostitutes to the perversion of democracy in city halls, statehouses, and the United States Senate. Their output varied greatly in quality. Some writers, like Ida M. Tarbell, who carefully documented the impersonal ruthlessness of John D. Rockefeller and his associates in the *History of the Standard Oil Company* (1904), established standards of research and reporting that few journalists have ever surpassed. Others resembled David Graham Phillips, author of *The Treason of the Senate* (1906), whose innuendo and misrepresentation obscured much of the real truth that underlay his work.

One muckraker, Lincoln Steffens, brought to his work extraordinary insight into contemporary practices of American politicians, businessmen, and ordinary citizens. His two chief contributions were *The Shame of the Cities* (1904) and *The Struggle for Self-Government* (1906). Steffens was neither unaware of the defects of character that made public officials accept bribes nor indifferent to the moral lassitude that made average citizens indulgent of bad government, but he was much more interested in the bribe givers than in the bribe takers. Refusing to cater to anti-immigrant biases, he revealed that in Rhode Island rural Yankee legislators, not urban Italians, had sold out to the streetcar and other interests. He described how the Pennsylvania Railroad in New Jersey and the Public Service Corporation of that state had contrived to have the New Jersey legislature perpetuate low taxes and other special privileges for railroads and public service corporations.

Ida Tarbell, whose exposure of the dubious business dealings of the Standard Oil Company earned her the reputation of "muckraker." *(Library of Congress)*

The muckrakers' analysis of business and political corruption confirmed progressive leaders' belief that the American republic must be reformed or become a businessman's oligarchy, and the widespread circulation of their articles helped to create the support necessary for successful progressive political action.

ARCHITECTURE, PAINTING, AND LITERATURE

ARCHITECTURE

The two most innovative architects of this period, Louis Sullivan and Frank Lloyd Wright, were perhaps too sophisticated for popular taste, but their work has stood the test of time and is still studied by students of architecture in the twenty-first century. Although Sullivan continued to do distinguished work until after World War I, his commissions became more and more infrequent. Meanwhile, a number of talented designer-engineers built functional and often esthetically inspiring bridges and factories of steel and reinforced concrete, but most architects and their businessmen-clients, however, emphasized form rather than function. The overwhelming majority of the buildings of the era were more banal than creative, more pretentious than graceful. The same held for private houses. Sullivan, Wright, and a few others did imaginative work, but most new construction was eclectic. When historical styles such as Cape Cod, Georgian, or Greek Revival were used, the end product almost invariably violated the lines and proportions that had given the originals their distinction.

Sullivan attributed this failure of taste to the appeal of the Roman façades, false monumentalism, and harmonious lagoons of the Great White City fashioned for Chicago's Columbian Exposition of 1893. "The damage ... has penetrated deep into the ... American mind," he wrote, "effecting there lesions of dementia." More likely, however, the Exposition's imperial style touched the same impulses for grandeur that ordained the acquisition of an empire after the war with Spain in 1898, to be discussed in Chapter 7.

Frank Lloyd Wright, Sullivan's student, also failed to exercise much immediate influence on the American skyline. "Early in life," Wright once wrote, "I had to choose between honest arrogance and hypocritical humility. I chose honest arrogance." Wright further developed Sullivan's concept of "organic" architecture. Professing a regional style (he was in fact influenced by the Japanese), he designed from the inside out, always emphasizing the unique texture of his materials. He used native woods, horizontal planes, and deep overhangs and often succeeded brilliantly in harmonizing his buildings with their natural surroundings. As early as 1900 the *Architectural Review* recognized Wright's genius, and by 1905 his work had deeply affected the modern movement in Germany, Holland, and France. Only as Europeans like Walter Gropius brought his ideas back to the United States, however, did Wright make a vigorous imprint on American architecture. Meanwhile, the skilled traditionalists Stanford White, Ralph Adams Cram, and their disciples continued both to form and to reflect the widespread preference for Roman and Gothic.

Ironically, the maligned Columbian Exposition had a much greater impact on progressive public policy than did the works of Sullivan and Wright, the true intellectual progressives. Its classic spaciousness sparked a nationwide movement to beautify American cities. Uncounted urban open spaces were converted into parks, and sums commensurate with the nation's wealth were poured into public buildings. Unfortunately, little attention was given to the flow of traffic, and even less to the needs, interests, and habits of pedestrians. Almost always, moreover, the buildings erected were more derivative than original in design.

PAINTING

"There is a state of unrest all over the world in art as in all other things," the director of the Metropolitan Museum complained in 1908. "It is the same in literature, as in music, in painting, and in sculpture." This was the year that eight young painters, spearheaded by the realists Robert Henri, George B. Luks, and John Sloan, protested against the National Academy's near blackout of their work and staged a private show in New York. They rebelled not against the old painting techniques—they never mastered the new ones—but against the class bias that failed to see reality in all human activity, including the seamy. Their work of social protest grew more out of the political ferment of the era than the revolution in art forms that had already swept Europe. Inevitably, Victorian-minded critics dismissed them as "apostles of ugliness," "the revolutionary gang," "the black gang," and, most often, "the ashcan school."

Meanwhile, more creative European currents were beginning to affect American artists. By 1912 the work of the Postimpressionists was familiar to sophisticated habitués of the New York gallery of the revolutionary camera artist Alfred Stieglitz. The next year 1,600 paintings, drawings, prints, and pieces of sculpture representing almost every mode in modern art appeared in a spectacular show at the New York Armory. Picasso, Matisse, Brancusi, Duchamp, Kandinsky, Cezanne, Van Gogh, Gauguin, and others had their work displayed, to the extreme discomfort of conservative critics. The *New York Times* labeled the show "pathological." *Art and Progress* compared many of its artists to "anarchists, bomb-throwers, lunatics, depravers." An official of the Chicago Law and

Charcoal illustration by John Sloan (*Library of Congress*)

Order League demanded that the exhibition be banned from his city because the "idea that people can gaze at this sort of thing without it hurting them is all bosh."

New York was the venue for introducing the new work, but it played another role, too, in the transition to modern art. In *The Great American Thing* art historian Wanda Corn demonstrates how much creative energy flowed from various artists' encounters with New York City itself in these years—the city then being a place where new urban forms were being pioneered. For perhaps the first time, avant-garde sensibilities were being shaped on this side of the Atlantic, as well as in Europe.

In hindsight, it is possible to conclude that the vehemence of conservative criticism and the desperation of these critics' counterattack served only to underscore their artistic bankruptcy. As the art historian Sam Hunter writes, "They were soon unable to pose with real conviction or enthusiasm a possible alternative, since even the art they defended was becoming a retarded and diluted academic derivative of some form of modernism." Nevertheless, the public proved as slow to accept the highly individualized abstractionism of the new painters (including the Americans Max Weber and John Mann) as it did the architecture of Sullivan and Wright.

THE NOVEL

The trend toward realism in literature, begun in part by Henry James, continued in his own late works and in the novels of Willa Cather, author of *O Pioneers!* (1913) and *My Antonia* (1918), and Edith Wharton's novels of manners—including *Ethan Frome* (1911) and *The Age of Innocence* (1920), a story of New York high society.

Meanwhile, Jack London and Frank Norris were writing the survival-of-the-fittest doctrine into a host of brutal novels ranging in subject from the individual's struggle against the elements to the battle with the trusts. It was in the writings of Theodore Dreiser, however, that naturalism—as literary determinism was called—proved most profound. The son of German Catholic immigrants who settled in Indiana, Dreiser early disavowed belief in religion and conventional morality. "Man was a mechanism," he wrote, "undevised and uncreated, and a badly and carelessly driven one at that." Yet Dreiser, no less than his predecessors, was a moralist at heart. All his work was charged by a tension between determinism and its antithesis. In the very act of denying free will and the importance of man, he affirmed them. "To have accepted America as he has accepted it, to immerse oneself in something one can neither escape nor relinquish, to yield to what has been true and to yearn over what has seemed inexorable," this, concluded critic Alfred Kazin, "has been Dreiser's fate and the secret of his victory."

Dreiser's publisher withdrew Dreiser's first novel, *Sister Carrie* (1900), because of its harsh reception. Critics, many of whom objected to the novel's sympathetic treatment of a "fallen woman," failed to see that its account of the purposelessness of life was counterbalanced by its emphasis on life's sheer vitality. His second book, *Jennie Gerhardt* (1911), like *Sister Carrie*

Frank Norris *(Library of Congress)*

the story of an otherwise virtuous "kept woman," struck at the failure of the conventional moral code to correspond to reality. Similar themes pervaded *The Financier* (1912) and *The Titan* (1914), though they were widely regarded as progressive indictments of the "robber barons."

POETRY

The years before World War I also witnessed a remarkable renaissance in poetry. Perhaps the most powerful voice was that of Edwin Arlington Robinson, a traditionalist who dealt with the abiding theme of the individual's search for God and truth amidst darkness and suffering. Robinson failed in his quest. Life and human destiny remained mysterious, yet in the "black and awful chaos of the night" he felt "the coming glory of the Light." Rescued from obscurity by Theodore Roosevelt, who gave him a government sinecure after reading his *Children of the Night* (1897), Robinson failed, nevertheless to receive full recognition until after the war.

In 1912, Harriet Monroe established the magazine *Poetry* in Chicago, and renaissance was at hand. Vachel Lindsay, now remembered more for his jazz-like odes than his sensitive lyrics, published his "General William Booth Enters into Heaven" in the first issue of *Poetry* and then went on to exalt the common people in numerous other works. Edgar Lee Masters, Clarence Darrow's law partner, startled traditionalists with his masterpiece, *Spoon River Anthology* in 1915. There he laid bare the sham and moral shabbiness of small-town America in a brilliant combination of irony, sadness, and humor which closed paradoxically, on an affirmative note. A year later Carl Sandburg's first important volume appeared. A Whitmanesque romantic who employed free verse, Sandburg glorified Chicago as the roaring, brawling butcher and steel-maker to the world. During these same years Robert Frost was writing deceptively simple verse against a rural New England backdrop that masked his passionate, almost terrifying, life-force.

At the same time another revolt against the genteel tradition was brewing among a group of American and English poets in London, the so-called imagists. Led by Ezra Pound and Amy Lowell, they asserted that the poet should re-create impressions caught in the fleeting image. Holding that meter and rhyme made the creation of a pure image difficult, if not impossible, they reject these confining conventions. They also dismissed Romanticism as being the literary expression of a decadent humanistic culture. They were soon joined by T. S. Eliot, whose now classic "The Love Song of J. Alfred Prufrock" met a hostile reception when first published in *Poetry* in 1915.

Both the novels and the poetry by these early twentieth-century writers reflected a new aesthetic, one that critics have called "modernism." Rejecting the sentimentalism of many nineteenth-century writers, the new voices constituted a definitive break with the past.

TWO MILESTONES

WOMEN AND WOMEN'S SUFFRAGE

The modest changes in the status of women, which had brought co-educational education to two thirds of the nation's colleges and universities by the 1890s, continued through the Progressive Era. The revolution in morals commonly ascribed to the 1920s had actually become a subject of social commentary well before World War I. Divorce became much more common; and though divorcees remained "tainted," by 1916 one marriage in nine was ending in divorce, as compared to one in 21 in 1880. Meanwhile, working-class men, especially Irish, were deserting their families in appalling numbers. By 1920, despite religious scruples and high legal costs, the working-class divorce rate equaled that of the middle class.

Concurrently, the percentage of married women employed outside the home rose to 10.7 by 1910, as the number of working-women passed 6 million. The concept of "equal pay for equal work" even received a brief trial during World War I, though the hostility of unions and the widespread belief that women's employment should be regarded as temporary or supplementary soon restored the old order.

Intellectually, Charlotte Perkins Gilman of the famous Beecher family leveled the era's most penetrating attack on prevailing sexual and familial arrangements. Woman's survival, wrote Gilman, depended on her ability to seduce and hold a husband—"men worked to live ..., while, women mated to live." Among many other solutions, Gilman proposed complete emancipation of women from domestic duties through the establishment of day nurseries and communal kitchens—though who would staff them remained somewhat murky.

Most working women labored out of economic necessity, and their particular concerns were addressed by the most celebrated feminists of the era—Jane Addams, Lillian Wald, Florence Kelley—and by thousands of less well-known figures. (See *"Florence Kelley: Social Reformer."*) Often working out of Chicago's Hull House, New York's Henry Street Settlement, and other settlement houses, they strove to help immigrant women adjust to American life while encouraging the immigrants to preserve the best of their own cultures.

More importantly—for the settlement movement reached only a comparative few—the social reformers in the broader circle both inspired and did much of the tedious research behind hundreds of state and federal laws prescribing working conditions for women, children, and even men. Time and again their testimony before state and congressional legislative committees tipped the balance. "If I wanted to put a measure through—no matter how silly or outrageous—," grumbled an arch conservative West Virginia assemblyman, "I would simply get a handsome woman—with a sort of cheerful ring in her voice—to come down here and lobby for it." Historian Robyn Muncy has referred to this social reform-oriented feminist network and the various agencies the reformers either ran or influenced as the "female dominion."

Meanwhile the long struggle for women's suffrage was drawing to a successful conclusion, with two discrete organizations each making its own unique contribution. A new voice came into the suffrage battle when, in 1909, Pennsylvania-born Alice Paul returned from studying in England at the height of the suffrage struggle there.

PEOPLE THAT MADE A DIFFERENCE

Florence Kelley: Social Reformer

Of Florence Kelley it was said that she projected so much energy and courage that when she came into a room, "Everyone was brave." Born in Philadelphia in 1859, she was a descendant of Quaker botanist John Bartram. Her father, Congressman William D. Kelley, was a former Jacksonian Democrat who left the party over slavery in 1854 and later earned the sobriquet "Pig Iron" for his vigorous defense of the protective tariff. An early advocate of woman's suffrage, he encouraged Florence, the only one of his six daughters to survive infancy, to attend Cornell.

Although Florence's senior thesis on the legal status of children was published in the *International Review* the summer of her graduation in 1882, she was refused admission to the University of Pennsylvania graduate school because of her sex. She then enrolled at the University of Zurich, the first European university to admit women. There she became a socialist in the belief that Marxism explained both the cruel treatment of children, which she had earlier observed in England, and American slavery, as her Quaker relatives had described it to her. She also entered into correspondence with Marx's collaborator, Friedrich Engles, and later translated his *The Condition of the Working Class in England in 1844*.

While in Zurich, Florence married a Russian socialist medical student, Lazare Wischnewetsky, and bore the first of three children. In 1886 the couple went to New York and Wischnewetsky tried, with mediocre results, to establish a medical practice. They joined the Socialist Labor Party, but the Europeans who dominated the local group mistrusted her and soon expelled both of them, perhaps because Florence could be as explosive and hot-tempered as she was dedicated and nondoctrinaire. Meanwhile she bore two more children. Then, following several years of estrangement from her husband, she moved to Illinois to obtain a divorce under the state's more permissive laws. At first she lived in Jane Addams' Hull House while the children lived at the home of the reformer Henry Demarest Lloyd in Winnetka. After the divorce Florence resumed her maiden name and reunited the family in an apartment near Hull House.

Kelley's energy, incisiveness, and wit won her quick entry into Hull House's inner circle. As Addams wrote, she "galvanized us all into more intelligent interest in industrial conditions about us." In 1893, largely as a consequence of Kelley's lobbying, the state legislature enacted a statute to limit hours of work for women, prohibit child labor, and control tenement sweatshops. Appointed Chief Factory Inspector by Governor John Peter Altgeld, Kelley braved a smallpox epidemic to inspect sweatshops and once received a warning shot outside a factory.

Although her annual reports kept conditions before the public, prosecution of violators proved so difficult that she took a law degree in the evening division of the Northwestern University Law School in 1894. Three years later Altgeld's conservative successor dismissed her. Kelley continued to work out of Hull House two more years, supporting her family by working evenings at the John Crerar Library. Then in 1899, she and the children moved to Lillian Wald's Henry Street Settlement in New York, and Kelley became executive secretary of the newly formed National Consumer's League.

The League strove to persuade consumers to press for improved working conditions, and under Kelley's forceful leadership it became one of the most effective reform agencies of the Progressive Era. At its height it had sixty leagues in 20 states. "No gentle saint," in the words of one of her intimates, Kelley gave her opponents no quarter. She favored "direct assault" but was not averse to "guerilla" tactics. Legislators shrank under the fury of her scorn and the power of her magnificent presence. "She had the voice and presence of a great actress," noted Frances Perkins, "though she was far from theatrical in her intentions."

By 1913, mainly because of Kelley's efforts, nine states had adopted minimum wage legislation for women. Meanwhile she had assembled much of the medical and sociological data on the differences between men and women that Louis D. Brandeis incorporated in his defense of Oregon's ten-hour-day law for women in *Muller v. Oregon* (1908). (It should be noted that the new feminists of the 1970s repudiated much of this logic, that is, that the differences between men and women are so vast as to warrant special treatment for women workers).

The death of Kelley's only daughter from heart disease in 1905 seemed to give a special urgency to her abiding interest in the welfare of children. She played an important role in marshalling support for a federal children's bureau in 1912, the child labor bill of 1916, and the Sheppard-Towner maternity-aid measure of 1921. Irritated by Samuel Gompers' lack of interest in social legislation, she wrote him off as an "aged Dodo." Nor could she contain herself when the Supreme Court struck down state minimum wage legislation and the second child labor act early in the 1920s. Why, she asked, are "seals, bears, reindeer, fish, wild game in the national parks, buffalo, migratory birds, all found suitable for federal protection; but not the children of our race and their mothers?"

Kelley long served as vice-president of the National Woman Suffrage Association, partly in the conviction that municipal government and services would not be cleaned up until women got the vote. She had felt since 1885, however, that the suffrage movement was preoccupied with problems of the middle-class women, and she feared that the proposed Equal Rights Amendment of the twenties would wipe out the hard-won protective legislation for lower-class working women by eliminating laws based on the physical differences between men and women. "How cruel ...," she wrote, "is the pretension of certain organizations of professional and business women to decide for the wage-earners ... what statutory safeguards they are henceforth to do without."

Kelley was equally scornful of the new Woman's Party's refusal to fight against the disfranchisement of blacks in the South. "An inglorious ideal of equality this!" she expostulated. "Acquiescence in the disfranchisement of millions of women, provided only that the men of their race also are deprived of their constitutional rights."

Kelley continued her leadership of the National Consumers' League and her campaign for social justice till her death. She maintained a nominal socialist affiliation over the years, prompting one conservative United States senator to declare in the 1920s that her proposed child labor amendment "derived straight from the communist manifesto of 1848." Yet, partly because of her Quaker heritage, she lacked the requisite temperament to be doctrinaire on anything but pacifism. More an activist than a theoretician, she believed that the moral sensibilities of the middle classes—especially women—would eventually bring the reforms she sought. She died from anemia in 1932, too early to see the partial harvest that came with the New Deal.

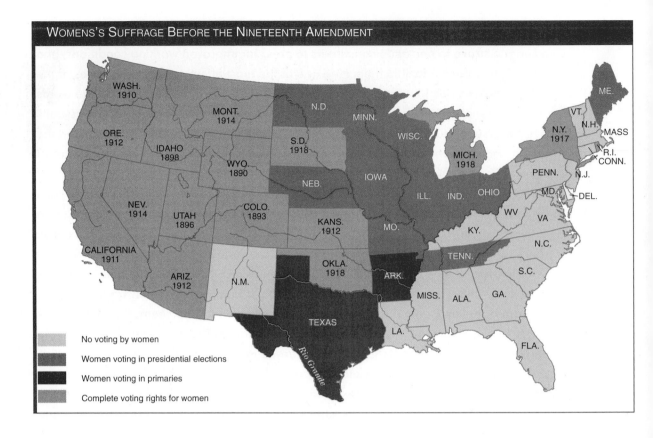

WOMENS'S SUFFRAGE BEFORE THE NINETEENTH AMENDMENT

No voting by women

Women voting in presidential elections

Women voting in primaries

Complete voting rights for women

Having observed the militant tactics employed by British suffragists, Paul joined the National American Woman Suffrage Association, but quickly became unhappy with what she saw as too tame an approach. She then organized a group of like-minded women into what would eventually become the National Woman's Party in 1917. Paul and her colleagues began picketing the White House in 1913 during Woodrow Wilson's first term in office. Arrested for picketing, they then went on a hunger strike, the same tactics used by British suffragists. It is difficult to parse how much the eventual victory owed to Paul and her group, but at the very least President Wilson—who long opposed suffrage—began to find NAWSA more attractive when he considered the alternative.

As for NAWSA, its fortunes improved under the leadership of Carrie Chapman Catt. A superb organizer and skilled politician with broad social concerns, Catt had served from 1900 to 1904 as Susan B. Anthony's successor as NAWSA's president. She then put her unflagging energies into mobilizing suffrage sentiment in the states and, in 1915, to helping Jane Addams organize the Woman's Peace Party. Catt returned to the presidency of NAWSA the following year to combat what she saw as the divisive tactics of Alice Paul's group and to confront the mounting opposition of conventional women to the movement for suffrage.

Suffrage parade in New York City on October 23, 1915 *(Library of Congress)*

Publicly, at least, the suffragists justified the vote for women in terms of broad social and political policy. Their arguments frequently overlapped, and their emphasis shifted with time and place; but in general, several distinct approaches emerged. The social-reformer feminists contended that suffrage would produce a more just and compassionate society and even eliminate war. As Addams said, a woman cannot care properly for her family if she has no voice in making the laws and electing the officials who determine whether her home has pure water, fresh food, proper sanitation, and adequate police protection. Others, more politically conservative and probably more representative of suffragists as a whole, argued that suffrage would reestablish Anglo-Saxon domination of urban politics and clean out corruption. Professional women tended to put the case almost solely in terms of career discrimination. Protestant churchwomen, and most social reformers as well, argued that the women's vote would assure national prohibition legislation. Only a small minority of fervent radicals boldly declared that suffrage would enable women to free themselves of male domination within marriage.

Opposition to women's suffrage came from some Protestant fundamentalists, however, who argued that God had created for women

Women suffragists marching on Pennsylvania Avenue in Washington *(Library of Congress)*

a separate, exclusively female role in society and that women did not belong outside of this female "sphere" of "wifery" and childbearing. In this mindset, suffrage was, therefore, viewed as a threat to the "God-ordained" natural order of society where women were assigned a subservient place as "man's helper." Both Protestant fundamentalists and traditional Catholics also opposed women's suffrage as a measure linked to the movement for birth control—which they equated with promiscuity, loose morals, and the erosion of family values.

Nevertheless, by 1917, Catt's tactics had already won substantial support in the states, and the suffragists were urgently pressing most of the above considerations on Congress. Many congressmen—probably most— were privately unsympathetic. By mounting pressure on these congressmen from within their home districts, however, shrewdly aligning themselves with the prohibitionists, and capitalizing on the Wilson administration's desire for wartime unity, Catt's forces persuaded the House to approve a federal suffrage amendment in January 1918. Eighteen months later a lobby-wearied Senate also submitted, and within 15 months three fourths of the states had ratified the Nineteenth Amendment. In simple declarative language it stated that the right to vote should not be abridged "on account of sex." Women would vote for the first time in federal elections in 1920, and their presence in the electorate was part of the reason that the Republicans nominated Warren G. Harding that year on the belief that he was physically attractive to women. The overall impact of women in the electorate was less than some expected, however, because women did not vote as a cohesive group and had just as many political divisions among them as men.

MARGARET SANGER AND BIRTH CONTROL

The swirling cross currents of the turbulent women's movement engulfed the movement for birth control. In 1873, Congress passed what became known as the "Comstock Law," which banned the sending of obscene materials through the mail. A special postal agent named Anthony Comstock determined at his discretion what did or did not violate the law; and, as a result, contraceptives and information concerning contraception or any anatomical drawings and many medical terms were deemed to be obscene and subject to seizure by the United States Postal Service. Until well into the Progressive Era, Protestants and Catholics alike had regarded artificial contraception as a violation of the law of God, and by 1914 twenty-two states had anti-birth control statutes on their books. By then the shift to an industrial society had made large families an economic liability, especially in towns and cities. This latter reality had already induced a decline in the birth rate, notably among old-stock urban whites in the middle and upper classes. For the most part, this decline reflected natural controls.

So strong was the consensus against contraceptives at this time that Congress banned the dissemination of birth control information in interstate commerce in 1914. This ban provoked a bitter reaction, in particular among younger radical feminists and political leftists—for different reasons. The feminists saw contraception as a form of emancipation or as a means to reduce men's sexual exploitation of women. Those on the political left believed that

Margaret Sanger was responsible for founding the nation's first birth control clinic. (*Library of Congress*)

capitalists wanted more births in order to create a surplus of labor and thus keep down wages. The views of these two groups fused in the early career of Margaret Sanger, who for 40 years served as the knife's edge of the movement for birth control.

Sanger was the daughter of an Irish-born workingman, an all-round iconoclast who had renounced his Catholicism, and a mother who bore 11 children. Sanger became a nurse with a practice in New York. In 1912, following the death of a working girl from a self-induced abortion, Margaret stripped off her nurse's uniform and emerged as *l'enfant terrible* of the birth-control campaign. Inspired at first by the anarchist Emma Goldman, she was also encouraged by William D. "Big Bill" Haywood of the radical Industrial Workers of the World, Eugene V. Debs of the Socialist party, and women's liberation groups.

Early concluding that the marriage bed was "the most degenerating influence in the social order" because it made sex-chattels of wives, Sanger declared that women "are determined to decide for themselves whether they shall become mothers, under what conditions, and when." Soon she was urging women to stop producing children "who will become slaves to feed, fight and toil for the enemy—Capitalism." Then, in 1916, she defied the law by opening a birth-control clinic in New York. Tried and found guilty, she won a partial victory on appeal in 1918 when the court's opinion gave physicians somewhat greater latitude to prescribe contraception.

Sanger's agitation broadened the movement's base. Partly in the conviction that smaller families would raise the standard of living of the poor, middle-class reformers organized the National Birth Control League in 1915. Two years later the philosopher John Dewey drafted a measure to make contraceptives freely available—to which the New York State legislature refused to give serious consideration.

Meanwhile, eugenicists took up the cause in the belief that mental defectiveness was transmitted through the genes and could be greatly reduced through birth control. The ranks of these eugenicists included some of the most blatant racists and conservative elitists in the country—as well as people with a genuine concern about hereditary disease. Buoyed by the support of these and other respectable figures, Sanger began to abandon her socialist rationale for birth control. "More children from the fit, less from the unfit—that is the chief issue," she announced in 1919. Marxism, she contemptuously asserted in 1922, is "purely masculine reasoning."

Nevertheless, religious opposition to contraception remained vigorous—and among the lower classes, effective—through the 1920s. The Catholic Church became increasingly militant in its defense of the Papacy's standing disapproval of contraception, and it was not until 1931 that a major Protestant body—the Federal Council of Churches of Christ—formally endorsed birth control. Long before then, however, large numbers of Protestant clergymen had become silent converts to the movement.

By the mid-20s the use of contraceptives was commonplace among middle-class Protestants, Jews, and non-church people. Old-line radical feminists like Charlotte Perkins Gilman were continuing to hold that only procreation justified intercourse, but there was wide acceptance among non-Catholics of the newer generation's contention that it should also be indulged in for reasons of pleasure.

THE TRIUMPH OF NATIONAL PROHIBITION

The informal alliance of the suffragists and prohibitionists arose out of considerably more than convenience. As Norman H. Clark observes in his perceptive revisionist synthesis, *Deliver Us from Evil*, the prohibition movement aimed to "protect the values sheltered by the American nuclear family" at a time when it seemed that its security was more urgent to society's well-being than were the rights of individuals. Alcoholism had been a "WASP" (White Anglo-Saxon Protestant) problem since the founding of Jamestown, and Southern Baptist and Northern Methodist women had long been in the vanguard of the movement to restrict the indiscriminate use of liquor. By 1900 thirty-seven mainly rural Protestant states had enacted local option laws. In 1907 Oklahoma, an old-stock territory with a minuscule foreign population came into the union with a completely dry constitution, and by 1919 ten of the 12 states in which women could vote had outlawed the saloon.

These facts suggest that Prohibition's much remarked anti-ethnic and anti-Catholic thrust was more incidental than causal. Only because many Germans happened to be heavy beer drinkers and many Irish heavy whisky drinkers did the movement become identified as a "nativist" crusade. It should be mentioned, however, that the *Baptist Standard* in 1917 proclaimed, "Prohibition is an issue of Anglo-Saxon culture versus the inferior civilization of niggers in the cities." Therefore, nativism and racism were most certainly present in the movement.

Nevertheless, pietist immigrants from Sweden supported prohibition vigorously, as did many Reformed and other non-Lutheran Germans. A group of priests organized the Catholic Clergy Prohibition League, and Father J. J. Curran served 25 years as a national vice-president of the Anti-Saloon League. The bishop of Montana, a state where hard drinking was notorious among Irish miners, even observed that prohibition would contribute to the "spiritual progress of the Catholic Church" in America.

Neither was prohibition an essentially rural phenomenon, despite its successes in rural states. Most sponsors of local option laws were town or city people, and most members of the W.C.T.U. and the Anti-Saloon League were urban. As Clark writes, "behind them in solid support were the deep ranks of urban business leaders, labor leaders, attorneys, physicians, teachers—both Catholic and Protestant." They stood behind them because, like their counterparts in Finland, Scandinavia, Germany, Britain, France, and the province of Quebec—all of which had serious temperance movements—and they perceived alcoholism to be a grave social problem.

They realized, of course, that saloons served as workingmen's clubs, but they also saw that many embodied the worst features of urban industrial culture: "blatantly and aggressively masculine to the mood of a sneering *machismo*, linked sordidly to organized crime, organized prostitution, and the organized herding of mercenary voters." Hardly a social reformer with first-hand knowledge of the saloon's impact on family life and urban politics failed to support prohibition, probably with the silent support of hundreds of thousands of workingmen's wives.

Women tended to favor prohibition because for many women, their husbands were their sole source of financial support for them and their children. Alcoholic husbands were less likely to remain employed, thus threatening the well being of the wife and her children. Thus, women allied with big business owners who favored prohibition for the creation of a sober and, therefore, more productive workforce. Additionally, it was well known that some men have a tendency to become abusive when under the influence of alcohol, and the women who were the victims of that abuse sought a remedy through prohibition.

Protestant fundamentalists tended to favor prohibition as well, not only as an anti-Catholic measure but also due to strict interpretations of the Bible that viewed the consumption of alcohol, especially to excess, as sinful. An alcohol-free society in their view would, therefore, be a more Godly society.

New scientific evidence on the linkage between alcoholism and brain damage further strengthened the prohibition movement in business and professional circles. Physicians prescribed alcohol less frequently, and in 1914 a national meeting of psychiatrists and neurologists actually pronounced it a poison. At the same time, numerous investigations by social scientists revealed relationships between alcohol and crime, prostitution, and poverty. By 1916, as Clark concludes, science, no less than organized religion, had prepared the way for total abstinence.

The entry of the United States into World War I also produced a general moral crusade linked to the moralistic views of President Woodrow Wilson. Many Americans viewed the American role in World War I as one of bringing the superior "American way" and democracy to the rest of the world. If the United States were to embark on a moral crusade, it would be a contradiction to do it while drunk.

Nevertheless, the moderate prohibitionists would probably have settled for a ban on hard liquor; but the so-called wets, who were liberally financed by the hard liquor industry as well as by German-American beer interests, stiffened dry lines by refusing to compromise. Soon after the United States entered the war, the War Department gave the prohibitionists an important victory by banning the sale of alcoholic beverages near army camps. When the Eighteenth Amendment—banning the manufacture, sale, and transportation of intoxicating liquor—still left it to Congress to define what was "intoxicating," prohibitionists won inclusion of beer and wines by playing up the need to conserve grain. The amendment, adopted by Congress in December 1917, went into effect in January 1920.

THE INSTITUTIONS OF CHANGE

TECHNOLOGY AND BUSINESS

Chief among the many forces that made the Progressive Era a period of extraordinarily rapid change were technology and scientific management. In manufacturing, mechanization and time-and-motion-saving techniques pioneered by Frederick Winslow Taylor helped production to increase 76 percent between 1899 and 1909, while the labor force expanded only 40 percent. In organization and distribution, managerial innovations created nationwide markets.

By the early 1900s, the internal combustion automobile, powered by gasoline, had won the day over steam or electric-powered vehicles. In the automotive industry that soon developed, assembly-line production enabled Henry Ford to cut the price of his Model T from $950 in 1912 to $290 by 1924. Ford also pioneered "just-in-time" technology where he synchronized with his suppliers just how much of each item he needed at what time so that he could have tires delivered the day he needed them for his cars, etc. Ford standardized and simplified as much as he could so as to keep down costs. Every Ford Model T looked just like every other Model T so that the running

Henry Ford's development of assembly-line production of the Model T Ford, shown here, enabled him to make the car's price more affordable.
(Library of Congress)

joke was that Model T buyers could have "any color they wanted, as long as it was black." Ford also pioneered the idea of paying his employees more than the going rate, "$5 per day," so that they could actually purchase one of the cars they built. In so doing, Ford essentially created his own market for his cars. By 1917 almost 5 million vehicles were clogging a partially macadamized highway system. In addition, the automobile industry produced huge spin-offs, thus boosting the iron, steel, oil, paint, glass, copper, textile, and rubber industries as well as a host of others.

Automobiles, however, were not the only technological innovation driving economic growth. Orville and Wilber Wright launched their successful airplane flight at Kitty Hawk, North Carolina in 1903, and the aviation industry was born. By the time of the American entry into World War I, a 7-million telephone network had wrought a revolution in communication, and some 50 corporate research laboratories were forging another revolution in product development. Meanwhile the use of electricity grew so fast that by the end of World War I it powered more than half of American industry—whereas only two percent of American industrial power had been supplied by electricity at the turn of the century. Electricity in turn had spawned a booming home appliance industry. Among the most important new electrical powered items was the radio—which brought mass culture, national advertising, and national news. By 1920, Americans owned 10 million radios, and the number was growing rapidly.

Not all the effects proved salutary. Skilled workers were downgraded in older industries like steel and textiles, and the dehumanizing efficiencies of the assembly lines and of Taylorism made virtual automatons of everyone but supervisors in many of the newer industries. On the other hand, real wages in manufacturing rose 37 percent from 1897 to 1914 and rose again during the war. Outside the factories, moreover, the number of skilled workers—electricians, plumbers, carpenters, toolmakers, automobile mechanics, and heavy equipment operators—grew greatly. An increase in the clerical and sales work force from 3 percent in 1880 to 8 percent by 1910 also raised the number of reasonably challenging jobs. Nor was that all. Increased wages, together with the spread of truck gardening, the rise of the citrus industry, and increased use of refrigerated railroad cars, produced a marked improvement in diet. By the early 1900s the average American worker and his family were consuming twice as much meat as their British counterparts, in addition to increasing amounts of citrus fruits.

MODERNIZING THE GOVERNMENT

Years before the Progressive Era began, thoughtful observers of the American scene agreed that the art of government had not kept pace with the science of industry. Progressives proposed, consequently, to apply the techniques of business management to the bewildering complexities of the new urban and industrial society. With remarkable unanimity, they turned to experts—scientists, engineers, economists, physicians, political scientists, and social workers—for information, political support, and personnel to staff new or enlarged departments and regulatory commissions.

By the end of the era much of American government had become thoroughly modernized and professionalized. Graduate engineers were planning and operating municipal sewer and water systems. Trained medical personnel were combating disease by enforcing public health measures. Experts with Ph.D.s in agronomy, chemistry, and other sciences were engaged in research sponsored by the Department of Agriculture at land-grant universities and experimental stations. Even police and fire department recruits, traditionally trained on the job, were attending newly founded academies.

Politically, the modernization of government increased the distance between the average citizen and the decision-makers, and the move to a more merit-oriented civil service system of government recruitment diminished the "spoils" associated with politics and, therefore, direct vested interests of many in political outcomes. Progressives viewed party reforms as crucial since the primary tool of reform used by progressives was government. It was assumed by progressives that government would not be a good tool for reform if the political party system remained based on patronage and corruption. This doubtless contributed to a decline in voter turnout, one of the most pronounced trends of modern times, but the social benefits were almost incalculable.

Among the political reforms that progressives championed was a shift to secret ballots so as to minimize coercion at the polls. Prior to the introduction of the secret ballot, since others knew how one voted at the polling place, violence and intimidation of voters were rampant. The secret ballot was initiated on a state-by-state basis beginning as early as the 1880s.

In reaction to the corruption in government at local levels, such as the famous political machine of Boss Tweed, progressives reformed local government structures to decentralize power away from the mayor's office. Stanton, Virginia introduced the council-manager format in 1908 where an elected city council performed legislative duties, but executive powers were vested in an appointed, professional city manager that was responsible to the council, thus separating legislative and executive powers at the local government level and introducing professionalism to local government. Some cities made local elections nonpartisan so as to diminish party influences and further hinder the building of corrupt political party machines.

Other democratic reforms included the provisions of ballot initiatives whereby citizens could, through petition, place items on the ballot for public referendum (vote). Nineteen states had provisions for ballot initiative and referendum by 1918. Some states also implemented recall elections whereby citizens could, through petition, force an elected official to face an electoral challenge before the end of a prescribed term. Twelve states also passed restrictions on lobbyists, 22 banned corporate political contributions, and 24 states banned free passes on railroads for politicians.

Progress was also being made in the areas of health and sanitation. Louis Pasteur developed his germ theory of disease in 1869, and the discovery eventually led to a revolution in health and sanitation. In 1900, 50 percent of Americans did not live beyond the age of five due to poor sanitation and infectious diseases. In American factories, the drinking supply was often an open water barrel where all employees would simply dip their

Louis Pasteur *(Library of Congress)*

cups until the water was gone. Employees were sometimes told to dig their own latrines with no instruction and without pay. In the 20 years before the United States entered the war, advances in medical science and sanitation based on Pasteur's germ theory combined with improvements in diet to reduce the death rate from 17 to 12.2 per thousand and to increase life expectancy from 49 to 56 years.

THE SOCIAL SCIENCES

PSYCHOLOGY AND ECONOMICS

By undermining classical economics, the psychology of this period powerfully influenced progressive thought and attitudes. Freed from its old metaphysical and theological commitment by the Darwinian revolution, psychology had begun to explore the whole range of human activity. By World War I two definite schools—the instinct and the behaviorist—had emerged. Both were European in origin, and both found a receptive audience in the United States.

The founder of the instinct school in America, William McDougall, felt strongly that psychology should concern itself with social behavior. He contended that humans were ruled by deep-seated instincts rather than by rational or moral considerations; and his charge that classical economic theory was "a tissue of false conclusions drawn from false psychological assumptions" reinforced the insights Thorstein Veblen had already written into his *Theory of the Leisure Class* (1899). In *The Instinct of Workmanship and the State of the Industrial Arts* (1914), Veblen echoed McDougall's strictures against the inadequate psychological base of classical economics. He especially charged that modern industrial institutions had failed to play upon people's constructive instincts. F. W. Taussig argued in *Inventors and Money-Makers* (1915) that the instinct of contrivance, or workmanship, did not depend necessarily on prospective gain, as the defenders of the profit-making system contended, but rather on the satisfaction of making something. However much instinct psychology undermined classical economic thought, it produced no systematic theory of its own as a substitute.

The behaviorist psychology of the Russian Ivan Pavlov and the Americans E. L. Thorndike and John B. Watson proved both more receptive to, and more reflective of, progressive thought because it supported an environmentalist interpretation of society. Passing over everything that could not be verified by direct observation, the behaviorists sought to measure all human behavior in terms of stimulus and response. "It is the business of behavioristic psychology," wrote Watson, "to be able to predict and control human activity." Since consciousness was not observable, it should not be studied; thought was to be treated as latent speech.

Behaviorism offered too restricted and shocking a view of human nature to win universal acceptance. Humanists rejected it angrily. Nevertheless, it sired a school of psychology and markedly influenced all subsequent social science. It also contributed enormously to both the hard and soft sides of progressivism—to the production efficiencies of Taylorism—and to the reformers' belief that the poor were the victims of their environment. Behaviorism further contributed to the rise of the consumer society by giving an intellectual base to the manipulative skills of advertisers.

THE NEW HISTORY

The writing of history proved no more immune to progressive currents than did other disciplines, nor did it escape their paradoxes. The influence of German methodology, first felt at Johns Hopkins, continued as historians now severed their ties with literature almost completely. Seeking scientific truth by the use of rigorously exact techniques, they destroyed hallowed beliefs, stripped history of its individual drama and romance, and lost their popular audience. Yet they added immeasurably to the general body of knowledge and contributed important new insights about the forces that had molded America.

One of the foremost characteristics of the new history was present-mindedness. As James Harvey Robinson and Charles A. Beard confessed in their path finding *The Development of Modern Europe* (1907), they had "consistently subordinated the past to the present" in the "ever-conscious aim to enable the reader to catch up with his own times." Implicit in this approach was a belief in laws of behavior as formulated by social scientists. The insights of philosophers, poets, and observers no longer sufficed. Implicit, also, was a desire to use history to create a better future. This last was not new; from Thucydides on, historians had concerned themselves with the usable past. By Robinson and Beard's time, however, probably a majority of America's professional historians had conceived their task as being merely descriptive. It was against them and their failure to search for causal explanations that might indirectly bear on the present—to be, in the new view, truly scientific—that Robinson and Beard revolted.

As an instance of the new work, Beard authored one book that is still being debated. "The Constitution," he wrote in *An Economic Interpretation of the Constitution* (1913), "was essentially an economic document based upon the concept that the fundamental private rights of property are anterior to government and morally beyond the reach of popular majorities." He then set forth data to substantiate his contention that through their interest in public securities, money, manufacturing, trade, and shipping, the framers of the Constitution had stood to gain directly from the establishment of the new government.

Beard insisted that his work was American-inspired. James Madison, he repeatedly pointed out, had offered "one of the earliest, and certainly one of the clearest" statements of economic determinism. As Morton G. White observes, however, Beard's *An Economic Interpretation of the Constitution* actually reflected the worst, or at least the simplest, aspects of thought by both Marx and Madison. Thus Marx neither denied man's capacity for high-minded action nor accepted the idea that every political action derived directly from an economic interest. Conversely, Madison believed with Aristotle that factions and interests were rooted in human nature—not, as Marx contended, in economic systems. In Beard's analysis the framers had been moved by a narrow Marxist view of the deterministic force of economic systems and a similarly narrow Madisonian view of a direct relationship between self-interest and action. Recent scholarship has seriously challenged the evidence on which Beard based his economic thesis.

Beard always denied that he had written a tract for the times. "I simply sought to bring back into the mental picture of the Constitution," he said, "those realistic features of economic conflict, stress and strain, which my masters had, for some reason, left out of it, or thrust far into the background as incidental rather than fundamental."

PROGRESSIVE EDUCATION

PUBLIC EDUCATION

The higher educational level required for entry into business and government inevitably transformed the public school system. Every strand of progressivism—from the quest for order through the cult of efficiency to the belief in equal opportunity—entered into the transformation. By the end of the era the foundations and much of the superstructure of modern education had been firmly established.

In 1900 the upper classes sent their children to private schools or had them tutored, and except for a few middle-class sections of large cities the public school system was in deplorable condition. Politics,

The beginning of the twentieth century saw an increase in both public school budgets and student enrollment. (*Library of Congress*)

corruption, and incompetence were rife. Rote instruction, oversized classes, and an out-of-date curriculum were the rule. Teachers were poorly prepared and even more poorly paid, averaging $42.15 a month—less than the wages of a day laborer. In the South, three years schooling was the norm, and in the North, seven years. Southern states spent $9.72 per pupil each year; Northern states spent $20.85.

The most pronounced changes occurred in the South, which experienced an educational revival comparable to the one that had swept the North before the Civil War, though mainly for white children only. By 1910 school budgets had doubled, the enrollment of white children had risen almost a third, and the school term had lengthened from five to six months. White illiteracy had also declined from 11.8 to 7.7 percent.

Nowhere, however, did the increase in expenditures affect all social and economic classes equally. Even in the richest states of the North, dependence on local taxation produced wide disparities between rural, small-town, suburban, and metropolitan appropriations. Old-stock whites in the remote areas of upper New England and western New York frequently fared worse than immigrants in the large cities. Within the urban systems, the middle-class composition of school boards also produced inequities. Almost invariably, facilities tended to be poorer and student-teacher ratios higher in lower class and ethnic neighborhoods.

Discrimination fell heaviest, of course, on blacks. Although they managed to decrease their illiteracy rate from 44.5 to 30.1 percent during the first decade of the century, no Southern state (and no Northern one either) made a conscientious effort to give black people equal facilities. By 1910 only 8,251 black youths were attending high school in the entire Southeast. As late as 1915 South Carolina was spending $13.98 annually for each white child and only $1.13 for each black one.

Meanwhile, an exceptionally high dropout rate, especially among immigrants' children, prompted a wave of compulsory attendance laws and curriculum changes. Some progressives believed that early employment deprived children of their birthright. Others feared that lack of schooling would create a permanent urban proletariat.

Virtually all recognized that the technological society required greater education for everyone. Vocational and commercial high schools were established in the larger cities with strong business support and, after 1917, federal subsidization. In single-high-school towns, manual training and commercial courses were offered. For numerous reasons, including the failure of equipment and instruction to keep abreast of developments in industry, the vocational schools never flowered, but for years thereafter, the commercial courses produced a steady flow of male bookkeepers and female typists and stenographers.

In keeping with the spirit of the times, basic changes in the aims and methods of teaching accompanied the upgrading of physical facilities in the public schools. The most distinguished educational theorist of this period was philosopher John Dewey, a disciple of William James (see Chapter 2). Born in 1859 in Vermont, Dewey taught at the Universities of Michigan, Chicago, and Columbia and remained an influential and active force in American thought until his death in 1952.

To Dewey, valid thinking and understanding had to be based on one's own experience. Thus he abandoned authoritarian teaching methods and the use of rote practice. Subject matter, he felt, should be adapted to the needs and capabilities of children, and learning processes should be centered on their own experience and discovery. They should "learn by doing," inquiring and drawing their own generalizations instead of memorizing someone else's.

To foster such learning, he wrote in *School and Society* (1899), "means to make each one of our schools an embryonic community life, active with types of occupations that reflect the life of the larger society, and permeated throughout with the spirit of art, history, and science." Such schooling, he believed, would advance democracy and develop intelligence as a tool for social reform. The development of vocational education was in keeping with Dewey's interest in practical education.

Against the sustained opposition of traditionalists, Dewey and his followers accomplished one of the major cultural revolutions of the century. By the end of World War I, Teachers College of Columbia University was well on the way to inculcating a new generation of teachers with a potentially creative approach to teaching. Dewey's most influential work, *Democracy and Education*, appeared in 1916. Three years later the Progressive Education Association was organized to advance the dynamic new program.

As in most creative changes, the costs proved high. Traditionalists within the universities failed at first to grasp the intellectual foundation of the reconstruction of primary and secondary education, thus forcing departments and colleges of education to organize without the help of the liberal arts faculties, who might have exercised a leavening influence on the new education curricula. At the same time, state teachers' colleges began to supplant the two-year normal schools. Directed by professional educators, they offered so many overlapping education courses as to make a mockery of the word *education*. On no level—B.S., M.S., or Ph.D.—did the quality of an education degree compare favorably with that of a degree in one of the traditional disciplines.

HIGHER EDUCATION

Colleges and universities were favorably influenced by the deepening of knowledge, the specialization induced by the new technology, and their own growing commitment to excellence. The quality of graduate and professional study rose notably. States greatly expanded their aid to higher education. Municipal colleges and universities multiplied. Major strides occurred in adult education. Between 1900, when the Association of American Universities was founded, and 1914, the total enrollment in colleges and universities nearly doubled—increasing from 109,929 to 216,493.

Concurrently, the status and salaries of college professors rose and the percentage of Ph.D.s increased. The principle of academic freedom was also receiving wider and wider acceptance, except for some notorious violations during World War I. The improvements reflected in part the influence of the American Association of University Professors, organized in 1915. But in the main they marked the coming of age of American higher education.

Increased specialization, expanded research opportunities, and freedom to create led to great contributions to almost all areas of knowledge. By the end of the Progressive Era American scholarship had surpassed European scholarship in some fields and equaled it in many others, but once again the cost proved high. The social sciences developed their own vocabularies, often unnecessarily, and scientists, physicians, and engineers lost contact with the humanities and social sciences because of their need to specialize early in their undergraduate careers.

Legal education was beset by the same paradoxes. Pre-law training was steadily upgraded; by World War I two years of undergraduate work was a common requirement for admission to reputable law schools. Except in a handful of schools attached to the great universities, however, the nature and theory of law were largely neglected. Even though a law degree became a virtual prerequisite for election to public office, most law schools turned out little more than competently trained technicians.

Medical education, which had become a national scandal, underwent a dramatic upgrading following publication of Abraham Flexner's searching report for the Carnegie Endowment in 1910. Medical care, however, was a different matter. For a few years, progressive elements of the medical profession showed interest in institutionalizing medical service to the poor. By 1919, however, entrepreneurial attitudes had become dominant within the already powerful American Medical Association. Proposals for the mildest forms of socialized medicine (Medicare) were fiercely repelled, and the United States' record of treatment for the poor, both black and white, became one of the worst in the Western world. Conversely, advances in medical science, education, and technology, including an enormous hospital-construction program, put American care of the middle and upper-middle classes among the world's best.

In agriculture, federal grants-in-aid to land grant colleges underwrote invaluable research in crops, soil properties, and conservation practices. County agents and farmer's institutes sponsored by university extension services also brought scientific knowledge to farmers themselves, though the more poorly educated and less prosperous farmers generally resisted it. In the long term, these developments sharply increased the quality and quantity of agricultural production, but they also spurred the growth of commercial farming and the increase in tenancy earlier noted.

CHURCH AND SOCIETY

PROTESTANTISM

The social and intellectual ferment of the Progressive Era affected religion and its institutions in profound and sometimes paradoxical ways. Organizations like the Young Men's Christian Association, the International Sunday Schools Association, and the American Bible Society blurred denominational lines, while fundamentalism, modernism (the attempt to reconcile contemporary scientific thought and traditional religion), and the Social Gospel cut across them. After 1908, the formation of the Federal Council of Churches of Christ in America by 33 evangelical bodies created a loose unity among their 17 million members.

Yet the Northern Presbyterian Church preserved the purity of its doctrines only by expelling several of its most distinguished ministers and losing control of its leading seminary, Union, in New York to the modernists. Modernist clergymen also captured many Northern Baptist, Congregational, and Methodist congregations, while perhaps a majority of intellectuals left the church in spirit.

Rural migrants to the city decisively rejected modernism. Uncomfortable in sophisticated urban congregations and uninterested in theological subtleties, they throve on the thundering fundamentalism of the Reverend Billy Sunday and a wave of revivalism that swept the established evangelical churches. Many became enthusiastic converts to Pentecostalism, to Holiness churches, and to the Jehovah's Witnesses. Many also responded to exhortations by spellbinders, like the Baptist Russell Conwell, to accept the prevailing social and economic order. In a thousand sermons the country over, Conwell affirmed the virtue of getting rich—"to make money honestly is to preach the gospel."

Conversely, a small but growing minority of urban ministers and laymen transformed the Social Gospel into a powerful progressive force during the prewar years. In general, supporters of the Social Gospel believed that churches should become more involved in alleviating societal suffering. Consequently, they offered political support to progressive programs aimed at curbing social injustices and developed essentially social welfare functions of their own. They agreed with the Congregational clergyman George Herron that the dualism of contemporary life was intolerable:

> A corporation, greedy, godless, vicious in many of its operations, consists of men famous for their piety and benevolence. A nation governed by men of eminent Christian character goes mad with the spoils of unrighteousness. ... A church containing many sincere, teachable, self-sacrificing Christians is as powerless a moral institution in the community as the town pump.

In 1908, one year after the publication of Walter Rauschenbusch's most important work, *Christianity and the Social Crisis*, the Methodist Episcopal Church came out for abolition of child labor and for a host of other reforms. Though Methodists rejected his Christian Socialism, they accepted his graphic analysis of the brutalizing impact of the new industrial order. During that same year the newly organized Federal Council of Churches of Christ called for the end of exploitative capitalism by a program of social-welfare legislation.

The Social Gospel movement quickened many lay consciences and raised profound questions about business ethics and the morality of the laws of the marketplace. It thus broadened and strengthened the moral foundations of the progressive movement. Other volunteer organizations also arose with goals of alleviating the plight of the poor. Perhaps the most well known and most successful of these is the Salvation Army, which grew to 23,000 members by 1920. Nevertheless, the counter-truth remains: Evangelical Protestants spent more energy campaigning for prohibition and against parochial schools than they did in fighting exploitation of their fellow men and women.

CATHOLICISM

Partly because of the Roman Catholic Church's authoritarian structure and partly because of the still low educational level of most of its members, the Catholic Church in America remained clear of the conflict over modernism that rocked Protestantism. For millions of immigrants, it was the one familiar institution in an alien culture. Despite the drop in membership during the Gilded Age, Poles and other workers supported the Catholic Church with much greater zeal than was being shown in Europe.

Assuredly, Catholicism was beset by other problems. A group of dissident Poles founded the National Polish Catholic Church in 1907. Italian American males gave the Church only nominal support and broadly refused to send their children to parochial schools. There developed an acute shortage of priests of the same ethnic background as their parishioners. Then, after that problem began to be resolved, conflict ensued over whether instruction in the parochial schools should be in English or in the language of ethnic origin.

New immigrants also resented bitterly the reluctance of the Irish to share their domination of the Church hierarchy. Finally, public support of parochial education was resisted by non-Catholics and not sanctioned by American legal institutions, subjecting many Catholics to a heavy financial burden. In spite of these difficulties, however, church membership and parochial education grew rapidly throughout the entire period.

Although Catholic working people gave greater support than Protestants to the welfare aspects of progressivism, the Social Gospel movement had slight impact on the Catholic Church as an organization. The Paulist priest, economist, and political scientist, John A. Ryan, did emerge as one of the era's more influential reformers following publication of his *A Living Wage: Its Ethical and Economic Aspects* in 1906. Moreover, Pope Leo XIII's charge in *De Rerum Novarum* (1891) that "a small number of very rich men have been able to lay upon the masses of the poor a yoke little better than slavery itself," also spurred uncounted parish priests to compassionate works. The hierarchy's militant philosophic and theological conservatism, however, and especially its sharp perception of the Church's need for acceptance by the conservative Protestant business establishment, caused most bishops to continue to ignore the encyclical.

JUDAISM

Some developments within the Jewish community paralleled those within Protestantism and Catholicism. By 1900 the mainly German-Jewish immigrants of earlier years had risen in extraordinary numbers into the middle, upper-middle, and professional classes. Fearful that the great influx of Jews from Eastern Europe would compromise their own hard-won social position, they were repelled by the political radicalism of many of the newcomers combined with what they regarded as the newcomers' "crude" religious Orthodoxy. They turned first to immigration restriction, then to paternalistic programs of uplift. Although tension persisted into the next generation and beyond, it was eased by modifications in Orthodox practices as the east Europeans became Americanized and educated. Late in the period, moreover, many of the more successful Orthodox Jews moved to the suburbs and joined Conservative congregations in a blend of Orthodoxy and German Reform Judaism. Furthermore, large proportions of highly educated Jews—even more than Protestants—abandoned religion in all but name.

No comparable Social Gospel-type movement emerged within Judaism in America, partly because Jews came to the United States with a more refined sense of community than most old-stock Americans. Proudly, the German-Jewish social agency, the United Hebrew Charities, reported in 1900 that it had taken care of almost every poverty-stricken Jew it had found. Just as Jews made a disproportionately large contribution to the nation's cultural and intellectual life, they also supported the humanitarian aspects of progressivism with an intensity and strength out of all proportion to their numbers.

LEGAL AND POLITICAL MAIN CURRENTS

SOCIOLOGICAL JURISPRUDENCE

The vast changes in American thought and institutions wrought by progressivism were mirrored in the law. Admittedly, the old absolutes died hard. Not until the new industrial problems became acute did the liberating force of Oliver Wendell Holmes' The *Common Law* begin to be felt. Not until judges came abreast of the new psychological and sociological currents did a progressive synthesis begin to be formed.

In crudest form the new accommodation reflected the judiciary's realization that since it lacked the power of the purse or sword, it could not indefinitely hold back a nation bent on reform. As the humorous newspaper commentator "Mr. Dooley" phrased it, "Th' Supreme Court follows th' ilection returns." In its broadest and highest form it reflected the same impulses that had inspired the progressive

Oliver Wendell Holmes *(Library of Congress)*

movement in general—the quest for social justice, the belief in progress, the urge to create, and the faith in science. Thus Harvard's Dean Roscoe Pound, who synthesized the historical insights of Holmes, the methodology of the social scientists, and the pragmatism of James and Dewey, conceived of the law as an agency for social reconstruction:

> The sociological movement in jurisprudence is a movement for pragmatism as a philosophy of law; for the adjustment of principles and doctrines to the human conditions they are to govern rather than to assume first principles; for putting the human factor in the central place and relegating logic to its true position as an instrument.

In spite of lingering opposition, the force of these and similar ideas was immediate and widespread, though hardly pervasive. Judges began to probe beyond the crime into its social or psychological origins and to view juvenile delinquency as environmental rather than hereditary in origin. Children's courts, modeled on one that Judge Ben Lindsey established in Denver, spread throughout the nation.

The law also began to adjust creatively, though again slowly, and inadequately, to labor problems. The common law concepts of "fellow-servant rule," and "contributory negligence" had made workers, not employers, liable for most industrial accidents; but these concepts withered away as the courts upheld liability and workmen's compensation laws grounded on sociological realities. No one put the case more graphically than President Theodore Roosevelt in a remarkable message to Congress on January 31, 1908:

> It is hypocritical baseness to speak of a girl who works in a factory where the dangerous machinery is unprotected as having the "right" freely to contract to expose herself to dangers to life and limb. She has no alternative but to suffer want or else to expose herself to such dangers. ... It is a moral wrong that the whole burden of the risk incidental to the business would be placed with crushing weight upon her weak shoulders.

Nevertheless, the Court struck down the Child Labor Act of 1916, and it ruled numerous state statutes unconstitutional. Yet, as a recent student of the Supreme Court concludes, many constitutional historians exaggerate in calling the period one of unrestrained judicial conservatism. The Court did uphold most of the basic progressive legislation of the period even though much of this legislation restricted some elements of the free enterprise system—for example, an employer's right to fix prices and wages.

POLITICAL THOUGHT

While Dewey, Pound, and Beard were reconstructing education, law, and history, Herbert Croly, later one of the founders of the progressive weekly, *The New Republic,* was calling for a reconstitution of politics. He charged that the existing system was geared to the interests of the wealthy minority. The remedy, he concluded, was to infuse the political order with the new social and psychological concepts.

In *The Promise of American Life* (1909), Croly accepted the charges of Veblen and the instinct psychologists that industrialism had repressed the finer human instincts. He directed his fire, accordingly, at laissez-faire capitalism's basic precept—the belief that freedom to pursue individual gain leads inevitably to social progress. In words that came close to paraphrasing Theodore Roosevelt's presidential messages of 1907 and 1908, Croly called for the replacement of individualism by social togetherness. By the exercise of self-discipline, said Croly, people must create a community loyal to an ideal—a nation-state that would fulfill humanity's great promise.

Believing in big business' potential for good and despairing of the Democrats' devotion to states' rights, Croly at first fastened on the Republican Party as the vehicle to achieve his purposes. He considered

Roosevelt almost the ideal statesman: "The whole tendency of his programme is to give a democratic meaning and purpose to Hamiltonian tradition and method. He proposes to use the power and resources of the Federal government for the purpose of making his country a more complete democracy in organization and practice." Like Roosevelt, however, Croly finally concluded that Republican nationalism served big business interests almost exclusively.

By the end of the Progressive Era, most of these social, intellectual, and economic currents were influencing Washington in greater or lesser degree. Moving upward from the unions in some cases, downward from business in others, and in from the universities in almost all, they usually affected local and state politics first. Often, as in education and birth control, local and state influences remained strongest. On other matters, notably regulation of national corporations, Congress became preeminent, but in most instances, local, state, and federal governments divided responsibilities. We will now explore in more depth the new style of governance then being constructed.

6

THE FORGING OF MODERN GOVERNMENT, 1900–1918

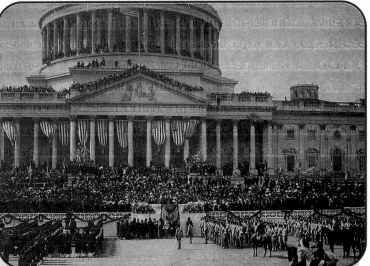

(Library of Congress)

PROLOGUE TO CHANGE

ENTER THEODORE ROOSEVELT

On a September afternoon in 1901, at the Pan-American Exposition in Buffalo, New York, a young anarchist named Leon Czolgosz, proclaiming that he was killing an "enemy of the people," shot President William McKinley at close range while the President was standing in a receiving line. Eight days later the President died of complications from gangrene. Vice-President Theodore Roosevelt took the President's oath, and the old order began to give way to what was to become known as the Progressive Era. It was symbolized at first by Roosevelt, at 41 the youngest man to occupy the White House, then by Senator Robert M. La Follette of Wisconsin and followed by President Woodrow Wilson.

The Republican Party had not planned for it to be this way. Roosevelt had been elected governor of New York in 1898 following his heroism in the Spanish-American War. Republican Party leaders in the important state of New York viewed Roosevelt as a meddlesome loose cannon and desired to remove him from the office of the governor; but his popularity, stemming from his status as a war hero, dictated that he could remain governor of New York as long as he desired. As a consequence, New York Republican Party leaders had urged William McKinley to make Roosevelt his running mate in 1900, thus removing him from New York and placing him in a position from which he could do no harm.

Republican Party leader Mark Hanna opposed Roosevelt's selection as Vice President because he feared that Roosevelt could use the office as a stepping-stone to the Presidency. Upon McKinley's untimely death, Hanna reportedly exclaimed, "I told William McKinley that it was a mistake to nominate that wild man at Philadelphia. I asked him if he realized what would happen if he should die. Now look—that damned Cowboy is in the White House."

Roosevelt, however, was much more than a "cowboy." While it is true that Roosevelt had spent time in the Dakotas as a rancher in the 1880s in an effort to recover from the sudden death of his young wife, and it is also true that he fought in the Spanish American War with the "Rough Riders" at San Juan Hill, Roosevelt was born into a wealthy New York family and should also be considered one of America's "scholar-Presidents." A reader of thousands of books and a writer of several of his own, Roosevelt dedicated himself to both physical and academic pursuits with equal vigor. As a child, Roosevelt had been sickly, asthmatic, and weak with poor eyesight, but as an adult, Roosevelt made up for lost time as an avid swimmer, cowpuncher, military man, and big game hunter. Essentially, Roosevelt glorified warfare, and what he termed as the "strenuous life," as a route to true "manhood." In an 1899 essay entitled "The Strenuous Life," Roosevelt urged Americans to extinguish "the soft spirit of the cloistered life" and "boldly face the life of strife." Roosevelt advocated enjoying the outdoors and exercising, but also he advocated competitive athletics. Roosevelt's boisterous personality excited the American public, and he eventually became the only twentieth century President immortalized on Mount Rushmore.

Though Roosevelt was viewed by conservative Republicans as a radical and a loose cannon, in reality, Roosevelt was a conservative at heart and viewed reform less as a vehicle for remaking society and more as a means of protecting society against more radical changes. Nevertheless, Roosevelt would bring about numerous reforms during his Presidency and gain the reputation as a progressive. Two and a half months after being sworn in, President Roosevelt sounded the dominant note of twentieth-century American politics. The old system, he said in his first annual message to Congress, must be changed to meet new social and economic problems. "When the Constitution was adopted, at the end of the eighteenth century, no human wisdom could foretell the sweeping changes ... which were to take place by the beginning of the twentieth century. At that time it was accepted as a matter of course that the several States were the proper authorities to regulate, so far as was then necessary, the comparatively insignificant and strictly localized corporate bodies of the day. The conditions are now wholly different and wholly different action is called for."

PRESIDENTIAL INITIATIVE

Action soon followed words. On February 14, 1902, Roosevelt invoked the Sherman Antitrust Act against the Northern Securities Company, a mammoth railroad holding corporation controlled by the bankers J. P. Morgan

J. P. Morgan *(Library of Congress)*

and Company and Kuhn, Loeb and Company and the railroad operators, James J. Hill and Edward H. Harriman.

Morgan was stunned. He exclaimed that Roosevelt had not acted like a "gentleman" and later tried to treat the President like a rival operator. Hill was even more embittered. "It really seems hard," he complained, "that we should be compelled to fight for our lives against the political adventurers who have never done anything but pose and draw a salary." In spite of these complaints, however, the proceedings continued. Two years later the Supreme Court, in a five to four decision, ordered the Northern Securities Company to dissolve.

By the time the Northern Securities case was settled, Roosevelt had added another dimension to presidential leadership. In May 1902, John Mitchell, the moderate leader of the United Mine Workers, had called anthracite miners of northeastern Pennsylvania out on strike. The strikers demanded an eight-hour day, wage increases, and recognition of their union. The eight railroad companies, which dominated the industry, would neither recognize the United Mine Workers nor mitigate the workers' near subhuman conditions of life. "(The miners) don't suffer," the operators' chief spokesman expostulated at one point. "Why, they can't even speak English!" With the mine owners used to getting their way, often with government intervention on the side of the mine owners, management refused to budge, so the strike continued through the summer and into the fall.

Fearful of a coal shortage and infuriated by the operators' arrogance, Roosevelt considered filing an antitrust suit against the coal combine. When the Attorney General advised that it would fail for lack of evidence, however, Roosevelt decided to invite the contesting parties to the White House. The operators deeply resented this implied recognition of the U.M.W. and vehemently refused to make any concessions at the ensuing conference in October. In contrast, the U.M.W. was more open to Roosevelt's mediation because the union was used to the federal government immediately taking the side of the mine owners rather than taking the middle ground.

Roosevelt was so determined to end the strike in the interest of the American economy that he issued secret orders to the army to prepare to seize the mines. He then warned prominent business leaders on Wall Street of his intent. These measures sufficed, and the operators agreed to accept the recommendations of an independent arbitration committee appointed by the President. Their plan to crush the U.M.W. had failed. "This is the great distinguishing fact," the Springfield Republican proclaimed at the time, "for while the operators still nominally refuse to recognize the mine workers' union, that union nevertheless is a party to the President's plan of arbitration and is so recognized by him."

The political importance of both the Northern Securities Company suit and the President's intervention in the coal strike far transcended their immediate economic significance. By striking out boldly on his own, Roosevelt had asserted his independence of big business, revitalized the executive office, and helped prepare the way for the progressive movement to reach the national level. He had also given meaning to the Sherman Antitrust Act and had created the impression that the Republican Party could become a viable instrument of progressive reform.

THE REVOLT OF THE MIDDLE CLASSES

THE NEW CONSENSUS

The program that Theodore Roosevelt and Woodrow Wilson pressed on Congress and the nation from 1905 to 1916 was neither revolutionary nor original since many reforms of the Progressive Era had been spelled out originally in the Populist Party platform of 1892. Theodore Roosevelt campaigned for re-election in 1904, offering every American what he termed as a "square deal." The slogan and Roosevelt's personality resonated enough with voters that he won a record 57 percent of the vote in 1904 over Democratic candidate Alton B. Parker; but many Republican backers of Roosevelt did not realize that they had just re-elected a progressive reformer. William Jennings Bryan had suggested, earlier, almost every major measure that Roosevelt and his successors would sign into law. Even the attack on the Northern Securities Company was based on a law enacted 12 years before. Why, then, did progressivism succeed when Populism and Bryanism had failed?

Many historians argue that the middle-class character of progressivism's constituency and leadership made the crucial difference. Populism, despite its attempt to win labor support, had been essentially a movement of rural protest. Bryan's Populism had been broadly based, but Bryan's identification with prohibition and evangelical Protestantism had alienated many normally Democratic Catholic and Jewish workers. In 1896 Bryan had generally failed, however, to win middle-class support—even among well-to-do farmers.

Middle-class voters had been frightened mainly by Bryan's allegedly "wild" financial ideas. "How intellectually snobbish I was about 'sound economics,'" the editor William Allen White wrote later.

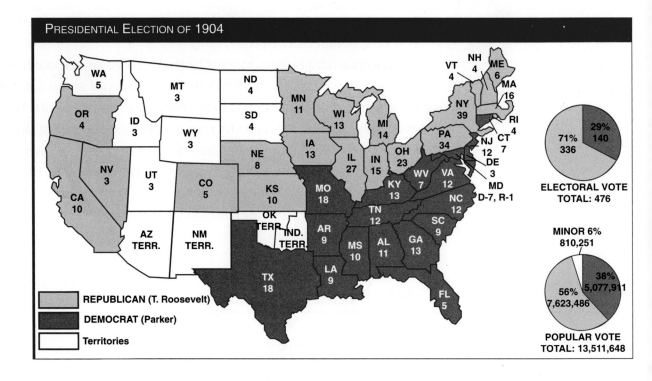

PRESIDENTIAL ELECTION OF 1904

"... It seemed to me that rude hands were trying to tear down the tabernacle of our national life."

Progressivism triumphed because tens of thousands of civic-minded Americans who shared White's virtues and prejudices were drawn into the environment of change. "Populism shaved its whiskers, put on a derby and moved into the middle of the class—the upper middle class," White wrote. That, of course, was poetic license, but progressivism did appeal more to educated, prosperous farmers than to uneducated, unsuccessful ones. It also exerted a powerful pull on skilled laborers, however. Urban blue-collar workers of old stock or of northern European origins gave it disproportionate support, especially on economic issues. Even in the Middle West, progressivism's voter strength lay more in cities and medium-size towns than in the countryside.

Assuredly, most first-echelon progressive leaders came from the old-stock middle or upper-middle classes. The secondary leadership was of similar background though it contained some minor union officials, some old-line politicians, and a number of Jewish professionals. It was augmented, moreover, by the female social reformers, without votes (except in certain states) until 1920 but extraordinarily influential nonetheless.

On the average, the men who would "march to Armageddon" with Theodore Roosevelt in 1912 and form the Progressive ("Bull Moose") Party were 10 years younger than the conservatives who remained with the G.O.P. They had been college students or impressionable young men of affairs when the intellectual revolution of the Gilded Age challenged the economic and social values of their fathers. Although they might not have heard of Lester Ward and his *Dynamic Sociology*, they were thoroughly familiar with Henry George's indictment of poverty and Edward Bellamy's utopian vision of the potentialities of the new technology. They accepted the postulates of reform Darwinism, and they believed with varying intensity that the environment could and should be shaped to bring out the best in humankind and its institutions.

Despite their broad identity of background, few progressives thought alike on all issues. As we have already seen, the progressive movement was at once positive and negative, liberal and conservative, democratic and elitist. It possessed both a soft side and a hard side, both a social justice wing and a business wing; thus, many of the urban businessmen—who joined early citizen's movements for local control, city manager government, and efficient administration—had scant sympathy for much of the social justice progressives' economic program. They had no desire to reform the tax structure or create a welfare polity through minimum wage laws, workmen's compensation, and health insurance systems. Neither did rural and small town progressives evince much concern for social justice. In Connecticut, for example, small town state legislators voted down workmen's compensation in the same session in which they enacted a strong measure to regulate public utilities. In Congress, too, rural progressives gave considerably more support to measures regulating business than to those affecting workers.

Even the urban, middle-class professionals who comprised the heart of the progressive movement had divided allegiances. The narrower moralists among them wanted mainly to clean up politics by destroying "bossism" and its attendant evils. They believed that the Australian (secret) Ballot, the direct primary, and numerous other procedural reforms would shift power from the boss-manipulated masses to themselves and people like themselves. They fumed over soaring tax rates and gas, electric, and streetcar monopolies. They also, mistakenly, attributed the increasingly high cost of government to corruption rather than to the root cause—expanding services, and they blamed rising prices on the "trusts" rather than on market forces.

The moralists also feared the aggrandizement of power by organized labor, though they sympathized with individual workingmen and women. Many felt that they were being squeezed between the upper and nether elements of society. A few of the aristocrats among them may even have been moved by desire to regain a status and prestige lost to the new business leaders, those *nouveaux riches* that one critic described as being "without restraints of culture, experience, the pride, or even the inherited caution of class or rank."

Yet to view progressivism through one or another of its constituent parts is to miss the thrust of the movement as a whole. All but the most opportunistic progressives shared a vision of society that impelled them, within limits, to put what they saw as the public good above their private interest. Whatever their personal ambitions—even the purest idealists among them possessed normal drives for prestige and power—their breadth of outlook enabled them to transcend short-range economic and social considerations in pursuit of long-range civic goals.

As political activists, they forged a series of shifting political coalitions based on the mainly material concerns of labor, farmers, white-collar workers, and businessmen. As educated and highly informed citizens, they based their program on the ostensibly objective findings of social scientists. As pragmatic idealists, they gave their designs unity and purpose by evoking the moral impulses roused by the Social Gospel and by the muckrakers' exposures of corruption and exploitation. In short, despite their differences and inconsistencies, they mobilized the new public interest philosophy in three areas of American life: social, economic, and governmental.

SOCIAL PROBLEMS

Everywhere that progressives looked they saw poverty, injustice, and political corruption in the midst of growing abundance and seemingly limitless opportunity. One percent of the nation's families owned seven eighths of its wealth, and 10 million Americans lived in abject circumstances. Many workers still toiled 60 hours a week, and almost 2 million children worked in the fields or in factories, frequently on night shifts. Thousands of workers were killed annually on the railroads alone—by one estimate over 7,000. As late as 1913, industrial accidents caused 25,000 deaths a year.

Nor did there seem to be much hope that employers would or could cope with these problems. Wages were fixed by supply and demand; and in the absence of a strong labor movement or minimum wage laws, even those manufacturers who wished to be humane were forced to keep wages at the subsistence level in order to survive competition. Thus Massachusetts, which had pioneered in strong child labor laws, steadily lost textile mills to the South where child labor helped keep production costs low.

Labor's attempts to organize and strike for higher wages and shorter hours had been systematically weakened by injunctions and,

Child laborers in a factory *(Library of Congress)*

more importantly, by management's use of immigrants as strike breakers. There was no pension system, no automatic compensation for injuries or death sustained on the job. In such an environment, the widow who received $250 from her late husband's employer could consider herself blessed. Relief, when available, came largely from private sources.

THE POWER OF BUSINESS

The consolidation of several firms into large industrial combines, a movement described in Chapter 3, threatened to make conditions worse rather than better. By 1904 combinations of one form or another controlled two fifths of all manufacturing in the United States. Six great financial groups dominated about 95 percent of the railroads, and some 1,320 utilities companies were organized under a handful of giant holding companies. As early as 1902, the United States Industrial Commission reported, "In most cases the combination has exerted an appreciable power over prices, and in practically all cases it has increased the margin between raw materials and finished products." The Commission added that the cost of production had probably decreased and that profits had doubtlessly increased. A subsequent report revealed that the cost of living actually increased 35 percent between 1897 and 1913.

As we have seen, efficiency was the economic justification for these developments; but the consolidation movement, like the protective tariff movement, was based primarily on fear of competition and its attendant instability. No one, not even J. Pierpont Morgan, whose very gaze "forced the complex of inferiority ... upon all around him," was immune. Fear of competition had driven him and his associates to buy out Andrew Carnegie and organize the United States Steel Corporation in 1901. The desire for stability and assured profits had also prompted him and James J. Hill to organize the Northern Securities Company in 1901.

The consolidation movement tended both to destroy competition and, more importantly, made it difficult for the nation to solve its festering social and political problems. Great corporations not only had the power to prevent labor from organizing basic industries but also used this power ruthlessly. They also transformed economic power into political influence in various ways. If railroad, sugar, oil, and steel interests could not "buy" state legislatures as openly as they had 25 years earlier and if they could no longer send as many hand-picked men to Congress as they once had done, they nevertheless exerted great influence over both elections and legislative decisions. They made huge contributions to the Republican Party, controlled countless newspaper editors and publishers, and kept lobbies in Washington and in state capitals.

Small industrialists, organized in 1895 as the National Association of Manufacturers (NAM), also fought social and economic change. They and other comparatively small businessmen and real estate promoters shared responsibility with big business for the already widespread pollution of America's cities and desecration of the countryside. Small industry fought minimum wage, child labor, and factory safety bills. Small businessmen lobbied most vigorously for low local and state taxes and, thus, for inadequate schools and social services.

STRANGLEHOLD ON GOVERNMENT

The obstructionist role of small business should not obscure the major issue that Roosevelt and progressives faced on the national level. The inescapable fact was that big business in 1901 constituted the most potent threat to American democracy. The post-Civil War shift of power from Washington to Wall Street had accelerated under President McKinley. By Roosevelt's ascension, the presidency had become a kind of branch brokerage office, with the President himself little more than the Washington director of a nationwide financial operation. There was nothing particularly sinister or even secret about the system. Republican politicians, such as McKinley and his friend

Mark Hanna believed that national welfare depended upon cooperation between business and government.

In such an environment, no national progressive movement could gain political power until the reign of big business was effectively challenged. This was why Roosevelt's action against the Northern Securities Company had such great symbolic importance. Progressives continued to emphasize direct democracy—the primary, initiative, referendum, recall of judicial decisions, and, above all, direct election of senators (United States Senators were elected by State Legislatures until the passage of the Seventeenth Amendment). These devices, they believed, would enable them to introduce bills in boss-dominated legislatures, undo the work of conservative legislatures and judges, and replace business-oriented senators with people more representative of the general citizenry.

THUNDER IN THE CITIES AND STATES

ORIGINS OF URBAN REFORM

The catalyst behind the shifting coalitions that formed the progressive movement was the prolonged depression of the 1890s. A business editor wrote at the time:

> It is probably safe to say that in no civilized country in this century, not actually in the throes of war or open insurrection, has society been so disorganized as it was in the United States during the first half of 1894; never was human life held so cheap, never did the constituted authorities appear so incompetent to endorse respect for the law.

Appalled by the people's hardships and fearful of their social implications, the middle and upper-middle classes had begun to become politically active in large numbers for the first time. As we have seen, clergymen were trying earnestly to apply the Social Gospel, Women's literary societies developed an interest in social and economic problems, and men's civic clubs turned their sights on public utility monopolies. Furthermore, untried reform politicians challenged conservative business leaders, and most importantly of all, farmers' organizations, labor unions, church clubs, and other civic groups formed common fronts. In so doing, they regularly crossed—though they rarely severed—the class, ethnic, and religious lines that had heretofore separated social units.

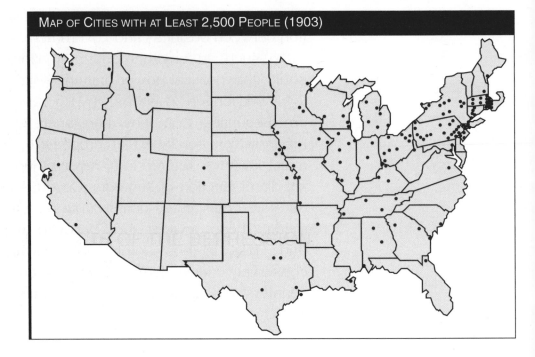

MAP OF CITIES WITH AT LEAST 2,500 PEOPLE (1903)

Between 1894 and 1897, municipal reform movements erupted across the nation. In city after city during the next decade, reform candidates—both Republican and Democratic—campaigned successfully for commission or city manager government, for local control, and for honest elections. Invariably, they found that the trail of privilege and corruption led from the city hall to the statehouse and thence to powerful business interests. Government, they gradually—and often reluctantly—concluded, must be transformed from a negative to a positive force. Only then could insurance and utility companies be brought under control, exploitation of men, women, and children stopped, and the power of the bosses destroyed.

STATE REFORMS

As governor of New York in 1899, Theodore Roosevelt pushed through a corporation tax, strengthened factory and tenement inspection laws, and flouted business interests on so many other counts that the G.O.P machine eased him out of the state and into the vice-presidential nomination in 1900. In the same year, Robert M. La Follette abandoned Republican orthodoxy and won the governorship of Wisconsin. Much of his program had developed piecemeal in the East, especially in Massachusetts and New York; but La Follette, drawing on a general shift of progressive support from the countryside to urban centers, implemented his program so imaginatively that it became a model and gained renown as the "Wisconsin Idea." There and elsewhere, progressives won the direct primary, the short ballot, the initiative and referendum, and the recall of elected officials.

Progressives in state legislatures strengthened child labor laws, created commissions to regulate utilities and railroad rates, and began to impose inheritance, corporation, and graduated income taxes. They also made increasingly large appropriations for schools, state universities, mental and penal institutions, and welfare programs in general. Maryland enacted the first

Robert La Follette *(Library of Congress)*

workmen's compensation law in 1902, protecting workers against on-the-job injuries. Oregon limited women workers to a 10-hour day in the next year, Illinois established a public assistance program for mothers with dependent children in 1911, and Massachusetts created a commission to fix wages for women and children in 1912. By the end of the Progressive Era, the number of students in high schools had almost doubled, most of the great industrial states had workmen's compensation laws, and the number of industrial accidents had been dramatically reduced by the forced or voluntary adoption of safety procedures. The epilogue that Senator La Follette wrote in his *Autobiography* in 1913 was in reality a prologue:

> It has been a fight supremely worth making, and I want it to be judged ... by results actually attained. If it can be shown that Wisconsin is a happier and better state to live in, that its institutions are more democratic, that the opportunities of all its people are more equal, that social justice more nearly prevails, that human life is safer and sweeter—then I shall rest content in the feeling that the Progressive movement has been successful.

PROGRESSIVISM MOVES TO WASHINGTON

By 1904 President Roosevelt was girding for a mighty struggle with conservatives in his own party. He had come into office well aware that his party was a hostage to business and its spokesmen in Congress and that this situation placed limits on his ability to act. As he explained to intimates, he could do something about either the tariff or the trusts, but not both. He had opted for trust reform as the more popular issue, the issue less offensive to Congress, and the issue more vulnerable to executive leverage.

On the legislative side, the record of his first administration had been modest. A Democratic-sponsored reclamation measure, The Newlands Act, which provided federal funds for the construction of dams and canals in the West and for the construction of hydroelectric power plants, had been passed in 1902 with the President's support. The Elkins Act to prohibit railroad rebates had gone through in 1903 because the railroads favored it; and a Department of Commerce and Labor, including a Bureau of Corporations with investigatory powers, had been created the same year. A handful of conservatives, however, called Old Guardsmen—Nelson W. Aldrich of Rhode Island, William B. Allison of Iowa, Marcus A. Hanna of Ohio, Orville H. Platt of Connecticut, and John C. Spooner of New York—had otherwise kept the legislative hatches closed.

Wealthy, able, and intelligent, these senators were also arrogant and dogmatic. Only Mark Hanna had sought to make peace with labor in 1900 by joining Samuel Gompers in forming the National Civic Federation to promote settlement of labor disputes. Other senators were insensitive to social and economic injustice. They supported governmental subsidies and other favors to business, even while invoking the principle of laissez-faire to prevent even the mildest reforms, and not want Roosevelt to run for a full term in 1904. After Roosevelt captured the party machinery, however, they and the financial and business interests helped him win a rousing victory over the conservative Democratic candidate, Judge Alton B. Parker of New York, who actually believed that the trust problem should be left to the states. As the New York *Sun* put it, better to

Judge Alton B. Parker *(Library of Congress)*

have "the impulsive candidate of the party of conservatism than the conservative candidate of the party which the business interests regard as permanently and dangerously impulsive." Significantly, not even Roosevelt's extraordinary popularity reversed the downward trend in voter turnout that had started in 1900 and would continue until 1928. This decline was strong in the North as well as in the South, especially among workers and marginal farmers.

THE PARTY STRUCTURE

The key to the conservative domination of the Republican delegation in Congress was malapportionment in the states and the election of United States senators by their legislatures. In every state east of the Mississippi, the small towns and rural areas had become grossly overrepresented as the cities grew. Districts were not generally equal in population, and rural districts with much smaller populations would have the same representation as urban districts with many more people, especially in state legislatures. In almost every state, a handful of entrenched leaders with close ties to an intricate network of business lobbyists dictated the selection of senatorial candidates, and by gerrymandering congressional districts, they assured the election of conservative Republicans to the House. Only in the northwest central states and on the Pacific Coast did progressive Republicans control the selection of senators and representatives with any consistency.

At no time, therefore—not even during the height of progressive Republican insurgency between 1910 and 1912—was as much as a fourth of the Republican delegation in Congress progressive, yet neither was this dominant conservatism truly representative of rank and file Republicanism. "If I thought the Republican organization under the dome of the Capitol represented the Republican Party of the country," a Wisconsin progressive protested in 1909, "I would be ashamed of being a Republican."

Roosevelt could find little support for his legislative program by turning to the Democrats, however. Most Southern state legislatures were gerrymandered in favor of rural "Tories," conservative ideologically, but members of the Democratic Party due to the sectionalism that followed the Civil War and continued into the mid-twentieth century. Thus, progressive thought was far weaker in Congress than outside it; and though Southern Democrats willingly abandoned states' rights on issues that redounded to the South's advantage, they remained basically unsympathetic to Roosevelt's centralizing tendencies. Furthermore, the Democrats' strength in the Senate was too slight for Roosevelt to have forged a viable coalition with them and the small minority of progressive Republicans. He had no choice, therefore, but to work through those who controlled the party—the conservative Republican leaders.

Still, there were offsetting factors. The President controlled the patronage, and he could enforce acts of Congress vigorously or indifferently. He could also appoint fact-finding commissions, and he could use the vast moral force of his office to influence public opinion and thus, indirectly, the Congress. Reinforced by his understanding of these powers and emboldened by his popular mandate and the angry excitement whipped up by the muckrakers, Roosevelt prepared in December 1904 to present a full program of reform to Congress.

RAILROAD REGULATION

His first major achievement was the Hepburn Act to strengthen the ratemaking power of the Interstate Commerce Commission (ICC). Following publication in *McClure's* of a devastating account of railroad malpractices, a concerted demand for action arose in the Middle West and the South. It came not only from farmers but also from merchants, manufacturers, and civic leaders, whose national organizations protested less against high rates than against the discrepancies between charges for long and short hauls, the curtailment of services induced by the consolidation of lines, and similar abuses.

These powerful pressures drove a number of conservative Republican senators part way to Roosevelt's side. Spurred by brilliant presidential maneuvering, a coalition then passed a compromise measure in 1906. Although La Follette cried "betrayal" because the bill failed to authorize evaluation of a railroad's worth in determining rates, the Hepburn Act had many progressive features, including extension of the Interstate Commerce Commission's jurisdiction to oil pipeline, sleeping-car, and express companies. This act also strengthened the regulatory authority of the ICC over railroads, enabling them to set rates and inspect the books, and ended free railroad passes to politicians.

PUBLIC HEALTH CONTROLS

Shortly after adoption of the Hepburn Act, the President signed two other significant measures—the Pure Food and Drug Act and the Meat Inspection Amendment to the Agricultural Appropriations Act. Each was necessitated by the callous disregard for the public's health by the industries concerned. Each reflected a growing conviction that only federal regulation could safeguard the people's health against avaricious business.

The Pure Food and Drug Act was a testament both to the new scientism and to the single-minded dedication of the Department of Agriculture's chief chemist, Dr. Harvey W. Wiley, "a very mountain among men, a lion among fighters." Wiley had long been pressing for a law to prevent the manufacture and sale of adulterated, misbranded, or poisonous foods and drugs. With powerful help from President Roosevelt, the American Medical Association, and muckraker Samuel Hopkins Adams, his bill finally came to the floor of the Senate in the spring of 1906. Sneering openly at chemists in the Department of Agriculture, Senator Nelson W. Aldrich said that "the liberty of all the people" was at stake, but Senator Porter J. McCumber of North Dakota rejoined that the real issue was the public's right to receive what it asked for and "not some poisonous substance in lieu thereof." An imperfect but pioneering pure-food-and-drug measure became law on June 30, 1906.

The fight for the Meat Inspection Amendment offered an even more penetrating insight into the business mind. Upton Sinclair's muckraking novel, *The Jungle* (1906), graphically exposed conditions in the meatpacking industry:

> There was never the least attention paid to what was cut up for sausage, there would come all the way back from Europe old sausage that had been rejected, and that was mouldy and white—it would be doused with borax and glycerine, and dumped into the hoppers, and made over again for home consumption. There would be meat that had tumbled out on the floor, in the dirt and sawdust, where the workers had tramped and spit uncounted millions of germs. ... [A] man could run his hand over these piles of meat and sweep off handfuls of the dried dung of rats.

Upton Sinclair *(Library of Congress)*

After reading *The Jungle,* according to Finley Peter Dunne's humorous character

"Mr. Dooley," Roosevelt rose from his breakfast table crying "I'm pizened" and threw his sausages out the window. Actually, the President ordered an immediate investigation. Meanwhile, lobbyists for the meatpacking industry charged that an inspection measure drawn by Senator Albert J. Beveridge of Indiana was "unconstitutional" and "socialistic." When European sales dropped precipitously, however, the meat packers abruptly reversed themselves. They demanded, in the words of Mark Sullivan, "an inspection law ... strong enough to still public clamor, while not so drastic as to inconvenience them too greatly." The result was compromise in the Roosevelt pattern.

FOR GENERATIONS YET UNBORN

By then the President was also deep in a bitter struggle for rational control and development of the nation's natural resources. On his side stood a great host of governmental scientists and experts headed by Gifford Pinchot, uncounted public-spirited citizens from all over the nation (but especially from the East), numerous homesteaders, and the great lumber corporations. Arrayed against him were small lumber companies, grazing, mining, and power interests of all types, most Western state governments, and, in the end, a decisive majority in Congress.

The issues were simple in some instances and complex in others. Should homesteaders be sacrificed to big cattle and sheep men for reasons of efficiency? Should giant lumber corporations, which had the means to pursue scientific forestry, be favored over small companies, which did not? Should the moralistic and scientific assumptions of Roosevelt and his supporters prevail? These assumptions were that the country's natural resources belong to the people as a whole; that "the fundamental idea of forestry is the perpetuation of forests by use"; that the federal government should reclaim arid lands; that "every stream is a unit from its source to its mouth, and all its uses are interdependent"; and that the electric monopoly is "the most threatening which has ever appeared."

Early in his administration Roosevelt saved what would become the heart of the Tennessee Valley Authority in the 1930s by vetoing a bill that would have opened Muscle Shoals on the Tennessee River to haphazard development by private interests. He then set aside governmental reserves in Nebraska for a tree-planting experiment that would serve as a model for a more comprehensive program under the New Deal. In 1905 he rehabilitated the Bureau of Forestry, renamed it the Forest Service, and appointed Gifford Pinchot as its chief.

A small revolution followed. Trained and dedicated foresters staffed the new agency. Enlightened controls directed the development of waterpower sites by corporations, and the President vetoed numerous bills injurious to the public interest. More than 2,500 potential dam sites were temporarily withdrawn from entry in order to assure orderly and constructive development. In addition, 150 million acres were added to the national forests. Half as many acres with coal and mineral deposits were transferred to the public domain, and most large lumber corporations (though not the small ones) were persuaded to adopt selective-cutting techniques that alone assured the perpetuation of timber resources.

Western congressmen beholden to private interests responded with near-hysterical charges of "executive usurpation" and destruction of states' rights, but Roosevelt was undaunted. He skirmished for the preservation of the country's natural monuments even as Congress passed laws depriving him of authority to create new national forests. Before he left office in March 1909, the number of national parks had doubled. Sixteen National Monuments, like California's Muir Woods and Washington's Mount Olympus, had been created and 51 wildlife refuges established. "Is there any law that will prevent me from declaring Pelican Island a Federal Bird Reservation?" Roosevelt asked. "Very well, then I so declare it."

The President also appointed a commission to investigate and make recommendations for multipurpose river valley developments such as the Tennessee Valley Authority later became. Then in May 1908, he urged the first conference of governors to implement the conservation movement in their states. No governor espoused the movement with Roosevelt's zeal and understanding, but spadework for moderate state programs had, nevertheless, begun. "When the historian ... shall speak of Theodore Roosevelt," Senator La Follette later wrote, "he is likely to say ... that his greatest work was inspiring and actually beginning a world movement for ... saving for the human race the things on which alone a peaceful, progressive, and happy life can be founded."

VARIATIONS IN ANTITRUST POLICY

Neither La Follette nor most other progressives were altogether enthusiastic about Roosevelt's later attitude toward big business. The President had followed up action against the Northern Securities Company with a spate of suits, and by the end of his second term 25 indictments had been obtained and 18 proceedings in equity had been instituted. His successor, William Howard Taft, intensified the

William Howard Taft *(Library of Congress)*

pace, bringing 43 indictments in four years and far exceeding Roosevelt's "Trust-busting." Unlike Roosevelt, who merely wanted to regulate the trusts for the purpose of staving off revolutionary reform, Taft was a legalist who viewed the trusts as in violation of the Sherman Act and, therefore, illegal. In 1911 the Supreme Court implicitly reversed the Knight decision of 1895 in two verdicts, decreeing dissolution of the Standard Oil Company and the American Tobacco Company. These decisions made it clear that manufacturing combinations were not exempt from the Sherman Antitrust Act, even though the Court qualified its position somewhat with the so-called rule of reason, which acknowledged that bigness *per se* was no crime.

"The example of these basic decisions served as a powerful negative factor in business affairs," concludes one recent scholar. "Certain lines of development were denied to ambitious men." They wrought few basic changes in the American economy, however. Price leadership continued as the producers in an industry followed the lead of a few dominant corporations. Moreover, control over credit remained highly concentrated in Wall Street.

As his administration progressed, Roosevelt himself experienced a metamorphosis in his attitude toward the "trusts." Because he appreciated the advantages of large-scale production and distribution, he sought to distinguish between "good" and "bad" trusts. Putting his faith primarily in regulation, he repeatedly called on Congress to strengthen and expand the regulatory Bureau of Corporations. Then, after he left office, he came out openly for government price-fixing in basic industries.

Otherwise, from this time on Roosevelt maintained cordial relations with the Morgan-U.S. Steel axis. In order to prevent the spread of a severe financial panic that struck New York in 1907, he went to the aid of the banks and acquiesced in U.S. Steel's absorption of a Southern competitor, the Tennessee Coal and Iron Company, financed by J. P. Morgan. Then, in the next year he accepted without protest the inadequate Aldrich-Vreeland banking bill, which progressives and agrarians bitterly opposed as banker-oriented.

TROUBLE ON THE LABOR FRONT

Labor continued to make modest advances during the Roosevelt and Taft administrations, mainly because of the progressives' work in the states. The American Federation of Labor grew by fits and starts, and the standard of living of its highly skilled members rose appreciably. In manufacturing, we have seen, wages increased while the average work-week declined from 60 to 50 hours.

The AFL failed, however, to organize basic industry, mainly because of the massive counteroffensive by employers, spearheaded by the National Association of Manufacturers. To prevent labor from organizing, the NAM resorted to weapons ranging from propaganda to violence. Its most effective tactic was maintenance of the open shop (a shop in which union membership is not a precondition of employment), and its most important ally was the middle class. The employers understood that in practice an open shop meant a nonunion shop, but middle-class progressives often did not. Even when they saw the point, a lingering devotion to natural law and individual rights made it difficult for them to accept the idea of the closed shop. Roosevelt was unsure on the issue, and men like Woodrow Wilson, then president of Princeton, and Charles W. Eliot, president of Harvard, were adamant in their opposition to the closed shop. Eliot actually acclaimed the strikebreaker as "a very good type of modern hero." In consequence, labor received virtually no support during the Progressive Era for the one measure that would have assured it success—active governmental support of the organizing process.

To compound labor's difficulties, the basic right to strike was often grossly impaired by management's private police forces, the actions of corporation-dominated state governments, and the indiscriminate issuance of injunctions by judges who cared more for property than for human rights. In speech after speech from 1905 to 1912, Roosevelt inveighed mightily against the abuse of the injunction (six special messages to Congress between 1905 and 1908), but the NAM was so influential in Republican councils that he failed even to get an anti-injunction plank in the party platform in 1908.

Members of the Industrial Workers of the World union *(Library of Congress)*

Campaigns to organize the steel industry, meanwhile, suffered a series of setbacks and finally collapsed altogether. The United Mine Workers were successful in the East, but they failed in two bloody efforts in Colorado. The first, in 1903–1904, ended in a rout climaxed by the deportation of strikers to the desert. The second, in 1913–1914, ended in tragedy when National Guardsmen burned a strikers' tent colony at Ludlow on April 20, 1914, accidentally killing 11 women and two children.

Against this background the formation in 1905 of the freewheeling and sometimes violent (especially in rhetoric) Industrial Workers of the World ("Wobblies") was almost predictable. Concentrated in the West, the I.W.W. fought the battles of frontier miners, lumberjacks, and migrant workers.

FORECASTS OF THE WELFARE STATE

By 1907 the Republican majority in Congress had had their fill of Theodore Roosevelt. They approved no major domestic legislation during his last two years in office and repudiated him openly on several occasions. Nevertheless, the executive power under Roosevelt continued to expand. The President appointed numerous investigatory commissions, and he made further advances in conservation. Furthermore, he repeatedly lectured Congress and the people on the need to mitigate the harsh inequities of capitalism by welfare measures. The Supreme Court's ruling in *Lochner v. New York* (1905), which held a maximum-hours law for bakers to be unconstitutional on the grounds that it was an unreasonable interference with the right of free contract and an unreasonable use of the state's police power, outraged him. After a New York tenement law was invalidated and a workmen's compensation law declared unconstitutional, Roosevelt wrote Justice William R. Day that, unless the judiciary's spirit changed, "we should not only have a revolution, but it would be absolutely necessary to have a revolution, because the condition of the worker would become intolerable."

On January 31, 1908, Roosevelt sent Congress the most radical presidential message to that time. He charged that businessmen had revived the doctrine of states' rights in order to avoid all meaningful regulation. Furthermore, he observed that there was "no moral difference between gambling at cards ... and gambling in the stock market." He called for stringent regulation of securities, imprisonment of businessmen who flouted the law, and a comprehensive program of business regulation. In addition, he upbraided "decent citizens" for permitting "those rich men whose lives are evil and corrupt" to control the nation's destiny. He lashed the judiciary for "abusing" the writ of injunction in labor disputes; and he contemptuously dismissed editors, lawyers, and politicians who had been "purchased by the corporations" as "puppets who move as the strings are pulled." Moreover, Roosevelt came out for workmen's compensation, compulsory arbitration of labor disputes, and acceptance of big unionism as a countervailing power to big business.

In doing so, Roosevelt lost the support of big business conservatives that was needed if he were to secure the Republican nomination in 1908. Laissez faire conservatives also erroneously believed that the Panic of 1907 was a result of Roosevelt's meddling in the economy. Finally, Roosevelt was limited by his own words since he had promised in 1904 that he would only run for one term, since he had served most of William McKinley's term as well as his own. Consequently, to run again in 1908 would mean going back on his word, which Roosevelt was loathe to do. Consequently, at age 50, Roosevelt decided that he could not run again in 1908 and briefly retired from public life. Nevertheless, the crowd at the Republican National Convention in 1908 chanted "Four More Years" for 49 minutes until Henry Cabot Lodge finally came forward and announced that the President's decision was irrevocable.

The Disruption of the G.O.P.

TAFT'S BACKGROUND

Roosevelt's chosen successor, William Howard Taft, unfortunately lacked the energy, conviction, and political skill to carry on Roosevelt's policies. He seemed to be sympathetic to Roosevelt's progressive views, but he had marked limitations. He believed implicitly in natural law, and he was a good but painfully conventional lawyer. Furthermore, he had no zest for the give-and-take of politics, and he possessed a strain of courage but lacked political boldness and energy.

Big and small business heartily concurred in Taft's nomination in 1908, and he handily defeated William Jennings Bryan's third unsuccessful bid for the Presidency by 321 to 162 electoral votes in what was billed as the "fattest election in history" since both candidates probably weighed well over 300 pounds, giving America a solid "third of a ton" of Presidential candidates. A story surfaced from when Taft had been governor of the Philippines in 1902 that he had sent a cable to Elihu Root from Manila, stating, "Took a long horseback ride—feeling fine," to which Root reportedly replied, "How is the horse?"

At any rate, no sooner were the election returns in than Taft's troubles began. Taft's personality was a great contrast with that of the energetic Roosevelt, whose popularity may have exceeded any President's since George Washington. Teddy bears, Teddy glasses, and Teddy stories permeated American life, and any person following Roosevelt may have found the shoes difficult to fill. For Taft, however, the contrasts were even greater. While Roosevelt had been energetic and athletic, Taft was sedentary and obese. He received much bad press when a wall had to be knocked down at the White House to install a special, oversized bathtub for his oversized body. Taft was also prone to falling asleep at inopportune times and dozed off in an open car while campaigning in New York; and on another occasion, he nodded off at a State funeral.

Politically, Taft conceived his mission to be to consolidate the Roosevelt reforms (giving them the "sanction of law," as he privately phrased it), not to embark on new ventures. Actually, he was too steeped in legal traditionalism to accept Roosevelt's dynamic conception of the Constitution; and he, therefore, failed to seize the executive reins. Taft believed that the counsel of lawyers was superior to that of scientists and other experts, and he deplored Roosevelt's reliance on investigatory commissions. Taft also tended to adhere strictly to the letter of the law and preferred not to see gray areas where Roosevelt had done so, including in the areas of anti-trust and separation of powers.

THE TARIFF FIASCO

By 1908 so many Midwesterners were blaming rising prices on the high schedules of the Dingley Tariff (1897) that Taft implied during the campaign that his administration would revise the tariff downward. Faithfully, he called a special session of Congress for the spring of 1909, but instead of lowering the duties, Old Guardsmen in the Senate raised them. This forced the President to accept a compromise (the Payne-Aldrich Tariff) that left the old schedules more or less intact. Then, to the disgust of progressive Republicans in the Midwest, he defended the measure as "the best bill that the Republican Party ever passed." Two years later he negotiated a reciprocity agreement with Canada that the Canadians subsequently rejected because of loose talk that it presaged annexation of their country.

THE RISE OF INSURGENCY

Meanwhile, Taft was besieged with troubles on other fronts. In 1910 a group of progressive Republicans in the House, led by George W.

Norris of Nebraska, stripped Speaker Joseph G. Cannon of his arbitrary and partisan control over legislation and committee appointments. Taft was secretly pleased, but both the insurgents and the public continued to link the President with the uncouth and reactionary Speaker.

Taft's rather curious stand on conservation led to even worse difficulties. He believed in conservation, but he abhorred the freewheeling methods that Roosevelt had used to achieve his objective. Taft replaced Secretary of the Interior James R. Garfield with Richard A. Ballinger, an honest conservative who had earlier resigned from the Land Office because

George W. Norris *(Library of Congress)*

he disagreed with Roosevelt's view that the public's interest in natural resources should be given priority over that of entrepreneurs. Construing the law rigidly when government interests were at stake and loosely when private interests were at issue, Ballinger soon provoked Gifford Pinchot, Chief of the United States Forest Service, to charge a "giveaway" of Alaskan mineral lands to the Guggenheims, the great mining industrialists. Ballinger had removed approximately one million acres of forests from public land reserves created by Theodore Roosevelt. Interior department investigator Lewis Glavis charged that Ballinger had engaged in a plan to turn over public coal reserves in Alaska to private investors for profit. Glavis took his evidence to Theodore Roosevelt ally Gifford Pinchot, who was still head of the forest service. Pinchot presented the evidence to Taft, who also heard Ballinger's rebuttal and announced that the charges were groundless. Pinchot then leaked the story to the press and to Congress, and an enraged Taft dismissed Pinchot for insubordination. In the end, Taft alienated progressives and Roosevelt supporters who viewed Pinchot as a defender of the public interests against greedy industrialists.

Ballinger was eventually exonerated, but President Taft was fatally stamped as anti-conservationist since he fired Roosevelt's man, Gifford Pinchot. The characterization was not wholly unfair. Although Taft withdrew more lands from public entry (closing them to exploitation by private individuals and corporations) than Roosevelt and put millions of acres of forest lands into new reserves, he never did grasp the Roosevelt-Pinchot concepts of controlled development or of multipurpose river valley projects.

ROOSEVELT CHALLENGES TAFT

Roosevelt returned from abroad in 1910—characteristically, he had gone big game hunting in Africa—in high indignation over Taft's ineptitude and the implied repudiation of his conservation policies. At Osawatomie, Kansas, on September 1, the former President developed further the social welfare program he had set forth in his memorable messages of 1908, calling it the "New Nationalism" because it put the national need "before sectional or personal advantage." Roosevelt quoted Lincoln's assertion that "Labor is prior to, and independent of, capital." He asserted that the judiciary's primary obligation was to protect "human welfare rather than ... property" and he called for graduated income and inheritance taxes, workmen's compensation legislation, a federal child labor law, tariff revision, government health insurance, and more stringent regulation of corporations. Furthermore, Roosevelt denounced Taft for "completely twisting around the policies I have advocated and acted upon."

The congressional elections in the fall of 1910 produced the most sweeping changes since the great realignment of the mid-90s. From East to West, stand-pat Republicans were turned out of office as the G.O.P. lost 58 seats in the House, 10 in the Senate, and a total of seven governorships. Furthermore, progressive Republican candidates ousted conservatives in 40 districts, creating a majority progressive House. Most contemporary observers blamed the tariff and Taft's failure to project a dynamic progressive image; but recent scholarship suggests that resentment among normally Republican Germans against other Republicans' increasingly fervent support of prohibition figured importantly and perhaps decisively.

Taft attempted to pacify progressives with vigorous anti-trust legislation and, in October 1911, filed an anti-trust suit against U.S. Steel, alleging that the 1907 acquisition of Tennessee Iron and Coal that had been facilitated by Theodore Roosevelt violated the Sherman Act. Roosevelt was incensed since the suit essentially inferred that Roosevelt's approval of the purchase back in 1907 was improper. Roosevelt followed by announcing his candidacy for the Presidency in February 1912.

THE "BULL MOOSE" PARTY

Early in 1911 Republican progressives began to call for the nomination of Robert La Follette or Roosevelt in 1912. The Wisconsin senator made an early and earnest bid and then refused to bow out gracefully after his most devoted followers concluded that he could not win. Roosevelt's entry into the race in February 1912 precipitated one of the bitterest preconvention campaigns in Republican history. The primary election system was relatively new, and only 13 states held Republican primaries. Roosevelt outpolled Taft two to one in the 13 states that held primaries, winning all 13 states; but the Old Guard refused to let him have the nomination, awarding 90 percent of the unassigned delegates at the Convention to Taft. "We can't elect Taft," a Kansas regular confessed, "but we are going to hold on to this organization and when we get back four years from now, we will have it and not those d---- insurgents."

Faced with these attitudes, more than 300 Roosevelt delegates stormed out of the convention hall in Chicago in a dispute over the seating of delegates. Six weeks later they returned to form the Progressive or "Bull Moose" Party (so named because Roosevelt

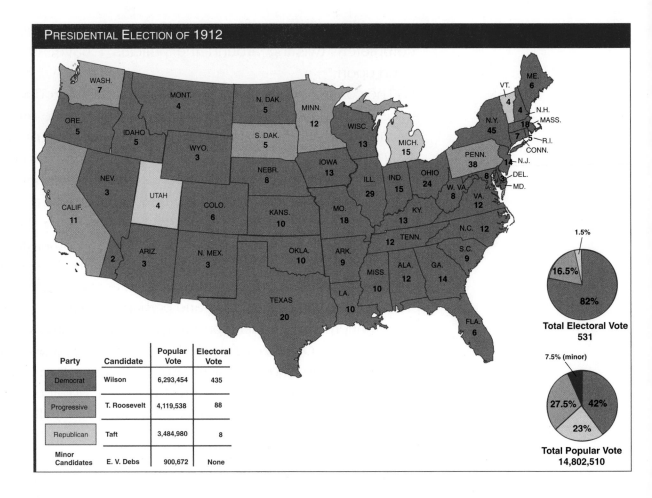

PRESIDENTIAL ELECTION OF 1912

WASH. 7
MONT. 4
N. DAK. 5
MINN. 12
ORE. 5
IDAHO 5
WYO. 3
S. DAK. 5
WISC. 13
MICH. 15
VT. 4
ME. 6
N.H. 4
MASS. 18
N.Y. 45
NEV. 3
UTAH 4
NEBR. 8
IOWA 13
ILL. 29
IND. 15
OHIO 24
PENN. 38
R.I. 5
CONN. 7
N.J. 14
CALIF. 11
ARIZ. 3
COLO. 6
KANS. 10
MO. 18
KY. 13
W. VA. 8
VA. 12
DEL. 3
MD. 8
N. MEX. 3
OKLA. 10
ARK. 9
TENN. 12
N.C. 12
S.C. 9
MISS. 10
ALA. 12
GA. 14
LA. 10
TEXAS 20
FLA. 6
2

Total Electoral Vote 531
82%
16.5%
1.5%

Total Popular Vote 14,802,510
42%
27.5%
23%
7.5% (minor)

Party	Candidate	Popular Vote	Electoral Vote
Democrat	Wilson	6,293,454	435
Progressive	T. Roosevelt	4,119,538	88
Republican	Taft	3,484,980	8
Minor Candidates	E. V. Debs	900,672	None

proclaimed himself as fit as a bull moose), nominate their hero, and synthesize their program for a just society.

Roosevelt's following included Social Gospel clergymen and laymen, college presidents and professors, liberal businessmen and editors, Gifford Pinchot and his fellow conservationists, and social workers by the hundreds. Jane Addams gave one of the speeches seconding his nomination; but when the Democrats nominated a moderate progressive, Governor Woodrow Wilson of New Jersey, Roosevelt and his party were doomed. Wilson's platform differed from Roosevelt's primarily only in that Wilson opposed the "largeness" of big business in and of itself and favored complete destruction of the trusts, rather than merely regulating them as Roosevelt proposed.

The election of 1912 has been described as a three-candidate election, but only a two-candidate campaign, as Taft quickly recognized that he had no chance of winning and essentially did not even try. When asked why he was not campaigning like the other two candidates, Taft's response was, "There are so many people in the country that do not like me." In the election that autumn, Wilson won 40 states and 42 percent of the popular vote while Roosevelt ran second with 27 percent and Taft a poor third with 23 percent of the popular vote. It was the largest defeat of a sitting President in United States History as Taft won only eight electoral votes.

Actually, by the time Taft left office in March 1913, his administration had compiled an impressive legislative record. It included safety regulations for miners, an Employers' Liability Act for work done under government contract, and a measure to establish a Children's Bureau. The Interstate Commerce Commission's authority had been extended to telephone, telegraph, cable, and wireless companies, and a postal savings system had been established to serve farmers and others in remote rural areas. Congress had also adopted two of the progressive movement's most cherished proposals, the Sixteenth Amendment, giving Congress the power to levy an income tax, and the Seventeenth Amendment, providing for direct election of senators. Taft himself had given warm support to some of these measures, perfunctory support to others, and little beyond his signature to one or two. All owed their passage more to a coalition of Democrats and progressive Republicans than to the regular Republican majority.

IRONIES OF AMERICAN SOCIALISM

The election of 1912 also drew the largest Socialist vote to that time although not wholly for reasons of ideology. Probably half the 900,000 voters who cast their ballots for the charismatic Socialist Party candidate, Eugene V. Debs, were simply disaffected by the middle-class character of the Bull Moose leadership and, especially, by the unofficial commitment of the three major parties to prohibition.

The Socialist Party itself was hardly more radical in practice than the Progressive Party was in theory. Socialist leaders believed firmly in evolution, not revolution, and most of the 1,200 party members who held office in railroad, mining, and industrial towns during the era pushed progressive-type programs, including efficiency and economy. Furthermore, the conservative German contingent headed by Victor Berger of Milwaukee was avowedly racist. Not until after the northward trek of blacks at the end of World War I made it politically expedient to appeal to them did the party do so, although Debs and many others had long been sympathetic.

Conservative Socialists also differed little from organized labor and the major parties on immigration. "Slavonians, Italians, Russians, and Armenians," said Berger before a House committee in 1911, were the "modern white coolies" of the steel industry and had "crowded out the Americans, Germans, Englishmen, and Irishmen." Even Morris Hillquit, leader of the party's strongly Jewish eastern wing, favored selective restriction of immigration. More ironic still, the dirt and tenant farmers of Oklahoma and Texas, who constituted the party's largest faction stood strongly for individual rather than communal ownership of land.

Yet, for all its internal inconsistencies, socialism made a significant impress on American life. As the memoirs of numerous progressives attest, socialist values influenced the social justice wings of the Republican, Democratic, and Progressive parties alike. They also served as a central inspiration to Jane Addams, Florence Kelley, and many of the other great reformers.

THE TRIUMPH OF PROGRESSIVISM

WILSON'S BACKGROUND

Woodrow Wilson was born in a Presbyterian manse in Virginia in 1856 and reared in a South (Georgia) convulsed by Civil War and Reconstruction. Wilson, like Roosevelt, should certainly be considered one of America's scholar-Presidents as he graduated from Princeton in 1879 and went on to obtain a law degree and practice law in Atlanta. Wilson became dissatisfied with the legal profession and returned to school to earn a Ph.D. in political science from Johns Hopkins University. As a Ph.D. candidate at Johns Hopkins, he argued in a brilliant dissertation, *Congressional Government* (1885), that the basic weakness in the American political system was its separation of executive from legislative leadership. Wilson obtained a spot on the faculty at Princeton and following a distinguished tenure as a professor, worked his way up to be president of Princeton University in 1902. Wilson gained a reputation for progressive academic reforms at Princeton and used that reputation to propel himself to the New Jersey governor's office in 1910. As governor, Wilson shifted from being an academic conservative into a practical progressive. He boldly seized control of the Democratic state machine, pushed a comprehensive reform program through a divided legislature, and gave eloquent voice to high ideals and moderately progressive aspirations.

Wilson was the first Southerner elected to the White House since 1844 and the only Democrat elected to the White House, besides Grover Cleveland, since Reconstruction. Wilson was a moralist and a teetotaler who called for a day of prayer after his inauguration. With a keen intellect and high education, but a strict religious upbringing, Wilson had strong political convictions and was rarely open to compromise.

Wilson was also a single man for a portion of his Presidency and courted his second wife, Edith Gault, while in office, creating a

Woodrow Wilson on his daily ride in the outskirts of Washington *(Library of Congress)*

tabloid media circus. Love letters from the President to Edith eventually were published where the President proclaims, "You are my ideal companion, my perfect playmate, with whom everything is gay," and "How deep I have drunk of the sweet fountains that are in you." One Secret Service agent reported that after seeing Mrs. Gault one night, the President skipped down the street singing, "Oh, you beautiful doll." It is perhaps little wonder then that the *Washington Post,* after the President spent an evening on the town with his "perfect playmate," printed the famous gaffe, "The President spent much of the evening entering Mrs. Gault."

After the two married, Edith remained at the President's side at all times, evidently viewing herself as a true partner in all things, even the presidency. When Wilson traveled to Europe to sign the Versailles Treaty after World War I, Edith Wilson was by his side. This brought out Wilson's critics in full force. In the early part of the twentieth century, it was not customary for First Ladies to take an active role in the President's official duties.

In contrast, Edith Wilson believed that being with her husband at all times, to counsel him and give him support and her advice, was

President Woodrow Wilson and First Lady Edith Wilson *(Library of Congress)*

her right as his wife; and she, therefore, ignored the critics. Similarly, it appears that President Wilson felt comfortable consulting with his wife on the issues of the day; and it appears that she was his confidant, and he respected her opinion as much as that of most of his other advisors.

THE NEW FREEDOM PROGRAM

The program Wilson called the New Freedom was grounded in the theory that no group should receive special privileges. It differed from Roosevelt's New Nationalism in two essentials. First, it advocated regulated competition rather than regulated monopoly. Second, it turned most of the social programs of progressivism back to the states and municipalities. The first goal was to be achieved by downward revision of the tariff, strengthening and relentlessly enforcing the antitrust laws, and freeing the banks from dependence on Wall Street.

TARIFF AND BANKING REFORM

Wilson aimed to destroy the Republican system of special privilege for industry and for the producers of raw materials by reducing tariff protection and, thereby, increasing competition. He used patronage to hold wavering Democrats in line; and he marshaled opinion against the G.O.P. Old Guard by charging publicly that Washington had seldom seen "so numerous, so industrious or so insidious a lobby" as had invaded the Capitol. This masterful exertion of leadership resulted in the first substantial reduction of the tariff since before the Civil War.

Wilson began auspiciously by calling a special session of Congress the day of his inauguration and then addressing a joint meeting of the Senate and House in person. In doing so, Wilson became the first President since Thomas Jefferson to make an appearance before Congress in a situation that was neither mandated by the Constitution nor emergency, but simply to argue for the passage of particular policies. Again, being a major fan of the British Parliamentary system, Wilson desired to approach Congress much as a Prime Minister would in England and take the lead in legislation. Wilson's first action as President was, therefore, to appear before Congress and argue for a reduction of the tariff, and Congress, now with a Democratic majority, passed the lower tariff.

After the ratification of the Sixteenth Amendment, Congress under Wilson also passed a modest income tax (10 percent on income over $4,000 and six percent on income over $500,000) along with the lower tariff. In October 1913, however, Wilson was embroiled in conflict over banking legislation. Conservative Republicans wanted a single central bank controlled by private bankers, while conservative Democrats insisted on a decentralized reserve system under private control. Bryan Democrats and progressive Republicans called for a reserve system and currency supply owned and controlled by the government. (The latter were roused especially by sensational revelations of Wall Street's influence over the nation's financial and investment system.) Finally, after consultations with Louis D. Brandeis, his most influential adviser on domestic matters, Wilson worked out a series of constructive compromises that were adopted as the Federal Reserve Act in December 1913.

The measure created 12 Federal Reserve Banks, each to be owned and controlled by the individual private banks in its district but responsible to a seven-member central Federal Reserve Board appointed by the President. The Federal Reserve Banks would hold a percentage of the assets of their member banks in reserve and use those reserves to support loans to banks at a discount rate. Federal Reserve Banks could also issue Federal Reserve Notes and shift them to imperiled banks to provide them with the funds necessary to meet loan demands in times of currency shortages. Provision was also made to meet the seasonal needs of agriculture. The Federal Reserve System was not intended to destroy private ownership and initiative in banking, but it did create new centers of financial power to offset the overweening influence of New York bankers.

Wilson planned to round out his program by revising the antitrust laws. There were to be no special benefits to labor, no aid to agriculture, no such conservation program as Roosevelt had envisaged. Child labor, woman suffrage, workmen's compensation, and all the rest would have to come, if they came at all, by haphazard state action. Indeed, when a bill sponsored by the National Child Labor Committee passed the House in 1914 over the protests of states' rights Southerners, Wilson refused to push it in the Senate.

MOVING TOWARD THE NEW NATIONALISM

By 1914, the progressive movement had gathered too much momentum to be long halted by presidential indifference. While the child labor forces were regrouping for a second assault, new pressures were bearing so heavily on the White House that Wilson had either to accommodate them or risk loss of his office in 1916.

These pressures were first felt when the administration introduced its program in 1914. Wilson's original measures included legislation to outlaw specific, unfair trade practices and to create a federal trade commission with only fact-finding powers. Progressives in both parties thought little of the former and refused to support the latter because it did not grant the commission power to act on its findings.

Finally, Brandeis and others persuaded Wilson that it was impossible to outlaw every conceivable unfair trade practice and that something like Roosevelt's proposal for continuous regulation was the only workable alternative. Wilson, therefore, signed the Clayton Antitrust Bill despite its ambiguities and qualifications, but he put his energy and influence into Brandeis' measure to create a federal regulatory agency empowered, in effect, to define unfair trade practices on its own terms and to suppress them on its own findings, subject to broad court review. As a consequence, the final component of Wilson's New Freedom was the passage of the Federal Trade Commission Act, which created the Federal Trade Commission (FTC), a new federal regulatory agency that was given the authority to prosecute business for unfair trade practices and the investigative authority necessary to carry out such prosecution. After the creation of the Federal Reserve banking system and the FTC, Wilson considered his New Freedom complete.

Meanwhile, Wilson engaged in a bitter quarrel with organized labor over the Clayton Antitrust Bill. Samuel Gompers and the AFL hierarchy

Samuel Gompers *(Library of Congress)*

demanded provisions to exempt labor unions from prosecution for the secondary boycott, the blacklist, and other weapons the Supreme Court had declared in violation of the Sherman Antitrust Act. In effect, labor wanted special privileges to offset management's power.

Wilson held rigidly to the New Freedom line against special privilege for any group, but he did accept an affirmation of rights that labor already possessed in law, if not always in fact, and a few other moderate provisions. His adherence to the New Freedom program on this one point did not signify that he was ordinarily unsympathetic to labor. On the contrary, the AFL lobby spoke with greater effect in Washington during Wilson's administration than did the National Association of Manufacturers.

"WE ARE ALSO PROGRESSIVES"

As Wilson's tenure lengthened, it became evident that the New Freedom's opposition to special privilege and commitment to states' rights made it too confining to permit fulfillment of the President's own expanding concept of social justice. For example, Wilson opposed an amendment to impose women's suffrage on the states because of states' rights. It also became clear that the Democrats would have to attract a substantial portion of Roosevelt's disintegrating "Bull Moose" Party to retain the presidency in 1916. Against this background, Wilson again became more progressive. He began by signing the La Follette Seaman's Act of 1915, which freed sailors from bondage to labor contracts. Then, early in 1916, he nominated Louis Brandeis to the Supreme Court over bitter opposition by Old Guard Republicans and leaders of the legal profession. (Brandeis, a Kentucky-born Jew known as the "people's lawyer," had broken legal tradition in 1908 by presenting a mass of sociological data—with help from Florence Kelley and her colleagues—to the Court in his defense of an Oregon bill establishing maximum working hours for women.)

Next, the President came out in support of a languishing rural-credits bill that he had condemned as class legislation two years before. Wilson also won approval of a model federal workmen's compensation bill. He successfully urged creation of a tariff commission because he feared that surplus European goods would be dumped in America at the end of World War I, and he threw strong support behind the Child Labor Bill and won its adoption. Enacted in the summer of 1916, the bill made it illegal to transport goods manufactured by child labor across state lines. The Act was declared unconstitutional two years later, however, in *Hammer v. Dagenhart*.

The flow of legislation continued until the very eve of the election. A measure to extend federal assistance to the states for highway construction rolled through Congress, and the revenue act adopted in the late summer of 1916 increased income taxes sharply and imposed a new estate tax. In September, the President personally drove through Congress the Adamson bill to establish the eight-hour day for railroad workers; and finally, during his second administration, Wilson signed both the prohibition and woman suffrage amendments, though his heart was in neither.

Altogether, Wilson's first administration embodied an imposing and important program of reform legislation. Wilson could truthfully claim, as he did during the presidential campaign of 1916, that he and his party had put a large part of the Progressive Party's platform of 1912 onto the federal statute books.

POLITICS AND BLACKS

For the vast majority of African Americans, progressivism proved more an illusion than a reality, regardless of who occupied the White House. Violence or the threat of violence continued to be the ultimate means of race control. Although the total number of lynchings decreased nationwide because of a sharp decline in the North, the number increased in the South. As often as not, moreover, the burnings and hangings were for imaginary or concocted offenses. In 1906 12 persons were slaughtered in a race riot in Atlanta. Similarly, two years later an anti-black riot occurred a half mile from Lincoln's home in Springfield, Illinois. Meanwhile Southern orators, like South Carolina's "Pitchfork Ben" Tillman, carried the message of white supremacy to receptive Northern audiences. The production in 1915 of *The Birth of a Nation*, which was based on Thomas Dixon's blatantly racist book, *The Clansman*, brought more violence.

Roosevelt had been moderately sympathetic to blacks. His original objective had been a biracial Southern Republican party led by patrician whites and educated blacks—his immediate end the securing of his own nomination in 1904 through control of the Southern delegations. He had maintained close relations with Booker T. Washington, head of the Tuskeegee Institute, and, unlike McKinley, he had appointed eminently qualified blacks to federal offices in the South. He had also denounced lynching and ordered legal action against peonage, in which a worker, usually black, was forced to pay off a debt through the court-rigged assignment of that debt to a private employer.

By 1904 these actions by Roosevelt had produced a vicious reaction in the South. With the tacit acquiescence of Bryan, Southern editors and politicians inflamed the region over "Roosevelt Republicanism" and, thereby, forced enlightened white Southerners on the defensive. After Roosevelt entertained Booker T. Washington at the White House, newspaper headlines included: "Roosevelt Dines a Darky" and "Our Coon Flavored President." Nor was the situation much better in the North, where "scientific" racial theories that taught the innate inferiority of blacks had penetrated even the universities.

Against this background, Roosevelt equivocated. He appointed a few more African Americans to medium-level offices and continued to denounce lynching, but during the race riot in Atlanta in 1906, he provided no moral leadership. Then in the aftermath of an affray at Brownsville, Texas, erroneously thought to involve blacks, he arbitrarily discharged three companies of black soldiers. By the end of his presidency he had concluded that the hope of a viable biracial Republican Party in the South was an idle dream. As he sadly reflected, "the North and the South act in just the same way toward the Negro."

His successor, William Howard Taft, had no interest whatever in solving the race problem or in helping black people. "I will not be swerved one iota from my policy to the South ...," Taft snapped. "I shall not appoint Negroes to office in the South. ... I shall not relinquish my hope to build up a decent white man's party there."

In 1912 many Northern blacks went over to Woodrow Wilson and the Democratic Party, but they were soon disillusioned. Under Wilson, blacks were segregated in some federal departments, and virtually no blacks were appointed to any but the lowest-level offices in either the South or the North. Wilson also reversed Roosevelt's integrationist policies in the United States armed forces and favored the continued segregation of railroad cars. Never in his memory, wrote Booker T. Washington, had he seen his people so "discouraged and bitter." During World War I, discrimination became so extreme in the military service that the Federal Council of Churches of Christ established a commission to investigate.

A few small advances—most of them of greater long-range than short-run significance—punctuated this otherwise dreary record. A handful of Northern philanthropists expanded their support of black colleges, and a small number of Northern progressives—many the descendants of abolitionists—also formed a common front with blacks. On Lincoln's birthday in 1909, a group of white educators, clergymen, editors, and social workers joined a group of black intellectuals in forming the National Association for the Advancement of Colored People. They dedicated the organization to the abolition of all forced segregation and to the promotion of equal justice and enlarged educational opportunities for blacks, but for tactical reasons, only one black, W. E. B. DuBois, served as an official during the NAACP's early years. (See "*William E. Burghardt DuBois: Black Intellectual*.")

Two years after the founding of the NAACP another group of black intellectuals founded the National Urban League. Neither organization made much headway at first, but they were gathering expertise and resources that would permit a frontal assault on Jim Crow after World War II.

On the legal front, the Supreme Court struck down peonage in separate decisions during the Taft and Wilson administrations though the system actually continued with modifications into the late 1920s. It also overturned an amendment to the Oklahoma Constitution—the so-called Grandfather Clause that allowed certain illiterate whites, but not illiterate blacks, to vote.

THE PROGRESSIVE ERA IN RETROSPECT

Neither the impressive achievements of the Roosevelt, Taft, and Wilson administrations nor the remarkable flow of legislation in the states fulfilled the best hopes of the social justice progressives. In 1920 the distribution of wealth was roughly the same as it had been in 1900, the social and economic status of African Americans was only marginally better, and that of women only modestly so. Basic industry remained unorganized, and thousands of steelworkers labored 12 hours a day, seven days a week. Farm tenancy was continuing to rise, and most farm youths still lacked access to secondary schools. The calls of progressives for social security and unemployment insurance systems were as yet unheeded, and good medical care, like good legal service, remained more a function of the marketplace than a fundamental right.

Civil liberties were no less subject to the whim of the crowd, the local authority, or the business-oriented judge than they had been 20 years earlier. City manager and city council forms of government had altered little more than the face of urban politics, and no perceptible change in the quality of candidates had been wrought by the direct election of United States senators. Neither had the conservation movement halted the abuse of privately owned natural resources or the despoliation of the countryside by individuals and businesses, both large and small.

Despite the highly publicized attacks on trusts, corporations were larger and monopoly or near-monopoly was more widespread at the end of each presidential administration than at its beginning. Many of the regulatory agencies had already become virtual captives of the industries they were supposed to regulate, and, close ties had developed in other agencies between the experts who ran them and the interests that sought their favors. By any reasonable measure, America in 1920, like all other advanced technological nations, had become a partially formed bureaucratic, corporate society.

Nevertheless, as we have seen, the majority of people led somewhat more comfortable and more interesting lives in 1920 than they had in 1900; and their opportunities for self-fulfillment were also much greater. Technology relieved some of the drudgery of housework, and the increase in leisure time that resulted from the rise in productivity was generating new forms of entertainment and diversion. Government regulations had reduced the industrial accident rate and eased slightly the severity of labor in factories and mines. Modernization of municipal government made cities more manageable, and advances in public health made them more livable.

The growth of urban colleges and evening courses had opened professional careers to thousands of ethnic youths, and the parallel expansion of state colleges and universities was putting higher education within the reach of small town youngsters and the sons and daughters of well-to-do farmers. More important still, the explosion of knowledge sparked by the development of graduate education was

PEOPLE THAT MADE A DIFFERENCE

William E. Burghardt DuBois: Black Intellectual

W. E. B. DuBois *(Library of Congress)*

The most intensely intellectual black spokesman of the first half of the twentieth century was W. E. B. DuBois, whose greatest achievement, perhaps, was to awaken interest in the black past, both African and American. He was born in Great Barrington, Massachusetts, with, as he phrased it, "a flood of Negro blood, a string of French, a bit of Dutch, but thank God! no Anglo-Saxon." His paternal grandfather, a restless and embittered man, had been the offspring of a wealthy French Huguenot American and a Bahamian mulatto slave. His father, no less restless and embittered, had married Mary Burghardt, whose partly Dutch family were among Great Barrington's earliest settlers; he left her permanently soon after their child was born.

Short and bronze-skinned, with sharp features and an aloof personality that gave him an aristocratic mien, DuBois in his teens was hardly aware that he was "different" until he offered his calling card to a white girl and was rejected "peremptorily, with a glance." Feeling that a "vast veil" had shut him out, he knew "days of secret tears" thereafter. The black man, he wrote in 1903, "feels his two-ness—an American, a Negro, two souls, two thoughts, two unreconciled strivings, two warring ideals in one dark body."

DuBois began to develop an interest in racial matters while still in high school, and at the age of 15 he became the local correspondent of the black New York Globe. His principal, Frank A. Hosmer, recognized his precocity and encouraged him to prepare for college. (DuBois often wondered, he later said, what his fate would have been had Hosmer been "born with no faith in 'darkies.') Financed by local white church goers, DuBois went to Fisk University, an all-black college in Tennessee in 1885. He completed his degree in three years and entered Harvard with Junior standing as a scholarship student. There, as one of his biographers writes, he came to think of the institution "as a library and a faculty, nothing more." Contemptuous of the lack of purpose of most of Harvard's white students, DuBois took an active part in black affairs in Boston during his first years. His aloof personality caused resentment, however, and in time he withdrew into himself. Meanwhile, he was awarded a fellowship to the University of Berlin.

Study in Germany strengthened DuBois' interests in scientific social and historical research, though he had done brilliantly in the natural sciences as an undergraduate. Never—

not even after he renounced his American citizenship late in life—did he lose faith that social science would some day triumph over the mythology of racism and the pathology of discrimination. After two years in Germany, DuBois returned to complete a degree in history under Albert Bushnell Hart (one of the leading figures in sociologically-informed history) in 1895 and to become Harvard's first black Ph.D. Forced to accept a teaching position at Wilberforce College in Ohio, a black institution with a strongly religious orientation, he deplored "the wild screams, cries, groans, and shrieks" of the revival meetings. Only his marriage to Nina Gomer of Cedar Rapids, Iowa, brightened his life. Then, following a temporary appointment in sociology at the University of Pennsylvania, he published one of his finest works, the pioneering Philadelphia Negro (1889). It marked the founding of black sociology.

DuBois differed radically from pragmatic Booker T. Washington, who was tied to Southern roots. Harvard and European educated, living in two worlds yet belonging to neither, DuBois believed fervently in the immediate need to prepare the "Talented Tenth" of blacks for the professions and general leadership. "The Negro race," he wrote, "is going to be saved by its exceptional men." From his new urban base at Atlanta University, the faculty he joined in 1897, he came to deplore Washington's emphasis on vocational and industrial education. In 1903, in a moving and at times poetic book of essays entitled The Souls of Black Folks, DuBois criticized Washington as a compromiser whose ideology "practically accepts the alleged inferiority of the Negro." Not only does Washington apologize for injustice, DuBois wrote, "He belittles the emasculating effect of caste distinctions, and opposes the higher training and ambition of our brightest minds." Negroes should realize, he also said, that "Beauty is black."

Two years later DuBois invited a select group of black intellectuals to meet at Fort Erie, Ontario, where they formed the Niagara Movement. Condemning racism as "unreasoning human savagery," they called for federal aid to education, and denounced the discriminatory politics of employers and labor unions alike. They also demanded suffrage for blacks on the same basis as whites. The organization was short-lived. DuBois then played a role in founding the interracial National Association for the Advancement of Colored People, the most important civil rights organization of the twentieth century

Subsequently, as editor for 22 years of the NAACP's monthly magazine, The Crisis, DuBois explored a whole range of racial issues and personalities. "He does do dangerous things," wrote Mary Ovington, his most loyal white supporter on the NAACP board. "He strikes at people with a harshness and directness that appalls me, but the blow is often deserved and it is never below the belt." Meanwhile DuBois became increasingly frustrated by his inability to resolve the paradox of Negro life in the United States: Should blacks regard themselves as Americans or as Afro-Americans? Should they strive for complete integration or for separatism? Incremental reforms or fundamental changes?

In 1912 DuBois had resigned from the Socialist Party, partly in disgust over its racism but mainly in the vain hope that the election of Woodrow Wilson would bring modest gains to his people. When the country entered World War I, DuBois suffered the contempt of radical black integrationists for urging creation of a separate Negro Officer candidate's School. During the 1920s, he charged Robert M. La Follette's Progressive presidential campaign with "deliberately dodging" the black question, and he fought with Communist Party leaders for the same reason.

William E. Burghardt DuBois: Black Intellectual, *continued*

DuBois resigned his editorship of The Crisis in 1932 after a series of policy disputes and returned to Atlanta University. There he edited the Encyclopedia of the Negro (1933–1945) and in 1935 published Black Reconstruction in America. This brilliant work did much to wrench white historians from the pro-South bias that marred most histories of Reconstruction until that time.

In 1961, angered by the Cold War and the government's harassment of him for his opposition to it, DuBois joined the Communist Party. But by then he had already committed his mind and heart to Africa—"the Spiritual Frontier of humankind," as he called it. He accepted an invitation from the government of Ghana to supervise compilation of the Encyclopedia Africana and died in Accra in 1963 at the age of 95. He had become a Ghanian citizen just a few months before his death.

In the early twenty-first century, the outstanding African American scholar Henry Louis Gates, Jr. holds the W. E. B. DuBois Chair of Humanities at Harvard University, a concrete example of the way in which DuBois's stature has grown since his death.

creating an almost entirely new professional class and giving both business and government their guiding intelligence.

Philosophically, progressivism raised the level of political discourse far above that of the late nineteenth century and probably to the highest level since the time of the Founding Fathers. Educationally, it inculcated the belief that advanced training was both a societal need and a public responsibility. Sociologically, it put into the political realm an environmental and behaviorist interpretation of society that, for all its oversimplifications, was and remains the moral rationale for social reform. Psychologically, it changed the perception of government from a negative to a positive force—a view that prevailed for many decades until the advent of Ronald Reagan as a force in American politics—and promoted the view that the federal government should serve as a countervailing power to the large business corporation. Administratively, progressivism demonstrated both the government's dependence on experts and the apparent impossibility of completely insulating them from the influence of powerful private interests. Constitutionally, it raised important, and partly effective, challenges to the concept of state's rights and to the prerogatives of manufacturers engaged in interstate commerce. Economically, it established a revenue base for the society's current and future needs by winning broad acceptance of the general principle of graduated corporation, income, and inheritance taxes.

Just as important, perhaps, progressivism greatly stimulated rising expectations and a dependence on government for the solutions of social and economic problems; but these years in which modern governance was being invented were also years of transformation in American foreign policy. As we shall soon learn, both Roosevelt and Wilson left their mark in this arena in ways that few other presidents have had the opportunity so to do.

7

THE RISE OF AMERICA AS A WORLD POWER, 1898–1919

(Library of Congress)

ANOTHER FRONTIER

Several decades before the historian Frederick Jackson Turner proclaimed in 1893 that the Western frontier had closed, an influential minority of Americans was straining to extend the nation's power and influence to the remote reaches of the globe. Their motives and emphases varied. Some feared that Europe's penetration of South America threatened the United States' security, while others felt that it was the manifest destiny of a "superior" people to extend their influence. Still others believed that expansion would divert the people's attention from slavery or pressing industrial problems. In almost all cases, however, there was an underlying conviction that assured access to the markets of the world was essential to long-term prosperity and that the possession of outlying territories was one of the hallmarks of greatness.

"Rome expanded and passed away," wrote Theodore Roosevelt, "but all western Europe, both Americas, Australia and large parts of Asia and Africa to this day continue the history of Rome. ... Spain expanded and fell, but a whole continent to this day speaks Spanish and is covered with commonwealths of the Spanish tongue and culture. ... England expanded and England will fall. But think of what she will leave behind her. ..."

The foremost early expansionist was William H. Seward, Secretary of State under Lincoln and Andrew Johnson. "Give me ... 50, 40, 30 more years of life," he declared in Boston in 1867, "and I will give you possession of the American continent and control of the world." Two months later the United States took over the unoccupied Midway Islands far out in the Pacific, and then, in April 1867, the Senate ratified a treaty with Russia, negotiated by Seward, for the purchase of Alaska for $7,200,000. Most Americans, however, were still too anti-imperialistic to give Seward his rein; and he went out of office in 1869 with his major objectives unfulfilled—annexation by one means or another of Hawaii, Cuba, Puerto Rico, the Danish West Indies (now the Virgin Islands), St. Bartholomew's Island (now St. Barthélemy), Greenland, Iceland, and Canada.

Nevertheless, the expansionist impulse continued to grow. Under President Grant an annexation treaty with Santo Domingo was signed, only to be rejected by the Senate, 24 to 24; and only the consummate diplomacy of Seward's successor, Hamilton Fish, prevented the United States from becoming embroiled in Cuba where a rebellion against Spain broke out in 1868. Meanwhile the expansionist minority was formulating the intellectual underpinning of its case. As early as 1847 the New York Sun had begun to argue that annexation of Cuba would be commercially advantageous, and many Americans subscribed to these sentiments.

More significant in the long run was the growing rapport between naval officers, congressmen, intellectuals, and businessmen. During the 1870s the United States' exports exceeded its imports for the first time, and in the 1880s the aforementioned groups combined forces to promote the revitalization of the navy. Again and again, congressmen justified requests for naval construction in commercial or expansionist terms. "The time has come ...," Senator John F. Miller of California declared in 1884, "when manufactures are springing up all over the land, when new markets are necessary to be found in order to keep our factories running." Congressmen also deferred to the professional officers' expertise. "We assembled at the Navy Department," the chairman of the House Naval Affairs Committee explained, "and listened to the advice of naval officers, and our bill was changed in obedience to their views." Finally, in 1890, Captain Alfred T. Mahan published *The Influence of Sea Power upon History*. A brilliant synthesis of ideas current in naval circles for 10 years or more, it argued that only a large navy could protect the trade that would be the lifeblood of the new American empire.

Many businessmen agreed. The National Association of Manufacturers devoted much of its initial program to promoting expansion of the merchant marine, the navy, and foreign trade, and expansionist intellectuals and politicians continued to trumpet for territorial acquisitions. In 1885 the Reverend Josiah Strong in *Our Country* equated Christianity with those "peculiarly aggressive traits" that would impose Anglo-Saxon civilization "upon Mexico, down upon Central and South America, out upon the islands of the seas, over upon Africa and beyond." That same year John Fiske, the most persuasive of the Social Darwinists, predicted that "every land on the earth's surface that is not already the seat of an old civilization shall become English in its language, in its religion, in its political habits." A

Alfred Mahan *(Library of Congress)*

decade later Henry Cabot Lodge, a disciple of Captain Mahan, put forth the commercial rationale for naval expansion in categorical terms:

> Commerce follows the flag. The great nations are rapidly absorbing for their future expansion and their present defense all the waste places of the earth. ... The United States must not fall out of the line of march.

SAMOA

Hard on the completion of the first transcontinental railroad in 1869, American business and naval groups arranged a treaty for a naval station and commercial coaling rights in Samoa in expectation of a quickening of the Asian trade. A decade of jockeying for control of Samoa by Germany, Great Britain, and the United States followed. Open conflict was narrowly avoided in 1889. The German government proposed that the islands be divided, but at the United States' insistence they agreed instead to establish a tripartite protectorate. Rivalry continued, and in 1899 the fiction of Samoan independence ended. Germany and the United States divided the Samoan Islands, and Great Britain took the Gilbert and Solomon Islands in compensation.

HAWAII

By the mid-nineteenth century, American investors in Hawaii had developed a prosperous American-owned sugar industry on the Islands. In 1875, the United States signed a Reciprocity Treaty with Hawaii that essentially created exclusive free trade between Hawaii and the United States on sugar. Then in 1887, Hawaii granted exclusive use of Pearl Harbor to the United States Navy. In 1890, however, the McKinely Tariff Act removed the American tariff on all foreign raw sugar, thus opening the United States sugar market to Hawaii's competitors and destroying the advantage enjoyed by Hawaiians since the Reciprocity Treaty. Simultaneously, the McKinley Tariff Act also granted American sugar producers a two-cent per pound bounty on sugar. American sugar growers in Hawaii called for annexation to the United States since annexation would award Hawaiian sugar growers the same two-cent per pound bounty enjoyed by American sugar growers.

Hawaiian Queen Liliuokalani was a Hawaiian nationalist who desired to sever the United States relationship and, therefore, opposed annexation. A group of American naval officers conspired with Hawaiian-American business interests to depose the obstructive queen. American Minister to Hawaii John L. Stevens ordered 160 marines from the *U.S.S. Boston* in Pearl Harbor to help the rebels depose the queen in a near bloodless coup to give the United States sugar growers control of Hawaii. Stevens immediately recognized the new Hawaiian government controlled by American sugar growers, and the new government sent a mission to Washington to negotiate a treaty of annexation. President Benjamin Harrison signed the Treaty of Annexation in February 1893, but the Senate refused to ratify the treaty on the grounds that the new

President Grover Cleveland *(Library of Congress)*

government did not really represent the Hawaiian people. When new President Grover Cleveland took office, he sent a fact-finding mission to Hawaii that determined that most of the Hawaiian public supported Queen Liliuokalani. Cleveland, therefore, withdrew the treaty on the grounds that the provisional government in Hawaii did not represent the Hawaiian people. Cleveland desired to restore Queen Liliuokalani to the throne; but to do so he would have had to use the same American troops, which had ousted her, against the American sugar growers in Hawaii. Cleveland well understood that using American troops against American citizens in Hawaii would be bad politics. He decided, instead, to extend recognition to the Republic of Hawaii in 1894, and Congress passed a new tariff law that restored Hawaii's favored position.

This, however, did not produce a final resolution to the Hawaii question. Instead, President Cleveland's refusal to approve the treaty set off a four-year debate. American strategists contended that possession of Hawaii would give naval protection to the Pacific Coast, prevent annexation by Japan, and enable the United States to penetrate the Far East commercially and militarily. Annexation, in their view, was part of a "Large Policy" embracing construction of a Nicaraguan canal and acquisition of Canada. Meanwhile, a puppet government ruled Hawaii for white businessmen.

President McKinley announced on taking office that he opposed all acquisition of territory, but he soon changed his mind. Three months after his inauguration he submitted a new treaty of annexation to the Senate. The treaty was rejected; but later, after naval operations in the Pacific during the Spanish-American War dramatized Hawaii's usefulness as a naval base, Congress annexed the islands by joint resolution in July 1898. "As I look back upon the first steps in this miserable business and as I contemplate the outrage," ex-President Cleveland wrote to his former Secretary of State Richard Olney, "I am ashamed of the whole affair."

VENEZUELA AND THE MONROE DOCTRINE

Yet Cleveland himself had contributed to the jingoism that made the imperialists' triumph possible. Angered by Great Britain's refusal in 1895 to accept American arbitration of a boundary dispute between British Guiana and Venezuela, Secretary of State Olney had bluntly informed the British Foreign Secretary that "... the United States is practically sovereign on this continent, and its fiat is law." The British testily replied that the Monroe Doctrine was not recognized in international law and did not apply to boundary disputes in any event. Cleveland then warned that failure to accept the findings of an American investigation would constitute "a willful aggression." Four years later an international commission fixed the boundary largely in accord with Britain's original claims.

Cleveland's rude threat of force had ironic implications. Until then, enforcement of the Monroe Doctrine had actually been dependent on the might of the Royal Navy because the British opposed any new wave of European colonialism in Latin America almost as much as the Americans did. Now, however, the Doctrine became an instrument of American initiative. More ironic still, the President's action prompted Great Britain to reappraise its relations with the United States in the context of Germany's rise as a world power. This was to lead, in time, to a decision of momentous importance—agreement during the administration of Theodore Roosevelt on a kind of unofficial naval alliance between the United States and Great Britain.

THE GREAT DEPARTURE

TROUBLE IN CUBA

In spite of the increasingly strong thrust of the imperialists, American foreign policy until 1898 had been generally grounded on a realistic appraisal of the national interest—one that reflected a sharp awareness of both the possibilities and the limitations of American power. The festering crisis in Cuba during the 1890s precipitated the first fateful departure from this policy.

Cubans had always resented Spain's misrule of their island. When their sugar economy collapsed under the weight of European competition, the international depression of 1893, and the restrictive duties of the Wilson-Gorman Tariff of 1894, their smoldering hostilities flamed into a full-scale revolt. Determined to suppress it, Spain sent over its ablest general, Valeriano "Butcher" Weyler, who soon drove much of the civilian population into concentration camps at an estimated cost of 200,000 lives.

An outpouring of propaganda from a revolutionary junta in New York and by the yellow journalism of the New York *World* and New York *Journal* intensified the American people's sympathies for the Cuban people. "You furnish the pictures," *Journal* publisher William Randolph Hearst wired one of his artists who reported that there was no war in Cuba to portray, "and I'll furnish the war." It was the press as a whole, however, feeding voraciously on the junta's releases and reprinting indiscriminately the *World's* and the *Journal's* atrocity stories, that incited the nationwide hysteria.

Genuine sympathy for the Cubans combined with less altruistic attitudes to create growing demand for a war to liberate the Cubans. Conservative Republicans and Democrats hoped that a war would divert attention from liberal or populist issues such as free silver. Others saw commercial benefits. "Free Cuba would mean a great market to the United States" and "an opportunity for American capital," Senator Lodge asserted. Protestant clergymen felt that American intervention would alleviate suffering and, incidentally, open Cuba to Protestantism. Ultranationalists saw war as a means of testing the nation's military might, uniting the North and South, and even resolving the unemployment problem. As one Atlantan wrote the President, "The South dearly loves a fighter; if you will show yourself strong and courageous in defense of Cuba, you will have a solid South at your call. ... Strengthen the Army and Navy of this country and in this way give employment to the thousands of idle men who need it." Furthermore, by 1896, Cuban rebels under Maximo Gomez controlled two thirds of Cuba and had destroyed millions of dollars worth of American property in the process. American business, with some $50 million in Cuban assets, favored intervention to protect their investments.

President Grover Cleveland, however, had a different conception of his duty. Convinced that the Cuban insurrectionists were as barbarous as the Spaniards, Cleveland did not favor war with Spain and

General Maximo Gomez (Library of Congress)

announced that he would not send the United States to Cuba to fight the Spanish if Congress declared war. Cleveland thus left office in March 1897 without having yielded to the passions of the times.

ESCALATION OF CONFLICT WITH SPAIN

Cleveland's successor, William McKinley, had won the Presidency in 1896 with New Manifest Destiny as part of his foreign policy platform, but McKinley lacked Cleveland's stubborn courage and iron principles. Neither McKinley nor his industrialist and banker friends wanted war, but McKinley's minister to Spain, Stewart Woodford, was nevertheless instructed to demand Spanish withdrawal from Cuba. Under such American pressure, Spain recalled General Weyler in the summer of 1897 and promised a cease-fire. The Spanish government also promised to abolish the concentration camps and to grant Cuba autonomy similar to that of Canada (then a member of the British Commonwealth). Nevertheless, McKinley gradually locked himself into a policy of full independence for Cuba because he understood that the Cuban rebels would not accept some form of home rule and remained determined to fight for full independence.

The war fever mounted in early February 1898, when the Hearst press published a stolen letter written by the Spanish Minister Dupuy de Lome to a friend in Spain, which called McKinley a "peanut politician" and a "bidder for the admiration of the crowd." The New York Journal called the letter the "worst insult to the United States in its history," in spite of the fact that in democratic politics pretty much all elected officials could be called "bidders for the admiration of the crowds" and Theodore Roosevelt had once described McKinley as "having no more backbone than a chocolate éclair." Nevertheless, Western Republicans responded by introducing three separate resolutions to give the Cuban insurrectionists the status of a warring power, and McKinley dispatched the battleship U.S.S. Maine to Ha-

Wreck of the *U.S.S. Maine* in 1898 *(Library of Congress)*

vana in a gesture designed to display the American government's resolve to force a settlement.

On February 15 an explosion destroyed the *U.S.S. Maine* in Havana Harbor, killing 260 Americans. The cause was never determined, but the Hearst papers, the New York *Tribune* and a few others blamed the disaster on Spain and called for war. The navy originally concluded that the ship had hit a mine, but this conclusion makes little sense because Spain would be unlikely to mine their own harbor. The most usual purpose of mining harbors was to disrupt the trade of an enemy, not disrupt the trade of one's own country. Later reconstruction of the event suggested a coal explosion in the engine room, boiler explosion, or explosion of the ship's magazine would have been much more likely causes. Regardless, American newspapers exclaimed, "Remember the *Maine*, to Hell with Spain," and politicians such as Henry Cabot Lodge and Senator Albert J. Beveridge of Indiana joined them in a pro-war chorus. The *Maine* "was sunk by an act of dirty treachery on the part of the Spaniards," then Assistant Secretary of the Navy Theodore Roosevelt charged; but President McKinley was not yet so moved, and he along with much of the financial establishment still hoped for peace. The President's more cautious response was to appoint a commission of inquiry and resume negotiations with Spain.

As passions mounted, administration circles began to fear that McKinley could not be reelected if he refused to submit to the war cries. Reluctantly, important business and financial leaders, who had little interest in expansion and none whatever in liberating the Cubans or avenging the destruction of the *Maine,* now joined the war hawks. Thus presidential adviser Elihu Root warned: "Fruitless attempts to hold back or retard the enormous momentum of the people bent upon war would result in the destruction of the President's power and influence, in depriving the country of its natural leader, in the elevation of the Silver Democracy to power." Under the weight of such counsels McKinley lost the will to resist. "I think ... possibly the President could have worked out the business without war," one of his intimates later wrote, "but the current was too strong, the demagogues too numerous, the fall elections too near."

On March 27, 1898, the United States sent an ultimatum to Spain demanding an immediate armistice, closing of the concentration camps, and Cuban independence if the United States decided it was advisable. McKinley did also send a note to Spain offering to arbitrate a settlement in Cuba; but before Spain could respond, the President began to compose his war message. On March 31, Spain ordered the end of its "reconcentration policy," agreed to an armistice if the rebels made the request, and agreed to submit the *Maine* issue to international arbitration. Spain did not, however, offer full independence for Cuba. On April 9, Spain announced a unilateral cease-fire.

On April 11, two days after Spain had offered a unilateral armistice, McKinley sent his unrevised war message to Congress, adding only that Spain had agreed to an armistice. On April 19, Congress enthusiastically passed, and the President then signed, a joint resolution authorizing use of force to compel the Spaniards to evacuate and secure Cuban independence. Neither McKinley nor Congress considered the Spanish offer of a unilateral armistice to be sufficient since they believed that the rebels would not cease hostilities with anything less than full independence. Senator Henry Teller of Colorado attached the "Teller Amendment" to the Resolution whereby the United States forever renounced any future annexation of Cuba.

The spirit of the Teller Amendment was to demonstrate that the United States was not going to war out of self-aggrandizement or an imperialistic desire to acquire territory through military conquest, but for the liberation of the oppressed Cuban people.

Spain responded by breaking diplomatic relations with the United States on April 21st, and William McKinley then gave Spain three days to withdraw from Cuba before it would be forcibly removed. Spain declared war on the United States on April 24th, and the United States declared war on Spain the following day. Although it is clear that Spain could not have avoided military hostilities with the United States without withdrawal from Cuba, the Spanish war declaration proved to be an error since it allowed the United States to attack Spanish possessions throughout the world. Without a declaration of war, it is possible that the war could have been limited to Cuba; but with the war declaration, the war would become much more costly to the Spanish than they had envisioned.

THE SPANISH-AMERICAN WAR

Due to Assistant Secretary of the Navy Theodore Roosevelt's advanced planning, only the American navy was prepared for hostilities. When Spain declared war, the United States army had only 28,000 men—enough to put down Native American uprisings, but insufficient for fighting a foreign war away from American soil. Modernization and expansion of the American naval fleet, however, had roughly paralleled the rise of interest in the Far East. By 1898 the United States navy was the fifth largest in the world and the Asiatic squadron was especially strong. Ten days before the destruction of the Maine, in accordance with standing plans put in place by the Assistant Secretary of the Navy Theodore Roosevelt, Commodore George Dewey was ordered to prepare to attack the Philippines in the event of war with Spain.

On May 1, in less than seven hours, Dewey destroyed an antiquated Spanish fleet in Manila Bay and changed the course of history, as he sunk the entire Spanish fleet in Manila without losing a single American ship. The United States would then dispatch 11,000 United States troops to the Philippines in an attempt to gain control of the Islands. Six weeks later 17,000 regular army troops and volunteers, including Theodore Roosevelt's "Rough Riders," landed in Cuba amidst incredible confusion. They were short of every basic supply from arms to medicine, but the Spanish army essentially had to wait for orders from Spain and did not engage the American troops during their five day disorganized landing at Daquiri. Nevertheless the American forces drove forward toward Santiago, winning a fierce engagement at El Caney and a major battle at San Juan Hill. San Juan Hill would become famous as the battle where future President Theodore Roosevelt and his "Rough Riders" took out a Spanish garrison. The strategic value of the assault on San Juan Hill by the Rough Riders is questionable, but the courage of Theordore Roosevelt during the battle was not. To his dying day Roosevelt would refer to the battle of San Juan Hill as, "That great day in my life."

At any rate, after the American victories at El Caney and San Juan Hill, the Americans besieged Santiago. Out of these engagements emerged the usual complement of heroes, but none so dramatic as Colonel Roosevelt. "The instant I received the order I sprang on my horse," he wrote, "and then my 'crowded hour' began."

The end of the war swiftly followed. On July 3 an American squadron commanded by Rear Admiral William T. Sampson destroyed the Spanish fleet after it emerged from Santiago Harbor under orders from Spain. Back in the Pacific, American forces took Wake Island the following day. On July 17 the Spanish ground force in Santiago was surrounded, and eight days later American troops occupied Puerto Rico with little opposition. An armistice ended further hostilities on August 12. In the Armistice, Spain agreed to cede Puerto Rico and Guam to the United States and withdraw from Cuba, thus giving the Cubans their independence and eliminating the primary reason America had to wage war with Spain. In September, the United States sent a delegation to Paris to negotiate with Spain the fate of Cuba and the Philippines.

All told, the United States lost 379 men in battle and 5,462 from disease and other causes. "It has been a splendid little war," Secretary of State John Hay remarked. Most Americans agreed, but at least 5,462 found it not so "splendid." American soldiers were sent into sub-tropical warfare with blue flannel clothing and rations that included "embalmed beef" and canned salt pork left over from the Civil War that had ended 33 years previously. Antibiotics had not yet been invented, so minor war wounds became life-threatening infections overnight and amputations of infected limbs were frequent. Due to sub-tropical microbes and rancid food rations, the most common cause of death, however, was diarrhea.

JUSTIFICATION FOR IMPERIALISM

The self-denying Teller Amendment had reflected the American people's humanitarian strain as distinct from their romantic imperialist impulses, but expansionist sentiment had grown to gale-like proportions

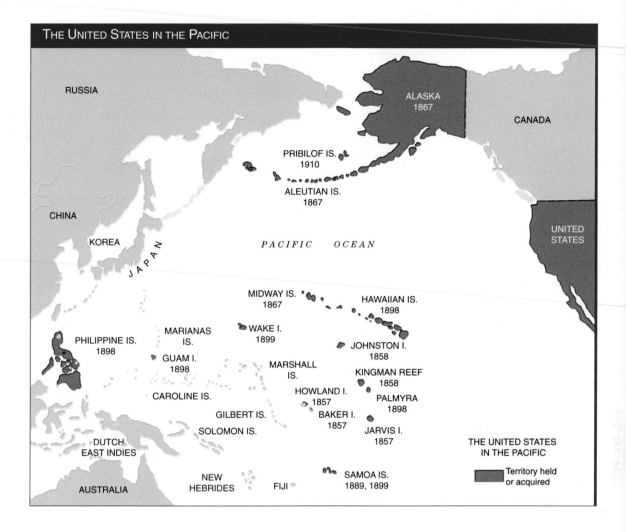

THE UNITED STATES IN THE PACIFIC

RUSSIA

ALASKA
1867

CANADA

PRIBILOF IS.
1910

ALEUTIAN IS.
1867

CHINA

KOREA

PACIFIC   OCEAN

UNITED
STATES

JAPAN

MIDWAY IS.
1867

HAWAIIAN IS.
1898

WAKE I.
1899

MARIANAS
IS.

PHILIPPINE IS.
1898

GUAM I.
1898

JOHNSTON I.
1858

MARSHALL
IS.

KINGMAN REEF
1858

CAROLINE IS.

HOWLAND I.
1857

PALMYRA
1898

GILBERT IS.

BAKER I.
1857

SOLOMON IS.

JARVIS I.
1857

DUTCH
EAST INDIES

THE UNITED STATES
IN THE PACIFIC

NEW
HEBRIDES

FIJI

SAMOA IS.
1889, 1899

Territory held
or acquired

AUSTRALIA

during the war. The Hawaiian annexation resolution rolled through Congress three months after hostilities began. Soon afterward the President also decided that Puerto Rico and Guam should be ceded to the United States.

The acquisitions quickly presented the American public with the question of what to do with the new possessions. In general, Americans were divided between imperialists, who desired American colonization and control of the newly acquired territories, and isolationists that wanted to keep the United States out of the "trappings of empire." In the case of Cuba, the Teller Amendment prevented the United States from directly annexing the island. In the case of Puerto Rico, there was little opposition to making it an American colony due to its close proximity to the United States, and most Americans, therefore, viewed its annexation as "natural." In addition, there was little opposition to the annexation of Guam, which was generally viewed as an insignificant and distant coaling station for the United States navy. The Philippines, however, became a major subject of debate, and significant opposition developed against bringing the Philippines into the United States as an American colony.

Anti-imperialists argued that the logic and spirit of the Teller Amendment was that the United States did not take foreign territory by force. For the same reasons that the United States relinquished any claim to Cuba, it should also absolve any claim to the Philippines. Anti-imperialists also argued that the annexation violated the United States Constitution, which did not authorize expansion by military conquest. Furthermore, the colonization of the Philippines was said to violate the spirit of the Declaration of Independence since there was not talk of the Philippines ever becoming an American state, and the United States would be governing the Philippines without the consent of the governed. Nativists opposed annexation of the Philippines for xenophobic reasons, arguing that no nation of non-whites should be placed under the American flag or the American race would surely be mongrelized. Finally, labor unions opposed annexation out of fear of cheap labor competition.

In contrast, big business favored annexation for increased trade and investment opportunities. The main argument of the imperialists, however, was that the Philippines could not be returned to Spain due to Spanish oppression; but it also could not be granted independence immediately because the Filipino people were incapable of ruling themselves. Consequently, the only alternative was annexation and colonization. President McKinley was persuaded by these arguments and made plans to retain Manila, finally deciding to annex the entire Philippine archipelago.

McKinley later explained his decision to a delegation of Methodist clergymen:

> I went down on my knees and prayed God Almighty for light and guidance more than one night. And one night late it came to me this way—I don't know how it was, but it came: (1) that we could not give them back to Spain—that would be cowardly and dishonorable; (2) that we could not turn them over to France or Germany—our commercial rivals in the Orient—that would be bad business and discreditable; (3) that we could not leave them to themselves—they were unfit for self-government—and they would soon have anarchy and misrule over there worse than Spain's was; and (4) that there was nothing left for us to do but to take them all, and to educate the Filipinos, and uplift and civilize and Christianize them, and by God's grace do the very best we could by them, as our fellow men for whom Christ also died. And then I went to bed and went to sleep and slept soundly.

Evidently, McKinley was convinced that "Christianization" of the islands had not occurred under the rule of Catholic Spain, but McKinley's most fundamental reason was the third: desire for a commercial outpost in the Far East. As Mark Hanna declared, "If it is commercialism to want the possession of a strategic point giving the American people an opportunity to maintain a foothold in the markets of … China, for God's sake let us have commercialism."

All through the summer and autumn of 1898 newspapers, religious publications, and civic leaders called for retention of the Philippines for the same reasons the President gave the Methodist clergymen. McKinley sensed the force of this opinion, but he wanted to be certain that the people as a whole would approve such a radical break with tradition. So in October, with a stenographer at his side to time the applause given his various soundings, he toured the Middle West. Convinced finally that national sentiment favored annexation, he cabled his peace commissioners in Paris to demand cession of the entire Philippine archipelago. In December, the American delegates signed the Treaty of Paris, officially ending hostilities.

THE TREATY OF PARIS

By the terms of the treaty signed on December 10, 1898, Spain ceded the Philippines to the United States for $20 million. Spain also acknowledged Cuban independence and ceded Puerto Rico and Guam outright to the United States. Spain also agreed to the assumption of some $400 million in Cuban debt, much of which was owed to Spanish companies. Inhabitants of all the territories were ensured religious freedom, and Congress would determine the civil rights of all citizens in all the territories. Two months later the Senate ratified the treaty. It would probably have been defeated had not a substantial number of anti-imperialist Republicans put party loyalty above conscience. It would also have been defeated if Bryan had not influenced a handful of Democrats to support it in the hope that imperialism would then become the dominant issue in the presidential campaign of 1900.

THE AFTERMATH OF CONQUEST

The ramifications of the Spanish-American War were that the United States had suddenly become recognized internationally as a world power. In the words of the French Foreign Minister, "The United States is now seated at the table where the great game is played and cannot leave it." For the first time in American history, the United

States had acquired colonies in the form of Guam, Puerto Rico, and the Philippines.

By 1900, however, the United States tasted the first bitter fruits of imperialism. Filipino partisans had begun a fierce fight for independence from Spain before the Americans arrived. They turned against their new American masters in 1899 and inflicted losses on the American occupation troops heavier than those suffered in the war with Spain. Filipino rebels had fought with the Americans against Spain during the Spanish-American War and felt betrayed by the American refusal to withdraw and the failure of the United States to grant Filipinos their independence. What resulted is perhaps the least remembered, but seriously deadly, war in American history. The war to subdue the Filipino uprising involved 200,000 United States troops (only 17,000 Americans landed on Cuba), and cost the lives of 4,300 United States soldiers—more than ten times the battle deaths in the Spanish-American War. The war against Spain had lasted only three months, but the war in the Philippines would last from late 1898 into 1902; and an estimated 200,000 Filipinos were killed.

Americans at first believed that the rebel faction under Emilio Aguinaldo was a minority renegade faction; but by 1900, General Arthur MacArthur wrote, "I have been reluctantly compelled to believe that the Filipino masses are loyal to Aguinaldo." The rebels did not confront the superior American force head on and, instead, used guerrilla tactics. The United States army viewed such tactics not as warfare, but as murder, and their enemy not as an army, but as murderers. Consequently, captured Filipino rebels were tried by the United States army in military tribunals and executed. In general, American soldiers viewed the "little brown men" as subhuman and unworthy of mercy. General Arthur MacArthur perpetuated these sentiments with orders to United States soldiers to "Kill and burn, the more you kill and burn, the better it will please me. Shoot everyone over age ten." Not until the Americans resorted to methods as ruthless as those used by the Spanish in Cuba were the Filipinos finally defeated formally in 1902. Finally, Emilio Aguinaldo was captured in 1901 and forced to issue a call to the rebels to put down their arms in exchange for his life. Governor William Howard Taft implemented some home rule reforms, and the guerilla warfare slowly dissipated, though some activities continued through 1906.

Partial restitution followed. McKinley, and especially Theodore Roosevelt, took literally the poet's charge to "Take up the White Man's burden—Send forth the best ye breed." McKinley instituted and Roosevelt greatly strengthened a political system designed to prepare the Filipinos for self-government. Schools were built, small farmers were installed on lands purchased from the Catholic Church, and numerous other reforms were instituted.

Major criticisms of the American activities in the Philippines, however, were widespread. Mark Twain suggested painting black over the stars and stripes and adding a skull and crossbones. Yale professor William Graham Sumner stated, "We talk of civilizing lower races, but we have never done it yet. Instead, we have exterminated them." *The New York World* printed the poignant short political poem with the lines, "We've taken up the white man's burden of ebony and brown; Now will you kindly tell us, Rudyard, how we may put it down."

Meanwhile, the United States observed the form of the Teller Amendment by granting nominal independence to Cuba, though that independence involved temporary rule by the United States military. Certain benefits to the Cuban people followed, above all in public health; but in addition, insisting that Cuba accept an agreement to this effect—the Platt Amendment—the United States assured itself control of Cuba's foreign affairs and the right to intervene to protect Cuban national independence and just government. The Platt Amendment, which Congress passed in 1901, became attached to the Cuban Constitution. The amendment forbade Cuba from signing foreign treaties or borrowing money without approval from the United States. This amendment also allowed the United States to intervene militarily, at any time, to preserve order or property. As a consequence, the United States would intervene militarily in Cuba four times by 1921, including assuming control of the government from 1906–1909. The United States was also granted a permanent naval base in Cuba at Guantanamo Bay. In May 1902, American forces withdrew, but the United States retained the naval base at Guantanamo Bay under what became a permanent lease.

Anti-imperialists in the United States condemned the new Cuban Constitution and the Platt Amendment, but President Theodore Roosevelt denounced the opposition as "unhung traitors, liars, slanderers, and scandal mongers."

In 1902, an American Reciprocity Treaty with Cuba lowered duties on Cuban exports to the United States, and United States trade with Cuba quadrupled by 1913. The economic advantages as accrued to the United States from its new island possessions were offset, somewhat, in the long run by vast American expenditures for civic and social improvement. From the outset, moreover, the Philippines were a military liability—"our heel of Achilles," as Roosevelt was calling them by 1907, due to the distance across the Pacific and difficulty for America in defending the islands if they were attacked by their much closer and powerful neighbor, Japan.

Although the United States slowly instituted democratic forms of government on those islands it owned outright, it remains an open question whether on balance native peoples fared better or worse under American rule. Hawaii prospered, but largely as the virtual fief of a half-dozen giant American corporations. Puerto Rico, short of natural resources, suffered from absentee ownership and overpopulation induced by American public health measures, and the Philippines concentrated too much on the production of raw materials for the American market. Everywhere, to be sure, the material standard of living improved considerably; yet the old social structures and extremes of wealth and poverty persisted, while much of the islanders' cultural integrity disintegrated.

THE FAR EAST

THE OPEN DOOR

The quest for trade together with missionary zeal soon drove the United States into the vortex of Far Eastern affairs. Senator Albert J. Beveridge summed it all up in January 1900:

> The Philippines are ours forever. ... And just beyond ... are China's illimitable markets. We will not retreat from either ... will not renounce our part in the mission of our race, trustees under God, of the civilization of the world. ... The power that rules the Pacific is the power that rules the world.

Senator Albert J. Beveridge *(Library of Congress)*

In another sense, American policy was grounded more on fear than on the aggressive territorial designs of businessmen and romantics. All the great powers—Japan, Russia, France, Britain, and Germany—and two of the smaller ones, Belgium and Holland, were more stridently imperialistic than the United States during this period. Virtually all Africa had already been taken over by Europeans with an agreement drawn up dividing Africa between the powers of Europe at the Conference of Berlin in 1884. Southeast Asia had become the province of the British, the Dutch, and the French. Japan was bursting to take over Korea, and Germany aspired to whatever was available in the Far East, North Africa, or South America. However great the ultimate tragedy of the United States' acquisition of the Philippines, McKinley had correctly assayed French and German designs in making his decision to acquire them.

Alone among the great powers, the United States did not have a colony in Africa, nor did it have a "sphere of influence" in China where the great powers had been carving out spheres of influence in that unhappy land for several years. The United States feared that it could be denied commercial opportunities, both in the realms of trade and in natural resource extraction in any country's sphere of influence. In 1899 the British began to evade payment of the tariff, the Chinese government's main source of revenue. Such action, if adopted by the French, Germans, Russians, and Japanese (Italy also sought, but failed to get, a sphere of influence), would have forced the collapse of the Beijing government and the dismemberment of all China. Concerned by the implications to American business and persuaded, in any event, that freedom to trade was in the interest of everyone, Secretary of State John Hay sent a round of "Open Door" notes to the powers in 1899 and 1900. The notes proposed, in summary, that Chinese officials continue to collect tariffs and that all nations be guaranteed equal trade rights throughout China. Although most of the powers simply ignored Hay's note, and Russia outright rejected it, Hay baldly announced their unanimous acceptance.

BOXER REBELLION

The European attitudes toward the Open Door principle would change in 1900 when a Chinese revolutionary group known as I Ho Chuan (Righteous and Harmonious Fists) or "Boxers" staged a rebellion against foreigners in China. The Boxers' goal was to expel all of the

In 1900 the Boxers staged a rebellion against foreigners in China (*Library of Congress*)

foreign influences from China. The Boxers declared, "The will of heaven is that the telegraph wires be cut first, the railways torn up, and then shall the foreign devils be decapitated." The Boxers seized the British Embassy in Beijing and captured the entire diplomatic corps, of not only Great Britain but also the United States, Japan, Russia, and France.

The United States, France, Russia, Germany, and England responded by sending an international expeditionary force of 20,000 soldiers (5,000 of whom were American) to China to put down the rebellion. In August 1900, the Boxers were defeated, and the diplomatic hostages were rescued. Following this successful international cooperation among the great powers during the Boxer Rebellion, both England and Germany agreed to the Open Door principle. While each country favored their own access and special privileges in China, all feared most the dominance of China by any one power. Consequently, the Open Door principle worked because it was consistent with the balance of power game that the great powers were engaged in.

The weakness of the Open Door notes was less one of principle than of power. As Admiral Mahan pointed out at this time, the United States lacked the will and the military strength to enforce them. Nevertheless, they marked a heady triumph for the proponents of the "Large Policy," commanding, in the words of one historian, "a measure of interest and support over the years second only to that accorded the Monroe Doctrine." In particular, they led to deep and continuing involvement in the Far East by the United States and, ultimately, to conflict with Japan.

ROOSEVELT'S POLICY

More than any other twentieth-century American President, Theodore Roosevelt viewed the Open Door policy with a measure of realism. He felt that the United States could maintain a legitimate interest in the Far East only by recognizing Japan's need for raw materials and markets. He also believed—even more strongly— that Japan was a natural counterpoise to Russia, whose failure to withdraw from southern Manchuria until 1907 he termed an act of "well-nigh incredible mendacity." Thus he approved the Japanese-British naval alliance of 1902, and he privately accepted Japanese suzerainty in Korea in 1905.

By then Roosevelt was mediating the Russo-Japanese War of 1904–1905 at the request of the victorious but nearly insolvent Japanese. In 1895, Russia had played a role in preventing the lease of a port on the Liaodong Biao (Liaotung Peninsula) in southern Manchuria from China to Japan. Russia also left their troops in Manchuria after the Boxer Rebellion. Since Japan desired control of Manchuria, it attempted unsuccessfully to negotiate a settlement with Russia that would secure Japanese interests. In 1904, Japan launched a surprise attack on the Russian Pacific Fleet and sunk it in the Harbor of Port Arthur (Dandong) in Southern Manchuria at Korea Bay. Japan then launched a ground war, attacking the Russian troops that were stationed in Korea and Manchuria. Both sides rushed massive armies to the area, and soon a full scale ground war developed with over 400,000 troops involved on each side. Nevertheless, the Japanese pushed the Russians out of Korea and captured Mukden (Shenyang), the principal city in Manchuria. In May 1905, the Russian Baltic Fleet, the pride of Russia, arrived from Europe, but the superior Japanese navy sunk it upon arrival in the Korean Strait.

Though Japan had won most of the battles and accomplished most of their objectives, it found itself embroiled in an expensive ground war with Russia and sought a negotiated settlement. Consequently, the Japanese Minister to the United States, Kogoro Takahira, asked Roosevelt to intervene to mediate a peace settlement.

The American position had been basically neutral; but, in reality, Theodore Roosevelt had originally favored Japan because the Russians had refused to accept the Open Door, and he believed that Japan would do so. Roosevelt was heard to exclaim that it was "Bully the way the Japs started that war," and he referred to the Russian Czar Nicholas II as a "preposterous little creature."

Peace talks were held at Portsmouth, New Hampshire, in August of 1905, with Theodore Roosevelt as the mediator. Basically, he sought to preserve the balance of power and to protect the Open Door, but he also deemed it his moral duty to end the carnage as soon as possible. He further hoped to cement Japanese-American relations. Roosevelt decided

Czar Nicholas II *(Library of Congress)*

to divide the disputed Sakhalin Island (North of Japan and East of the Russian Pacific coast) between Russia and Japan, and both countries accepted the solution. As the victors in the conflict, Japan demanded $600 million in war reparations from the Russians, but the Russians refused. Japan finally relented on the reparations issue essentially to cut their losses and prevent spending more on the costly ground war. Japan did, however, gain the Liaotung Peninsula, and Russia agreed to recognize Japanese interests in Korea. Manchuria was returned to China, and both Russia and Japan were to withdraw their troops from Manchuria.

Roosevelt's mediation fulfilled the first three of his goals in ending the war, preserving the balance of power, and protecting the Open Door in China; but it failed in the fourth goal of improving American-Japanese relations because the Japanese blamed him for Russia's refusal to pay a war indemnity or to cede to them all of Sakhalin Island. Japan viewed the results as unfair because they had taken all of Sakhalin Island in the war and, as the victors, they believed they were due reparations. Japan did, however, emerge from the conflict as the dominant power in Asia; but the relations between both Japan and Russia and the United States worsened, as both Japan and Russia were discontent with the results of the Treaty of Portsmouth and America was their scapegoat.

A decision by the San Francisco board of education to segregate the 93 Japanese students in the city's public schools, noting the "yellow peril," dealt Japanese-American relations a more serious blow in October 1906. Roosevelt labeled the segregation order "a crime against a friendly nation" and threatened to use "all the forces, civil and military," at his command to rectify it. He then called the board members to the White House. They agreed to reverse the order if Japan would curb the emigration of peasants and laborers. A "Gentlemen's Agreement" to that effect was arranged in 1907. Japan agreed to voluntarily prohibit issuing passports to persons seeking to come to the United States for employment, but the Japanese again had reasons for animosity against the United States.

Having thus deferred to Japanese sensibilities, Roosevelt characteristically decided to flaunt American strength by sending the battle fleet on a world cruise in 1907. Roosevelt perceived that the United States could not successfully defend the Philippines in case of a Japanese attack; therefore, he pushed Congress unsuccessfully to grant Philippine independence as quickly as possible. At the same time, Roosevelt desired to show Japan that the United States had the power to hold on to its possessions. The United States had embarked on a naval building program (as had Japan) during Roosevelt's presidency. Persuaded by the arguments of Alfred Thayer Mahan that naval power was most important, the United States Navy budget increased from $56 million in 1900 to $117 million in 1905.

To impress the Japanese, Roosevelt had the navy painted white, to make it appear more impressive, and ordered it to sail around the world, especially to Japan along the way, in a show of strength. Congress refused to fund the expedition as both wasteful and provocative, but Roosevelt ordered the fleet to Japan anyway. Roosevelt stated that he had enough funding to get the navy half way around the world, so Congress could worry about getting them back. Before the fleet returned, however, the President made another realistic concession to Japan. By the Root-Takahira Agreement of November 1908 the United States probably, though not certainly, recognized Japan's economic ascendancy in Manchuria in return for a reaffirmation of the status quo in the Pacific and the Open Door in China.

The sail of the "Great White Fleet" also violated Roosevelt's own policy of "Speak softly, but carry a big stick." The show of force certainly was "big stick," but it hardly qualified as "speaking softly." Roosevelt was also fond of saying, "Don't flourish a revolver unless you intend to shoot." The sail of the "Great White Fleet" then appears to be a violation of Roosevelt's own advice.

NEW FAR EASTERN POLICIES

Neither Taft nor Wilson shared Roosevelt's view that the United States should accept Japanese preeminence in East Asia. As early as 1910 Roosevelt warned Taft that China was "weak and unreliable" and 'that the United States should abandon its commercial aspirations in Manchuria. Taft, however, believed too strongly in the fiction of Chinese independence and was too enamored of trade possibilities to agree. He followed instead a policy of "active intervention to secure for our merchandise and our capitalists opportunity for profitable investment." He permitted his Secretary of State, Philander C. Knox, to demand American participation in an international bankers' consortium to build a network of railways in China. Taft also allowed Knox, who was alarmed by the consolidation of Japanese and Russian influence in Manchuria, to propose internationalization of that province's railways.

President Wilson proved no less determined than Taft to maintain the Open Door. "Our industries have expanded to such a point that they will burst their jackets if they cannot find a free outlet to the markets of the world," he declared in 1912. "Our domestic markets no longer suffice. We need foreign markets." Essentially, however, he conceived of China, which had been penetrated by Christian missionaries, in moralistic terms. He opposed the bankers' consortium because he feared that it would result in European domination, not because he intended to withdraw from the Far East. The United States, he declared at the time, intends "to participate, and participate very generously, in the opening to the Chinese and to the use of the world the almost untouched and perhaps unlimited resources of China." He then urged American bankers to act independently.

Wilson perceived that the outbreak of World War I in 1914 created a power vacuum in China because of the great powers' involvement in Europe. When Japan tried to make China into a satellite by imposing 21 far-reaching demands in 1915, the President vigorously defended Chinese integrity and independence. To forestall Japanese economic domination of China, Wilson and Secretary of State Robert Lansing proposed formation of a new four-power consortium to supply China with private capital. With Wilson's approval, Lansing also rejected Tokyo's demand that the United States recognize Japan's paramount interest in China just as Japan had recognized America's in Mexico. Finally, they arranged a *modus vivendi*—the Lansing-Ishii Agreement of November 1917. By this document the United States recognized Japan's special interests in China while Japan reaffirmed its support of the Open Door and agreed not to use the war situation to seek new privileges in China.

THE CARIBBEAN

PANAMA

President Roosevelt's Caribbean diplomacy aimed to establish stability, security, and U.S. supremacy in the area. Soon after taking office he arranged negotiation of the second Hay-Pauncefote Treaty (1901), by which Great Britain granted the United States the right to build and defend a canal across Central America. Early American planning envisioned a Nicaraguan route, but volcanic activity near the proposed Nicaraguan canal zone, combined with a drop in price from the bankrupt French New Panama Canal Company from $110 million to $40 million to purchase the rights to a canal route through Panama, caused Roosevelt to seize the opportunity to buy the French company's rights. The President also had Secretary of State Hay draw up a treaty to grant $10 million and $250,000 annual 100-year rental for the proposed six-mile wide canal zone to Colombia, which owned Panama. The United States would also pay $40 million to the French New Panama Canal Company for their assets.

The construction of the Panama Canal *(Library of Congress)*

After signing the treaty, Colombia's foreign minister was told to delay signing until he received further instruction. It was too late, however; the Treaty had been signed, and the United States Senate quickly ratified the Treaty. Colombia's Senate, however, rejected the Treaty and demanded $15 million up front instead of $10 million; and they also demanded $10 million of the $40 million that was earmarked for the New Panama Canal Company. The Colombian senate's indignant rejection of this arrangement infuriated Roosevelt. Privately castigating the Colombians as "Dagos" and "inefficient bandits," he tacitly encouraged agents of the French company to stimulate a Panamanian revolution against Colombia. The Panamanians quickly reasoned that they could become independent and then reap the benefits of the canal for themselves, separate from Colombia. When the revolution broke out on November 3, 1903, Roosevelt sent an American warship to the scene under conditions that assured the revolutionaries' success. In a near bloodless coup (two deaths—a man and a donkey), the Panamanian rebels took over the government by bribing Colombian military and government officials that had been in charge of Panama. A 500-man Colombian army sent to Panama to put down the insurrection never made it to Panama City because the Panama Canal Company, suspiciously, had no railroad cars available to transport them and travel through the Panamanian rain forest was virtually impossible without the railway. Three days later Roosevelt recognized the new Republic of Panama and approved a treaty, negotiated by Panama's new minister (Philippe Vunau-Varilla, an agent of the French company), authorizing the United States to build the canal. The treaty was similar to the original Canal Treaty with Colombia except that the United States Canal Zone was widened from six miles to 10, and the United States assumed all rights, power and authority within the zone to the exclusion of Panama. The United States also guaranteed the independence of Panama, thus making Panama a United States "protectorate."

Roosevelt later claimed that "our course was straightforward and in absolute accord with the highest standards of international morality." Then in 1911, however, he blurted, "I took the Canal Zone and let Congress debate, and while the debate goes on the canal also does." Ten years after that confession, the United States agreed to pay Colombia $25 million. By then Roosevelt was dead, but the memory of his high-handedness lived on.

Meanwhile, the first great government corporation in American history overcame extraordinary health and engineering problems to complete construction of the Panama Canal. It was opened to the commerce of the world on August 15, 1914, on equal terms to all nations—but only because President Wilson had persuaded Congress to repeal an act of 1912 that exempted American coastwise traffic from payment of tolls. The Panama Canal was completed at a cost of $352 million. Fifty-six hundred people died in constructing the canal, most from malaria or yellow fever.

THE ROOSEVELT COROLLARY

The need to defend the Panama Canal soon drew the United States deeply into the affairs of the Caribbean. Neither Roosevelt nor his successors wanted this. As the President said of the Dominican Republic, he had "about the same desire to annex it as a gorged boa constrictor might have to swallow a porcupine wrong-end-to." The poverty, instability, and corruption of the Caribbean countries invited European penetration, however, and even such an apostle of peace as William Jennings Bryan saw no recourse but to make the Caribbean Sea an American lake.

The first serious incident occurred in December 1902, when the Germans, cooperating with the British in a blockade of Venezuela, bombarded a port town and threatened to take control of Venezuelan

THE UNITED STATES AND LATIN AMERICA

customs in order to force payment of debts owed their citizens. Roosevelt and the American people reacted militantly. Theodore Roosevelt referred to Venezuelan leader Cipriano Castro as "an unspeakable villainous little monkey," but offered arbitration of the dispute, which Venezuela rejected, as did Germany until Roosevelt threatened to send the United States Navy to Venezuela.

Kaiser Wilhelm II, reluctant to add the United States to the growing list of nations hostile to Germany, accepted Roosevelt's suggestion for mediation, as did Britain. The Hague Tribunal settled the dispute in 1904, and ruled against Venezuela. Latin Americans feared the consequences of the Hague decision because they feared it would encourage the use of force in international disputes and increase the likelihood of the use of force in international disputes, therefore increasing the likelihood that European powers would use force to achieve their goals in Latin America.

By 1904 the Dominican Republic had been forced by the German, Italian, and Spanish governments to sign protocols for the payment of debts, totaling $32 million. The Dominicans thereupon requested Roosevelt "to establish some kind of protectorate over the islands," as the President phrased it. Roosevelt recognized that the Europeans could be expected to intervene militarily as they had done successfully in the Venezuelan crisis. In 1905 the United States assumed control of Dominican customs so that funds could be allotted to the European creditors. The United States collected the customs duties for the Dominican Republic, using 55 percent of the duties collected to pay debts and leaving the remaining 45 percent for the government of the Dominican Republic.

To preclude future intervention in the Caribbean by Europeans, Roosevelt also declared that the United States was empowered to serve as an international police force in the event of "chronic wrongdoing, or an impotence which results in a general loosening of the ties of civilized society." This, the so-called Roosevelt Corollary to the Monroe Doctrine, transformed the original doctrine from an external protective device to a justification for internal intervention by the United States. Two years later the President sent American troops into Cuba to avert a revolution. Then in 1911, the President of the Dominican Republic was assassinated, and rebels from neighboring Haiti were pillaging the country. The United States had to shut down the customs houses until September 1912, when United States marines arrived to restore order. The United States would militarily occupy the Dominican Republic until 1920.

Also in 1911, the Nicaraguan government threatened to cancel mine concessions to the United States and executed two Americans. President William Howard Taft sent 2,500 United States marines to Nicaragua to depose the government and help establish the Samoza regime that would be friendlier to the United States. The United States signed a treaty with Nicaragua, similar to the one with the Dominican Republic, which would have placed the United States government in charge of the Nicaraguan customs house. The United States Senate, however, rejected the Nicaraguan treaty along with a similar one with Honduras, but the State Department helped private New York banks take over the Customs House of Nicaragua in 1912. In 1912, the United States sent another 2,000 troops to put down another Nicaraguan revolt, and United States troops would stay in Nicaragua until 1933.

DOLLAR DIPLOMACY

President Taft expanded upon Roosevelt's imperialistic policies. Meanwhile he and Secretary of State Philander Knox devised a program called "dollar diplomacy"—use of private American capital, often against both the desire and the judgment of the bankers concerned—to displace European bondholders and concessionaires in Latin America. The idea of Dollar Diplomacy was to wield influence in Latin America through trade and investment rather than direct military control. Over the years this drive for stability and protection of the Panama Canal resulted in a clear pattern of American support of ultraconservative and often dictatorial governments in much of Central America and the Caribbean.

Philander Knox *(Library of Congress)*

WILSON'S MISSION: IDEAL AND REALITY

Woodrow Wilson's vision in foreign policy was to create a progressive world built on capitalism, free trade, and moralism. Wilson's foreign policy was, in part, a reflection of his own, personal, inflexible moralism. Wilson referred to his foreign policy as "releasing the intelligence of America for the service of mankind." Like those before him, however, Wilson pushed for the Open Door in China and sought to resist Japanese expansion in Asia. Wilson denounced both Roosevelt's "big stick" and Taft's "Dollar Diplomacy." President Wilson was not averse to using dollar diplomacy when circumstances seemed to require it, however; and he and Secretary of State William Jennings Bryan also conceived that they had a mission to democratize the corrupt and revolution-ridden Caribbean republics. "We can have no sympathy with those who seek to seize the power of government to advance their own personal interests or ambition," Wilson warned in a public statement on March 11, 1913. "As friends, therefore, we shall prefer those who act in the interest of peace and honor, who protect private rights and respect the restraints of constitutional provision."

Wilson, however, simultaneously adhered to the Monroe Doctrine and the Roosevelt Corollary, a path that produced policy decisions that would be every bit as "big stick" as Roosevelt but one linked to Wilson's own sense of moral idealism. Unparalleled diplomatic and military intervention in the Caribbean and Mexico followed. The Wilson administration regularized the occupation of Nicaragua, which remained occupied by United States marines until 1933. It sent marines to Haiti and, by imposing a puppet but nominally democratic regime in 1915, made that state a virtual protectorate of the United States. It dispatched marines to the Dominican Republic in 1916 and there governed it directly through military officers. It also fostered road building, school construction, and public health projects. In 1913, the Wilson administration attempted to make amends to Colombia for the Panama affair and signed a treaty whereby the United States agreed to pay Colombia $5 million in damages. The Senate, however, was less apologetic and voted down Wilson's Treaty of apology.

TRIUMPH AND TRAGEDY IN MEXICO

Meanwhile, Wilson embarked on a bold new policy toward Mexico where the classic Latin American alliance of dictator, Church, and foreign investors had provoked a convulsive political upheaval. By 1911 more than half of Mexico's oil, two thirds of its railroads, and three fourths of its mines and smelters were owned by Americans. Much of the remaining oil was British-owned. The Catholic Church was the largest landowner although William Randolph Hearst and other Americans also had huge holdings. The average Mexican peon or industrial worker lived in abject poverty.

Against this background, a revolution erupted in 1910. The dictator Porfirio Díaz, who had ruled Mexico for 40 years, was finally driven out in May 1911 by a group of middle-class intellectuals headed by a constitutionalist named Francisco Madero. Madero promised to bring democracy to Mexico, but American conservatives opposed Madero because he had brought instability that threatened American investments in Mexico. Americans owned 40 percent of the property in Mexico at the time, more than was owned by the people of Mexico. Less than a year later, and one month before the inauguration of Woodrow Wilson, the United States Ambassador to Mexico Henry Lane Wilson (no relation to Woodrow) gave support to a conservative military general Victoriano Huerta, who planned to oust Madero in a coup. Huerta asked Ambassador Wilson what he should do with Madero, and Wilson replied, "Take whatever steps are necessary to bring peace."

Before Madero could institute his "democratic reforms," counter-revolutionary forces under the army's chief general Victoriano Huerta overthrew Madero. Huerta, then became president of Mexico amid revolutionary upheaval; and men working for Huerta executed Madero when he was shot "trying to escape" on the way to prison.

Wilson's first break with tradition came when he withheld recognition from Huerta on the grounds that the United States should henceforth cooperate only with governments based on the unquestioned consent of the governed. Unaware of America's tacit approval of Huerta's execution of Madero, Wilson referred to the Huerta government as a "government of butchers." Wilson announced that the United States would extend recognition only to those governments built on "orderly processes of just government based on law, not upon arbitrary or irregular force." This marked the first time in American history that human rights influenced the recognition of a foreign government. In the words of Wilson, "morality, not material interest, must guide United States foreign policy." Wilson denounced Huerta as a "drunken brute" and publicly called for his resignation. Next, he persuaded the British to withdraw their support from Huerta. Wilson informed the British foreign minister that the United States intended to not only depose Huerta, but also to "exert every influence it can to secure Mexico a better government under which all contracts and business concessions will be safer than ever." Wilson pressured other European governments to denounce and sanction the Huerta government; but the Europeans refused, viewing Huerta as another Diaz who would bring stability to Mexico.

In the meantime, Wilson sought a means by which he could depose Huerta militarily. Then he brought his new policy to fruition by offering to aid Huerta's chief antagonist, the constitutional reformer Venustiano Carranza. Carranza wanted only arms, and on February 3, 1914, Wilson lifted an arms embargo instituted by Taft.

Huerta's strength nevertheless continued to increase, partly as a result of resentment over United States interference. Wilson's sense of frustration became more acute. Seizing finally on a trivial incident at Tampico, where several United States naval officers from the *U.S.S. Dolphin* were arrested by Mexican authorities for selling fuel to enemies of the Huerta government. Seeking to avoid a confrontation with the United States, the Mexicans at Tampico quickly released the U.S. soldiers. Even though the Mexican officer in command personally apologized, the commander of the *U.S.S. Dolphin* demanded a 21-gun salute as an official apology. When Mexico refused the 21-gun salute apology, Wilson used the opportunity to order a blockade of Vera Cruz on the Southeast Mexican coast to prevent arms shipments from Germany from reaching Huerta's army. Wilson asked Congress for authority to move against the Mexican dictator. Congress had not responded by April 21, 1914, when Wilson ordered the

The *U.S.S. Dolphin* (Library of Congress)

fleet to occupy Vera Cruz to prevent a German ship from unloading ammunition. In the resultant action, 800 United States troops engaged Huerta's Mexican federal troops, and 19 Americans and 126 Mexicans were killed. Over 3,000 more Americans landed on April 22, and over 7,000 United States troops were in Vera Cruz by the end of April to take control of the city. United States troops would occupy Vera Cruz until November 1914.

Simultaneously, Wilson was supplying arms to the opposition rebels of Venustiano Carranza. Wilson offered the use of American troops to Carranza for the purpose of ousting Huerta, but Carranza refused them, knowing he could never have popular support in Mexico if he appeared to be a puppet of Wilson and the United States.

The President's militant action horrified peace-loving Americans and provoked even Carranza to threaten full-scale resistance should American troops march on Mexico City. Abandoned by the liberals of both Mexico and the United States, Wilson resolved his dilemma by agreeing to mediation by the "ABC powers"—Argentina, Brazil, and Chile. Huerta eventually resigned in favor of Carranza, who became *de facto* president of Mexico on August 20, 1914, and Huerta fled to Germany.

Yet Wilson continued to press Carranza to accept his guidance, pushing for democratic reforms. He warned against mass executions and made it clear that he would oppose expropriation of the vast holdings of Americans and other foreigners. Carranza delayed the implementation of democratic reforms, however, arguing that the rebellions of Pancho Villa and Emiliano Zapata continued unabated against the government and putting down these revolts took precedent. Wilson became disenchanted with Carranza over his failure to quickly implement reforms; and then, putting much faith in the unpredictable Pancho Villa—about whose role in history debate still rages—Wilson began to support him against Carranza. Armed with Wilson's weapons and provisions, Villa at one point captured Mexico City and ousted the Carranza government. Villa also was slow to implement democratic reforms, however, causing Wilson to once again aid Carranza. Thereupon, Carranza broadened his own reform program while his leading general, Alvaro Obregon, crushed Villa's armies in the field and restored Carranzas government.

Back in Washington, American conservatives put the President under tremendous pressure to mount a full-scale invasion of Mexico. The Catholic hierarchy, the Hearst press, oil and other corporate interests, and ultranationalists like Theodore Roosevelt all urged him to act, but Wilson held firm and in October 1915 extended *de facto* recognition, but not full recognition, to the Carranza regime.

Reduced to banditry, Villa now strove to regain his power by inciting the United States to war. Early in 1916 he murdered 18 American engineers in northern Mexico when he stopped a train carrying the American citizens; and Wilson once again braved a nearly overpowering call for war. Then, in a bold sortie into New Mexico, Villa killed 17 more Americans when he crossed the border into the United States and burned the town of Columbus, New Mexico.

The President thereupon ordered Brigadier General John J. Pershing and a United States expeditionary force of 7,000 troops to pursue Villa into Mexico. Villa fled south and evaded the pursuing United States army, which penetrated some 300 miles south of the Mexican border. Though the United States army never did find Villa, they engaged Carranza's regular Mexican troops on several occasions, killing 40 of Carranza's federal troops at Parral in April 1916. In late June, Carranza's troops killed 12 Americans and captured 23 in a skirmish at Carrizal. More incidents followed, and for the third time conservatives and ultranationalists called angrily for an all-out invasion.

Wilson responded by mobilizing the National Guard along the Mexican border, but he refused to change the expedition's limited objective. Carranza accused Wilson of secretly planning to occupy northern Mexico and wrote a letter to Wilson threatening war if Wilson did not withdraw. Wilson at first refused. Finally, in late January 1917, he ordered the withdrawal of what was now called the "perishing expedition" in the media because of the escalating problems surrounding World War I in Europe and what appeared to be impending conflict with Germany. In March 1917, one month before the United States entered World War I, Wilson granted full recognition to the Carranza government. The move was perhaps an indicator of the direction that Wilson intended to lead America as he became convinced that America could no longer remain neutral in the Great War. The instability in Mexico would have to be ignored so that Wilson could turn his attention to the larger problem looming in Europe.

8

AMERICA AND THE GREAT WAR, 1914–1918

(Library of Congress)

WORLD WAR I: EUROPE BEFORE THE WAR

Prior to World War I, the major powers of Europe were divided into two great military alliances. The "Triple Entente" united Britain, France, and Russia. If any of the three were attacked, the others were bound to come to their aid. The purpose of the alliance was to deter any other country from attacking any of the three and thus, supposedly, preserve the peace. The Central European powers of Germany, the Austro-Hungarian Empire, and Italy were allied in a similar arrangement known as the "Triple Alliance."

Each country had its own security concerns, and several had expansionist desires that could be expected to be resisted by other countries. England had been the dominant power in the nineteenth century and still had the world's largest colonial empire from which to draw resources and the most powerful navy. To enhance its advantage, England converted its navy from coal to oil in 1913, a move that made ships faster and more efficient, while oil-deficient Germany retained its inferior coal-driven navy.

France was inferior in a naval sense to Britain, also, but had maintained the largest army in Western Europe until the rise of Germany in 1870. Germany unified as a country from a collection of some 30 principalities in 1870 and experienced 40 years of rapid industrial growth. By 1914, Germany had surpassed England to become the leading industrial power in Europe, and their army constructed under Kaiser Wilhelm II was larger than that of France.

Germany had defeated France in a war at the time of its unification in 1870 and taken the coal rich area of Alsace-Lorraine from France. Germany also humiliated the French by forcing them to pay $50 million in gold bullion in reparations. As a result, the French wanted revenge for the debacle of 1870 and the return of Alsace-Lorraine.

The Austro-Hungarian Empire was a conglomeration in decline at the time of the outbreak of the war, primarily controlled by the Austrians. The empire included not only Austria and Hungary, but also most of what is now Poland, Czech Republic, Slovakia, Slovenia, Bosnia, and Croatia. Austria, though German in ethnicity, had been left out of German unification due to their ambitions to the east since Austria's principal commercial river, the Danube, flowed east into the Black Sea; hence, Austria's principal trade partners were to the east along the Danube. German Chancellor Otto Von Bismarck had disdain for the land to the east, most of which was populated by slavic people instead of Germans. Consequently, he opposed Austria's unification with Germany in spite of the fact that the Austrians were German in ethnicity and spoke German. In the words of Bismarck, "The entire Balkans are not worth the hair on the head of one Pomeranian Grenadier."

Though Bismarck clearly underestimated the value of the land and people to the east, he did not underestimate the potential for trouble. In 1906, Austria-Hungary defeated Serbia in a war and annexed the territory of Bosnia from Serbia. Bosnia was an area of many competing factions, but it included both factions that favored Bosnian nationalism and those that desired a return of Bosnia to Serbian control. These sentiments would fester in Bosnia for eight years until a spark in Sarajevo would ignite World War I.

Giuseppe Garibaldi (*Library of Congress*)

Elsewhere, Italy was unified as a country in 1870 from a collection of city states through a "revolution from above" led by Giuseppe Garibaldi and Giuseppe Mazzini; but an area of the Alps with a large Italian-speaking population remained under the control of Austria. Italians that wanted all Italians united under one flag argued for the annexation of this Austrian Tyrol.

Russia ever since Peter the Great had considered itself the "Defenders of the Slavs" and was essentially sworn to come to the aid of any slavic country, if that country were attacked, in what was essentially the Russian version of the Monroe Doctrine. Thus, any problems in the slavic Balkans were likely to bring Russia into a war.

Finally, Belgium, a small defenseless country of low relief on the western European coast, was internationally recognized as a "neutral" country by virtue of a treaty signed by all the great European powers. Violation of Belgian neutrality would result in its playing a role in World War I.

OUTBREAK OF HOSTILITIES

On June 28, 1914, an obscure Serbian nationalist named Gavrilo Princep shot the heir to the Austro-Hungarian throne, Archduke Francis Ferdinand, and his wife in Sarajevo, Bosnia. The resultant crisis between Austria-Hungary and Serbia might have been localized if Europe had not been organized into a network of alliances that reflected deep divisions of militant nationalism, and if the Russian and Austrian governments had not been spurred to reckless action by dangers of national revolt.

After Ferdinand's assassination, Germany guaranteed Austria-Hungary its full support and guaranteed victory if the Austrians would attack Serbia in retaliation for the assassination. Germany feared the breakup of the Austro-Hungarian Empire, their friends to the east whom they viewed as a buffer between themselves and Russia; and they urged the Austrians to make an example of the Serbs so as to dissuade anyone else in the Austro-Hungarian Empire who may have similar nationalist intentions. After Serbia rejected impossible demands by Austria, the Austrians opened hostilities against the Serbs. Russia then went to the aid of Serbia. When Russia mobilized its army to defend Serbia out of its role as "Defenders of the Slavs," Germany declared war on Russia, prompting France to enter the war on the side of Russia—both to honor the Entente, and also to regain Alsace Lorraine as revenge for 1870. When German troops pushed through neutral Belgium in a vain effort to knock out France immediately, Great Britain went to war against Germany—ostensibly to defend Belgian neutrality and honor the Entente. This prompted Germany's Chancellor Theobald von Bethmann Hollweg to remark that the English were "going to war over a scrap of paper;" but, in reality, the British were merely playing the "balance of power" game and making a move to prevent Germany from becoming the dominant power in Europe. The Ottoman Empire (Turkey) entered the war on the side of Germany out of fear of Russian dominance and a desire to gain territory in southwestern Soviet Union where Muslims of Turkish ethnicity resided. Japan entered the war on the side of the Allies, desiring to gain Germany's possessions in the Pacific. Bulgaria entered the war on the side of Germany out of ethnic hatred and a desire to gain territory held by Serbia. Italy eventually broke with the Triple Alliance and entered the war in 1915 on the side of the Triple Entente for the purpose of gaining the Tyrol from Austria. Four years and three months later, a generation of Europeans—almost 8.5 million—lay dead.

President Wilson believed, at first, that geography would save the United States from the holocaust. He issued a proclamation of neutrality and then adjured the American people to be "impartial in thought as well as in action." Despite an initial resolve to avoid military involvement, however, the American public was never disposed to be neutral in thought. The dominant British and French bias was compounded by ethnic, business, and cultural ties and was intensified by a vaguely formed feeling that a German victory would adversely affect American interests by putting an aggressive military regime in control of Europe and possibly of the high seas. Key foreign policy spokesmen, too, believed that the preservation of the European balance of power by Britain had long served American interests and that, as Senator Henry Cabot Lodge phrased it on September 23, if "Germany conquers France, England, and Russia she will dominate Europe and will subsequently extend that domination, if she can, to the rest of the world." "The principle of Anglo-Saxon liberty seems to have met the irreconcilable conception of the German State," wrote Elihu Root at the time, "and the two ideas are battling for control of the world."

In these circumstances, Germany's violation of Belgian neutrality and later resort to indiscriminate submarine warfare simply solidified standing fears. Similarly, British propaganda served mainly to sharpen perceptions and inflame passions already present. The British cut the Atlantic Cable, making communication with Germany difficult and creating a situation where the only war news received in America was biased coverage from Britain. American papers then simply published the biased British versions of what was going on so that many more Americans supported the British.

These sentiments were far from unanimous. The great majority of the country's eight million Germans and German-Americans were strongly attached to the fatherland. The spokesmen of the nation's 4.5 million Irish-Americans were almost universally anti-British, and several million Poles and Jews were almost fanatically anti-Russian. From the outset these groups fed on German propaganda in their foreign-language or diocesan newspapers, and neither the pro-Allied cast of the regular press nor German actions changed their sympathies during the period of 1914–1916. Because most of these groups were lower or lower-middle class, however, they never exercised an influence proportionate to their numbers.

The divisions among the American people were accentuated by the impossibility of genuine neutrality. German might was based on dominance of the land mass of central Europe, Great Britain's on control of the seas. To impose an embargo, as the pro-Germans and many pacifists demanded, would be to deal Britain a paralyzing blow. To supply the Allies, as the United States soon did, was to strengthen them in relation to Germany—hence the impossibility of substantive, as distinct from formalistic, neutrality.

President Wilson's decision to accept Britain's control of the seas seems to have been based on two factors: his desire to adhere to traditional rules of neutrality and his fear of a German victory. As he said to his Cabinet in 1915, "The Allies are standing with their backs to the wall fighting wild beasts. I will permit nothing to be done by our country to hinder or embarrass them ... unless admitted rights are grossly violated." In short, Wilson's own democratic ideals were at stake. As an admirer of the British parliamentary system, he was loath to see it put asunder by what he viewed as an undemocratic government of Kaiser Wilhelm. In Wilson's words, "Everything I love is at stake. A German victory would be fatal to our form of government and American ideals." Assuredly, he protested Britain's expansion of the contraband list (goods which they could intercept under international law) to include even food; but at no time did Wilson consider military action against Britain to uphold his shifting and, in some cases, historically untenable construction of neutral rights.

As the war progressed, the President authorized positive action to assure the flow of supplies to the Allies. Anticipating a strain on American gold reserves in the summer of 1914, he had permitted Secretary of State Bryan to declare that the administration disapproved of loans to the Allies because they violated the spirit of neutrality. He modified this policy in March 1915, by allowing the Morgan banking house to extend a $50 million credit to the French government. He rejected a German-American proposal to prohibit the export of all war materials. Then, in the summer of 1915, he completely lifted Bryan's ban on loans. By 1917, Allied debt to the United States exceeded $2 billion, which the United States banks stood to lose if the Allies lost. An Allied loss, therefore, could have crumbled the entire American banking and monetary system.

The President's realization that war orders had boosted American prosperity undoubtedly influenced these decisions. By 1916 exports to the Allies exceeded $3 billion in value, four times their 1914 level. "To maintain our prosperity, we must finance it," Secretary of the Treasury McAdoo warned Wilson in August 1915. "Otherwise it may stop and that would be disastrous."

GERMAN SUBMARINE WARFARE

Very quickly, World War I bogged down into a stalemated trench warfare that neither side could win on the battlefield. Neither Britain nor Germany were self-sufficient in food and fuel, however, so if either power could cut off the food and fuel supplies to the other, it would ultimately win the war by starving the other side. Britain, with a superior navy, instituted a blockade of Europe with the intent of starving Germany and cutting off their fuel supplies. Although Germany's navy was inferior and could not challenge the British blockade, the

The "undersea boat" or "U-boat" was used by Germany to sink merchant ships during World War I. *(Library of Congress)*

Germans had invented the "undersea boat" or submarine (commonly referred to as the "U-boat") that it could use to sink cargo ships bound for England and thus prevent England from getting its supplies. On February 4, 1915, the German Admiralty marked out a broad war zone around the British Isles in which neutral vessels would run the risk of being sunk without warning by German submarines.

Technically, the British blockade violated international law since under international law neutral countries, such as the United States, had the right to sell nonmilitary goods to belligerents (warring nations). In other words, the international law allowed the United States to sell nonmilitary goods to Germany as well as England, but the English blockade prevented the United States from selling anything to Germany—thus violating American rights as a neutral under international law and provoking a protest by American President Woodrow Wilson. International law also required, however, that military ships provide fair warning by firing shots over the bows of ships before sinking them. The ship under attack would be then given time to evacuate and have its men paddle off in lifeboats before the attacking ship shelled it to the bottom of the ocean. The international law, however, was antiquated in that it was written before the invention of the submarine. The German U-boats were very vulnerable on the surface, even to small arms fire, and could not surface and give fair warning without risk of being sunk or damaged. Consequently, in order to be effective, the German submarines had no recourse but to fire torpedoes at merchant ships without warning, thus violating international law. Six days after Germany's announcement that they would sink ships without warning, Wilson replied that Germany would be held to "strict accountability" for illegal destruction of American ships and American lives.

The issue was first addressed in March when an American was lost on a British liner torpedoed without warning. Arguing passionately that the United States should not indulge the technical right of its citizens to sail through war zones on belligerent ships, Bryan proposed that the government warn them against it. Before a decision was reached, an event of tragic proportions virtually destroyed all hopes of such a solution. On May 7 off the coast of Ireland, the British liner *Lusitania*, the largest passenger liner in the world at the time with a length of over 700 feet, was sunk without warning—with a loss of 1,198 lives, 124 of them American. The sinking of the luxury liner could be seen from the coast of Ireland, but in waters of 43 degrees, people die of hypothermia in approximately 10 minutes—thus making it impossible for anyone to save the passengers of the *Lusitania*. Germany argued that it had published warnings in the United States newspapers implor-

The British ship *Lusitania*, sunk in 1915 by a German U-boat, was the largest passenger liner in the world at that time. *(Library of Congress)*

ing people not to travel on the *Lusitania* because Germany intended to sink it, believing it to be carrying four million rounds of ammunition.

The immensity of the disaster appalled the nation, and violated the American collective conscience, but few voices called out for war. From all over the country, in fact, came fervent appeals for peace; and from Democratic leaders in Congress came a warning that Wilson probably could not obtain passage of a war resolution. As a Kansas progressive leader informed Roosevelt, the Midwest's sense of outrage "died down as suddenly as it had risen." When the President soon afterward declared, "There is such a thing as a man being too proud to fight," Roosevelt was almost alone in denouncing him.

Determined to find a peaceful solution, Wilson called on the German government to renew its allegiance to "the rights of humanity" by conforming to the traditional rules of war. The second of his three notes was so stern that Bryan, who feared that it would provoke Germany into hostilities, resigned in protest. Bryan also denounced Wilson's policies of shipping military goods on passenger ships as "tantamount to protecting an army with women and children at the front." The President was prepared, at the most, to sever relations; but fearing war, the Germans proved unwilling to gamble on his intent, and on June 6 the Admiralty ordered U-boats to spare large liners. Wilson demanded that the Germans make reparations and apologize for the *Lusitania*. Germany argued that they had given fair warning in the American newspapers and that the *Lusitania* was aiding the enemy; therefore, Germany owed neither reparations nor apology.

When a German submarine commander provoked a more severe crisis by violating orders and sinking the British liner *Arabic* on August 19, 1915, killing two Americans, the German government avoided a break with America only by pledging that liners would not be sunk "without warning and without safety of the lives of noncombatants"— providing they did not offer resistance or try to escape. Following the torpedoing of the French steamer *Sussex*, thus injuring a number of Americans in March 1916, Wilson sent the Imperial Government an even stronger ultimatum, demanding reparations and the cessation of Germany's "sink all ships" policy. The Germans again pledged restraint, subject to British observance of international law. Germany pledged to stop sinking merchant ships without warning and agreed to pay reparations for the *Lusitania*. Essentially, Germany decided that the advantage gained from sinking merchant ships bound for England was not worth the disadvantage of bringing the United States into the war. Germany, however, refused to admit to any wrongdoing in the *Lusitania* incident. Wilson accepted the German pledge but not the qualification; and the crisis was temporarily resolved.

STEPS TOWARD UNITED STATES PREPAREDNESS

Meanwhile, Wilson began to prepare the nation for the hazards of an uncertain future. He was reluctant to do so, believing that a military buildup by the United States would violate American neutrality and be viewed as provocative by the Germans. Under the hammering of a bellicose former president Roosevelt and a substantial element of the Republican Party, however, he finally faced the implications of his "strict accountability" policy. He took the first tentative steps in the summer of 1915, came out for major increases in the navy and army in December, and then toured the Middle West in January and February 1916 to whip up support for his new preparedness program. Despite his proposed half billion dollar military buildup, the Democratic Party's slogan in the campaign of 1916 became, "He kept us out of the war."

No other issue of the period proved to be so revealing of the configuration of isolationist sentiment. Progressives of all three parties, including the secondary leadership of the disintegrating Bull Moose organization, opposed preparedness as a movement of munitions makers, in particular, and capitalists, in general. Farmers in upstate New York, in California, on the Carolina Piedmont, and in the valley of Virginia—no less than on the plains of Kansas and Nebraska—charged that preparedness would lead to war. Organized labor all over the country—in New York and San Francisco as well as in Chicago, Milwaukee, and St. Louis—agreed.

Conversely, conservatives from every section of the nation supported preparedness enthusiastically. The Chamber of Commerce in almost every state endorsed it overwhelmingly. Bankers' and manufacturers' associations in the Midwest and South came out militantly for it.

The main opposition in Congress came from Bryan Democrats and a few Republican progressives. Attributing the movement to conservative Republicans, they resolved to make them bear its cost. "I am persuaded to think that when the income tax will have to pay for the increase in the army and navy," wrote Claude Kitchin of North Carolina to Bryan, "they will not be one-half so frightened over the future invasion by Germany." Not until Wilson agreed to accept their inheritance, munitions-profits, and progressive income tax program did they relax their opposition. Even then, it was to approve a severely compromised program as the defense legislation of 1916 provided for only moderate increases in the army.

THE ELECTION OF 1916

Prewar progressivism had reached full flower by the spring and summer of 1916. In the convention at St. Louis in mid-June, the progressive-agrarian Democrats ignored the President's orders to make "Americanism" their keynote and indulged instead in one long and tremendous demand for peace. "He kept us out of war" became their campaign theme, and Wilson had little recourse but to accept it. Compared to the extreme measures advocated by the Roosevelt and Old Guard wings of the reunited Republican Party—the so-called jingoes—Wilson's was in fact the policy of moderation. This was widely recognized at the time, and along with the Democrats' remarkable legislative record, it exerted a powerful pull on independents and ex-Bull Moosers.

Divisions within the Republican Party also worked to Wilson's advantage. Although the G.O.P. platform criticized the Democratic preparedness program as inadequate, and virtually called for war against Mexico, it deferred to the sensibilities of the more than 100 German-American delegates at the Republican convention by equivocating on neutral rights. As a result, the Republican campaign lacked consistency. The Republican presidential candidate, former Justice Charles Evans Hughes, was forced, on the one hand, to call for a hard policy toward Germany and to contend, on the other hand, that such a policy would assure peace. Graphically, the *St. Louis Post-Dispatch* described his dilemma:

> To satisfy the pro-Germans he must quarrel with the pro-British, who demand war with Germany. To satisfy Wall Street, he must quarrel with the western radicals. To satisfy the jingoes and the Munitions Trust, he must quarrel with most of the country. To satisfy privilege and plutocracy, he must quarrel with the people. Even as a candidate Mr. Hughes dare not have a policy, because to have a policy is to antagonize one element or another of his followers.

Charles Evans Hughes *(Library of Congress)*

Wilson squeezed through by a narrow, half-million plurality and just 23 electoral votes. On election night it appeared that Wilson had lost, but Wilson won every state west of the central time zone except Oregon and was declared the winner the next day. The resentment of Irish-, German-, Jewish-, and Polish-American voters possibly cost him much of the East and such Midwestern states as Illinois and Wisconsin, though some recent scholars dispute this. At any rate, he swept most states where isolationism reflected agrarian rather than ethnocentric views and where the progressive impulse was strong. He also carried most of the Western states in which women could vote.

THE FAILURE OF MEDIATION

Hardly were the returns in when the President sought to end the war. At the time of his electoral victory, Wilson was perhaps as neutral as he had been at any time since 1914. The Germans had stopped sinking merchant ships without warning, and the British had elevated his irritation by their restrictions on neutral trade with their blockade. For almost two years he had been striving to persuade the belligerents to accept a negotiated peace. His efforts had failed because both the Allies and the Central Powers still aspired to victory in the field. Taking new hope in a German peace overture of December 12, 1916, Wilson six days later called on the belligerents to define their war aims. The British replied privately that they would negotiate on liberal terms (even though the Allies had returned a belligerent public answer); but the Germans answered evasively—and understandably so—for their real terms included control of Belgium and a strip of the French coast.

The President, thereupon, appealed to world opinion in a speech before the Senate on January 22, 1917. He asserted the right of the United States to share in laying the foundations for a lasting peace, set forth his plan for a League of Nations, and added the noblest of all his perorations: "It must be a peace without victory. Victory would mean peace forced upon the loser, a victor's terms imposed upon the vanquished. ... Only a peace between equals can last." Wilson also called for the principle that all states are equal and the principle of self-determination. Wilson called for international disarmament and called for "freedom of the seas," an American principle dating back almost to the American Revolution.

People of good will the world over were intoxicated by Wilson's great vision, but realists knew that it was hopeless to expect the German military party to will its own destruction. On January 31, the German government submitted terms that would have assured its hegemony in Europe. It also announced resumption of unrestricted submarine warfare as they launched a major offensive in France in a dramatic gamble to win the war before the United States could arrive. The Germans were low on food and fuel, and they knew they needed to win the war quickly; consequently, they hoped to cut off supplies to the British and then defeat their enemies before help arrived. The President responded by severing diplomatic relations with Germany after German U-boats sunk the *U.S.S. Housatonic* on February 3.

Although Wilson still hoped to avert war, the onrush of events soon overtook him. From British intelligence on February 25, he received a transcript of the "Zimmermann note"—a diplomatic message from German Foreign Secretary Zimmermann, proposing to Mexico that in the event of war between the United States and Germany, Mexico should join Germany against the United States. As a reward, Mexico should recover "the lost territory in Texas, New Mexico, and Arizona." The same day, German U-boats sunk the passenger liner *Laconia*, killing two Americans.

The next day the President asked Congress for authority to arm American ships for defense and to employ other measures to protect American commerce on the high seas, but the bill died by filibuster in the Senate. Bolstered by the public's militant reaction to the Zimmermann note, he castigated progressive senators who prevented adoption of the armed-ship bill as "a little group of willful men representing no opinion but their own." He then ordered merchant ships armed by Executive Order on March 9.

Events now moved swiftly to a climax. On March 19, three American ships went down with heavy losses. That same week a liberal revolution in Russia overthrew the czar. This softened the pro-German stance of Russian-American Jews and made progressives everywhere more willing to support the Allies. Great throngs of people now called for war in mass meetings in New York and other cities. Meanwhile, the White House received reports from London that the Allies were in such desperate straits that only American intervention could save them.

Weighed down by these pressures, the President sorrowfully decided for full-scale war. As his biographer, Arthur S. Link, concludes, he did so mainly for two reasons. First, he believed that the war was already in its final stages and that American participation would bring it to a quick conclusion. Second, and much more important, he believed that Allied war aims posed such a threat to enduring peace that only a decisive American presence at the peace conference could assure a rational reconstruction of the world order. For these reasons, the United States became an Associate power rather than an Ally.

At 8:30 in the evening on April 2, 1917, Wilson asked a joint session of Congress to recognize that Germany was at war against the

Jeannette Rankin *(Library of Congress)*

United States and mankind. "The world must be made safe for democracy," he said, "... for the right of those who submit to authority to have a voice in their own Governments, for the rights and liberties of small nations, for a universal domination of right by such a concert of free peoples as shall bring peace and safety to all nations and make the world itself at last free."

Four days later, on April 6, 1917, the Senate voted for a war resolution 82 to 6 and the House, 373 to 50. How much this vote reflected Congress' acceptance of Wilson's concept of a world democratic mission, how much a purely nationalistic reaction against the loss of American shipping, and how much a conviction that British naval supremacy in the Atlantic was in the United States' continuing interest is impossible to say. All that is clear is that many Republican interventionists conceived the war as a power struggle involving American interests and disparaged the proposed League of Nations from the outset. "I am an American," expostulated Congressman Augustus P. Gardner of Massachusetts. "I want no internationalism. I want no conglomerate flag of all nations, with a streak of yellow down the middle." Among the 50 who voted against the war was Jeannette Rankin of Montana, who not only voted against the War Declaration in 1917, but also would be the only member of the House to vote against the War Declaration that marked the American entry into World War II.

THE CARNAGE AND STALEMATE OF WORLD WAR I

At the time of the United States entry into the war, the German offensive had again failed, and the war continued its stalemated trench warfare into its third year. Almost the entire war on the Western Front had been fought along a 500-mile front, at essentially the same place after the original German offensive had failed outside Paris in 1914. In 1914, the German army made it to the outskirts of Paris in six weeks with well-planned precision; but the inexperienced German troops panicked and retreated when they saw the French army advance to meet them from Paris in a barrage of civilian vehicles that made the French army appear larger than it was. The Germans fell back, the war stalemated, and three years of bloody trench warfare followed.

The development of military machinery had outpaced battle tactics; and both sides were able to kill the enemy faster with machine guns and new heavy artillery than anyone could advance. Generals ordered their men to hurl themselves into machine gun fire across open fields, wasting literally millions of lives in the process. A million men died in the battle of Verdun and another 600,000 died at the Somme, yet nothing was settled. It was into this lunacy that President Wilson was sending the United States Army.

A PEOPLE AT WAR

The President and his advisers soon learned that disaster loomed on almost every side. On the Western Front a French offensive had been stopped, and 10 French divisions had already mutinied. In the Balkans the Allies were being pushed back. In Italy the Austrians, reinforced by the Germans, were soon to win a great victory at Caporetto. In the East the Russian armies were withdrawn from the war after the Bolshevik Revolution, where V. I. Lenin and the Bolsheviks took over the government of Russia with the promise of "bread, land, and peace" to the Russian people. While ending famine would prove more difficult for Lenin, he quickly signed a separate peace with Germany—withdrawing Russia from the war, allowing the Germans to shift 600,000 troops from the Eastern front to the Western front, and thus tipping the balance in German favor. On all fronts the Allies were running out of reserves. More ominous still, the Germans were destroying three times as much shipping each month as the Allies were building. Britain faced starvation unless something could be done.

The Washington administration responded boldly. The navy at once began to patrol the Western Hemisphere and to give assistance to the antisubmarine campaign around the British Isles. By July 1917, 35 American destroyers were based at Queenstown, Ireland. By the end of the war, almost 400 American ships were overseas. Meanwhile, the American navy virtually coerced the British into adopting the convoy system. The results of this critical decision were spectacular. Shipping losses fell from 881,027 tons in April 1917 to half that figure in December. By May 1918, they had dropped to 200,000 tons per month, thus destroying the calculations on which the Germans had based their decision to risk hostilities with the United States.

WORLD WAR I

U.S.A.
1917

NORWAY

NORTH SEA

Oslo

Stockholm

SWEDEN

FINLAND
Indep. July, 1917

Helsinki

Lake Ladoga

Petrograd

Edinburgh

**Battle of Jutland
May-June, 1916**

DENMARK

Copenhagen

BALTIC SEA

ESTONIA
Indep.
Feb, 1918

LATVIA
Indep.
Nov, 1918

Riga

**Riga offensive
Sept, 1917**

RUSSIA

GREAT
BRITAIN
1914

London

Kiel

Hamburg

Amsterdam

NETH.

Memel

LITHUANIA
Indep. Feb, 1918

Konigsberg

Vilna

Danzig

Smolensk

Minsk

Brussels

Cologne

BELG.
1914

Berlin

GERMANY
1914

**Masurian
Lakes
Sept, 1914**

**Tannenberg
Aug, 1914**

Paris

**GERMAN INVASION
AUG-SEPT, 1914**

Leipzig

Dresden

POLAND
Indep. Nov, 1918

Pinsk

Brest-Litovsk

Kiev

Metz

Mainz

Warsaw

Lublin

LUX.

Strasbourg

Danube River

Prague

Cracow

Lemberg

GALACIA

FRANCE
1914

Berne

SWITZ.

BAVARIA

Munich

Vienna

UKRAINE

Rhine River

Piave June, 1918

Pressburg

Graz

Budapest

AUSTRIA-HUNGARY
1914

Odessa

Milan

**Vittorio-Veneto
Oct-Nov, 1918**

Venice

Trieste

Genoa

RUMANIA
1916

Marseilles

ITALY
1915

Bucharest

BLACK SEA

SPAIN

**Withdrew from
Triple Alliance
1914**

CORSICA

Rome

BOSNIA

Sarajevo

Belgrade

MONTENEGRO
1915

SERBIA
1914

BULGARIA
1916

Sofia

Constantinople

PORTUGAL
1916

SARDINIA

Naples

ALBANIA

OTTOMAN EMPIRE
1914

Salonika

Gallipoli

Smyrna

GREECE
1916

**Dardanelles campaign
1915-1916**

SICILY

Athens

CRETE

MEDITERRANEAN SEA

Central Powers

Allied Powers

Neutral Powers

1916   Date of entry into the war

————   Maximum advance of the Central Powers

– – –   Maximum Russian advance

·········   Line of the Brest-Litovsk Treaty Mar, 1918

————   Armistice lines, eastern front Dec, 1917

0   500

MILES

N

MOBILIZATION FOR VICTORY

President Wilson rejected the idea of an all-volunteer army, and Congress passed the Selective Service Act, which eventually provided over 3 million United States soldiers, in May 1917. Another two million Americans volunteered for service. Over two million Americans eventually made the voyage to Europe virtually unmolested as the German high command made the decision to sink supply ships instead of troop carriers, believing the British supplies to be of greater value.

The typical American "doughboys" or soldiers were small, in ill health, and poorly educated by the standards of the twenty-first century. The average soldier was 22 years of age, 5'7" tall, and weighed 141 lbs. The median education for whites was 6.9 years, and 2.6 years for blacks, with 31 percent testing illiterate. The army rejected a full 29 percent of recruits as physically unfit for service.

The doughboys were all forced to shave and hair was cut short—so as to reduce head lice and body lice that they were to endure in trench warfare. Soldiers were issued safety razors and were given cigarettes as part of their rations so as to help calm nerves on the battlefield. Soldiers were also issued wristwatches with the result that fashions in America changed to clean-shaven and shorthaired for men. All American Presidents since World War I have been clean-shaven with relatively short hair. Cigarettes, which were considered feminine prior to World War I (men smoked pipes and cigars), have been just as masculine as feminine, if not more so, ever since. Similarly, wristwatches, which were considered as "jewelry" and "feminine" prior to World War I, have been standard male accessories for almost an entire century since World War I.

America was the only country that did not provide government prostitutes for their troops. Europeans were shocked when the American troops showed up in Europe without any females to tend to their needs. The French Premier offered to Secretary of State Newton Baker to supply French prostitutes for the American troops. Baker's famous response was, "Yes, but for God's sake don't tell Wilson; he'll stop the damn war."

Even though Wilson had pushed his military preparedness bill through Congress, the United States was not ready for a war of the magnitude of World War I. The United States military shipbuilding program was unable to complete the construction of any major new vessels until after the war ended. Similarly, the American army supplied only 8,000 of 8.8 million artillery shells fired by the United States army during the war. Congress authorized the production of 20,000 airplanes; but less than 50 were actually completed, shipped to Europe, and used in the war. Instead, American pilots flew British and French-made planes.

Three months after American intervention, the administration created the War Industries Board (WIB) to coordinate purchases, allocate (ration) raw materials, control production, set prices (prices were set high in an effort to boost production and companies made record profits), and supervise labor relations. The WIB made rapid progress in some areas but failed to control military purchases. "The Military Establishment ... has fallen down," a Democratic senator exclaimed in January 1918. "It has almost stopped functioning ... because of inefficiency in every bureau and in every department of the Government." Rejecting a Republican demand for a coalition cabinet, Wilson boldly conferred such sweeping authority on the WIB's new head, Bernard Baruch, that the industrial machine was soon hammered into shape.

Meanwhile Herbert Hoover, director of the War Food Administration, stimulated dramatic agricultural increases by pegging prices. Food exports to the Allies doubled in 1917–1918 and tripled in 1918–1919. The War Food Administration encouraged conservation through "wheatless Monday" and "Meatless Tuesday" campaigns. The War Fuel Administration was not so spectacularly successful, but it too performed effectively. The War Fuel Administration rationed coal and other fuels, including "coal holidays" where citizens were forced to go without fuel on certain days.

Conversely, the shipbuilding program proved a failure, with less than a half-million new tons being afloat by the end of the war. Only by commandeering three million tons already under construction in private yards and by seizing a million tons of German and Dutch shipping did the United States acquire the fleet that saved the Allies.

For a while the railroad situation was even worse. The eastern freight system nearly collapsed in December 1917, but conditions rapidly improved after the President put all railroad transportation under the control of William G. McAdoo. The demands of the great military effort of 1918 were fully met.

William G. McAdoo *(Library of Congress)*

Conservatives objected to Wilson's wholesale economic intervention; but since prices were typically set artificially high to encourage production, big business complaints were minimized. Furthermore, vehement condemnation of Wilson's policies placed one at risk of being labeled unpatriotic.

THE WAR ON LAND

Six weeks after adoption of the war resolution, a selective service law that applied to rich and poor alike was enacted, and by the summer of 1917 a great army was being formed. The following winter a small American expeditionary force held a quiet sector of the front and served generally to bolster sagging Allied morale. The first American troops reached the Western Front in October 1917, a full six months before the Germans had anticipated.

Meanwhile the American commander, General John J. Pershing, systematically prepared a major offensive. The Americans fought as separate units from the Allies, and the United States was never formally "allied" with the Allies—merely "associates." Appalled by the defense-mindedness of Allied generals, Pershing was determined "to draw the best German divisions to our front and consume them." Before he could do so, he had to throw two divisions into Chateau-Thierry to support the French in May 1918. Two months later 85,000 Americans helped the Allies turn back the last great German drive to break through the Marne pocket and take Paris.

Finally, in mid-September Pershing's army, now greatly reinforced, took the offensive at Saint-Mihiel in its first independent action. It attained its objective after a two-day battle that cost 6,000 in dead and wounded. Then, more than half a million strong, the Americans turned west and won a fiercely fought battle in the Meuse-Argonne area. Nevertheless, it was British and French successes in the central and northern sectors, not the American offensive, which brought Germany to its knees. Only in the sense that American involvement convinced the Germans that they would eventually lose did the United States' military contribution prove crucial. By November of 1918, Germany was out of food and out of fuel; and its leaders knew that they could not continue through the winter. Hence, Germany surrendered, and an armistice was signed on November 11, 1918. The German army had not been defeated on the battlefield, and the Allies were not on German soil at the war's end; but the British blockade had created food and fuel shortages so acute that at war's end house cats in Germany had become known as "roof rabbits."

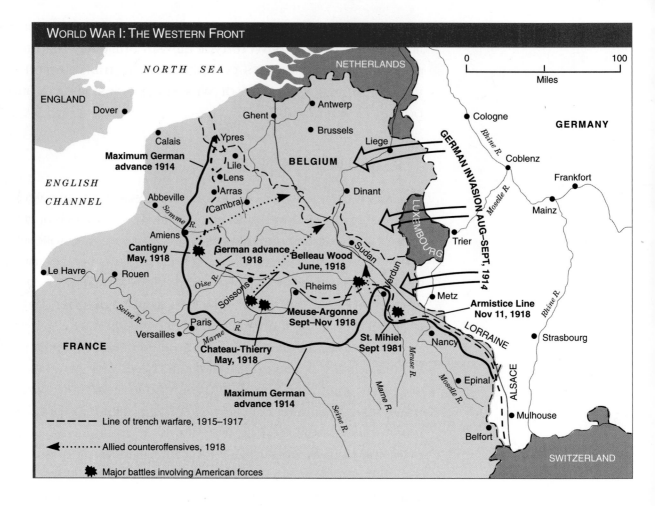

WORLD WAR I: THE WESTERN FRONT

HEROES AND WEAPONRY

The Great War (as it was called prior to World War II) produced new weaponry and heroes on both sides in the greatest struggle the world had ever known. In was in World War I that airplanes were first introduced into war. In the beginning, airplanes were used only for reconnaissance, and opposing armies were known to wave at the pilots in the enemy planes. Later, planes were armed with bombs and machine guns and used in battle; but their contribution was not significant, though the press celebrated it.

Planes in World War I were primitive and tended to put off toxic carbon monoxide fumes, poisoning pilots so quickly that flights had to be limited to one–two hours. Planes often crashed from mechanical failures and were generally inaccurate in bombing missions. Poorly synchronized machine guns even, on occasion, shot off the planes' own propellers. Nevertheless, Baron Manfred Von Richtoven, the "Red Baron," became the toast of Germany for shooting down 80 Allied planes in his red Fokker tri-plane. Similarly, American Ace Eddie Rickenbacker was credited with 27 kills and shot down enemy planes at a rate even faster than the Red Baron.

The greatest hero of World War I, however, was Sergeant Alvin York, a Tennessee sharpshooter who single-handedly captured 132 Germans and 35 machine guns after killing with 17 bullets the 17 Germans who dared to raise their heads out of a trench. York explained his incredible feat with humility, stating that, "Of course, it weren't no trouble no how for me to hit them big army targets. They were so much bigger than turkey's heads."

The war also produced other new weapons including tanks, which would make trench warfare obsolete in the next war; Zeppelins, which were ominous, but obviously too slow and too easy to shoot down; and poison gas, which was so horrible that no army used it in World War II. Some gasses were heavier than air; consequently, persons during gas attacks had the choice of staying in the trench and being killed by gas or coming out of the trench and being killed by bullets. Mustard gas burned the lungs of those who breathed it, while nerve gasses not only killed people, but also left others crippled with disorders of the central nervous system. It was these horrible lung and nervous system injuries that, in part, prompted the United States government to fund the Veteran's Administration (VA) and the chain of VA hospitals across the country as a way of meeting the health care needs of the returning doughboys.

PROGRESSIVISM IN WAR TIME

Over the bitter protests of conservatives, almost a third of the $32 billion total war bill was raised by war profits, income, corporate, and luxury taxes. In total, new taxation produced over $9 billion in government revenue. Borrowing essentially financed the rest of the war. The United States government introduced "liberty bonds," which were purchased by private citizens. Through an aggressive campaign, the bonds eventually raised $23 billion.

The National War Labor Board was placed in charge of labor relations and promoted harmony between labor and management. In return for a guarantee of no strikes, the National War Labor Board pressured companies to provide eight-hour days, equal pay for women, the recognition of the right of collective bargaining, and to set wages high so as to attract workers. For example, wages in the steel mills doubled during World War I. Women and blacks were also recruited to the workforce to perform jobs previously occupied by the five million men who went off to war. As a result, the AFL increased its membership from 2,072,702 to 3,260,168. Hours of labor declined from 53.5 per week in 1914 to 50.4 in 1920. In addition, real wages rose sharply—14 percent above the prewar level in 1917 and 20 percent in 1918.

Unfortunately, many of the gains proved temporary. The administration failed to devise and implement a viable reconversion plan, and upon the end of hostilities management resumed its old practices. After a series of long and bitter strikes, labor failed to organize steel and other industries. On the other hand, as we have seen, the progressives won their long struggle for prohibition and woman suffrage with the ratification of the Eighteenth and Nineteenth Amendments in 1919 and 1920.

PROPAGANDA AND CIVIL LIBERTIES

The record on civil liberties proved far less exemplary, partly because of Wilson's belief in the need to create a solid front. In some respects, World War I whipped the American public into a frenzy of hyper-patriotism that was perhaps unparalleled in American history. On the other hand, millions of Americans believed on April 6, 1917, that the United States should not have entered the war. In 1917 mayoral candidates of the antiwar Socialist Party polled close to half the vote in Dayton, Ohio, more than a third in Chicago, and nearly a quarter in New York and Buffalo—impressive evidence of both the magnitude and the geographic spread of antiwar sentiments.

The administration struck back with a vast propaganda program and legislation to discourage criticism of the war. Fanning the flames of this pro-war frenzy, President Wilson created the Committee on Public Information (CPI), essentially a federal war propaganda agency, and endowed it with the responsibility for selling the war to the American public. The CPI, under George Creel, induced the press to accept voluntary censorship and organized some 15,000 writers, scholars, and businessmen into a public speaking and pamphlet-writing bureau. Under such an atmosphere, free speech and truth and accuracy in the news media became seriously compromised as the news media essentially published the CPI's accounts of the war without question or criticism. The CPI painted the war as a crusade for freedom and democracy, and the German enemies were simplistically portrayed as cruel, savage, anti-democratic thugs bent on destroying the American way and dominating the world. The CPI placed ads in magazines and newspapers asking Americans to keep watch on their neighbors and report evidence of disloyalty, pessimism, or yearning for peace.

The American people generally accepted the draft, subscribed liberally to numerous bond drives, and adjusted reasonably well to the dislocations and inconveniences wrought by mobilization. They came also to believe the President's reiterated assertions—echoed again and again by Creel and his speakers and writers—that Americans were fighting to make the world safe for democracy.

At the same time, however, they indulged in an orgy of intolerance and bigotry. With the urging from the CPI, persons against Wilson's war policies became subject to public ridicule and attack. School boards outlawed the teaching of the German language. The German department at the University of Texas was closed so as to promote "purer Americanism." The University of Wisconsin censured progressive Senator Robert LaFollette for his anti-war views. The director of the Boston Symphony was fired simply for being German. German books and music were removed from library and retail store shelves, and German-Americans changed their names so as to conceal their ethnicity and avoid ridicule and attack. State committees of public safety persecuted pacifists, pro-Germans, and radicals almost capriciously. One German-American was lynched. Conservatives read "Bolshevist" and "German socialist" into almost any sign of labor strife. Meanwhile, black servicemen were proscribed from full participation in the "crusade for democracy."

VIGILANTES

Vigilante organizations quickly developed to enforce American patriotism. The most important of these was the American Protective League, a group whose purpose was to "mobilize respectable members of the community to root out disloyal members." The American Protective League claimed over 250,000 members at its peak in 1918. Other similar organizations—including the National Security League, American Defense Society, and Boy Spies of America—collectively claimed another 250,000 members. The organizations opened mail, tapped telephones, subjected targeted citizens to shakedowns, and engaged in lynching and violence against suspected disloyals. In Cincinnati, a pacifist clergyman was pulled from his bed, dragged to a nearby hillside, and whipped—"in the name of the women and children of Belgium." In Indiana, a man was acquitted of murdering an alien who had yelled, "To hell with the United States." In Montana, one member of the Industrial Workers of the World (IWW), a left-leaning labor organization that conservatives viewed as communist and un-American) was hanged and another was dragged to death behind a truck. IWW leader Big Bill Haywood fled to the Soviet Union rather than face potential lynching at the hands of vigilantes.

ESPIONAGE AND SEDITION ACTS

From the outset, the administration was determined to suppress opposition that might hinder the war effort. Congress fanned the flames of hysteria with several acts that essentially criminalized political dissent. The Espionage Act of June 1917 made it a crime to "aid the enemy" or "obstruct the United States war effort." On the surface, these items do not appear to be out of the ordinary, but in practice, they became launching pads for oppression and the erosion of freedom. This restrictive approach was broadened as the war progressed, partly because the activities of the "Wobblies" (the Industrial Workers of the World) caused production of copper to decline precipitously. The Trading-with-the-Enemy Act of October 1917 forbade trade with Germany and its Allies. In May 1918, however, Congress took things a step further with the passage of the Sedition Act, which declared that it was illegal to utter, print, write, or publish, any disloyal, profane, scurrilous, or abusive language about the government, Constitution, or armed forces. Furthermore, "saying anything" to discourage the purchase of war bonds was declared to be criminal activity. The Sedition Act of 1918 imposed virtual closure on free speech in the United States. By war's end, some 1,500 people had been convicted for violating the provisions of either these measures or the Espionage Act. The similarities between the Alien and Sedition Acts of 1798 and the Congressional actions of World War I are uncanny, and the results of the twentieth century acts were just as oppressive as those in the eighteenth century—if not more so. Under the Sedition Act of 1918, communist and socialist parties (who criticized the United States government effort in the war) were effectively silenced and over 500 communists were deported. The Justice Department initiated over 2,000 prosecutions under these acts, resulting in the incarceration of 900 persons during the 19 months of American involvement in World War I. Many of the famous radicals—Eugene Debs and Emma Goldman, for example—were imprisoned.

The oppressive rampage was not limited to the socialists and communists, however. Anarchist Ricardo Flores Magon was sentenced to 20 years in prison for publishing a statement criticizing Wilson's policies in Mexico (where there was much to criticize, but space limits us from elaborating here) that were completely separate from the issue of United States involvement in the Great War. One woman, Sarah Parker, received a five-year prison sentence for writing, "I am for the people, and the government is for the profiteers." Movie producer Robert Goldstein, who had made a film about the American Revolution entitled *Spirit of 76*, was sentenced to 10 years in prison because his film's depiction of atrocities committed by the British during the American Revolution was deemed by a judge to be a violation of the Espionage Act under the pretense that it might lead the public to "question the good faith of our ally, Great Britain"

THE LOST PEACE

As early as the spring of 1916, President Wilson had committed himself both to a liberal peace and to American participation in a postwar league of nations. He had amplified this program

Emma Goldman *(Library of Congress)*

in his "Peace without Victory" speech of January 22, 1917, and had spelled out its details in the memorable "Fourteen Points" address a year later.[1] He set out for the peace conference in Paris in the first week of December 1918, and a crowd of over one million people greeted him to a hero's welcome. Wilson was less of a hero both to

---

[1] Wilson's "Fourteen Points," pronounced on January 8, 1918, may be paraphrased as follows:

I.   "Open covenants openly arrived at"

II.   Freedom of the seas in peace and in war alike

III. The removal of all economic barriers and the establishment of an equality of trade conditions among all nations

IV.   Reduction of national armaments

V.   A readjustment of all colonial claims, giving the interests of the population concerned equal weight with the claims of the ruling government

VI.   The evacuation of foreign troops from Russian territory and the independent determination by Russia of its own political development and national policy

VII. The evacuation of foreign troops and restoration of Belgium

VIII. The evacuation of foreign troops and restoration of France and the return of Alsace-Lorraine

IX.   A readjustment of the frontiers of Italy along national lines

X.   Self-determination for the peoples of Austria-Hungary

XI.   Evacuation of foreign troops from Rumania, Serbia, and Montenegro and access to the sea for Serbia

XII. Self-determination for the peoples under Turkish rule and freedom of the Dardanelles under international guarantee

XIII. The independence of Poland, with free access to the sea guaranteed by international covenant

XIV. The formation of a general association of nations (i.e. the League of Nations) under specific covenants for the purpose of affording mutual guarantees of political independence and territorial integrity to great and small states alike

the Republicans in the United States Senate and to the European diplomats, however. The Republican-controlled Senate was miffed that Wilson had ignored the "advice" portion of the "advice and consent of the Senate" provision of the United States Constitution, in spite of the fact that no President had sought Senate advice in making a treaty since George Washington. Even when Washington had done so, he remarked, "I'll be damned if I ever go in there again;" and he never did. European leaders, Georges Clemenceau of France and David Lloyd George of England, favored punitive measures against Germany in direct contradiction of Wilson's "peace without victory" principle. Nevertheless, Wilson remained determined to impose this program on the Allies in spite of their secret treaties for the division of the German, Austro-Hungarian, and Turkish empires.

The President faced imposing obstacles. A narrow Republican victory in the congressional elections in November 1918 had weakened his moral authority. Many Republicans had already expressed opposition to his program; and Roosevelt and Lodge would soon write Prime Minister David Lloyd George of Great Britain and Premier Georges Clemenceau of France that Wilson did not speak for the American people. Clemenceau perhaps best summed the European attitude when he proclaimed, "God has given us 10 Commandments and we have been unable to keep them. Wilson has given us 14 points. We shall see."

The President reached France convinced, nevertheless, that he might well deliver all Europe from the tyranny of history. Triumphal tours of Paris, London, and Rome confirmed his sense of mission. "Wilson heard from his carriage, something different, inhuman or super human," wrote a correspondent who had seen other leaders of the age on parade. Hardly conscious of the fear, lust, and vindictiveness that would shatter his hopes, he sat down with Lloyd George, Clemenceau, and Vittono Orlando of Italy to forge a lasting peace.

The President first rejected a proposal by the French, who were obsessed with the need for security against Germany, to convert the west bank of the Rhine into buffer states under French control. He did agree, however, that the west bank should be permanently demilitarized and occupied by the Allies for 15 years. He also acquiesced in the return of Alsace-Lorraine to France, the reduction of the German army and navy to cadre strength, and the mandating of Germany's colonies to victor nations under the League of Nations. Finally, he won Clemenceau's acceptance of the League idea by agreeing to join Britain and France in a defense treaty against Germany.

At Paris, Wilson also opposed expansion of intervention in Siberia, where the British, Americans, French, and Japanese had sent troops in the summer of 1919. Point VI of the Fourteen Points had called for the evacuation of foreign troops from Russia in order to give that country "an unhampered and unembarrassed opportunity for the independent determination of her own political development and national policy." Though Wilson had reluctantly supported the anti-Bolshevik campaign in Siberia with American troops, he feared that the intervention would backfire by strengthening the Russian people's support of the Bolsheviks.

Actually, he hoped that the Bolshevik government would be supplanted by a liberal-democratic-capitalist regime such as he envisioned for the entire world, including Japan and China. To that end he instituted a policy of non-recognition of Soviet Russia that persisted until 1933.

More victories and more concessions followed. A new Poland was created without violating unduly the principle of self-determination. Italy gained control of the Brenner Pass for security reasons, but not of a long strip of the Dalmation coast, including Fiume, which it had requested. Finally, the Covenant of the League of Nations was firmly embedded in the peace treaty. On the other hand, though Wilson desired "peace without victory," England and France demanded—and achieved—a settlement of $56 billion in war reparations against Germany. Germany, therefore, faced a potentially astronomical reparations bill and was compelled to admit war guilt. German Pacific colonies were given to Japan, who had taken them in the war and refused to relinquish them to the League of Nations. More important still, economic barriers within Europe and throughout the world remained intact.

Wilson did get, however, his League of Nations, and he prevented the Allies from breaking up Germany into several smaller states. The Versailles Treaty created new states of Yugoslavia, Poland, Austria, Hungary, and Czechoslovakia based on Wilson's principle of self-determination; and the League of Nations would manage the German and Ottoman possessions until they were ready for self-rule. Thus Wilson had won considerably more than his critics later conceded and a great deal less than he had hoped.

The President returned to the United States on July 8, 1919, and threw down the gauntlet two days later. "Our isolation was ended 20 years ago," he warned the Senate. "There can be no question of our ceasing to be a world power. The only question is whether we can refuse the moral leadership that is offered, whether we shall accept or reject the confidence of the world."

Wilson's words fell on a divided country. The German-Americans and their powerful journalistic ally, the Hearst press, opposed the

EUROPE AFTER VERSAILLES

Allied Occupation Zone

New independent nations

Plebiscite area

treaty's harshness toward Germany. Italian-Americans were unhappy over Wilson's refusal to allow Italy to take Fiume. Irish-Americans mounted a virulent opposition because of President Wilson's failure to support the movement for Ireland's independence. Furthermore, a small group of sincere and irreconcilable isolationists in the Senate pledged themselves to the complete defeat of the treaty because of the provision for the League of Nations. Many intellectuals and idealists also revolted. "The European politicians, who with American complicity have hatched this inhuman monster," said the New Republic, "have acted either cynically, hypocritically or vindictively." Opponents argued that the treaty ignored freedom of the seas, a major principle that brought the United States into the war in the first place. Conservatives opposed the idea of disarmament as a violation of sovereignty and a naïve measure that sacrificed America's security. In the words of Senator Albert Beverage of Indiana: "The League of Nations is the work of amiable old grannies, who over their afternoon tea, are planning to denationalize America's manhood." Conversely, some progressives argued that the League of Nations could not possibly work if it excluded Bolshevik Russia.

Nevertheless, Wilson might still have won the fight for ratification had he not been so uncompromising. Wilson revealed his attitude in the matter by stating, "Anyone who opposes me I'll crush. The Senate must take its medicine." Senator Henry Cabot Lodge and a small group of pro-war Republican nationalists feared that the League, by raising false hopes, would compromise the balance-of-power foreign policy that they had always deemed essential to the nation's security. William Borah of Idaho perhaps best summed up the feelings of the opposition when he stated that, "I would vote against the League if Jesus Christ returned to the earth to argue in its behalf."

More than two thirds of the Senate approved the League Covenant in broad principle; and the President received a tremendous response as he traveled through the West in September 1919. It looked as though he must win. "My clients are the children; my clients are the next generation," he exclaimed with tears in his eyes to a cheering throng in Pueblo, Colorado. "I intend to redeem my pledges to the children; they shall not be sent [to France]." Seven days after this memorable peroration, the President suffered a stroke that paralyzed his left side. Wilson would remain bed-ridden for the rest of his presidency.

The battle now ground slowly to its tragic end. Lodge, as chairman of the foreign relations committee, presented the treaty to the Senate on November 6 for approval, subject to 14 Reservations to match Wilson's 14 Points. Lodge's Reservations essentially allowed the United States to opt out of the treaty's provisions in cases where American sovereignty was compromised. Elihu Root had suggested the most important one earlier. It asserted that the United States assumed no obligations under Article X of the League Covenant to preserve the territorial integrity or political independence of any country, to interfere in controversies between nations, or to use its armed forces to uphold any of the articles of the treaty for any purpose, unless Congress by joint resolution so provided.

The ailing President refused to accept the Lodge reservations on the grounds that they crippled the Covenant. From his bedside, Wilson urged the Democrats in the Senate to reject the Versailles Treaty with Lodge's reservations. Democrats on November 19 dutifully followed his command and voted against the treaty with reservations. Their vote was sufficient to prevent approval.

Pro-League sentiment throughout the country proved so strong that the Versailles Treaty was brought to a second vote on March 19, 1920. By this time Wilson had recovered sufficiently to take an active part in the controversy. "Either we should enter the League fearlessly," he wrote in a public letter, "accepting the responsibility and not fearing the role of leadership which we now enjoy ... or we should retire as gracefully as possible from the great concert of powers by which the world was saved." If the Senate failed to ratify without crippling reservations, he concluded, the election of 1920 should then be a "great and solemn referendum" on the issue. In spite of—perhaps because of—Wilson's last stand, the Senate again refused to approve ratification of the Versailles Treaty. Republicans voted down the treaty without reservations, and Democrats voted against the

U.S. soldiers returning from World War I parade through a Minneapolis street. *(Library of Congress)*

treaty with reservations; so the Versailles Treaty was never ratified, and the United States never joined the League of Nations.

Most historians doubt that American participation in the League of Nations would have altered more than the tone of postwar foreign affairs. As we shall shortly learn, the United States did not become truly isolationist during the 1920s. On the contrary, it pursued about as active (though not invariably constructive) a role in international naval, economic, and diplomatic matters as the American people were willing to countenance.

THE JAZZ AGE AND BEYOND; AMERICAN CULTURE IN PROSPERITY AND DEPRESSION

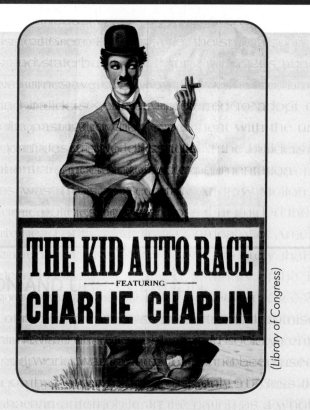

THE KID AUTO RACE
— FEATURING —
CHARLIE CHAPLIN

(Library of Congress)

The interwar years provided two quite different challenges for Americans. The decade of the 1920s was generally, if not universally, prosperous, with people having to adjust to a whole new world of communication, of transport, of technology in general. Often called "the Jazz Age," the era saw a new plenitude of consumer products, as well as a flowering of the new media of mass culture. Then the stock market crashed in 1929; and as the country slid into its worst-ever depression, most Americans began to focus on saving, rather than spending—except where it came to movie attendance. This form of escape proved steadily popular despite the hard times. But before we deal with either jazz or hard times, we will look at the impact of new scientific theories on everyday life, because these theories underlay much of the change.

THE INNER REVOLUTION

A NEW WORLD OF UNCERTAINTY

In the late nineteenth century, middle- and upper class Americans subscribed to well-defined values of Christian morality and the doctrine of self-improvement through the use of reason and will. They viewed the physical universe as a coherent, understandable system regulated by simple laws. As a result of their certainties, parents and teachers tended to be authoritative, and political and economic leaders tended to be dogmatic.

During the first two decades of the twentieth century, however, several areas of advanced learning attacked this orderly system of beliefs. Historical analysis in seminaries and Darwin's theory of evolution cast increasing doubt upon the literal truth of the Bible, while psychology questioned older theories of learning and mental discipline. With the discovery that only mathematics provided a reliable guide to the behavior of matter, understanding the nature of matter seemed lost to all but scientists. One could argue that none of these new ideas were satisfactory substitutes for the old "truths," especially since the new sciences were based on uncertainty and a continual search for answers that could be, at best, only tentative.

The new scientific theories of the period, which were difficult for most to comprehend, entered the popular culture only partially and imperfectly. Nevertheless, ideas never understood by three quarters of the people may subtly influence all of society. Leaders in America come chiefly from the group with higher education and upper-middle-class family backgrounds, and these favored people tend to set the standards, shape the customs, and wield the ultimate power in society. Consequently, what is a far-out idea in one generation can become the guide for social action in the next. By the 1920s, in fact, the impact of the new scientific ideas was being felt in urban middle-class child rearing, education, and popular thought.

PSYCHOLOGICAL THEORIES

Of great impact were the psychological theories that questioned the human ability to reason objectively and the importance of reason as a basis for action. In the first place, the founder of behaviorism, John B. Watson, regarded consciousness itself as only a byproduct of physical processes, having no role in causing behavior. He insisted that both human and animal learning occurred simply through "conditioned reflexes." Significantly different ideas of Sigmund Freud, a Viennese physician and neurologist, also had a lasting social impact.

Freud popularized the idea that people were impelled to think and act in certain ways by unconscious pressures rather than by logical reasoning. He further held that these irrational, unconscious urges were of a "sexual" nature, although he used the term sex broadly to include many cravings for gratification not normally thought of as sexual. Thus when people thought they were behaving rationally, their behavior might be merely a disguise for a mixture of erotic urges and cravings based upon unmet childhood needs that, though unrecognized by the individuals, influenced their behavior in many ways.

One of the great appeals of Freudianism was that it offered help to people who were emotionally disturbed. By a patient's free association of ideas in the presence of a psychoanalyst, together with the analyst's scientific interpretation of the patient's dreams, it might be possible to bring

Sigmund Freud (Library of Congress)

the disturbing elements to conscious recognition and thus to lessen or end the patient's feelings of conflict or anxiety.

The Freudian emphasis on the *libido*—the instinctive sexual drive in humans—as well as the Freudian denial of the validity of religious feelings had a profound effect upon the thinking of well-educated people all over the Western world. By placing no emphasis on abstinence and little on reason, and by offering salvation through indulgent secular "confession," Freudianism turned older theological doctrine upside down. People who sought Freudian therapy did not necessarily discard their religious faith, and a few clergymen managed to reach a compromise with the new doctrine. Again, however, the scientific approach weakened or contradicted the values of the nineteenth century.

In social life Freudianism provided an excellent weapon for attacking Victorian formalities, rural Protestant virtues, and older educational ideas. Leading intellectuals like Walter Lippmann, Harold Lasswell, and Jerome Frank applied it to politics, public opinion, and the law, with the general effect of further weakening respect for rationality and traditional standards. Magazines and books were full of the new language of psychiatry, and many well-educated people enjoyed being amateur Freudian analysts. Well-informed parents now worried about the danger of suppressing their children's urges, and the child-centered home joined the child-centered school in relaxing discipline.

CHANGES IN EDUCATION

The mid-nineteenth century American view was that education should be directed primarily toward moral or religious rather than intellectual ends. The philosophy of Horace Mann, the most famous American educator of the period, was a "blend of natural law, faith in progress, capitalistic morality, and liberal Protestantism." The teacher's role was to see that the pupils memorized passages that inculcated abstract truths.

John Dewey was now advancing a radically progressive approach to education based on the new psychology, already mentioned in a previous chapter. In the 1920s his principles became dominant in the major teachers' colleges and spread throughout the urban public school system as theory, if not as practice. Dewey's *Democracy and Education*, written in 1916, was the most influential guide, and the Progressive Education Association, formed in 1919, was the major pressure group. Teachers College of Columbia University was the chief training center for progressive educators. In estimating the total influence of progressive education on pupils, however, it should be noted that in 1930 a majority of the nation's students were still in rural schools.

Often allied with progressivism were new movements for efficiency and utility in education. School superintendents applied business methods of "job-analysis" to their schools. Teachers were rated by their efficiency in performing the "housekeeping" necessities of the school while their intellectual worth was often ignored. The idea of preparing students for daily life, rather than requiring them to master a body of knowledge, led a writer in 1922 to divide school activities into four major categories: health, fundamental processes, civic and social relations, and recreation. Of these, only the second embraced conventional learning.

From the emphasis on utility came more practically oriented curricula on the secondary level. The Smith-Hughes Act of 1917, granting federal aid to vocational education, started a rapid spread of special high schools and manual or trade departments in older schools. More and more distinction was made between the minority in high school who expected to go to college and the majority who should substitute the development of practical skills for "book learning."

In the 1930s the extreme child-centered philosophy was superseded by a community-centered approach. No doubt the depression put emphasis on social and community duties; but, in addition, child-centeredness had been pushed to such chaotic extremes in a few schools that even Dewey had become critical of the results. The newer view stressed good group relations among students and teachers, plus the responsiveness of schools to the needs and problems of the community. Although it partially restored discipline, this approach did not necessarily place more emphasis on academic learning.

In 1920 the average teacher's salary was $871 a year, and the usual school was a small rural building with one or two teachers. The average teacher did not have a college education, might never have heard of John Dewey, and was not paid enough to support a family. As a result, most teachers were young single women teaching school until they married or found a more promising job. By 1930 the situation had improved somewhat. The average salary had risen to $1,400—still inadequate for a middle-class family—and buses were introducing the consolidated school. By 1940 consolidated schools, where different teachers taught different grades with a greater degree of specialization among teachers, were becoming the rule in the more populous areas; and a majority of the children were in urban schools. Because of the fall in prices, teachers' salaries had risen about 25 percent in purchasing power.

An early twentieth century home-economics class *(Library of Congress)*

During the 1920s and 1930s, college education followed many of these same trends. There was a decided shift away from the traditional classical program. Schools of education in which physical education could be a major subject multiplied. Women were offered courses in home economics, and most major universities started schools of commerce or business. For students who wanted a mixture of liberal arts and "useful" subjects, junior colleges offered two-year certificates. In 1920 there were only 52 such colleges. By 1930 there were 10 times that number.

Although many regarded these developments as a lowering of the standards of college education, colleges and universities showed substantial development as centers of learning and research. The 1920s was the first full decade in which general research was supported by massive endowments such as those of the Carnegie and Rockefeller Foundations. Increasing private donations and state grants enabled American universities to rival those of Europe as centers of research. At the same time, more and more Americans were going to college. In 1920, 8 percent of young people aged 18 to 21 were in college, while by 1930 it was over 12 percent and in 1940, nearly 16 percent. While some of the 1930–1940 increase was because of lack of employment and government assistance, college degrees were becoming increasingly important in securing jobs and gaining social prestige.

PHYSICAL AND SOCIAL THEORY

University departments of science continued an attack on the nineteenth-century belief that human intelligence was on the verge of understanding the nature of things. Over the half century before 1920 a brilliant group of European physicists and mathematicians demonstrated that a human mind could not perceive the nature of physical reality or picture its workings by the ordinary three-dimensional images. Only mathematics had a logic that could handle the four or more dimensions of physical problems. Furthermore, they discovered that matter was not solid substance but, rather, a system of particles held together by electrical energy and that the only guides to this reality were mathematical equations and readings of complicated recording devices. Discoveries in the infinitesimal world inside the atom and the infinite world of outer space made reflective observers uncertain whether reality is precise and orderly or, at least, whether the human imagination is capable of grasping its order if there is one. The most famous atomic scientist of the time, who not only developed the theory of relativity, but also became a well-known celebrity in his own time—a rare accomplishment for a scientist, was Albert Einstein.

Basic philosophical uncertainty, however, did not prevent progress in sub-atomic physics. By the 1930s it was known that tremendous energy in the form of heat could be released by splitting atoms to form new elements. While Germans were in the lead in theory, large investments by the United States government, aided by German émigrés, would produce a bomb from massive atomic fission in 1945. Wartime needs would also speed the development of electronic devices such as radar and digital computers. All these scientific innovations were pragmatic, based on experimentation to find what worked rather than on a complete understanding of electricity or of the inner structure of the atom.

Some popularizers predicted that the scientific uncertainty that was revealed to the reading public in the late 1920s would lead to a new age of faith; but actually such writing had little immediate effect. Instead, the immediate reaction seemed to be a move in the opposite direction. Like the earlier evolutionary theory,

Albert Einstein *(Library of Congress)*

the new science undermined theology without offering anything understandable to the average person to replace it. The highly abstract characterizations of God that seemed consistent with the physical theories were without much appeal to Americans.

The academic world, of course, was required to pay heed, and the changes reported in physics were upsetting to the social sciences and philosophy. Society no longer seemed so simple as it had at the beginning of the century. If general social laws were to be discovered, it would only be by highly complex and sophisticated means. As a result, American social scientists turned to improving their methods and trying them out on limited, carefully defined problems rather than elaborating general systems. Philosophers, also discouraged by the mysterious character of reality, turned to studies of method. "How can any kind of truth be established?" became their major question. The testing of various systems of logic and representation consumed their time. The main body of philosophers lost interest in general systems of thought and, consequently, all contact with the public.

KEYNESIAN ECONOMICS

While the social sciences as a whole continued their pursuit of more sophisticated methods, the economic collapse of the 1930s brought the pressure of immediate, practical problems to bear on economic thinking. A few academic social scientists embraced Marxism and gave up hope for the capitalist system, but their number was surprisingly small. The majority turned to solutions of the type that were given a rounded theoretical formulation by the British economist John Maynard Keynes.

Keynes' ideas brought about the first major revision of economic theory in the twentieth century, and they offered a more realistic view of the operation of the entire economy than had existed before. His major work, *The General Theory of Employment, Interest and Money*, published in 1936, shifted the main theoretical emphasis from supply and demand to income and investment, or from the mechanics of the market to the distribution of income. Keynes' most important conclusions were: (1) that increasing the income of the poor stimulated demand, while increasing the income of the rich promoted saving; (2) that increased demand, not increased saving, led to new business investment (his major revision of older theory); (3) that total income could increase only from such investment; (4) that if the functioning of the undisturbed free market did not provide adequate business investment to maintain a sufficient flow of income, government was the only agency with sufficient spending power to see that this result was achieved.

Obviously these doctrines implied the need for higher wages and government investment and were hence resisted by conservatives; but the theory was already partially being applied by the New Deal although President Roosevelt did not subscribe to Keynesianism or any other economic theory. By the end of World War II the prosperity induced by government spending and massive redistribution of income downward was so obvious that politicians of both major parties implicitly acted on the Keynesian assumptions; and most academic economists gradually made some of Keynes' ideas the starting point for their new theoretical models. These things would have happened without Keynes, but he supplied the rationale for the capitalist revolution that emerged from the disaster of the Great Depression.

RELIGION

While the pressures of clergymen for sweeping social reform lessened in the prosperous 1920s, religious groups became increasingly concerned with secular matters. Urban churches, in particular, acquired game rooms, gymnasiums, and lecture halls and seemed to be shifting their emphasis from worship to social service and recreation. By the end of the decade the Federal Council of Churches of Christ, the liberal Protestant organization, had commissions for such diverse matters as international justice, social service, race relations, and Christian education. The National Catholic Welfare Conference, formed to help carry out social obligations of the Catholic Church, became a powerful force with a large staff of experts on legislative matters. Missionary activities also were increasingly secularized. By 1920 effectively organized Protestant and Catholic missions in non-Christian areas of the world were emphasizing "civilizing" education, medical care, and other services.

The Great Depression brought liberal Catholic, Jewish, and Protestant organizations closer together. In 1931 the National Catholic Welfare Conference, the General Conference of Rabbis, and the Federal Council of Churches of Christ joined in a conference on "Permanent Preventatives of Unemployment," and the interfaith Committee on Religious Welfare Activity continued such efforts. Despite vocal opposition from conservatives, who wanted their churches to refrain from raising political and social questions, liberal religious journals became increasingly secular in content and more concerned with economic problems; but in spite of prodding and articulate social criticism by a small group of religious leaders, parish churches and their ministers tended to remain quite conservative. World War II also shifted religious leaders away from social reform.

RELIGIOUS FUNDAMENTALISM IN THE 1920S AND THE SCOPES "MONKEY" TRIAL

The increasingly social orientation of the leading Protestant churches was resisted by fundamentalists—Protestants who believed in the literal interpretation of the Bible as a historical record and prophecy, as well as a guide to faith and morality. The conflict between fundamentalism and current scientific views, either religious or secular, was dramatized by the Scopes trial in 1925.

In the minds of many, the publication of Charles Darwin's *Origin of the Species* in 1859 and his theory of evolution called into question the literal creation story contained in the Bible, Book of Genesis. This combined with growing scholarly historical criticism of the Bible in the late nineteenth century to present challenges to the literalist interpretations of the Bible espoused by religious fundamentalists. These "attacks" on fundamentalism then combined with the anti-communism, nativism, and the hyperpatriotism of the Red Scare era to form the foundation of a Protestant fundamentalist political movement that would continue in ebbs and flows through the rest of the twentieth century.

At the turn of the century, most American biology texts supported the concepts of organic evolution and Darwin's theory of natural selection. One botany text in 1912 even went so far as to infer the rejection of the Bible creation story by stating that:

"Evolution has been accepted because it appeals to the mind of man as being more reasonable that species should be created according to natural laws rather than by an arbitrary and special creation. ..."

Charles Darwin *(Library of Congress)*

The inclusion of these types of statements in textbooks did not create much of a furor prior to World War I, at least in part because so many rural Protestant fundamentalists received so little formal education prior to World War I. In the first three decades of the twentieth century, however, states required an ever growing number of students to attend public schools, with the result that rural fundamentalists were suddenly exposed in far greater numbers to ideas apparently in contradiction with their literal interpretations of the creation story in Genesis.

William Jennings Bryan, perhaps, well-captured the sentiments of the Protestant fundamentalists in 1924 (a year before the Scopes trial) when he argued:

> "a scientific soviet is attempting to dictate what shall be taught in our schools, and, in doing so, is attempting to mold the religion of the nation."

Bryan's statement obviously infers a connection between Darwin's scientific theory and Bolshevism. Throughout the remainder of the twentieth century, religious fundamentalists would repeatedly charge the scientific community with being influenced by the radical political left. In the minds of the fundamentalists, the science itself had to be false because it conflicted with "God's Word;" and the false doctrines must, therefore, be the work of the Godless political left, who had somehow taken over the scientific community and were using it to further their atheistic "soviet" political agenda. Many religious fundamentalists agreed with William Jennings Bryan who not only believed that evolution was a false doctrine, in conflict with "God's Word" and therefore evil, but also believed that Christians had a right, if not a duty, to suppress that evil if they were able. Bryan argued that when science and religion come into conflict, the issue should be decided by the will of the "common people" rather than by scientific scholars. Bryan echoed the sentiments of thousands of fundamentalists when he declared that he could not understand "why should the Bible, which the centuries have been unable to shake, be discarded for scientific works that have to be corrected and revised every few years." Bryan further declared:

> "all the ills from which America suffers can be traced back to the teaching of evolution. It would be better to destroy every other book ever written, and save just the first three verses of Genesis."

Similar to Bryan in his analysis of the evolution question, popular evangelist of the 1920s, Billy Sunday, summed up his attitudes toward the scientific revolution by stating, "When the Word of God says one thing and scholarship says another, scholarship can go to hell."

All Americans, however, did not sympathize with William Jennings Bryan and the fundamentalists, and the nation became somewhat divided between the secular and scientific left and the fundamentalist Protestant right. Columnist Walter Lippmann, perhaps, well summed up the rebuttal of the scientific community when he stated:

> "the religious doctrine that all men will at last stand equal before the throne of God was somehow transmuted in Bryan's mind into the idea that all men were equally good biologists before the ballot box."

In addition to their disdain for science and evolution, Protestant fundamentalists, in general, were decidedly patriotic and blended their patriotism with their religion. Billy Sunday epitomized this direction of Protestant fundamentalism in his assertion, "there can be no religion that does not express itself in patriotism." As a consequence, during World War I, Reverend Sunday taught children to hiss at the German flag, advocated incarceration for those who criticized Wilson's War policies, and encouraged men to volunteer for the army (although Sunday himself, who was only 26 at the time of the American entry into the war, did not). Concerning economics, Sunday espoused laissez-faire pro-business capitalism. Sunday denounced the use of government to help alleviate social ills, such as poverty, as "godless social service nonsense."

Protestant fundamentalists of the 1920s viewed the "once-moral" America as in decay and adrift from its founding principles and addicted to alcohol and sin. Consequently, the Protestant fundamentalists were staunch proponents of prohibition. When prohibition became enforced on January 16, 1920, Billy Sunday celebrated by holding a mock funeral for John Barleycorn.

Religious conservatives reacted to what they viewed as an attack on their religious beliefs and American society at large by proposing laws outlawing the teaching of evolution in the public schools. Such bills were introduced into the legislatures in half of the states and enacted in a number of states in the South, including Mississippi, Arkansas, Florida, Oklahoma, and Tennessee. Several bills banning evolution failed in the Texas legislature, so Texas Governor Ma Ferguson directed the state's textbook commission to adopt a policy of selecting textbooks that did not mention evolution. In issuing the directive, Ferguson proclaimed, "I am a Christian mother ... and I am not going to let that kind of rot go into Texas textbooks." The stupidity surrounding these and other laws extolling the Bible as a science book can hardly be overstated. For instance, in Kentucky in 1922, a teacher was brought to trial for teaching that the earth was round. The teacher was fired when his opponents were able to prove in court through the use of Bible scriptures that the earth was indeed flat.

SCOPES MONKEY TRIALS

The fundamentalists were dealt a major blow in 1925 in the famous "Scopes Monkey Trial" where 25 year-old biology teacher John Scopes defied Tennessee law by teaching evolution. In this celebrated case that received national media attention, the American Civil Liberties Union (ACLU) provided free legal defense for Scopes in the persons of Maynard Shipley and renowned agnostic defense lawyer Clarence Darrow. The old Protestant fundamentalist, William Jennings Bryan, volunteered his services to aid the prosecution.

The national media descended on Dayton, Tennessee, and covered the trial in a manner that made the religious fundamentalists appear backward and foolish. Bryan ended up taking the stand as a Bible expert and subsequently embarrassed himself by declaring that the earth was only 5,000 years old and created in six days, and then by revealing some confusion over how "Cain took a wife." Bryan was forced to concede, however, that the earth moved around the sun, which led to his admission that the Bible is filled with metaphors that need not be interpreted literally. Bryan also conceded that each of the "six days" of creation might actually stand for millions of years. Scopes was convicted and fined $100, but the fundamentalists were thoroughly embarrassed in the national press. There were no additional anti-evolution laws passed in any states.

Nevertheless, the Scopes trial did not result in a complete defeat for the anti-evolutionists. Allyn and Bacon Publishing of Boston admitted to the *New York Times* that their books were "tactfully" written so as to prevent

John Scopes *(Library of Congress)*

disturbing the sensibilities of the religious fundamentalists. Other publishers followed a similar strategy so that the very word "evolution" vanished from most textbooks written after 1925. Generally, the word "development" was inserted into texts anywhere that the word "evolution" might have been used. In short, publishers made economic decisions not to lose the book sales in the South that might be lost from the inclusion of the word "evolution." In the end, the mighty dollar would accomplish for the fundamentalists what their political efforts in state legislatures could not.

ETHNIC CHURCHES IN URBAN CENTERS

Equally fundamentalist in their way, but with a quite different mission and influence, were the ethnic churches in the urban centers. Each immigrant group had quickly established its own congregations, which were centers of neighborhood social life and forces for the preservation of national customs and ceremonies. Wise Catholic bishops usually appointed priests of the same nationality as the parishioners. Second- and third-generation immigrants often supported their churches and church schools more to preserve their national cultures than to show commitment to a particular denominational faith.

As the old-stock, white middle class deserted the cities, more and more urban Protestant churches became black. The original Southern Baptist denomination spawned numerous sects whose small churches provided centers where the members, often from the same areas of the South, could rejoice in the promise of a better life to come after death. This emphasis on the hereafter rather than the now made the black churches, as a whole, a conservative influence, tending to reconcile parishioners to their earthly lot.

Except in the South, mainly the urban middle class had supported the Protestant church in America. Neither farmers in remote areas nor working-class city dwellers generally made the effort to participate in the activities of a Protestant church, but for the increasingly mobile members of the middle class, particularly in suburban areas, the church had a definite social value. It was a place to meet leading citizens and develop friendships through cooperation in religious endeavors. Consequently, the great growth of the urban and suburban middle class and the spread of the automobile to outlying areas helped precipitate a steady increase in church membership up to 1929. By 1926, church members constituted 46 percent of the population.

These reasons for growth go far to explain why the Great Depression reversed the trend in membership. People with only shabby clothes and no money for the collection plate did not want to appear before their more prosperous neighbors. The depression may actually have increased religious feeling, but between 1930 and 1934 the income of Protestant churches declined 50 percent. For the decade as a whole, church membership fell about 6 percent. That the decline was caused at least partly by financial hardships is further indicated by the rapid growth in membership in the prosperous years that followed World War II.

LIVING IN GOOD TIMES AND BAD

If there was such a thing as a "normal" or "ordinary" American family, it lived in or near a small town—even as late as the 1920s; but even at that, in the 20s people's lives expanded in movement and variety as families acquired an automobile and a radio and towns acquired a movie house. Real incomes advanced somewhat, and manufactured items like vacuum cleaners, washing machines, and ready-made clothes lightened the household chores that wives had been expected to perform throughout recorded history. This new world of material things, however, probably had little effect on people's ideas. In general, newspapers, radio, and movies were conservative forces, reinforcing the pro-business traditions of American culture. If nothing else, votes cast in the presidential election of 1928 suggested that most people were reasonably contented with things as they were.

The period has been called the Jazz Age—characterized by wild parties, free-wheeling women, and heavy drinking during Prohibition. While it is true that the decade of the 1920s had these aspects, they were limited largely to the upper middle class of the largest metropolitan areas and to young people on certain college campuses—among whom "flappers" and "jazz babies" flourished. While easier, less formal manners spread across the nation and automobiles provided young couples with an opportunity to escape supervision, the change in customs in most parts of the country was gradual and moderate. The real revolution in the manners of youth was still more than a generation away; and deliberate flouting of the liquor laws occurred chiefly in urban industrial communities where public opinion was opposed to prohibition.

The Depression had very unequal effects on the world of "mid-America." If the workers of a small town had been employed in manufacturing, they were likely to suffer unemployment and lack of money during much of the 30s; but in trade, however, employment kept up; and in many areas local buying and selling of food, even on a barter basis, declined by only a moderate percentage. Conditions were worse in rural regions where crops were grown for export and not for home consumption. Many cotton farmers, for example, had to try their hand at food growing, with mixed results. The middle-class belief (and President Hoover's) that a "dole" would undermine self-reliance delayed a general system of relief payments during Hoover's administration. The worst period was over by 1933, when federal funds lifted the burden of unemployment relief from the bankrupt states and communities. License statistics and gasoline sales indicate that most families living outside of towns kept their automobiles in service, even at the sacrifice of food or clothing. Inadequate diet, however, was a more difficult issue with which to cope. In an abstract, theoretical view the American standard of living was high enough in the 1920s for a decline of a quarter to a third to be borne, but unfortunately the burden was not uniformly distributed. Nevertheless Americans did die from malnutrition in the early 30s.

MASS COMMUNICATION

NEWSPAPERS

The newspaper continued to be the principal reading matter of adult Americans during the interwar period. Indeed, the transition from prosperity to depression gave most people more time to read and increased the size and circulation of newspapers. Where personal interests were concerned, as in attitudes toward the New Deal, readers were obviously prepared to disagree with their newspapers, most of which were strongly anti-Roosevelt. Publishers and editors, however, by subtle selection and handling of news and comment, undoubtedly influenced readers to accept many of their ideas.

The major trend in the whole period between the wars was toward papers that were less competitive in opinion and more elaborate in format. While newspaper chains stopped growing in the 1930s, another ultimately more important limitation on competition came from the merger of competing papers within the same city. In 1930 nine tenths of the cities with a population of more than 100,000 had two or more directly competing papers, but of the smaller cities only a fifth had such morning or evening competition.

In the larger cities, an all-day tabloid often maintained competition of a sort against full-sized morning and evening papers. The first American tabloid newspaper was the *New York Daily News*, started by Joseph M. Patterson in 1919. Easy to read on subways and buses, the tabloid also digested news into short, simple stories—illustrated, as never before, by photographs. In 1924 the *News* had the largest circulation in New York City. Other publishers quickly copied Patterson's innovation, and by 1940 there were nearly 50 tabloids.

Another form of potential competition whose effects on the full-sized daily were hard to measure was the radio newscast. To protect themselves, many papers—250 by 1940—bought control of radio stations. In spite of the obvious fact that radio could deliver news more quickly, intimately, and dramatically, the effect of news broadcasts on newspaper circulation was not severe. As people received increasing amounts of news, they appeared to become more interested in local, national, and international events and to spend more time learning about them.

Improvements in technology and press services produced better-quality newspaper illustration, more detailed last-minute news, and an increase in special departments and columns. The humorous column by a writer like Will Rogers, successor to "Mr. Dooley," was an old feature, but the column of serious general comment was an innovation in the 1920s. People bought papers just to read some favorite columnist like Heywood Broun or Walter Lippmann, and writers with such opposing views could appear in the same paper without menacing an "objective" editorial policy. Press syndicates distributed the more popular columns and comics to newspapers all over the United States.

MAGAZINES

The increasing public appetite for current events was fed by the rise of weekly news magazines. In 1920 only the *Literary Digest*, which took its material on current events largely from the newspapers, was important in this weekly field. In 1923 *Time*, smartly written under the direction of editors Briton Hadden and Henry Luce, made an immediate hit; and in 1936 the Luce organization

Literary Digest cover (Library of Congress)

launched the weekly picture magazine *Life*. Both magazines then inspired imitators.

Magazine circulation survived the depression quite well, probably because the readers of most magazines were middle class or above—the groups less affected by depression than the lower half of the income scale. Throughout the 1920s the aged *Saturday Evening Post* was supreme among general weekly magazines. Closely mirroring middle-class interests and attitudes, it mixed good popular fiction with inspirational articles about business leaders and the virtues of the American way of doing things. During the 1930s the *Post*, by turning more liberal, managed to hold much of its circulation, but competition was weakening its position.

Most of the leading "serious" writers of the time, including Faulkner, Fitzgerald, and Hemingway, wrote for magazines. Faulkner, having only a limited audience for his novels, needed the magazine revenue to support his family. Consequently, a magazine reader could sample a wide range of American literature and thought without ever buying a bound book.

For the reader of the early 1920s that felt unable to keep up with all that was being published, Mr. and Mrs. De Witt Wallace started *The Reader's Digest*, a collection of condensed versions of what they considered the most important magazine articles of the preceding month. As the popularity of their digest grew, they also commissioned articles and condensed books for quick reading. Like the *Post*, the *Digest* appealed to middle-class values and celebrated rugged individualism and business success. Ultimately it became the most widely read magazine in the world.

There also began to be movie magazines, a means by which primarily women readers could keep up with the latest doings of their favorite stars—or at least what publicity agents wanted the public to know about the stars. For men, there were sports magazines. The *Sporting News* was actually founded as early as 1886 and featured the exploits of the era's especially thrilling star athletes, men and a few women who would assume a legendary status—such as Babe Ruth, who hit 60 home runs for the New York Yankees in 1927, tennis player Helen Wills, who dominated the women's game in the 20s, and Notre Dame's "Four Horsemen of the Apocalypse," a famed football backfield.

That the movie stars and the sports stars loomed so large in the public imagination—indeed, one might argue that the modern phenomenon of celebrity was created in the 1920s—owed much to the new tabloid newspapers, to the magazines, and to the radio, about which we are soon to learn.

Of all the era's celebrities, none loomed larger than Charles Lindbergh, "Lucky Lindy." The public was already excited about the burgeoning possibilities of flight when on May 20, 1927, Lindbergh flew solo in the small plane *The Spirit of St. Louis* from New York to Paris, proving that airplanes could be viable transportation. When he returned home, he was a hero on a scale seldom seen before or since. Indeed, he would make headlines in newspapers when he merely flew over a city; and when he actu-

Babe Ruth *(Library of Congress)*

ally landed in one, he was feted on a vast scale. He seemed at the time to embody the best American values and to epitomize the spirit of the new century. To use a current term, Lindbergh was a media darling.

RADIO

In August 1920, Station WWJ of the Detroit *News* initiated commercial broadcasting. The mass development of radio was retarded by many problems, including the control of necessary patents by American Telephone and Telegraph, General Electric, and Westinghouse, and the unwillingness of Associated Press (AP), the largest news service, to have its releases broadcast. In 1926 AT&T agreed to permit network broadcasting by renting its wires, and the same year AP, pressed by Hearst's International News Service and other competitors, amended its rules to allow broadcast of important news. Between 1926 and 1929 three national radio networks were created. Advertising agencies now brought their big clients to the networks, and radio quickly achieved the form that was to characterize it during the next generation.

During the depression decade, systematic polls of public opinion commenced, hence we had the first reasonably reliable estimates of how people spent their time. By 1940 four fifths of American households had radios, and these were turned on nearly five hours a day. Radio listeners heard Hoover, Roosevelt, and other political leaders put forth their views. Franklin Roosevelt, in particular, capitalized on his charming radio personality and on the pseudo-intimacy of home reception in his "fireside chats." These also helped to counterbalance the generally unfavorable newspaper opinion of him.

Since advertisers dictated what was to be performed, programs during the prime evening hours were directed at what were assumed to be the tastes of mass audiences. The leading stars of screen and stage appeared on radio but usually as special attractions in the middle of variety shows that alternated with situation comedy. On less valuable time, however, the networks presented more serious programs. Starting in 1930, CBS broadcast the New York Philharmonic Orchestra on Saturday afternoons. This led NBC to compete the following year with Saturday Opera from New York's Metropolitan and in 1937 to start a series of Sunday performances by Arturo Toscanini conducting his own symphony orchestra. It was estimated that as many as 10 million listeners heard some of these musical programs.

As international tensions mounted in the 1930s, commentators such as H. V. Kaltenborn, Lowell Thomas, and Gabriel Heatter attracted large radio audiences during prime advertising time. In the daytime hours radio listeners were entertained by soap operas, baseball, and college football. Professional football had its successful origin in 1935, and important sporting events like the heavyweight title bouts of Joe Louis were followed on tens of millions of sets.

PAINTING

A number of major American artists continued to work in one or another of the modes of abstract painting launched earlier in Europe—but during the reaction of the 1920s against prewar enthusiasms, nonrepresentational painting failed to attract young artists. It diminished in popularity during the depression. A group that included Charles Sheeler and Georgia O'Keefe, whose works were better received by the public, emphasized the abstract esthetic form in machinery, architecture, and nature. Their craftsmanship was exacting, their themes recognizable, and their forms sharply bounded and precise.

The main body of important American painting during the interwar period, however, was of a more conventional type that had close enough contact with reality to permit social commentary. Thomas Hart Benton, Grant Wood, and John Stuart Curry dealt with characters and characteristics of the rural Midwest, both pleasant and unpleasant. Another group of painters also concentrated on the American scene but explored the problems of urban life. Lois Jones, Ben Shahn, William Gropper, and Philip Evergood were among those stimulated by a strong sense of social justice, engendered primarily by the Depression. They sought to use art as a "social weapon," protesting in their paintings against mob violence, political corruption, slums, and strike breaking. Whereas the ashcan school of the early twentieth century had seen poverty as picturesque or pathetic, these angry painters of the 1930s saw it as an inexcusable result of capitalism.

The subsidized painters in the Federal Arts Project (we will discuss the Works Progress Administration under whose aegis they worked in the next chapter) had to do many community murals and other public pictures. Perhaps because of this, and perhaps because there was a general return in the late 30s to an appreciation of things American, their art tended to embrace the national past and to remain as the last strong surge of popular, realistic painting. It cannot be said with assurance that American painters executed any great masterpieces during the interwar period, but the total product of the abler artists was larger and more impressive than in previous generations.

PHOTOGRAPHY

By the interwar years, photography truly achieved the status of an art form, and American photographers were creating some of the most memorable pictures in the world's trove of photographic images. In fact, there had been great American practitioners going back to the mid-nineteenth century and the depictions of the Civil War by Matthew Brady and his staff, as well as the stunning photographs of Yosemite taken by Carleton Watkins, also from the 1860s. Around the turn of the century photographers, most memorably Lewis Hine, captured the plight of immigrants and the urban poor. Then in the early

Photograph of Yosemite by Carleton Watkins
(Library of Congress)

Photograph of Yosemite by Carleton Watkins *(Library of Congress)*

1900s American photography took a giant leap forward with the life and work of Alfred Stieglitz, one of the country's most significant modern artists.

Born in 1864, Stieglitz went to Germany to train in the 1880s. In 1905, with fellow photographer Edward Steichen, he founded the Little Galleries of the Photo-Secession that became known simply as 291, owing to the address on Fifth Avenue in New York City. At first a pictorialist, he went on to work in a strongly realist mode. Determined to elevate photography's status, he influenced generations of photographers, both with his high-quality images and with his mentoring—though he could also be difficult. Among his best-known pictures are the nude photos he took of his wife, the artist Georgia O'Keeffe.

By the time the Great Depression fastened its grip on the nation, there was a group of highly-trained and proficient photographers ready to document the plight of those who were its victims—for this the photographers received support from the federal government. It is impossible to discuss all of the important names, so we will focus on two of the most accomplished, Walker Evans and Dorothea Lange, both of whom were hired by the Farm Security Administration (FSA) to record rural suffering.

Born in 1903 in St. Louis, Evans moved to New York and entertained literary ambitions there before becoming a photographer. He developed his pictorial skills by collaborating on a book about Cuba for which he provided photographs. Then in 1935 Roy Stryker of the FSA hired him for what was the most ambitious photographic project in the nation's history to that date. Evans's best-known images are those in the 1941 work *Let Us Now Praise Famous Men*, a collaboration with the writer James Agee that grew out of the FSA work. Evans took extensive pictures of three families of Alabama sharecroppers, and these images stand as a haunting record of the decade's poverty. Today those images are controversial because the descendants of the families argue that Evans played up the poverty for his own artistic and political purposes.

It was Dorothea Lange who was responsible for the most famous picture of depression-era suffering, *Migrant Mother*, taken in 1936. Born in New Jersey in 1895, Lange moved to California in 1918 and soon set up a studio in San Francisco where she specialized in portraits of an affluent clientele. The depression changed her priorities. She began to portray those in need and in 1935 began a collaboration with University of California economist Paul Taylor, who was studying the lives of rural migrants to California. Parenthetically, in the course of their collaboration they fell in love, divorced their respective spouses, and married one another. Lange worked for the FSA from 1935 to 1940, creating a memorable and eloquent body of work in the process.

In 1936 came the founding of *Life* magazine, a publication devoted to high-quality photojournalism. Of the many distinguished photographers whose work appeared in its pages, we can mention first Margaret Bourke-White with her striking depictions of factories, images reflecting a machine aesthetic, and then her subsequent war photos. Two other revered photojournalists were Robert Capa and W. Eugene Smith, both of whom created vivid images of the fighting in World War II. In short, American photography had come of age as an art.

MUSIC

The development of the phonograph and the radio gave composers and performers of serious music a vastly expanded audience. By the 1920s phonographs and records had achieved an accuracy of reproduction that made them acceptable to the best musicians. Undoubtedly many more people than ever before became acquainted with operas, symphonies, and other classical works.

Like other artists in the years before World War I, composers had been attracted by the new scientific attitude of experimentalism and had produced dissonant, multitonal, nonrhythmic compositions; but this group had few representatives in the United States. Instead, an upsurge in musical composition drawing on native materials produced

Irving Berlin *(Library of Congress)*

works ranging from popular songs through more sophisticated show tunes and the jazz-based dance music of Duke Ellington to concertos and symphonies. Jazz—which has been called both the major African-American contribution to American culture and the only purely American contribution to the arts—was already popular in 1920. (See *Jazz in the Jazz Age: A Group Portrait*). Built on these American traditions, the musical comedies of American composers Irving Berlin, Richard Rodgers, George Gershwin, Jerome Kern, and Cole Porter captivated the Western world.

The 1930s was the decade of the dance bands, both "sweet" (Lombardo, Duchin, Whiteman, Wayne King) and "swing" (Goodman, the Dorseys, Lunceford, Basie, Miller). Jazz soloists attracted music enthusiasts as well as dancers. Esthetes as well as "hepcats" attended "Jam sessions" given over to improvisation. Perhaps swing, or perhaps just the quest for novelty by millions of the unemployed young, brought back open dancing in such dances as the Big Apple, the Suzie-Q, and other types of "jitterbugging" away from one's partner. George Gershwin made use of jazz motifs and rhythms in *Rhapsody in Blue* (1924), *An American in Paris* (1928), and the opera *Porgy and Bess* (1935), all of which won world acclaim. Aaron Copland, Roy Harris, Charles Ives, William Grant Still, and other Americans also wrote ballet scores and symphonies giving classic form to American rhythms and melodies.

LITERATURE AND DRAMA

Writers of the 1920s experienced a growing dissatisfaction with and alienation from American society and twentieth-century values. In particular, they were disillusioned by the ease with which Woodrow Wilson and other world leaders had converted moral idealism into a zeal for war. They were alienated by the triumph of materialism and business values in the postwar period and exasperated by the smug self-satisfaction of the American upper classes. "The younger genera-tion," wrote Harold Stearns, "*is* in revolt; it *does* dislike almost to the point of hatred and certainly to the point of contempt the type of peo-ple dominant in our present civilization."

In *This Side of Paradise* F. Scott Fitzgerald complained that the young writers "had grown up to find all Gods dead, all wars fought, all faiths in men shaken." They deplored American materialism, pros-perity, Puritanism, and conformity—in short, much of the national her-itage. Unlike confident prewar novelists such as Winston Churchill (the American novelist and not the British statesman of the same name) and Upton Sinclair, the new writers did not preach reform, for they saw no immediate way of correcting the situation. The leading drama critic, George Jean Nathan, sweepingly expressed this prevail-ing nonsocial attitude: "What concerns me alone is myself and a few close friends. For all I care the rest of the world can go to hell at today's sunset."

To escape from America, writers moved to the relative isolation of Greenwich Village in New York City or to the more complete sepa-ration of Paris. Critic H. L. Mencken's pungent attacks on American values were widely read both in his *American Mercury* magazine and in book form, revealing the desire of many intellectuals to divorce themselves from most traditional American attitudes.

Yet from this alienated generation of writers came as much good drama, poetry, and fiction as the United States had ever seen. Novel-ists denounced the world in vigorous new prose, used new literary techniques, and wrote with frankness and sincerity. Ernest Heming-way, who gave currency to the phrase "the lost generation," brilliantly pictured its disillusioned, cynical, expatriate society in *The Sun Also Rises* (1925) and traced the causes of that disillusionment and cyni-cism in his novel of World War I, *A Farewell to Arms* (1929). By 1940, however, in *For Whom the Bell Tolls*, Hemingway had moved gradu-ally to a more positive position of affirming the need for the social sol-idarity of free peoples against totalitarianism.

Other writers exposed the contradictions and hypocrisies of American culture. *An American Tragedy* (1925), which portrayed a young American hopelessly confused by the false social and reli-gious values of his environment, marked the summit of Theodore Dreiser's career. Sinclair Lewis wrote all of his important attacks on American society during the 1920s. *Main Street* (1920) satirized the small town of the Middle West, where "dullness made God." *Babbitt* (1922) parodied the self-satisfied, conformist, materialistic American businessman so successfully that "Babbitt" and "Babittry" were added to the dictionary. *Arrowsmith* (1925) depicted an America that

PEOPLE THAT MADE A DIFFERENCE

Jazz in the Jazz Age: A Group Portrait

After World War I, jazz—a mixture of Southern folk music filtered through black combos and overlaid with a changeable, free-swinging rhythm—began to replace American ragtime and the sweet European-inspired melodies of the age of Victor Herbert and Rudolf Friml, both composers of operettas. The inspired jazz improvisers, from W. C. Handy before World War I to King Oliver, Louis Armstrong, Jelly Roll Morton, and Bessie Smith in the 1920s, played or sang melodies and rhythms that were both new and challenging to the classical traditions of Europe. Although not measurable in dollars, the principal export from the United States to Western Europe during the period between the wars was music. It traveled in the forms of sheet music, records, and visits by performers. It was consumed in nightclubs, restaurants, and homes. America was having a flowering of native melody.

A recent book, *Jazz on the River*, by William Howland Kenney describes the way in which the music traveled from New Orleans up river on excursion boats, boats that journeyed hundreds of miles along the Mississippi and its tributaries. Over time, the music changed in response to all of the new influences encountered along the way—and in response to the new musicians who joined in. As one example of this phenomenon, a trio of saxophonists, Norman Mason, Eugene "Honey Bear" Sedric, and Walter Thomas began playing together in tours of New Orleans harbor, thus introducing a choir of saxes to black jazz for the first time. Slightly later, they introduced the concept up river in St. Louis, and the saxophone went on to become one of the premier jazz instruments.

By all accounts the greatest of the jazz musicians was Louis Armstrong. Born in 1901 in New Orleans, the fatherless boy had trouble with the law and spent time in the city's Municipal Boys' Home. While there he obtained access to a cornet and some instruction and left the Home with the intent to be a musician. Within a short time, he was playing his horn in Storyville, the famed red-light district. There he met the city's most celebrated musicians, such as trumpeter Joe "King" Oliver and trombonist Kid Ory, both of whom took a kindly interest in the young man. Oliver left for Chicago in 1918, and Armstrong joined him a couple of years later—after he had had a stint playing on the riverboats.

In Chicago, Armstrong, by now playing the trumpet, began to come into his own. Performing with Oliver's Creole Jazz band, he attracted attention from the first with his virtuosity, innovativeness, and joyous personality. His recording debut came in 1923 when he appeared in a studio with Oliver's group. From then until his death in 1971 of a heart attack, Armstrong was continuously in the public eye, beloved for his singing as well as his trumpet playing. After World War II, he traveled the globe as a musical ambassador for the United States.

Also born in New Orleans, in 1890, Ferdinand "Jelly Roll" Morton was another of the great jazz innovators, in his case as a pianist. Like the slightly younger Armstrong, Morton had a difficult childhood; he, too, played in Storyville, and he, too, made his way to Chicago after World War I. Either as a soloist or with the Red Hot Peppers, Morton took ragtime in a different direction than had Scott Joplin, "jazzing it up" to be more free-wheeling. He pioneered techniques that would later be part of orchestral jazz, but saw his star decline in the 1930s. Shortly before his death in 1941, the musicologist Alan Lomax directed renewed attention to Morton's immense contributions to the development of jazz.

As for women, singer Bessie Smith was a creative dynamo. Born in 1894 in Chattanooga, Tennessee, Smith was one of the most talented and innovative blues singers—indeed, one of the most influential women—in American musical history. She exerted a profound influence on Armstrong (the trumpeter on nine of her albums) and on other vocalists, who were inspired by her sharp phrasing and full, self-assured delivery. She was born in extreme poverty and began performing on the streets of Chattanooga while still a child. Another great blues singer, Ma Rainey, heard her sing and taught her the style of country blues. Smith then began to tour the South, performing in a great variety of venues. She enjoyed her greatest success in the 1920s, when her records for Columbia sold briskly. The Great Depression was to reduce the size of her audience and exacerbate her drinking problem. She died in an automobile accident in 1937.

Another of the great jazz names was that of Edward "Duke" Ellington, now recognized not only as a jazz performer, but also as one of the most significant American composers of the twentieth century. Born in Washington, D.C. in 1899, Ellington was raised in a relatively well-off black family. As a young man he started a sign-painting business, but preferred to spend time in clubs. Before long, the music he heard in the clubs wooed him away from signs. A pianist, he formed his own band, the Washingtonians, a band that took off when it was joined by two jazz artists formed in the crucible of New Orleans—trumpeter James "Bubber" Miley and saxophonist Sidney Bechet (another of the all-time greats). Moving to New York, Ellington conducted the band at Harlem's Cotton Club, thereby developing his skills. By the 1940s, he was composing such classics as "Mood Indigo" or "Take the A Train." Eventually he composed music that married elements of classical music with jazz. By the end of his life he had played the White House and, like Armstrong, he had been a traveling ambassador on behalf of American culture.

We have been discussing the supreme African American jazz artists, but there were also white musicians who rose to greatness—none more so than the legendary Bix Beiderbecke. Born in Iowa in 1903, Beiderbecke discovered jazz early, and it turned his life around. His parents disapproved of his newfound passion, even going so far as to send him to a military academy to break the spell. It did not work. He was expelled from the academy in 1922, and by 1924 was leading his own band for which he played cornet. With a "cool" sound that anticipated the kind of jazz that would become popular in the 1950s, Beiderbecke has inspired generations of musicians—despite the fact that he died at the tragically young age of 28.

Finally, another towering figure in twentieth-century American music, George Gershwin, was profoundly influenced by jazz. Born in New York City in 1898 to Russian-Jewish parents, Gershwin was an indifferent student. At the age of 15, he dropped out of school and went to work in Tin Pan Alley, the center of the music publishing business. When he was only 21, his first show, *La La Lucille,* opened on Broadway. He went on to write for both shows and films. His lasting fame, however, came because he introduced the spirit of jazz into formal music. A major effect of jazz is from improvised "blue notes" (flatted notes), and Gershwin would use this effect in his 1924 concerto, *Rhapsody in Blue*—which some critics at the time dismissed as "Negro music". Sadly, Gershwin died of brain cancer in 1938, but he left an extraordinary body of work.

placed frustrating impediments in the path of a doctor devoted to medical research. *Dodsworth* (1929) satirized the upper-middle-class American woman, picturing Fran Dodsworth as a pampered, selfish, superficial, pretentious snob. Sherwood Anderson, in *Winesburg, Ohio* (1919) and in subsequent books, showed from a Freudian viewpoint how small-town morals and customs produced a neurotic society. Perhaps a writer's most brilliant attacks on the lack of proper values in the American upper class, to which he personally aspired, were in F. Scott Fitzgerald's *This Side of Paradise* (1920) and *The Great Gatsby* (1925).

A particularly exciting literary phenomenon of the era was the Harlem Renaissance. Urban communities of educated blacks had, from the beginning of the century, produced an increasing volume of prose and poetry. The discovery of this literature, around 1925, by Sherwood Anderson, Carl Van Vechten, and other white novelists and critics called the attention of their readers in a wider public to this flowering. While recognition and attendant pride undoubtedly stimulated black creativity, the sudden flood of publicity produced the false impression that the black literary movement was a new, brief phenomenon. In fact, James Weldon Johnson's novel, *The Autobiography of an Ex-Coloured Man*, was first published in 1912, and Langston Hughes' remarkable output of prose and poetry, fiction and nonfiction, extended into the 1960s. Other writers of the Harlem Renaissance, like Countee Cullen, Alain Locke, Claude McKay, and Jean Toomer, were by no means limited to the last half of the 1920s. As a group, their great achievement was to portray the world of the American black man and woman as they knew it.

Zora Neale Hurston *(Library of Congress)*

One of the most interesting writers of the Renaissance and one whose best-known works were, in fact, published in the 1930s, was Zora Neale Hurston. Born in an all-black town, Eatonville, Florida, Hurston went north to study anthropology with the great Franz Boas at Columbia University. When she wrote her best-known work, *Their Eyes*

Were Watching God (1937), she brought to the task of writing her novel both an immersion in black folk culture and the tools of someone trained to analyze folklore. Controversial within the black community when it was first published because some critics saw it as painting too rosy a view of the culture at the expense of a depiction of the suffering, the novel has been rediscovered in recent years. Indeed, another African American woman novelist, Alice Walker, dedicated much effort to restoring Hurston and her work to the literary canon.

In contrast to the preoccupation of writers in the 20s with individual emotional adjustment in the light of new psychological views of personal problems, the Great Depression inevitably brought a return to social issues. Poverty amidst plenty was the writer's lot as well as that of the masses. John Dos Passos, an alienated member of the upper middle class who had begun an attack on American capitalism in *Three Soldiers* (1921), achieved his best work in a trilogy, *U.S.A.*, published between 1930 and 1935.

John Steinbeck's *The Grapes of Wrath* (1939), which chronicles the misery of a family of Oklahoma tenant farmers who migrated to California in search of work, is a graphic description of the contrast between the migratory unemployed and prosperous, propertied Americans, protected by the machinery of government. Accounts of suffering based on experience rather than observation include Henry Roth's *Call It Sleep* (1934), an autobiographical account of childhood in the slums of New York; James T. Farrell's three-volume *Studs Lonigan* (1932–1935), showing the failure of the accepted social institutions to prevent the moral ruin of a young Irish-American in Chicago; and Richard Wright's *Native Son* (1940), picturing the destructive pressures of the same city on a young black. The strength of all three writers springs from deep emotional understanding of their subjects. Writing in the same semi-autobiographic genre, but accepting rather than damning his environment, Thomas Wolfe produced four novels between 1929 and his death in 1938. Characterized by an obsession with his own emotional responses, his long, loose-jointed books were unique in a decade largely given over to novels of social analysis.

The work of one writer, judged by critics in later decades to be the greatest of this period, virtually ignored the passing environments of war, prosperity, and depression. William Faulkner was concerned with the ultimate meaning of human existence; and while he found it in the individual's inescapable relation to nature and the land, his immediate focus was the problem faced by the traditional South in adjusting to the twentieth century. More daring as a writer than his contemporaries, he did not hesitate to depict the world through the eyes of an idiot, to manipulate time, and to imply emotional meanings beyond the range of rational communication. His great period, which ultimately won him a Nobel Prize for Literature, was from *The Sound and the Fury* in 1929 through *Light in August* (1932) and other books in the first half of the 1930s.

American poets of the 1920s—also trying to deal with ultimate, or existential, problems—achieved substantial world acclaim. In 1922 T. S. Eliot, expatriate but still an American citizen, published *The Waste Land*, a poem of despair with modern civilization that exerted tremendous influence. Hart Crane's major work, *The Bridge*, a difficult-to-decipher commentary on time, appeared in 1930. In addition to some of the older poets, Wallace Stevens, William Carlos Williams, Robinson Jeffers, Robert Frost, E. E. Cummings, and Marianne Moore were all writing poetry of the first rank.

In drama the postwar rebellion against the world, in general, and America, in particular, also produced important work. The 11 plays of Eugene O'Neill, from *Beyond the Horizon* (1920) to *Mourning Becomes Electra* (1931)—all strongly influenced by Freudian psychology—marked the first major American contribution to serious theater. A number of other dramatists, including Sidney Howard, Maxwell Anderson, Elmer Rice, and Robert Sherwood, joined in this remarkable upsurge. During the depression a new playwright, Clifford Odets, wrote a strong drama, *Waiting for Lefty* (1935), in praise of collective action and the labor movement, and late in the decade there was a shift from anticapitalist plays to antifascist and antiwar themes. Another talented playwright of the times was Lillian Hellman, a severe critic of much in American life.

MOTION PICTURES

D. W. Griffith's silent movie *Broken Blossoms* (1919), starring Lillian Gish, was widely acclaimed by critics as marking the emergence of a new art form, said by the *Literary Digest* to be as important as music or poetry. Unfortunately, technological success and the work of this one middle-aged pioneer were not followed by a great burst of high-quality motion picture composition, directing, and acting.

The motion picture as an art medium was subordinated to the business interests that marketed the film. The major production studios owned chains of theaters and controlled the circulation of pictures. By 1930, with an investment by the owners of $2 billion to protect, the managers of the companies were unwilling to risk financing films that might not appeal to a major segment of the American

Cover illustration for *Life Magazine*, February 18, 1926, depicting a flapper dancing with a well-dressed man

public. Consequently, motion pictures of the 20s were massive spectacles of courts and armies directed by Cecil B. De Mille, sentimental
melodramas starring Mary Pickford, breathtaking exploits by Douglas

Fairbanks, Sr., or romantic seductions by Rudolph Valentino. Comedy, however, remained as one genre that could reconcile profit-oriented producers and talented actors. Most famous of the comedians was Charlie Chaplin who, producing and directing his own pictures, continued in his comedies of the underdog to protest against many of the values of American society.

Whether or not they were art, movies began to enjoy an extraordinary influence, especially on the young. What girl could escape wanting to be as glamorous, as sexy, as vivacious as, for example, Clara Bow, the "It Girl"? What boy did not gaze in envy at the suave way with women exhibited by Rudolph Valentino?

In the last three years of the 1920s sound began to make the motion picture potentially the equal of the stage. As a result, stock companies and vaudeville practically disappeared, and the professional stage became restricted to a few of the largest cities. From the 1920s to the 1950s the motion picture was the standard form of visual dramatic entertainment for the great majority of Americans.

In the 30x the Hollywood production line turned out a steady stream of highly polished, star-laden escapist films—glittering musicals, gangster stories, westerns, heroic costume dramas, and comedies, from slapstick to sophisticated. Snubbed by most highbrows, they were embraced by millions of ordinary Americans, for whom the movies—at prices as low as 10 cents—provided a warm, dark refuge from reality. The grimmer aspects of depression were treated in a few commercial films and in some excellent documentary films produced by the federal government. In the early twenty-first century many of the films of the 1930s—the social commentary comedies of Frank Capra, the westerns (and *The Grapes of Wrath*) of John Ford, the screwball comedies, especially those directed by Howard Hawks—are seen by film scholars and critics as some of the most significant American art of the twentieth century. The great stars—Fred Astaire and Ginger Rogers, Marlene Dietrich, Clark Gable, Greta Garbo, Cary Grant, Katherine Hepburn, Jimmy Stewart, to name only a few—are still iconic figures in American culture.

ARCHITECTURE

The towering American skyscraper, created in part because of the narrow confines of the Chicago Loop and downtown Manhattan, was regarded as an architectural innovation of worldwide importance. It was a monument to American ideas of marketing. As land values rose in all U.S. cities, it became economical to increase the height of buildings in the most valuable locations; but the altitudes achieved in the 1920s far exceeded this economic need. The advertising value that accrued to the company that built a towering building and the extra amount that tenants were willing to pay for the prestige and convenience of such lofty offices led to a race for height that culminated for that era in the 1,200-foot Empire State Building.

The architectural design that was dominant in skyscraper architecture by the late 1920s resulted partly from the New York Zoning Act of 1916, which forced setbacks in buildings rising above certain heights. The plan of the Finnish-born architect Eliel Saarinen, which called for a series of blocks diminishing in size as the building rose and with windows set in vertical panels between continuous strips of stone or concrete, became a general model for skyscraper design.

During both prosperity and depression, older styles of architecture dominated in most public buildings and homes. The Capitol in Washington, D.C., was rebuilt by the Hoover and Roosevelt administrations in the classical Greco-Roman style, the style also chosen for most post offices and state buildings. During the 1920s hundreds of thousands of new homes were built by the well to do, but they or their architects and builders generally preferred to adopt or adapt some style from the past rather than experiment with the unfamiliar problems of "modern" design. Needless to say, the builders of small homes, many without architects, avoided experimentation.

SOCIAL CHANGE

MOTORIZATION AND URBANIZATION

While the advent of radio and progress in electronics promised great future changes, immediate changes in American society centered on the automobile. Until World War I automobiles had been used chiefly for the recreation of the upper middle class. In 1917 less than one farm family in six had an automobile. In the nation as a whole, there were fewer than five million cars. As forms of transport, trucks and buses were negligible economically and socially.

By 1930 two thirds of America's farms—probably all the prosperous commercial farms—had automobiles, and the nation had about 23 million passenger cars. Since there were only about 26 million households, and many families in big cities did not need private automobiles, the United States was approaching the goal of a car in the garage of every family that wanted one. Even more spectacular than the fivefold increase in passenger cars was a nine-fold rise in the number of trucks. Nearly 4 million commercial vehicles, of which

40,000 were buses, signaled the beginning of the change to a society built around motor transport.

In the new geography, main highway intersections would replace villages as shopping centers, cities would be within easy reach of farms, factories would move from congested cities to the country, and consolidated grammar and high schools would collect children by bus from miles around. Few places would remain remote from the pressures, advantages, and disadvantages of an urbanized culture.

While the spread of slums had shown the inadequacy of American municipal planning for nearly a century, the automobile, more than the slum, lay back of the rapid rise of city planning commissions and authorities. Although zoning was initiated in New York in 1916 without particular regard to motor transport, that transport—by potentially opening all areas to all types of use—led to the rapid spread of zoning to other cities. The steady migration to major metropolitan areas during the 20s also forced planning on reluctant municipal authorities. By 1930, 37 percent of the city population of the United States lived in zoned communities.

Automobiles and trucks required new bridges, tunnels, and thoroughfares into central city business districts. The Port of New York Authority, established by a "treaty" between New York and New Jersey in 1921, initiated interstate agencies to plan transportation. Generally, however, urban efforts to alleviate both traffic problems and slum congestion in the prosperous 20s could be characterized as too little and too late.

THE "AUTOMOTIVE SOCIAL LADDER"

One of the cultural pressures directly connected with the automobile was its rise as a sign of social status. The American automobile, to be sure, depreciated rather rapidly; and for reliable service, replacement was desirable in about five to seven years; but social considerations worked for even briefer ownership. A new car was a symbol of success and prosperity, and the bigger and more expensive the car, the higher the presumed status of the owner. For urban and suburban apartment dwellers the automobile took the place of an elaborate house as a mark of social standing. Only farmers and the very rich seem to have been relatively immune to such pressures.

Quickly observing this "automotive social ladder," automobile manufacturers began to differentiate each year's model and to carry on the most intensive advertising of any makers of durable goods. While there were real physical and psychological satisfactions to be gained from a swift, smooth ride in a heavy, powerful car, the lure of social approval was perhaps the strongest force behind the continuous demand for new and bigger machines. Since buyers seldom had saved the money to pay cash, the automobile became the most important item in a rapid growth of installment buying.

THE EMANCIPATED WOMAN

At the time that the Nineteenth Amendment of 1920 gave women the right to vote, upper-middle- and upper class women in and around the largest urban centers were shaking off the decorum of Victorian customs. They were smoking in public, drinking illegally in speakeasies, talking freely about sex, and—in general—creating the appearance of demanding equal social rights and privileges. The publicity accorded the suffrage movement and the "emancipated woman" was highly misleading, however. Failing to establish a bloc of voters that could be used to influence legislation, as the Anti-Saloon League had done in the prohibition movement, women soon found that their influence on party politics was minimal.

By the mid-1920s the Women's Joint Congressional Committee was losing power, and the appropriation for the new Women's and

Women voting *(Library of Congress)*

Children's Bureau was cut. The mere right to vote in federal elections did not seem to have given substantial new power to the women's movement. In fact, political victory and a decade of general prosperity may have lessened the drive for other forms of equality.

The emancipated upper class women were too few in number, particularly among the mature and influential, to have an effect beyond journalistic publicity. World War I produced no significant change in the definition or status of "women's work." Although the percentage of women engaged in professional life rose almost 20 percent from 1920 to 1930, women were still substantially excluded from professorships in major universities, from the medical profession, and from the most prestigious law schools.

The proportion of women in the labor force was about the same in 1930 as it was in 1910. In the latter year, 57 percent of working-women were blacks or immigrants, which is equivalent to saying they were in low-paying occupations. The percentage of women in clerical jobs remained about the same during the prosperous 20s. Women continued to be paid less than men for doing the same job. There was, in effect, an openly expressed intention by most political, trade union, and business leaders to keep women in their traditional roles, which would avoid difficult adjustments and limit female competition with men. The very fact of lower pay, however, helped many women keep their jobs in the depression although it lessened their militancy.

For the middle-class women who were homemakers, the trend to smaller houses and apartments and the availability of electrical housekeeping aids such as vacuum cleaners and refrigerators lessened the drudgery of housework. For the few married women who could secure good jobs, there was less social stigma attached to working than in earlier decades, but strong economic and cultural barriers still blocked the road to equality with men.

AN URBAN BLACK SOCIETY

Since the beginning of the century there had been a steady migration of rural blacks to the cities, but World War I so increased the movement that the largest Northern cities—New York, Chicago, Philadelphia—became America's major centers of black population. Although frequently able to earn more money than they ever had before, the occupants of these black urban communities soon realized that they had not achieved the Promised Land. Usually they had to move into overcrowded, run-down tenements where they replaced the most recent, poorest immigrants. Although blacks were usually of old American stock, they found themselves looked down on by the foreign-born whites just as they had always been looked down on by the native whites. For a time in the 1920s the singers, dancers, and musicians of black Harlem, and some of its writers and artists, as well, were "taken up" by white sophisticates and bohemians. This fad did not last, however, nor did it touch the average black person.

There had never been much feeling of labor solidarity in the United States, and black workers in industrial centers were often resented, just as women were, as intruders who threatened white male employment and wage standards. Similar resentment led to attacks on blacks as the ghettos overflowed into white neighborhoods. In 1919 racial violence broke out in a score of cities all over the nation, and blacks learned that they could not rely on either police protection or justice in the courts.

In the early 1920s, black activist organizations moved in two directions. With the support of white middle-class liberals, the National Urban League and the National Association for the Advancement of Colored People (NAACP) sought to establish for blacks the civil and political rights guaranteed by the Constitution. On this front, temporary legal victories were won in the *Sweet* case (1925) that upheld the right of blacks to defend themselves against violence, and in the *First Texas Primary* case (1927) that declared exclusion of black voters at the primary election stage in the democratic process to be unconstitutional. The organization that represented the hopes and dreams of many working-class blacks was the Universal Negro Improvement Association, founded by the charismatic Jamaican, Marcus Garvey. He called on black people to take pride in their race and its history, to turn their backs on white America, and to return to their African homeland. The practical NAACP worked for integration, the romantic Garvey for black unity. The same twin stream has run throughout African Americans' long history.

PROHIBITION

Superimposed on this society that was undergoing or resisting confusing changes was America's greatest experiment in more government control over personal habits. Few nations have had a history of more consistent attachment to the consumption of alcohol than the United States. In the decades prior to 1918, however, there had been a trend toward more drinking of beer and wine and less recorded consumption of hard liquor, as well as a trend toward various types of state prohibition. It seems possible that banning the purchase of hard liquor or making it difficult to obtain might have produced a more temperate nation without much public resistance,

Illegal liquor *(Library of Congress)*

but this experiment was never tried. Instead, the combination of war hysteria over a shortage of grain, anti-German sentiment against the brewers, and the financing of temperance organizations by important businessmen opposed to beer for workers led to an effort to ban all alcoholic drinks.

The Eighteenth Amendment left interpretation of what was an "intoxicating" beverage to Congress. The Volstead Act of 1919, vetoed by Wilson and then passed again by the necessary two-thirds majority, set the limit of alcoholic content at .5 percent. While farmers would continue to make wine and other drinks at home, as they always had, city dwellers were now denied the opportunity of legally buying even the weakest form of beer. As a result, the big urban areas that had opposed the prohibition movement now refused to abide by the law. As is usual under such circumstances, there was no difficulty in finding entrepreneurs ready to supply illicit demand.

It is an interesting paradox of the triumph of the prohibitionists in Congress that, having passed the amendment and the Volstead Act, they settled back and made no great effort to see that the law was enforced. The number of federal agents began at about 1,500 and rose to only a little over 2,800 at the peak. With a top salary of around $3,000, it was not surprising that these men were often corruptible; but even had they been entirely diligent, they were too few even to check the imports of liquor. Furthermore, the local authorities in wet areas gave them little or no help. In 1923 the state of New York State repealed its law for local enforcement, and politicians in other big metropolitan areas connived, almost openly, with those supplying the liquor.

As a result, an illegal traffic in whiskey, wine, and beer, worth hundreds of millions of dollars annually, fell into the hands of underworld leaders. The terms "racket" and "racketeer" came into use, and the newly powerful gangsters quickly branched out into other criminal activities—including bribery, extortion, arson, and murder.

"Where were the police?" one would logically ask. The answer often was: in the pay of racketeers. Al Capone, head of the liquor racket in Chicago, was as powerful politically as anyone in the municipal government of that metropolis, and he was the undisputed ruler of the suburban city of Cicero. In the suburbs of New York and other great cities, the liquor interests often controlled county or municipal politics. The sheriffs and police chiefs received a portion of the weekly collections from speakeasies and worked against the occasional federal agent who sought to get evidence of violation of the law.

The national picture was confusing. In dry areas prohibition appeared to work at least as well as it had before the amendment. In wet urban areas, relatively less well represented in Congress, prohibition seemed to be undermining the moral values of both the young elite and honest government. Some manufacturers thought there was less drinking among their employees, while others were sure there was more. The Republican administration continued vaguely to sponsor "the noble experiment." The Wickersham Commission, appointed by Hoover, gave an unfavorable report in January 1931, but illogically concluded that prohibition should be continued.

In the end it was not moral or temperance issues but the Great Depression and need for government revenue in the desperate year of 1932 that apparently tipped the balance in favor of legalizing the liquor business. There was no serious effort to substitute a new law permitting beer and wine for the unworkable Volstead Act. In 1933 the Eighteenth Amendment itself was quickly repealed by the Twenty-first, and the temperance problem was returned to the states.

THE PERIOD BETWEEN THE WARS

By 1940 the scientific and technological base for the highest level of consumption in the world's history had been achieved, but corresponding institutional adjustments had not taken place. The two decades following World War I were merely an interlude in a much longer period of change from the relatively stable commercial society of Western European nations in the eighteenth century to some new stage that may also have its periods of relative stability. In this transition the 1920s in the United States marked the world's highest peak of material well being up to that time and the 1930s the greatest depth of politico-economic failure to make use of existing facilities. It was hardly surprising that each decade produced unusual problems and unique reactions.

Depression inevitably upset most Americans more than any problems caused by prosperity. In 1932 they felt the deep sense of frustration that must come from seeing people starving while crops are being burned for lack of a market; but basic rebellion against capitalism or traditional American values was rare. To a remarkable degree people suffered deprivation in silence, comforting themselves with whatever was left. The majority warmly supported Franklin Roosevelt in his programs to provide greater material security; and the protest that feebly sprouted in the dark days from 1931 to 1934 was smothered under a reaffirmation of belief in traditional American values.

There was, however, a fundamental change: it would no longer be expected that individual citizens, or at least individual families, were solely responsible for their own welfare. A new tradition of public responsibility for the welfare of private citizens was in the process of creation, a tradition that would last for many decades. We now turn to a closer look at the politics of the 1920s and 30s, with special attention to the New Deal.

PROSPERITY AND DEPRESSION, 1919–1929

(Library of Congress)

THE SWING TOWARD CONSERVATISM

Nineteen-nineteen was a year of disillusionment. During the war progressives, once satisfied with social legislation and national regulation of trusts, had raised their hopes for such fundamental changes as federal control of railroads, shipping, prices, and employment. John Dewey, America's most famous philosopher, had predicted in 1918, "No matter how many among the special agencies for public control decay with the disappearance of war stress, the movement will never go backward." During 1919, however, the movement toward a publicly regulated economy not only receded but also was lost altogether in a wave of reaction.

Like all sweeping changes in opinion, the swing to conservatism between early 1919 and 1920 had many causes. The unsatisfactory peace in Europe, publicized in the worst light by opponents of the League of Nations, cooled the popular enthusiasm that President Wilson had temporarily aroused. The result appears to have been apathy about America's role in world affairs that carried over into domestic issues as well.

Along with this indifference to further reform there was undoubtedly a real fear on the part of middle-class Americans that revolution on the Russian model might spread. Socialism had ceased to be a utopian goal, safe to discuss at social club meetings, and had instead become a gray, alien world of commissars and secret police. As a result, the unprecedented series of strikes used by labor in 1919 to keep wages abreast of soaring prices was widely regarded as a dangerous indication of revolutionary sentiment, inspired by the subversive activities of a foreign power. In some cases management publicly condemned the strikers as Reds.

DEMOBILIZATION

At the close of the Great War, the war boards that Wilson had hastily put together—to convert the economy to wartime production—quickly relinquished control of the economy to the free market with predictable harsh dislocations. Wilson had naively assumed that the economy would adjust itself without complications; but the war had brought high wages and record profits, which along with a shortage of consumer goods produced record personal savings. When the free market was unleashed, the buying public was all too eager to unleash their savings in the form of consumption with the result that there were too many dollars chasing too few goods in the marketplace, thus creating rapid inflation. The American cost of living increased 50 percent from the end of the war to 1921, but wages were unable to keep pace, thereby precipitating a wave of strikes. Over four million American workers, some 20 percent of the workforce, were on strike at one time or another during 1919, in some cases paralyzing American industry and international trade.

Calvin Coolidge *(Library of Congress)*

In spite of the fact that the primary reason for the strikes was that wages had not kept up with inflation, American business managers generally argued, the media reported, and the public believed, that the strikes were the result of communist agitation. Perhaps the most famous strike of all in 1919 was the strike of the Boston police force. Massachusetts' governor, Calvin Coolidge, became a hero among conservatives during the strike by putting down the strike with a force of Harvard University students and United States Army veterans. Coolidge dismissed the striking policemen and refused to reinstate them, proclaiming— "There is no right to strike against the public safety by anybody, anywhere, any time."

THE RED SCARE

Though communist agitation was not the precipitant for the strikes in 1919, it is true that communist activity in the United States at the time was perhaps greater in scope that at any time in American history, though it was greatly overblown by the media and a paranoid public on the heels of the Bolshevik Revolution in Russia and World War I. Political demagogues were, of course, ready to ride to power by playing upon such fears.

The political violence that precipitated the conservative reactionary backlash that became known as the "Red Scare" began during an international shipping strike in 1919 when a bomb was sent to the home of the mayor of Seattle, who had opposed the labor union activity in Seattle shipyards. Although the Seattle bomb did not detonate, it provided more evidence for the American people that dangerous left-wing radicals dominated the labor unions. Labor Unions had been connected with bombs, political radicalism, communism, and anarchism in the minds of American conservatives ever since the Chicago Haymarket riot of 1886, where four anarchist labor leaders were executed for a bomb that killed seven policemen at a labor rally. The Haymarket affair combined with other violence-filled strikes, such as the American Railway Union sympathetic strike against the Pullman Palace Car Company and the Homestead Steel strike (both in 1892), to indelibly etch into the minds of Americans the connection between labor unions and left-wing political violence.

In 1919, the conservative perception of labor unions as organizations of communist and anarchist "bomb-throwing radicals" was greatly reinforced not only by the Seattle bomb, but also by the discovery by the United States Post Office of 16 bombs that were not delivered due to insufficient postage. A subsequent examination revealed that each was addressed to prominent persons such as John D. Rockefeller, Oliver Wendell Holmes, and Attorney General A. Mitchell Palmer. In April, 1919, a bomb was delivered and detonated that blew the hands off of the maid of a former Georgia senator, Thomas Hardwick, who was known to be anti-union. In June, a bomb destroyed the front of the home of United States Attorney General, A. Mitchell Palmer. The damage to Palmer's home could have been much worse; but the bomber's plan went awry when he apparently tripped on Palmer's porch, dropped the bomb, and blew himself to pieces. The bombing of Palmer's house was followed by several other bombings, suggesting to many that the terror activity was widespread. In all, seven bombs were detonated in five states.

Congress and the American public demanded that something be done about the terror, and the United States Senate passed a motion of censure against Attorney General Palmer for his inaction. After the bombing of his home, however, Palmer launched an unparalleled crusade against the terrorists and organized an anti-radical division within the Justice Department. Palmer then put J. Edgar Hoover in charge of coordinating the anti-radical division's activities and ensuring that safeguarding the Constitutional rights of the terror suspects received a low priority. In November 1919, the Justice Department rounded up and detained 250 members of the Union of Russian Workers. Thirty-three of the Russian workers were severely beaten by Justice Department officers, suggesting gross rights violations, but the raids were popular with the public. The next month, 249 aliens were deported for being "threats to the government," including the famed left-wing feminist, Emma Goldman. Palmer's raids were a tremendous success with the American people and the American press who applauded Palmer's actions. The *Washington Post* perhaps summed the views of many Americans up well when it argued, "There is no time to waste on hairsplitting over infringement of liberty."

On January 2, 1920, Palmer ordered hundreds of federal agents to 33 American cities to destroy the imagined Bolshevik conspiracy. In all, Palmer and Hoover's agents arrested 6,000 individuals on charges of conspiracy to overthrow the United States government. In furtherance of his crusade, Palmer attempted to alter basic criminal rights protections, a clear sacrifice of principles in the service of a desired end in a manner consistent with the arguments of the *Washington Post*. Specifically, Palmer attempted to persuade Secretary of Labor William B. Wilson to amend a portion of the deportation law that allowed suspects to secure counsel. He also requested a blanket deportation warrant to cover any aliens discovered once a raid had commenced. President Wilson refused these abuses of individual liberties; but while the President was on sick leave, one of Wilson's underlings, John W. Abercrombie, provided the changes that Palmer requested. Rights to counsel and habeas corpus, along with the rule that suspects had to be informed of the charges against them, were suspended for those arrested by Palmer's men.

Armed with the blanket suspensions of civil liberties, Palmer's abuses were legion. In Detroit, carrying with them 3,000 blank mimeographed warrants (with the names to be filled in later), Palmer's men arrested and jailed 800 people. It is certain that the experience was at least uncomfortable for those arrested since 800 detainees were allowed access to only one toilet for the entire group. In Boston, similar raids jailed another 800 people. In New Jersey, one man was arrested simply because he "looked like an alien," and the practice of arresting people simply because of how they looked was essentially encouraged by the Attorney General himself. In the words of Palmer:

> "Out of the sly and crafty eyes of many of them leap cupidity, cruelty, insanity, and crime; from their lopsided faces, sloping brows, and misshapen features may be recognized the unmistakable criminal type."

In all, 6,000 people were arrested, and 556 were deported by the end of 1920; and Palmer had lists with over 200,000 names as suspects. In spite of his gross abuses, Palmer briefly became a national hero for "ferreting out communists." Many Americans agreed with

Christian evangelist Billy Sunday, who argued, "The best solution is to shoot aliens rather than deport them."

Regardless, all of the activity from Palmer's Justice Department was carried out without any supporting or enabling legislation from Congress. Palmer appeared before a Congressional committee and asked for legislation authorizing the suppression of sedition during peacetime, and 70 bills were pending in Congress within five months of his request; but none of the measures passed. Palmer's paranoid zeal, however, would eventually become his own undoing as his over-reactive brutal raids began to stir the public conscience. In the words of William Preston:

> "The net was so wide and bureau detectives were so careless that some ten thousand persons were arrested including many citizens and many individuals not members of either party. Abuse of due process characterized the early stages of the drive. This ill-treatment proceeded from the official decision to protect under-cover informers. Indiscriminate arrests of the innocent with the guilty, unlawful searches and seizures by federal detectives, in-timidating preliminary interrogation of aliens held incommuni-cado, high-handed levying of excessive bail, and denial of counsel were the government's response to stiffening alien radi-cal resistance to deportation."

Additionally, less than 10 percent of arrests led to deportation, suggesting that the threat was overblown. Palmer's raids uncovered no explosives and confiscated only three pistols in 6,000 arrests.

Finally, Palmer discredited himself by making the mistake of play-ing the role of false prophet in predicting the day of the apocalypse. Palmer announced in April 1920, that the communists were going to launch a major revolt on May Day (May 1), 1920. In New York and other major United States cities, the police were put on round-the-clock alert, and National Guards were called out to head off the crisis. May Day passed without a single incident, however, and Palmer's ac-tions made him appear paranoid and ridiculous. As a consequence, public support for his reactionary tactics evaporated, and the Red Scare dissipated as the economy adjusted to the end of the war. The American public came to realize that the communist threat had been greatly overstated.

Nevertheless, 17 states passed "criminal syndicalist" laws provid-ing for the arrest of agitators proposing other forms of government. The New York state legislature carried out a lengthy investigation of revolutionary radicalism and refused to seat Socialist representatives from New York City. Meanwhile, Congress refused to admit Victor

Supporters of Italian anarchists Nicola Sacco and Bartolomeo Vanzetti *(AP Associated Press)*

Berger from Wisconsin until his Milwaukee constituents had again elected that very moderate Socialist.

One final tragedy did result from the "Red Scare," however, in the form of the arrest and conviction of two alien anarchists, Nicola Sacco and Bartolomeo Vanzetti, for the murder of a factory paymaster and guard during a robbery in South Braintree, Massachusetts. The Sacco and Vanzetti cases turned out to be the *cause célèbre* of the 1920s. Eyewitnesses were unable to positively identify Sacco and Vanzetti, and most of the evidence against the two men was circumstantial. Because of the alleged bias of the judge, Webster Thayer, who had privately referred to the two defendants as "those anarchist bastards" and the prejudicial tactics of the prosecuting attorney at the trial, many liberals protested that the men had been convicted for their radicalism rather than for the stated crime. In the six years following their conviction in 1921, protest meetings took place all over the world, and people of international prominence like Albert Einstein and novelist Anatole France gave their support to petitions urging clemency or a retrial. In Massachusetts, however, public opinion remained hostile. A special commission headed by the president of Harvard found that the trial had been fair and that the defendants were guilty. On August 23, 1927, Sacco and Vanzetti were electrocuted in an atmosphere of martyrdom. Supporters of the prosecution were vindicated in 1960 when ballistics experts with more advanced crime technology concluded that Sacco's revolver was the murder weapon. Supporters of the defendants, however, were also vindicated in that the same ballistics experts concluded that Vanzetti's revolver did not fire the fatal shots. In any case, most historians agree that the two men were executed as much for their political views (anarchism) as the evidence against them.

Perhaps the most alarming aspect of the wave of anti-Red hysteria in the 1920s, however, was not the injustices visited upon a few hundred leftists and aliens (though those people themselves may beg to differ), but the general suppression of free thought that accompanied the unrelenting efforts of the Attorney General and certain "patriotic" societies. Teachers became afraid to impart normal, necessary criticisms of American leaders and American society. Business employees were afraid to be associated with people or organizations branded by the super-patriots as subversive. Liberal journals were called revolutionary, and people were afraid to be seen reading them. Compared to the Red Scare of the 1950s, that of the early 1920s was less serious in its impact on government but probably more repressive in its effect on ordinary citizens.

REPRESSION OF AFRICAN AMERICANS

Over 400,000 black Americans had served in World War I, half of whom served in Europe and 40,000 served in combat roles. Additionally, an estimated half million African Americans migrated from the South to the northern cities during the war to engage in factory employment traditionally held by whites and contribute to the home front war effort. Blacks hoped that the war experience would secure for them greater citizenship rights; but after the war, there were mass layoffs of blacks in both the North and South as whites returned from the war to occupy the jobs they previously held.

Blacks in both the North and South were subjected to a new round of racial oppression as whites pressed to "keep them in their place." In 1919 alone, some 70 African Americans were lynched and killed by whites in the South. Urban centers, both north and south, experienced a new round of violent racial unrest. In East St. Louis in 1917, 49 people were killed in a race riot, including 39 blacks and 10 whites. In Chicago in 1919, a race riot killed 15 whites and 23 blacks in a week of rioting that destroyed over 1,000 homes and injured over 500 people. The Chicago riot was precipitated by an incident on Lake Michigan in which a young black swimmer swam too near a white beach, resulting in whites pelting him with rocks until he was rendered unconscious by the stoning and drowned. Race riots also transpired in Houston and in Philadelphia in 1919, with the result that 120 people died during 1919 as a result of urban racial unrest. Two years later in Tulsa, Oklahoma, whites dropped dynamite from airplanes on the black section of town, killing 75 people and destroying 1,000 homes.

THE KLAN

With the defeat of the "evil" Huns secured sooner than anticipated, the end of World War I found the American people essentially whipped into an emotional patriotic and moral fervor that was suddenly without direction. In the words of *Life* magazine Editor Robert Coughlan, the American political mindset was essentially in a state of "coitus interruptus." The general emotion among the American people at the time was one of continued chauvinistic patriotism and hatred for the devil they had been fighting; but the evil entity had essentially cheated them by surrendering before it could be obliterated. Into this void would step the KKK to provide substitute devils to slay in place of the old ones and to provide different means by which to slay them.

William J. Simmons, a Methodist minister from Georgia, and 15 like-minded followers reorganized the KKK on Thanksgiving night, 1915. At first, Simmons experienced difficulties in recruiting members, although he claimed over 1,500 recruits by the end of World War I; but in 1920 he enlisted the help of wealthy Atlanta widow Elizabeth Tyler and former newspaperman and solicitor for the Woodmen of the World, Edward Young Clarke. The KKK fortunes would abruptly change.

With Simmons as the front man, Clarke as the organizer, and Tyler as the financier, the KKK quickly

William J. Simmons *(Library of Congress)*

rose to prominence, playing on American moralism, nativism, religion, patriotism, greed, and the social energy and inertia that followed World War I. Simmons and Clarke developed what they termed as the "four major tenets of the Klan philosophy" or "character" of the Klan as a white man's organization, a gentile organization, an American organization, and a Protestant organization. Anything that the Klansmen did not view as "white gentile" and American Protestant in character would become a Klan target.

The Klan was modeled loosely after religious organizations, and much attention was given to titles, symbolism, and ceremony. Any room could serve as a Klan meeting place, but all meetings would have an altar, upon which there would be an American flag, a Bible open at Romans chapter 12, an unsheathed sword, and a container of initiation water that was sprinkled over new members to ceremonially cleanse them of any "alien" defilement.

The Klan's rapid growth in the 1920s is, at least partially, explained by its financial aspects in that it was essentially an early twentieth century political version of a multi-level marketing scheme. New members were required to pay a $10 initiation fee, of which $4 went to the Klansman that recruited the new member. The Cyclops (local leader) of the Klavern (local group) joined by the new member received $.50. The Imperial Kleagle, Edward Clarke, received $3, and the remaining $1.50 went to the Imperial Wizard, William J. Simmons. Klansmen also had to purchase the official robes for $6.50, a figure that included a minimum profit of $3.50 for the Klan. Initiation water had to be purchased at $10 per quart from the Imperial Wizard, who admittedly drew the water straight from the Chattahoochee River in Georgia. Other Klan profits were made from the robes for the Klansmen's horses, carrying cases for the costumes, pocketknives, and other "official" Klan paraphernalia. Given that the Klan estimated its membership before a Congressional investigation in 1921 at 700,000, it is not difficult to determine that Simmons and Clarke (as well as others) reaped tremendous windfalls. A postal inspector testified before Congress that Clarke's department alone received $860,393.50 from June 1920 to September 1921.

This, however, was only the beginning. Publicity in 1921 caused by an undercover investigation of the Klan by the *New York World,* and a Congressional investigation that followed the *New York World* piece provided a boost to Klan membership as nativists that had not known about the organization prior to the publicity rushed to join. The Klan was essentially swamped with 1.2 million applications for membership in the year following the Congressional investigations. In 1922, Simmons boasted that the Klan's membership increased daily by 3,500 new members, and the Klan's average daily income was $45,000 at a time when GNP per capita was under $1,000. The Klan also claimed membership in all 48 states, Alaska, and the Panama Canal Zone.

The stated goals of the Klan were to "return America to its Godly heritage and purge America of un-American and un-Godly influences." The Klan also claimed that it existed "to enforce law at a time of lawlessness." Hence, the Klan's appeal had as much to do with conservative reactions to the "immorality" of the roaring 20s with its excesses of alcohol, uptempo dancing, shorter skirts, and shorter hair for women, along with perceived greater sexual promiscuity. Similar to other nativist groups, the KKK integrated elements of conspiracy theory into their teachings. In the words of Emerson Loucks:

> "The belief in the minds of the nativists that there was a serious plot against American ideals and institutions, the success of which only immediate organization and united action could prevent, was as important for the growth of the Ku Klux Klan as the belief in the Devil and his angels was for the growth of the medieval Christian Church. It was the sine qua non of its existence."

For example, D. C. Stephenson, a prominent northern Klan leader, argued that World War I was the result of a conspiracy by Jewish bankers and part of a systematic plan designed to limit Christianity. Other Klan arguments included the contention that Jews had organized the Bolshevik Revolution in Russia and were the driving force behind international communism. The KKK also espoused conspiracy theories concerning the death of Warren G. Harding and the assassinations of Presidents Garfield and McKinley, essentially arguing that Harding's death was in reality a Catholic assassination plot, as were the assassinations of Lincoln, Garfield, and McKinley. In *Searchlight*, the national publication of the Klan, it was proposed that a secret Catholic army of a million Knights of Columbus were secretly arming themselves for a takeover of the country.

Another consistent Klan theme that conforms to the conservative extremist pattern was anti-intellectualism. In particular, college professors were accused of encouraging communism. In the words of one Klan leader:

> "In a nation toleration becomes a vice when fundamentals are in danger … The American liberals … have extended their liberality til they are willing to help the aliens tear at the foundations of the nation. They have become one of the chief menaces of the country, instead of the sane intellectual leaders they should be

... They give an almost joyous welcome to alien criticism of everything American. The unopposed attack on the Puritan conscience is only one illustration; our liberals today seem ashamed of having any conscience at all. Tolerance is more prized by them than conviction."

This Klan leader's message contains one further theme that is consistent among conservative extremists, and that is, it is they (Klan members) that are being somehow persecuted. In the words of Lipset and Raab (1970, 140):

"Most successful spokesmen found that the best way to appeal to prospective followers was by casting 'the native white Protestant—not as belonging to the predominant and controlling group ... but as the oppressed poor, oppressed sufferer, plundered by foreigners, tricked by Jesuits, and robbed of his birthright by scheming descendants of Abraham.'"

In doing so, the Klan appealed to the sympathy that the American masses tend to have for the "underdog;" hence, the Klan was able to link itself to anti-elitist and egalitarian populist traditions while simultaneously fostering bigotry and hate (Lipset and Raab, 1970, 140).

Selling bigotry and hate is much easier if it is cloaked in morality and patriotism. As a consequence, the KKK advocated specific curriculum for school children that would include the Golden Rule, the

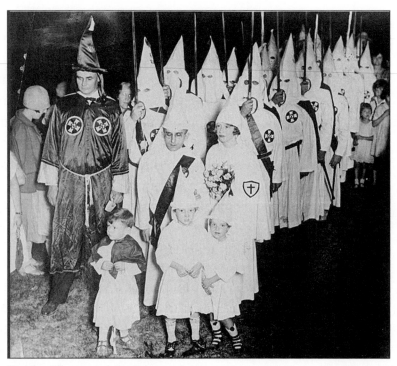

Ku Klux Klan members *(Library of Congress)*

Ten Commandments, opposition to Charles Darwin's theory of evolution, and opposition to the evils of alcohol—as part of their stated goal of fostering "morality" (Mecklin, 1924, 13, 28). The Klan was not the first, nor would they be the last, conservative group to cloak their bigotry under the guise of "morality": but in the 1920s, they were perhaps the most successful. It is worthy of note, however, that in these Klan positions, as well as in their persecution syndrome and anti-intellectualism, the Klan's views, goals, and platform of the 1920s are almost indistinguishable from that of the Christian Coalition of the early twenty-first century, with the exception that the Christian Coalition is much less noteworthy for racial bigotry.

The targets of KKK activities in the 1920s were not exclusively racial, and certainly included blacks, but they also included everything and everyone else that conservative extremists at the time viewed as unchristian, un-American, or immoral. The list of targets, therefore, also included Catholics, Jews, Mexicans, immigration in general, short skirts, abortions, all forms of sexual immorality, adultery, divorce, "demon rum," dance halls, movie theaters, businessmen charged with corrupting young women, husbands who abandoned their wives, divorcees who set "immoral" examples, pimps, prostitutes, gamblers, thieves, bootleggers, and doctors who performed abortions. The KKK also identified paintings and books that they considered to be immoral and argued for their censorship. Among other things, the Klan opposed beauty contests, carnivals, and jazz clubs as activities that led to immorality.

The KKK (along with other Protestant fundamentalist groups) also led the fight for state laws that required the closing of businesses on Sundays. Municipal laws were passed against "public flirting," women smoking in public, and the playing of jazz after midnight. Other municipal laws imposed restrictions on the brevity of bathing suits. In Texas, a bill was introduced in the legislature banning women's heels to no more than one inch.

The fact that the KKK and Protestant fundamentalism were intertwined in the 1920s is testified to by the fact that two thirds of the national Klan lecturers were Protestant ministers. The Klan's tirades against evolution and immorality were attractive to fundamentalist Protestant ministers, who regularly filled their sermons with similar messages. One of the Klan's most effective tactics to enlist the support of Protestant ministers was to have its members appear unannounced at Sunday Church services in full regalia. Klansmen would march solemnly and silently down the aisles, hand the minister envelopes full of cash, and then silently march out of the church as quickly as they had arrived. The tactics were evidently effective. In Knoxville, Tennessee, for example, Klan files of membership applications showed that 71.2 percent were Baptist and 24.4 percent were Methodist.

The Klan's solicitation of ministers was part of an overall effort to recruit members from the "top" of society down. The strategy was to recruit the leaders of communities, including political and religious leaders—as well as the prominent businessmen of the communities, and then enlist their help in getting others to fall in line. As a result, Klan leadership in any town often mirrored the leadership of the community. The Klan also recruited the police in every town, an obvious advantage for a group that engages in illegal activities. It is estimated that 10 percent of the policemen in California, including the police chiefs in Los Angeles and Bakersfield, and the sheriff of Los Angeles County, belonged to the Klan in the 1920s. The rank and file of the Klan, however, were predominantly the blue collar, uneducated, working class. Hiram Evans, the Grand Wizard in 1926 described the Klan thusly:

> "We are a movement of the plain people, very weak in the matter of culture, intellectual support, and trained leadership. We are demanding, and we expect to win, a return of power into the hands of everyday, not highly cultured, not overly intellectualized, but unspoiled and not de-Americanized, average citizen of the old stock ... This is undoubtedly a weakness. It lays us open to the charge of being hicks and rubes and drivers of second hand Fords. We admit it."

Whether "hicks and rubes" or not, with money and numbers comes political influence, and by the 1920s, the Klan had accumulated its fair share. Retail merchants were told to display a TWK (Trade With Klansmen) sticker in their window or expect to suffer a boycott by the Klan, and Klansmen were instructed to frequent businesses owned by other Klansmen. By economic boycott, the Klan could (and did) bankrupt merchants that opposed it. The Klan became so economically powerful at one point that it purchased its own college, Lanier University in Atlanta, and attempted to purchase Valparaiso University in Indiana as well, for the purpose of providing a place where one could receive a "proper" education.

The Klan also used its economic might to provide political backing for electoral candidates, and numerous Klansmen were elected to political office throughout the South. In Georgia, United States Senator William J. Harris won a bid for re-election after his opponent produced a letter signed by Elizabeth Tyler to Harris in which she addressed him as "Hon. W. J. Harris, A.K.I.A." (A Klansman Am I). Clifford Walker, the governor of Georgia in 1924, admitted that he was a Klansman and addressed the Second Imperial Klonvokation of the Klan in 1924. In Alabama in 1926, a United States Senate seat was won by future United States Supreme Court Justice Hugo Black, who had resigned from the Klan just prior to the election. The other Alabama Senator was another Klansman, the rabidly anti-Catholic Tom Heflin. In Texas in 1922, Earle Mayfield, an admitted Klansman, won a United States Senate seat. Two years later, Klan candidate Felix Robertson, who claimed he stood for the "God-given right and supremacy of white Christian men," almost won the governorship of Texas; but on the day of the primary election, a white-sheeted crowd threw rocks at the home of his female gubernatorial opponent (Ma Ferguson). Unfortunately for Robertson, the attack backfired since conservatives in Texas viewed the attack as an unmanly attack on a woman. Robertson garnered more votes than Ferguson in the primary that day, but the KKK rock-throwing incident helped Ferguson gain enough votes to force a runoff and defeat Robertson in November 1924 by 98,000 votes.

Perhaps the apex of Klan political strength was at the 1924 Democratic Convention where it is estimated that 300 Klan members were present as delegates. The Klan proved that it essentially controlled the convention when William H. Pattengall of Maine introduced an anti-Klan plank in the Democratic platform. Chaos ensued following Pattengall's proposal, and Madison Square Garden was filled with the hissing and booing of Klansmen along with fistfights, chair tossing, and destruction of convention decorations. Among the notables that came out opposed to the anti-Klan plank was the old populist warrior from Nebraska, William Jennings Bryan. The anti-Klan plank was defeated along with the Presidential nomination bid of Al Smith of New York, whom the Klan opposed due to his Roman Catholicism and anti-prohibition stance. Smith would win the Democratic nomination four years later only after the Klan had begun to subside.

In August 1925, the Klan further demonstrated its political strength when it held a national parade in Washington, D.C. where over 50,000 Klansmen participated in a four-hour march down Pennsylvania Avenue. Although the march was peaceful, the sight of 50,000 robed Klansmen filing past the White House provided an ominous symbol less than a decade before the National Socialists of Adolph Hitler took power in Germany.

After 1925, however, the KKK began to decline, with the result that the organization would become a shadow of its former self by World War II. There are numerous reasons why the Klan in the United States, in spite of its comparatively superior strength in 1925, was unable to take over power completely as did their German Nazi counterparts in Europe. The fact that the United States was on the winning, rather than losing side in World War I (World War I being the primary precipitant for the right-wing backlash in both the United States and Europe) was certainly one reason that the Klan failed in the United States while Hitler's Nazis succeeded; but Klan violence also clearly violated the sensibilities of millions of Americans who clamored for their government to act against Klan threats to stability. In response, states began ushering "Anti-Mask" bills through their legislatures that prevented Klan members from wearing their hoods in public, with the result that the "undedicated" members of the KKK quickly abandoned the organization in an overt sense. The Klan was also certainly guilty of over-reach. Put simply, if all of the people and all of the activities that the Klan were supposedly against were combined, (all minorities, immigrants, all non-Protestants, consumers of alcohol, anyone who had sex outside of marriage, etc.), it clearly represented the majority of Americans. It should be a fairly safe assumption that persons who were potential Klan targets would be less inclined to support the Klan.

Some of the decline of the Klan, however, is perhaps best explained by the fact that the Klan did experience some successes and achieve some of its goals. In fact, the major political parties and other groups (religious fundamentalists in general, for instance) took up many of the issues as part of their platforms, issues that concerned the Klan. In 1924, for example, the passage of strict immigration restrictions limiting immigration to a total number of 150,000 persons should be considered a Klan victory, but it also in part diffused the anti-immigration elements that were drawn to the Klan. Similarly, numerous Southern states passed laws outlawing the teaching of evolution, and prohibition was firmly embedded. In these instances, the Klan's demise falls into the pattern of other interest groups, such as the anti-nuclear protesters of the 1980s, whose demise is at least partially due to their own success. Finally, as the decade of the 1920s came to a close, the passage of time allowed the nation to distance itself from the hyper-patriotism and "100 percent pure Americanism" that had accompanied World War I. As they had before, however, these patterns of nativism, moralism, and bigotry would resurface again during the next political crisis.

Against the ominous rise of lower-middle-class reaction, the stuff of which fascism was to be made in Germany, must be placed the continuation of liberal and even radical farmer movements in the Upper Midwest and the Northwest. Led by the old Non-Partisan League, a Farmer-Labor Party ran second to the victorious Republicans in the election of 1920 in Minnesota, South Dakota, and Washington. Thus, the decentralized character of American politics sustained minority movements while making it difficult for them to win national power.

IMMIGRATION QUOTAS

A major change in American political policy in the early 1920s was the regulation of immigration on a quota basis. While a law in 1882 excluded the Chinese and diplomatic agreements had excluded the Japanese, other Asian and African people had not attempted to immigrate in any large numbers. Meanwhile the door had been held open for most Europeans although organized labor and "old stock" Americans had long tried to restrict the vast flood of newcomers, which in peaceful and prosperous years comprised more than a million annually. Finally, a combination of factors—resumption of heavy immigration from Eastern Europe, unemployment at home, and the Red Scare—led Congress to establish quotas based on the number of foreign-born residents in the United States in 1910. Opposed vigorously in Congress only by Catholics, the bill met a veto by Wilson. Passed again in the special session of 1921, it was signed by Harding. During the first year of operation the restrictions reduced yearly immigration from around 1 million to 300,000.

To organized labor, nativists, and those who feared communism, the number of "undesirable" or "unassimilable" immigrants from Eastern Europe still seemed too large. The National Origins Act of 1924 set up a temporary quota of two percent of the foreign-born residents in 1890 (a time when immigrants were still largely of British, German, or Scandinavian origin) and established a commission to work out quotas by a formula based on numbers of foreign-born over the whole range of the United States on the basis of census data. The bill excluded "Orientals."

Japan, which had been voluntarily restricting emigration to the United States, regarded this as an affront to its national dignity and declared a "National Humiliation Day" in response; but the Japanese protest was brushed aside by Congress. Enacted into law in 1929, the final report of the Commission on National Origins reduced southern and eastern European quotas to negligible size and held the total of restricted immigrants to about 150,000 annually. Citizens of countries in the Western Hemisphere were exempted from restriction. During periods of high employment, like the 1920s, the diminished pool of immigrant labor led to the hiring of more blacks and poor whites in the growing industrial centers.

TRIUMPH OF THE CONSERVATIVES

In the middle of the confusing year 1920 the Republican and Democratic conventions met to nominate candidates for the presidency. The leading Republican contenders—Governor Frank O. Lowden of Illinois and General Leonard Wood—fought each other to a deadlock. The compromise candidate supported by a group of business representatives and conservative congressional leaders was Senator Warren G. Harding of Ohio, a man virtually unknown to the American public but one who had the gracious, commanding look of a President.

Harding was nobody's first choice for President. He essentially received the Republican nomination when the Republican Convention became gridlocked between warring factions, and Harding seemed an inoffensive "second choice." Harding himself perhaps best summed up the situation when he exclaimed, "We drew a pair of deuces and filled."

In 1920, Harding's nomination made sense to the Republicans because his candidacy seemed to offend no one; and he was, in the words of Ohio boss Harry Daugherty, "a handsome devil ... and women could vote." In other words, Harding received the Republican nomination at least partially because he "looked like a President," rather than because of immense talent. Harding and his successor Calvin Coolidge would essentially be a return to the precedent set in the Gilded Age—that of choosing mediocre Presidents of average talent, but men who possessed the correct conservative ideological leanings.

Warren G. Harding *(Library of Congress)*

Harding's campaign promised what Harding referred to as a "return to normalcy." The "normalcy" campaign resonated with Americans in the upheaval following World War I, complete with economic and labor unrest along with the excesses of the Red Scare. Furthermore, Americans had experienced 20 years of progressivism that had brought prohibition, women's suffrage, and government economic and social regulation. By 1920, perhaps progressivism had merely run its course, and

Americans were ready to return to conservatism. In the words of progressive journalist William Allen White, Americans in 1920 were "tired of issues, sick at heart of ideals, and weary of being noble." At any rate, the election of Harding would signal that the Progressive Era was over.

Harding took a non-controversial approach to the 1920 campaign and straddled the fence on divisive issues so as not to alienate progressives. For example, Harding avoided the issue of segregation and neither attacked nor endorsed the KKK.

The Democrats had even greater difficulty in choosing a candidate. During 37 indecisive ballots, Attorney General Palmer, the anti-Red champion, fought William G. McAdoo, the liberal ex-Secretary of the Treasury and son-in-law of Woodrow Wilson. Then the convention compromised on a progressive who had been twice elected governor of Ohio, James M. Cox. While Cox was as little known to the general public as Harding, the Democratic ticket was strengthened by the vice-presidential nomination of Assistant Secretary of the Navy Franklin D. Roosevelt.

The election of 1920 also marked the last hurrah for Socialist leader, Eugene V. Debs, a particularly remarkable candidacy in that Debs ran for president from prison and obtained about one million votes. A strong critic of American participation in World War I, Debs had attempted to confine his remarks in speeches to those that would not be illegal under the Espionage Act of 1917; but he was arrested for saying that the master classes declared war, while the lower classes fought it—and he was subsequently convicted. In 1921, President Warren Harding would pardon him. This was the last of Debs's five presidential runs.

Partly in deference to President Wilson, the two major-party candidates Cox and Roosevelt made entry into the League of Nations a major issue of the campaign. The Republicans avoided commitment on the League question and, instead, advocated higher tariffs and tax reduction. Reading the popular temper correctly, they were extremely confident. During the campaign Harding stayed on his front porch in Marion, Ohio. His speeches, according to McAdoo, were "an army of pompous phrases moving across the landscape in search of an idea." In spite of—or perhaps because of—the assurance of victory, the Republicans were aided by a campaign fund of $8 million.

The Republican landslide was the greatest since the second election of James Monroe. Harding carried every state outside the "solid South," and there he carried Tennessee. He received 61 percent of the popular vote, as much as Franklin D. Roosevelt was to poll in his greatest victory. In Congress, the Republican majority was 167 in the House and 22 in the Senate. Although this was the first election following women's suffrage, no significant changes were apparent as a result of women's vote.

WARREN G. HARDING

Warren Harding as President would be an abrupt change from his predecessor Woodrow Wilson. Unlike Wilson, Harding had few strong convictions, was open to compromise, and could be easily persuaded to change his position on most issues. Harding was also non-confrontational and indecisive by nature; therefore, he did not enjoy the Presidency, an office that epitomizes confrontation and decision-making.

Harding is perhaps unique among Presidents in that he possessed an overwhelming awareness of his own incompetence. For example, Harding once stated, "I am not fit for this office and never should have been here." Similarly, to Judge John Barton Payne, Harding once exclaimed, "I don't think I'm big enough for the Presidency." In a similar vein, to Calvin Coolidge, Harding once offered, "I am a man of limited talents from a small town. ... I don't seem to grasp that I am President." To compound matters, Harding was generally ignorant of policy issues and realized the situation as such. For instance, he once stated his frustration on a tax issue by proclaiming, "I don't know what to do or where to turn on this taxation matter." Although generally ignorant in most policy areas, Harding was particularly ignorant on foreign affairs. When asked once by a reporter about European affairs at the time, Harding replied: "I don't know anything about this European stuff."

Harding's doubts about his own abilities were widely shared by contemporary intellectuals and astute politicians. Harding frequently butchered the English language in his speech and made frequent misstatements. Republican Senator Bose Penrose of Philadelphia perhaps best summed up the Republican Party's position on Harding when he argued that the Republicans should:

> "Keep Warren at home. Don't let him make any speeches. If he goes out on a tour, somebody's sure to ask him questions, and Warren's just the sort of damn fool to try to answer them."

Due to these shortcomings, Harding did not enjoy being President. In the words of Harding, "The White House is a prison and I cannot get away from the men who dog my footsteps." As a counter balance, Harding focused on the positive input from the public in the way of letters he received from his adoring fans; and he spent much of his time writing letters to citizens and greeting ordinary people at

President Warren G. Harding and Vice President Calvin Coolidge *(Library of Congress)*

the White House. When one White House aide questioned the amount of time Harding spent in his letter-writing and small-talking with the public, Harding responded with, "I love to meet people. It's the most pleasant thing I do; it is really the only fun I have. It does not tax me, and it seems to be a very great pleasure to them."

HARDING AND THE OHIO GANG

While Harding enjoyed the public support from Protestant fundamentalists and the prohibitionist KKK, a few blocks from the White House at the "House on K Street," Harding and the "Ohio Gang" drank mass quantities of bootleg liquor during Prohibition while they gambled, entertained women, sold government favors, and bribed Congressmen. Alice Roosevelt (Theodore's daughter) once came into the White House study and found the air "heavy with tobacco smoke, its tables cluttered with bottles containing every imaginable brand of whiskey and cards and poker chips at hand." The Ohio Gang plundered the government, private business, and taxpayers in almost every way imaginable. Jesse Smith, a top aide to Daugherty in the

Attorney General's office, used his office to sell pardons, government contracts, and government access. As a result of his misdeeds, Smith was accused of influence peddling and committed suicide in 1923. After the incident, Harding is reported to have stated:

> "My God, this is a hell of a job. I have no trouble with my enemies. I can take care of my enemies all right. But my damn friends, my God-damn friends, they're the ones that keep me walking the floor nights".

Similarly, Charles R. Forbes, head of the Veterans Bureau, pocketed millions of dollars appropriated for construction of veterans hospitals. Forbes fled to Europe, later eventually returned, and was sentenced to two years in prison. Forbes, however, fared much better than his assistant, Charles F. Cramer, who escaped the prosecution by committing suicide. Thomas W. Miller, the Alien Property Custodian, who was in charge of seized German assets from World War I, was sentenced to prison for accepting bribes in exchange for the release of assets to their original owners. Attorney General Harry Daugherty was implicated in the scandals, but took the Fifth Amendment on the stand and was not convicted.

The most celebrated of the scandals during the Harding Administration, however, was the Teapot Dome Scandal involving Secretary of the Interior Albert Fall. Fall arranged with Navy Secretary Edwin Denby for the transfer to the Department of the Interior of Navy oil reserves in Elk Hills, California, and Teapot Dome, Wyoming. Fall then leased the reserves to Edward L. Doheny's Pan-American Petroleum and Harry F. Sinclair's Mammoth Oil Company. Doheny "loaned" Fall $100,000 in cash (handed over in a "little black bag") while Sinclair gave Fall $300,000 in cash and securities. Sinclair was given nine months in jail for tampering with a jury, but acquitted of defrauding the United States government. Fall was fined $100,000 and given one year in prison for accepting a bribe, while Doheny went unpunished. President Harding evidently knew nothing of the scandal and it did not become public until after his death; hence, the scandal did not harm Harding's reputation during his lifetime.

Also in 1927 (some four years after Harding's death), it became publicly known that Harding had had an extramarital affair with Nan Britton, a young woman 30 years his younger. She began seeing Harding in 1917 after she wrote him from her home in Harding's hometown of Marion, Ohio, asking him for a job. Harding was able to secure employment for Britton in a clerical position at U.S. Steel in Washington, and they then commenced with their affair, which continued until Harding's death. Britton gave birth to Harding's daughter,

Elizabeth Ann, in 1919; and Harding made child support payments to Britton from the White House that were hand-delivered by the United States Secret Service. After his death, Britton sued Harding's estate to gain a trust fund for her daughter. Britton then wrote a book entitled *The President's Daughter,* which she dedicated to "all unwed mothers and to their innocent children whose fathers are usually not known to the world." Britton recounted details of the affair in the book, including accounts of trysts with Harding not only in the Oval Office, but also in a White House closet.

Harding also had a 15-year relationship with Carrie Phillips, the wife of his longtime friend, James Phillips. The affair began in Marion, Ohio, in 1905 and continued until Harding was running for President of the United States. This is in spite of the fact that in 1917 Phillips, a German sympathizer who had lived in Berlin, tried to blackmail then Senator Harding into voting against a Declaration of War on Germany. In 1920, the Republican National Committee removed Ms. Phillips from the picture so as to avoid any possible embarrassment of their Presidential candidate by paying Mr. and Mrs. Phillips $20,000 in cash and providing them with a free, slow, trip to Japan, along with monthly hush money.

By the summer of 1923 there was a rumor that the House, now controlled by Democrats and Progressives, might try to impeach the President; but on August 2, in the midst of the increasing revelations of corruption, Harding died of an apoplectic stroke. With Vice-President Calvin Coolidge now succeeding to the presidency, the Republican Party had a man superbly qualified to make amends for the laxity of the Harding administration. Coolidge, a slight, dry-looking, diffident Vermonter who after graduation from Amherst had won success in Massachusetts law and politics, seemed to personify the traditional virtues of thrift and frugality. His intimate friends would not betray him because he had none. At a time when business and most of the middle class seemed satisfied with the status quo, Coolidge could be relied upon not to rock the boat.

REPUBLICAN NATIONAL POLICY

Led for eight years either by Harding, who had been installed by the right wing of the party, or by Coolidge, whom Hoover called a "real conservative," the Republican administration tried to lessen or remove controls over business activity. In this policy the President was often at odds with Democratic-progressive coalitions in the House and the Senate, but the presidential powers of appointment and veto proved effective weapons in cutting down federal activities.

The Republican Presidents appointed conservative, business-minded members to federal regulatory commissions. This led to such a relaxation in vigilance that, in the words of a famous authority, the Federal Trade Commission "tried to commit *hara-kiri*"—to cease functioning as a regulatory agency. The antitrust division of the Justice Department seldom prosecuted mergers. The Federal Power Commission, established in 1920 to regulate interstate electric power, did little to justify its existence, and the efforts of the Interstate Commerce Commission to bring about railroad consolidation and recapture excess earnings were without significant effect.

Ocean shipping in the 1920s presented special problems. At the end of the war, the government owned some two million deadweight tons of hastily constructed freighters which were slow and inefficient in comparison with new turbine or diesel electric vessels coming from British and Continental yards. In addition, United States wages and manning requirements made it impossible for American ship owners to compete on an equal basis with foreign operators. To keep some of the ships at sea the Shipping Board for a decade pursued a policy of selling the freighters for $5 to $10 a ton and granting mail subsidies for operation on strategically important routes.

One of the first conflicts between the conservative President and the less conservative Congress was over the soldiers' bonus bill. This proposed legislation provided a 20-year endowment policy totaling $1 for each day a veteran had served in the United States and $1.25 for each day overseas. President Harding in 1921 and President Coolidge in 1924 vetoed the bill. The Harding veto was sustained, but a more generous Congress overrode that of Coolidge.

Freed from fear of federal regulation, businessmen also were gradually relieved of the higher taxes of the war period. In terms of economic policy, Harding was essentially a standard laissez-faire and pro-business conservative. Harding perhaps well summed up the mood of the times when he stated, "What we need is less government in business and more business in government." In 1921, Harding exhibited his conservative pro-business and anti-labor stripes when he called in the National Guard to put down a United Mine Workers' Strike in West Virginia and Pennsylvania. As a result of the federal government's tilt back toward management, Union membership nationwide dropped from 5 million in 1921 to 3 million in 1929.

Harding proved to be a "compassionate conservative," however, in that he pardoned radical dissidents imprisoned during the Wilson years, including Eugene V. Debs, the Socialist Party leader imprisoned for his anti-war stance against World War I. Harding also denounced lynching in a message to Congress in 1921, but did not follow up with initiative for an anti-lynching bill. In most cases, however, Harding personally was able to provide little in the way of policy direction, with the result that leadership flowed to Congress and Harding's executive appointees.

Harding concentrated on appointing what he believed were capable aides and cabinet members and delegating most of his authority. Harding rewarded Party leaders who had helped him gain the nomination with important positions, however; and Harding's trust in what eventually came to be known as the "Ohio Gang"

Eugene V. Debs *(Library of Congress)*

turned out to be partially misguided as Harding's appointees plundered the government for personal gain. Among Harding's most important appointees was Treasury Secretary Andrew Mellon, whose laissez-faire economic policies became those that guided the nation.

Mellon, formerly head of the Aluminum Company of America and one of the richest men in the world, believed sincerely that high income taxes retarded economic growth. As Secretary of the Treasury he immediately sponsored a tax bill that repealed the excess profits tax and sharply reduced the surtaxes on personal income. After amendments by the Republican farm bloc and by Democrats in the Senate, the Revenue Act of 1921 repealed the excess profits tax but cut the maximum surtax on personal income only from 65 to 50 percent. Nevertheless, since federal revenues steadily exceeded expenses, there was increasing pressure for tax reduction. By 1929 four subsequent revenue acts had reduced the maximum surtax to 20 percent and the effective initial rate to less than half of one percent. The tax on corporate income was slightly reduced, to 11 percent.

These tax reductions, which retarded repayment of the national debt and left it at $16 billion at the beginning of the Great Depression, have been vigorously criticized; yet Republican administrations faced a real economic dilemma. To have repaid the debt more rapidly would have released to the money markets as much cash as came from the untaxed savings of high incomes, if not more. Only if the government could have found a way to use the money so as to increase lower incomes or to pay it to some of the two million unemployed could the surplus have been kept from feeding the inflation in stocks and mortgage bonds. Such a fiscal policy would have been directly contrary to the firmly held beliefs of the conservative majority and, as an explicit policy, probably beyond the imagination of most of the more liberal minority.

One proposed use for federal funds that would not have involved the government in new types of business or competed with private industry was the support of farm incomes. Farmers had been led by the demands of World War I to expand wheat acreage, which in view of long-run trends was already excessive in 1914. After the collapse of the reconstruction boom in 1920, farm prices fell more than those of things the farmer had to buy, and both foreign and domestic markets for such staples as wheat and cotton declined. Farmers were not participating in the general prosperity.

A plan put forward by two farm machinery manufacturers in 1922 did not involve federal subsidy but merely required a federal marketing agency that could maintain a domestic price in excess of the world price. Written into the McNary-Haugen Bill and endorsed by practically all farmer organizations, the proposal was resisted by conservative Republicans as a dangerous extension of federal power. The bill was passed in 1926 and again in 1927, but killed both times by a Coolidge veto.

Although by the late 1930s the Farm Bureau Federation, the chief agricultural pressure group, was to seem conservative, in the 1920s it formed a rallying point for liberals. In spite of the conservative presidential leadership, progressives of both parties maintained their strength in Congress. The greatest obstacle to liberal victories during the decade was probably not the relatively small group of conservatives with substantial incomes but rather the general political apathy bred by prosperity from 1923 to 1929. Presidential elections drew only a little more than half the voters to the polls. Coolidge was sustained in the 1924 presidential election by a mere 28 percent of the possible electorate.

EXPANSION OF GOVERNMENT

FEDERAL, STATE, AND LOCAL CHANGE

Even within the administration, men like Charles E. Hughes and Herbert Hoover did not share the Coolidge stand-pat type of conservatism. Hoover, as Secretary of Commerce, tried to bring more efficiency into business operations. To avoid destructive competition he urged small companies to have trade associations administer their mutual concerns, and he invited them to post their prices with the Commerce Department and to refrain from secret rebates. To lower production costs he put his influence behind the movement for standard sizes. The number of shapes of bottles and the various sizes of bricks, for example, were both cut 90 percent. After unsuccessfully preaching self-regulation to the young air transport and radio industries, his department established regulatory agencies in 1926 and 1927, respectively. He and Andrew Mellon also took leading parts in introducing federal budgeting of income and expenses. In these directions Hoover was a planner but as he saw it, he was using the power of government primarily to suggest better voluntary planning to private industry.

State and local authorities, still the most important forms of government, were led to expand their operations greatly. Increasing high-school attendance, in particular, demanded new buildings and bigger school budgets. Skyscrapers concentrated so many workers in the centers of the largest cities that new public transportation was required. On the other hand, automobiles moved so many families to the open areas of the cities or suburbs that new streets and sewers were continually needed. New York and some other states increased the scope and size of their expenditures for welfare. New laws or municipal ordinances regulating business practices, sanitation, and housing required new bureaus and squads of inspectors. From all these needs of a growing industrial society the expenses of government soared. Between 1922 and 1927 the annual cost of state and local government rose nearly 40 percent, and the rise had undoubtedly passed 50 percent by 1929. The debts of these governments increased even faster, up nearly 50 percent from 1922 to 1927 and perhaps by two thirds, had figures been collected, by 1929.

It is also worth remembering that in 1929 these governments cost about two and a half times as much to

Andrew Mellon *(Library of Congress)*

run as the federal government and had about twice as many civilian employees, exclusive of schoolteachers. Thus what appears on the federal level to have been a period of low government expenditure and reduction of debt was *in toto* one of rapid increase in expenditure and dangerous accumulation of local indebtedness.

SECURITY IN THE PACIFIC

While there was a vigorous movement for the League of Nations and world peace, most of the minority of Americans who thought about foreign relations probably wanted to avoid being involved in either European or Far Eastern affairs. The war against Germany was ended by a resolution of Congress on July 2, 1921, and separate treaties were negotiated with the new governments of Germany, Austria, and Hungary; Far Eastern problems were not settled.

Meanwhile the Navy Department had plans for building the world's largest battle fleet. In spite of congressional refusal to pass the big-navy bills, England and Japan were deeply worried over the possibility of having to compete with the United States in naval construction. Therefore, they readily accepted Secretary of State Hughes' invitation to meet in Washington in 1921 to discuss naval disarmament. Since a naval agreement would have to be linked with treaties establishing and guaranteeing Far Eastern arrangements, France, Italy, Belgium, the Netherlands, and Portugal—nations with Asian territories—were invited to the conference together with China.

Early in 1922 Secretary Hughes led the way to a naval agreement whereby the United States, England, and Japan scrapped hundreds of thousands of tons of battleships afloat or in construction and agreed to a 5–5–3 ratio for capital ships, with Britain and the United States at equal strength and Japan held to 60 percent of that tonnage. To secure Japan's interests in the western Pacific each party agreed not to fortify new bases or enlarge old ones. World War II was to demonstrate that this arrangement, as planned, gave Japan an initial supremacy in its nearby waters.

After some argument, France and Italy joined in the treaty, each limiting the tonnage of its capital ships to 35 percent of the Anglo-American maximum. A new Four-Power Pact (United States, British Empire, France, Japan) replaced the Anglo-Japanese Alliance and pledged the powers to respect each other's possessions and rights in the Pacific. A Nine-Power Pact, also concluded during the Washington Conference, affirmed the sovereignty, independence, and administrative and territorial integrity of China. The American policy of an "open door" for Chinese trade was reaffirmed. The Washington treaties established a system of security for Asia such as the Treaty of Versailles was presumed to have provided for Europe.

HIGH TARIFFS

High tariff continued to be a major Republican policy. Ironically, the Midwestern farmers who feared Canadian, Irish, and Argentine competition led the protectionist group in Congress in the early 1920s. Wilson vetoed their first bill for increased agricultural duties on the grounds that American farmers also needed foreign markets.

The Harding administration favored higher duties, but the increases in the Fordney-McCumber Tariff of 1922 were generally moderate. Although agricultural products gained protection, the principle of a tariff that would equalize prices of domestic and foreign products was generally maintained. The farm bloc managed to get manufactures like shoes and wagons on the free list, but some industries received very high protection. The Tariff Commission still had the right to recommend changes, and the President had the power to alter the rates by 50 percent. Neither Harding nor Coolidge made important use of this power.

WAR DEBTS

The Treaty of Versailles had a number major weaknesses, but perhaps paramount among them was an unrealistic structure of reparations and war debts. In 1921 Germany was forced to accept a reparations commission bill for $33 billion, but no such sum could be transferred in a few decades from one European country to the others without severely disrupting the economies involved. Germany attempted to meet its obligations by issuing massive amounts of paper money, which had the impact of devaluing the German currency. By 1923, Germany experienced inflation rates of 26 billion percent, and their economy suffered an economic meltdown. Prices were altered in German stores by the hour, and people were paid hourly in piles of cash. It was said that Germany was the only country where a wheelbarrow full of money could buy a wallet full of goods. As a consequence, the Allied European powers were unable to collect their full reparations from Germany.

Similarly the United States tried to collect war debts of $4.6 billion from England, $4 billion from France, and $2 billion from Italy. The European states, arguing that they had paid for World War I with their lives while Americans were only out money, advised a cancellation of all international payments that would endanger normal economic growth; but Presidents from Wilson to Roosevelt insisted on the principle of collection. Calvin Coolidge, in particular, refused the European request to forgive the debt, quipping, "They hired the money, didn't they?"

Since such sums could be paid only in goods and since Mellon's high United States tariffs limited European exports to the United States, thus further hindering the European ability to pay, debt payments were regularly more than balanced by new American lending and investment abroad. Throughout the decade bankers sold annually about $1 billion worth of foreign government, municipal, and corporate bonds to American investors. This was a profitable system for the bankers; and by giving foreigners dollars to spend, it allowed United States manufacturers to maintain large exports. It meant, however, that world financial stability depended on continued prosperity and an easy money market in the United States.

Congress took several measures in the 1920s to try to alleviate the global currency crisis. In 1921, Congress lowered the interest rates on the debt and extended the terms, but the European nations remained unable to meet their obligations. In 1924 the so-called Dawes Plan, devised by Owen D. Young and Charles G. Dawes of the United States, cut reparations to what seemed like a manageable level. In 1925, the United States Foreign Debt Commission cancelled 80 percent of the Italian debt, 60 percent of the French debt, and reduced interest rates even further. By now the $33 billion bill had shrunk to about $2 billion. During the 1920s the Allies paid the United States about $2.6 billion in war debts, and the Americans loaned Germany some $2.5 billion, 80 percent of which was paid to the Allies.

Therefore, in fact, there was nearly a mutual balancing. The Allies paid the United States, which loaned to Germany, which paid reparations to Allies, and the cycle continued. But the American investors and banks that had advanced the money, however, were left with foreign bonds that soon defaulted on their interest payments. After the onset of the Great Depression, the system collapsed, causing President Herbert Hoover to suspend debt payments for one year in December 1931. In 1932, the European nations collectively cancelled 90 percent of Germany's reparations, hoping that the United States would then cancel the debt. Hoover refused to do so, with the result that when the moratorium on European debt payments ended in December 1932, the Europeans could not pay and all but Finland defaulted by 1934.

Meanwhile, the United States pursued a rather uncertain course of international cooperation. Secretary of State Hughes started the practice of sending "unofficial observers" to League of Nations sessions and to meetings of the principal League committees, but isolationists in the Senate prevented the United States from joining the World Court. This, however, did not prevent Americans, as individuals, from serving as justices.

In 1921, the United States, Britain, France, Italy, and Japan signed the Five-Power Treaty that placed a 10-year moratorium on the construction of battleships and other large naval ships. Maximum "tonnage" of large naval ships was set for each nation with the United States and Great Britain receiving limits of 525,000 tons, Japan 325,000, and France and Italy each 175,000 tons. The United States and Great Britain agreed to prevent any further fortifications of their Pacific possessions; and this, along with the fact that Japan's Pacific fleet would actually be the largest of the three, induced Japan to sign the treaty. A major flaw in the treaty, however, was that it set no limits on the building of smaller ships—including submarines, destroyers, and small cruisers. Within a year after signing, all nations violated the spirit of the Five-Party Treaty by embarking on the construction programs for these smaller ships.

The next year, the United States, Japan, and seven European powers signed the Nine-Power Treaty where all agreed to respect the Open Door in China. The treaty had a major flaw, however, in that it permitted intervention by any of the signatories in China if China did not develop and maintain an effective and stable government. There was also no provision for enforcement or sanctions on the violators of the treaty.

In 1925, the United States and other world powers signed the Geneva Convention of 1925 that established the rules for war, including the rights and treatment of POWs during wartime. In 1928, French Foreign Minister Aristide Briand invited the United States to join France in a bilateral treaty renouncing war. The French were considering occupation of parts of Germany near the French

Aristide Briand *(Library of Congress)*

border and wanted to prevent the United States from intervening on the side of Germany if hostilities erupted. Secretary of State Frank B. Kellogg thought that the proposal was folly; but a pact outlawing war had popular support in the United States and refusal would make America appear belligerent. Consequently, Kellogg declared that Briand's proposal was so laudable that the United States would invite all nations to join America and France in outlawing war. Kellogg then took the lead in negotiating a general agreement to outlaw war as an instrument of national policy. The Pact of Paris, or Kellogg-Briand Pact, was signed ultimately by 63 nations, including all the great powers, but Kellogg regarded the pledge as more valuable for appeasing peace sentiment at home than for influencing foreign nations. Providing no means of applying collective sanctions against an aggressor, the pact was an idealistic but empty gesture, much pressure for which had been generated by the activism of women's organizations.

Paradoxically, the idealistic foreign policy of Woodrow Wilson had left the United States deeply involved in the affairs of Caribbean countries. United States troops were in Haiti, Nicaragua, and the Dominican Republic, and diplomatic relations with Mexico had been suspended. On the South American mainland, hostility toward these United States occupations interfered with both trade and investment.

REPUBLICAN LEADERSHIP REAFFIRMED

In the depression year of 1922 discontented agrarian and labor elements met in a Conference for Progressive Political Action. Continuing its meetings into 1924, the conference agreed to support the presidential nomination of Senator Robert M. La Follette at the Republican convention and, if defeated there, to organize a third party with La Follette as its candidate.

Obviously the progressive minority had no chance of winning the Republican nomination, but it might have swung over to the Democrats if that party had supported an advanced liberal ticket. The Democratic Party, however, was disastrously split over such issues as prohibition, the Ku Klux Klan, Catholicism, and immigration restriction. Hampered additionally by a rule requiring a two-thirds majority for nomination, its convention took 103 ballots to select a relatively unknown New York corporation lawyer, John W. Davis, who failed to inspire enthusiasm in any faction.

When the Republican convention met and nominated Coolidge on the first ballot, the Progressives held their own convention and put forward La Follette. Supported by the American Federation of Labor, many Western farm organizations, and the Socialist party, La

Follette ran on a platform advocating the type of action that Europeans called social-democratic. Nationalization was to apply only to railroads and hydroelectric power. Injunctions in labor disputes were to be effectively forbidden. And Congress was to be given power to overrule the Supreme Court.

Coolidge swept the election with 15,718,000 popular votes to 8,385,000 for Davis and 4,831,000 for La Follette. Davis won only the solid South, and La Follette carried only Wisconsin. The Progressive party had failed to develop the strength necessary for survival.

CALVIN COOLIDGE

Calvin Coolidge was a standard conservative clone of Harding in regard to economic and social policy, but a great contrast on a personal level. Coolidge's conservative laissez-faire ideology was perhaps best summed up by Coolidge himself when he stated, "The chief business of the American people is business. The man who builds a factory, builds a temple. The man who works there, worships there."

On the personal level, however, Coolidge differed greatly with Harding in that he was quiet, detached, sober, endowed with a Puritan moral ethic, and considered to be honest beyond reproach. In these things, unlike Harding, Coolidge was at least consistent with the ideals of his conservative Protestant fundamentalist supporters. Coolidge's ethical standards, however, proved to be much more than window dressing; consequently, he quickly forced the resignation of Attorney General Daugherty and others tainted by scandal during the Harding administration.

Coolidge would be less quick to action in other areas, however, since his stated goal was "to become the least President that the country ever had." Coolidge's statement is a reference to his Hobbesian conservative laissez-faire philosophy of government, but he may have achieved his goal in more ways than one. Coolidge was non-energetic, both in policy and in his personal life, and generally chose to confront crises by taking long naps in the White House. Those around Coolidge described his disposition as "eternally tired." Coolidge's "Silent Cal" nickname was earned by keeping appointments and meetings to a minimum, engaging in as little conversation as possible. Coolidge himself acknowledged his own preference for "silence" and once remarked to reporters, "I don't recall any candidate for President that ever injured himself very much by not talking." Comedian and political commentator Will Rogers perhaps summed it up best when he observed of Coolidge, "Silent Cal. He don't say much, but when he does say something, he don't say much."

When Coolidge did choose to speak, he sometimes revealed that he was actually better off remaining silent. A good example of this is Coolidge's assessment of the economy in 1928, prior to the onset of the Depression when he stated, "The future may be better or worse. … I am certain of one thing, however, when people are thrown out of work, unemployment results." On another occasion, Coolidge astutely observed, "The final solution for unemployment is work."

Few American Presidents have enjoyed four such prosperous, peaceful, and generally pleasant years as those from 1924 to 1928. Coolidge could easily have been renominated and reelected had he chosen to run for a second elected term in 1928, but after keeping the bosses in doubt long enough to preserve his influence in the convention, Coolidge announced simply that he chose not to run. With this announcement, the energetic Commerce Secretary Herbert Hoover became the obvious Republican choice for President. Hoover won the Republican nomination at the Republican National Convention on the first ballot despite a stinging rebuke from Coolidge, who labeled the more progressive Hoover as a "spendthrift," with "bad ideas." Coolidge further exclaimed, "That man has offered me unsolicited advice for six years, all of it bad."

Hoover was supported both by big business and by conservative moralists, who favored his "dry" position on Prohibition. Quickly nominated, Hoover ran on a platform of continuing the Harding-Coolidge policies. With these, he said, "We shall soon, with the help of God, be in sight of the day when poverty shall be banished from this nation."

The Democratic managers probably had little hope of defeating a strong Republican, but they thought that an unusual candidate might bring new voters to the polls. Such reasoning may explain the swing to Governor Alfred E. Smith of New York, a Catholic of Irish immigrant parentage who emphasized his origins by wearing a brown derby. Other than prohibition, the Democratic platform scarcely differed from the Republican, and on economic questions Smith differed little from Hoover. Smith made John J. Raskob, a fellow Catholic and chairman of the Finance Committee of General Motors, manager of the Democratic campaign. Raskob gave the utmost assurance to business that there would be no upsetting changes.

Aside from the immense support given the Republicans by the boom prosperity, the issues came to be Catholicism and prohibition. Smith could do nothing about the former except give assurances of his independence from Rome and his religious tolerance, and these apparently had little effect in the strongly Protestant back country. In the belief that labor and many businessmen were now in favor of repeal of the Eighteenth Amendment, Smith departed from the plank in

Herbert Hoover *(Library of Congress)*

the party platform that had been inserted to win the support of the dry South and campaigned strongly against prohibition.

While probably no candidate could have defeated Hoover in the year 1928, Smith lost or miscalculated on all fronts save one. His "me-tooism" in support of business probably changed few votes. His Catholicism and anti-prohibition sentiments lost seven Southern states and, at the most, gained only two Northern ones. Smith even lost his home state of New York and lost the electoral vote 444 to 87. Smith did, however, have an appeal for the urban masses; and this urban swing, scarcely noticeable in the Hoover landslide, was a portent of the basic change in party strength that was to come from the increase in urban Democrats in the decades ahead.

HIGH HOPES FOR A PROSPEROUS NATION

In his inaugural address Hoover said, "I have no fears for the future of our country, it is bright with hope." His *Memoirs* also show the high hopes with which he started his administration: "Mr. Coolidge was reluctant to undertake much that was either new or cost money, and by 1929 many things were already 14 years overdue." Hoover had a number of plans for bringing more efficiency into government activity, but his first major act, calling a special congressional session to redeem Republican promises to farmers, unfortunately misfired. The President sponsored the Smoot-Hawley Tariff bill to raise the rates on agricultural products; but when the bill finally passed the Senate in June 1930, it carried higher rates on numerous manufactured products and raised the general level of rates on dutiable articles about 25 percent. Although this was not what the President had intended, he signed the bill to give assurance to business. Meanwhile, other nations had been raising their tariffs, some in retaliation for the United States' action; and the outlook for world trade and repayment of international obligations steadily grew darker.

In place of the McNary-Haugen scheme, passed twice by Congress but vetoed both times by Coolidge, the administration planned to help the farmer by the Agricultural Marketing Act of 1929. This originally provided for loans to aid cooperative selling, but progressives added a provision for the use of federal money to stabilize the market price of grain. For these purposes a Federal Farm Board was given a revolving fund of $500 million, the largest single appropriation up to that time for nonmilitary purposes. The plan for buying grain to raise domestic prices and reselling when the market could absorb the surplus might have worked for a time had there been rapid worldwide recovery in 1930. Since the trend toward oversupply in wheat already seemed clear, however, this cure through manipulating the market was, at best, a makeshift expedient.

After the onset of the depression in 1929, most of President Hoover's plans for efficiency and mild reform were abandoned in the effort to bring back prosperity. "Instead of being able to devote my four years wholly to these purposes," he lamented, "I was overtaken by the economic hurricane. ... Then the first need was economic recovery and employment." Fearing that reform would upset business and deepen the depression, the President became as conservative as his predecessors.

POSTWAR ECONOMIC CHANGE

THE DECLINE OF CRAFT UNIONISM

World War I and the postwar boom brought union membership to a peak of 5 million workers in 1920, about 12 percent of the total labor force. While this was a record for the United States, the level of organization was low in comparison with western Europe. A major reason was that American labor organizations were limited largely to the skilled crafts and older types of industrial activity, thus excluding millions of workers, not only white men with poor skills but also people of color and white women. The new mass production industries of the twentieth century, such as automobiles, chemicals, and electrical equipment, had successfully resisted efforts at organization.

The union situation of 1920 was essentially unstable. Many union members in war industries and postwar construction soon had to seek other jobs. Employer organizations, held back since 1917 by government policy and competition for workers, were now ready to marshal business-minded people against organized labor. During the Red Scare it was easy to convince the middle class that unions had radical intentions. The Supreme Court dealt unions a major blow in 1921 when they ruled that "Dangerous strike activity" was illegal. Furthermore, the court defined picket lines as "dangerous strike activity" when they declared that any picket placed within 50 feet of another to be "dangerous activity" and, therefore, illegal. Under this definition, all picket lines, in the traditional sense, were illegal and strikers could not block the entrance of scab workers into the workplace without being arrested. The same year, President Harding called in the National Guard to put down a United Mine Workers' Strike in West Virginia and Pennsylvania.

Unions also faced political pressure from big business. The American Plan, representing small and medium-sized business, was sponsored by the National Association of Manufacturers and vigorously pursued by various trade and employer organizations. It called for the open shop—a shop in which workers could be hired without joining a union. Some of the organizations associated with the movement insisted that their members should not enter into any union contracts. Advertisements were placed in newspapers, denouncing the closed shop (one restricted to union members) as un-American. Labor spies were hired in larger numbers than before to detect union organizers.

One important "welfare" device for preventing national unions from organizing workers was the employee representation plan or company union. The government demand that contractors in World War I enter into collective bargaining with their employees led 125 of the largest companies to organize their own unions with some 400,000 members. Since these unions and their officers were controlled and supported financially by the companies, they were not generally regarded as true representatives of labor. Yet in the 1920s they constituted the one growing area of labor organization. By 1928 it was estimated that company union membership had grown to 1.5 million, half that of the AFL.

In addition to the American Plan and competing company unions, independent unions may also have been weakened by reforms in employee relations. In some big companies, the personnel departments that had been established during the war sought to decrease turnover and increase productivity by improving working conditions and proposing various measures to bolster workers' morale. It may still be argued, however, that the independent unions declined because of the depression of 1920 to 1922 and because business was growing away from the old skilled crafts. The immediate drop in union membership during those two years of depression was 1.4 million. Another 200,000 members were lost during the prosperous years from 1923 to 1929. By 1930 less than seven percent of the labor force was organized in independent unions.

Only in coal and textiles were white labor leaders engaged in vigorous campaigns during the mid-20s. Both industries had the same basic problems: Southern areas were not unionized, and Communists were undermining the existing union leadership. Although John L. Lewis was able to preserve the United Mine Workers' bargaining position in the older areas, he had to agree to wage cuts during the years of high national prosperity. Neither the United Textile Workers nor its Communist-led rival, the National Textile Workers' Union, was able successfully to invade the South and unionize the new mills. With lower wages in that region, the industry continued to drift away from New England and the Middle Atlantic states.

As militancy declined in the ranks of labor, there was a trend toward cooperation with employers. Where an employer had a small business and was often poorly informed, as in the garment industry, unions could help to improve shop practices and overall efficiency. Even some of the large railroads found that union-management cooperation increased productivity in their shops; but looking at the labor scene as a whole, the areas of advancing cooperation were small.

Another trend in this period was toward surrender of union leadership to racketeers. In unions where the complacency of the mid-20s made the members careless about attending meetings, dishonest local officials, supported by so-called gorillas, built up machines that the rank and file dared not oppose. Often these labor racketeers dealt secretly with employers, taking payments from them to prevent the union members from demanding wage increases. The 20s were not a decade of pleasant prosperity for organized labor.

INDUSTRIAL DISTRESS

In the 1920s, reformers increasingly criticized that symbol of modern mass production, the automated assembly line. The speed of the line was set by management, and with no independent unions to protect the workers, those who could not maintain the pace were summarily fired. In addition, such plants generally had many workers under a single supervisor or foreman, who consequently had little contact with the workers as individuals. While such big-plant assembly-line jobs involved only a small fraction of the labor force, to many artists and intellectuals they dramatized the plight of the individual in an impersonal, mechanized society.

Blacks who had come to industrial centers during the war and the postwar boom faced problems of a special type. Many companies would not hire them for anything but menial service jobs, and AFL unions would not accept them in the skilled crafts. This discrimination made many blacks quite ready to act as strike breakers against organized white labor. A. Philip Randolph, one of the few influential black labor leaders, organized a union of Pullman Company maids and porters in 1925, but in spite of the all-black personnel on the cars, the Brotherhood of Sleeping Car Porters was unable at that time to displace a company union and force collective bargaining. Other efforts by Randolph to create a national organization of black unions were even less successful.

AGRICULTURAL DEPRESSION

The poorer and the less efficient farmers also failed to share in the prosperity of the 1920s. Those who had been encouraged by the government to borrow money in order to bring more land under cultivation to meet the wartime demand now found themselves with heavy debts and a declining market. The hardest hit were wheat farmers in the Western prairie and plains states and cotton growers in the South. Mortgage foreclosures forced owners to become tenants, and losses on farm loans led to the closing of thousands of small banks in country towns. In the South black sharecroppers, particularly, were forced off the land and had to seek jobs in the growing cities.

During the decade, advances in soil biology and chemistry made diversification of crops much safer than formerly. Hybrid seeds were developed which could increase the yield and resistance to unfavorable weather of both corn and wheat, and all-purpose tractors were reduced in cost. Since few farmers had extra capital and the overly competitive situation failed to interest other investors, the new knowledge and technology were little used until World War II again brought high prices, rural prosperity, and a shortage of labor. Nevertheless, the development of the internal combustion engine-driven tractor increased American agricultural production at the same time that European demand for American farm products diminished as Europe recovered from the devastation of World War I. The development of synthetic fibers further depressed prices of cotton and wool so that by the end of the 1920s, when GNP per capita was $873, farm GNP per capita was only $223.

A SLOWER RATE OF GROWTH

In the long run, economic growth depends upon the making of more and more capital goods such as buildings, factories, roads, and machines. For the decade 1919 to 1928 net capital formation (that is, the creation of new capital goods) in relation to national income was 14 percent less than in the previous decade and nearly 18 percent less than two decades earlier. During the years 1924 to 1929 the annual investment in new capital goods was actually falling. On the other hand, lower taxes were increasing the net income of the wealthiest classes, and their savings were rising. These savings of funds for investment were, by 1924, beginning to run ahead of the needs of industry and business for capital for physical expansion. In other words, the upper-income groups had more savings each year than there were productive new securities to be bought. As a result, investors were competing for the available securities, and the price of securities went up. A large part of the nation's savings was being used for speculation, while rising interest rates in 1929 were attracting unneeded billions in bank loans from Europe.

Why should the rate of creation of capital goods slow down when there was plenty of saved money to pay for them? Two explanations can be offered. One is that since there was little change in real wages or salaries from 1924 to 1929, consumer demand did not rise rapidly enough to encourage industrial expansion. The other explanation is more speculative. Changes in technology occur in incalculable ways. Some that promise substantial profits require large new investments, as in the case of railroads, while others do not, as in the case of the phonograph. A series of technological innovations requiring large investment absorb savings and labor and produce an expanding economy, but in the 1920s few major capital-absorbing innovations in technology occurred. While some older developments such as electrification, roads for automobiles, and improvements in steel production were still going forward, there was a slowing down of the combined rate of growth after 1927.

TECHNOLOGICAL ADVANCE

Although the new technological developments of the 1920s did not actually increase the rate of capital investment, new devices were sought more vigorously than ever before. By 1929 about a thousand large firms were supporting some type of research. Better control of industrial products through careful cost accounting, spot testing, and laboratory analysis (collectively referred to as "quality control") also led to higher efficiency and productivity.

Radio broadcasting and air travel first reached the general public in this decade, and automobiles and electricity came into general use. Until 1919, the federal government forbade private use of radio. Broadcasts by Westinghouse's station KDKA of the results of the presidential election of 1920 demonstrated the great public possibilities of the new medium of communication; and within the next few years the industry assumed the general pattern that was to remain for decades—competing national networks would subsist on substantial revenue from large advertisers, and high-priced performers would offer variety programs. By 1930, 12 million American families, about 40 percent of the total, could tune in stars like Rudy Vallee, Eddie Cantor, and sports announcer Graham McNamee on their radio sets.

The airplane, invented before World War I, had never attracted much interest in America. During the war the government made an effort to catch up with European development but produced few planes before the Armistice led to cancellation of contracts. The Post Office started an experimental airmail route between New York and Washington in 1918 and after six years extended service to Chicago and San Francisco. Meanwhile, commercial plane production was negligible, and flying was limited to selling rides at airfields and local fairs. In 1925 the government first made an effort to build commercial transport by allowing the Post Office to grant airmail contracts to private firms. The following year Congress gave general regulatory authority to the Commerce Department.

The regular use of air service in Europe and a series of spectacular overseas flights culminating in Charles A. Lindbergh's solo crossing of the Atlantic in 1927, gave some Americans confidence enough to travel by plane. Between 1928 and 1930 passengers increased from 1,400 to 32,000, and revenue miles flown multiplied about 30 times to a total of 4.3 million. Although the young industry continued to grow during the

Charles A. Lindbergh *(Library of Congress)*

depression, the 100 million passenger miles flown in 1940 were almost negligible compared to the 24 billion passenger miles by rail and the incalculable travel by private cars.

In the automotive industry, even in the prosperous years of the 1920s, the smaller assemblers of cars had been dropping out. The early years of the depression reduced the number of competitors to fewer than a dozen, all producing similar cars within four or five price ranges. Ford finally had to give up his famous Model T in 1927 and bring out the Model A, a car similar to those of his chief competitors. This episode temporarily convinced American manufacturers that the public wanted size and luxury in new cars rather than cheapness. No one was more easily convinced than Walter P. Chrysler, who had a passion for fine cars. (See "*Walter P. Chrysler: Lover of Fine Cars.*")

Both homes with electricity and total consumption of electrical energy doubled from 1920 to 1930. In urban and suburban areas five sixths of all residences came to have electricity, but farm electrification was only beginning. In 1920 1.4 percent of farms had electricity and by 1930 only 10 percent.

THE NEW ERA IN BUSINESS

MANAGERIAL ENTERPRISE

As usual in times of business prosperity, the number of firms grew faster than the population as a whole. In 1920 there were probably fewer than 2.5 million firms, in 1929 over 3 million. About two thirds of all firms were in trade and service, and very few of these had more than two or three employees. The overall growth figures, however, conceal a great deal of routine change. Every year of the 1920s thirty to fifty thousand new firms started, and every year a slightly smaller number left the business scene. While adequately capitalized small companies that were started by people who knew the business they were entering had good chances of success, a large percentage of entrepreneurs lacked both qualifications. At the top, a few medium-sized or large firms disappeared each year through mergers, but these equaled only one or two percent of the new firms starting up.

The American business structure appeared to have reached a plateau of stability. Big companies continued to dominate highly capitalized manufacturing industries, railroads, and utilities. Antitrust laws had checked the rise of true monopoly, however. In industries dominated by a few companies, competition in price was avoided, but competition in quality and marketing was generally vigorous.

By the 1920s the stock of most very large companies was widely held. Neither the officers nor the directors of the company owned any considerable percentage of the shares. The chief officers were chosen from among men who had made successful careers in management and were professional executives, rather than either relatives of an owner or large personal investors. The connection of such men with profit was indirect. Profit for the company was a mark of success, a guarantee of security, and a fund from which larger salaries could be drawn, but it did not directly enrich the professional manager. These men were interested in building strong organizations capable of weathering bad times, rather than in reaping quick profits in the market. They favored spending earnings for research, expert advice, and improvement of company morale, rather than using them to pay extra dividends to the stockholders. As a result, the common stock dividends of the biggest companies tended to move toward moderate, stable rates rather than to fluctuate with profits.

While scarcely a thousand companies were big enough to have professional, bureaucratic management remote from control by owners, the thousands of top executives of these big companies were leaders of business opinion. Executives commanded specialized knowledge and expert staff work. They hired the best lawyers, lobbyists, accountants, and engineers. Their assistants wrote speeches and articles for them analyzing business problems. Hence America seemed much more a land of big business than was the case statistically.

SHAPING PUBLIC OPINION

George Creel's Committee on Public Information, similar to European agencies for propaganda during World War I, provided a new emphasis on creating favorable

George Creel *(Library of Congress)*

PEOPLE THAT MADE A DIFFERENCE

Walter P. Chrysler: Lover of Fine Cars

Early in the century Henry Ford had first supplied sturdy, homely, reliable automobiles at moderate prices. By the 1920s Walter P. Chrysler had brought luxury cars within the financial reach of the middle class. In the long view, the high performance of Chryslers from 1924 to after World War II typifies the trend of American automobile design much more than the stark, bare Model Ts. Chrysler's role in setting the pattern for the principal American industry of the twentieth century makes him one of the most important men of his time.

When Chrysler was born in 1875, his father was a locomotive engineer living in Wamego, Kansas. Even such aristocrats of labor, however, couldn't afford to send their children to engineering school. After high school Chrysler went into the railroad shops to learn by doing. His rise was rapid and his devoted wife and young children moved often as he climbed up the ladder of railroad shop positions to a top rung as Superintendent of Motive Power for the Chicago Great Western.

Chrysler was a big, broad-faced, genial man with an emotional power that often controlled his own decisions as well as impressing those around him. Fortunately his intuitive reactions usually turned out to be right. In 1908 he saw a white Locomobile with red upholstery, four cylinders, and chain drive at the Chicago automobile show. It shared with half a dozen other makes the highest prestige in the luxury part of the market. Chrysler promptly fell in love with fine cars. For a man making $4,200 a year to buy a $5,000 automobile was madness. Yet Chrysler, with the help of a banker friend, managed to do it. He didn't want the car to drive and it was weeks before his family even had a ride. Instead, he wanted to take the car apart. He wanted to learn everything about it, which he proceeded to do during nights and weekends.

Meanwhile, to learn more about the problems of production, still unconsciously driven, no doubt, by his dreams of creating motor cars, he quit his railroad job in 1910 and took one in manufacturing with the American Locomotive Company in Pittsburgh at 20 percent less salary. Within two years the chance came to make automobiles. Although American Locomotive wanted to keep him at $12,000 a year—real wealth in the last year before federal income taxes—he became Works Manager for the Buick division of General Motors at $6,000.

Now he was on the main track of his career in a prodigiously expanding industry. Buick, a medium-price car, was the most popular of the General Motors lines. An offshoot of William C. Durant's wagon works, Buick construction was still being supervised by men who had originally been craftsmen in wood. Chrysler quickly introduced the techniques of large-

opinion. About 1920 Edward Bernays and Ivy Lee began to call themselves public relations counselors. Soon the major advertising scale metalworking he had learned at American Locomotive and actually had part of the works on an assembly line earlier than the Ford Plant.

Chrysler was so successful in both making and marketing cars that in 1915 Durant, the founder of General Motors, who had regained control of the company with help from the du Ponts, made Chrysler President of Buick at a salary of $500,000, payable largely in G.M. stock. By 1919, his division was forging ahead of the others at General Motors, and Chrysler was one of the key men in the industry. He had come to be respected for his great ability at selling and finance as well as in production, and he had enough money in G.M. stock to be independent. Consequently, when Chrysler thought Durant was overexpanding early in the inflationary years of 1919, he decided to leave the company and dispose of his stock. Selling out near the peak of the boom, he put the cash in trust for his wife and children and prepared to retire.

General Motors was not the only major automobile company to be caught with too much inventory and too little cash in the rapid market decline of the spring and summer of 1920. Chrysler was soon drawn back into industry affairs, first as a "doctor" for Willys-Overland at an incredible $1 million-a-year salary, and two years later as Chairman of the Reorganization Committee for the ailing Maxwell Motor Company. Meanwhile, in talking with design engineers Fred M. Zeder, Owen Skelton, and Carl Breer, Chrysler succumbed to the overwhelming urge to bring out a new car with its own name and design, using the Maxwell facilities.

Over numerous difficulties, chiefly financial, Chryslers were displayed to large crowds at the Commodore Hotel in New York during the 1924 annual automobile show at nearby Grand Central Palace. Besides being attractive and well made, the Chryslers were the first to combine high-compression engines (which meant higher speed), four-wheel hydraulic brakes, and a shorter wheelbase—a majority of the most important engineering innovations that would be made during the next fifteen years. And the cars sold for no more than Buicks of comparable size.

As young people, particularly, swung toward Chryslers, the company quickly took steps to move beyond medium-priced cars sold to hundreds of customers to cheap cars sold to millions. To compete with Ford and Chevrolet, which dominated this market, Chrysler purchased Dodge Brothers in 1927 in one of the largest financial deals in American automotive history. This marked the formation of the "big three" in the American automobile market, with Chrysler for many of the early years ahead of Ford in sales.

Chrysler's emphasis on engineering and performance permanently shifted sales efforts toward attractive new models offered at relatively uniform, noncompetitive prices. Chrysler's new ideas created the American automobile market, whose features were to last with little change until the advent of the compact in the late 1950s, and in many respects without much alteration until the gasoline crisis of the 1970s. Few other twentieth-century Americans have been so responsible for shaping the everyday utilities of life.

agencies also had public relations departments. The usual techniques were to publicize events that showed the client in a good light and to plant favorable stories in magazines. Much of the content of newspapers in the peaceful years of the 20s originated in public relations offices.

The value of the stockholder as a public relations resource was also exploited. By lowering the price of shares through splitting them two or more ways, and by aggressive selling to small investors, often through agents of the company, it was possible for a big corporation to acquire tens of thousands of new stockholders. American Telephone and Telegraph, which took a leading part in this movement, increased the number of its owners from 50,000 in 1920 to 210,000 in 1930. Stockholders were sent attractive annual reports and letters from the president designed to make them feel that they were an important part of the organization. In return, many stockholders undoubtedly used their votes and influence for government policies favorable to the company.

Whether as a result of the new public relations, or prosperity, or for other less obvious causes, the American public seemed to have given up much of its traditional hostility to big corporations. Articles in praise of business signed by corporate leaders made popular reading in mass-circulation magazines, and business periodicals boasted of the dominance of the businessman and his values. Advertising executive Bruce Barton even pictured Christ as a businessman. In this friendly atmosphere business was bold in the use of direct influence in legislatures, in community pressures through business clubs, and in the use of advertising contracts to influence editors. A basic danger, as illustrated in the 30s, was that business developed few new progressive policies to go with its added power.

STOCK MARKET BOOM AND BUST

Besides lacking a suitable social philosophy, businessmen and their economic advisers lacked understanding of relationships in the economy. Consequently, the stock market boom from 1927 to 1929, though not reflected in any corresponding upswing in real capital formation, was not regarded as dangerous. Confidence that the severe business cycle was a thing of the past pervaded American finance.

The wealthiest class (about 5 percent of the population) received about a third of all income and were taxed at very low rates. Thus, their savings were tremendous. Low corporate taxes allowed big companies to accumulate unprecedented cash surpluses. Both personal savings and corporate surpluses were used for speculation. Moreover, brokers, by means of loans, made it easy for investors of even modest income to purchase securities beyond their means. Investors could buy "on margin"—that is, deposit only a small percentage of the total price of a block of securities, with the broker advancing the rest of the money. The hope was, of course, that the price of the securities would rise and enable the investor to make a large profit on his small equity. Often brokerage houses and banks would lend three quarters of the cost of new securities, the customer depositing only a 25 percent margin. In practice, margins often were allowed to go down to 10 percent or less. Not only were both domestic and European banks happy to lend on this type of "demand" or "call" loan, but big business companies also employed unused reserves for stock market loans.

Since investors would readily buy the shares of railroad and public utility holding companies, ambitious entrepreneurs like the Van Sweringen brothers in Cleveland, Samuel Insull in Chicago, and S. Z. Mitchell in New York set up pyramids of one holding company on top of another. By selling stock in these companies to the public, the empire builders got the money to buy dozens of operating companies while keeping personal control of the organization through the top holding company. In theory, economies were being achieved through removal of wasteful competition, but in fact the savings were often consumed by greater managerial costs.

High-pressure selling by the agents of bankers and brokers led investors into buying many other questionable securities. Mortgages on the new urban hotels, apartments, and office buildings that were rising all over the nation were divided into small bonds for sale to investors. Ultimately these buildings would be needed, but in 1929 construction was already outrunning the demand for such space. United States investment firms literally coaxed foreign governments into issuing bonds that could be marketed to the American public; and, in spite of all this manufacture of new securities, the demand exceeded the supply and boosted the price of existing stocks higher and higher.

By the summer of 1929 many insiders, convinced that stock prices were too high in relation to earnings, started to sell; but thousands of speculators could only cling to the limb they were on and hope for some miraculous support. Late in October the limb broke. In a series of panic days on the New York Stock Exchange, stocks sank so fast that holders on margin were generally wiped out. Efforts by J. P. Morgan and Company to stabilize the market failed, and European banks began withdrawing $2 billion they had loaned on call. On October 29, the day of most extreme panic, 16 million shares were traded, and at times stocks could not be sold for want of buyers at any reasonable price. By November stocks had lost 40 percent of their September value.

Stunned by this disaster in what appeared to be stabilized prosperity, business and political leaders insisted that the economy was sound and that the market break would not affect industry. Only about half a million people had margin accounts, and only a million and a half had brokerage accounts of any kind. But since this small group included most of the chief accumulators and users of capital, their importance was not to be measured in numbers. Furthermore, the whole economy had become more closely geared to the stock market than ever before. In the collapse of values, corporations lost their surpluses. Brokerage houses were unable to sell fast enough to cover their loans. Banks in turn were left with demand loans that could be liquidated only at a fraction of their value, and foreign governments were no longer able to borrow on Wall Street.

THE GREAT DEPRESSION, 1929–1939

(Library of Congress)

THE GREAT DEPRESSION

INCREASING FORCE OF THE DEPRESSION

In August 1928, Herbert Hoover campaigned for the Presidency proclaiming, "We in America today are nearer to the final triumph over poverty than ever in the history of any land. The poor house is vanishing from among us." Hoover, as it turned out, had only six months in which to apply his management skills to the American economy before the stock market crash of 1929 that signaled the beginning of the Great Depression. Prior to the crash, however, there were numerous economic problems that had been ignored due to the robust, overall economic growth of the 1920s.

For instance, as previously mentioned, the international debt situation from World War I was never fully resolved, and farming had been suffering throughout the 1920s due to overproduction. Simultaneously, coal mining had been depressed due to the global switch to petroleum as the primary fuel source. The economy had become oligopolistic and automobile driven, with just a few companies controlling numerous major industries and Ford, General Motors, and Chrysler already dominant in the automobile industry. The 200 largest corporations in America controlled 50 percent of American GNP. The automobile industry, the engine of American growth, was an industry that was particularly subject to recession since the purchase of a new automobile could often be put off by any household by simply repairing the existing car. The 1920s were also a time of great income inequality—the wealthiest 27,000 Americans held the same assets as the poorest 11 million. When the depression did hit, in such a scenario, consumption would be difficult to jump-start. Finally, the stock market was greatly overvalued, increasing 450 percent from 1925–1929, and was due for a major adjustment. The credit structure was also overburdened, with small banks overextended due to difficulties in the agricultural sector and large banks overextended due to foreign debt and investments in the stock market. To top it all off, demand for United States goods abroad was softening as Europe recovered from World War I, yet the foreign debt situation contributed to an American currency crisis. Over 9,000 American banks failed between 1930 and 1933, resulting in $2.5 billion in losses to depositors. As a result, economists estimate that the total United States money supply diminished by as much as one third from 1930–1933. The Federal Reserve, failing to grasp the consequences of their actions and the causes of the monetary collapse, raised interest rates in 1931, further diminishing an already shrinking money supply.

Though the stock market panic of October 1929 that signaled the beginning of the Great Depression was abrupt and severe, the Great Depression itself began more gradually. At the end of 1929 and the beginning of 1930 employment declined only slightly more than was seasonally normal. A Wall Street economist thought the collapse of inflated security values "a favorable development from the point of view of general business." Secretary of the Treasury Andrew Mellon saw nothing "in the present situation that is either menacing or warrants pessimism. All evidence indicates that the worst effects of the crash on unemployment will have passed within the next 60 days." Mellon believed that the economy should be allowed to slide unchecked until it hit bottom in what he viewed as a normal business cycle occurrence. Mellon argued, "let the slump liquidate itself, liquidate labor, liquidate stocks, liquidate farmers. People will work harder, live a more moral life, values will be adjusted, and enterprising people will pick up the wrecks from less competent people."

President Herbert Hoover, initially, concurred with Mellon's optimism and laissez-faire approach due to his own ideological belief in the free market and a patriotic confidence in America itself. Hoover regarded individualism as the most important element in the development of American economic and social life, and he tenaciously believed in the power of voluntarism. In general, Hoover was ideologically opposed to federal involvement in welfare programs because he believed that they would erode individual and community responsibility and encourage a "dole mentality." As late as April 1931, Hoover argued in his memoirs that the country was recovering from a "normal recession due to domestic causes." Hoover's ideological leanings are reflected in his statement of November 15, 1929, (after two devastating months of stock market crash) when Hoover argued, "Any lack of confidence in the economic future or basic strength of business in the United States is foolish." Influenced by the prevailing expressions of optimism, President Herbert Hoover sought to end the mild recession by encouraging appropriate business action and by implementing favorable government policies. In conferences with business leaders he urged them to maintain wages, prices, and plans for expansion. In return he promised to continue a normal program of public works, to raise tariffs, and to lower the Federal Reserve System's rediscount rate (the rate of interest at which banks could exchange customers' notes for currency at Federal Reserve Banks) in order to stimulate business activity by making credit more readily available. Unfortunately, the magnitude of the economic crisis quickly made voluntary efforts by the business sector untenable, and Hoover was soon forced to abandon the conservative principles of laissez faire in favor of government economic intervention.

HOOVER'S ACTIVE CONSERVATISM

First, Hoover attempted to jump-start the economy with a tax cut; but the volume of dollars returned to consumers for consumption through a tax cut was insufficient to remedy the cash shortage in the economy. In June 1930, Hoover attempted to attack the Depression from another traditionally conservative direction and reverted to the nineteenth century Republican Party posture of economic prosperity through tariffs. Despite a petition signed by a thousand economists warning Hoover against increasing tariffs, Hoover signed the Smoot-Hawley Bill increasing tariffs on imports to the United States. The tariff, of course, led to retaliatory tariffs by European nations and contributed to a precipitous decline in international trade. The Smoot-Hawley tariff would later become notorious among most free market economists as a factor that contributed further to the economic malaise by depressing trade and, therefore, hindering international debt repayment.

Hoover also adhered to the nineteenth century Republican monetary position of remaining on the gold standard, thus putting the United States at a trade disadvantage with the Europeans that abandoned the gold standard in late 1931. When the Bank of England defaulted on gold payments in September 1931, the American Federal Reserve Board responded by raising interest rates in an effort to prevent a drain on American gold reserves. The raising of interest rates, in turn, further hindered the American economy by discouraging borrowing and thus further reducing the money supply. Hoover exacerbated the capital shortage even more by stressing the traditional conservative belief in the importance of a balanced federal budget—his reasoning being that since citizens had to live within their means, and the government should lead through the example with fiscal responsibility. Hoover also vetoed the Bonus Act of 1931 that was slated to give almost $1 billion to veterans; but Congress passed the measure over his veto. In Hoover's conception, economic crisis was not reason enough to abandon the conservative economic principles of the balanced budget and fiscal responsibility.

Hoover did not, however, strictly adhere to all conservative economic budgetary principles. By June 1931, Hoover's federal budget was $500 million in the red since the economic decline had also produced declining federal revenue. Hoover supported increased public works programs, favored federal loans to banks, businesses, farmers, and homeowners, and called for expansion of state and local relief programs—though he continued to oppose federal involvement in direct relief. In addition, Hoover created the Federal Farm Board (created under the Agricultural Marketing Act of 1929) to establish semipublic stabilizing corporations with the authority to purchase excess farm products and thus prop up prices. The Federal Farm Board was expected to support agricultural prices by lending funds to marketing cooperatives or to corporations set up by the cooperatives to stabilize the market. The loan funds would be used to purchase basic farm crops and livestock at marketing time so that markets would not be glutted.

Such a program was consistent with the principles of the Agricultural Adjustment Act of 1933, a major part of Franklin Roosevelt's New Deal, championed by the liberal Democrats and opposed by conservative Republicans after Hoover was voted out of office. The Federal Farm Board efforts, however, failed to stop the collapse of agricultural prices because farmers continued to overproduce.

The President, however, refused to face realistically the condition of the unemployed and, probably unaware of the weakness of the banks, continued to manipulate figures to encourage a false optimism. In the spring of 1930, just before business unemployment climbed sharply, he assured the nation: "The worst effects of the crash upon unemployment will have passed during the next 60 days."

Hoover justified federal loan programs on the premise that such loans eventually would be repaid; hence, to Hoover, loans were not the same thing as the government dole. Direct grants or relief, however, were anathema to Hoover. By 1932, Hoover's federal government spending was a very "New Dealish" $500 million per year on public works; but because of the coincident decline in state and local spending on public works, total public outlays on public works in 1932 were almost $1 billion below the levels of 1929. Hoover also refused to allow the federal government to become involved in local relief efforts due to his belief that welfare was a state, rather than federal, responsibility under the United States Constitution. Hoover's refusal to initiate direct federal relief programs was viewed by many Americans as evidence that Hoover neither understood nor cared about the plight of the common person. Furthermore, Hoover's offhand remarks that "no one is actually starving" and that "the hoboes are better fed now than they've ever been" were proof enough to many that Hoover lacked compassion; consequently, many Americans came to identify the calamities of the Great Depression personally with Hoover. Makeshift shantytowns outside of cities became known as "Hoovervilles" and an empty pocket turned inside out became known as a "Hoover Flag."

In the final analysis, historians John Garraty and Robert McCaughey argue that Hoover's policies to combat the Depression failed due to the limitations of his conservative ideology. In the words of Garraty and McCaughey:

> "Hoover was too rigidly wedded to a particular theory of government to cope effectively with the problems of the day ... flexibility and a willingness to experiment were essential to any program aimed at restoring prosperity. Hoover lacked these qualities."

In other words, the chief barrier to effective action in dealing with the advancing depression was that President Hoover, most economists, and practically all businessmen adhered to the traditional laissez-faire view that government should not interfere with business. Thus they considered voluntary private investment the only road to national economic recovery. They did not regard public works projects or other government programs as means of recreating prosperity through increasing demand for workers, goods, and services. Furthermore, allied to the general political failure to appreciate the possibilities of artificially increased employment and demand was the traditional attitude that helping individuals by federal food or relief payments would undermine the initiative of the American people.

A slight upturn in early 1931 supported President Hoover's "wait-and-see" policy. The business indexes soon started down again, and the international financial structure began to disintegrate. In June 1931, banks on the European continent failed. Reparations and debt payments soon stopped, and by September England went off the gold standard (refused to pay its foreign obligations in gold). In July President Hoover, with the agreement of England, France, and Germany, declared a one-year moratorium on European debt and reparation payments. He hoped that such a temporary lifting of the burden of intergovernmental debts would promote world trade and stimulate economic recovery. However, the European crisis resulted in continued gold withdrawals from banks in the United States, European sale of American securities, and the freezing of most foreign short-term loans owed to banks in this country. These events forced a further contraction of bank loans in the United States and an end to the possibility of a quick return to prosperity. While the collapse of 1929 was initiated in the United States, descent into the deep trough from 1931 to 1933 was, as President Hoover claimed, precipitated by European events.

INITIATION OF THE WELFARE STATE

Those in "the business world," wrote President Hoover, "threw up their hands and asked for government action." As voluntary action proved inadequate to counteract the deepening depression, Hoover moved step by step toward federal legislation. In December 1931 and January 1932 the President cooperated with leaders of the politically divided Senate and the Democratic House in creating the Reconstruction Finance Corporation (RFC). This conservatively managed agency, with resources of $2 billion, was to make loans to companies such as banks and railroads to prevent bankruptcy and forced liquidation and provide funds to state and local governments for public works. Aid was given to some 5,000 medium-sized to large businesses to help them meet their pressing obligations, such as bond and mortgage interest or short-term debts. The philosophy of aid was to preserve those institutions whose operation was essential to the public and to other businesses. Consequently, banks and railroads received the most aid while small business, in general, was not initially helped. Critics argued that the RFC helped only those businesses that needed it the least and ignored those that needed it most. Critics dubbed the RFC as the "Breadline for Big Business."

Nevertheless, the RFC only provided loans and not grants to business, could not purchase stock or provide no-strings capital to businesses or financial institutions. The RFC also provided money only for those public works programs that could be shown to eventually pay for themselves such as a toll road or public housing. In addition, the RFC was also stingy in allocating the resources under its control. For example, Congress appropriated $300 million for support of local relief efforts, but the RFC had spent only $30 million by the end of 1932.

Until this time the "general welfare" clause of the Constitution had never been interpreted to mean maintenance of the economic system by congressional action. While later Democratic acts continuing the RFC and extending aid to agriculture and individuals were to push the doctrine much further, the nonpartisan RFC Act can be considered the beginning of the federal "welfare state" or "social capitalism." It demonstrated in the sphere of big business that an advanced industrial economy was so complexly interrelated that government could not stand by and see any essential parts break down.

Other recovery measures enacted in the spring of 1932 included the Glass-Steagall Act, which made government bonds and additional types of commercial paper acceptable as collateral for Federal Reserve notes—thus liberalizing the lending powers of banks—and made available to business about $750 million of the government gold supply. In July the Federal Home Loan Bank Act created 12 regional Federal Home Loan Banks to extend federal financial assistance to building and loan associations, savings banks, and insurance companies that were in trouble because of falling prices. Democratic congressional efforts at direct aid to individuals were defeated by presidential vetoes, however. Hoover continued to view relief as a function of state and local governments; consequently relief limped along on the basis of small RFC loans to the states.

EFFECTS OF THE DEPRESSION

By the spring of 1932, conditions in the United States reached what seemed to be an intolerable impasse. Then, after remaining relatively unchanged for some nine months, the situation grew even worse. Historians essentially agree that American capitalism had failed in 1932 with thousands roaming both the countryside and the city streets searching for food. Food prices were so low that farmers in Iowa and Nebraska burned their corn for fuel while millions had not enough to eat. In Birmingham, Alabama, landlords ceased evictions to prevent people from burning their abandoned dwellings for fuel. Federal Immigration officials in the Southwest began deporting all Mexican aliens in an attempt to reduce the labor force and create jobs for the whites that remained. An estimated half million Mexicans left the United States for Mexico from 1931–1933.

Yet in all this year of material, social, and moral prostration, there was never any threat of revolution, or even any important rise of radicalism in American politics, at least initially. The American cultural traditions of self-help and individual responsibility seemed, for the most part, to make the sufferers feel guilty, and perhaps sullen and resentful, but not ready to fight for a new order. By the end of the decade, however, a small but significant minority of Americans had moved in a more radical direction, either joining the Communist Party or becoming what was called a "fellow traveler," though actual Communist Party membership may never have eclipsed 100,000 people during its peak in 1934. Nevertheless, Communist Party parades on May Day between 1932 and 1934 drew an estimated 50,000 people in New York. The radicals were disproportionately located in certain sectors, such as among artists and intellectuals or among those active in the labor movement.

Beginning in 1935, however, the American Communist Party shifted its strategy away from the goal of communist revolution and ceased to work independently from other organizations. Instead, the

Communists worked through the labor unions with a focus on increasing wages and improving working conditions. The efforts of the Communists and the labor unions paid off in 1938 when the Supreme Court upheld the right, in *NLRB v. Jones and Laughlin Steel*, to bargain collectively. As a result of this success and the fusion with the labor unions, the Communist parades in New York in 1938 drew only 2,000 people.

The overall statement that unemployment rose somewhere to a quarter or a third of the labor force gives too optimistic a picture of the effects of the depression on human beings. To begin with, total man hours worked in mid-1932 were only about 40 percent of those in 1929, and many experienced workers were being paid only five to ten cents an hour. Furthermore, destitute farmers were not considered unemployed; and people who had given up seeking work and students who stayed in school or college solely because they had no hope of finding jobs were not part of the "labor force." In general, the most easily replaceable workers, such as the unskilled, lost their jobs first. What work remained was apportioned between management and skilled labor. Both managers and women office employees kept their jobs more often than workers in plants.

One-industry towns could be paralyzed by the failure of two or three local companies. By early 1932 the entire county of Williamson in southern Illinois had almost no employment. Some Appalachian mining cities had two or three hundred employed out of many thousands. If a community depended on industries that made goods for other industries, it usually suffered mass unemployment.

Without income or housing to hold them together, many families disintegrated. A father without a job—who washed dishes, made beds, sat around, and failed to provide food—lost status in his family. Sometimes his position became intolerable, and he was driven to suicide. Many more unemployed fathers and older children started drifting around the country, presumably looking for work but perhaps really seeking escape through activity. The drift of a million or more of these "migrants of despair" was aimless but generally toward warm areas, where each city tried to keep the wayfarers moving to somewhere else. In many cities they could get a meal but could not stay.

In the larger cities the major burden of relief fell first on private donors and then on voluntary organizations, like the Red Cross, Salvation Army, Community Chest, and, as these exhausted their resources, on small local and state appropriations. Before the end of 1930, people who administered relief recognized that these resources were inadequate. "Local organizations," said C. A. Dykstra of Cleveland in 1932, "have tried to make $400 million play substitute for

$20 or more billion, formerly paid in wages." In small cities conditions were often worse than in the major centers. A survey of 59 cities of upstate New York in the winter of 1930–1931 revealed that most of them had no relief programs. "By the fall of 1931," says Professor Irving Bernstein, "municipal relief—private and public—was bankrupt in virtually every city in the United States," and it is estimated that unemployment rose 50 percent in the next 18 months.

Recipes developed and circulated on the best way to cook violet tops, various weeds, flowers and dandelions. Some municipalities planted municipal gardens in attempts to feed people. Communities in west Texas sponsored rabbit hunts and snake hunts with the kills distributed to the poor as food. Crowds often developed around garbage cans, behind groceries and restaurants as people searched for food. Despite the despair, an estimated 50 percent of the jobless declined any sort of state aid out of pride.

The Depression altered family structures by forcing extended families to move in together. Young couples put off marriage for lack of a way to support themselves; and marriage rates, divorce rates, and college attendance—all declined 20–30 percent as people could not afford changes to their living arrangements. The American birthrate was 27.7 per 1,000 in 1920, but dropped to 18.4 per 1,000 in 1930's United States.

Virtually every economic indicator reflected a similar decline. American GNP was $104 billion in 1929, but declined to $76 billion in 193—a 25 percent decline. In 1929, $16.2 billion was spent on capital investment, but by 1933 the aggregate of all capital investment was a paltry $330 million. Wholesale prices fell 43 percent from 1929–1933, and by 1932 unemployment is estimated to have been over 20 percent with an estimated 13 million unemployed.

The farming country presented the most outrageous paradox of all. With no effective means of controlling prices or production, farmers literally ruined each other. To keep his income up when prices were falling, each farmer tried to produce more and more, thus driving prices down still further until the value of some crops and animals was too low to justify taking them to market. Because gifts of food would potentially compete with sales, no permissible way was found to distribute and use agricultural supplies. As a result, a sheep raiser cut the throats of young lambs and threw them into a canyon because he could not afford to feed them while the families on so-called "bread lines" had watered-down soup. Southern sharecroppers fared worst of all. Owners unable to finance new crops left former tenants without food, and these rural areas generally lacked charitable or other relief organizations.

FARM HOLIDAY ASSOCIATION

With the economy in shambles, especially in agricultural areas, a certain level of political unrest perhaps should have been expected. Though there was some political unrest in the Great Depression, the degree of political unrest given the economic circumstances should be considered mild at best. Nevertheless, Midwest farmers in the summer of 1932 became politically active with the creation of the Farm Holiday Association. The Association endorsed the idea of withholding farm products from the market—in effect, a farm strike—in an effort to increase agricultural prices. The strike began in August 1932 in Iowa and spread to the surrounding areas. Over the short term, the strike was effective in keeping some farm products from reaching the market; however, the scope of the strike was too small to impact farm prices as a whole, and most farmers did not comply with the strike. Consequently, some farmers turned to violence in efforts to enforce their strike. Rail lines were blocked, and trucks carrying farm products were attacked and overturned in efforts to enforce the strike. These activities, however, were too little and too isolated to impact prices, and the strike dissolved by the end of 1932.

BONUS ARMY

World War I veterans were scheduled in 1945 to receive a bonus for their services in the Great War. In 1932, a group of veterans organized and demanded that the Government pay the bonus immediately rather than delay until 1945. President Hoover was opposed to early payment because he believed it would prevent the government from running a balanced budget.

In June 1932, 20,000 veterans, calling themselves the "Bonus Army," marched into Washington, built a crude camp, and announced their intention to stay until the bonus was paid. In July, Hoover ordered the D.C. police to remove the protesters from some abandoned buildings where they had been staying with the result that the veterans threw rocks at the police when they attempted to evict them from the empty dwellings. The police then retaliated with gunfire, killing two.

Hoover then became convinced that the veterans were radical and dangerous, and called in the army to help the police. General Douglas MacArthur, army Chief of Staff, carried out the operation himself. In full battle dress, MacArthur led the 3rd Cavalry (under the command of General George S. Patton), two infantry regiments, six tanks, and a machine gun unit down Pennsylvania Avenue to disperse the bonus

General George S. Patton *(Library of Congress)*

army, which fled in terror under a barrage of tear gas and bayoneted, rifle-carrying troops. MacArthur then followed the protesters across the Anacostia River and burned their camp. At least 100 demonstrators were injured and one infant was trampled to death by the fleeing protesters.

The majority of United States newspapers supported Hoover's use of troops, but the photos of the United States Army chasing unarmed veterans with tanks and tear gas were not well received by the American public. The entire affair was proof to many Americans that Hoover was insensitive to their plight. Hoover further damaged his reputation with a series of insensitive and inaccurate statements, such as, "Nobody is actually starving," and "The hoboes are better fed than they have ever been."

By the summer of 1932, the patience of various groups throughout the nation was becoming exhausted. In addition to the Farm Holiday Association and the Bonus Army, police had killed numbers of unemployed in riots around Detroit, and some conservative editors were calling for a dictatorship to preserve the state. A majority of the leaders of both major parties, however, conservatively opposed any substantial change in policy. Of the Democratic leaders only Governor Franklin D. Roosevelt of New York seemed to lean toward a more progressive approach, favoring the use of government power to whatever extent necessary, and in whatever ways necessary, to reverse the trend of economic events.

THE ELECTION OF 1932

Franklin Delano Roosevelt (FDR), the son of a wealthy railroad tycoon and a fifth cousin of Theodore, had been brought up on a country estate above Poughkeepsie, New York, and educated at Harvard and at Columbia Law School. In 1910 he entered politics and was elected to the New York state assembly, where he stood for progressivism and reform and was an ardent supporter of Woodrow Wilson. President Wilson, aware of the personal charm of the big, strong-jawed, smiling young man, appointed Roosevelt Assistant Secretary of the Navy, the same post that had been occupied by his cousin Teddy in 1898. The 1920 Democratic convention, needing the magic of the Roosevelt name, nominated him for the vice-presidency. Teddy's children, Ted and Alice, were offended that their distant relative was running on the family name and campaigned against FDR believing that it was Ted, not Franklin that should be the torchbearer of the Roosevelt name in politics.

Shortly after his defeat as Cox's running mate, Roosevelt contracted infantile paralysis (polio), but by 1924 he had recovered sufficiently to appear, supported by crutches, at the Democratic convention and make the nominating speech for Alfred E. Smith. As much as possible, Roosevelt would do his best to shield the public from his infirmity, however, under the premise that many Americans at the time would hesitate to vote for a "cripple."

While he was recovering, his wife Eleanor (niece of Theodore Roosevelt) maintained the visibility of the Roosevelt name by her own hard work in the Democratic Party of New York. Franklin had married Eleanor in 1904, and the couple had four children together before Eleanor discovered a briefcase full of love letters between Franklin and Lucy Mercer in 1918. Eleanor was heartbroken, but agreed to remain by his side due to their mutual political ambitions. Eleanor would later become, perhaps, the most political and influential First Lady in American history.

Eleanor also had to deal with Franklin's overbearing mother, Sarah, who meddled in the Roosevelts' lives and attempted to drive a wedge not only between Eleanor and Franklin, but also between Eleanor and her own children. Sarah built Franklin and Eleanor a house in New York next to her own with the two houses open to one another on all four floors. To the children, Sarah reportedly stated, "I am your real mother; Eleanor merely bore you."

In spite of the challenges at home, in 1928, at Al Smith's insistence, Roosevelt ran for governor of New York. Carrying the state by 25,000 votes while Smith lost it for the presidency marked Roosevelt as one of the coming men in the Democratic Party. As governor of New York, Roosevelt gained a reputation for using government to solve social problems. Under Roosevelt's tutelage, New York enacted unemployment insurance, old age pensions, and public works projects. In 1930, after one term as a rather easygoing, liberal governor, he was reelected governor of New York by a record-breaking 725,000 votes.

These repeated victories made him the party's logical candidate for the presidency in 1932, but Roosevelt, fearful of a strong undercurrent of conservative opposition, left nothing to chance. His able secretary, Louis M. Howe, planned and advised, and New York Democratic chairman James A. Farley toured the country and talked to politicians. At the Democratic convention Farley skillfully negotiated with William Randolph Hearst and William C. McAdoo for California's support on the fourth ballot in return for the nomination of conservative House Speaker John Nance Garner for Vice-President. This shift swung Garner's state of Texas and other Southern states to the Roosevelt bandwagon, but Al Smith held on to his delegates and left Chicago without congratulating the nominee.

The Republicans had no recourse but to nominate Hoover again; and in truth, the prosperous people who financed and ran the national machinery in both parties probably thought that Hoover had done all that could be expected. Yet everyone knew he would not be a strong candidate with the public.

Alice Roosevelt openly campaigned for Hoover and publicly made fun of Eleanor's poorly aligned teeth. Later, Alice would publicly state in reference to Franklin, "I would rather vote for Hitler." Not to be outdone, Eleanor followed Ted Roosevelt at campaign stops with a teapot, representative of Ted's involvement in the Teapot Dome scandal.

The campaign mirrored the complete confusion in both parties regarding acceptable economic policy. The two platforms were nearly the same, and both candidates talked of public works and relieving misery while reducing spending and balancing the budget; but Garner was no doubt right when he told Roosevelt that to win "all you have to do is to stay alive until election day." FDR was not a miracle worker in New York, and the state suffered from the Great Depression along with the rest of America; but FDR appeared to most Americans to be more energetic and open to different approaches than Hoover, who probably gained no votes with his weary and often bitter campaign. FDR lacked any concrete plan for attacking the Depression, but won over Americans with his "Try Something" approach. FDR—"The country needs bold, persistent, experimentation. It is common sense to take a method and try it. If it fails, admit it frankly and try another, but above all, try something." FDR and the "Try Something" approach carried all but six states and 57.4 percent of the popular vote, while Hoover polled only 15,759,000 votes to Roosevelt's 22,800,000.

While many middle-class voters supported Socialist party candidate Norman Thomas as the only candidate with a constructive program, Thomas failed utterly to attract the masses. His 881,951 Socialist votes were fewer than in 1920—when Eugene Debs had campaigned from prison—and relatively less than half the Socialist vote in 1912. Some artists and intellectuals desiring a stronger protest supported William Z. Foster, the Communist, but his meager 102,785 votes indicated that few workers had supported him.

BOTTOM OF THE DEPRESSION

The Great Depression reached its lowest ebb in the four months between the election and Roosevelt's inauguration. During this critical period there was little constructive leadership. Hoover

Norman Thomas *(Library of Congress)*

thought that everything justifiable had been done in the domestic field and was interested in stimulating foreign trade. Roosevelt could not accept Hoover's analysis of the domestic situation and was not prepared to work for return to an international gold standard, the keynote of Hoover's plans. When FDR had accepted the nomination at the Democratic convention in the summer of 1932, in his acceptance speech he offered Americans a "New Deal." "I pledge you, I pledge myself, to a New Deal for the American people." "The "New Deal" was a vague reference to government economic and social intervention; but before FDR could even take office, the depression worsened with a major bank panic and a rash of runs on banks and bank failures. In Michigan, its governor temporarily closed all banks for eight days. Other states followed. By the March 4 inauguration, 40 states had ceased all banking operations, and all but one had imposed some type of banking restriction. Hoover wrote to FDR insisting that the panic was the result of a lack of confidence in the policies of the incoming administration, and Hoover asked FDR to announce that his new administration would stay on the gold standard and balanced budget. FDR intended to do neither and refused. The result was a rift between the two men that all could see during their famous ride down Pennsylvania Avenue on the way to the inauguration—as a gleeful Roosevelt waved to the crowd while a sulking Hoover looked the other direction.

The final breakdown of commercial banking was responsible for bringing the economy to its lowest ebb. Of the 16,000 state banks of 1929 that were not members of the Federal Reserve System, nearly half had closed their doors by 1933. These banks had no system to save them, and many of their officers knew little about banking. Of the 7,500 members of the Federal Reserve, about 1,400 disappeared during the depression, demonstrating that even these banks were too small and poorly connected to stand the strain. Banks that failed drew away deposits kept in the banks of the larger cities. The first major metropolitan area to buckle under the pressure was New Orleans. Early in February 1933 the governor of Louisiana declared a temporary "bank holiday," freezing loans and deposits.

Meanwhile, a Senate committee investigating banking practices had uncovered dishonesty and evasion of responsibility in the highest circles. Major banks had lent money to their officers on no proper security, and bad securities had been sold to banks to save investment subsidiaries or affiliates from disaster. Federal examiners had overlooked these and other questionable practices. Faced with such uncertainties, depositors began to withdraw their surplus cash from the banks and stuff it into safe deposit boxes.

Closing of the banks in Michigan in mid-February started a chain reaction that ended on March 4, 1933—the day of Roosevelt's inauguration—when Governor Lehman of New York and other governors joined in declaring a "bank holiday" to stop destructive runs as depositors rushed to withdraw savings. The banking crisis had, in turn, hurt business, driving unemployment up to somewhere between 14 and 17 million, perhaps as much as a third of the labor force. The economy was producing at about half the rate of 1929, and the trend was downward.

As the nation drifted without leadership, the Silver Shirts, White Shirts, Khaki Shirts, and other fascist organizations strove unsuccessfully for mass support. "Technocracy," a vaguely defined plan for placing control of the nation's means of production in the hands of technicians in order to realize the full efficiency of industrial equipment, created a midwinter furor; but it died quickly from lack of immediate, practical proposals. In general, the people waited patiently, putting their hopes in the new administration.

FDR: The First Term

THE HONEYMOON

When FDR took office, the mood of the people, Congress, and even big business, was generally in favor of drastic government action. The first change was in February 1933, when Congress passed the Twenty-first Amendment repealing Prohibition. The necessary three

Franklin Delano Roosevelt *(Library of Congress)*

fourths of the states ratified the amendment by the end of 1933, and Prohibition on the nationwide scale was ended.

Roosevelt's inaugural address on March 4, 1933, struck a note of hope. The nation was strong, he said, and would recover from this crippling depression. "The only thing we have to fear is fear itself—nameless, unreasoning, unjustified terror which paralyzes needed efforts to convert retreat into advance." Roosevelt gave an indication as to his direction by stating that "This nation asks for action, and action now." He closed by affirming, "The people of the United States ... have asked for discipline and direction under leadership. They have made me the present instrument of their wishes. In the spirit of the gift I take it."

The nation and Congress, which Roosevelt immediately called into emergency session, responded to his appeal; and quickly the pattern of the "New Deal" began to reveal itself. "Our greatest primary task," Roosevelt declared in his inaugural address, "is to put people to work." Preferably the employment should be private firms, but if necessary the federal government should use its resources to provide employment on the most useful work projects that could be quickly devised. Second, the abuses that aggravated the depression must be corrected. Anyone guilty of criminal acts of financial or corporate manipulation must be punished. Banking laws should be made stricter in some respects, controls over the stock exchanges and the commodity markets should be tightened, and abuse of the holding-company device should be corrected by closer control of its use, especially in public utilities. After these emergency corrective measures had been taken, Roosevelt proposed a series of permanent steps to bring about a fuller development of the country and to make the lives of most Americans more secure and prosperous. Roosevelt referred to these three objectives of the New Deal as "Relief, Recovery, and Reform."

On March 6, before Congress met in special session, the President proclaimed a four-day national bank holiday and a four-day embargo on the export of gold, silver, and currency. Congress, convening on March 9, began what perhaps should be considered the most productive 100 days in the history of the United States Congress. With a Democrat majority, FDR essentially faced no opposition in Congress, and there was almost complete unanimity in favor of greater federal economic intervention. First, Congress provided for the reopening of banks to relieve the financial emergency. The Emergency Banking Relief Act—enacted that day—confirmed the President's earlier actions and provided for Treasury Department inspection of all banks before they could reopen. The act also provided federal assistance to unstable banks in the form of loans and the absorption of bad loans by the federal government. At the same time Congress prohibited the use of gold except under license for export.

FDR then restored the American confidence in the banking system through his "fireside chats" over the radio where he declared to the American public that the banks would be safe when they re-opened. FDR explained to Americans over the radio, "It is safer to keep your money in a reopened bank than under the mattress." Though no major substantive changes had been made to the banks, Americans believed the President; and by April 10, 1933, over $1 billion in hoarded currency returned to the banks. Importantly, the banks had not been nationalized since FDR had chosen reform rather than revolutionary change.

The special session of Congress subsequently was fed a stream of recovery measures drawn up by groups in the administration, often with differing philosophies, but with the force of the President behind them, sweeping bipartisan majorities. The Economy Act, in March 1933 cut federal salaries 15 percent and cut veteran's pensions 15 percent in an effort designed to help balance the budget since the government faced a $1 billion deficit without the cuts. FDR was trying to convince both the public and the business community that the economy was in safe, responsible hands. The Economy Act was problematic, however, in that it also had the effect of shrinking the money supply even further in a cash-short economy and, therefore, worsening the depression.

Congress established the Federal Deposit Insurance Corporation (FDIC) to ensure bank deposits and guard against further runs on banks. The Federal Securities Act required full public information on new stock issues and appointed the newly created Securities and Exchange Commission to regulate securities transactions.

By the time this famous "Hundred Days" or political "honeymoon" ended in June 1933, the basic emergency legislation was complete. The Federal Emergency Relief Administration (FERA) was created with $500 million in funds to be granted to states for direct relief. A Civilian Conservation Corps (CCC) was set up to put unemployed young men into camps to carry out various reforestation and erosion-control projects. The demand for relief in the states was so great that the FERA had already spent the majority of the $500 million by the end of 1933.

THE SPIRIT OF THE NEW DEAL

It did not take long for the new administration to reveal an utterly unprecedented approach to governing—and not only because of the legislation it pushed through Congress. Appointments to major positions drew in an unusual mix of college professors and former settlement house workers—such as Secretary of Labor Frances Perkins, the first woman to be appointed to a cabinet position—as well as career politicians and bureaucrats. Indeed, more women were appointed to influential governmental positions than ever before in the nation's history. Moreover, FDR was eager to encourage new ideas although he did not necessarily always decide to employ them. Nothing embodied the new spirit more than the character of First Lady Eleanor Roosevelt. Born to privilege, she had been a neglected and underloved child. Scholars have suggested that this phenomenon helped give her the capacity to identify with the many victims of the depression to the extent that she did. With her husband still suffering from the effects of polio, she traveled the country in his stead, becoming, in effect, his eyes and ears. She descended into coal mines or visited the rural poor; and when she would return to Washington from one of these trips, she would bring with her the conviction that government could do something to help. Further, she reached out to African Americans in a way no other White House resident ever had. Many people called her "the conscience of the New Deal."

FARM RELIEF

From the standpoint of loss in money income, farmers were the hardest hit of any occupational group. From 1925 on they were in a vicious circle of increasing overproduction of staple crops and declining prices. Earnings were so low that grain and cotton farmers could not afford the investment needed to shift to other produce for which there was a better market. Depression turned hardship into disaster. Total cash income for farmers fell from an average of nearly $11 billion per year in the late 1920s to $4.7 billion in 1932. Even these figures fail to suggest however, the desperate straits of marginal cotton, corn, and wheat growers.

By May 1933, FDR was perhaps more concerned about the plight of the farmers than any other segment of society. The Agricultural Adjustment Act created the Agricultural Adjustment Administration (AAA), which was charged with reducing agricultural production in order to increase prices. The AAA controlled seven base commodities (wheat, cotton, corn, hogs, rice, tobacco, and dairy products) and would decide production limits for each crop. Then, the AAA would allocate to each farmer how much he could plant, paying subsidies to farmers to leave some of their land idle in an effort to curb production and increase prices.

The Agricultural Adjustment Act of June 1933 contained the basic principle of subsequent farm legislation. The government should pay staple crop farmers to plant fewer acres, thus reducing output and raising the prices on farm products. Money to subsidize the farmers was to come from a tax on millers and other processors of staple products. In this way the law would be self-supporting. To get the program going quickly, the Secretary of Agriculture arranged for the plowing up of millions of acres of cotton and the slaughter of six million pigs of less than usual market weights—the pigs to be put to uses other than providing human food. Although many Americans considered the destruction of food and cotton positively sinful when millions were hungry and poorly clothed, farm prices and income did improve in 1934 and 1935.

There were multiple problems with the AAA, however, as it led to sharecropper unemployment as landowners would remove land from production (in effect laying off sharecroppers that had been working the land) and accept government subsidies. With less land to tend, wage-earning field hands also suffered layoffs. The drops in agricultural production hurt other areas of the economy, such as the railroads that carried fewer products to market. Finally, the Supreme Court struck down the AAA in 1936 as unconstitutional, arguing that Congress had no authority to limit production.

In February 1936, Congress responded by passing the Soil Conservation and Domestic Allotment Act, which permitted the government to pay farmers to "conserve soil" and prevent erosion. Although the final result was much the same as that of the AAA, the Soil Conservation Act survived Court challenges.

MORTGAGE REFINANCING

The government had to try not only to revive farm income but also to take care of hundreds of thousands of defaulted mortgages, both farm and non-farm. In two initial acts creating the Federal Farm Mortgage Corporation and the Home Owners Loan Corporation, the government offered to refinance mortgages on long terms at low interest.

In addition, the Federal Housing Administration Act of 1934 introduced the guaranteed packaged mortgage—one that could be paid, principal and interest, by uniform monthly payments. This government guarantee of loans for a high percentage of the total cost of homes in the low-price range constituted the most important change in the history of American home ownership. Now people with steady jobs could afford to build or buy, where they had had to rent before, and payment was much easier. This new system also marked an important step in the development of less expensive homes and long-term installment buying.

REGIONAL DEVELOPMENT

One of the most revolutionary of the acts passed by Congress during the Hundred Days initiated the redevelopment of an entire region—the economically ailing seven-state Tennessee valley area. The Muscle Shoals–Tennessee Valley Development Act of May 1933 created an independent public corporation, the Tennessee Valley Authority, which was given control of the government property at Muscle Shoals, Alabama, and the power to build and operate other dams and power plants on the Tennessee River and its branches wherever the authority thought advisable. In addition to generation and distribution of electric power, TVA was charged with controlling the floodwaters of the Tennessee River and improving its navigation facilities, promoting the conservation of soil in the valley, aiding reforestation, and producing nitrates and other fertilizers for the improvement of the valley's agriculture. Government-financed improvements in the valley continued over the next generation, leading ultimately to industrial development as well as greatly increasing animal husbandry. The TVA eventually built 20 new dams and improved five others. Flooding was controlled on the Tennessee River, and the TVA became the largest and cheapest producer of electricity in the United States. Other power companies were forced to lower their rates to compete with the TVA.

The power dams, plants, and distribution systems of TVA were criticized by private power companies as unfair competition, since the public facilities were not required to pay the same taxes as private companies and received other government subsidies. The Supreme Court upheld the constitutionality of the TVA, however, in 1936. The following year President Roosevelt asked Congress to set up six additional regional river valley authorities, but Congress declined. The areas in which they were to be located were not quite such distinct units as the Tennessee valley, nor were the people of these other areas in such a distressed condition as those of the Tennessee valley had been in 1933. The general business outlook was brighter in early 1937, and the business community supported the widespread contention that private capital could develop these valleys as effectively as the federal government.

Partially thwarted in his larger conservation and development plans, the President succeeded in having the Civilian Conservation Corps plant a tree belt across the Great Plains, while the Department of Agriculture checked soil erosion by urging farmers to plow furrows at right angles to the slope of the land, a practice called contour plowing. Thus the New Deal period may be looked upon as the beginning of a heightened federal consciousness of ecological problems.

INDUSTRIAL RECOVERY

While banking, currency, mortgages, and agriculture had occupied the President's attention during the first weeks of his administration, he learned in April 1933 that unless he acted quickly Congress would pass a uniform 30-hour-a-week law governing all industry. Because he regarded such a law as impractical, the President had his advisers prepare a substitute. The resulting National Industrial Recovery Act (NIRA), though hastily improvised, actually was the outgrowth of much thought by business, labor, and government about how to reconcile "free" private enterprise with effective governmental control of wages and competition.

In many industries excess industrial capacity, unemployed labor, and nearly bankrupt firms had reduced the market to chaos. With women receiving as little as $5 for a full week's work, companies that tried to maintain fair labor standards found themselves undersold. The solution proposed in the act was to have each industry, probably through its trade association, agree to a code of "fair competition" defining wages, hours, and minimum prices. Industries were encouraged to set minimum wages at $.30 per hour, maximum hours at 40 per week, and place severe restrictions on child labor. Labor would be represented in the making of such industry agreements by representatives of its own choosing without any pressure from the employer. The NIRA guaranteed workers the right to bargain collectively through representatives of their own choosing. The public would also be represented so that the interests of consumers would not be lost sight of. When all three parties were represented in the determination of policies for an industry, the government could overlook the fact that a price agreement would appear to be a clear "conspiracy to restrain trade" under the terms of the Sherman Antitrust Act. The National Recovery Administration (NRA) was set up to administer this section of the law.

The second section of NIRA set up the Public Works Administration (PWA) and authorized the expenditure of $3.3 billion for public works projects designed both to provide work for relief and to stimulate recovery.

The bill became law in June 1933, and the President appointed retired General Hugh S. Johnson as administrator of the first section. The negotiation of codes proved difficult and time consuming. In July 1933 President Roosevelt, in an attempt to speed matters, announced a blanket President's Reemployment Agreement (PRA) governing wages and hours for those industries that could not agree upon a code. A blue eagle was adopted as the symbol of the cooperating firms.

Those that signed codes or the PRA were allowed to display it on their stores, plants, or merchandise, and the public was strongly urged not to patronize those who didn't have the symbol. Within months millions of Americans were working under the blue eagle. The original idea of cooperation between the employer, organized labor, and consumer representatives, however, was all but lost in the difficulties of reaching agreements. Furthermore, consumers were unorganized and unable to protect their interests as management and government drew up a flood of codes. As time passed, thousands of cases of noncompliance with codes were reported. Labor was extremely restive because the union organization as authorized by NIRA was often opposed by industry. The country was plagued by strikes. The dominant corporations in each industry often wrote codes under the NIRA; and, therefore, the codes were criticized for helping big businesses more than small businesses. Employers began to fear that they had made a mistake in agreeing to negotiate with labor in drawing up the codes. The public also began to feel that it was being fleeced by prices that were rising faster than income.

Although the NRA contributed to the raising of wages from the low levels of 1932, did away with child labor, and in some industries helped small business stay alive, the NIRA experiment illustrated the difficulty of suddenly regulating a complex economy. More important, it failed to bring back prosperity. Limiting production had a negative effect on employment, and higher prices had a negative impact on consumption. Industrial production declined 30 percent in the third quarter of 1933, in spite of higher prices. By the spring of 1935, there was widespread cheating by firms who could no longer financially abide by the codes. Businesses cut wages and cut prices to reduce costs and gain market share.

To make matters worse, the PWA was slow to act and had not spent the majority of its appropriations after five years. Blacks complained that the PWA was discriminatory as it prohibited blacks from public works programs and the PWA constructed segregated housing. Blacks mocked the NRA by joking that the acronym really stood for "niggers rarely allowed." Nevertheless, the United States Chamber of Commerce and labor leaders as diverse as William Green, John L. Lewis, and Sidney Hillman continued to support the NRA until the Supreme Court ruled, in *Schechter Poultery v. United States,* that the act (along with collective bargaining) was unconstitutional. Business in general, and the rising leaders in the Roosevelt administration lost interest in the NRA or had become hostile toward it. Roosevelt himself denounced what he termed as the "sick chicken" decision by the Court and denounced the Court for their "horse and buggy" interpretation of the United States Constitution. FDR would have to seek another direction in trying to combat the depression.

DEVALUING THE DOLLAR

Controllable inflation, the President hoped, would raise farm prices and in general lighten the burden of debts in relation to income. The administration felt that such inflation could be stimulated either by heavy government spending or by altering the value of the dollar. Of the two possibilities, devaluing the dollar had the immediate advantages of not adding to government costs and of stimulating exports.

While the President was supporting the inflationist group in Congress, the United States, Japan, and European nations were meeting in June and July 1933 in London to attack the worldwide depression by attempting to agree on stabilizing national currencies and restoring the international gold standard. Contrary to this spirit, however, an amendment to the Agricultural Adjustment Act of May 1933 gave the President the right to inflate U.S. currency by issuing $3 billion in paper currency, freely coining silver, and devaluing the gold content of the dollar up to 50 percent. For the time being he did none of these things, waiting to see whether the AAA and the NRA would do the inflationary job, but neither would he enter into any international

agreement fixing the value of the dollar. European delegates at the Economic Conference in London angrily accused Roosevelt of undermining the conference. As a result, the London Economic Conference was a failure. The conference had been further undermined by the behavior of American delegate Key Pittman of Nevada, the Chairman of the United States Senate Foreign Relations Committee. While Belgium, Italy, and France were seeking stabilization of currency through the gold standard, Pittman—from a silver mining state—called for the international

Key Pittman *(Library of Congress)*

monetization of silver. Pittman also went on a drinking binge in London (during prohibition in the United States) and on one occasion shot out streetlights in London with a pistol. On another occasion, he was seen naked in the halls of a posh London hotel with a whiskey bottle in one hand and a bowie knife in the other, chasing terrified delegates through the halls and screaming about the silver standard.

Although there was a sharp increase in manufacturing production, employment, and prices between March and July 1933—in part, the result of an effort to produce before the restrictive NRA codes went into effect—by autumn manufacturing and employment were declining, and wholesale prices had again leveled off. At this point the President decided to use his power to devalue the dollar in the expectation that the resulting inflation would lead to higher prices. The Treasury Department began purchasing gold on the open market in July in an attempt to drive up the price of gold and thus devalue the currency. The efforts failed to significantly alter gold prices, so Congress passed the Gold Reserve Act in January 1934. The Gold Reserve Act allowed the President to arbitrarily set the price of gold. Once endowed with this power, FDR increased the price of gold from $25 an oz. to $35—an increase of 40 percent—and thus the currency was devalued—a degree of devaluation calculated to restore the price level of 1926. Prices rose slightly, but not nearly so much as the administration had expected.

RISE OF CONSERVATIVE OPPOSITION

Early criticism of the New Deal had come primarily from advanced liberals and labor leaders. Some members of Congress, for instance, would have nationalized banking and railroads. They and even more moderate liberals regarded the restoration of the banking system in relatively unchanged form as the loss of a great opportunity for progress toward a more stable economy. Organized labor was particularly dissatisfied with its treatment by the NRA, which in labor circles came to be called the "national run-around."

On the other hand, monetary manipulation during the last half of 1933 lost the President the support of many conservative Democratic leaders, who opposed any tinkering with the monetary system. Efforts at permanent reform of financial operations, as distinct from mere recovery, widened the rift between liberals and conservatives.

The reform program really began with the Federal Securities Act of 1933, by which the Federal Trade Commission was given the power to see that underwriters fully disclosed to investors all essential details pertaining to new securities issues. A further reform was effected by the Banking Act of June 1933, which divorced investment banking from commercial banking on the premise that the promoting and selling of new securities by commercial banks gave them an improper amount of power over other businesses and was inconsistent with the policy of caution and prudence which banks should follow. The Banking Act also created the Federal Deposit Insurance Corporation (FDIC) to insure bank deposits up to established limits and prevent losses to depositors. Because it involved more governmental regulation, leading bankers vigorously opposed deposit insurance, and more general business opposition was aroused by the stricter regulation of the securities markets.

The battle between liberals and conservatives was intensified when the Securities Exchange bill was before Congress in the spring of 1934. This bill called for the establishment of a three-member Securities and Exchange Commission to regulate the practices of stock exchanges, including the size of margins; to require full disclosure of details about all securities; and to enforce other parts of the Federal Securities Act of 1933. Stockbrokers and investment bankers complained strongly about the restrictions this legislation would place on them. But despite bitter debate in Congress the bill was passed in June 1934, and the die-hard opponents of all governmental regulation of the financial community were decisively defeated.

Another development in the spring of 1934 that alarmed some businessmen was adoption of the Reciprocal Trade Agreements Act, which gave the President power to make separate agreements with foreign nations to alter U.S. tariff rates by 50 percent in either direction. Even moderate Republicans denounced it as a surrender of power to the President, but the Democrats, with strong Southern support, held firm and enacted this change in American tariff policy.

In the course of debates over the Securities Act and the tariff, business arguments against the New Deal took their permanent shape. The government was condemned for creating a vast and irresponsible bureaucracy, for depriving individuals of their freedom and initiative, and for increasing the national debt. Direct relief, in particular, was condemned as running contrary to the deeply ingrained tradition that self-help was the basis of American greatness.

In August 1934 a group of wealthy Republicans and conservative Democrats formed the Liberty League to defend the rights and liberty of the individual against the New Deal. Backed by Du Pont and General Motors executives, the League won the support of previous Democratic presidential candidates John W. Davis and Alfred E. Smith and many other conservative political leaders in both parties. The big city daily newspapers were moving in the same direction. Within a

John W. Davis *(Library of Congress)*

year, at least two thirds of the metropolitan dailies were strongly in opposition to the New Deal, and their influential columnists were attacking the "third-rate college professors" and other "impractical intellectuals" of the "Brain Trust" that was held to be guiding the policies of the administration. Moreover, the activist First Lady Eleanor Roosevelt became a lightning rod for criticism.

RELIANCE UPON THE MASSES

The business attack on the New Deal, though backed by adequate finances and the support of major newspapers, had the fatal weakness of lacking a positive philosophy. Business leaders could only ask the public again to put its faith in the self-regulating economy. That, in fact, the public would not trust self-regulation was shown in the election of 1934. Normally the administration party loses strength in Congress in the non-presidential elections. Instead the Democrats gained nine seats in the House and nine in the Senate, with nearly 57 percent of the popular vote—an off-year administration victory unmatched since before the Civil War.

What had built the Democratic majority? The answer of a number of presidential advisers was that it was the voters' desire for security— for assurance that when unemployed or old they would be cared for. At this point, therefore, the New Deal became more equalitarian and humanitarian than any of the previous progressive movements.

PUBLIC WORKS

In November 1933, Congress created the Civil Works Administration (CWA) that provided public works employment. By January 1934, four million were employed for the CWA. Congress spent one billion dollars in five months of operation of the CWA, causing the President to cancel the program due to cost since FDR was afraid of running massive deficits prior to the Congressional elections of 1934. In the spring of 1935 Congress created the Works Progress Administration (WPA), which essentially took over where the CWA left off. Jobs ranging from mixing concrete to painting murals were to be created from an appropriation of nearly $5 billion. Pay would be at rates above relief but lower than approved for private employment. The Works Progress Administration lasted until World War II and spent some $11 billion from 1935–1943. Although it could employ only from two to three million workers, it kept those with the more valuable skills from deteriorating through idleness. Congress also created the National Youth Administration, which employed over two million persons between the ages of 16 and 21 in public works projects. Other minor forms of aid were instituted to help students stay in school and to provide potential farmers with subsistence homesteads.

Disliked by the conservative opponents of the New Deal, the various arts projects supported by the public works programs, in fact, left a remarkable legacy for the nation. Many public buildings were adorned with murals, and such distinguished artists as Jackson Pollock, Alice Neel, Willem de Kooning, and Louise Nevelson received support from the WPA. Aaron Copland wrote his two ballets, *Billy the Kid* (1938) and *Rodeo* (1942) for the WPA. The Federal Writers' Project sponsored guidebooks to each of the then 48 states, books rich with material that might have otherwise gone unrecorded. African Americans with memories of slavery and the southern poor were interviewed. Hundreds of American folk songs were catalogued, and the creative lifeblood of the country was kept in circulation.

SOCIAL SECURITY

In the President's mind, the most important legislation of this administration was the Social Security Act of 1935. This act created a Social Security Board to administer unemployment compensation, old-age security, and various social services. Payroll taxes of 1 percent were levied on both employers and employees to finance old-age pensions of from $10 to $85 per month for retired workers. Pensions under the new system would not begin until 1942, but meanwhile the federal government would assist the states in paying small pensions. In the beginning many groups, including farm and educational workers, were not eligible for pensions, but in succeeding years coverage was broadened and rates rose to compensate for inflation. The Social Security Act also extended federal-state unemployment insurance to 28 million workers and authorized money grants to states to assist them in relief of the blind, the crippled, delinquent children, and other dependents. Now the power of Congress to legislate for the general welfare had a new meaning.

THE SUPREME COURT: CHALLENGE AND RESPONSE

Early in 1935, with the Social Security bill on its way through Congress, the President regarded his program as virtually complete. Had the Supreme Court upheld the legislation of 1933 and 1934, the Roosevelt administration, like that of Woodrow Wilson, might have turned its attention to matters other than domestic reform. The Supreme Court had four justices, however, unalterably opposed to the New Deal, and two others, Owen J. Roberts and Chief Justice Charles E. Hughes, who were very doubtful about the constitutionality of delegating congressional power to administrative agencies and using the commerce power to regulate conditions of production and trade within the states.

The crucial tests came in the spring of 1935, when the Court declared the NIRA and a number of other basic acts of the New Deal unconstitutional. There was little hope that those still to be tested, such as the Agricultural Adjustment Act, would fare any better. Indeed the Supreme Court invalidated the first AAA in January 1936.)

The Court's failure to interpret the Constitution flexibly and to support the type of laws initially planned in cooperation with business leaders pushed the President toward further regulation. The influence of the administration was already behind Senator Robert F. Wagner's National Labor Relations Act to replace the labor provisions of the outlawed NIRA. The Wagner Act created a new National Labor Relations Board (NLRB) for administrative purposes and upheld the right of employees to join labor organizations and to bargain collectively through representatives of their own choosing.

This support of labor was accompanied by other New Deal measures that antagonized conservatives. A new tax bill introduced in June 1935 had the announced purpose of shifting the tax burden from the poor to the rich. The "Soak the Rich Act" of 1935 actually made few changes in taxes on income under $50,000 a year, and the graduated corporation income tax stopped at 15 percent; but high taxes on big incomes and on inheritance of estates further alarmed the wealthy over the "communistic" trend of the New Deal.

The attack on the New Deal by the rich probably strengthened support for the President. More politically dangerous, however, was the attack on his policies by radical reformers. In his weekly radio broadcasts Father Charles F. Coughlin, a demagogic Catholic priest, first criticized the President for failure to take care of the rural poor and then progressed to a fascist type of attack on Jews and international bankers. Coughlin had supported the New Deal at first and then turned against it with a vengeance, viewing it as part of an international communist conspiracy. Coughlin contended that Adam Weishaupt, the founder of the Illuminati, was the inspirer of Karl Marx, essentially tying the global communist threat to an Illuminati conspiracy. Also in cahoots with the communists in Coughlin's conception were international bankers, Jews, and Masons, but especially Jewish Masons. Coughlin was decidedly anti-Semitic and generally denounced those with whom he disagreed politically as being Jews. Coughlin even went so far as to argue that Alexander Hamilton, a founding father that favored national government economic intervention, was actually Jewish and his original name was Alexander Levine. Coughlin also published a newspaper, *Social Justice,* where he denounced FDR as "stupid," referred to him as "Franklin Double-crossing Roosevelt," and called for his impeachment. Coughlin wielded tremendous influence with conservatives in the 1930s and used his radio show to organize a political lobby of five million members. In 1934, his lobby group was responsible for sending 200,000 letters to Congress in protest of the establishment of the World Court. In 1934, Coughlin received more mail than any person in the world and took in over $500,000 in donations at the height of the Great Depression.

In a more constructive vein, Dr. Francis Townsend of California advocated pensions of $200 a month for the elderly, but the most comprehensive political and economic appeal of the day came from Senator Huey P. Long of Louisiana. A mixture of machine politician and shrewd administrator who believed the depression could be cured by government spending, Senator Long advocated a guaranteed minimum income and a capital levy on the rich to provide every family with a home, a car, and a radio. His simple country-boy manner and his slogan, "Every man a king," made him a real threat to Roosevelt's control of the Democratic Party until Long was killed by a personal enemy in September 1935. Coughlin and other unorthodox reformers continued to keep the administration under fire, but without Long they lacked a strong political leader.

THE ELECTION OF 1936

The election of 1936 was clearly a national referendum on the New Deal. Republicans were deeply divided over the New Deal with the more staunch conservatives violently opposed to all aspects of it and a more moderate faction that supported the New Deal for the most part, but rejected its deficit spending. Many Republicans felt that with Alfred M. Landon, ex-governor of Kansas, they would defeat Roosevelt in 1936. The *Literary Digest's* poll of telephone subscribers, which indicated a Landon presidential victory, helped sustain this view. (Overlooked was the fact that Roosevelt supporters were not adequately represented among telephone subscribers.) Landon promised to do everything that the New Deal was doing for the common man, but to do it in ways more satisfactory to business. The President responded with a more advanced liberalism than in earlier campaigns. In his speech accepting renomination, he denounced the "economic royalists" and said that Americans, in their achievement of economic and social democracy, had a "rendezvous with destiny." The result was the greatest landslide since 1920. Landon with 16.7 million votes (36 percent) to the President's 27.8 million (61 percent) carried only Maine and Vermont. The Democrats increased their majority in both houses while the fascist Coughlin group, supporting a radical farm leader, polled less than a million votes; and the Socialists' and Communists' votes were negligible. No President since Monroe had received such strong second-term support from the people.

LAST PHASE OF THE NEW DEAL

BATTLE OVER THE COURT

In a surprise move after the election of 1936, Roosevelt boldly attempted to use his great political strength and national popularity to alter the composition of the ultraconservative Supreme Court—and thus to liberalize the Court's attitude toward New Deal legislation. In eight of 10 major New Deal cases from 1933–1936, the Court struck down New Deal legislation as unconstitutional. The New Deal programs consistently lost on the Supreme Court by a 6-to-3 vote.

Roosevelt believed that in 1937 the Court would also strike down a number of major provisions of his New Deal. Lawyers were so confident that the Courts would rule against the New Deal that they were advising corporations to ignore the Social Security Act. In reaction, the President presented Congress, in February 1937, with a bill to reorganize the federal judiciary by adding up to 50 judges to the federal court system as a whole. The bill further proposed to increase the membership of the Supreme Court from nine to a maximum of 15 by permitting the President to appoint one new justice for each justice over 70 who refused to retire. Roosevelt's ostensible argument for the bill was that federal judges were overworked and decisions too long delayed because the judiciary was "handicapped by insufficient personnel." Furthermore, the President contended that the aging judges were antiquated in outlook—"little by little, new facts become blurred through old glasses fitted, as it were, for the needs of another generation." For the lower courts Roosevelt's argument was valid; but the highest tribunal was not far behind in its casework, and the justices over 70 included some of the most vigorous and liberal members of the Court.

The magnitude of the change from nine to 15 justices when no previous Congress had ever altered the size of the Court so drastically, and the doubtful sincerity of Roosevelt's argument for the major provision of the bill, created unexpected Congressional opposition to the administration. Liberal Democrats and progressive Republicans joined conservatives in opposing the measure. The press was violent in its denunciation, and public opinion polls showed popular distaste for so arbitrary an action by the President.

While Congress debated the President's "Court-packing" bill, the Court itself removed much of Roosevelt's reason for the bill by voluntarily liberalizing its stand on New Deal legislation. Justice Roberts and Chief Justice Hughes abandoned the conservative camp and joined Justices Brandeis, Cardozo, and Stone in reversing the legal doctrines of 1935 and 1936. In March 1937 the Court, by a five-to-four decision, upheld a Washington state minimum wage law for women although the previous year it had declared unconstitutional a similar law of the state of New York. In April the Court declared the National Labor Relations Act constitutional, and the next month it upheld the Social Security Act. Furthermore, Justice Van Devanter's resignation from the Court in May 1937 gave Roosevelt a chance to appoint a justice who would convert the liberal minority of the Court to a majority in future decisions. To succeed Van Devanter, Roosevelt appointed Senator Hugo L. Black of Alabama, an enthusiastic supporter of the New Deal.

In June 1937 the Senate Judiciary Committee reported the court reform bill unfavorably, and the Senate, after bitter debate, subsequently rejected the proposal by voting 70 to 20 to return it to the Judiciary Committee. Congress did, however, pass a Supreme Court Retirement Act permitting Supreme Court justices to retire, with full pay, at age 70. It also passed a Judicial Procedure Reform Act that established reforms in the lower courts.

New Dealers found consolation for the defeat of the administration bill in the fact that the few years after defeat of the "Court-packing" plan saw a radical change in the complexion of the Supreme Court. A succession of deaths and resignations enabled Roosevelt to make eight new appointments to the Court and gave him the liberal tribunal that Congress had denied him.

A GOVERNMENT-PROTECTED LABOR MOVEMENT

Early in 1933 the total independent union membership in the United States had fallen to less than 2.7 million, including about 2 million in the AFL. Unemployment had reduced company union membership to less than a million. The morale of union leaders was at low ebb. In general their proposals for recovery were no more imaginative than Hoover's.

Section 7(a) of NIRA (granting to organized labor the right of collective bargaining through representatives of their own choosing) and the subsequent upswing in employment gave unions a chance to expand. Organizing drives and some help from the National Labor Board of the NRA raised total union membership to 3.6 million in 1935. Meanwhile, faced with the threat of being forced by code authorities to bargain collectively, the larger employers were setting up new company unions. By 1935 this type of membership had passed 2.5 million.

In the same year a group within the AFL, led by John L. Lewis of the United Mine Workers, was urging the organization of all workers in a given industry—skilled or unskilled—into a single union. The AFL as a whole, however, was dominated by craft unions and continued to be officially opposed to all moves toward unionization by industries.

The Wagner Act of 1935 gave industrial organizers new and potentially effective weapons. The powerful National Labor Relations Board created by the Act could hold a plant election at the request of a union but not of an employer. If the union received the vote of a majority of workers, it became the bargaining agent for all. Furthermore, the Board could determine the unit—plants, companies, or industries—for election purposes, and it could prevent employers from interfering in any way with organizers or trying to influence the election. If the winning union was able to negotiate a closed-shop agreement, the employer was required to deduct union dues from the pay of all workers. In view of the decisions of the Supreme Court in 1935 and 1936, however, even labor leaders regarded the law as probably unconstitutional.

Encouraged somewhat by the opportunities the new law might offer and much more by the sweeping reelection of a friendly President, the leaders of eight AFL unions defied the parent body and formed a Committee for Industrial Organization. Led by John L.

Lewis, the CIO refused to compromise with the crafts, and the AFL expelled the unions involved in 1937. The following year the committee became the Congress of Industrial Organizations with Lewis as president and a membership roughly equal to that of the AFL.

While Lewis in 1936 wanted to use the government-supported power of labor to organize steel workers, the local unions in the automotive industries initiated action on their own front. Late in the year, when General Motors refused to recognize and bargain with the United Automobile Workers, union members in Flint, Michigan, occupied their plants. The sit-down strike left the workers in possession of valuable machinery, while their families brought in food. Efforts by local authorities failed to dislodge the workers, and the newly elected Democratic governor, Frank Murphy, refused to enforce court orders to remove them by using the state militia. Meanwhile, orders for cars were mounting as the motor industry enjoyed a return to prosperity, and President Roosevelt kept a steady pressure on General Motors to bargain with Lewis. As a result of both factors, a settlement was reached that established a pattern of collective bargaining with the UAW. During the prosperous spring of 1937 similar agreements were worked out with the other motor companies except Ford.

In April the Supreme Court, under pressure from the judicial "reform" bill in Congress, reversed its previous attitude and declared the Wagner Act constitutional. Even before this, the two major steel companies, also anxious to avoid a costly and perhaps useless strike, had signed agreements with the CIO. While Ford and the smaller steel companies violently resisted organization for some years more, by World War II they had all been forced into line by government action.

In spite of the sharp downswing of business and employment from mid-1937 to 1939, union strength continued to increase. Enthusiastic young organizers, government protection of the processes of organization and election, and compulsory bargaining were building a labor movement of unprecedented strength. In self-defense the AFL was forced to adopt the principle of industrial unionism and compete vigorously with the CIO. That led to the AFL successfully organizing, for example, a union among the female-dominant canning industry in northern California, just the kind of work force that the AFL had previously ignored. In 1940 there were nearly 9 million organized workers: over 4 million in the AFL, 3.5 million in the CIO, and 1 million in independent unions. Although substantially less than the 28 percent organized in Great Britain, the 30 percent in France, and the 50 percent in Australia and Denmark, the total of nonagricultural unionized employees was at a peak for the United States.

A 22-year-old mother and her children in a migrant resettlement camp (*Library of Congress*)

WOMEN IN THE DEPRESSION

In most of its unions the AFL would not accept women members, but the new CIO would. Therefore, division in the ranks of labor worked in favor of women's rights. The fact that women worked for lower wages than men also kept a few more of them at their jobs in the worst years of the depression, but with partial recovery the situation returned to about that of 1930.

The inevitable effect of hard times was to move feminist activity from direct efforts to compete more equally with men in the job market, which could scarcely succeed in the face of high unemployment, to national legislative reforms. Eleanor Roosevelt took her place as leader in this movement. She encouraged Mary Dewson, head of a Women's Division of the Democratic Party, to work hard for FDR and his reform legislation. She also recruited women to run for Congress.

In spite of making Frances Perkins Secretary of Labor, it seems doubtful that FDR personally was a strong advocate of women's rights. His pressure on the Supreme Court seems partly responsible for a decision in 1936 upholding state minimum wage laws for women, and one in 1941 validating the equal pay provisions of the Fair Labor Standards Act of 1938. Yet even by 1940, in many states women had not become the legal equals of men. Twenty states still prohibited women from serving on juries, 16 denied a wife the right to make contracts, and 11 forbade a wife to retain earnings without her husband's consent. Thus women entered the war period with few realized gains from the previous decade, but with a potential in both the labor movement and the job market to make some lasting progress.

THE SURVIVAL OF THE INDIAN

In 1924 Congress passed the Indian Citizenship Act, granting citizenship to Native Americans on a systematic basis. Before this time, Native Americans had become United States citizens on a piecemeal basis and by a variety of means—such as military service, marriage, or by receiving allotments under the Dawes Act of 1887. This reform notwithstanding, by the mid-20s it was obvious that, in general, government policy concerning the 325,000 Indians scattered across the nation had failed. The Dawes Act, providing for individual ownership of tribal land, had reduced tribal land acreage by some 60 percent through subsequent white fraud, high-pressure sales, and a variety of illegal schemes to steal more land from the Indians. Indians had been given the land individually, without the equipment to farm it, or schooling on how to use it for grazing, farming, or timber cutting. They were an impoverished people, but psychologically they may have been in still worse shape.

Indian health was a national disgrace. The plains Indians, for example, were forced to cease their nomadic way of life, yet were not taught to handle the sanitation problems of sedentary living. Indians were made to depend on a government diet that was lacking in vitamin C, proteins, and roughage. Often if they were "unruly," local administrators withheld even this food. They were given a very few doctors and nurses when, in fact, they needed many more than the average white population; and the ones they got were quite often incompetent. Consequently Indians suffered from rampant diseases, high infant mortality, and rates of suicide and alcoholism much higher than those for the rest of the population. Nevertheless they responded to the army volunteer drive of World War I with enthusiasm, and were conspicuous for their bravery in battle. It is believed this war record sparked another reform drive in behalf of the Indians.

Reform was a complex problem. Generally speaking, legislators from states with many Indians fought against giving extra federal funds earmarked for their states to a largely nonvoting minority, who even if they did vote, did not have the numbers to elect anyone. The rest of Congress was generally lacking in knowledge about the variety of problems each of the 250 to 300 tribes faced.

The Bureau of Indian Affairs, run by the Executive branch of the government also had an extremely poor reputation among the Indians, because its policies, usually administered by patronage employees, changed with every new President. These administrators naturally knew and cared very little about Indian cultures. Boarding school education, promoted by the Bureau of Indian Affairs, alienated many children from their hereditary culture, while it equipped them for participation in white society that, in most states, did not want them.

To reformers such as John Collier and the American Indian Defense Association, the best hope for the future appeared to be in strengthening tribal organization and restoring communal land holding. Collier was influential in getting the Wheeler-Howard Indian Reorganization Act through Congress in 1934. For those tribes who voted to accept it, the Act ended further individual allotments and restored all remaining lands to tribal ownership. More land was to be purchased by the government to resettle landless Indians. Tribes were to be set up as corporations, able to draw on a $10 million revolving fund for new economic enterprises. Each cooperating tribe was also to draw up and ratify a constitution that would restore government by tribal council.

Although education improved, the policies pursued by the Bureau over the next generation were, on the whole, unsuccessful. By congressional mandate, the Act was not applied in Oklahoma, where the "Five Civilized Tribes" lived and enjoyed some unevenly distributed wealth from oil. The Navajo tribe, suspicious of white benevolence—with good historic reasons—numbered about a quarter of all Indians and refused to join. Applying the Act to most of the remaining tribes, who were given over 7 million acres of poor land, led to no considerable gain in their prosperity. It led, however, to a great deal of trouble between the Indians, the paternalistic local agents, and the remote Bureau. In all, this well-intentioned policy came too late in the history of Indian-government relations to alter the results of decades of neglect and abuse in both policies and administration. By the mid-twentieth century, Indian grazing culture and white industrial society were so far apart that any assimilation could only be slow and diffi-cult. Reconstitution of tribal society, on the other hand, was both arti-ficial and—given the great differences among the Indian peoples—extremely difficult.

BLACK AMERICA

The depression decade was nearly spanned by a particularly well-publicized and flagrant denial of justice to nine young blacks. On March 25, 1931, on the railroad line from Chattanooga to Memphis, a fight developed between white and black youths on a boxcar that re-sulted in the white boys being expelled from the train. The white boys alerted local authorities; and when police arrested the black youths for assault at the next stop, two white women who had also been in the railcar accused nine young black men, ranging in age from 12 to 19, of rape in the railroad boxcar. The black youths were charged with rape and held in a jailhouse in Scottsboro, Alabama. An all white jury found all nine guilty and eight were sentenced to death. One woman later recanted her charge, and a new trial was held in 1937. Four of the Scottsboro Boys were released in 1937, four more in 1944, and the final man escaped in 1944. During the 30s, the case achieved worldwide notoriety—thanks in part to the action of the legal bureau of the Communist Party, yet the case had pointed out the kind of "justice" blacks often received.

President Roosevelt appointed white race-relations counselors in many government departments; and from 1932 on, as the urban black vote shifted dramatically from Republican to Democratic. Mary M. Bethune became Director of Negro Affairs in the National Youth Administration, and Robert C. Weaver, adviser to the Department of the Interior—the highest federal posts held by blacks since World War I. In *United States v. Classic* (1941), the Supreme Court made the state governments responsible for the conduct of party primaries and hence for the enforcement of constitutional rights in these contests, which were in fact the real elections in the solidly Democratic South. On the whole, however, the President was not prepared to battle Southern congressmen over enforcement of the rights of blacks, and New Deal housing policies actually increased segregation. The suc-cessful struggle of the poor black—and of the impoverished and neg-lected Indian—to survive, however, was continued as before with growing spiritual strength. As a result, that spirit won allies such as the President's remarkable wife Eleanor.

Toward the middle of the 1940s some progress was made toward equality of economic opportunity. The NAACP, directing its energy toward winning equal pay for black schoolteachers, had little immediate success, but in 1941 the federal district court for Virginia, at least, ordered equality in pay by 1943. The CIO in principle admitted blacks to all its unions, though in the South they were often put into separate locals and denied true job equality. The growth of the new labor movement brought black workers into the mass production industries and in a few cases to minor administrative positions in big white companies. Although still largely impoverished, blacks were making new efforts to improve their condition.

MEXICAN AMERICANS

The Mexican American population in the United States grew substantially during the early twentieth century, owing to the political instability in Mexico. Mostly concentrated in the Southwest, immigrants and their families typically made their living as agricultural workers. Given that the agricultural sector was hit so hard by the Great Depression, it is not surprising that farm workers were among the groups to suffer the greatest problems. In addition to such market-driven difficulties as falling wages and deteriorating working conditions, the Mexican workers also faced the wrath of those who blamed them for stealing jobs that might have gone to others. As a consequence, some 500,000 Mexicans and Mexican Americans were repatriated to Mexico during the 1930s. Some—but not all—left voluntarily. It is important to note that of those who were sent to the mother country, there were a good many American citizens, some of whom had been born in the United States—which was, in fact, their true mother country.

THE DUST BOWL MIGRATION

During the mid and late 1930s, nature added to the woes of farmers in a swath of states in the Midwest and Southwest: severe drought, compounded by summer heat waves and poor agricultural practices, laid waste their land and created the conditions for what became known as the Dust Bowl. The drought essentially continued on the Great Plains for an entire decade, converting once fertile farmland into desert. Since three fifths of the farmers on the Great Plains went bankrupt, millions of acres went uncultivated and without crops to keep the soil in place. The combination of these factors, along with plagues of locusts, resulted in interstate dust storms that carried millions of tons of topsoil into the atmosphere. During the Dust Bowl, dust from the Great Plains was carried by prevailing winds all the way to the Atlantic Ocean, dropping dust on the coastal cities of New York and Washington as well as on ships over 300 miles off shore in the Atlantic Ocean. Dust storms on the Great Plains during the Dust Bowl were so intense that the sky would be dark at noon, and people could not see their hands in front of their faces in some cases. The Dust Bowl would not come under control until 1941 when demand for agricul-

Two migrant children *(Library of Congress)*

tural products increased, the rains returned, and the land became cultivated again.

Faced with the impossibility of farming their land profitably, some 300,000 people migrated to California, where they were categorized as "Okies" and treated harshly. Indeed, for a brief time the city of Los Angeles (illegally) posted guards at the state line to turn away indigent migrants. Scholars estimate that during this period about one third of the farms in the Dust Bowl states of Kansas, Missouri, Arkansas, Oklahoma, and Texas were abandoned.

This tragic movement of people—tragic because what they encountered in the Golden State was often little better or even worse than what they had left behind—inspired some of the greatest and most profound of American art: John Steinbeck's novel *The Grapes of Wrath*, John Ford's film based on the novel, songs by the folksinger Woody Guthrie (himself an Oklahoman), and the photographs of Dorothea Lange. The historian James Gregory wrote *American Exodus: The Dust Bowl Migration and Okie Culture in California*, a prize-winning account of the Okies' travail. It would take at least a generation before the Okies and their descendants began to fit into their new home and be accepted as Californians.

RETURN TO DEPRESSION

Aided by increased federal spending for the WPA, more state spending for public works, and payment of the remainder of the World War I soldier's bonus certificates (over the President's veto), 1936 and early 1937 saw returning prosperity; but at this point the lack of any clear economic policy by either the administration or most of its critics was disastrously illustrated. To suit the conservatives in Congress, whose votes were needed to pass the Supreme Court bill, the President promised a balanced budget for 1937–1938. His own fear of too strong a boom, even though 6 million were still unemployed, was shown when the Federal Reserve System took steps to tighten the money market.

National income, which was $82 billion in 1929, and dropped to $40 billion in 1932, had rebounded to $72 billion in 1937. The economic improvements convinced FDR that it was time for a retreat from his government spending programs, and it was time to attempt to balance the federal budget. FDR feared the mounting deficits, and leading economists were now more concerned about inflation than with unemployment (which was still over 10 percent). Consequently, FDR pushed the Federal Reserve to raise interest rates in an effort to curb inflation. In doing so, the money supply would diminish, and the economy would slow. FDR attempted to balance the budget by instituting sweeping budget cuts in New Deal Public Works and Relief programs. As a result, the index of industrial production was 117 in August 1937, but dropped to 76 by May 1938, and four million more Americans were added to the lists of unemployed. As a result of this drastic reversal in federal policies, the sharpest business decline in American history began in July 1937 and reached bottom about mid-1938. Not until the beginning of 1940, when the European war and American rearmament had become important economic factors, was there a return to the business volume of 1937. The severity of the depression was about equal to that of late 1931. Unemployment rose above 10 million—a fifth of the labor force. Even with the return toward prosperity in 1940, over eight million people were still looking for jobs.

FDR was certain that his actions had produced the new recession, and in April 1938 he asked Congress for an additional $5 billion for public works and relief. Congress complied. By 1940, unemployment returned to the level of 1937 and GNP returned to the level of 1937 by 1939.

NEW POLICIES

The renewal of the depression forced the government to institute new policies to promote recovery. Agricultural production had been sharply cut by the severe drought in 1934 that had created the "dust bowl." It had been checked again by a more moderate drought in 1936. In the latter year Congress had passed a soil-conservation act to check planting of soil-depleting crops and encourage planting of soil-restoring crops. As a result of these developments agricultural income, including government payments, stood up during the renewed depression better than did the income of some other sectors, but in 1938 the well-organized farmers won substantial new support in the Agricultural Adjustment Act.

Soil conservation was to be encouraged by payments to staple crop producers who agreed to acreage allotments. Marketing quotas could also be imposed by the vote of two thirds of the growers of a staple crop; and whenever actual prices fell below "parity prices," government-determined prices intended to keep the farmer's purchasing power in relation to nonfarm commodities at the 1909–1919 level, farmers conforming to these regulations would be given "parity payments" if Congress appropriated the money.

Crop loans were also available to all farmers of crops with marketing quotas, but those who did not accept the quota could borrow only 60 percent as much as could the cooperators. In spite of many loopholes and much subsequent criticism, this law remained the basic plan of agricultural support.

Wage and hour guarantees attempted in the NIRA were now incorporated in a Fair Labor Standards Act. The labor of children under 16 was prohibited, the minimum wage was set at 25 cents an hour, and overtime was to be paid beyond 44 hours a week. The Housing Act of 1937, now in operation, began the great task of slum clearance. With increases in other parts of the federal budget, including public works and defense, federal expenditures in 1939, more than 25 percent above 1938 were the highest of any peacetime year in previous American history.

ASSESSING THE NEW DEAL

While the New Deal had greatly improved stability and security in the national economy, it had not brought satisfactory recovery. For the first time the gross national product per capita had failed to achieve a level higher than in the previous decade. What had been wrong? Several different answers were possible, depending upon different economic theories.

It was possible, first of all, to emphasize the fact that from beginning to end President Roosevelt, either from conviction or for political expediency, held down spending and tried to balance the budget. Prior to the renewed depression of 1938, only 1934 and 1936 showed substantial increases in government spending in relation to receipts, and in both cases the level of spending dropped the following year. The failure of the New Deal to end the depression was largely because the economy needed a larger infusion of capital than was supplied by the New Deal. The depression was instead halted by World War II, which provided that capital infusion in the form of massive deficit spending and increased demand. In short, the New Deal failed because it was too conservative and its balanced budget constraints hindered its effectiveness. Put another way, the administration failed to make a clean break with the idea of the self-regulating economy and failed to develop a philosophy of where and how to spend. Yet while failing to spend at the level necessary to promote expansion, the government did not announce policies that encouraged expansion through investment by business.

Another line of reasoning pointed to the failure of NIRA and other legislation to redistribute income enough to create sharply increased consumer demand. Still another was that by chance too few technological innovations had been occurring that would offer profits in return for large capital investment.

Whatever approach one took, the disturbing question remained: How could a healthy economy be assured in time of peace.

LASTING EFFECTS OF THE NEW DEAL

Nevertheless, the New Deal produced lasting effects on the American political system. The New Deal and the Great Depression created a precedent for federal government intervention in the economy that has never been abandoned. For example, when the economy slipped into recession in 2008, Republican President George W. Bush and the Democratic Congress responded with a tax rebate in an effort to stimulate the economy. The New Deal also permanently established the right to collective bargaining, which benefits labor unions through the present. In addition, the New Deal increased the regulatory functions and the scope of the federal government, responsibilities that have never been relinquished. Moreover, the New Deal created the beginnings of the federal welfare state and increased the general welfare responsibilities of the United States government. Even under conservative President George W. Bush in the twenty-first century, federal entitlements (Medicare) have been expanded. The New Deal also altered the state-federal relationship from "dual federalism" or "separate spheres of influence" to "cooperative federalism" with shared state and federal responsibilities. Furthermore, Democrats were propelled to dominance in American politics, especially in the United States House of Representatives, until 1994 when Newt Gingrich and the Republicans took over the House in a conservative "revolution." Finally, the New Deal elevated the President to a position as the nation's foremost policy leader that has never been relinquished.

12

WORLD WAR II

(Library of Congress)

THE ROAD TO WAR

BREAKDOWN OF THE SECURITY SYSTEM

Americans had become decidedly isolationist in their foreign policy outlook in the aftermath of the Great War, during the 1920s and the Great Depression. Many Americans, among them American hero Charles Lindbergh, viewed World War I as a mistake and were determined to remain out of any future European squabbles. Despite prevailing isolationist sentiment, the United States in the 1920s was part of a system of international security which rested on the Washington Treaties of 1922 governing Far Eastern relations; on the structure of international debt and reparations payments worked out in the Dawes and Young Plans; and on the ability of the League of Nations—or its leading members, England and France—to police the settlement of Versailles. Between 1931 and 1935 this entire security structure was demolished, leaving the world perennially on the verge of war.

Partly because Russia had not been invited to take part in the Washington Conference, the treaties of 1922 did not bring peace to China. During the next decade Russia and China first combined to reunify China by defeating local warlords and then fought each other in an undeclared war. When peace was restored with Russia, the Chinese Nationalist leader Chiang Kai-shek tried to assert his power in southern Manchuria, long a Japanese sphere of influence. This gave the strongly imperialist Japanese army the excuse to overthrow the liberal ministry in Tokyo and to wage a war for complete control of Manchuria. The islands of Japan are volcanic, poor in natural resources, and the Japanese sought to remedy their deficiencies in food, fuel, and the precious metals needed for a developed industrial economy through control of foreign territory. The League of Nations, as well as individual countries like Britain and the United States, condemned the Japanese aggression, but did not impose economic sanctions. Japan ignored the protests and established a puppet government in Manchuria known as Manchuko. The United States and the League of Nations responded with American Secretary of State Henry L. Stimson's "Doctrine of Nonrecognition," whereby the United States and the League of Nations would not recognize governments established by force. In response, Japan completed its conquest of Manchuria, and, in 1933, withdrew from the League. This demonstration that a great power could embark on aggression without meeting effective opposition from the strong members marked the beginning of the disintegration of the League, exposing the fatal flaw in the peacekeeping treaties that had been signed after the Great War—the West lacked the will to enforce them. It also marked the beginning of the Japanese view of the United States as the central obstacle to its ambitions in Asia. Japan's foreign minister Yosuke Matsuoka summed up the Japanese view by stating, "The United States taught Japan the game, and now wants to take up contract bridge."

International debt and reparation payments depended upon continuing loans from the United States. With the collapse of the Wall Street security market it was only a question of time before payments would end. President Hoover's moratorium in 1931 temporarily eased the debt burden on European nations, but neither the Hoover nor the Roosevelt administration was ready to profit from the inevitable by canceling the war debts. After 1934 only Finland continued to pay, and another part of the World War I settlement had come to an end.

GROWING DANGERS IN EUROPE

A single man, Adolf Hitler, however, must bear the most responsibility for the end of world peace. By 1933 a German democracy—weakened by economic and political chaos that followed the Great War and stark internal political conflicts between conservatives, liberals, Socialists, and Communists—invited the rise of a man who could impose order and bring back prosperity. Supported by much of labor, by patriots who wanted to undo the hated Versailles Treaty, by the military, by rural religious conservatives, and by business conservatives who viewed him as a check against communism, Hitler's party won a plurality of the vote in the German Parliament

Adolf Hitler (*Library of Congress*)

(Bundestag). Hitler, thus, became Chancellor. Shortly thereafter, the Bundestag voted to dissolve and passed an Enabling Act that allowed Hitler to rule Germany by decree. The German experiment in democracy during the interwar period had come to an end.

Hitler began an industrialization and militarization program backed through massive government deficits. The government spending boosted the economy and softened the harshness of the depression in Germany, thus increasing Hitler's popularity. Hitler pulled Germany out of the League of Nations and the Geneva Disarmament Conference in October 1933.

MEIN KAMPF

In a book he wrote while serving time in prison for treason in 1924 for his role in what is known as the Beer Hall Putsch—a failed attempt at government overthrow, Adolph Hitler outlined his plans for creating a superior German State in his autobiographical work entitled *Mein Kampf*. In *Mein Kampf*, Hitler explains the German loss in World War I as the result of German inadequacies in food and energy, as well as due to treasonous acts by Jews. As a consequence, Hitler argues that Germany must secure land with agricultural production to ensure that it is self-sufficient in food (the wheat fields of Poland and the Ukraine) and must secure access to energy (the oil fields of the Caucuses in the Southwestern Soviet Union). Hitler viewed the German people as racially superior and viewed it as a problem that all persons of German ethnicity were not united within the borders of Germany. Hitler, therefore, called for a uniting of all the German people (Anschluss) that included the absorption, by Germany, of areas in France, Austria, Czechoslovakia, and Poland that were predominantly German in ethnicity. Hitler also argued that the expansion of Germany's borders was necessary to give the German people needed "Lebensraum" (living space) and secure their food and energy supplies. Furthermore, Hitler argued that Germany was never defeated on the battlefield in World War I, and the war was never fought on German soil. Hence, Hitler perpetuated the Dolchstoss myth (backstab myth) that Germany had not actually lost the Great War, but instead was sold out by traitorous Jews.

Although his aim, set forth in *Mein Kampf*, was to gain control of Europe by war, British and French leaders chose to regard his statements as mere political slogans. Even by 1938, when Hilter had already annexed unresisting neighboring territories and commenced his deadly Jewish pogroms, the conservative leaders of Western Europe valued him as a defense against communism while President

Roosevelt—hindered by the depression and isolationism in America—took no decisive action.

Meanwhile, Italy followed Japan's lead in aggressive expansion. In October 1935, the Italian fascist dictator Mussolini launched a wholesale invasion of the African kingdom of Ethiopia (Abyssinia). The League of Nations, under British pressure, condemned Italy as an aggressor and imposed economic sanctions; but because Britain and France were afraid of driving Germany and Italy into an alliance, the embargo did not include coal and oil. Furthermore, the League had little machinery for enforcing economic sanctions, and nonmembers like Germany and the United States largely ignored the prohibitions. As a result, the conquest of Ethiopia was quickly completed, and the authority of the League was totally undermined.

The conflict over Ethiopia gave Hitler his first big opportunity to use the military force he had been building up in defiance of the Versailles Treaty. In March 1936 Nazi troops marched into the Rhineland, which had been demilitarized by the Versailles Treaty. France mobilized 150,000 troops, but Britain refused to support the use of force to compel German withdrawal. Another World War I agreement had been smashed.

Why had the major military and naval powers of the world failed to enforce the peace? In the first place, Russia, the nation most feared in the long run by Great Britain, was not a party to the Western agreements. (The Soviet Union was not even recognized by the United States until 1933.) The fact that Hitler was a professed enemy of Russia made it difficult for British governments, particularly the Conservative ones, to decide where the ultimate national interest lay. Yet even if the British decided to let Hitler gain strength, they did not want him too strong; and this weakened them in dealing with Italy. Another factor faced by both Britain and the United States was the strength of pacifist and neutralist movements in their own countries. A government embarking on vigorous policies that risked war might find itself lacking in the necessary legislative support. In France many conservatives in the army and the government feared communism much more than they feared Hitler's fascism.

ISOLATION AND NEUTRALITY

The breakdown of the world order led the United States both to strict isolationist legislation and to an effort to weld the Western Hemisphere into a self-sufficient defense system. The latter presented many difficulties. Aside from Canada, the nations of the Western Hemisphere were further removed from the United States by tradition and national culture than were the nations of western Europe. The capitals of the three largest South American powers—Argentina, Brazil, and Chile—were also farther removed geographically. Economically, as well, the United States had more ties with Europe, and so did each of the major South American nations. Upon his becoming President, FDR's initial concerns were in producing reciprocal trade agreements that would boost the economy. President Roosevelt's inaugural address in 1933 dedicated the United States to "the policy of the good neighbor"—nonaggression, nonintervention, and friendly cooperation to solve mutual problems in the Western Hemisphere. His first attempt was at the International Conference of American States in 1933 in Montevideo, Uruguay. In order to create better relations in Latin America, Secretary of State Cordell Hull signed a convention that stated, "No state has the right to intervene in the external affairs of another." The initiative was designed to eliminate interventionist fears in Latin America and produce attitudes more receptive to trade with the United States. Congress followed with the Reciprocal Trade Act of 1934 that authorized the President to take the initiative in lowering tariffs on a reciprocal basis, up to 50 percent, with any country. As a result, United States trade with Latin America increased—from 30 percent to 50 percent of all Latin American trade by 1940. Nevertheless, the attitude of the United States toward social democratic governments in the Caribbean area remained ambiguous. In the same year that the new pact was adopted, Washington withheld recognition of a liberal government in Cuba that was opposed by the island's landed and business interests, and American warships surrounded the island. These actions, engineered by conservative State Department officials rather than by President Roosevelt, led eventually to the overthrow of the liberal government by the military dictator Fulgencio Batista.

The President's long-range policy was reaffirmed the next year by abrogation of the Platt Amendment authorizing intervention in Cuba and by withdrawal of marines from Haiti. In 1936 the

General Fulgencio Batista (AP Photo)

United States ratified a treaty restoring sovereign powers to Panama. Reciprocal trade agreements negotiated with six Latin American nations strengthened economic ties. While the bonds between "good neighbors" 5,000 miles apart remained somewhat tenuous, the Roosevelt administration policy marked a great improvement over inter-American relations of the previous 30 years.

Though Americans in the mid-30s were fully cognizant of the onrush of fascism in Europe, most of them were confident that the United States could remain a neutral bystander in the impending conflict. As Europe's crises deepened, determination mounted in the United States to "sit this one out." At the time of the Nazi takeover of Germany, Roosevelt's Republican opposition was divided over what should be the proper American role. For the conservative "nationalist" wing of the party, sound foreign policy was based on isolationism with regard to European affairs, unilateralism, protectionism, anti-communism, and the Monroe Doctrine in the Western Hemisphere. In the words of historian Lewis Gould:

> "Disillusion with the outcome of World War I, antipathy toward Great Britain, some degree of anti-Semitism, and sympathy for Germany moved together in various degrees to feed the argument on behalf of continued isolation. Senators such as William Borah of Idaho and Gerald Nye of North Dakota led the block of Republicans in the upper house who wanted to stay out of European disputes."

In furtherance of these foreign policy guides, Republicans had generally opposed Roosevelt's recognition of the Soviet Union in 1933 (which Roosevelt did as much to boost American grain exports as to counterbalance the emergence of Nazi Germany in Europe), regardless of whatever benefits trade with the Soviets might bring to the American economy. While conservatives typically supported the free market, the support did not extend to doing business with communists. Rural Republicans, in particular, tended to support isolationism and opposed alliances and any encroachments on sovereignty embodied in international organizations such as the League of Nations. In 1935, Republicans had thwarted Roosevelt's effort to secure American participation in the World Court under the premise that it would erode American sovereignty. Similarly, rural Republicans tended to view foreign aid and loans to foreign countries as idealistic utopian fantasies outside the parameters of American national interests.

The hastily improvised Neutrality Act of 1935, reluctantly signed by Roosevelt, prohibited the export of arms or ammunition to belligerents and required the President to forbid American citizens to travel on the ships of belligerents except at their own risk.

A "permanent" Neutrality Act in 1937 retained the earlier restrictions on loans and munitions in time of war and declared travel on belligerent vessels unlawful for American citizens. In addition, it provided that for a period of two years belligerent nations could purchase goods, other than munitions, from the United States only on a "cash-and-carry" basis. The intent of these two acts was to prevent the recurrence of the events that had led to the American entry into the Great War, debts incurred by belligerent nations and the deaths of American civilians on the high seas.

During the Spanish Civil War of 1936–1939, in which Germany and Italy lent aid to the forces of the right-wing Generalisimo Francisco Franco and the Soviet Union supported the other side, the United States remained resolutely neutral. Americans generally had sympathy for the Spanish government in their struggle against Franco's fascist rebel; but since the Soviet Union supported the Spanish government, the United States could not become involved in the struggle on the same side as the communists.

RISE OF THE AXIS

In 1936 the last safeguards of the World War I diplomatic structure were finally swept away. In October and November Germany, Italy, and Japan entered into an anticommunist pact that became known as the Rome-Berlin-Tokyo Axis. These powers, having built new mechanized armies, were now too powerful for England and France to attack. Helped by German military engineers and scientists, Hitler had worked a diplomatic revolution that made defeated and penalized Germany the strongest nation in Europe.

Why had this happened? Causes may be traced far back, but three were abundantly clear in 1936: (1) Mutual distrust between England and France on one side and Russia on the other prevented revival of the old World War I alliance against the central powers; (2) the United States could not be relied upon for active support; and (3) England and France had not kept up with military development. To make their plight worse, England and France guaranteed the independence of Czechoslovakia and, in 1939, of Poland, which they could not possibly defend against Germany. Faced with the choice of arming for possible war or muddling along in the hope that some change would occur in the German situation, the conservative leaders of the Western powers chose the latter course.

Tension in the Pacific also increased in the summer of 1937 when Japan expanded its six-year-old war in China and attacked five other Chinese provinces. The Japanese invasion was full scale and brutal, and over 100,000 Chinese were killed in 1937 alone. The large-scale Japanese inroads in northern China led President Roosevelt, in a speech of October 1937, to test American sentiment by advocating a "quarantine" of aggressor nations. The term "quarantine" had no official meaning in international law, but rather was a general reference by FDR to a severing of diplomatic relations and a trade embargo. He quickly found that Congress was two to one against cooperation with the League of Nations in bringing effective sanctions against Japan. Additionally, public reaction to FDR's quarantine speech was so overwhelmingly negative in an America dominated by isolationism that FDR decided that he could not proceed with any further action. Underlying much of this isolationist attitude was an implicit confidence that England and France were still capable of controlling the situation. From 1938 on, however, as Germany continued to build up its mechanized army, the European situation was beyond the control of England and France. Hitler was ready to embark on a daring program of expansion, and his territorial demands were to prove limitless, all the while the Japanese continued their belligerence in Asia.

PANAY INCIDENT

On December 12, 1937, Japanese planes bombed and sunk the United States gunboat *Panay* on the Yangtze River in China. The

Gunboat *Panay* (AP Associated Press)

attack occurred in broad daylight, with clear visibility, and a large United States flag was painted on the deck of the boat. The only logical conclusion to draw is that the attack was deliberate. Three Standard Oil tankers under the *Panay's* escort were also sunk. Two Americans died and 30 were wounded, some by the planes' machine guns as the planes made a second pass while their victims attempted to swim to safety.

Japan claimed that the attack was accidental, formally apologized, and agreed to more than $2 million in reparations. The American public was satisfied with Japan's apology by about two thirds, according to opinion polls. In July 1938, FDR had Secretary of State Cordell Hull send letters to United States manufacturers urging a voluntary "moral embargo" on Japan. To this Japan responded with the announcement that there was a "New Order" in Asia, and the Open Door in China was no longer in effect.

ANSCHLUSS AND LEBENSRAUM

Beginning in 1936, Adolph Hitler began the implementation of his plans as outlined in *Mein Kampf* for Anschluss, involving the annexation of the ethnically German areas outside of Germany's political borders and the expansion of Germany's Lebensraum or living space. In 1936, Hitler informed foreign ambassadors in Berlin that he would no longer abide by the Locarno Agreement of 1925 that set Germany's western borders. Hitler then moved his army into a demilitarized zone of western Germany known as the Rhineland without first consulting the Reichstag (Parliament). The Rhineland had been in German hands prior to World War I, but in French hands before 1870 and in French hands after World War I. Hitler's bold move defied the Versailles Treaty, which had required the area to be demilitarized, and the Locarno agreement of 1925 that had the security of the borders to the countries to Germany's west. International reaction was somewhat ho-um, however, since a large percentage of the population of the area were German in ethnicity and people could justify the Nazi control of the area as "natural."

Hitler then turned his attention to the annexation of entire countries. Hitler's first victim was his neighbor Austria. First Hitler demanded that Austrian Chancellor Kurt von Schuschnigg award positions in his government's cabinet to members of the Austrian Nazi Party. Schuschnigg did so, but also called for a plebiscite that he expected to be a public rejection of the German annexation of Austria. Hitler then mobilized his army along the Austrian border and called for Schuschnigg's resignation. Facing a Nazi invasion, Schusschnigg resigned on March 11, so as to prevent the destruction of Austria by Hitler's war machine. The following day his successor, Arthur Seyss-Inquart of the Austrian Nazi Party, invited Hitler's army into his country, ostensibly to keep order. Germany then announced the Anschluss (annexation) of Austria on March 14, 1938. Less than a month later, Austrian voters approved of the annexation by 99.75 percent in an obviously fraudulent election controlled by the Nazis.

After the Austrian coup, Hitler moved on to his next objective—the annexation of the Sudetenland, a German-speaking portion of Czechoslovakia. Czechoslovakia favored war instead of submission if they could secure help from France and England; but they, also, realized that resistance was futile against the German war machine without outside help. Hitler bluntly informed English Prime Minister Neville Chamberlain that he was determined to secure self-determination for the Sudeten Germans. Chamberlain in turn persuaded Édouard Daladier, the French premier, that a sacrifice on the part of Czechoslovakia would save the peace. In September 1938 Hitler, Mussolini, Daladier, and Chamberlain met in Munich—without any representative from Czechoslovakia present—and worked out the details of the surrender of the Sudentenland in return for Hitler's promise that he had no further territorial ambitions. Neville Chamberlain returned to England to a hero's welcome and rode down the streets of London in an open car to cheering crowds, while waving the agreement and declaring that it had secured "peace in our time." Chamberlain's conservative opponent in Parliament, Winston Churchill, however, denounced the agreement as "appeasement" and argued, "Tyrants should not be appeased, but thwarted at the outset." After the onset of World War II in Europe, the Munich accords became known as representing the policy of "appeasement" and have been condemned by scholars and politicians worldwide ever since.

While the Munich Pact gave Britain precious time to build up its air force, British and French hopes that the agreement would appease Hitler's expansionistic cravings were shattered, just six months later, when in March 1939 the German army invaded and seized the remainder of the Czech nation. Mussolini seized Albania, the poorest and weakest country in Europe, the following month, and the two dictators celebrated by signing a military alliance, the "Pact of Steel." France and England reacted by assuring Romania and Greece that the Allies would come to their aid if Mussolini attacked them next. Albania, however, would be the only country during World War II that Mussolini's Italy would be able to attack and conquer without assistance from the German army.

The shock of Hitler's callous violation of the solemn pledge made at Munich ended the appeasement policy of France and Great Britain. Britain launched a tremendous arms program, and in Paris Daladier obtained special emergency powers to push forward national defense.

It was Germany's aggression against Poland, however, that finally precipitated the Second World War in Europe. During the summer of 1939 Hitler had made increasingly insistent territorial demands upon Poland. Poland refused the cession and appealed to France and Germany for help. France and Germany assured the Poles that they would come to the aid of Poland if Hitler attacked. Chamberlain, with the French government concurring, also warned the Nazi government that "in the event of any action which clearly threatened Polish independence" the British would "at once lend the Polish government all support in their power." Hitler viewed the area of northwestern Poland, which had been formerly known as East Prussia, as no different than the Rhineland, Austria, or the Sudetenland because it had a large ethnic German population and sections of it had actually been part of Germany prior to the Great War. Hitler did not believe that the French and the English really cared about Poland; and if the annexation of the Rhineland had been viewed as "natural," why not Poland?

As German threats against Poland increased, Britain and France sought an alliance with the Soviet Union but refused to assent to its reannexation of the Baltic states. Meanwhile, the Nazi and Soviet foreign secretaries were secretly working out an agreement of their own. On August 23, 1939, Russia and Germany signed a nonaggression pact. Stalin, perhaps, correctly surmised that he could not count on the Western powers to come to the aid of the communist Soviet Union if the Nazi belligerents turned their war machine to the east. Stalin knew that his military status as of the summer of 1939 was greatly inferior to that of the Germans and reasoned that an agreement with his traditional and ideological enemy would provide him the best chance at security. Furthermore, a conflict in Western Europe after Germany invaded Poland would give the Soviet Union time to build up its armaments. Hitler well understood the traditional Russian position as "defenders of the slavs" from the German experience in World War I and sought to avoid conflict with the Soviet Union in 1939 if he sent the German army into Slavic Poland. The Soviet Union also secured German recognition of Soviet claims in eastern Poland and the Baltic states, thus in the process securing Hitler's recognition of long-standing Soviet foreign policy. In essence, Hitler had agreed to recognition of Stalin's Slavic interests, but Stalin and Hitler had agreed to divide Poland between them.

Now Hitler could attack Poland without fear of intervention by his great rival to the east, but he also had to legitimate his planned invasion of Poland with the German people. In order to do so, Hitler dressed German soldiers in Polish uniforms and had them stage an attack on a radio station in Germany near the Polish border. Hitler then denounced the Polish aggression to the German people; and without a declaration of war, Nazi troops crossed the Polish frontier on the morning of September 1, 1939, and the *Luftwaffe* began to bomb Polish cities. Hitler hoped that the appeasing governments of France and Great Britain would wring their hands and do nothing, but he had miscalculated. Hitler was in the process of building his war machine to be the most formidable and technologically advanced force the world had ever known, but he was not yet finished. His war machine was not on schedule to be fully constructed until some time in 1942 or 1943. The two Western democracies, knowing that their own time would come sooner or later, declared war on Germany on September 3 The Second World War had begun. Hitler had begun World War II in Europe with his invasion of Poland, but that had not been his intention. Instead, he had merely intended to take Poland—as he had the Rhineland, Austria, and Czechoslovakia—and then cease his expansion until his military buildup was fully completed. Beginning World War II three to four years ahead of his own schedule was perhaps the first of Hitler's many major miscalculations that would eventually lead to his own demise, but not before six years of the most devastating war in human history would be waged against him.

BLITZKRIEG

Germany unveiled its new type of war strategy in the Polish invasion that became known as Blitzkrieg or "lightning war." Blitzkrieg was essentially rapid armored advance accompanied by massive air support, an approach to warfare that has been employed by advanced armies ever since. Neither planes nor tanks were well developed as military tools in World War I, but they proved in Poland to be the most important weapons of modern warfare in 1939. Poland's air force was small and vastly inferior, and the Poles lacked anything that proved effective at stopping the advanced German tanks.

The Poles had known before the war that help from France and England would be required if the Poles were to successfully halt a Nazi invasion. The French and English, however, were not ready for war and help would, therefore, not arrive quickly. Thus, Germany subdued Poland in six weeks (with help from the Soviets who

German advance guards and scouts in a Polish villa during the Nazi blitzkrieg and occupation of Poland, September 1939. *(AP Associated Press)*

invaded Poland from the East) before the Allies could provide any significant assistance to Poland. Hitler then ceased any further attack.

THE AMERICAN QUANDARY

Beginning with Germany's invasion of Poland, the political debate in the United States over intervention into the war in Europe dominated foreign policy discussions. American public opinion quickly shifted in favor of support for Britain and France—short of war—thus leaving conservative isolationism at odds with the opinion of the majority. Congress quickly voted to repeal the arms embargo portion of the Neutrality Acts and allowed belligerents to purchase military goods from the United States, but the "cash and carry" limitation that had been imposed under the Neutrality Acts remained. The United States would not extend credit to the warring nations, and belligerents would have to pick up the military goods in United States ports using their own ships. Republicans opposed the end of the arms embargo and other subsequent aid to the Allies by an average of 85 percent on the key votes in Congress. Conservative Southern Democrats, however, broke with the isolationist conservative Republicans and favored war intervention, thus helping to shore up support for Roosevelt in 1940 for his record third term.

While the Western powers were preoccupied with Germany, Stalin used the opportunity in the fall of 1939 to overrun Latvia, Estonia, Lithuania, and Finland. Stalin's invasion of Lithuania violated his Non-Aggression pact with Hitler where they had secretly divided Europe into spheres of influence. Lithuanians are Germanic in language and ethnicity, and Hitler had planned to put them under his sphere of influence.

In retaliation against Soviet aggression, the United States placed a "moral embargo" on the shipment of arms to Russia. The moral embargo was completely ineffective, and the Soviets had secured Finland and the Baltic States by March of 1940. Furthermore, United States exports to the U.S.S.R. actually doubled during the Soviet campaign against Finland.

After the rapid conquest of Poland, Germany remained virtually inactive during the winter of 1939–1940. This "Phony War" ended abruptly on April 9, 1940, when Germany simultaneously invaded Denmark and Norway. A month later Nazi armies invaded Belgium, France, and Holland, and in six weeks all had surrendered. The French had staked their security on the Maginot Line, a complicated series of trenches, tunnels, bunkers, stationary guns, and subterranean rails along the German border. Essentially constructing defenses in anticipation of an advanced version of the trench warfare of World War I, the French had invested in a defense for the war of yesteryear. The French did not, however, build fortifications along the border with Belgium; and the German army simply went around the Maginot Line and invaded France through Belgium as they had in World War I. Without the Maginot Line to protect them, the outmoded French army was overwhelmed by the German Blitzkrieg and lost 110,000 men in a month. France surrendered on June 22, 1940, and Hitler's Nazi army goose-stepped through Paris.

After the fall of France, the British rescued over 300,000 of their troops from the beach at Dunkirk through a heroic civilian flotilla called for by Winston Churchill via radio, as England lacked the necessary means to evacuate their army before the Nazis overran them. The British had to abandon practically all their equipment, however, as the civilian flotilla could carry soliders, but little ease. The British army then returned to an island without land defense against armored columns. On June 10, when the defeat of France was certain, Italy came into the war on the side of Germany. As of June 22, Britain stood alone against German and Italian aggression.

FDR reacted by freezing the assets of conquered countries to keep them out of Hitler's control. FDR was also concerned that the colonial possessions in Latin America of conquered countries could

Winston Churchill *(Library of Congress)*

fall into German hands. As a result, Congress passed the "no transfer resolution" whereby the United States opposed "the transfer of territory in the Americas from one non-American to another non-American power," thus denying Germany control over the colonial possessions of the conquered powers of Western Europe.

BATTLE FOR BRITAIN

In August 1940, Germany launched an air war against the British, attacking English air bases in preparation for an invasion. At one point, it appeared that the German strategy might be successful as the British were losing planes and pilots faster than they could be replaced. FDR cancelled a previous American purchase of 350 planes from Britain, which had already been delivered and paid for, and sent them back to England to help the British replenish the Royal Air Force (RAF). FDR also traded the British 50 outdated American destroyers for American naval bases on British territory in the Caribbean, Bermuda, and Newfoundland.

As fate would have it, the character of the battle for Britain would change when on one raid, German pilots got lost over cloudy English skies and accidentally bombed a residential section of London. In retaliation, Churchill launched a daring 500-plane raid, bombing Berlin and shocking the Germans. The bombing of Berlin provided a morale boost to the British and proved to the British people that Germany was not invincible. Hitler was enraged and let his rage get in the way of good military sense, and he retaliated by shifting his air strategy away from targeting air bases and instead to punishing the British by bombing residential London. Although the German raids on British cities were devastating, the British minimized civilian deaths through the employment of underground bomb shelters; and the shift in German strategy allowed the British to rebuild their air force and airfields. The BBC kept British spirits high through a propaganda campaign full of erroneous information and exaggerated claims. BBC reports of British "kills" of German aircraft were typically triple American estimates. The British perpetuated the myth of the superiority of the British spitfire fighter plane as a German killer due to its unique-shaped wings; but, in actuality, more German planes were shot down by the more conventional looking British hurricane. The British accuracy in anticipating and intercepting German raids was also greatly enhanced due to the new invention of radar. RAF pilots remained on 24-hour alerts for months, prompting Churchill to proclaim that "never has so much been owed by so many to so few." Against odds that seemed to many to be impossible at the time, Britain did not fall.

A YEAR OF DECISION

What should American policy be now that Hitler with his ally, Italy, controlled western Europe, and military men regarded the conquest of England as likely? The joint planners of the War and Navy Departments thought that the United States should husband its resources at home to prepare for attack. Isolationists, including many leading citizens and scholars, opposed any action that went beyond defense preparations.

The leader of the Nationalist Republican faction, Senator Robert Taft, for example, continued to oppose intervention in the European war even after the fall of France in June 1940. Nationalist Republicans argued that United States intervention in the war would increase the power and scope of the national government, as it did in World War I, and thus institute a form of "national socialism" in the United States and destroy American freedom, the supposed purpose for intervention in the war in the first place. Furthermore, the Nationalist Republicans argued that the expansion of Nazi Germany posed no threat to the security or economic well being of the United States. Nationalist Conservatives also argued that Britain and France had made a mistake in declaring war on Germany after the Nazi invasion of Poland. The argument was that the Allies should have allowed Hitler to take Eastern Europe—with the result that the totalitarian dictators, Hitler and Stalin, would eventually come to blows and slug out between themselves to the benefit of the free world. Hitler's army then would have bogged down in the Soviet Union, thus preventing an invasion of western Europe and eliminating any necessity of another war between Germany and the powers of western Europe. Furthermore, intervention in the European war would be unlikely to advance the causes of freedom and democracy any more than did World War I. Instead, World War I had created the chaos and destruction that led to the germination and growth of Communism and

Fascism, the current scourges of international politics. Why would another war be expected to do anything different?

Robert Taft echoed the sentiments of leftist war protestors in the conflicts of later decades in Southeast Asia (1960s) and Iraq (2000s) when he argued that the Republican Party:

> "should be opposed to risking the lives of five million American boys in an imperialistic war for the domination of Europe, Asia, and Africa, and the supposed 'manifest destiny' of America."

Taft argued that it was the Eastern Wall Street wing of the Republican Party that favored intervention while the farmers, working men, and small businessmen opposed the war. In Taft's words:

> "The war party is made up of the business community of the cities, the newspaper and magazine writers, the radio and movie commentators, the Communists, and the University intelligentsia."

AMERICA FIRST COMMITTEE

In the summer of 1940, Nationalist Republicans organized the America First Committee to lobby and produce propaganda against war intervention. Backed by the financing of Robert E. Wood, Chairman of the Board of Sears, and William H. Regnery, President of the Western Shade Cloth Company, the America First Committee had over 800,000 members by the end of 1941, including Charles Lindbergh, a bonafide American hero and the first man to fly nonstop across the Atlantic in 1927. Lindbergh himself was an isolationist that viewed the interventionists' position as part of a grand conspiracy, the primary forces behind which were "the British, the Jewish, and the Roosevelt Administration."

It is clear from the arguments of the America First Committee and others that conservatives generally preferred Nazi Germany to the communist Soviet Union and were essentially comfortable with, and unthreatened by, the Nazi presence. Nationalist Conservatives argued that the entry of the Soviet Union in the war against Germany in 1941 took the pressure off Britain and eliminated the need for United States intervention. Furthermore, entrance in the war on the side of Britain would now aid the communists in Russia; hence, the war could not be a war to end totalitarianism. In essence, the policy that the nationalist/isolationist conservatives pursued is the policy that would later be condemned by American conservatives, in general, as "appeasement."

Republicans did, however, typically support the British in principle against Nazi Germany and believed that there was a need for military preparedness. The America First Committee argued that military preparedness would prevent war because with an impregnable defense, no foreign power could dare attack the United States. Similarly, Herbert Hoover in 1940 argued, "We are determined to be armed to the teeth to defend ourselves and the Western Hemisphere."

Military preparedness, in turn, did not necessitate aid to the British, and it most certainly did not necessitate aid to the Soviet Union. The America First Committee argued that "aid short of war" weakened military preparedness at home by siphoning off resources. Furthermore, "aid short of war" was likely to cause the United States to cross paths with Nazi Germany and thus drag the United States into the war. Aid to the communist Soviet Union, on the other hand, was complete anathema. On August 5, 1941, a group of Republican leaders—including Herbert Hoover, 1936 Presidential nominee Alf Landon, former Vice President Charles Dawes, and former RNC Chairman Henry P. Fletcher—issued a statement criticizing what they viewed as "unauthorized aid to Russia" and arguing that American aid should be "utilized only to protect the independence of 'democracies.'"

The President was for as much aid to Britain as he could arrange without being overridden by the antiwar majority in Congress. The President's decision to take a chance on British survival through all-out United States aid was probably the most fateful one of the entire period. He could have pursued a more isolationist policy without alienating his political support, and the policy he elected to pursue led almost inevitably to war. In the decisions of both Roosevelt and Wilson, the overriding fact appears to have been an unwillingness to permit a Europe in which a militaristic Germany was the dominant power. FDR's neutrality, however, was overtly different than Wilson's as FDR from the beginning told Americans that he could not ask them to be neutral in thought.

In a contest over policy involving military action the President has a great advantage over Congress. He can act and seek support later, whereas Congress, as a non-administrative body, is always behind a rapid march of events. This is in effect what happened from June 1940 on. The President went ahead administratively to give England as much aid as possible. In so doing, he educated the public toward his point of view, and Congress was usually presented with actions already taken that would be hard to reverse.

In June, for example, Congress thought to restrict the President by passing a law forbidding him to give away military equipment unless the Army Chief of Staff and the Chief of Naval Operations certified it as not essential to the national defense. On September 2, an executive agreement was signed with England transferring 50 overage American destroyers in return for British bases in Newfoundland, Bermuda, and the Caribbean. Since the bases increased American security, this action was obviously not a violation of the law; yet it tied the United States to the defense of the British Empire and marked the end of any pretext of neutrality. Germany did not declare war at this time because it did not want the United States in the war; but later in the same month Germany, Italy, and Japan formed a military alliance obviously aimed at the United States.

These critical strokes of foreign policy took place during the presidential campaign of 1940. Four days before the Republican Convention met in June, the President appointed Republican leaders Henry L. Stimson and Frank Knox to his cabinet as Secretaries of War and of the Navy. Two days before the convention, France surrendered. The general confusion favored the internationalists. As none of the leading Republican contenders developed decisive strength, Wendell L. Willkie, a businessman who sympathized with Roosevelt's foreign policy, was skillfully maneuvered to victory. As in 1936, the Republicans had gone far away from the principles of their center and right wing to attract marginal Democratic votes.

Henry L. Stimson *(Library of Congress)*

The national emergency led the President to seek a third term. Through the manipulations of Harry Hopkins, representing the President, the Democratic bosses were reluctantly forced to accept Henry A. Wallace, the liberal Secretary of Agriculture, for the vice-presidency.

During the campaign both those favoring all-out aid to Britain and those opposed to risks that might lead to war were nationally organized. The journalist William Allen White of Kansas headed a Committee to Defend America by Aiding the Allies, in direct opposition to Robert F.

Wood's isolationist America First Committee. The effect of the controversy on the campaign was not immediately clear since both candidates were internationalists.

By October, however, as Great Britain withstood Germany's bombing attacks and was not invaded, the argument that aid to Britain was more important than keeping out of war lost its immediate urgency. When public opinion pollsters found that the number of those favoring foreign aid had declined to less than half the voters, Willkie shifted his ground. Having failed to gain support on the issues of the third term and mismanaged defense, Willkie now attacked Roosevelt as a warmonger. Alarmed by the apparent success of the Willkie strategy, the President was pushed further and further away from his true beliefs. Just before election he told his listeners, "I have said this before, but I shall say it again and again and again. Your boys are not going to be sent into any foreign wars." In his mind, conflict resulting from an attack on the United States would not be a "foreign" war.

The Democratic vote was slightly below that of 1936 and the Republican 5.5 million larger, but Willkie won only 82 electoral votes to Roosevelt's 449. The total minor party vote fell below 200,000. It was hard to call the result a referendum on any policy since there had been no substantial disagreement; but it could be read as a vote of confidence in Roosevelt personally, or, as Republicans saw it, as proof of the strength of habitual patterns of voting and the Democratic political machine. To the President, it was support for more vigorous foreign aid and military preparation.

Characteristically, the President had put political and foreign problems ahead of domestic ones. By August Congress had appropriated some $16 billion for defense—enough, if it could be used, to move toward a war footing. The following month Congress agreed on a bipartisan basis to a selective service (draft) act, but meanwhile the economic organization essential for defense faltered. Production, the President felt, could be called into existence later when needed.

This was, of course, far from true. Coordination of production was in the hands of a nearly powerless National Defense Advisory Commission. In the words of Donald Nelson, its coordinator for procurement, the commission "began to stagger in the late summer and early autumn of 1940. In November it was punch drunk. It did not fall flat on its face until five days before Christmas." Its successor, the Office of Production Management, had little more success.

The basic difficulty was that private industry did not want to be regimented in time of peace, and, for fear of strengthening the isolationists, the President was reluctant to ask Congress for the necessary power. Fortunately, however, the United States had great capacity for manufacturing the automotive and other steel equipment needed for this war. Incentives such as quick tax write-offs and long-term contracts stimulated big business to undertake much of the new construction that had to precede mass production of military equipment.

LEND-LEASE

By December 1940 the opinion polls indicated that around 60 percent of the American people were in favor of helping Great Britain even at the risk of war. Thus, when Churchill told Roosevelt that British credit for the purchase of war supplies was nearing exhaustion, Roosevelt believed he had popular support for extending more liberal, outright aid. Polls suggested that public opinion in America was approximately two thirds in favor of aid to England. A bill was quickly drawn up and introduced in Congress calling for "munitions of war and supplies of many kinds to be turned over to those nations which are now in actual war with aggressor nations," to be paid back in goods and services at the end of the war. In support of the bill, FDR argued, "When your neighbor's house is on fire, you loan him a hose." Senator Robert Taft quipped that it was actually, "More like loaning someone your chewing gum. After it is used, you don't want it back." Others, such as America's Irish-American Ambassador to London, Joseph Kennedy, opposed aid to England as a waste of America's resources on the British lost cause. Though opposed by Republican leaders in Congress, the Lend-Lease bill had the compulsion of the situation behind it. On March 11, "Lend-Lease" became law, and the next day the President asked Congress for an initial $7 billion to implement the policy.

The United States had already broken the laws of neutrality beyond repair by aiding only one side and keeping the vessels of the other out of the western Atlantic. Lend-Lease marked the point of no return on the road to war. The bill committed American industrial power, nearly equal to that of all the rest of the world, to the defeat of Germany.

ROOSEVELT'S DILEMMA

The Lend-Lease Act of March 1941 was only the first step that President Roosevelt was prepared to take in a broader effort to help Britain resist German aggression. Although he probably overestimated the strength of the vocal isolationist minority, he estimated correctly the great reluctance of most Americans to become directly involved in a war. As a result, in his pursuit of what he thought was the defense of American interests, he was not always open and candid. Sometimes he acted secretly, as he did in late April 1941, when he ordered a naval patrol of the North Atlantic to help the British detect German submarines. Other times he acted as boldly as he thought the majority of the people would permit, as in July 1941, when American troops were ordered to Iceland to relieve the British in protecting it from German invasion.

When Hitler, in a surprise move, invaded the Soviet Union on June 22, 1941, Roosevelt followed Churchill in welcoming a new fighting force in the war against Germany, even though few military advisers believed the Russians could hold out more than three months against the German blitz. Acutely aware of the weakness of British and Russian defenses, Roosevelt, in early July, asked Congress for an extension of the draft law and repeal of the prohibition on overseas service for draftees. Isolationists branded the request as yet another of the President's covert efforts to get the United States into war, but after acrimonious debate the draft extension passed by a single vote in the House of Representatives.

HEMISPHERIC DEFENSE

Despite Lend-Lease, FDR had further problems in getting arms to the British in that German U-boats were sinking British shipping at a rate of 500,000 tons per month—faster than England could build ships. Much of the Lend-Lease shipments would be going to the ocean floor unless British shipping could be protected. Consequently, in July 1941, FDR declared that the Western Atlantic was a "neutral zone" and the collective responsibility of the "American Nations" under what he termed as "Hemispheric Defense." Under the policy of "Hemispheric Defense," United States ships patrolled the Atlantic as far east as Iceland and reported to the British the location of German submarines.

One month prior to FDR's implementation of "Hemispheric Defense," (June, 1941) Hitler made perhaps his greatest error of the war and invaded Russia without first defeating England. In doing so, Hitler opened the war on two fronts. Hitler expected to overwhelm Russia within six weeks, but the massive operation over a 4,000-mile front overwhelmed his ability to supply his army. Consequently, the advance slowed, and Russia did not fall as Hitler had planned. FDR reacted to the German invasion of Russia by extending Lend-Lease to the U.S.S.R. in the beginning of what would, eventually, grow to become a formal alliance.

From August 9–12, Roosevelt and Prime Minister Churchill met secretly on the U.S.S. *Augusta* in Placentia Bay, Newfoundland. The result was the Atlantic Charter, setting forth the aims of the war: No territorial changes would be made in favor of the victors, and all nations would be protected in their right to choose their own governments, without fear of aggressive threats. FDR and Churchill also agreed that their mutual goals included the final destruction of Nazi Germany. When announced on August 15, this meeting between a technically neutral country and an active belligerent brought loud protests from isolationists in the United States. Nevertheless, upon his return home Roosevelt asked for increased appropriations for aid to Britain and the Soviet Union.

UNDECLARED WAR

When in September a German U-boat attacked the American destroyer *Greer*, which, unbeknown to the American public, was sending the British navy information about German submarines, Roosevelt seized the opportunity to issue a "shoot-on-sight" order to the navy and asked Congress for authority to arm American merchant ships. With American naval vessels shooting without even waiting to be attacked, it was only a matter of time before a serious incident would occur. On October 17, the American destroyer *Kearny* was torpedoed and damaged off Iceland, and 11 Americans were killed. Less than three weeks later the *Reuben James* was sunk by a German U-boat with the loss of 115 lives. Yet most Americans seemed to support the President's policy, and in early November Congress authorized Roosevelt to arm merchant vessels and permit their entry into the war zone. Congress also authorized American ships to escort Allied cargo ships all the way to their home ports. Although the fight in Congress had been bitter, the House victory was 212 to 94, far greater than the single-vote margin of the previous summer. With the approval of these actions by Congress coupled with FDR's orders for American ships to shoot German submarines on sight, the result was essentially an undeclared naval war on Germany.

By the end of November 1941 Hitler's armies were deep inside the Soviet Union, seemingly on their way to an early victory, and Japan was obviously readying itself for an offensive against the British and Dutch colonies in Southeast Asia. The President's dilemma was acute. He could not dispel the nagging fear that the Germans might yet overwhelm Russia and Britain, despite American aid, an event that would leave the United States alone to face Germany. At the same time, he knew that Americans were so divided over the struggle in Europe that he dared not try to lead them immediately into full-scale war against Hitler.

THE END OF HESITATION

JAPANESE-AMERICAN RELATIONS, 1940–1941

Ever since the early 1930s, Japanese expansionism on the Asian mainland had met gradual but increasing American opposition. Finally in 1939 the United States began to restrict the flow to Japan of some strategic war materials, including oil and scrap iron; but Roosevelt would not embargo all war materials as some of his advisers urged. He believed some measures were necessary to warn Japan of American opposition to aggression, but he feared that too strong a stand would push the Japanese into an adventure against the oil-rich and defenseless Dutch East Indies. The Japanese response was to move into northern Indochina in the summer of 1940 and to join the Tripartite Pact with Germany and Italy in September 1940.

By early 1941 the Japanese and American positions in Asia were irreconcilable. Japan's minimum demand was that the United States cease its aid to Chiang Kai-shek, while the United States insisted that Japan end its war against China. The Japanese refused to do so because a pullout of China would not only deny Japan the resources it needed for self-sufficiency, but would also cause the Japanese to lose face. Japanese soldiers had been dying in China for a decade. Culturally, the Japanese leaders viewed a pullout of China as meaning that all of those soldiers had died in vain. Therefore, during 1941 diplomatic efforts aimed at softening the two positions proved to be equally in vain. Japanese militarists believed that war was the only answer to America's interference with Japanese ambitions in Asia; and the military's hand was strengthened in April 1941 when the Soviet Union promised to remain neutral in the event of a Japanese-American war. Japan's fear of a two-front war was thus reduced while Hitler's earlier promise to support Japan in a war against the United States made it clear that the United States would be the one forced to fight on two fronts.

Japanese ambitions became clearer and more alarming in July, when Japanese military units invaded southern Indochina in obvious preparation for an attack upon the Dutch East Indies. Indeed, American code breakers had broken the Japanese codes and knew that the Japanese planned an invasion of the Dutch East Indies. In retaliation the United States, Britain, and the Netherlands cut off all vital military supplies to Japan.

On September 6, 1941, Japan's Supreme War Council voted for war if American aid to China did not cease within six weeks. The Japanese hoped that an impressive attack on the United States followed by a series of military victories would force the United States to end the embargoes of oil and other materials needed by Japan for their military campaign in China. Japanese military leaders argued that the United States was unprepared for war and that Japan could deal the United States serious military setbacks in the Pacific for six months. After six months, however, Japanese military experts cautioned their leaders that Japan would fail to win a protracted struggle with the United States. Consequently, Japan's political leaders would have six months to negotiate open trade with the United States after the beginning of the war, after which Japan would only lose.

President Roosevelt refused to meet with the liberal Japanese Prime Minister in the fall of 1941, and before the six weeks elapsed after the Japanese Supreme War Council meeting of September 6, the militant General Hideki Tojo became premier. Though now convinced that war was inevitable, Tojo sent a personal representative, Saburo Kurusu, to Washington in early November for further fruitless talks with the Americans. By the end of the month Americans knew from their breaking of the Japanese codes that war was coming; but they did not know where in the Pacific it would start.

On November 24, American naval authorities sent out warnings of war with Japan to commanders at Pearl Harbor and Manila. On November 27, these bases were warned again, this time with "an aggressive move by Japan is expected within the next few days." Unfortunately, the authorities at Pearl Harbor had not been aware of military code changes in Washington; and the message sent to Pearl Harbor that was intended to warn of an impending air raid was misinterpreted as a warning to prepare for sabotage attacks. Consequently, planes were lined up on the runways in the open where they could be easily watched, making them very good targets for an air raid.

On December 1, the Japanese emperor gave his consent to war. Already a Japanese task force was steaming across the northern Pacific for a surprise attack on Pearl Harbor. In Washington, the two Japanese envoys, Kurusu and Ambassador Nomura, continued their inconclusive talks with Secretary of State Cordell Hull.

PEARL HARBOR

Two new technologies would play roles in the American disaster at Pearl Harbor. First, American military intelligence believed that American ships in Pearl Harbor were safe from attack by aerial torpedoes because the torpedoes would hit the bottom of the shallow harbor, only 45 feet deep, before they could correct their paths and hit their targets. The Japanese, however, had discovered that the attachment of wooden stabilizers to the torpedoes' fins would allow them to be dropped in depths of less than 40 feet and not hit the bottom. Second, early on Sunday morning, December 7, 1941, two young radar operators noted an unusually large number of blips on their radar screen about 130 miles north of Oahu; but the blips were misinterpreted by the radar operators' superiors as American B-17s due to arrive that morning, and no warning was issued.

The time was 7:50 on Sunday morning, December 7, 1941. In the sky over the island of Oahu, Captain Nakaya of the Japanese navy wrote in his log:

> Pearl Harbor is still asleep in the morning mist. The orderly groups of barracks, the wriggling white line of the automobile road climbing up to the mountaintop; fine objectives in all directions. ... Inside the harbor were important ships of the Pacific fleet, strung out and anchored two ships side by side in an orderly manner.

Ten minutes later the first wave of Japanese planes struck the great American base. The surprise was complete. Some American sailors thought the first bombs were accidentally dropped from American planes. Although the Americans fought back fiercely, the losses sustained were enormous—all eight battleships, the main object of the attack, were put out of action. Two never saw action again. Except for three aircraft carriers, which happened to be at sea, the whole Pacific fleet was damaged or destroyed. Almost all the aircraft, most of which did not even get off the ground, were knocked out. More than 2,400 Americans were killed and 1,200 wounded. The Japanese lost 29 airplanes, five midget submarines, and one fleet submarine. Considering the extensive damage, the attack on Pearl Harbor was one of the cheapest victories in the history of warfare.

For the Americans, it could have been even worse. The Japanese attacked for two hours and then stopped. They could have refueled and attacked again, but they did not. America's four aircraft carriers under William F. "Bull" Halsey were not in the harbor at the time of the attack, and Japan's Vice-Admiral Chuichi Nagumo did not even order any attempt to find them. Some of Nagumo's decision was evidently influenced by Japanese cultural factors. Given that Japan was attacking without a declaration of war, many Japanese viewed the idea of a surprise attack as dishonorable and akin to a sucker punch. Those who opposed such action forced a compromise where the Japanese military would hit the United States hard in one lightning surprise attack and then cease attacking until war could be declared later in the day. The aversion to the idea of a surprise attack was so strong among the Japanese pilots that some were found weeping in shame after the attack at Pearl Harbor, believing that they had committed acts of cowardice. Hence, despite the devastating success of the raid, the decision to attack Pearl Harbor was a colossal blunder. First, the Japanese had allowed America's most important ships stationed at Pearl Harbor, the aircraft carriers, to escape—a factor that would come back to haunt the Japanese the next year at the Battle of Midway. Second, the idea that Japan could attack the United States and somehow force trade concessions by launching a devastating war is perhaps the greatest cultural misunderstanding of the twentieth century. For some time Roosevelt had feared that if the Japanese attacked British and Dutch possessions in Asia without involving the United States, it would be impossible to unify America behind a war to halt their aggression. After December 7, however, Americans were not only united in their opposition, but also in the goal of the unconditional surrender of Japan.

The strike against Pearl Harbor was only one part of an audacious grand plan to destroy British, Dutch, and American power in the western Pacific. Soon after the bombing of Pearl Harbor, Japanese planes attacked the Philippines. Though this time there had been specific warning, the Americans—because of bureaucratic tie-ups—were again caught unready. On December 8 the Japanese attacked Hong Kong, Borneo, the Malay Peninsula, and the American island outpost of Guam.

The boldness and power of the Japanese advance were brought home on December 10, when Japanese land-based bombers sank the British battleship *Prince of Wales* and the battle cruiser *Repulse* off the coast of Malaya. Never before had air power destroyed a free-moving battleship; the age of the airplane in naval warfare had arrived. Successful amphibious landings in the Philippines and elsewhere also attested to the Japanese' command of the most advanced methods of offensive warfare.

The day after the attack on Pearl Harbor, Congress, at the President's request, voted for war with Japan with a unanimous vote in the Senate and only one dissenting vote in the House, Jeannette Ranking of Montana. On December 11, Hitler made another of his ill-fated decisions and fulfilled his promise to the Japanese by declaring war on the United States. Italy followed soon thereafter. Hitler's reasoning was that war with the United States would allow him to attack British and Soviet shipping without restraint and thus cut off American supplies to England. Without American supplies, Hitler believed that Britain would quickly be defeated. Any dilemma FDR might have had over whether the United States should go to war with Germany after the attack on Pearl Harbor was resolved by Hitler himself; and the United States was now in a position to use to the fullest its great power against aggressor nations in both Asia and Europe.

After the initial shock had passed, many Americans grew suspicious that the astonishing success of the Japanese assault must have resulted from traitorous acts, and staunch isolationists blamed Roosevelt for somehow selling out America to the Japanese. Exhaustive investigations on the part of both the navy and Congress, however, produced no evidence to support such allegations. The fact is that most military experts seriously underestimated Japan's ability to mount the kind of elaborate, multi-pronged assault of which Pearl Harbor was but a part. The commanders at Pearl Harbor were lax in taking precautions after the war warnings of November, but these defects add up to nothing more sinister than inefficiency and carelessness.

WAR IN TWO HEMISPHERES

CREATION OF THE GRAND ALLIANCE

Within two weeks after Pearl Harbor Winston Churchill and his chief military advisers arrived in Washington for extended discussions with the President and American military leaders about the long-range strategy of the two-front war in which both countries were now engaged. The basic decision of the conference, as General Marshall later reported, was that "Germany is still the prime enemy and her defeat is the key to victory. Once Germany is defeated the collapse of Italy and the defeat of Japan must follow." Roosevelt, despite pressure to do otherwise, never deviated from this decision, even though Japan appeared to be the greater immediate menace to the United States. The two allies also agreed to pool their resources and military equipment for the duration of the struggle.

Finally, the conference created a Combined Chiefs of Staff in Washington to plan and coordinate global strategy. As a public manifestation of the new association, Churchill, Roosevelt, Maxim Litvinov (representing Stalin), and the representatives of 23 other nations at war with one or more Axis powers signed the Declaration of the United Nations on New Year's Day, 1942.

As the arsenal of the alliance, the United States in subsequent months worked out new Lend-Lease agreements with the principal allies. According to these agreements, the costs of the war were to be borne in proportion to ability to pay. By the end of the war in 1945, the United States had contributed over $50 billion in Lend-Lease, the bulk of which went to Great Britain. In return, the Allies provided $8 billion in goods or services to the United States.

HOLDING THE LINE

The first months of 1942 were filled with one Japanese success after another. (As a gesture of defiance, the United States dispatched General James Doolittle to lead a small, carrier-borne air strike against Tokyo in April to boost morale, but its military value was nil.) In a matter of months the Japanese overran all of Southeast Asia. In February, they took the great British naval base of Singapore and in March, Java, the main island of the Dutch East Indies. Another Japanese army, meanwhile, had overrun Siam (now Thailand) and Burma and now stood poised on the borders of India.

By the end of March the Japanese controlled the western half of the Pacific from the Kuriles in the North to the Solomons in the South as well as the islands and mainland of Southeast Asia from Indochina to India. Japan captured American outposts on Guam and Wake Island and launched a major offensive against Americans in the Philippines in January 1942. American forces under General Douglas MacArthur retreated first to the Bataan Peninsuala and then to the Island of Corregidor before all resistance in the Philippines ceased on May 6. The Japanese then marched the American army and their Filipino allies 60 miles across the Bataan Peninsula, abusing them en route in what became known as the Bataan "death march." Of the 11,000 Americans taken prisoner on the Philippines, only 1,000 would survive the war. As many as 26,000 Filipinos would also die during the death march and the brutal months afterward when they were subjected to malnutrition and brutality in Japanese prison camps. Living to fight another day, however, was American General Douglas MacArthur, who issued the famous personal vow, "I shall return," upon his departure from the Philippines.

The Japanese had to hold off the United States until they could develop Netherland Indies iron and oil. Not knowing that Americans had broken their naval code, the Japanese made the fatal error of trying to expand their defensive perimeter. In May of 1942, the naval-air Battle of the Coral Sea halted the Japanese southward advance, and the following month an American victory over a large Japanese naval task force off Midway Island ended the eastward thrust. In the Battle of the Coral Sea, off the Southeast Coast of New Guinea, United States aircraft carriers turned back the Japanese Navy. A new kind of warfare was unveiled as Japanese and American ships attacked each other by airplane while the ships themselves remained, out of sight and out of range from each other. The United States lost the carrier *Lexington*, causing the Japanese to be "encouraged" and consider the engagement a victory; but the United States also considered the battle a victory because it had, for the first time, halted the Japanese advance.

On June 3, 1942, the Japanese launched a major naval offensive aimed at taking the Midway Islands northwest of Hawaii. The Midway Islands were imminently important because they were close enough to the United States that Japan could use them as a base from which to bomb the United States.

The United States knew of the Japanese plan from interceptions of coded transmissions and rushed every available ship and plane into the area.

Both sides suffered enormous losses. The United States lost every pilot, except one, from its aircraft carriers at Midway, and that one pilot was also shot down and watched the entire battle floating in the ocean. On the plus side, however, the United States sank four Japanese aircraft carriers while the Japanese only sank one of the United States. Hence, despite the heavy American losses, the Battle of Midway was a major American victory as the Japanese did not accomplish their objective of taking the Midway Islands. The battle also proved to be the turning point in the Pacific. Prior to Midway, the Japanese had virtually won all the battles in the Pacific theater. After Midway, Japan would lose them all. Midway also displayed the importance of the American aircraft carriers surviving the attack on Pearl Harbor since the United States surely would have lost at Midway if the aircraft carriers stationed at Pearl Harbor had not been present at Midway. Finally, Japanese losses at the Battle of Midway were so critical that, thereafter, the Imperial Navy suddenly was on the defensive and would remain so throughout the rest of the war.

ISLAND HOPPING

With General MacArthur pushing northward and westward from Australia and Admiral Chester Nimitz pushing west from Hawaii, the United States planned to advance toward Japan by capturing Japanese strategic outposts in each Pacific island chain that had come under Japanese control. Instead of attacking every island with Japanese soldiers on it,

Admiral Chester Nimitz (*AP Associated Press*)

American military strategists decided to attack only the most important supply islands and air bases in each island chain, effectively leaving the rest of the Japanese forces on other islands to live off the land without supplies. Each island to be invaded was to undergo an amphibious assault with massive air support, a method that the United States would use repeatedly through D-day. The first test of the amphibious assault, island-hopping strategy was at Guadalcanal in the Solomon Islands. The first precarious American landing on Guadalcanal took place on August 7, 1942, but it was not until the fifth major sea and air encounter on November 13–14, 1942, that the southern Solomons rested securely in American hands. Superior American air power was the deciding factor in the battle; but American deaths were over 3,000 and the struggle for the island took much longer than expected. Over 20,000 Japanese were killed on the island, and the Japanese fought essentially to the last man as the United States took only 156 prisoners, of whom many were wounded. On Guadalcanal, the Americans quickly discovered that all of the fallen Japanese soldiers on the battlefield were not necessarily dead; some were merely "playing possum" and would shoot Americans from the ground as they passed the positions of the "possum" Japanese. Americans then assigned "Possum Squads" of men to make the rounds of bodies lying on the battlefield and shoot them in the head or engulf them with flamethrowers. Some quickly battle-hardened Americans made personal items from the skulls and

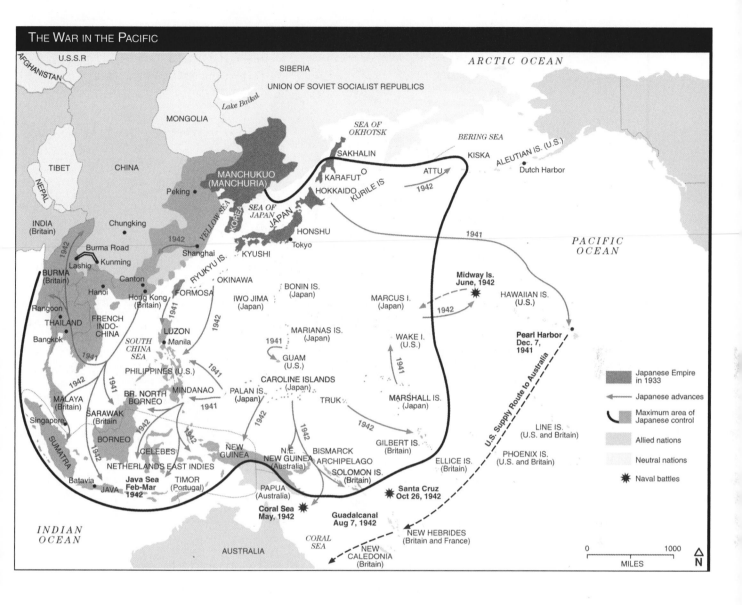

THE WAR IN THE PACIFIC

bones of Japanese soldiers. The gruesome pattern of Guadalcanal would be repeated throughout the Pacific in 1943, 1944, and 1945—on the islands of Tulagia, Gavutu, Tarawa, Makin, Kwajalein, Eniwetok, the Philippines, Iwo Jima, and Okinawa. For instance, on Tarawa, a tiny coral cay of less than three square miles, 3,000 Japanese and 1,000 Americans were killed in three days. Two thousand more Americans were wounded and only 17 Japanese survived, a survival rate of barely more than half of one percent.

EUROPEAN THEATER

Unlike the war in the Pacific, the first year of war in Europe brought almost uninterrupted setbacks for the Allies on both land and sea. That spring and summer German submarines sank Allied tankers and merchantmen before the eyes of civilians on the shores of New Jersey

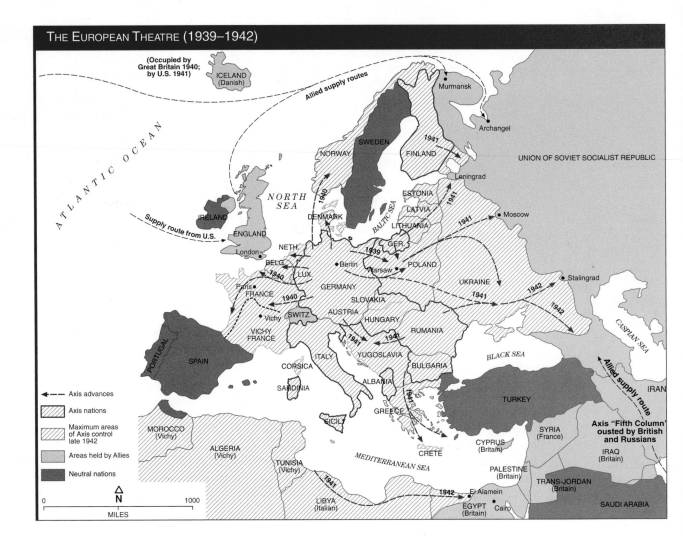

THE EUROPEAN THEATRE (1939–1942)

and Florida. By the middle of 1942 shipping losses reached a new peak of 4.5 million tons, or more than in all of 1941. Yet in the same six months only 21 U-boats were sunk. At the conclusion of eleven months of war and after a furious program of shipbuilding, Allied tonnage was still less than it had been on the day Pearl Harbor was bombed. Although losses were gradually reduced, the submarine menace hung over Allied preparations for counteraction until the middle of 1943. In North Africa, Nazi forces under General Erwin Rommel (The Desert Fox) took Libya and most of North Africa from the English and were within 100 miles of Cairo and the Suez Canal. Meanwhile, the Germans had advanced deep into Russia, taking the wheat fields of the Ukraine and nearing the oil fields of the Caucuses. By the fall of 1941, German troops were within 40 miles of Moscow and the city was within eyesight.

From December 1941 when America entered the war until the summer of 1943, the army of the Soviet Union was the only army fighting the Germans on the European continent. The Soviet Union might have been over-run in the fall of 1941 had it not been for the onset of the brutal Russian winter that stopped the advance of the German army in its tracks. The Germany army had left Germany for the assault on the Soviet Union in the spring of 1941 with no winter coats, expecting the Soviets to be defeated by mid-summer. By October, the German army was engulfed in a winter cold front that plunged temperatures as low as 40 degrees below zero. German tanks, trucks, and other military vehicles would not start, fuel in some cases turned to jelly, and horses brought by the German army to pull heavy equipment froze to death along with humans. Some German soldiers perished when the metal helmets on top of their heads froze the blood on the top of their skulls.

The Russian winter bought the Soviets time to build their army. Entire factories in the western Soviet Union were dismantled and shipped east to the Ural Mountains for reassembly as the Germans advanced. By the time the weather relented in the spring of 1942, the Soviet army would be sufficient to resist the German advance.

In contrast, the United States army would not engage the Germans on the ground anywhere until November 1942, almost a year after Pearl Harbor. This lack of a second front would be a bone of contention between the Allies until "D-day" on June 6, 1944. During these two and a half years, Stalin would repeatedly complain that his allies were leaving him to fight the Germans himself. The Americans and British argued that if they tried to invade Europe before they were ready, they would suffer unacceptable casualty rates and were doomed to failure. Stalin, however, was unimpressed with the Allies' complaints since an estimated 28 million people would perish in the Soviet Union during the war compared to 321,000 Americans.

Though formally allied, the Soviets rarely shared military strategies with their American and British Allies, and Stalin feared throughout the war that the British and Americans might settle for a separate peace with Germany. The United States and Britain also failed to share their nuclear weapons research with the U.S.S.R.

ALLIED WAR STRATEGIES/DIVISIONS

Despite the fact that FDR had told Soviet Foreign Commissar Vyacheslav Molotov that a second front in Europe was possible in 1942, FDR and Churchill believed that no such invasion could be launched with success until the spring of 1943, since the United States would need a full year to achieve the necessary military readiness. Churchill wanted to avoid the catastrophic British casualties of World War I; otherwise, he feared that the British people might lose heart and surrender. United States General Eisenhower believed that a lack of a second front would doom the U.S.S.R.

In the spring of 1942, the German army began to move again and make progress on the Russian front. In May, Soviet Foreign Commissar Vyacheslav Molotov visited Washington and warned the Americans that unless at least 40 German divisions could be diverted, the Soviet effort suffered imminent collapse. Molotov again urged the Allies to open a Western Front in Europe, and Stalin again criticized the Allies for allowing him to fight the war by himself. In response, Churchill met with FDR in Washington in June and urged an invasion of North Africa instead of Europe. FDR reasoned that the United States was not ready for an invasion of Europe, and ordered the U.S. forces to join the British in defending North Africa.

THE TURNING POINT

Near the end of 1942, Allied forces around the globe assumed the offensive, which they never lost thereafter. November witnessed the victory on Guadalcanal. At about the same time the Russians, after a heroic defense of Stalingrad on the Volga, seized the offensive against the Germans. On November 8, 1942, 11 months after Pearl Harbor, American forces commanded by General Dwight D. Eisenhower invaded the French colonies of Morocco and Algeria with surprise landings from a giant armada of 500 warships and 350 transports and cargo ships. United States forces landed at Casablanca, Port Lyamtey, and Safi in Morrocco and Algiers. The Germans, before Eisenhower's landing, had gained control of the North African coast as far east as Egypt. The immediate purpose of the North African landings was to catch the German armies, under General Erwin Rommel, in a giant squeeze. Only a week before, General Bernard L. Montgomery's British Eighth Army had begun an offensive at El Alamein in Egypt. As Rommel's forces retreated westward before Montgomery along the North African coast in December and January, they backed up against the now well-established American forces in Algeria and Tunisia.

An agreement was signed with fascist Spain, which stated that Spain would not interfere in the Allied invasion of Spanish Morocco. In return, the United States supplied Spain with oil and purchased Spanish metal ores at a price above that of the free market. Churchill explained the Allied strategy by arguing, "My children, you are permitted in time of great danger to walk with the Devil until you have crossed the bridge."

For the first three months of the invasion, the Americans fought Vichy French troops who were in great disarray. The German-controlled Vichy French offered only scattered resistance, and total Allied casualties amounted to fewer than 2,000. The Americans made an agreement with Vichy France for it to withhold naval assistance from the Axis in exchange for United States shipments of coal, sugar, and cotton. The Americans also made an agreement with Vichy French Admiral Jean Darlan whereby the United States would recognize Darlan as the leader of Vichy France in Africa if Darlan would help with the Allied invasion. Darlan ordered his men to cease firing on the Allies as they approached the shore during the invasion of the North African coast. A supporter of the Free French Government of Charles De Gaulle, who had not known of Darlan's secret collaboration with the Allies, assassinated Darlan a few weeks later.

Simultaneously, while the Americans were invading in Morocco and Algeria, the British under Field Marshall Montgomery launched a counteroffensive against the Germans from Egypt. In their first major engagement with the Germans, however, the Americans were defeated and retreated from Kasserine Pass in Tunisia, February 14–22, 1943. The defeat at the hands of the Germans proved that the American troops were inexperienced and that American tanks were not superior to those of the Germans.

General George S. Patton was given command and regrouped the United States troops and, together with the British under Montgomery, drove the Germans from North Africa in May 1943. Rommel's once invincible Afrika Korps was no more, and German losses in Africa reached 350,000.

Though eventually successful, the North Africa campaign had been more costly than anticipated and had taken six months. This combined with the continued Atlantic sinking of Allied shipping caused FDR to delay his planned invasion of France that had been tentatively scheduled for May 1943.

In April 1943, the Germans unearthed and made public 10,000 Polish soldiers in a mass grave in the Katyn Forest of Poland. They had been killed by Stalin's troops in 1940. Stalin denied the atrocity, and the Americans chose to believe Stalin, even though he refused to approve a request by the Poles to have the international Red Cross investigate. Stalin then broke relations with the Polish government in exile in London.

EASTERN FRONT

While the United States and British were driving the Germans from North Africa, Stalin's army turned the tide against the Nazis in the winter of 1942–43. Hitler was within reach of his goal—the oil fields of the Caucuses—but ordered his army to destroy a Russian army that was dug in at Stalingrad. After three months of intense, costly, house-to-house fighting, 600,000 members of the cold and starving German army surrendered in February 1943. Hitler's army on the Eastern Front would never recover. After the defeat at Stalingrad, the German army would lose all major battles on the Eastern Front.

The German army lost perhaps another 500,000 troops in another urban siege at Leningrad. The siege of Leningrad began in January 1941 and lasted 872 days until January 1944. During that time, the city witnessed the starvation of 1.2 million civilians in Leningrad, the evacuation of another estimated 1.4 million, and the bombing of the children of Lenningrad by the Luftwaffe as the children were evacuated on sleighs across the frozen Lake Ladoga. The undersupplied Russians at Leningrad ate frozen human bodies, both German and Russian, drank human blood, and ate wallpaper paste after pealing the wallpaper off the walls. In spite of the unspeakable suffering, the Soviet city never fell to the Germans; and by the time the siege ended, the German effort on the Eastern Front was all but lost.

ITALY

Throughout 1943, even though the Red army had turned the tide in the East, Stalin continued to clamor for a Western Front; but the Allies delayed a planned invasion of France in favor of an invasion of Italy. The United States and British armies landed at Sicily on July 9, 1943, and secured the island on August 16. Then on September 3, British and United States forces attacked the Italian mainland. Mussolini's government quickly collapsed, and the dictator attempted to flee to Germany. Mussolini was eventually captured and executed by his own people; and his body put on public display in Milan where thousands of Italians could pass by daily to spit upon his remains.

Mussolini's successor, Marshall Pietro Badoglio, surrendered to the United States and Great Britain, thus signing a "separate peace" without the participation of the U.S.S.R. The United States and Britain had set a precedent in Italy that Stalin could use later. Essentially, the armies that liberated a country from the Germans would determine its postwar status.

Mussolini's empire had been a paper tiger built on show and bravado but with little real substance. Mussolini had once boasted that the Italian army would have a "million bayonets," but his army was never larger than 600,000; and the Second World War would not be won with bayonets. Italy's armor and air force also proved insufficient to the task; and opposing forces repeatedly repelled the Italians when not accompanied by the German army.

After the fall of Italy, Germany immediately shifted eight divisions to Italy and continued the fight on the rugged Italian peninsula. The American and British advance quickly ground to a halt in Italy due to the mountainous terrain. Rome would not fall to the Allies until June 4, 1944, two days before D-day, and the Germans would not be totally pushed out of Italy until 1945. The Italy invasion was so costly that it caused Churchill to urge FDR to delay the invasion of France for a year—a delay that angered Stalin, who again believed that the Allies were evading the true war and leaving the real battle up to the Russians.

SETTING THE GOALS OF WAR

In January 1943, soon after the consolidation of the Allied landings in North Africa, Roosevelt and Churchill met in the Moroccan city of Casablanca to discuss war aims. It was at this meeting that Roosevelt, after consulting with Churchill, announced that only unconditional surrender of Germany and Italy would be acceptable to the Allies. Later critics would argue that such uncompromising terms stiffened German resistance and prolonged the war. Certainly the Nazi propaganda machine played upon the argument that victory for the Allies spelled annihilation for the Germans; but at the time Roosevelt was careful to say that unconditional surrender "does not mean the destruction of the population of Germany, Italy, and Japan, but it does mean the destruction of the philosophies of those countries which are based on conquest and the subjugation of other people." Actually, it appears doubtful that the statement influenced German resistance very much. Certainly it produced exactly the opposite effect upon the Italians, who surrendered with alacrity nine months later.

Late 1943 saw several meetings of the Big Three powers. At the end of October the foreign ministers of the United States, Great Britain, and the Soviet Union met for the first time in Moscow. There it was agreed that the three nations would consult on "all matters relating to the surrender and disarmament" of their common enemies. They also recognized a need for setting "the earliest possible date" for the planning of an international organization of the "peace-loving states." Victory, in short, was already being anticipated.

En route to a meeting with Stalin in Teheran, Iran, Churchill and Roosevelt stopped at Cairo on November 22–26, 1943, to confer with the Nationalist Chinese leader Chiang Kai-shek. The three allies agreed to prosecute the Pacific war until Japan was forced into unconditional surrender. They also agreed that Manchuria, Formosa,

Stalin, Roosevelt, and Churchill on the portico of the Russian Embassy in Teheran, during a conference between November 28–December 1, 1943. *(Library of Congress)*

and the Pescadore Islands, earlier seized by Japan, should be returned to China after the war.

The Teheran Conference of November 28–December 1, 1943—the first personal encounter between Stalin, Churchill, and Roosevelt—resulted in few final decisions, although Roosevelt did secure from Stalin, as Hull had from Molotov a month earlier, a promise of Russian help against Japan soon after the end of the war against Germany. Stalin wanted Germany cut up into pieces after the war, and FDR wanted Germany to be ruled by the "Four Policemen"—the United States, Britain, Russia, and China—each with a sphere of influence. The "Four Policemen" idea was agreed upon in principle. The Big Three also agreed on a spring 1944 invasion of France.

Convinced of the need to have Stalin's friendship in the postwar world, Roosevelt did his best to charm the dictator and to dissipate Stalin's obvious suspicion of the two English-speaking allies. Stalin, on his part, was eager to get along well enough with his allies so that they would open up a second front in northern Europe, thereby relieving pressure on the Soviet Union, which was paying a fearsome price in civilian casualties because of the German invasion. Afterwards, FDR announced that he "got along fine" with Stalin and that the United States would "get along very well with him and the Russian people." At one point in the conference, Stalin suggested that after the war, the Allies should exterminate 50,000 German officers. Churchill was horrified; and FDR said that Americans could not accept such a figure, but the President added, "49,000 would be fine."

SUPPORT AT HOME

THE BATTLE FOR PRODUCTION

In a very real sense the turning of the tide of war from constant defeat to persistent victory was attributable to the astounding production that flooded from American factories and farms. At Teheran even Stalin acknowledged that without American production the Allies would not be winning the war.

Conversion of the economy to full wartime production did not really begin until after Pearl Harbor. During 1940 and 1941 Roosevelt had created several agencies, headed by businessmen and labor leaders, to speed up and coordinate production. When the Japanese struck, the level was still far from satisfactory. In January 1942, Roosevelt set up the War Production Board with Donald M. Nelson as chief; and though this more centralized control was the best arrangement yet, the organization of production did not achieve optimum efficiency until the creation of the Office of War Mobilization in May 1943 under James F. Byrnes, former Democratic senator from South Carolina.

While building up an armed force of some 15 million men and women, the United States undertook to expand its productive capacity to feed, clothe, supply, house, and transport this army as well as make sizable support contributions to the British and Russian armies spread around the globe. To meet this gargantuan assignment required not only the expenditure of billions of dollars but also the execution of a host of plans and arrangements. Priorities for materials had to be established, raw materials gathered, labor recruited to replace the men and women serving in the armed services, and civilian industries converted to war work. The automobile industry, for example, was given over entirely to the manufacture of tanks, trucks, and other military vehicles,

The aviation industry expanded its work force from 49,000 in 1939 to a peak of 2.1 million in November 1943, when it employed over 12 percent of the total number of workers in manufacturing. To keep supplies moving, the total tonnage of American shipping increased over five times between 1939 and May 1945. Whole new industries sometimes had to be created. The production of synthetic rubber was inaugurated when the Japanese cut off the major source of natural rubber from Southeast Asia. The volume of industrial production increased so rapidly that by October 1943 some cutbacks were made to prevent surpluses.

Between 1939 and 1946 agricultural production increased some 30 percent, even though the labor force on farms fell more than five percent. As a result, not only was the United States able to keep the armed forces well supplied with food, but the nation as a whole ate better than ever before, and the Allies were able to draw upon the American larder during the war and after.

In order to gear up for this level of productivity, the federal government took several steps; one of which, in particular, was to have long-term consequences. In the first place, the government suspended antitrust prosecutions, which had been in abeyance during the NRA period but then had been reinvigorated during the late 1930s. Secondly, it instituted cost-plus contracts, whereby firms with defense contracts were guaranteed a profit—their costs plus a profit—in order to offer incentives to firms to convert to production for the military. Both of these decisions meant that big business grew bigger during the war; and during the Vietnam era, critics of United States foreign policy pointed to the cost-plus contracts as a key element in launching the military-industrial complex.

CONTROLLING INFLATION

Simply because there was so much money and so few consumer goods, the control of prices was a major problem. Essentially, prices were kept under control by two methods—increased taxes and a price freeze. The Office of Price Administration, which was in charge of controlling inflation, failed to put a tight lid on prices until late in 1942 so that some prices, notably those of foods, rose alarmingly through most of that year. Thereafter, however, controls were more effective.

Because Congress would not follow through on legislation, taxation was not so steep as the administration had hoped. Only the Revenue Act of 1942, which increased corporate, private income, and excise taxes, took much of a bite out of civilian purchasing power. In that act, for the first time, the income tax reached into the pockets of the average citizen. About 50 million income-tax payers were recorded in 1943 as compared with 13 million in 1941. Congress refused to heed Roosevelt's demand for a further increase in taxes in 1943. Yet in spite of government spending at a rate as high as $100 million a year, about 40 percent of the ongoing cost of the war was paid for out of taxes, a proportion which had never been achieved in any previous American war.

CIVIL LIBERTIES

Fearful of sabotage, early in 1942 President Roosevelt issued Executive Order 9066, which authorized the rounding up of some 110,000 Japanese living on the West Coast, even though some two thirds of them were American citizens. Although no specific acts of sabotage could be charged against them, these people were held in "relocation centers" in the interior for most of the war. The camps were essentially POW quality, and people were housed together in buildings that contained little besides bunks. One six-year-old Japanese-American boy probably summed up the situation best when he repeatedly asked his mother, "Mother, when are we going back to America?"

Meanwhile their property was placed in the hands of often incompetent or unfriendly custodians. This action of the government, though generally supported at the time and subsequently upheld by the Supreme Court, was later condemned as an indefensible act of racism since mere Japanese ancestry was the basis for the internment. Ironically, the Japanese in Hawaii, who made up a much larger proportion of the population, were not affected by the order.

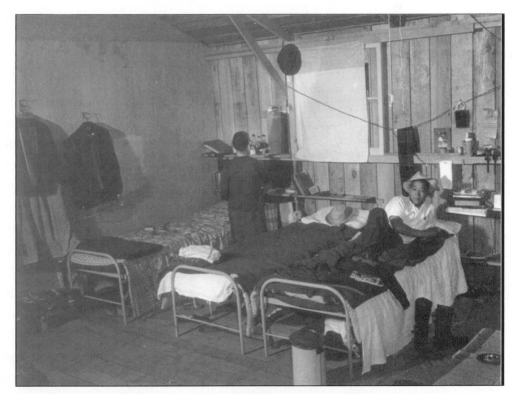

Japanese-American World War II relocation center *(Library of Congress)*

The best-known resister to the executive order was Fred Korematsu, who lived till 2005, long enough to receive the Presidential Medal of Freedom in 1998 from President Bill Clinton and to become a civil rights icon. Sent to a camp, Topaz, in the Utah desert, Korematsu began a legal case against internment, *Korematsu v. United States*, a case that made it all the way to the United States Supreme Court where he lost. Over time, however, American public opinion swung around to the position that internment had been a grave injustice, and Korematsu became a hero.

It should also be noted that despite the pain of internment one of the most decorated units in the war, the 442nd Battalion, was comprised of Japanese Americans. Fighting in the European theater, the battalion established a distinguished record of courage under fire.

No comparable interference with civil liberty was taken against Americans of German or Italian ancestry, nor did the population at large indulge in irrational attacks on Germans like those that had marred the domestic record during the First World War; but *Native* minorities, however, did suffer. Large numbers of whites attacked blacks in Detroit in 1943, and whites in other cities resorted to violence against blacks. During the last two years of the war, white servicemen and civilians also harassed young Mexican-Americans in the Los Angeles area in what came to be called the "zoot-suit riots," after the flamboyant styles worn by many Mexican-American youths. Later, these incidents were seen to mark the beginning of overt Mexican-American self-consciousness, which by the late 1960s became the Chicano movement.

SEEDS OF A MORE JUST SOCIETY

For all the suffering and death the war brought about and the violations of the civil liberties of loyal Japanese Americans, it also created substantial new opportunity for other disadvantaged groups. To cite two brief examples, Chinese Americans in San Francisco, heretofore almost invariably confined to employment in Chinatown itself, began to be able to get defense work; and unmarried Mexican American women in Los Angeles, hitherto closely chaperoned by their families, obtained gainful employment and more freedom. That both of these examples come from California is not a coincidence. The Golden State, more than any other state in the country, was transformed by its defense industries, aircraft in southern California and ship-building in northern California.

The two groups for whom the gains were the most significant were women—both white women and women of color—and African Americans. We begin with women. Because so many millions of men serving in the armed forces created an enormous manpower short-age. To meet the need, some 6.5 million women went to work, including 3 million who were married. Until this point there had been a strong taboo against the employment of married women, but the taboo never had the same force after the war. Moreover, the women who already had jobs were often able to move up to better jobs, due to the demand for more workers. This was especially beneficial for black women, many of whom had been employable only as maids. During the war, they could move into factory jobs. The United States government encouraged the employment of women in the defense industry with "Rosie the Riveter" propaganda. Not only were millions of women employed outside the home, but also and for the first time in American history on this scale, tens of thousands joined the military. There were 140,000 in the Women's Army Corps (WAC), 100,000 in the navy unit called WAVES (Women Assigned for Volunteer Emergency Service), and 23,000 in the Marine Corps Women's Reserve.

Though the war gave so many women a taste of gainful employment and greater opportunity, it also created many difficulties. Housewives had a hard time feeding their families the food to which those families were accustomed because of the rationing of food, for example. Childcare was often nearly impossible to obtain. Schools in areas with defense plants were usually overcrowded, sometimes on triple shifts. Although the war led to a great increase in the number of women in unions, the male-led unions often treated their new female

Women's Army Corps (WAC) *(Library of Congress)*

members less than fairly. On balance, however, most historians believe that World War II was truly transformative for American women.

Transformative is also a good word to describe the impact on African Americans. After World War I, though black troops had fought bravely in their segregated units, they came home to race riots in several American cities—Chicago, East St. Louis, and Tulsa saw the worst—and to a general lack of appreciation for their sacrifices. As war seemed increasingly likely in the months before Pearl Harbor, African American leaders determined not to repeat the mistakes of an earlier generation by rallying around the flag and then having nothing to show for the patriotic effort by their people. Led by A. Philip Randolph of the Sleeping Car Porters, African Americans threatened to march on Washington on July 1, 1941, to demand redress of their grievances. When attempts to persuade them to call off the march failed, President Roosevelt yielded to the pressure and issued Executive Order 8802 forbidding racial discrimination by recipients of federal contracts, setting up the Fair Employment Practices Commission to monitor hiring practices. Nevertheless, armed forces remained segregated, however.

As was the case for white women, there were abundant new employment opportunities for black men and women, but in this case, the discrimination by unions was even more flagrant than it was for white women. Unions took the dues of black people, for example, but sometimes relegated them to a separate category in which they received fewer benefits from union membership than did whites. In spite of these problems, overall, the war against Adolf Hitler, the arch racist, created a powerful momentum for social change, fed by activism such as in the March on Washington movement. Almost as soon as the war ended, President Harry Truman issued an order desegregating the armed forces; and in the 1950s, as we shall soon learn, a civil rights revolution took place.

THE ELECTION OF 1944

In the midst of the Second World War, as in the Civil War, the nation conducted a presidential election. The Republicans, who after Pearl Harbor strongly supported the war effort, now entertained high hopes for victory since in the congressional elections of 1942 they had gained 47 seats in the House and nine in the Senate, dropping the Democratic majority in the House to its lowest level since Roosevelt first took office. Prominently considered for the Republican nomination was Thomas E. Dewey, who had gained national renown as the first Republican since 1920 to be elected governor of New York State. Dewey spoke for the same internationalist wing of the party that had supported Wendell L. Willkie in 1940, but he did not suffer from Willkie's close identification with the administration. Moreover, Dewey, unlike Willkie, enjoyed the support of the professionals in the party.

As a result, the convention nominated Dewey on the first ballot—with only a single dissenting vote. John A. Bricker of Ohio, who as a Midwesterner and an isolationist brought balance to the ticket, received the vice-presidential nomination. The party platform was internationalist in content, but the convention's enthusiasm for Bricker betrayed the persistence of isolationism in Republican ranks.

Roosevelt waited until just a week before the Democratic convention met in July before he indicated his willingness to seek the nomination for a fourth term. The real battle in the convention then raged around the choice of his running mate. Roosevelt's own choice, though not a strong one, was incumbent Vice-President Henry Wallace, but Wallace was unacceptable to conservatives within the party. The President's second choice was James F. Byrnes, the efficient and capable Director of the Office of War Mobilization. Labor leaders and liberals in general, however, opposed Byrnes as anti-black and perhaps anti-labor. As a consequence, before the convention actually voted, party leaders and the President had decided upon Harry S Truman as a compromise candidate. Truman, a senator from Missouri, was chairman of a Senate investigating committee that had gained national acclaim for its honest and efficient policing of government war contracts.

His head filled with plans for the postwar settlement, Roosevelt's heart was not in the hustings. Nevertheless, early in the campaign he made one of the most effective political speeches of his career; and by the vigor of his few campaign speeches effectively countered Republican charges that he was physically incapable of enduring another term of office. As usual Roosevelt won, though by a smaller margin in the popular vote than ever before, receiving 25.6 million votes to Dewey's 22 million. The Democrats retained control of both houses, gaining 24 new seats in the House of Representatives.

PUSHING TOWARD VICTORY

ISLAND HOPPING IN THE PACIFIC

When the last Japanese resistance ended on Guadalcanal in February 1943, the United States began the long push northward toward Japan. The task was essentially one for the navy and the marines since the Japanese were dug in on a multitude of small islands scattered throughout the western Pacific. One by one through 1943, Japanese island fortresses fell to air and amphibious attack, often only after terrible loss of life—the central Solomons in the summer, eastern New Guinea in the fall, and the Gilbert Islands in the late fall. As the great naval task forces of the United States moved northward, other Japanese outposts were bypassed, their garrisons still intact. Cut off from supplies, they would eventually have to surrender without bloodshed. By the end of June 1944, the capture of Saipan in the Marianas placed the air force's giant new B-29 bomber within easy striking distance of Tokyo itself. Systematic bombing of Japan's home islands from Saipan began in November 1944.

THE INVASION OF EUROPE

Meanwhile, preparations were well under way for the long-awaited frontal assault upon Hitler's "Fortress Europe." Ever since the middle of 1942 Stalin had been urging the Western allies to open a second front; but aside from the invasion of Italy, which was obviously peripheral, their response had been confined to bombings of the Third Reich. Nevertheless, by the middle of 1943 these air attacks were formidable. In one week in July 1943, for example, the combined British and American air forces dropped 8,000 tons of bombs on Hamburg, devastating three quarters of the city. Later, 50 other large German cities each received a similar pounding. More than 300,000 Germans died in these uninterrupted raids, which by 1944 were deliberately aimed at workers' homes, as well as factories in an effort to destroy German morale as well as German industrial capacity. In one raid, Allied bombers killed an estimated 135,000 German civilians in the incendiary bombing of the German city of Dresden. Though the air campaign was devastating for Germany, the raids also cost the Anglo-American air forces thousands of bombers and their crews.

On December 6, 1943, in appointing Dwight D. Eisenhower Supreme Allied Commander of the West, the Combined Chiefs of Staff told him, "You will enter the continent of Europe and, in conjunction with other Allied Nations, undertake operations aimed at the heart of Germany and the destruction of her armed forces." For months before the actual invasion began and while supplies, shipping, and men were being accumulated in England, Allied planes bombed and strafed German positions along the Channel coast. The Nazis could not help but know in general what was impending; but thanks to superb Allied counterintelligence, they misjudged the exact point of the attack on D-day, June 6, 1944. On June 5, three divisions of American paratroopers

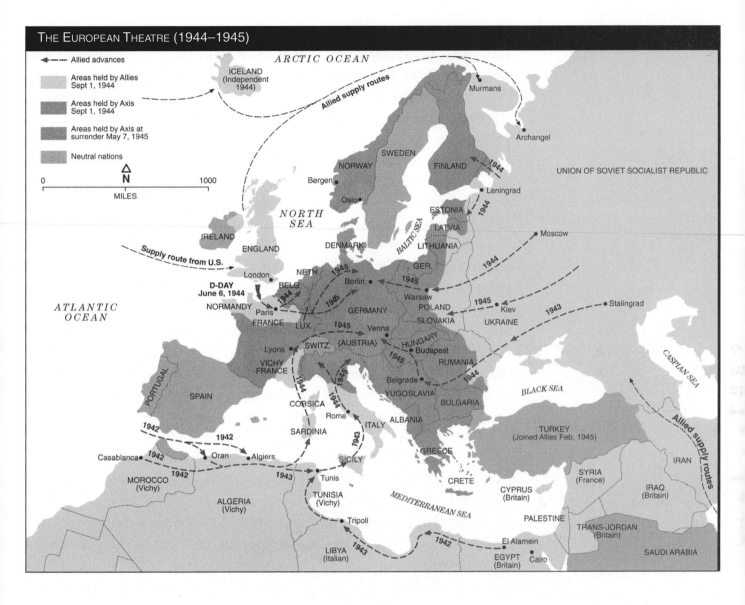

THE EUROPEAN THEATRE (1944–1945)

◄--- Allied advances

Areas held by Allies Sept 1, 1944

Areas held by Axis Sept 1, 1944

Areas held by Axis at surrender May 7, 1945

Neutral nations

0   N   1000
MILES

were dropped behind the German lines where they disrupted German communications and caused some general confusion. On June 6, 4,000 ships landed troops and supplies on the beaches of Normandy, France in the largest invasion in history. The main concentration of Allied troops was north of the Cotentin Peninsula in Normandy, where the massive invasion force quickly established five connected beachheads. Within two weeks, a million troops landed and moved inland. The United States suffered heavier casualties than anticipated because thousands of troops drowned in the rough seas. Furthermore, United States intelligence had missed German defenses at Omaha Beach where most of the United States casualties occurred; consequently, Eisenhower and the Allied commanders were sharply criticized for attempting the invasion in bad weather and for the intelligence failures. Nevertheless, by the end of July both the British and the American armies had broken out of their coastal positions and were striking north and west. On August 15, a new American army invaded southern France, and on August 25 Paris fell to French and American troops. Parisians greeted their American liberators with sweets and flowers in one of the greatest civilian celebrations of the war.

Concomitantly with the Allied invasion of June 6, the Russians launched a broad offensive on the eastern front, bringing their armies to the Baltic and into Poland and Romania by the end of the summer. By late autumn of 1944 the armies of the Grand Alliance were poised to strike into Germany from both east and west.

After the liberation of Paris, however, the Allied advance slowed due to the size of the operation that stretched from Switzerland to the Netherlands. British Field Marshall Montgomery argued for a massive assault and "Spearhead" drive to Berlin that could rapidly end the war. Eisenhower, however, felt that such a move was too risky and could leave thousands of Allied troops cut off and lost if it failed. Instead, Ike opted for a general advance along the entire 500-mile front.

Although the Allied and German armies on the western front were roughly equal in size in late 1944, the Allies had 20 times as many tanks and almost total control of the air. To compound matters further for the Germans, since they were retreating on the eastern front at the same time, they could not transfer resources from the east to the west. The Allied victory was merely a matter of time.

Despite the overwhelming land and air power being brought against it, Germany made two desperate attempts to forestall the inevitable. The first was a new secret weapon, a fast-flying rocket bomb, the V-2. (The V-1 or "buzz bomb," used somewhat earlier, was a jet-driven aerial bomb and not a rocket.) The first V-2s landed in England in August. Traveling faster than the speed of sound, the V-2 was impossible to intercept, and it hit without warning. Before Allied bombers could destroy the launching bases, the murderous V-2 attacks killed some 8,000 Britons

The other desperate German effort was a great counteroffensive mounted on December 16, 1944, against the American forces in the Ardennes forest of Belgium. In the fall and winter of 1944, bad weather slowed the Allied advance, and cloud cover rendered Allied air superiority almost useless on the battlefield. The adverse weather conditions provided Germany an opportunity to launch one last counteroffensive. The Battle of the Bulge, as it came to be called, caught the Americans by surprise and forced them to retreat. The offensive was planned by Hitler himself and was directed at the center of the Allied lines on the western front. The offensive was designed to divide the allied forces in two and capture the Allied fuel depot at Antwerp in Northern Belgium.

The Germans advanced rapidly using newly constructed tanks without fear of Allied aircraft because of the cloud cover. The United States suffered 77,000 casualties in the Battle of the Bulge, their largest losses in the European theater. Despite the casualties, the Allies prevented the Germans from taking the massive Allied fuel depot at Antwerp before the weather cleared just enough for Allied aircraft to bomb the German advance. Without the Allied fuel depot at Antwerp, the Germans did not have enough fuel to continue the offensive, and many of the Germans were forced to abandon their tanks and walk back to Germany.

During the battle, German morale suffered a setback at Bastogne, Belgium, where the heavily armored German Army surrounded a company of Americans. The Germans demanded surrender, but the Allied commander at Bastogne, General Tony McAuliffe, sent back a one word reply scrawled on a piece of paper—"Nuts." The Germans did not know how to interpret the response and were demoralized that the Americans did not give up when faced with certain death. The troops at Bastogne were saved by Patton's troops three days later. After the end of the German advance in the Battle of the Bulge on January 16, 1945, Germany would only retreat.

As a result of the Battle of the Bulge, however, the whole Allied timetable in the west was set back over six weeks. The first Allied troops did not cross the Rhine until March 7, 1945, when soldiers of the American Ninth Armored Division unexpectedly took the bridge of Remagen, one of the few remaining Rhine bridges. By that time the Russians stood on the banks of the Oder River, less than 45 miles from Berlin.

THE BIG THREE AT YALTA

As the coils of Allied power tightened around Germany, Roosevelt, Stalin, and Churchill met February 4–11, 1945, at Yalta, a resort town in the Crimea. Desirous of securing Russian aid against the Japanese and of bringing the Soviet Union into a new world organization, Roosevelt did his best to assure Stalin that the United States recognized Russia's special interests in Europe. It was agreed that the new government of Poland would be the one established at Lublin by the Russians and not the one in exile in London; but it was also agreed that final recognition of the Lublin government would await "free and unfettered elections." Also, pending the signing of a German peace, Poland would receive German territory to compensate for portions of eastern Poland taken by Russia in 1939.

Final dinner held in connection with the conference at Yalta, Crimean Peninsula, Russia, February 11, 1945. *(AP Associated Press)*

The Americans also favorably received Russian insistence upon a large figure for German reparations, although no final commitment was made. Stalin asked for and received cession of the Kurile Islands from Japan and concessions and bases in China. In return, Stalin agreed to participate in the new world organization and to enter the war against Japan within three months after the defeat of Germany.

Despite later criticism, the so-called concessions by Roosevelt do not seem excessive in the context of February 1945. Poland, after all, was in Russian hands, and Russian military assistance against Japan then seemed eminently desirable and worth the granting of Japanese territory to the Soviet Union. Furthermore, Chiang Kai-shek later consented to the concessions Roosevelt agreed to support in Stalin's behalf. Furthermore, it must be remembered, the Soviet Union lost an estimated total of 28 million lives, both military and civilian deaths. Hence Stalin could negotiate on the basis of widespread knowledge of his country's terrible price for Allied victory.

THE END OF THE THIRD REICH

Soon after the Yalta Conference, on April 12, 1945, Franklin D. Roosevelt died of a cerebral hemorrhage at Warm Springs, Georgia. A surprised and shaken Harry S Truman, who had only been Vice President for one month and had not been involved in any of the war strategy sessions, assumed the presidency the same day. Roosevelt's death plunged the nation and the peoples of the Allied world into sorrow, but the military machine he had helped to forge drove on to total victory over Germany and Italy.

With the Russians already fighting in flaming, bombed-out Berlin, Adolf Hitler on April 30 committed suicide in his underground bunker beneath the Reichs chancellery. Faithful guards burned his body. Nazi Germany outlasted its founder by no more than a week. On May 2, Admiral Karl Doenitz, whom

Harry S. Truman *(Library of Congress)*

Hitler had named as his successor, tried to surrender to the British while continuing the war against the Russians; but Field Marshal Bernard L. Montgomery contemptuously rejected this last attempt to divide the Western and Eastern allies. Germany surrendered unconditionally to all the Allied powers on the morning of May 7, 1945.

American forces under Patton advanced rapidly and could have beaten the Soviets to Berlin, but were halted by Eisenhower at the Elbe River. Eisenhower reasoned that the taking of Berlin would entail house-to-house fighting that would needlessly take thousands of American lives. Consequently, Ike left Berlin to the Russians. Estimated casualty figures from the Red Army's assault on Berlin proved Eisenhower correct. An estimated 300,000 Soviet troops died in the assault on Berlin, almost equivalent to the number lost by the United States in the entire war. Afterwards, Berlin devolved into chaos as Stalin allowed his troops three days of plunder, with the result that there were 100,000 reported rapes, countless murders of civilians, and a rampage of looting and mayhem in the Soviet sack of Berlin.

HOLOCAUST

As Allied troops overran Germany, they uncovered the Nazi death camps and confirmed the rumors that had reached the United States as early as 1942. As many as 14 million people (6 million Jews) died during the Holocaust, including an estimated 90 percent of Europe's Jewish population. FDR had dismissed the intelligence reports on the death camps as exaggerated propaganda from the Jewish Lobby. As early as 1943, the Jewish Lobby in the United States had pushed for the bombing of the Nazi death camps. FDR had refused, however, on the grounds that bombing the camps took men, planes, ammunition, and resources away from the defeat of the German Army, which took precedent. During the war, both the United States and England had denied immigration to most Jewish refugees fleeing Europe as the U.S. Department of State feared that German spies could hide among the Jewish refugees.

Upon uncovering the death camps, however, even the most hardened American soldiers were aghast at what they encountered. The camps were teeming with unfed human skeletons packed into crowded housing in inhuman conditions, awaiting execution. By the end of the war, the Nazis had made killing people in the camps into a scientific study of efficiency. Humans were brought into the camps in crowded railroad boxcars, jammed into the camps to await execution, stripped of all their possessions, and herded into buildings where they were killed with poison gas. The bodies were then burned in massive ovens. The Nazi death camp at Auschwitz accomplished the record for efficiency by exterminating 9,000 people in just one day.

The Nazis had adopted the death camp strategy after simply machine-gunning people proved to be too labor intensive (the bodies had to be buried, some people had to be chased down as they ran from machine gun fire, and German soldiers suffered from resulting mental problems). The Nazis attempted to remedy part of the problem by forcing non-Jewish townspeople in conquered territories to be the triggermen; but the excessive labor problem remained, thus leading to the death camp as the "final solution."

Evidently, it had been Hitler's intent to kill every Jewish person in Europe, if not the world. The crime was so heinous that Allied troops could hardly believe their eyes when they encountered the Holocaust operation. General Eisenhower ordered media and cameras to the death camps to document the atrocities and ordered that German townspeople be forced to tour the death camps to see what their country had done. Eisenhower remarked that such measures were necessary because the crime was so great that the world would later be unable to believe it if it were not well documented. Unfortunately, his words have proven prophetic.

THE UNITED NATIONS AND POTSDAM

With Roosevelt's death, President Truman was left to complete the task his predecessor had considered preeminent—the convocation of the representatives of the Allied and other nations at San Francisco to draw up a charter for a new world security organization. All 50 countries signed the completed Charter of the United Nations on June 26, 1945. Despite America's long history of isolationism and its rejection of the League of Nations after World War I, the Senate agreed to American membership in the United Nations after only six days of debate and with only two dissenting votes.

President Truman was also called upon to represent the United States at the last conference of the Big Three powers. Since no final decisions on Germany had been made at Yalta and since the United States still wanted Russia's support against Japan, Truman, Stalin, and Churchill (later replaced by Clement Attlee, representing the newly elected Labour government in Britain) met at Potsdam, outside ruined Berlin, on July 17, 1945.

Differences between East and West were more evident than before. Wrangling frequently occurred over details and the meaning of previous agreements. The two Western allies were deeply suspicious of Russian policy in Poland, which Stalin seemed intent upon making a Russian satellite despite agreement on its independence at Yalta. Stalin also insisted that the new border between Germany and Poland was final although at Yalta the border had been considered only temporary. Furthermore, Stalin now insisted that the tentative agreements on reparations were final.

All three powers agreed that Germany should remain united; but for purposes of temporary military administration, each of the three powers (later France was added) would occupy a separate zone. Berlin itself was to be occupied jointly by the victors. Even though Russia had not yet entered the war in the Pacific, the conference issued a demand for Japan's unconditional surrender. The Allies also agreed that after the war the leading Nazis would be tried as war criminals by an international tribunal.

Truman had attended the conference with the intention of dictating terms to the Soviets. Unknown to Stalin, the United States had performed its first successful nuclear test just 12 days prior to the Potsdam conference, and armed with the knowledge of the bomb, Truman entered the negotiations with confidence. Truman quickly discovered, however, that Stalin was not so easily manipulated. After the conference, Truman remarked that Stalin was "one smart as hell s.o.b."

THE END OF THE WAR WITH JAPAN

As the European war reached its climax in the summer and fall of 1944, the American air force and navy moved ever closer to the Japanese home islands. Admiral Chester Nimitz in command of the Pacific fleet wanted to use all available military strength to reach Iwo Jima, an island near enough to mainland Japan so that fighter escorts could protect bombers. He reasoned that with the conquest of the mainland all other Japanese-held areas would have to surrender.

General Douglas MacArthur, the commanding general of the Pacific area, however, wanted to divert planes and ships to reconquer the Philippines and make good on his promise from 1942 of "I shall return"; and he convinced the Joint Chiefs of Staff to divide American forces so as to pursue both policies simultaneously but necessarily, more slowly. In February 1945, the reconquest of the Philippines was completed and the island of Iwo Jima, 500 miles from Japan, was conquered in a bloody assault. On Iwo Jima the Japanese continued their policy of fighting to the last man, with the result that 50,000 Japanese soldiers were killed. American casualties were also heavy, with an estimated 20,000 killed or wounded. The action on Iwo Jima provided the most reproduced image in the history of photography, the raising of the American flag on Mt. Suribachi, a picture taken by Associated Press photographer Joe Rosenthal. In the Philippines, the Americans witnessed the first Japanese use of Kamikaze attacks (suicide bombers) at Leyte Gulf. There is no Japanese tactic that would be more damaging to the United States Navy for the rest of the war than the Kamikaze attacks, both in terms of lives lost and ships sunk. Kamikaze attacks were also damaging to American morale since it provided a vivid illustration of the Japanese dedication to defending their homeland. Ultimately, the Japanese would lose 3,500 pilots of planes and small submarines to Kamikaze attacks.

On March 9, B-29s from Saipan dropped a record load of firebombs on Tokyo, igniting the wooden and paper houses of the city. The resulting holocaust was rivaled only by that at Hiroshima five months later. The Japanese had dispersed their manufacturing into private homes in residential neighborhoods so as to avoid detection. Not knowing where to bomb in order to target Japanese industrial capacity, the United States made the decision to destroy entire Japanese cities with firebombing. In the Tokyo bombing, 16 square miles of densely populated Tokyo were destroyed, resulting in the deaths of 250,000 Japanese citizens in one night. The deaths in the firebombing of Tokyo would exceed those produced by either atomic bomb. Another 250,000 Japanese citizens would die in American firebombing of other Japanese cities, so that over half a million Japanese total would die in the incendiary bombings. Some historians have later condemned the attacks as atrocities, but there was little protest in the United States at the time. From Pearl Harbor to the Japanese surrender, the dominant view of the Japanese in America was one that considered the Japanese to be treacherous vermin, almost subhuman, and certainly deranged and evil. The image was reinforced by the surprise attack at Pearl Harbor while Japanese diplomats were pretending to negotiate in Washington, the fighting to the last man mentality in the island-hopping campaign, the Bataan Death March, deplorable Japanese treatment of POWs, and the Kamikaze attacks. Therefore, there was little remorse over the killing of such enemy civilians.

Even as fierce fighting continued in the Philippines, the Americans invaded Okinawa, close to the home islands. Once again, as at Tarawa in the Gilberts and Iwo Jima in the Bonins, the Japanese dug in and fought virtually to the last man, while Kamikaze hurled their planes at the Americans, sinking 34 ships of the invading fleet. By the end of the campaign in June 1945, some 110,000 Japanese had died on Okinawa. Fewer than 8,000 had been taken prisoner. The 49,000 American casualties were the heaviest of any engagement in the Pacific theater and a grisly prefiguring of the costs to be expected from the contemplated assault on the Japanese home islands.

ATOMIC BOMB AND SURRENDER

That dreaded encounter, however, never came. At 8:15 A.M. on August 6, 1945, a lone B-29, the *Enola Gay,* dropped a single atomic bomb ("Little Boy") on the industrial city of Hiroshima. Hiroshima was chosen because it was one of the few major Japanese cities that had not yet been fire bombed by the United States. The tremendous blast waves, fire waves, and radiation leveled 60 percent of the city and killed over 70,000 people outright; 10,000 more were never found. Another 100,000 people would die over the next year due to excessive exposure to radiation. Because the bewildered Japanese did not surrender immediately, a second nuclear bomb ("Fat Man") was dropped on Nagasaki on August 9, also with equally devastating consequences. Nagasaki was chosen actually as the bomber's fourth alternate target on August 9 because the first three cities on the pilot's list could not be found due to heavy cloud cover. Just before the pilot had to turn back due to low fuel supplies, he spotted Nagasaki through a hole in the clouds and released his deadly cargo. The bomb landed on the edge of town and was, therefore, less effective than the Hiroshima bomb. 25,000 people died in-

The atomic bombing of Nagasaki, Japan, on August 9, 1945. (*Library of Congress*)

stantly, however, and another 60,000 would eventually die of radiation and other injuries from the Nagasaki bomb. A day before, on August 8, the Soviet Union had fulfilled its promise by declaring war on Japan and invading Manchuria.

Japan's leaders, recognizing that their country faced certain destruction, convened their Diet and debated surrender. Given that the United States had dropped two atomic bombs in three days and the Japanese had no way of knowing that the United States could not drop another bomb every three days (the United States expected another bomb to be ready in six weeks), the choice faced by the government was one of either surrender or suicide. Conservative hawks in the Japanese government favored continuation of the fight to the last man mentality under which the Japanese military had been operating throughout the war. Their opposition, however, reasoned that there was nothing honorable in continuing the fight since the United States had proven that they could kill every man, woman, and child in Japan with no casualties of their own. The Japanese government was deadlocked over the surrender decision, and the Emperor Hirohito was asked to intervene and break the deadlock. The Emperor mournfully favored surrender. The Japanese government, heeding the emperor's pleas that no more lives be sacrificed, unconditionally surrendered on August 14 on the condition that Hirohito would nominally remain Emperor. The official surrender took place on September 2 aboard the battleship Missouri anchored in Tokyo Bay.

The story of the development of the nuclear bomb began in August 1939 when President Roosevelt received a letter from Albert Einstein informing him that the splitting (fission) of the nucleus of an atom of uranium seemed possible. The consequent release of energy, Einstein wrote, would be enormous. Fearful that Nazi scientists might develop such a bomb, the administration in 1940 began the Manhattan Project under the direction of Robert Oppenheimer to try to beat the Germans to it. Working secretly in a squash court under the stands of the football stadium at the University of Chicago, a team of scientists under the direction of Leo Szilard, successfully constructed the first atomic pile in December 1942. Once it had been shown that a nuclear reaction could be controlled, the engineers took over—constructing plants at Oak Ridge, Tennessee, and Hanford, Washington, for the manufacture of materials needed for assembling a bomb. After more than $2 billion had been invested in the great gamble, the first test of the bomb took place successfully on July 16, 1945, in the desert outside Alamogordo, New Mexico.

In the "Trinity Test," as it was called, no one knew exactly what to expect. Physicist Enrico Fermi was taking bets that the bomb would create a chain reaction that would incinerate the atmosphere, a bet that would have been difficult to collect had he been correct. Fermi also estimated that the blast would be 10 kilotons (equal to 10,000 tons of TNT); but after the blast, Fermi determined from measurements of blown scraps of paper he had placed on the ground that the blast was 20 Kilotons. The blast turned much of the gypsum New Mexico sand near the epicenter into transparent glass-like crystals. Generals on the site had soldiers collect the crystals to make necklaces for their wives, not knowing that the crystals would be radioactive and deadly (Manhattan Project scientists quickly put a stop to this folly).

In spite of the size of the project and the fact that literally thousands of people had been involved in the making of the bomb in one way or another, the secret of the project had been kept so well that Harry Truman did not learn of it until he became President upon Roosevelt's untimely death. At that point, Secretary of War Henry L. Stimson informed the former Missouri Senator of the Manhattan Project.

A crowd of people in Times Square on V-J Day during the announcement of the Japanese surrender in 1945. (*Library of Congress*)

The job of building the bomb was so complicated and time-consuming that the two bombs used against Japan were the total world supply. Later it was learned that the Germans had lagged far behind the United States and Great Britain in the development of nuclear fission and probably would not have been able to construct a bomb for months or perhaps years. Not only had Hitler's racist policies driven brilliant Jewish scientists out of Germany, but Hitler had also diverted scientists from his nuclear and missile programs into less productive efforts. One was to develop a giant lens that could be used to incinerate England, as one would burn insects with a magnifying glass, and the other—a sophisticated bell that could be used to kill the British with sound. The bell project did make enough progress that the Germans could use it to kill mice in a bathtub; but in retrospect, it appears that Hitler should have diverted these scientists to his nuclear project. No matter who made the first bomb, however, once its devastating power had been released, the world could not be the same again. Thus, simultaneously with the coming of peace, the world entered the age of nuclear power—an age that would be at once an era of promise and of fear.

In the more than half century since the dropping of the bomb, historians and other   American citizens have debated whether or not President Truman made the right decision when he authorized its use. It clearly ended the war with Japan sooner than might otherwise have been the case, thus saving an estimated one million American lives and perhaps five million Japanese—but at a fearful cost. Even some of the scientists who had developed it, most notably Leo Szilard, were queasy about its use, urging that a bomb be dropped as a demonstration before being employed against human beings. Furthermore, many critics have questioned the necessity for the second bomb dropped on Nagasaki. Why not wait a little longer for the Japanese to respond? Others point out that the Japanese had sent peace delegations to Sweden and Moscow and argue that the United States might not have been able to negotiate surrender with Japan if the Japanese had known about the bomb. These are issues of more than academic interest, especially in the early twenty-first century when the question of nuclear proliferation is so consequential.

Truman, who ultimately had the final decision on the bomb, decided against any such demonstration because such a demonstration would remove the element of surprise; and Truman believed "surprise" was necessary for maximum psychological impact. Furthermore, Truman believed that it would be embarrassing to the United States if the bomb used in any such demonstration were a dud; and such a disaster could only prolong the war. Truman also believed that the damage to the Japanese caused by the bomb would provide better leverage against the Russians in post-war negotiations. As to whether or not the bomb should be used at all, Truman never seriously considered that. Truman believed that the bomb could and should be used just like any other weapon that had been developed. The use of the bomb, Truman believed, could shorten the war and ultimately save lives, both American and Japanese.

Although it is true that the Japanese had already sent peace delegations to Sweden and Moscow before the atomic bombs were dropped, the fact that the Japanese Diet was deadlocked over the decision to surrender after the United States dropped the bombs suggests that the Japanese were not going to be persuaded by a nonmilitary demonstration. After all, those that favored peace in Japan were not the majority as of August 6th. After the surrender decision, there was a rash of suicides in Japan among the hawkish members of the government and the top Japanese military leaders. For these men, incineration by atomic bomb may have been preferable to the disembowelment they ultimately experienced at their own hands.

THE CULTURE OF THE POSTWAR ERA

(AP Photo)

THE RISE OF THE CONSUMER SOCIETY

THE PROSPEROUS AMERICAN

The hallmark of life in the United States during most of the 35 years after 1945 was the expanding prosperity of the ordinary citizen. The Great Depression had not ended immediately, of course, and even at the conclusion of the period, in the 1970s, millions of Americans, particularly those with dark skin, remained poor and disadvantaged. Yet, measured against any previous period, the economic pattern of life for most Americans distinctly improved during the 30 years after World War II. The economic abundance of these years calls for some understanding and explanation, for it was abundance that shaped the life of the ordinary American.

Who was this American? What was his life like? The first point to note is that the average American, in a statistical sense, was not a "he" at all. For the first time in the history of the country, the majority of Americans in the years after 1945 were female. The "average" American was white, married, and probably a mother. Although 80 percent of adult male Americans worked, most women during these years did not. By 1971, however, a majority of married women worked outside the home at least part of the time. That same year over half of married working women were mothers of children under 18.

The possessions of the average American and her husband reflected the prosperity of the times. They owned their own home, most likely in an urban area since well over half of all Americans lived in cities. By the end of the period it was likely that the house would be in a suburb rather than a metropolitan city. Regardless of where she lived, the average American would have a car, a telephone, and a television set. In 1974, almost two thirds of American homes contained a color TV, and 45 percent of them had two or more television sets.

So popular was television in the lives of Americans that more owned TV sets than owned washing machines and dishwashers together. Thus 94.4 per cent of families with incomes under $5,000 in 1974 had a TV and a refrigerator, but only 55 per cent of them owned a washing machine. Televisions and refrigerators were the only major appliances the ownership of which did not vary significantly by income.

Neither the average American, if she worked outside the home, or her husband worked with their hands at a machine in a factory. Both were likely to be white-collar workers in an office or performing some personal service for others. If she had been born before 1940, it was likely that her children would be attending college although even in the 1970s when about half the young people continued their education after high school, only about a third of college-age people actually graduated from college.

The recreation of the average American centered on her family, with a heavy dependence upon watching TV. Movies, which had once been a major form of popular entertainment, had become principally an entertainment of young people. Some spectator sports, particularly professional football, had burgeoned into a major popular entertainment. Attendance figures at the National Football League games alone jumped almost 500 percent between 1950 and 1973. In 1970 some 30 million people attended college football games.

Participatory sports—that is, those that cost money to participate in, such as bowling, golfing, riding, or swimming—also surged. In fact, in 1976 Americans spent more on such sports than on movies or on spectator sports. An equal amount ($3.9 billion) was spent on flowers, plants, and seeds, suggesting that gardening was another significant participatory sport.

Although Americans had never been avid book readers, they had once supported a large number of newspapers, but in the years between 1950 and 1970 the numbers of newspapers declined in the face of rising costs and declining revenues. During the 1970s, however, the number began to rise again. The number of periodicals increased throughout the period, too. They catered increasingly to such specialized interests and hobbies of Americans—like woodworking, sailing, gardening, hunting, sewing, and cooking—as well as prurient interests, with the rise of "men's" magazines such as *Playboy* and *Penthouse* that thrived in the 1960s and 1970s with photos of nude and semi-nude women, articles with sexual subject matter, and centerfolds.

The pursuit of recreation in a period of prosperity can be measured by the fact that 16 million Americans rode horses, 10 million played golf, and 7 million owned motorboats. Between 1950 and 1975 the number of people who took out hunting licenses doubled while fishing licenses more than doubled, reaching 35 million in 1975.

As the figures on appliances, possessions, and recreation imply, the United States of the 1950s and 1960s was a consumer society of the highest order. The production and acquisition of goods and services became almost an obsession. The very diversity of goods available was at once tantalizing and bewildering. Consumption threatened to outrun production as Americans sought to increase their leisure and reduce their work. Although millions of Americans

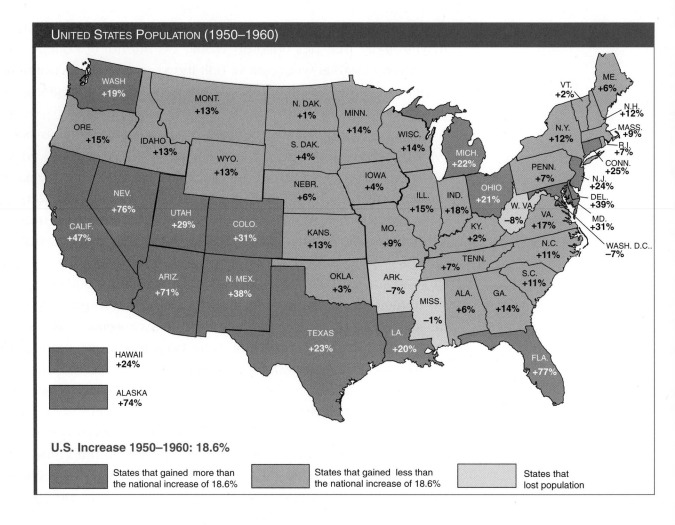

UNITED STATES POPULATION (1950–1960)

WASH.
+19%

MONT.
+13%

N. DAK.
+1%

MINN.
+14%

VT.
+2%

ME.
+6%

N.H.
+12%

ORE.
+15%

IDAHO
+13%

WYO.
+13%

S. DAK.
+4%

WISC.
+14%

N.Y.
+12%

MASS.
+9%

R.I.
+7%

NEV.
+76%

UTAH
+29%

NEBR.
+6%

IOWA
+4%

MICH.
+22%

PENN.
+7%

CONN.
+25%

N.J.
+24%

CALIF.
+47%

COLO.
+31%

KANS.
+13%

ILL.
+15%

IND.
+18%

OHIO
+21%

W. VA.
−8%

VA.
+17%

DEL.
+39%

MD.
+31%

MO.
+9%

KY.
+2%

WASH. D.C..
−7%

ARIZ.
+71%

N. MEX.
+38%

OKLA.
+3%

ARK.
−7%

TENN.
+7%

N.C.
+11%

S.C.
+11%

MISS.
−1%

ALA.
+6%

GA.
+14%

TEXAS
+23%

LA.
+20%

HAWAII
+24%

FLA.
+77%

ALASKA
+74%

U.S. Increase 1950–1960: 18.6%

States that gained more than the national increase of 18.6%

States that gained less than the national increase of 18.6%

States that lost population

still lived outside the urban environment, they did not escape city values or materialistic temptations, if only because they had a direct line to the city in their televisions. Few farmhouses were without the thrusting TV aerial to link them to the wider world.

Although more and more Americans traveled outside the United States—the number increased tenfold between 1950 and 1970—the average American spent her vacations with her family inside the United States, usually at the seashore, at lakes, in the mountains, or visiting the national parks in the West. In 1973 there were more visits to the national parks than there were people in the country, reflecting the visits of many people to more than one park or monument. Attendance at amusement parks reached unprecedented levels. Although the rising price of gasoline began to curtail that kind of vacationing in the late 1970s, the quarter century after the Second World War witnessed an ever-growing dependence upon the automobile for pleasure.

One reason Americans could become a nation on wheels in the summer was that vacations had become longer. Before 1940 the average annual vacation was one week. After the war the average doubled, and for increasing numbers of Americans vacation time stretched to three and four weeks.

During the years of prosperity Americans also ate differently. The near-full employment that prevailed during these years encouraged people to buy more prepared foods like TV dinners, pastry and other mixes, and frozen vegetables and juices, as well as more costly kinds and cuts of meat. Per capita consumption of frozen foods jumped 300 percent between 1950 and 1973, while per capita purchases of beef went up 150 percent and those of chicken and turkey more than doubled. The per capita intake of hard liquors rose almost 90 percent after 1950, and of wine, 74 percent. The change in wine drinking over 25 years reflected not only an increase in alcoholic intake but a broadening of tastes as well.

Despite the increasing richness of the diet and the rise in the consumption of alcohol and tobacco, the life expectancy of the average American significantly improved. In 1940 the average life expectancy at birth was 62.9 years. By 1976 it was up to 72.5. By 1977, it was 73.2. An even more significant measure of improvement was the increase in the life expectancy of black males—from 53 years in 1940 to 68.3 years in 1976. A large part of the improvement stemmed from the lowering of infant mortality rates during those years. A 70 percent drop in infant mortality for whites and 67 percent for blacks reflected not only improvements in medical care, but general prosperity as well.

Although the federal government and private medical organizations mounted extensive campaigns against cigarette smoking during the 1950s and 1960s because of the clear causal linkage between smoking and cancer, the per capita consumption of cigarettes actually increased from 175 packs a year in 1950 to 210 packs in 1973. It declined then, however, to 203 in 1977.

How was it possible for average Americans to have improved their standard of living so dramatically in the years following World War II? To understand that story let us look at the various segments of the economy and the society.

AN AFFLUENT SOCIETY

The striking fact about the 1950s and 1960s—in contrast with the 1930s and 1940s—was that unemployment, which as late as 1939 was running at 17 percent of the labor force, did not go above eight percent at any time in the following 30 years. This was true even though there were at least three rather severe recessions during those years. In the early 1970s economists were puzzled by an increase in prices in the midst of unemployment. In the preceding 30 years, however, they had at least understood the workings of the economy well enough to help prevent a return of the massive unemployment of the Great Depression. The principal single agency responsible for that achievement was the federal government.

After 1940 and until 1973 high productivity and prosperity were the dominant social facts. Goods spilled from American factories and farms in ever-increasing volume and variety. Between 1940 and 1960 the gross national product (GNP), after price changes are discounted, rose 114 percent, though the population grew less than 36 percent. In 1971 the GNP for the first time passed $1 trillion. As recently as 1960 it had been "only" half that. Even when the growth is measured in constant dollars—that is, taking inflation into account— the GNP increased 150 percent between 1950 and 1977. As rates of economic growth go among industrial nations, this was not spectacular; measured in quantity of goods, however, American production dwarfed that of any economy in the world. Only Sweden and Switzerland equaled the per capita production of the American economy at the beginning of the 1970s.

Other periods in American history—the 1920s, for example—had been notable for productive capacity and prosperity; but the novelty of the years between 1945 and 1970 was that lower-income groups, as well as upper-income groups, shared in the prosperity. Millions of American families moved up the income ladder. One sign of this rise is that the weekly wage of workers in manufacturing between 1947 and 1957 rose 16 percent—even after the rise in the cost of living is taken into consideration. Another is that since 1950 the average income of the bottom tenth of the population has gone up about 55 percent, after discounting price changes. A third measure is the increase in home ownership. In 1940 fewer than 44 percent of American families, including farmers, lived in homes they had bought. By 1973 the proportion was up to 65 percent. Moreover, the proportion of Americans who lived below the poverty line steadily declined from 22 percent in 1959, when the statistics were first compiled, to 11.4 percent 16 years later.

That the prosperity was as widespread as it was and that millions of Americans achieved middle-class status owed much to an unprecedented piece of legislation, the G.I. Bill of Rights, passed in the spring of 1944. Thanks to the G.I. Bill, returning servicemen, of whom there were millions, were entitled to help with a college education, help in purchasing a home, and unemployment benefits—should these be needed. Before the war, a college education had been reserved for the sons and daughters of relatively affluent families. With

G.I. Bill benefits about one half of the returning veterans were able to achieve at least some higher education. Thus the bill had a powerful impact in democratizing access to college, and thus in helping millions of families into the middle class. When coupled with relatively high, albeit regionally specific, levels of investment in public education, the Baby Boom generation (the children of the veterans)—and the economy as a whole—received a tremendous boost.

Nonetheless, millions of Americans still lived in want. As a result, federal outlays for welfare rose rapidly, especially in the 1960s as a "war against poverty" was mounted by the Johnson administration. In 1966 federal expenditures on behalf of low-income people amounted to $11.3 billion. By 1971, under the first Nixon administration, the figure had more than doubled to $25.5 billion.

Despite these aids to the poor and the move up the income ladder of millions of lower class and middle class Americans, the distribution of income barely changed in these years. In 1950 the top five percent of families received 17 percent of aggregate income, while the lowest 20 percent received 4.5 percent. Twenty-five years later the proportion of total aggregate income received by the top 5 percent was down to 15.5 percent, but the proportion received by the lowest 20 percent was up only to 5.4 percent. Furthermore, the top 20 percent of income receivers got about the same share in 1975 that they had in 1950—that is, about 40 percent. As might be expected in a competitive society, income distribution remained far from equal; but it was greatly improved from the Gilded Age and much better than it would be after the Reagan Revolution of the 1980s moved America away from the social welfare state model that was developed in the 1960s, and toward a model that favored greater reliance on the free market.

THE CORPORATE ECONOMY

The rapidly expanding economy of the 1950s and 1960s was highly institutionalized. Most people in the labor force worked for someone else, usually a corporation. In 1900, 36 percent of all members of the work force had been self-employed. By 1958 that figure was down to 15 percent. There were still millions of small businesses, but measured by income and production they constituted only a small proportion of the economy. In 1968 less than 3 percent of all corporations received almost four fifths of the total income of corporations. Corporate enterprises, with their large capital resources and heavy expenditures on research and development, were at once a cause and a consequence of the prosperity of the 1950s and 1960s.

Government, too, with its large outlays of funds, encouraged the corporations and stimulated the economy. Defense expenditures alone reached $50 billion a year in the early 1960s and surged to over $80 billion at the height of the Vietnam War. In fact, after the Second World War the federal government moved far beyond its largely regulatory role under the New Deal. It was now, with its huge budget, a significant participant in the marketplace as well. By 1970 the federal government alone spent a quarter of the nation's money and, with state and local governments, hired almost a fifth of the labor force.

The federal government was also one of the principal forces sustaining the housing boom of the 1950s and 1960s, a major stimulus of the prosperity of those years. Through agencies like the Federal Housing Administration and the Veterans Administration, the government helped finance mortgages for the construction of millions of homes and poured money as well into the housing industry, in general, through its support of low-income public housing. Since residential construction makes up between 20 and 25 percent of all private investment, the significance of government aid to construction can hardly be exaggerated in explaining the economic growth of the postwar years. The extent of the housing boom of the 1950s and 1960s can be measured in the simple fact that in 1971 two fifths of all the houses and apartments occupied in the country had been built in the preceding 20 years.

At the root of economic growth, of course, was the increase in the productivity of the labor force. Generally this gain was achieved through a greater use of machines and power. As machines became more sophisticated and versatile, workers became primarily feeders, supervisors, and operators. The machines did almost all the labor. Even in primary work like digging ditches, machines were used. Forklifts, cranes, and other types of equipment greatly reduced the heavy lifting by workers, which as recently as the 1930s was common in foundries, mills, and warehouses. Efficiency was further enhanced by new integration processes whereby interruptions in the manufacture of goods were eliminated. In the so-called continuous-flow processes, a sequence of operations now became a single operation. A result was that whereas in 1947 it took 310.5 hours to make an automobile, by 1962 the time had been cut in half. Single inventions like the digital computer and, later, the microchip made a whole range of clerical and arithmetical activities amazingly rapid, thus releasing money and labor for other tasks.

One consequence of the growth of industry and big business was the expansion of American enterprises abroad in the form of the multinational corporation. Industrial giants like Ford and IBM opened plants in foreign countries in order to tap foreign markets and cheaper labor more easily. Sometimes the products of these American-owned companies in foreign countries competed with American exports, thus arousing the ire of organized labor in the United States. At other times multinational corporations, not all of which were American by any means, encountered opposition from the host countries because they dominated or threatened to stifle local enterprises.

Some of the multinational corporations became enormous. The incomes of the largest dwarfed the national economies of two thirds of the countries of the world. Seen in historical perspective, the multinational corporation imposed a new stability and order on the international economy, not unlike that which the trusts and giant corporations of the nineteenth century had imposed on the national economy of the United States. Like the nineteenth-century trusts, they were great aggregations of economic power—but on an international rather than a national scale and consequently even more difficult to regulate or monitor. The size of the multinational corporations measured, too, how the technological advances of the affluent postwar era had tied together the United States and the rest of the world in a global economy.

RISE OF THE WHITE-COLLAR CLASS

As the emphasis upon machine production implies, the work performed in the United States in the postwar years was quite different from the industrial labor of previous years. During most of America's history the majority of workers had been farmers, miners, fishermen, and factory workers—that is, blue-collar workers. Ever since the opening of the twentieth century, however, an increasing proportion of the labor force has comprised white-collar workers—managers, clerks, professionals, government employees, and self-employed proprietors. Beginning in the 1950s more than half of American workers were white-collar and service workers rather than blue-collar workers. In 1970 white-collar workers alone constituted 50.8 percent of the nonagricultural labor force, blue-collars 34.5 percent, and service workers (policemen, bank tellers, domestics, and others) 10.5 percent.

The growth of a white-collar class meant that an increasing number of people were being supplied with goods by an ever-smaller proportion of agricultural and manufacturing employees. It also was a measure of the maturity of the economy, since only a highly mechanized and skilled society could achieve such a division of labor. By 1970 less than five percent of the work force was in agriculture, compared with 18 percent employed by government—in a society that prided itself on being the antithesis of socialistic! (In officially Communist Yugoslavia in 1972, 20 percent of the work force was employed by the government.)

White-collar predominance also testified to the consumer nature of the economy. Whereas in previous history most paid labor was employed in making new goods, by the end of the 1950s most working people were consuming goods, helping others consume goods, or performing a service.

Traditionally, white-collar workers have resisted joining unions, even though white-collar pay is often inferior to industrial wages. In 1972, for example, only 16.5 percent of all unionized workers were employed in white-collar occupations. The growth in the white-collar class thus seemed to explain, at least partly, the stagnation in labor organizing in the 1950s. Despite its organizing drives and its power, organized labor in the 1960s barely kept pace with the growing size of the labor force. In 1964, for example, about 30 percent of nonagricultural workers were in unions. Eight years later the proportion was down to 26.7 percent.

A large part of the white-collar class was composed of women, who after 1940 entered the labor force in ever increasing numbers. Indeed, between 1950 and 1970 some 13.2 million women joined the labor force, as compared with only 9.5 million men, and among these workingwomen were growing numbers of wives and mothers. By 1970 over two fifths of all married women were employed in paying jobs. Almost a third of women with children younger than six were working, counting only married women whose husbands were present. In short, women now constituted the largest source of new workers in the economy.

Women entering the labor force, however, were frequently compelled to accept jobs that paid less or were otherwise less rewarding than their education or training warranted. This was especially true of college-educated women, who, proportionately, returned to work in larger numbers than their non-college sisters. Furthermore, the needs of the economy apparently did not encourage women to develop their powers. In the 1950s women made up a smaller proportion of all college students than they had in the 1920s; and fewer women, proportionately, were entering graduate schools. By the 1970s, however, there began to be evidence that this pattern was changing.

A REVOLUTION IN AGRICULTURE

Like industry, farming experienced a revolution in productivity during the 1950s and 1960s. The increased ability to produce food was an important impetus to the prosperity and the high standard of living of those years. In 1960, for example, an hour of employment in manufacturing bought 2.2 pounds of round steak. In 1929 the same amount of labor had bought only 1.2 pounds. By 1969 an hour's work in a factory bought 2.4 pounds. (Even at the height of inflation in 1974, an hour of factory work bought 2.3 pounds of round steak.) In 1960 about seven minutes of work purchased a quart of milk. In 1969 less than five minutes would buy the same amount.

If, as these figures suggest, American farming was highly productive, it was also in some places backward, inefficient, and a cause of poverty for hundreds of thousands of people who could not afford the costly machines and costly methods that made the agricultural revolution of the postwar years. Even though the number of farmers had been steadily declining ever since the 1920s, as late as 1961 some 1.6 million farm-families, or 44 percent of the total, earned so little from agriculture that they had to engage in other kinds of employment to make ends meet. These people—black and white sharecroppers in the South, farmers on marginal lands in Appalachia and the Middle West—actually were as hard up as the poor of the central cities. Indeed, in 1968 it was estimated that 23 percent of the farm population lived below the poverty line, as compared with 12 percent of the urban population.

It was the highly efficient farms that produced the great bulk of food, thanks to the encouragement of high government price supports during the 1950s. Capital per farm in 1974 was about 6.6 times in constant dollars what it had been in 1950. Put another way, in the 1960s the amount of capital per farm work was about $5,000 more than the amount of capital per worker in manufacturing. It was this high capitalization that explained the enormous increase in farm productivity. In 1969 over 4.5 million tractors were in use on American farms; and thousands of mechanical cotton pickers had displaced hundreds of thousands of Southern black workers, who left agriculture to seek wider opportunities in Northern cities. New seeds, new machines, and new chemicals of all kinds also gave impetus to the farm revolution of the postwar years. Chemicals were used not only to kill harmful insects but also to hasten crop maturity, to kill weeds, to defoliate plants in order to facilitate harvesting, or to inhibit growth in crops like tobacco where only certain kinds of leaves are desired. The chemical industry also developed new feeds for chickens that speeded up growth and made it possible to raise broilers from egg to maturity in eight to nine weeks. The disastrous effects of some of these chemicals upon wildlife have posed a serious dilemma for a society wanting cheap and abundant food and wildlife at the same time. Perhaps the most notorious of these was DDT, a pesticide that proved to have a deleterious effect on the reproductive capacity of bald eagles and reduced the American National Bird to the status of an endangered species before DDT was banned by the federal government.

The most important consequence of the changes in agriculture after 1945, however, is that the family farm, as it has been known in the United States since the beginning, has almost disappeared. Between 1949 and 1959 some 1.2 million farm-families simply left agriculture. By 1960 less than eight percent of the American population lived on farms, and by 1970 that proportion was down to less than five percent; yet the value of total farm production rose about 20 percent in the same 10-year period. Thus, a farmer either was a large-scale operator with a large capital investment or would soon be compelled to withdraw from farming.

ADVANCES IN CHEMISTRY

A large part of the enormous increase in agricultural productivity derived from advances in chemistry. The new chemistry also had a profound effect in areas outside of agriculture. The breakthrough came just before the Second World War when artificial fibers, such as nylon, which had been created in the laboratory, began to replace cotton, linen, and silk in the manufacture of cloth. Then during the war, when the supply of natural rubber in Asia was cut off by the war with Japan, chemists were able to develop a new synthetic rubber industry. The discovery of how to create giant molecules called polymers allowed chemists to lay the foundation, after the war, of the plastics industry.

Plastics, it was found, could be used in place of wood, rubber, and metals, and had the decided advantage of being moldable. As a result, the shaping of objects made out of plastics did not incur high labor costs. Moreover, plastics were lightweight, resistant to corrosion, and good at insulating. Thus plastics came to be used in a myriad of ways, some of which were quite central to the economy. An automobile, for example, now contains about 100 pounds of plastics. Since almost all plastics are made from petroleum waste products, the dependence of the American economy on foreign oil derives from more than simply the American love affair with the automobile.

Chemistry also reshaped the field of medicine, for a whole range of new drugs and medicines have been developed for the relief of pain and the treatment of many diseases, including mental illness.

Tranquilizers, sleeping aids, birth control pills, fertility pills, and many other kinds of drugs and chemicals not only are new since the Second World War but also are now a part of the everyday lives of millions of Americans. It has been estimated that at least half of the current products of the giant chemical industry were unknown before 1950. In the drug branch of the industry, no more than 10 percent were known before 1955.

LITERARY AND DRAMATIC EXPRESSION

THE NOVEL

Not surprisingly, the Second World War fostered a number of novels by important American writers. Among them were John Hersey's *A Bell for Adano* (1944), Irwin Shaw's *The Young Lions* (1948), Norman Mailer's *The Naked and the Dead* (1949), James Jones' *From Here to Eternity* (1951), and—10 years later, for another generation—Joseph Heller's *Catch-22*. From a different angle, and still later, was Kurt Vonnegut's macabre *Slaughterhouse Five*, about the bombing of Dresden, which began his popularity among college students. Norman Mailer went on to write more novels and then moved over into a highly personal form of journalism that produced, among other works, *Armies in the Night* (1968), his remarkable account of his own participation in an antiwar demonstration at the Pentagon.

By 1960 the final works of a number of novelists of the first and second rank—Faulkner, Hemingway, Dos Passos, Steinbeck, and O'Hara—had appeared. Some of the best of the new writers carried on in the realistic tradition: Saul Bellow (*The Adventures of Augie March*, 1953; *Herzog*, 1964; *Humboldt's Gift*, 1975), for example, and Bernard Malamud (*The Assistant*, 1957; *A New Life*, 1961). In 1976 Bellow won the Nobel Prize

William Faulkner *(Library of Congress)*

for Literature. (That Bicentennial Year, in fact, Americans won all five Nobel Prizes.)

Other writers began in the realistic tradition and then moved away from it—Mailer, for one, and for another, Philip Roth, who followed a brilliant short story collection (*Goodbye, Columbus*, 1959) with two traditional novels before swerving to the wild sexual excess of *Portnoy's Complaint* (1969), and the vitriolic political satire of *Our Gang* (1971) that was about President Nixon. His interest in outrageous fantasy continued with *The Breast* (1972) and *The Professor of Desire* (1977).

John Updike, a virtuoso performer, moved in and out of the realistic tradition with *Rabbit Run* (1960), *The Centaur* (1963), and *Rabbit Redux* (1971). His rising interest in Africa was reflected in his *The Coup* (1978). Of a much more traditional character was the work of Isaac Bashevis Singer, written in Yiddish though Singer now lived in the United States. He recounted in compelling narrative and wry humor the joys and sorrows of Jewish life. His remarkably diverse body of work was recognized internationally in 1978 with the Nobel Prize.

The best-known African American writers in the opening years of the period were Ralph Ellison, whose *Invisible Man* (1952) became a classic, and James Baldwin (*Go Tell It on the Mountain*, 1953; *Another Country*, 1962). The most striking black talent in the second half of the century was female: Toni Morrison, whose *The Bluest Eye* (1970) captured attention immediately, would go on to win a Nobel Prize in 1993, and Maya Angelou, whose autobiography *I Know Why the Caged Bird Sings* (1970), was both popular and significant.

Though William Faulkner was in decline, the tradition of splendid writing emanating from the American South continued. Georgia-born Flannery O'Connor wrote short stories in a Gothic mode. Mississippian Eudora Welty also wrote highly regarded short stories. From Alabama came Harper Lee, whose 1960 novel *To Kill a Mockingbird* became one of the best-loved books of the twentieth century; and her childhood friend was Truman Capote, best-known for his 1966 work of non-fiction, *In Cold Blood*, about the murder of the Clutter family in Kansas. Capote and the book became the subjects of an Oscar-winning film in 2005, *Capote*.

Finally, in 1973, Erica Jong published *Fear of Flying*, which heralded a new voice in American literature by being a frank account of female sexuality. That it appeared when it did was no coincidence. The novel was both cause and effect of the feminist revolution then taking place, of which much more will be said.

TELEVISION AND THE MOVIES

By the early 1950s, there was a new form of entertainment that captivated most Americans, television. As previously noted, more households had a TV set than dishwashers and washing machines combined. Very soon patterns of family behavior began to change to accommodate the new medium: people gathered around the set to watch such beloved favorites as *I Love Lucy*—a cultural phenomenon in itself—or *The Ed Sullivan Show*. In those early decades, families typically had only one set, and the programming tended to appeal to people across a broad span of ages and interests. The Sullivan show provided a good example of this. There were animal acts for the children, Elvis or the Beatles for teenagers, and stars of classical music for those of more highbrow tastes. By contrast, in the early twenty-first century television sets abound in the typical household, and programming tends to reflect that pattern with cartoon networks for kids, MTV for teenagers, and so on.

As early as 1954, television began to demonstrate its potential for providing riveting, real-time programming that documented actual events, a demonstration that occurred when networks televised the Army-McCarthy hearings, of which more later. Then in 1963 a heartbroken nation followed the events surrounding the assassination of President John Kennedy, including the murder of the assassin, Lee Harvey Oswald, on live television. During the following decade the coverage of the Vietnam War played a large role in shaping public opinion; the network anchors, above all CBS's Walter Cronkite, were national icons. Today, an increasing number of Americans get their news online, and the anchors no longer have the same clout.

The initial impact of television, when it burst upon the entertainment scene, was to cause a decline in public interest in movies. Hundreds of movie theaters closed down during the 1950s and 1960s, and the Hollywood studios either went unused or were turned over to making movies for TV. In 1948 there were 18,600 movie houses in the country. By 1963 the number was a mere 9,200, but then a revival began as independent producers and moviemakers came upon the scene. By 1967 there were some 12,000 movie houses, and by 1977 the figure was 17,000. Moreover, by 1976 more money was being spent on movie tickets than for all spectator sport events, theater, and opera admissions put together.

By the late 1960s, in sum, it was evident that a sizable segment of the population did not want to stay home nights and stare at the TV set. Reared on television, the young were ready to leave the "tube" to their parents. Many members of the new movie audience were college students or recent graduates because during the 1960s there was a great increase in college attendance. To reach this expanding potential audience the movies had to grow up. The best of them did. As in the theater and the novel, censorship was virtually dead—a development that conservatives blamed on the "permissive liberalism" of the Supreme Court but which permitted a new realism and a new frankness of both theme and treatment. More significant, perhaps, was the new sophistication the audience demanded. Westerns could still succeed, but movies that laughed at the clichés (*Cat Ballou, True Grit*) or depicted three-dimensional characters instead of cardboard cutouts (*Butch Cassidy and the Sundance Kid*) did best. War, long the subject of romantic or chauvinistic epics, came in for ironic attacks in movies like *Dr. Strangelove, Catch-22,* and *M*A*S*H.* The Vietnam War was treated seriously—and critically—in the poignant *Coming Home,* starring, appropriately enough, the antiwar actress Jane Fonda, and in *The Deerhunter,* which unblinkingly depicted the cost of the war to those who supported it. *The Deerhunter* was also one of several movies dealing realistically with working-class life in America. Another was *Norma Rae,* for which Sally Field won an Academy Award.

Some of the best of the new movies were addressed directly to the young. *The Graduate* came to be considered a classic statement of what young people held against their parents and what they thought of themselves. *Easy Rider* offered a sympathetic view of the drug culture in idyllic settings, and *One Flew Over the Cuckoo's Nest* expressed many a young person's sense of the insanity of the conventional world and its institutions. If some older fans were troubled by the moral ambiguities in the new films and wondered whether there was, in fact, anything particularly grown up or sophisticated about clinical studies of loveless sex (*Deep Throat*) or celebrations of mindless violence (*Straw Dogs, Clockwork Orange*), by the 1970s the movies were an important emotional and intellectual experience for a great many young Americans. In *Saturday Night Fever* and *Grease* the importance of rock music and dancing in the lives of millions of young people was brought home to all who saw those films.

Older Americans also found certain films in the 1970s attractive, perhaps because they stirred remembrances of things past (*The Great Gatsby, The Sting*) or sentimental ethnicity (*The Godfather*) or the love of being frightened (*Jaws* and *The Exorcist*). Science fiction movies, the groundbreaker of which was the highly creative *2001: A Space Odyssey,* proved inordinately attractive to young as well as old. *The Man Who Fell to Earth* was not a great success in 1976, but in the next two years three science fiction movies each challenged all money-

Olivia Newton-John and John Travolta in *Grease*. (AP Photo/Ho)

making records: *Star Wars, Close Encounters of the Third Kind*, and *Superman*, the last based upon the old comic strip and TV serial. Was this new interest in science fiction a delayed reaction to the success of the 1960s in putting a man on the moon—or merely escape?

By the 1970s movies made about blacks and for blacks began to appear (*Shaft, Super Fly*, and *Sounder*). Blacks were increasingly a part of the mainstream of America and were recognized as such in the social mirror of the movies. Some blacks as well as whites deplored the separatism and racial chauvinism sometimes depicted in these movies, but others cheered the fact that there were beginning to be some black heroes and heroines with whom black fans could identify. Situation comedies on TV also began to feature African Americans; some of the top shows had primarily black casts and outlook, although generally written by whites.

The most spectacular success in all of television production concerned African Americans. It was the series running eight consecutive evenings called *Roots*, which told the story of a black family from its beginnings in Africa, through the darkness of slavery in America, and finally into freedom. Written by African American author Alex Haley, *Roots* was seen in January 1977 by almost three quarters of the owners of television sets in the country—in itself a powerful comment on the impact of the black experience on the consciousness of Americans, white as well as black.

THE DARK SIDE AND THE BEGINNINGS OF CHANGE

SOURCES OF ANXIETY

The unusual prosperity of these years obscured a number of nagging fears and broad dissatisfactions; these, too, were a part of the postwar social scene. As we shall see in the following chapters, the end of World War II did not mean the end of international suspicions or even of war for the United States. This was the time of the Cold War when the immense military power and broadened aspirations of the Soviet Union seemed to threaten first Europe and then Asia. Fear of Communist ideology during part of the 1950s so undermined the self-confidence of Americans that a "witch-hunt" was mounted for Communist spies and sympathizers. Hostilities between nations not only threatened, but also brought death to, thousands of Americans, first in Korea and then in Vietnam. Fear of nuclear war was sufficiently high in those years to put schoolchildren through bomb drills, and for many citizens to build home bomb shelters. Over one million private bomb shelters were constructed nationwide, and *Architectural Digest* reported that the bomb shelter would become as much a part of the American home as the garage.

The very prosperity was a source of anxiety and confusion of values. It encouraged many Americans to buy goods to "keep up with the Joneses," to choose goods over goals. Many adults who had grown up during the Great Depression sacrificed to give their children material advantages they themselves never enjoyed. In doing so, they laid the groundwork for the antimaterialism of the 1960s counterculture that, in turn, alienated many children from their parents. Since even poor people had television, they had first-hand knowledge of the goods they were denied by their poverty. The resentment of many erupted into violence in dozens of cities. For others, the resentment was kept hidden, but it was no less alienating and divisive.

The highly organized corporate economy and its burgeoning bureaucracy, which was in large part responsible for the prosperity, reduced the individual's feelings of significance and effectiveness. The efficient organization of work, on which the prosperity depended, made the work place for millions of Americans monotonous, impersonal, and dispiriting.

New sources of anxiety appeared on a global scale: rapid population growth; impending world shortages of food and irreplaceable resources like oil and gas; the deadly effects of pollution and toxic wastes; and the growing gap between the rich and poor nations, with the latter increasingly insistent upon a fairer share of the world's production. Behind all these threats stood the most immediate and ominous danger of all: the possibility of a nuclear war that might obliterate half the world. The arms race between the United States and the Soviet Union was still uncontrolled, and nuclear weapons by the 1970s were in the hands of at least four other nations as well, including communist China.

The bright and dark sides of the years after 1945 were summarized in the achievements and the problems of the nation's cities, then undergoing important changes.

THE TRANSFORMATION OF THE CITY

The trend toward urbanization had begun early in the nineteenth century. By 1970 almost three fourths of all Americans lived in urban areas, and the trend appeared irreversible, with each census reporting a further decline in the rural population. During the 50s and 60s, however, the kinds of urban areas in which Americans chose to live began to change. Central metropolitan districts did not keep up with the general urban growth. Between 1950 and 1960, for example, the aggregate total population of cities over 100,000 increased only 9.3 percent, and four out of five of the giant cities of over a million actually decreased in population.

Increasingly, people moving from the country or small towns were settling in the suburbs of the big cities rather than the cities themselves. Many people residing in the cities themselves were also deserting the central cities for the suburbs. This movement had begun in earnest in the 1920s, but by the 50s it was a mass exodus. In 1953 the editors of *Fortune* compared the suburban migration to the great immigration from Europe in the early years of the twentieth century. About as many people—1.2 million—moved to the suburbs that year as had entered the United States in 1907.

The census of 1970 made it clear that this trend was continuing. Between 1960 and 1970, 61 of the 153 cities of 100,000 or more lost population. For many it was the first loss of population since the beginning of the urbanizing movement. In 1970 less than a third of Americans lived in central cities, while more than two fifths lived in surrounding suburbs—which were now becoming places of work as well as residence. By comparison, in 1920, 19 percent of Americans had lived in New York City alone. Furthermore, by 1970 the suburbs were providing only slightly fewer jobs than the central cities. They were no longer simply "bedroom communities" although 85 percent

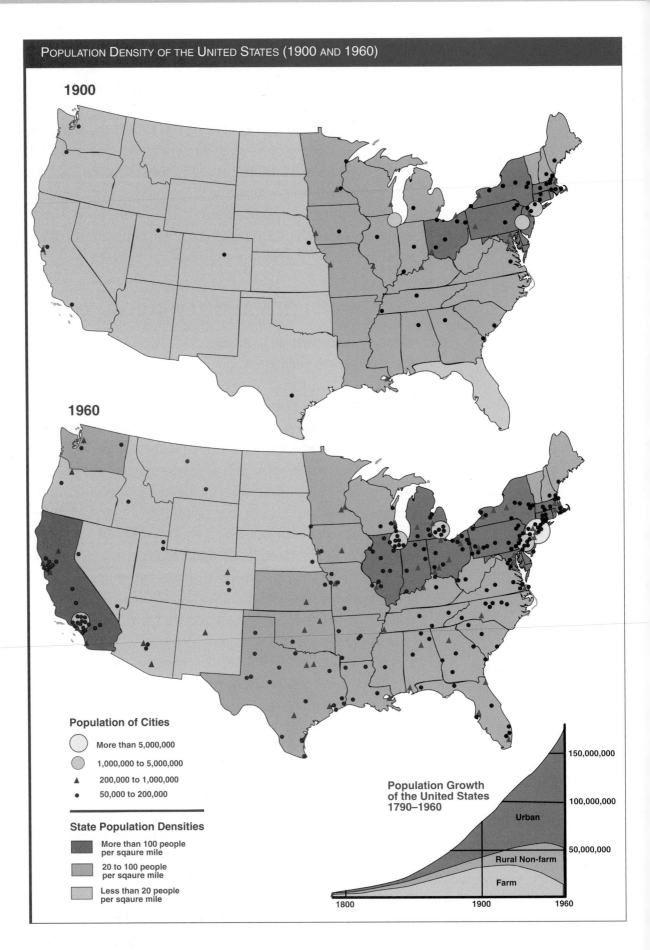

POPULATION DENSITY OF THE UNITED STATES (1900 AND 1960)

1900

1960

Population of Cities

More than 5,000,000

1,000,000 to 5,000,000

200,000 to 1,000,000

50,000 to 200,000

State Population Densities

More than 100 people per sqaure mile

20 to 100 people per sqaure mile

Less than 20 people per sqaure mile

Population Growth of the United States 1790–1960

Urban

Rural Non-farm

Farm

150,000,000

100,000,000

50,000,000

1800   1900   1960

of American workers used their cars to get to work, especially in the West, where cities developed after the invention of the automobile.

For the central city, commuters and their automobiles presented a growing problem. The demand for parking facilities alone—not to mention the multiplying demands for new expressways and freeways—ate significantly into the prime real estate of the great cities, thus cutting into the tax base that was needed for increased urban expenditures. Moreover, commuter trains, forced to compete with the automobile, found it more and more difficult to make a profit or even to survive; and many were forced to reduce or discontinue their service. Much of the metropolitan labor force still depended on the commuter lines for daily transportation, however. As a consequence, a number of state and local governments faced pressures to subsidize the commuter lines in one way or another.

The Urban Mass Transportation Assistance Act of 1970 brought some federal money for mass transportation to the beleaguered cities, but the need far outran the remedy. The automobile was still a difficult competitor to overcome—as San Francisco's computerized Bay Area Rapid Transportation (BART) discovered soon after it opened in 1972. In spite of an impressive multimillion-dollar engineering feat that included building a train tunnel under San Francisco Bay, seven years later it had not yet fulfilled the promise either to reduce auto traffic significantly or to pay for itself. Nevertheless, the need for mass transit was reflected, however, in the new subways that opened in the late 1970s in New Orleans, Atlanta, and Washington, D.C.—the last pronounced a practical and visual success from the outset—and in the plans for a Texas version of San Francisco's BART in Houston and later in Dallas.

The flight to the suburbs was both a symptom and a cause of the decline of the central city as a place of human habitation. As middle-class families fled the overcrowded schools, substandard housing, and polluted air, the city became the home of the poor and metropolitan areas deteriorated still more high land prices, caused in part by land speculation and by rapid, unplanned growth in the new areas, created a big obstacle to the construction of adequate low- and middle-income housing. Nonexistent or poorly enforced building and housing codes, haphazard zoning laws, and the profits to be made from slum real estate further contributed to the continual rotting of the core cities in America's metropolitan areas.

When the Housing Act of 1968 authorized the building of 1.7 million units—mainly low- and moderate-income—over the next three years, it was estimated that at least 6 million were needed. Added to the problems of housing were those of overcrowded, understaffed urban schools and the fact that large areas of modern cities were generating increasing rates of crime, including juvenile delinquency.

These perplexing urban problems stimulated attempts to restore the nation's cities to economic and social health. Under the generic term "urban renewal," many cities attempted to rehabilitate run-down neighborhoods by land clearance and new construction or by renovating existing structures and bringing such areas into conformity with zoning, housing, health, and safety standards.

Despite the success of urban renewal projects in several of America's metropolitan areas, progress was slow. Land clearance ran into vexing legal delays, the relocation of former tenants was a continuing source of irritation for all concerned. Renewal critics attacked everything from spiraling costs to the esthetic and social drawbacks of the new construction. They charged that several billions already spent to rejuvenate America's cities had helped only to destroy their individuality. They called the new middle-income housing "a marvel of dullness and regimentation." Furthermore, some correctly predicted that new low-income projects would themselves be slums by the 1970s. Moreover, urban renewal as it was then practiced gave scant attention to the wishes of slum dwellers themselves, hence was labeled by some critics, "Negro removal."

One device by which the Johnson administration in 1966 pushed better housing for the poor was to provide rent subsidies permitting people to live in non-governmental housing even if rents were higher than they could afford. Another was to provide federal funds for the renovation of older houses and tenements in established neighborhoods in order to escape the often starkly unattractive housing projects. These efforts, too, often resulted in ownership of still more slums by the federal government when the private owners defaulted.

Since coordination of the many efforts to deal with the problems of the decaying city was a paramount need, Congress in 1965 created a new cabinet post for urban development and, in 1966, another for transportation. The latter was designed to encourage and coordinate efforts in behalf of better intra- and interurban transportation, since the automobile had itself become a problem of urban living.

A NEW ETHNIC AND RACIAL SELF-CONSCIOUSNESS

Almost from its inception in 1776, the United States has been a broad mixture of peoples, but for most of those 200 years the national emphasis has been upon denying or suppressing that diversity in order to create a unified American people. The irony was often recognized in the observation that there were more Irish in Boston than in Dublin or more Germans in Milwaukee than in Heidelberg. Even in the 1970s it was true that there were more African Americans in New York City than in Lagos, Nigeria, and more Jews in Los Angeles than in Tel Aviv.

During the years after World War II the ethnic and racial diversity of America began to receive its proper due. Political scientists and historians, as well as movies, TV shows, and novels, began to emphasize the sense of loyalty, community, and identity that people felt toward their national, racial, or religious kin. Jewish humor, Italian families, and Irish political activity became the subjects of studies, novels, and entertainment. Young people took a new pride in their European roots and found no serious conflict, as once their parents had been warned, between their Americanism and their ancestry.

A large part of the reason for the new pride in ethnic and racial identity was the emergence into political and economic prominence of these once-submerged groups. The Irish, it is true, were prominent in urban politics in the late nineteenth century, but the Jews, Poles, and Italians and racial groups like African Americans, Mexican Americans, Japanese, and Chinese came forward only in the twentieth century and principally after World War II. This is partially due to changes in demographics that occurred after 1950, however, as at mid-century, nonwhites still made up only 10 percent of the American population. This would change greatly over the next several decades due to increases in immigration from Asia and Latin America. Part of the new attitude, too, reflected the recognition by the dominant majority that racial and ethnic prejudice had no place in a society that prided itself on equality of opportunity.

Undoubtedly the most conspicuous and immediate impetus to the belated recognition of religious, national, or racial identities in American life was the Black Revolution of the 1960s, which started as a nonviolent civil rights movement and was led by Martin Luther King, Jr. until his assassination in 1968. That movement, simply because of its power and its influence on politics, is treated in subsequent pages; but there can be no question that it was a catalyst, if not a model, for the rise in ethnic self-consciousness of other groups in the 1960s and after. Ironically, the success of the blacks' demands for recognition and a share in the national pie of prosperity caused some ethnic groups to react against black aspirations. In the 1970s, for example, the Irish in Boston and the Poles in Detroit were conspicuous in the demonstrations against busing to integrate public schools.

The new emphasis upon equality and group identity as well as impatience at the slow rate of progress from nonviolent methods,

Martin Luther King, Jr. *(Library of Congress)*

caused new black nationalist or separatist groups to come to the fore during the latter 60s. The Black Muslims, a religious society founded by Elijah Muhammad during the 1930s, attracted national attention in the mid-1950s when the very articulate Malcolm X became head of the Muslims in Harlem. The Black Muslims preached a form of Islam in religion and black separatism in social policy. After he had turned away from the narrow nationalism of Elijah Muhammad, Malcolm X died at the hands of an assassin in 1965.

The most militant of the nationalist groups was the Black Panther party, which began in the ghetto of Oakland, California, in 1966. The best-known spokesman of the party was Eldridge Cleaver, a former convict of some literary talent. His book *Soul on Ice* is one of the classics of the Black Revolution along with Malcolm X's *Autobiography*. Cleaver fled to Algeria in 1968 after a series of confrontations between police and the Panthers. By 1972 the Panthers were less involved in shoot-outs with the police and more concerned with educational and breakfast programs for black children in the urban ghettos. In 1975 Cleaver returned to the United States, prepared to stand trial on the criminal charges against him.

A third figure of prominence in the new black nationalism of the 1960s was Stokely Carmichael, who in 1966, at 24, became head of the Student Nonviolent Coordinating Committee (SNCC). His slogan "Black Power" aroused a new sense of self-awareness and pride among young blacks and a sense of identification and cohesion among blacks of all ages. As a leader, Carmichael did not last into the 1970s nor did the idea of Black Power, but both left a sense of positive identity among dark-skinned Americans in regard to their blackness and their African origins. Thenceforth, most preferred to refer to themselves as black rather than Negro. (See *"Muhammad Ali: Float Like a Butterfly, Sting Like a Bee."*)

The Black Revolution by its example spurred into visibility a large minority heretofore almost unknown to most Americans: the Mexican-Americans, who then numbered as many as 10 million. Though they were concentrated principally in the Southwest, hundreds of thousands lived in the Detroit-Chicago area, so that their disadvantaged social and economic position was not simply a regional concern. The new Chicano (as they were called to give an explicitly political self definition) organizations were most active in the Southwest, however. In Texas, for example, the Raza Unida party

Eldridge Cleaver *(Library of Congress)*

was sometimes successful in local politics.

Cesar Chavez was perhaps the best known of the Chicano leaders, principally because of his successful organizing of the California grape pickers, most of whom were Mexican-Americans. Chavez, like King, based his movement on principles of nonviolence, aimed at ultimate reconciliation with the dominant majority rather than victory of one group over another. His grape boycott in the years 1965–1969 compelled the grape growers to recognize the union and to bargain with it. In 1975 Chavez' Farm Workers' Union triumphed over the rival unions in gaining recognition among largely Chicano farm workers in California.

More Mexican-Americans were now entering the universities and politics, particularly in the Southwest, suggesting that soon they would play a role in the life of the region commensurate with their numbers. Both Texas and New Mexico sent Mexican-Americans to Congress; and President Carter appointed a Mexican-American to head the Immigration Service Bureau, an agency now confronting the issue of large numbers of Mexicans entering the United States illegally in search of jobs and a better life.

Another, but socially quite different Spanish-speaking minority in the United States had already made an impact on its region. That was the Cuban-American community of southern Florida that grew

PEOPLE THAT MADE A DIFFERENCE

Muhammad Ali: "Float Like a Butterfly, Sting Like a Bee"

Besides being enormously popular, spectator sports in America have become a big business and a source of cultural idols. In the turbulent sixties, sports figures became political figures as well. No figure in modern sports has been more successful, more popular, or more controversial than boxer Muhammad Ali.

Ali was born Cassius Marcellus Clay, Jr., in Louisville, Kentucky, on January 17, 1942, the son of a black sign painter. The Clays were proud of their lineage, claiming descent from the South's most famous white opponent of slavery, Cassius Marcellus Clay, a relative of the statesman Henry Clay. At the age of twelve, Clay began amateur boxing when Joe Martin, a local policeman, offered to train him. Later Martin would say Clay had been a model student—never smoking, drinking, or using foul language, and always working hard at the gym. After more than a hundred amateur fights, Clay won the competition to represent the United States at the 1960 Olympic games in Rome.

Clay early on exhibited a trait that would make him notorious: he talked incessantly, almost always boasting about himself. As a form of psychological warfare, he would predict the round in which he would defeat his opponent and often he made the prediction come true. Even before he went to the Olympics, fans booed him for his unabashed egotism. After he won an Olympic gold medal for boxing, he ostentatiously wore it around his neck for weeks. His triumphant return to Louisville brought out the whole town, and a group of local wealthy white men agreed to back him as a professional fighter. Clay had just completed high school.

That same year he teamed up with Angelo Dundee, who became both trainer and friend. Clay later summed up their relation with a piece of doggerel: "He's got the connection and the complexion to get me the right protection which leads to good affection."

One of the reasons Clay worked so hard at making himself controversial was that it bettered his chance at a heavyweight championship bout. Fight promoters look for boxers who can attract great numbers of paying spectators. In 1964, when he was just 22, Clay got his chance to fight the champion, Sonny Liston. After six rounds, a battered and stunned Liston could not respond to the bell. Clay was the new champ. In his dressing room a shouting, exuberant Clay taunted the reporters, who had long resented his boasting: "Who is the greatest?" he demanded. "You are," they reluctantly answered.

Soon thereafter he went on a tour of Africa and was received by the Presidents of Ghana and Egypt. Clay used the trip to announce that he was a member of the Black Muslims, a religious sect known for its hostility toward whites and its belief in black separatism. Suddenly Clay was no longer the All-American black but a critic, even an opponent, of the white establishment. He dropped his name, contending that white slave masters had given it, for one from his new religion—Muhammad Ali. Openly he associated himself with the rising civil rights movement and the new interest among blacks in Africa. Although his wife divorced him and his parents disapproved, he did not waver. Floyd Patterson's 1965 challenge to Ali's title seemed a defense of the establishment when Patterson proclaimed that he intended to bring "the championship back to America." Ali, however, kept the crown easily.

The most severe test of Ali's convictions came later over his induction into the Army. When first called up in 1962, Ali failed the achievement test and was deferred. His critics, particularly in the white South, were outraged; nor did Ali soften their wrath by quipping, "I only said I was the greatest, not the smartest."

The consequence was that in 1966 he was reclassified as eligible. By then over 150,000 Americans were fighting in Vietnam. In that context, Ali's remark, "I ain't got nothing against those Vietcongs," set off a barrage of protests. When early in 1967 he refused induction on religious grounds, the boxing authorities stripped him of his title. Within another two months he was indicted and convicted of draft evasion by a Texas jury. An indignant judge levied the maximum sentence: five years in prison and a $10,000 fine.

Although he did not go to jail while appealing the conviction, Ali could obtain no matches. Between 1968 and 1970 no promoter could find an opponent and no state would let him fight. By taking away his passport, the federal government prevented him from going abroad to seek matches. He earned what he could by speaking at antiwar rallies and on college campuses where he was a hero to the opponents of the war. Ultimately, in 1971, the U.S. Supreme Court unanimously upheld Ali's contention that he should have been exempt from the draft because of his religious convictions.

Even before this, the barriers to his fighting had begun to come down. He was still a heavy drawing card, the best known as well as the most-hated boxer of the century. In 1971 he was matched against Joe Frazier, the official champion. Because Frazier had never fought, much less defeated Ali, most boxing fans did not consider him the true world's champion. The fight was a sell-out, with the contestants each promised $2.5 million. After fifteen rounds of hard slugging, Ali lost by the decision of the judges.

Ali now determined to do what only one other American had done before—to win back the championship. He accomplished this in 1974, against George Foreman, an American, in Kinshasa, Zaire, the first time a heavyweight fight had been set in Africa. Although Foreman was also black, the 60,000 fans who came to watch rooted for the best-known challenger. "Ali, *bombaye*," they chanted, "Ali, kill him." Ali's victory was not only a spectacular comeback, but also an unprecedented one for a fighter over thirty.

Ali said he would soon retire as undefeated champion, but he could not resist the popular acclaim or the money that always came with being on top. The inevitable occurred. In February 1978 he lost his title to Leon Spinks, a man twelve years his junior. The urge to be the best would not die. Later that same year in a match televised around the world, Ali defeated Spinks to become the only man to win the world heavyweight championship three times—and at age 36, to boot! In 1979 he announced his "final" retirement while still champion.

out of the large number of refugees from Castro's Communist dicta-torship in the early 1960s. These largely middle-class refugees soon came to dominate large parts of Dade County (Miami) culturally, eco-nomically, and even politically. In 1980, for example, the mayor of Miami was a Cuban-American,

By June 1980, more than 110,000 refugees from Castro's Cuba had entered the United States in a flotilla of small boats, the operation being largely financed by the Florida Cuban community. The free-dom and economic opportunities available in the United States were still acting as a social magnet—this time for poor Mexicans and for Cubans of all classes.

The newest minority group to assert itself in the late 1960s was also the oldest—the Indians. Books by militant friends of the Indian such Alvin Josephy's *Red Power* (1971) or by Indians themselves such as Vine Deloria, Jr.'s *Custer Died for Your Sins* (1969) brought the Indians' outlook to a wider public, and the federal government took some steps to recognize the just claims of Indians for fairer treat-ment. (The occupation of Alcatraz Island in San Francisco Bay by a group of Indians in 1971 and a shoot-out between Indians and fed-eral authorities at Wounded Knee, South Dakota, in 1973 showed that some thought the government was moving too slowly.) Under President Johnson an Indian headed the Bureau of Indian Affairs for the first time.

In June 1970 President Nixon proclaimed, "the historic relationship between the Federal Government and the Indian communities cannot be abridged without the consent of the Indians." His announcement ended the policy, begun under the Eisenhower administration, of turn-ing the Indians off the reservations into society. That same year, as recognition of past injustices to the Indian, the Nixon administration returned to the Taos Pueblo Indians 48,000 acres of land around Blue Lake, New Mexico, which they had long held sacred. Indians were still often caught between two cultures, without much preparation or opportunity to move into the mainstream of American economic life—if that was what they wished to do—but at least more recognition was being given to their situation as a separate culture than at any time since the Indian Reorganization Act under the New Deal.

One of the purposes of the new ethnic and racial consciousness of the 1960s and 1970s had been the expansion of opportunities for mi-norities in American society. By the opening of the 1980s, however, minority appeals to the remainder of the society were considerably less effective, especially those made by blacks. Segregation had been officially ended with the Civil Rights Act of 1964, voting rights had been federalized and enforced by the Voting Rights Act of 1965, and numerous federal government programs put in place by the Johnson and Nixon administrations were designed to help the poor, many of whom were black. Consequently, believing they had done enough, the white majority was no longer finding Black Power or Black Nationalism of interest. The consequence was that many of the sources of funds on behalf of black advance were shrinking or drying up.

Even moderate organizations like the NAACP learned that indifference to the cause of racial equality presented serious problems in raising funds and support. In Ronald Reagan's America of the 1980s, few government programs for minority rights would be pushed. Affirmative action on behalf of ethnic and racial minorities and women would also come under attack. In the Bakke and Weber cases (to be discussed), the Supreme Court compromised on how the affirmative action principle should be carried out.

By the early 80s gains had certainly been made in the direction of greater equality under law, voting rights, and equality of opportunity—thanks to the new sense of racial and ethnic identification; but the day when color or race or ethnic origin would not matter in getting a job, making friends, or being accepted into a neighborhood was still far in the future. Furthermore, many ethnic and racial groups were doubtful whether they wanted to see the day when such distinctions did not count.

CHALLENGES TO THE EDUCATIONAL SYSTEM

The Russian launching into orbit around the earth of the first Sputnik, on October 4, 1957, dismayed Americans who liked to think of themselves as first in science and technology. Sputnik not only challenged this comfortable self-image but also seemed to mean that the Soviet Union was doing a better job than they in training scientists and engineers.

Actually, even before Sputnik began to circle the earth, some educators and others had been calling for more rigorous training and for more emphasis on science and mathematics in the curricula of the nation's schools. These critics now made much of reports on Russian education showing the large amount of time spent on science, mathematics, and languages in the Soviet schools. Soon after Sputnik went up, schools around the country began to revise their curricula to put more emphasis upon these subjects.

The administration and Congress responded to the national concern in September 1958 by enacting the National Defense Education Act (NDEA), which suggested in its title the newly discerned connection between schools and the defense of the country. The law originally provided for financial encouragement to instruction and study in science, mathematics, and modern foreign languages, but that encouragement was soon extended to virtually all fields. In the first 10 years of the law more than 1.5 million college students received some $1.3 billion in low-interest loans to continue their education, while some 27,000 fellowships were granted to graduate students for advanced work. The NDEA was the first major federal effort on behalf of higher education since the College Land Grant Act of 1862, but as would become apparent during the Johnson administration, the interest in federal support of higher education was only beginning. By the mid-1970s the reevaluation of the goals and methods of education sparked by the reaction to Sputnik was to become more urgent and less optimistic.

In any case, the impact of Sputnik on education in America was far-reaching, stirring a new interest in education on all levels. By the 1960s that interest had taken on a life of its own. Of students who entered the fifth grade in 1962, 47 percent went on to college in 1970, as compared with 21 percent of those who had entered the fifth grade in 1942. In 1970, 2.9 million students graduated from high school, and 2 million enrolled in some institution of higher learning, reflecting the fact that many older Americans were also signing up for college courses.

Between 1960 and 1976 the number of full-time students in four-year colleges increased 150 percent to 6.8 million. Never before had a college education seemed so necessary to the average American. In itself this drive to college was at once a sign of the affluence of American society and a measure of the need for highly trained personnel in an advanced economy.

To meet this rising demand, existing facilities were expanded and new institutions were founded across the nation during the 1960s. New York State, for example, by 1967 had surpassed California with the largest state system of higher education, enrolling 200,000 students in its several branches of a state university system that had started only in 1947. It was reported, moreover, that each week in 1967 saw a new institution of higher learning being founded in the United States. Indeed, the expansion of state systems—with junior colleges, liberal arts colleges, and graduate and professional schools—posed a new and serious threat to even the best of the long-established private institutions as they all competed fiercely for high-quality students and faculty. If higher education by the middle 1960s was one of the great "growth" industries of the economy, by the early 1970s that growth had slackened considerably, thanks in part at least to some of the unforeseen consequences of the unprecedented expansion.

The state systems, for example, became so large that students began to protest that they were being lost in the rush to "greatness." The first of several spectacular manifestations of student concern was a series of student protests on the Berkeley campus of the University of California in 1964, the Free Speech Movement, which brought classes at that huge educational complex to a halt for several days. The immediate cause was the fact that the administration had denied space to political activity on campus, this being an outrage to students, some who had recently returned from civil rights organizing in the South. Though the upheavals at Berkeley and other institutions caused administrators and faculty to think afresh about their enterprise, this did not prevent even more massive disruptions at Columbia University in 1968 and at Harvard in 1969, to mention only two of the more prominent. Indeed, between January and June 1968, the National Student Association counted 221 major demonstrations at 101 colleges and universities, involving some 40,000 students. By this time the protests were against not only the impersonality of the large educational institution and the alleged irrelevance of higher education but also the continuation of the Vietnam War. Suddenly the American student, long known for docility and lack of interest in social protest, was aroused. That the phenomenon was not simply related to the Vietnam War was evident from the riots and disturbances on many campuses in foreign countries in 1968 and 1969. For several days, for example, the whole university system of Paris was brought to a halt by student rebellion.

The student demonstrations in the United States, which had started as nonviolent protests, became more militant and reached a peak in September 1970, with the bombing of a computer center at the University of Wisconsin in which a researcher was killed. Thereafter, the demonstrations, as well as the violence subsided sharply. During the academic year 1972 most college campuses were undisturbed by the interruptions of classes and academic routine that had been almost standard at dozens of campuses for half a decade. The reasons for the decline of the demonstrations are not clear, though administrative and curricular changes along the way demanded by student protesters undoubtedly helped. Certainly the growing violence and the repeated interruptions of classes made many students increasingly intolerant of them. University administrations and faculty also became more adept at defusing or countering demonstrations than had been the case in the beginning. Moreover, the ending of the draft in 1973 removed a good deal of the force behind the student rebellion.

One consequence of the student demonstrations was a more fundamental rethinking of the goals and nature of university education than even Sputnik had spurred. Some educational authorities as well as lay citizens began to question seriously the value of a liberal arts education for all the high-school students who were going on to college each year. Despite the escalating tuition charges and the termination of many of the student amenities, scholarships, and curriculum programs that student activism had initiated—enrollments remained high. In the face of the rising competition for jobs in a weakening economy, however, the less-well-endowed institutions responded more than ever to student demands for practical education.

THE YOUTH CULTURE

Both the Berkeley protests and the society's apparent indifference to the injustices being dramatized by civil rights leaders in the South led to an increasing self-consciousness among affluent college youth. In increasing numbers they began to challenge the older generation's failure to live up to its professed moral and religious values and, by implication, to examine their own justification for existence. In 1962 Tom Hayden, who would become one of the best-known student leaders in the country, wrote "the Port Huron Statement" for presentation to the evolving Students for a Democratic Society. In the statement, one of the founding documents of the "New Left" that represented so much vitality and activism during the period, Hayden criticized the combined affluence and injustice of American society.

If any one date can be selected for the beginning of the increasing self-consciousness among young people who found American society hypocritical and misdirected, it was the summer of 1964. That was the time when hundreds of white students, predominantly from Northern and Western colleges and universities, descended on Mississippi and other parts of the South to work for the black civil rights movement. Although some were disillusioned by that foray against injustice, many went on to other causes, particularly the movement to end the war in Vietnam. It was this cause that most affected their generation, through the draft, the casualty lists, the emigrations to Canada, the desertions to Sweden; and it was this cause that mobilized their forces. In October 1967 a confrontation at the Pentagon involved some 35,000 people, most of them young. Later, several antiwar demonstrations attracted over 100,000 participants.

It would be a mistake, however, to see the rise of a self-conscious youth movement as simply a consequence of political events or as a political event in itself. At bottom, it was a criticism of American society; not infrequently it went beyond criticism to outright rejection of the values of that society and the embracing of a new "counterculture." For a tiny revolutionary minority, rejection came to mean destruction by bombing.

The most visible manifestation of the rejection of society was the revolution in dress and hairstyle. The dress that many young people assumed—pseudoproletarian blue jeans, denim shirts, and work boots; fringed jackets and Indian headbands; flamboyant colors and designs—set them apart from the "straight" world, even as it created a new uniformity. An even bolder rejection of contemporary mores by young men was the wearing of long hair, a practice that developed in the mid-60s. (Fashion designers and the straight society—including in many cases the parental generation—first fought the revolution in dress and hair styling and then adapted it to their own uses. Whether this was victory or a defeat for the young, it undeniably showed their influence and their ability to provide alternatives in lifestyle.)

Behind the casual dress, however, lay a greater significance—an emphasis upon equality and a denial of deference, rank, and hierarchy. People, many of the young insisted, should be recognized for their individual human dignity and not for what society said they were. The new equality was evident in the impatience of most college-age students with the traditional distinctions of race and sex. Even in many Southern universities young people were much less racially prejudiced than their elders.

Establishment spokesmen, like President Nixon and Vice-President Agnew, often stigmatized the decline in deference as a result of permissiveness. Yet it was clearly part of a broader world movement toward equal rights and empowerment of the powerless and disadvantaged everywhere. An important facet was the insistence that people have a voice in the making of decisions that would affect them whether they lived in "third-world" countries emerging from colonialism or in the inner cities of America. This outlook was seen in organizations among welfare recipients as well as in demands on behalf of various other minority groups, including homosexuals seeking respect and freedom from harassment and people with disabilities seeking societal support for better access on a variety of fronts.

Perhaps the most significant difference between the young people of the counterculture and their elders was the emphasis the young now placed upon feeling and emotion. It appeared most obviously in the interest among college students in mysticism, Zen Buddhism, and the works of radical psychologist R. D. Laing. It was also to be seen in the spreading use of hallucinatory drugs, particularly marijuana, which enhances feelings and imagination while dulling reason and rational thought. It is true that the consumption of alcohol—the

Marijuana plant *(iStock)*

most "successful" drug of all time—continued to exceed by far the use of all other drugs, but the rise in the use of marijuana and later cocaine among both old and young was yet another measure of youth's influence.

The new emphasis upon feeling was also indicated by the enormous popularity during the 1960s—and after—of the loud, rhythmic rock music and the vigorous, often explicitly erotic dancing that accompanied it. These dances were out of a different culture from the ballroom dancing of the previous generation, as many young people in the early 1980s well recognized when ballroom dancing began to come back onto college campuses.

The new emphasis on feeling and emotion also helps to explain the new freedom between the sexes that came to be called the *sexual revolution*. In 1960, the contraceptive pill began to be widely available, and within a decade there had been a sea of change in many Americans' attitudes toward abortion, a "birth-control" measure that had traditionally been seen as immoral. Given the new reproductive rights, many young people saw no reason to deny their feelings by postponing sexual relations until marriage. The traditional emphasis upon female virginity before marriage was widely abandoned, Living together out of wedlock was accepted in many areas of the country and on levels of society that, only a decade before, had uniformly viewed premarital sexual relations, especially for women, as immoral. Indeed, the whole society in the course of the 1960s and early 1970s came to accept a freedom of expression on sexual matters, on nudity, and in language that was striking considering the great scope of the change and the rapidity with which it had been achieved. Even in small towns in so-called Bible-belt states, pornographic literature and movies were readily available.

A less enduring side of the youth culture was the attitude toward careers and work. Since personal experience was deemed as of primary importance, many young people in the 1960s saw little reason to put off traveling or experimenting with vocations—or simply enjoying themselves. To many of the young, the good life was not represented by making and saving money or by working hard for a home in the suburbs. It was more likely to be found, they thought, in doing what interested them rather than in choosing what paid well, and in having satisfying relations with people rather than in competing with each other.

To many adults, particularly those with still-sharp memories of the Great Depression, this attitude seemed shockingly impractical. The onset of the recession in the 1970s made it evident that the prosperity of the 1950s and 1960s had been an important precondition for the youth culture. When faced with the need to confront a competitive world, many young people in the 1970s began to take those courses in high school or college that would prepare them for careers and would promise some economic security in a world no longer running at full employment. Moreover, the cessation of the draft and the ending of the American involvement in Vietnam cooled down the political and social concern of many young people.

The upsurge of the young in the 1960s left enduring marks on the country, however. The essential seriousness and responsibility of young people were acknowledged, for example, in 1971 when in record time the voting age was lowered to 18 by the passage of the Twenty-sixth Amendment. Even more significant was the fact that by 1972 over half the states, including California and New York, had also lowered the age of majority from 21 to 18 in all or almost all legal matters. Young people played a vigorous role in the primary campaigns of Eugene McCarthy and George McGovern, but political activity by the young in the election of 1972 was less evident than it had been in 1968. Despite the lowering of the voting age, young people did not exercise the franchise in the same proportion as older people in subsequent elections.

Although the youth culture embraced a large number of people in the 1960s and early 1970s, the majority of youth had not participated in the criticism of American society, values, and standards. Most had not demonstrated against the war in Vietnam or campaigned for Eugene McCarthy, Robert Kennedy, or George McGovern. The majority of those who went to college did so in order to get ahead and to do better than their parents. In fact, many young people worked for the reelection of Nixon and Agnew. By 1975 some of the most radical of the young leaders of the 1960s, like Tom Hayden, a founder of Students for a Democratic Society (SDS), were engaging in conventional politics. They were usually found within the Democratic Party, though they had derided the conventional parties in the 1960s.

THE WOMEN'S MOVEMENT

Like Chicanos, Indians, and young people, women also responded to the example of the Black Revolution. Although they constituted a majority of the population, women were like the racial and ethnic minorities in that their opportunities for jobs and prestige were arbitrarily limited. They resembled minorities, too, in that they often did not assert themselves. These were among the arguments in Betty Friedan's *Feminine Mystique* (1963), which helped spark the new feminist movement of the late 1960s and early 1970s. Beginning as only a weak voice in a society largely complacent about the denial of women's rights and opportunities, the movement by the mid-1970s was compelling a new recognition of women's quest for equality—fueled by women getting together amongst themselves to air their grievances, a process known as "consciousness-raising". Even older women, observers pointed out, began to call for equal occupational opportunities for persons of their sex, as well as equal pay. The spreading interest produced a wide range of organizations, some highly militant or politically radical, though the moderate National Organization for Women (NOW), which Betty Friedan founded in 1966, counted the most members. In 1972 the women's movement helped push through Congress a women's equal-rights amendment to the federal Constitution, an amendment whose fate will be discussed later. These years also saw the passage of much significant legislation on behalf of women, such as the Equal Credit Opportunity Act of 1974. The political scientist Ethel Klein has argued that it is no coincidence that, except for Title VII, all of the new legislation followed a huge national demonstration by women on August 26, 1970, the fiftieth anniversary of women's suffrage. Politicians pay attention to this kind of mobilization.

Thanks to the afore-mentioned Title VII of the Civil Rights Act of 1964 and executive orders prohibiting discrimination on grounds of sex as well as race or religion, the federal government forced open new jobs for women in private employment while insisting that public institutions increase their proportion of women employees, especially in high-level jobs.

Another highly significant piece of legislation was Title IX of the Education Amendments Act of 1972 that prohibited sex discrimination in educational programs receiving federal funding. This law has remade the nature of athletics for women, creating scholarships and other opportunities that were unheard of for earlier generations. The new drive to expand women's opportunities saw traditionally male occupations like those of army general, telephone lineman, jockey, air-tower controller, and FBI agent being filled by women either for the first time or in unprecedented numbers. The new women's organizations also mounted a successful campaign to change state laws to make abortions and birth control information easier to obtain; and they aroused a new popular demand for—and in some instances succeeded in gaining government support for—child-care centers, so that mothers could have a true choice as to whether or not to seek employment. These social changes have remade the demographic make-up of certain professions that had been nearly entirely male—such as medicine, law, and academia.

Although not many more women were actually elected to national political office than in previous years, women participated in politics on a greater scale than ever before. At the Democratic Convention in 1972, for example, about 35 percent of the delegates were women—a proportion previously unheard of—and a black woman, Representative Shirley Chisholm of New York, was placed in nomination for President. Even at the Republican convention, which had no minimum quota for women delegates, women made up almost 30 percent of the membership. In 1974 Ella Grasso was elected governor of Connecticut. She was the first woman to reach that level of government unaided by a husband's political prestige or power. Women were also elected to a number of mayoralties, including those of San Jose, California, a city of half a million, and Chicago, the nation's second largest city.

There were also monumental changes in the area of jurisprudence. It may be recalled that immediately after the Civil War certain suffragists had tried to use the Fourteenth Amendment as the basis for voting—but to no avail. In 1971, for the first time in American history, the United States Supreme Court employed the equal-protection clause of the amendment to strike down legislation on the grounds that it discriminated on the basis of sex. The case was *Reed v. Reed*, and it revolved around an Idaho statute that had given the preference to males in administering estates. This case then legitimated a whole new field of law, whereby women could now bring suit to overturn discriminatory laws or hiring practices.

Although women workers were still concentrated in low-paying and low-prestige jobs, the new interest among women and throughout the society in equality of opportunities of all kinds provided broader horizons for women than had previously been the case in the United States. Whether all women wanted to compete with men in the world was still an open question, if antifeminist women's groups were to be believed; but that many women welcomed the widening of their horizons, no one could deny.

GAY LIBERATION

On June 28, 1969, there took place an event that has been seen as the symbolic launching of the gay rights movement, the Stonewall riot in New York City. On that date, police raided a bar with a reputation of being frequented by gays, the Stonewall Tavern. At that time, in fact, such a bar constituted an illegal assembly of homosexuals under New York law, but on this occasion, the patrons fought back; and there was soon a new slogan: "Gay Power."

It must be pointed out that there had long been gay communities in major American cities—and even gay activism. The activism was, of necessity, discreet; and the communities' residents had remained closeted, fearful of losing their jobs—or of other forms of harassment. This did not represent paranoia on their part, inasmuch as consensual sex between adults of the same gender was illegal in most states. Moreover, until 1973 the American Psychiatric Association labeled homosexuality a mental disease. After Stonewall, and no doubt inspired by the civil rights activism of so many other groups, there began to be Gay Pride parades and flourishing—and uncloseted—gay and lesbian communities in big cities or bohemian smaller cities. The new attitude was perhaps best expressed by gay artist Andy Warhol, who stated that "I didn't think I should want to change. ... Others should change their attitudes, but not me."

A RESURGENCE OF RELIGION

In the early 1800s the French visitor Alexis de Tocqueville noted the importance of religion in the lives of Americans. Because of the long-standing importance of religion to Americans, their ways of worship have reflected—often quite closely—the social as well as the spiritual changes in their society. Therefore, it is not surprising that alterations in religious outlook and practices in the decades after World War II reflected both the prosperity and the anxiety that so strikingly characterized those years.

During the 1950s, for instance, there was a kind of religious revival among Protestants in which popular preachers like Billy Graham and Norman Vincent Peale extolled traditional Christian morality. Some 95 percent of Americans claimed some form of religious belief, and a full 60 percent claimed to attend church weekly, the highest percentages in American history. It was the time of the Cold War when contrasts between atheistic communism and religious America served political as well as religious purposes. Evangelists combined evangelical Christianity with the anticommunism of the cold war. Billy Graham and Billy Hargis argued that Americans must be converted to Christianity in order to stave off the threat from godless communism. With so many Americans displaying their religious beliefs, Congress reacted with a string of symbolic resolutions that reflected American religiosity. Congress declared a National Day of Prayer and made "In God We Trust" the national motto. "In God We Trust" was also added to American folded currency (It had been on coins since 1863 when Abraham Lincoln had it inscribed on Union coins to show the faith of the Union in juxtaposition with the Confederacy). It was also in the 1950s when the words "under God" were first added to the Pledge of Allegiance to the Flag. The original pledge had been written in the 1890s for the purpose of displaying national unity in a nation of immigrants.

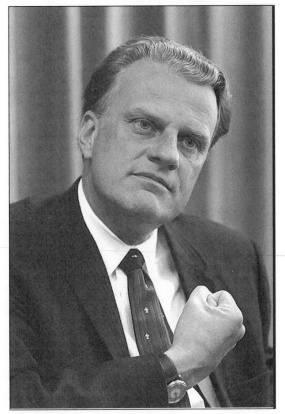

Billy Graham (Library of Congress)

It is not entirely evident, however, that the move to greater religiosity significantly altered other aspects of human behavior. For instance, the religious nation was stunned in 1948 when Alfred Kinsey published his controversial work, *Sex and the Human Male*, where his much-criticized survey data revealed that 67 percent of college-educated adult males and 84 percent of non-college educated adult males had experienced some form of sexual activity outside of the bonds of marriage. Furthermore, 37 percent reported that they had experienced some form of homosexual activity, and 18 percent of rural males reported that they had experienced sex with animals.

That turn toward popularizing traditional Christianity, however, proved to be short-lived in the face of the drive for social reform during the 1960s. Most of the established churches became caught up in the great civil rights movement and in the opposition to the war in Vietnam. The heavy involvement of Roman Catholics, both clerical and laypersons, was especially notable inasmuch as the Church had long been recognized as conservative in its outlook on both religion and social change. Efforts to democratize the Church internally were encouraged by liberal Pope John XXIII, whose two Vatican Councils marked a turning point in broadening the Church's outlook on the world. For the American Catholic Church, though, the effect of the changes seemed to be divisive, a sign of which was a drop of one third in the rate of church attendance among Catholics from 75 percent in 1957—among the highest for Americans—to 54 percent in 1975.

This substantial drift away from the traditional Catholic Church was experienced by many traditional Protestant denominations as well. One of the consequences of the churches' emphasis on social issues during the 1960s was that many Americans began to fear that the spiritual message of religion was being forgotten in the process. Moreover, the materialism of the consumer society apparently aroused in many a yearning for a spiritual balance.

As a result, by the 1970s those Christian churches that emphasized personal salvation and individual fulfillment rather than social action grew rapidly. Sometimes they were old denominations, like the Southern Baptists, but more often they were new evangelical churches like the Churches of Christ, the Churches of God, or what came to be called the Pentecostals. All of them emphasized forceful, emotional preaching, Christian fellowship, and personal conversion—that is, "being born again." At the same time, they minimized theological doctrines and encouraged a literal interpretation of the Bible. In 1976 a Gallup poll reported that a third of all Americans considered themselves as having been "born again."

The new stress on the search for personal spiritual meaning in an anxious, if affluent society also showed itself outside conventional religious groups. It could be seen in the six million people who took up Transcendental Meditation (T.M.) and in the three million who practiced yoga during the 1960s. The thirst for personal commitment was noticeable, too, among the young people who joined the studious Jesus Movement, the chanting, begowned Hare Krishnas, or the aggressively proselytizing Unification Church of the Reverend Moon.

Signs that this concern for personal religious commitment was making itself felt in secular politics were President Carter's proud announcement that he was a "born-again" Christian, a similar statement by John Anderson, one of Carter's rivals in the 1980 campaign, and the increasing attractiveness of the conservative politics of Republican candidate Ronald Reagan to the new evangelical churches of the South and Southwest, whose members had usually been Democratic.

In the 1980s religion was still clearly important to many Americans. Surveys showed that, of all the industrial nations of the world, the United States was the most religious. It should be observed, however, that it was precisely because Americans continued to place a high value on religion that they put pressure on the churches and synagogues to respond to social change. In July 1978, for example, the authoritarian Mormon Church for the first time permitted black men to become full-fledged members of the priesthood, and several Protestant denominations and Jewish synagogues in the late 1970s granted pastoral roles to women in response to demands from their members and the women's movement in general.

The social and economic changes in the United States during the postwar era owe much to the altered position of the United States in the world as a result of its total victory over its enemies in World War II. That victory helped to shape not only how Americans thought about their responsibilities in the world, but also what they believed about themselves as a people. In some ways the victory gave Americans a sense of mission and a sense of power that encouraged them to transform their society for the better and to assume a positive role in the preservation of freedom abroad. That same self-confidence and sense of mission, however, led them to undertake policies and actions that many would later deplore and regret—policies that not only imposed excessive burdens, but also threatened the life of the Republic, repudiated its ideals, and brought destruction upon thousands of people living far beyond the borders of the United States. In the next two chapters we examine those policies and actions at home and abroad that helped to shape the fateful years after 1945.

THE PRICE OF POWER, 1945–1963

(Library of Congress)

FROM PEACE TO COLD WAR

The surrender of Japan soon after the dropping of the two nuclear bombs in August 1945 caught most Americans, in and out of government, by surprise. Since the Nazi defeat in April, the army and the navy had been readying the great military machine for the final assault upon the Japanese home islands. Yet within weeks after the Japanese surrender, the dismantling of the military establishment, built up over four years of war, had begun. Public clamor to "bring the boys home" was insistent throughout the remainder of 1945. By January 1946 the government was discharging members of the armed forces at the rate of 35,000 a day. By the end of 1946 the military establishment was down to one fifth of wartime strength.

Simultaneously with the discharge of soldiers, the government began the cancellation of war contracts, and within a month after the surrender of Japan $35 billion worth were dropped. The end of war work and the glutting of the labor market with discharged veterans seemed to many to presage a severe depression, but billions of dollars of personal savings and the rapid transition to peacetime production made things turn out otherwise. Instead, inflation became the principal problem in the ensuing years.

THE ECONOMIC PROBLEMS OF RECONVERSION

The ending of overtime work at war plants and the upward movement of prices, in 1945 and 1946, provoked organized labor into a wave of strikes. In October 1945, for example, the number of worker days lost through strikes doubled over September. It continued to rise, and all told, about 4.5 million workers went out on strike in 1946. Since the strikes were usually for increased wages, the federal government ran into difficulties trying to hold the line on prices. Demands by Congress and the public for tax reductions also meant increased pressure on prices. In November 1945 Congress cut income taxes by some $9 billion and repealed the wartime excess-profits tax as an inducement to increased production.

Nevertheless, the big issues of 1946 were prices and labor unrest. The Truman administration tried to hold the line on prices by continuing wartime price controls, but businessmen, most Republicans, and other large sectors of the popu-lation were anxious to re-

Harry S. Truman *(Library of Congress)*

move all wartime restrictions. The results were inadequate price-control legislation and a steadily rising price curve as Americans attempted to spend their wartime savings in a marketplace that had experienced shortages of consumer goods during the war. In the resulting situation, American demands for consumer goods outstripped the capacity of American industry to produce them.

With the election of a Republican Congress in November 1946, the Truman administration gave up and abolished virtually all controls over prices. Nevertheless, shortages of all kinds of goods persisted with the result that prices in 1947 continued to increase to new heights almost every month. Despite the high prices, or perhaps because of them, employment remained high and business activity good. Undoubtedly many workers, especially unorganized labor and white-collar workers, suffered from the steady increase in the cost of living but the country as a whole enjoyed a post-war boom.

In February 1946, before it was clear that a boom would be the shape of the postwar era, Congress passed the Employment Act, which placed responsibility upon the federal government for the prevention of mass unemployment and economic depression in the aftermath of the war. Although no specific measures were spelled out in the act (because of the need to win conservative support), it did create the Council of Economic Advisors to the President. In a sense the Employment Act was a reflex from the days of the depression, showing the continuing effect of the New Deal revolution.

TRUMAN VERSUS A REPUBLICAN CONGRESS

Opposition to price controls, support of labor control bills, and demand for tax reductions marked a rising conservative tide across the country and in the Congress. This conservatism was clearly reflected in the congressional elections of 1946. Brandishing the slogan "Had Enough?" the Republicans elected majorities in both houses for the first time since 1928. First on the agenda of the new Eightieth Congress was legislation to control labor unions, which since the end of the war had been disrupting the economy through nationwide strikes. Earlier in 1946 Truman had vetoed a severe anti-labor law, even though he himself, beset by a national railroad strike in May 1946, had threatened to draft rail workers into the army. In June 1947 the new Republican Congress under the leadership of conservative Senator Robert A. Taft passed the Labor-Management Relations, or Taft-Hartley Act. Truman returned the bill with a stinging veto message, but Congress quickly overrode the veto.

The Taft-Hartley Act attempted to meet two public complaints against labor. In an effort to deal with nationwide strikes that disrupted the economy, the act empowered the President to force a union to accept a 60-day "cooling-off period" before striking. If at the end of the cooling-off period the dispute was not settled, the employer's last offer would have to be presented to the workers for a secret vote. The act was also intended to reverse the alleged favoritism of New Deal legislation toward labor by listing a number of unfair union practices. It banned the closed shop (the requirement that employees join unions), permitted employers to sue unions for broken contracts or strike damages, required unions to make their financial statements public, forbade union contributions to political campaigns, limited the "check off" system whereby employers collected union dues, and required union leaders to take oaths that they were not Communists. Despite the opposition of labor organizations and of many liberal Democrats, the Taft-Hartley Act has remained unchanged, a measure of the American people's conviction in the postwar era that national labor unions, like business, need some kind of public control.

Although Truman and the Republican Eightieth Congress rarely agreed on domestic policies, on defense and foreign policy they often did. Both Truman and the Republican Congress were staunchly anti-communist, and both would quickly begin waging a war against communism with vigor. Truman and Congress also agreed to reorganize the armed forces, and the army, navy, and air force were merged into the Department of Defense under the National Security

Act of July 1947. James V. Forrestal, former Secretary of the Navy, was named the first Secretary of Defense.

SOVIET EXPANSIONISM

Even before the Potsdam Conference in July 1945, there had been signs that the Allied unity displayed at Yalta was superficial. Before his death, for example, Roosevelt had warned Stalin that the Yalta agreements concerning Poland must not be ignored. Stalin's initial refusal to send Foreign Minister Molotov to the United Nations conference in April 1945 also aroused Western suspicions of Russian intentions about the postwar world. The abrupt end of Lend-Lease in early May (after the fall of Germany) raised doubts in Russian minds about Western friendship, though Truman reinstated a scaled-down version of Lend-Lease to placate the Soviets after their vehement protests. At Potsdam Stalin insisted on having his way in Poland and with German reparations, which the Russians considered imperative for the rebuilding of their devastated country. In Poland, Stalin refused to allow free elections because he knew that they would have resulted in the election of the Polish government-in-exile in London that would oppose Stalin's control. Stalin was also determined to render Germany powerless since they had twice invaded the Soviet Union in less than a quarter century. The British, in contrast, wanted a strong Germany allied with the West as a check on Soviet expansionism.

During the last half of 1945 and most of 1946, at the United Nations and at meetings of the Council of Foreign Ministers to draw up peace treaties with the lesser enemy states, the West and the Soviet Union clashed repeatedly, each viewing the other as increasingly threatening or uncooperative. Obviously the two sides had different security concerns and differing views of the future of Europe—especially of Germany. The Soviets also protested unilateral United States control of Japan and favored Soviet involvement through the United Nations. The matter was essentially solved when Secretary of State Byrnes agreed to recognize Soviet control in Romania and Bulgaria, in return for Russian acceptance of the United States role in Japan.

Particularly ominous for the peace of the postwar world was the Soviet Union's refusal to withdraw its troops from Iran, which the Russians and the British had jointly occupied during the war. Only vigorous protests by the United States and the United Nations impelled a Russian withdrawal in late May 1946. To the Russians the important point was that they had withdrawn under pressure. To the West, and particularly the Americans, it was the necessity to threaten the Russians that was significant. Two months later, in early August, the Soviets demanded slices of Turkish territory and a share in the control of the Dardanelles. To many Western observers Russian behavior announced a resurgence of historic czarist ambitions.

Actually, Soviet conquests already far exceeded any dreams of the czars. Russian armies stood as far west as Berlin and central Germany, and all of eastern Europe lay under their control. Indeed, throughout the 40s and early 50s it was the presence of large Russian armies in central Europe at a time when the West had long since demobilized its wartime forces that sustained the suspicions and aroused the fears of Western leaders. Today the likelihood of a Russian military advance against western Europe seems slight, but to a generation that had seen Russian power move west against Hitler, that likelihood was ever present.

Moreover, although Yugoslavia was not occupied by Russian troops, it was then firmly Communist under the leadership of Marshal Tito. Indeed, in 1946 Tito was more truculent in his dealings with the West than was Stalin himself. The same month that the Soviets served their demands upon Turkey, Tito's planes on two different occasions shot down unarmed American transport planes which had accidentally crossed the Yugoslav frontier. It was Yugoslavia, not Russia which was supplying Communist-led guerrillas fighting the British-dominated monarchy in a civil war that erupted in Greece following World War II.

Churchill, now out of office because of a Labour Party victory, gave voice to the concern of the Western nations. At Fulton, Missouri, on March 5, 1946, with President Truman sitting conspicuously on the platform, Churchill called attention to the "iron curtain" which "has descended across the continent" from "Stettin in the Baltic to Trieste in the Adriatic." Moreover, he went on, "Nobody knows what Soviet Russia and its Communist international organization intends to do in the immediate future, or what are the limits, if any, to their expansive and proselytizing tendencies."

Meanwhile, the Soviets in the United Nations turned down the American plan for international control of nuclear energy. Since under the plan the United States would have voluntarily surrendered its monopoly of nuclear power, Americans took the Soviet rejection as another sign that the Soviets were not interested in peace and order in the world. The Russians, apparently, saw the American plan as a way of denying them their own nuclear bomb. On both sides, suspicions grew.

THE PROBLEM OF GERMANY

The major European dispute between East and West concerned the future of Germany. In the view of the Western powers, particularly the United States, the revival of a united Germany had been agreed upon at Yalta and reaffirmed at Potsdam; but Russian insistence upon large German reparations could only mean that Stalin intended to keep Germany weak and without hope of recovery for the foreseeable future. As a result the Russians obtained very little in the way of reparations from the Western occupation zones, though in their own zone they carted eastward everything they could.

By the fall of 1946 Secretary of State James F. Byrnes was convinced that the Russians did not really want a reunited and independent Germany and were using the continued division of Germany as a means of impeding German recovery. He, therefore, persuaded the British to merge their zone with that of the Americans (The French, as skeptical of German unification as the Russians, did not join the other Western allies until 1949); however, in merging the Western zones, Byrnes was helping to divide Germany ever more decisively between East and West. Thus, in Germany as in the United Nations, the Cold War had obviously come into being by the end of 1946. Increasingly in the years ahead, West Germany (which became independent as the German Federal Republic in 1954) would be viewed by the West as the chief bulwark against Russian expansion into western Europe, while the Soviet Union would see it as the chief threat to Russian hegemony in eastern Europe.

THE CONTAINMENT POLICY

In 1946, Stalin publicly asserted his confidence in the eventual triumph of the communist system. Stalin argued that communism and capitalism were on a collision course and that capitalism would be torn apart. Stalin further stated that the U.S.S.R. would do without consumer goods, if it needed to do so, in order to strengthen its military and ensure its own survival. In response, United States Supreme Court Justice William O. Douglas referred to Stalin's speech as the "Declaration of World War III." Meanwhile, Churchill reacted to the Stalin speech by arguing in his Fulton Missouri Speech that the United States and England must work together to "contain Soviet aggression."

For a time after World War II, it seemed that the Russians might well be in a position to extend their influence into western as well as eastern Europe. Economically and militarily prostrate from their struggles, the nations of western Europe were in poor position to defend themselves against Soviet military force and subversion. In France and Italy strong Communist parties seemed on the verge of taking power either through the ballot box or by force.

In Greece Communist-led guerrillas fought pro-Western government forces for control of the country. Even Great Britain, presumably one of the principal victors of the war, was on the verge of bankruptcy. Economically bled, Britain could no longer sustain its traditional role as guardian of Greek independence. In February 1947 the British announced the imminent withdrawal of aid. In Turkey, too, an unstable government was being pressured by the Soviets for territorial grants and administrative concessions in the Dardanelles.

In Asia and Africa the steady drive for independence had already begun. With their lack of experience in democratic procedures and the difficulties of maintaining stability in the midst of poverty and strife, the new nations seemed ripe for Communist revolution or subversion—either of which, American leaders anticipated, would make them allies of the Russians.

The American response to this global Communist threat was the establishment and gradual implementation of the policy of "containment." As publicly announced in July 1947 in an article by State Department aide George F. Kennan, "The main element of any U.S. policy toward the Soviet Union must be that of a long-term, patient but firm and vigilant containment of Russian expansive tendencies." While accepting—though not happily—the accomplished fact of Soviet control over eastern Europe, the policy of containment sought to hold the line against the further extension of Soviet power, military or political.

Kennan, in a document known as his "Long Telegram" and in his article "The Sources of Soviet Conduct," argued that the U.S.S.R. contained internal political and economic contradictions that it could not stand over the long haul. Consequently, if the United States would merely contain the U.S.S.R., it would eventually crumble from within due to the internal contradictions. Kennan argued that the U.S.S.R. was

George F. Kennan *(Library of Congress)*

not a legitimate government to the people of the U.S.S.R. and, therefore, could only rule by massive coercion. That would take tremendous energy and be very expensive, and the Soviet Union would, therefore, eventually burn itself out. Furthermore, Kennan argued that the Soviet economy was untenable, partially due to the command nature of the economy that ignored the demand-driven principle, and partially because the allocation of 15 percent of its resources to military purposes would cause serious consumer shortages and eventual economic collapse. Kennan expected containment to last no longer than 20 years, but warned that it would be very expensive and that Americans would tire of the policy before it was over.

The same month that Kennan's article was published, Congress passed the National Security Act, which created the National Security Council to advise the President on domestic and foreign policy related to national security. The National Security Act also created the Central Intelligence Agency to gather and analyze intelligence. CIA activities were to include covert operations outside the country, including sabotage and subversion, as well as spreading untrue propaganda that would further American interests and undermine the interests of its enemies—primarily the Soviet Union.

THE TRUMAN DOCTRINE

Even before the containment policy was officially enunciated, the Truman administration had taken steps to stem the Communist advance. After much soul-searching and consultation with congressional leaders of both parties, President Truman urged the United States to take up the burden of aid to Greece and Turkey. In a historic address to Congress and the nation on March 12, 1947, he called for $400 million in economic and military aid for the two beleaguered countries to save them from "aggressive movements that seek to impose upon them totalitarian regimes." Liberals and left-wingers, who denounced his proposal as warmongering, and conservatives that protested its cost opposed Truman's proposal. All recognized that this "Truman Doctrine," pledging aid to nations resisting aggression or subversion, signaled a sharp departure from the whole previous practice of American foreign policy. For the first time in peace, the United States was being asked to commit its military might (though that part of the proposal was underplayed by the President) and economic power to the defense of countries outside the Western Hemisphere. George Kennan, the father of the containment policy, argued that the Truman Doctrine was "grandiose" and "sweeping" and might lead to a worldwide crusade that the United States was neither militarily nor economically prepared to support.

Nevertheless, Secretary of State Dean Acheson met with Congressional leaders and argued for United States aid to the imperiled Greek monarchy. Acheson argued that: "Like apples in a barrel infected by one rotten one, the corruption of Greece would infect Iran and all to the East." Although Acheson did not mention the word "domino," his speech was essentially the beginning of the "domino theory," which held that if one country fell to communism, others would also fall to communism, like "dominoes." Acheson argued that a communist victory in Greece would "open three continents to Soviet penetration." Acheson—"The major powers are now at Armageddon as the Soviet Union presses for advantage. Only the U.S. has the power to resist."

By votes of 67 to 23 in the Senate in April and 287 to 107 in the House in May, the Republican Congress sanctioned the new turn in foreign policy by voting the funds. Three hundred United States military and civilian advisors were sent to Greece to help the monarchy against the leftist rebels. Yugoslavia's Marshall Tito had aided the rebels, but Tito cut off aid to the Greek rebels in July of 1948. United States Navy planes dropped napalm on areas where the guerrillas were hiding in the Grecan Mountains, and the rebels were defeated. The Greek Monarchy upheld, and the first test of the policy of containment was a success.

THE MARSHALL PLAN

An immediate Soviet military invasion was not the greatest threat to western Europe in the first postwar years. It was the legacy of war—persistent poverty, widespread misery, and mass unemployment—in which communism found its greatest ally, especially in countries like Italy and France, where economic and political instability was an open invitation to subversion. A strong possibility existed in both countries that Communist parties would be voted into power. Many in both countries viewed the Communists as the true patriots because the Communists, unlike the French and Italian right-wing elements, never collaborated with the Nazis. If the capitalist economies failed, the Communists stood poised to seize power. Therefore, to stimulate European recovery and stave off communism, the Truman administration began plans for extending massive economic assistance. The idea—first suggested in a speech by Under Secretary of State Dean Acheson—was brought to the attention of the world, and Europe in particular, in a Harvard commencement address delivered by Secretary of State George C. Marshall on June 5, 1947.

Marshall's speech offered American economic aid to any European nation seriously interested in restoring the shattered economy of Europe, including those nations closely associated with Soviet Russia. The nations of western Europe accepted with enthusiasm, but Russia, after some preliminary exploration, compelled its allies to stay out of the scheme, suggesting that the Marshall Plan was a cover-up for American imperialistic designs. The proposal also evoked widespread opposition in the United States, from both the right and the left, but leading Republicans, notably Senator Arthur H. Vandenberg, championed it from the outset. Calling the idea a "calculated risk" to "help stop World War III before it starts," Vandenberg countered assertions that it was a gigantic "international WPA" or a "Socialist blueprint." As presented to Congress in December, the measure envisioned the expenditure of $17 billion over a four-year period, with $6.8 billion to be spent in the 15 months following April 1, 1948.

During the fall and winter of 1947 the continued decline of the European economy and the many stories of starvation and misery in western Europe gave substance to the argument for United States assistance. Equally influential, however, were the continued signs of Soviet pressure. For example, in February 1948 a Communist workers' coup thrust democratic Czechoslovakia behind the Iron Curtain, and in March reports of a Russian advance to the West circulated among government officials. Furthermore, a Communist victory appeared to be a real possibility in the Italian elections coming up in April. Responding to these pressures and to others from an anxious administration, Congress on April 2, 1948, passed the European Recovery Act, or Marshall Plan, granting to the President about 90 percent of the funds he had requested for the first year. Though Congress refused to commit the United States to anything thereafter, subsequent grants were made on an annual basis.

The full four-year plan was never carried out, however, because the Korean War intervened; but the $12.5 billion extended to 16 western European countries achieved the purpose of reviving the European economy. Between 1948 and 1951 production in all the countries rose about 37 percent. With a more prosperous economy and resultant political stability, the internal threat of communism receded noticeably. Moreover, the international cooperation fostered by the plan afforded the European nations a new insight into the advantages of closer economic union. That insight bore fruit in the 1950s with the formation of the European Coal and Steel Community and, later, the Common Market, or European Economic Community—leading eventually to the European Union.

NATO

In June 1948, the West established the West German Republic and introduced a new West German mark to curb the rapid inflation that had been rising in Germany due to the flooding of the German market with Russian-made currency in East Germany. Stalin retaliated by cutting off land access to West Berlin from West Germany. Without outside aid, West Berlin would starve. Stalin also cut off electric power to West Berlin from power plants in East Berlin. Stalin issued the Warsaw Declaration, which demanded a return to the four-power division of Germany stipulated at Potsdam.

President Truman was influenced by the arguments of Presidential Counsel Clark Clifford, in what was known as the Clifford Memorandum, where he argued that the United States must prepare for imminent atomic and biological warfare from the U.S.S.R. and that Soviet aggressions could be stopped only from counter-pressure from the United States. Consequently, Truman desired to implement "counter-pressure" against the Soviet action at Berlin. In considering courses of

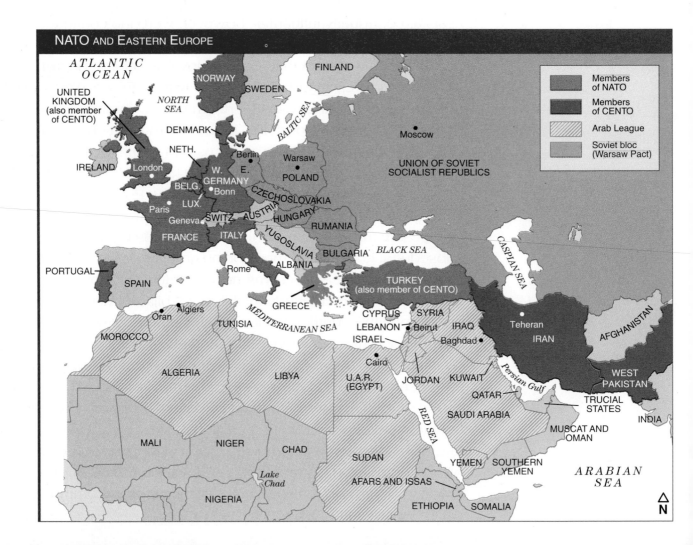

action, United States General Omar Bradley warned against a truck convoy of supplies to Berlin because the Soviet military in the region outnumbered NATO forces 3–1. Therefore, Bradley and the United States military commanders considered any such ground campaign to supply Berlin as unnecessarily risky. The dominant view was perhaps best expressed by Colonel Frank Howley, who argued, "We would have got our derrieres shot off." Faced with the prospect of a perhaps disastrous war if they forced their way overland to Berlin, the Western Allies instead instituted a gigantic airlift to fly in supplies and food. The food and supplies were flown to Berlin daily for over one year until May 1949, when Stalin lifted the blockade. Over two million tons of supplies were airlifted to Berlin—over 13,000 tons a day. Planes left for Berlin every three minutes and provided three times the amount of supplies needed to sustain the city.

In the event that the airlift failed, Truman appeared prepared to resort to the atomic bomb. Truman secured Britain's permission to accept 60 B-29 bombers and declared to the press that they were "atomic capable" (although they really weren't, and the United States did not even have 60 atomic bombs at the time). Although the Russians did not molest the airlift, they did not agree to end the blockade until May 1949. Meanwhile the airlift had proved its ability to sustain the West Berliners and the Western right of access to Berlin.

The Berlin blockade reinforced the American belief in the need for closer military cooperation among the western European nations. The Brussels Pact of March 1948 had already created a defensive alliance among Great Britain, France, Belgium, Luxembourg, and the Netherlands. Toward the end of 1948 the United States encouraged widening the Brussels Pact alliance to include other nations rimming the North Atlantic. In the spring of 1949, 12 countries, including Canada and the United States in the New World, joined the North Atlantic Treaty Organization, which in 1952 expanded to include Turkey and Greece and in 1955 West Germany.

With the signing of the treaty in April 1949, the United States obligated itself to come to the aid of the Europeans—the strongest commitment yet assumed in the course of the diplomatic revolution that had begun only four years earlier with the ratification of the United Nations Charter. The NATO treaty encountered only slight opposition in the Senate, which ratified it on July 21, 1949. Under the treaty, "an armed attack against one was considered an armed attack against all." The stated purpose of NATO was to maintain a ground force in Europe large enough to hold off Soviet attack until the United States could engage the Strategic Air Command—in other words, nuclear bombers. In early 1951 General Dwight D. Eisenhower was appointed Supreme

Commander of the new integrated NATO defense force to be fashioned out of the national armies of the 12 signatories.

Since the Soviet decision to blockade Berlin had been calculated to break the Western alliance, but had only made the alliance stronger, the Soviets called off their blockade in May 1949. The U.S.S.R. then countered NATO with the creation of the Warsaw Pact, a similar alliance between the U.S.S.R. and the states under its control in Eastern Europe. As it had been prior to World War I, Europe was again divided into two great opposing alliances.

THE ASIAN REVOLUTION

THE OVERTHROW OF COLONIALISM

If the results of the war in Europe dropped unexpected problems into the laps of Americans, the consequences of the war in Western Asia constituted a revolution. The great colonial powers, though victors in the war, lost virtually all their Asian possessions within five years after the defeat of the Japanese. (It should be mentioned that an end to colonialism might well have been seen as implicit in the Atlantic Charter of 1941). When the British returned to Malaya and Burma, the Dutch to the East Indies, and the French to Indochina, they were greeted with demands for independence and sometimes by open military rebellion.

One by one the European nations made the only reasonable response—granting independence to the former colonies and removing themselves from Asia. The United States, acting on a prewar promise, led the movement by granting final independence to the Philippines on July 4, 1946. Britain followed next, finally reducing its once vast empire in Asia to a few pinpoints on the map, the most important of which was Hong Kong. Not all the European powers, however, recognized the shape of the future as clearly as Britain. The Dutch did not transfer power to the new nationalist government of the United States of Indonesia until 1949, and the French sacrificed the flower of their officer corps and thousands of young men in a futile struggle to suppress the nationalist movement of the Viet Minh under their leader Ho Chi Minh in Indochina until 1954. The liquidation of colonialism was the first part of the Asian revolution.

THE TRANSFORMATION OF JAPAN

The second part of the revolution in Asia was the American occupation of Japan. Although ostensibly representing all the Allied powers, General Douglas MacArthur, the American occupation commander, in reality was the supreme authority in that country, and his policy was dictated by the United States. Aside from stripping Japan of all its colonies, including Formosa and Korea, the United States deliberately undertook to destroy the old Japan. Thoroughgoing land reform, which spread land ownership more widely than ever before, improved the lot of the peasantry. A new democratic constitution, in which the emperor was reduced from a god to a mere symbol of national unity, also removed the army from politics. In fact, Article IX of the Japanese Constitution eliminated the Japanese military for all purposes whatsoever, forever. Simultaneously, Japan signed a security treaty with the United States where the security of Japan became the exclusive responsibility of the United States. Women were enfranchised for the first time and given greater freedom in society and within the family. As Edwin O. Reischauer, an authority on Japanese history and ambassador to Japan under the Kennedy administration, once wrote: "During the early postwar years in Japan, MacArthur played the role not only of the most radical American revolutionary of modern times but also of the most successful."

When the Korean War broke out in 1950, the United States and its non-Communist allies in the war against Japan hastened to conclude peace with the Japanese, despite the objections of the Soviet Union. MacArthur ordered the Japanese to construct a 75,000-man security force for self-defense, an apparent contradiction with Article IX of the Japanese Constitution. The final peace treaty was signed in September 1951, and in a separate agreement the United States was permitted to retain military bases in Japan.

THE VICTORY OF CHINESE COMMUNISM

The third prong of the Asian revolution was the Communist conquest of China. When World War II ended, China was accorded the status of a great power, receiving, for example, a permanent seat in the Security Council of the United Nations. With the Japanese defeat, most people assumed that Generalissimo Chiang Kai-shek's Nationalists would reinforce their rule over all China. Even Stalin at the close of the war recognized Chiang's Nationalist government, not Communist leader Mao Tse-tung's (Mao Ze Dong), as the rightful regime.

The Chinese Communists, however, had a sizable army and a government in northwestern China and were stronger than many observers thought. The Communists had gained a reputation as true Chinese patriots for their efforts in World War II against the Japanese

Mao Tse-tung *(AP Photo/Hsinhua News Agency)*

invaders, and they gained more popular support by promising land redistribution to the peasants.

At first the United States helped Chiang in his effort to spread his military authority over all of China. When that failed, the United States attempted through most of 1946 and 1947 to find a basis for agreement between Chiang and Mao Tse-tung. In December 1945 President Truman had dispatched General George C. Marshall to China where he worked for over a year on such a mission, but without success. By late 1947 the two sides were fighting it out in open civil war, during which Chiang's lack of support from the masses of the Chinese people became increasingly evident.

By the close of 1949 the Nationalists had been forced to flee to the island of Formosa (Taiwan), some 100 miles off the coast. In October 1949 the Soviet Union extended diplomatic recognition to the new People's Republic of China, and in February 1950 the two Communist powers signed a mutual assistance agreement and pact of alliance. Thus, just as the end of the Berlin blockade and the creation of NATO marked the ebbing of the Communist danger in western Europe, the Cold War came to Asia.

At almost the same time in 1949, the Soviets shocked Americans by detonating their own Atomic bomb, 20 years prior to American expectations. In response, the United States formulated NSC-68 in 1947 and adopted by the National Security Council in 1950. NSC-68 contained several arguments that would guide American foreign policy for the coming years. First, the document stated that conflict between East and West is unavoidable and that amoral Soviet objectives were counter to United States aims. Furthermore, negotiations were considered useless because the U.S.S.R. could not be trusted to bargain in good faith; consequently, the United States must increase its military spending 40 percent.

THE DEMOCRATS STAY IN

THE MIRACLE OF 1948

By 1948 Harry Truman had warmed up well to the role of President, which had been thrust upon him so suddenly three years before, and he was eager to try himself before the electorate. Although opposed by many Democrats who thought he lacked popular appeal (according to opinion polls, his presidency was approved by only 36 percent of the people in April 1948), the President controlled the July Democratic convention, which dutifully nominated him on the first ballot, naming Senator Alben W. Barkley of Kentucky as his running mate. When the Republican Congress was called into special session by Truman that summer and refused to enact his program, Truman went into the campaign talking about the "do-nothing" Eightieth Congress.

In the election, Truman faced a serious loss of votes from both the right and left wings of his own party. Because the Democratic convention adopted a strong civil rights plank (following the desegregation of the Armed Forces in 1946 and that of major league baseball by Jackie Robinson in 1947), several Southern states bolted from the

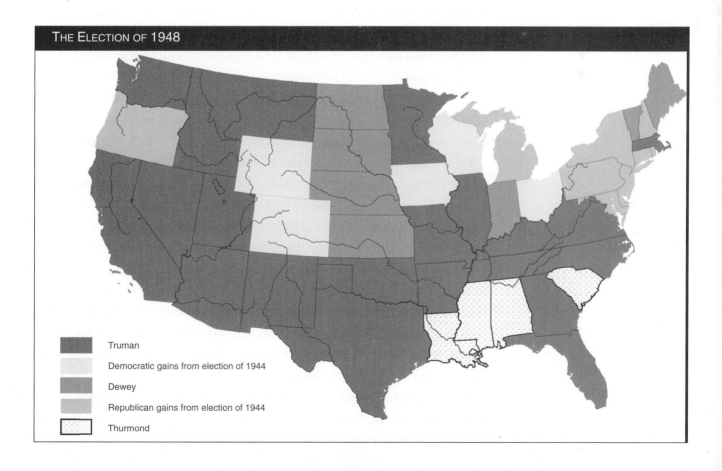

THE ELECTION OF 1948

Truman

Democratic gains from election of 1944

Dewey

Republican gains from election of 1944

Thurmond

Democratic Party and put forth their own States' Rights segregationist "Dixiecrat" party candidate, Governor J. Strom Thurmond of South Carolina. Thurmond, it was expected, would cut deeply into Truman's support in the Deep South. The candidacy of Henry A. Wallace, who favored negotiations with the Soviets rather than resistance, on the newly formed Progressive Party ticket promised to draw away left-wing and liberal votes for Wallace campaigned vigorously against the administration's containment policy, contending that it was anti-Russian and would lead to war instead of peace.

The Republicans, more confident of victory than at any time since the Great Depression, nominated for President their 1944 standard bearer, Governor Thomas E. Dewey of New York, with Governor Earl Warren of California as the vice-presidential nominee. Dewey's campaign was a model of caution. Sure of victory, he preached unity and the need for efficiency. Accepting all of the New Deal reforms, even though they were also Truman's stock in trade, Dewey simply said he would administer them better. Even commentators opposed to Dewey conceded, along with the public opinion polls, that a Republican victory was foreordained. Harry Truman, though, was not convinced. He barnstormed around the country, attacking the Republican Congress for being against the people's interests. Republicans, he said, were "old moss backs ... gluttons of privilege ... all set to do a hatchet job on the New Deal." He traveled some 32,000 miles and made 356 speeches, far exceeding the campaign effort of Dewey, his overly confident and much younger opponent.

Truman deflected charges from the right that he was soft on communism with the creation of the Loyalty Review Board that investigated and fired federal employees for supposed communist ties. Truman's anti-communist credentials were also boosted with the Berlin Air Lift as a response to Stalin's blockade of West Berlin. The Berlin crisis also created a "rally around the flag" effect that was beneficial to Truman and his administration. Furthermore, Truman's continuation of the New Deal was a political winner among both agricultural interests and the urban working class.

Election night brought the big surprise as Truman never lost the slight lead he gained in the early returns. By the next morning the miracle had occurred—Truman swept the late-reporting western states and was re-elected by two million votes. Some newspapers that had gone to press on election night ran headlines the next morning entitled, "Dewey Defeats Truman," but it was not to be so. Truman was elected by two million votes. Truman's vigorous appeals to popular memories of the Great Depression and his uncompromising defense of the New Deal had apparently struck fire in millions of voters (though 700,000 who cast votes for state candidates did not even bother to vote for President). Moreover, by emphasizing the decline in farm prices under Republican farm legislation, Truman actually recaptured the farm vote, which Roosevelt had lost in 1940 and 1944. Dewey, however, ran well, better than Republican congressional candidates, probably because of Truman's vigorous attacks on the Eightieth Congress.

Not surprisingly, the Democrats gained 75 new seats in the House and nine in the Senate. Although Truman lost four Southern states (39 electoral votes) to Thurmond, he had shown that a united South was not necessary for a Democratic victory, especially since his Southern losses were more than made up for in the North by urban black votes. Henry Wallace's candidacy, which at one time had been viewed as a threat to Democratic strength in Northern cities, affected Truman's total hardly at all.

THE FAIR DEAL

In his inaugural speech in January 1949, Truman spoke of his program as the "Fair Deal." In effect, it was a continuation and extension of the New Deal that called for civil rights legislation, a national health program, aid for public education, and support for low-income housing. Truman also asked for repeal of the Taft-Hartley Act and enactment of a new farm subsidy program (the Brannan Plan), but the Congress, despite its Democratic complexion, would agree to neither. A coalition of Republicans and conservative Southern Democrats killed off not only civil rights legislation but also most of the other measures of the Fair Deal. On the other hand, in 1949 Truman did succeed in obtaining a housing act and a minimum-wage increase to 75 cents an hour. In 1950 Congress also agreed to broadening Social Security coverage to cover dependents, largely due to the widows and orphans problem that resulted from World War II, placing some 10 million more persons under the benefits of the system. At the time, with only a 1 percent payroll tax, Social Security had accumulated a $9 billion surplus.

After 1949 Truman was increasingly plagued by revelations of corruption in his administration. Although none of the disclosures compared with the Teapot Dome scandals of the 1920s, many officials, especially in the Internal Revenue Service, were proved in court to be corrupt. Moreover, some White House officials turned out to have rather casual standards of proper behavior for government officers. In short, the Republican charge that the Democrats had been too long in control of the executive branch of government seemed to have some validity. An issue of foreign policy, however, was to supersede corruption as a Republican weapon against the administration. Truman himself would eventually leave office essentially broke, suggesting that he himself, at the very least, did not use his position for personal enrichment.

THE OUTBREAK OF THE KOREAN WAR

When in 1945 the United States and the Soviet Union occupied the former Japanese colony of Korea, they arbitrarily divided the country between them along the 38th line of latitude. Originally intended to be temporary, the line, in the suspicious atmosphere of the Cold War, hardened into a border between two Korean regimes—the North under Russian tutelage and the South under American. Because each of the Korean regimes wanted to unite the peninsula under its own rule, border clashes were frequent. When the Americans withdrew their troops from South Korea in 1949, they carefully refrained from leaving behind any offensive weapons like tanks or heavy artillery for fear that the strongly nationalist president of South Korea, Syngman Rhee, would attempt to conquer North Korea by force of arms.

The Russians, withdrawing at about the same time, left a well-trained and heavily equipped North Korean army behind, complete with Soviet T-34 tanks. After the withdrawal of American troops, low intensity conflict and border raids between North and South Korea increased in intensity. Over 100,000 Koreans died between 1946 and 1950 in border clashes and raids. Then on June 24, 1950, Communist North Korea, armed with Soviet weapons, attacked capitalist South Korea. Stalin denied any involvement in the North Korean action and even pulled his troops near Korea away from the borders to display his non-involvement. Instead, Stalin announced that North Korea was acting on its own. Nevertheless, the United States viewed the attack as "Soviet aggression" and responded through the UN.

In any event, the North Korean army stormed across the 38th parallel, quickly overwhelming the thin South Korean defenses. Before the rapidly advancing invaders, Rhee's government fled the capital of Seoul. The UN unanimously denounced North Korea as the aggressor and passed a resolution to militarily aid South Korea. The U.S.S.R. could have vetoed the measure had their representative been present, but the Soviet minister was absent that day in protest of the failure of the UN to admit Communist China to the UN. China had fallen to the Communist rebels of Mao Tse Tung the previous year, but the UN had recognized "Nationalist" China on the island of Formosa instead. The fact that the Soviets were absent at the UN the

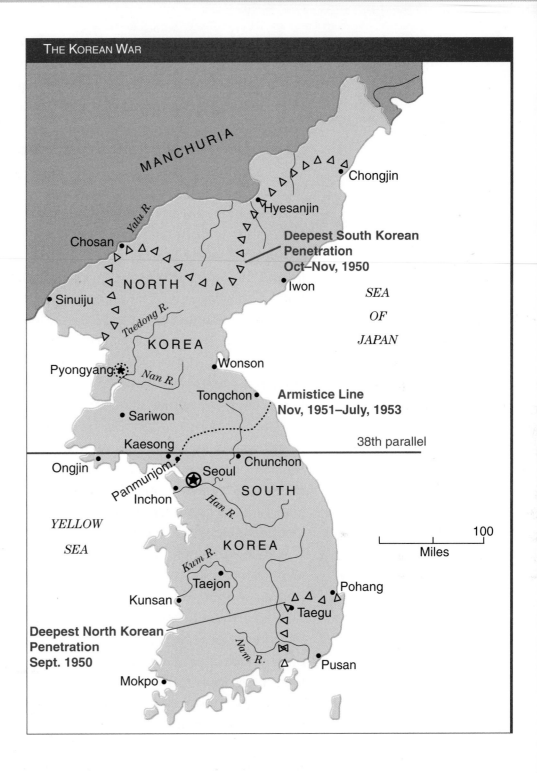

day of the vote on the use of force in Korea suggests that either the Soviet's fumbled or that North Korea, indeed, was acting on its own. If the Soviets had known of the attack in advance, surely the Soviet representative in the UN would have ended the Soviet boycott of the UN and registered a veto of the resolution to aid South Korea.

Thereupon, the Truman administration, faced with a naked act of military aggression, decided to commit the United States to South Korea's defense, even though the American army then comprised no more than ten and one half infantry divisions and one armored division. On June 30, when it became evident that American air and naval support alone could not save the South Koreans, the first United States ground troops landed in Korea.

Prodded by the United States, the United Nations on June 27 branded the North Koreans as aggressors and called upon all member states to "furnish such assistance to the Republic of Korea as may be necessary to repel the armed attack and to restore international peace and security to the area." On July 7, General Douglas MacArthur was designated United Nations commander in chief. Although all during the fighting in Korea, American and South Korean troops made up the great preponderance of UN forces, some 20 nations had sent some kind of support by the end of 1950. Truman did not ask Congress for a Declaration of War because he described the situation as a "police action." Truman recognized that Korea had no strategic importance, but had great symbolic importance in showing the Soviets that the United States would not allow the spread of communism.

The North Korean troops, using Soviet tanks, rolled through South Korea with ease before help could arrive in sufficient number—as the South Koreans had no weapons that could penetrate the armor on the Soviet Tanks. Seoul fell on June 28, 1950, and Truman responded with United States air strikes against targets in North Korea. General Douglas MacArthur recommended that the United States send an invasion force, blockade the coast, and launch air strikes wherever militarily necessary. For over two months the American and South Korean forces suffered uninterrupted defeats as the powerful North Korean armies pushed them down the peninsula into a small pocket around the port city of Pusan. Then on September 15, 1950, in a surprise maneuver, General MacArthur led a successful amphibious landing at Inchon on the west coast, far behind the North Korean lines. MacArthur's subordinates had argued against the Inchon landing due to high tides and rocky cliffs, but MacArthur believed that those same conditions gained him the element of surprise. A simultaneous drive from the Pusan area caught the Communists in a giant pincer movement. By the end of September, the United Nations forces were on the verge of crossing the 38th parallel into North Korea. When they did, a new phase of the war in Asia opened.

President Truman altered his war strategy from containment to "liberation" and began what was known as "Operation Rollback." The American military purpose suddenly was no longer merely "containment" of the spread of communism, but became one to liberate all of Korea from communism. Truman consequently approved the advance of MacArthur's troops north of the 38th parallel. George Kennan warned that the Soviets would resist such a move; and the People's Republic of China warned the United States that they would intervene if the United States approached the Chinese border.

The United States believed that the Chinese warning was merely bluster and that China was too weak to intervene. Dean Acheson, in particular, argued that Chinese intervention would be "sheer madness." Similarly, General MacArthur believed that the Chinese would not intervene because they had no air force and would, therefore, be completely vulnerable to the advanced United States air power, resulting in massive casualties. On September 29th, Secretary of Defense George Marshall gave MacArthur the authority to cross the 38th parallel. On October 9, 1950, two United States jets mistakenly strafed a Soviet airstrip near Vladivostok, Russia. The Soviets protested, and the United States apologized as the two superpowers attempted to avoid direct confrontation. Also on October 9, the United Nations General Assembly passed a resolution calling for a unified democratic Korea, thus authorizing MacArthur to invade North Korea and providing UN support for Truman's new goal of eliminating communism in all of Korea.

MacArthur's invasion forces pushed the North Koreans back across the 38th Parallel and into North Korea, but China's Communist leader Mao Tse Tung retaliated against the invasion by sending a group of "Chinese Volunteers" to attack the UN forces on October 26, 1950. The attack by Mao's "Volunteers" was a warning from Mao that he would not tolerate the proposed UN takeover of communist North Korea. In response, MacArthur called for an all-out offensive in North Korea on November 24, declaring that his men would drive the communists out by Christmas.

On November 26, as units of the United Nations forces approached the Yalu River—the border between Korea and Communist China—large contingents of Chinese "volunteers," perhaps as many as 600,000 in number ambushed the 20,000 American troops, compelling the UN troops to retreat. In temperatures as low as 30 degrees below zero, the American troops were simply overwhelmed by superior numbers. Thereafter, increasing numbers of Chinese poured across the Yalu, and the UN troops were once again pushed far south of the 38th parallel. In January of 1951, the Chinese invasion force pushed all the way to Seoul and retook the South Korean capitol. The UN denounced the Chinese invasion and called for their withdrawal, but the Chinese demanded the withdrawal of UN troops, the cessation of United States aid to Taiwan, and admission of the People's Republic of China to the UN. MacArthur then regrouped his forces and launched a counter-offensive that pushed the Chinese back to the 38th Parallel in March, 1951. Here the war stalemated.

Thus deprived of total victory, General MacArthur asked for permission to bomb the Chinese in what he called their "sanctuary" across the Yalu. The Truman administration turned down his request on the ground that such action might well invoke the Sino-Soviet mutual assistance pact and thus bring on a war with the two chief Communist powers. Furthermore, Truman authorized UN forces to bomb only the southern half of bridges on the Yalu River (the North Korean border with China), provoking MacArthur to reply sarcastically that he did not know how to bomb "half a bridge."

Truman favored a negotiated peace, but General MacArthur favored a military victory. MacArthur called for a blockade of the Chinese coast, bombings of Manchuria and China's major industrial centers, a Nationalist/American invasion of the Chinese mainland from Taiwan, and the dropping of a field of radioactive cobalt along the Chinese-North Korean border. MacArthur also favored the use of atomic bombs on the North Koreans.

Truman feared that MacArthur's strategies would lead to Soviet intervention and possibly World War III. Furthermore, United States allies were not in favor of expansion of the war. The Nationalists in Taiwan had already proven incapable of defeating the communists on the Mainland, and MacArthur's bombings would most likely not stop the Chinese intervention in North Korea.

If through Truman's strategy the nation was spared a world war, however, a limited war far from American shores produced frustrations that made the Korean struggle immensely unpopular. Public opinion polls indicated that after January 1951 Truman never again received the support of a majority of the American people. Many spoke bitterly of "Truman's War." A draft board in Montana went so far as to refuse to draft any more men until General MacArthur was authorized to bomb as he saw fit in China.

As the leading advocate of striking directly against China, MacArthur inevitably came into fatal clash with the administration. When a letter written by MacArthur to the House Republican minority leader was released to the press—a letter in which MacArthur charged administration "diplomats" with fighting the Asian war "with words" rather than "with arms" and declared that "there is no substitute for victory"—President Truman on April 11, 1951, summarily removed the general from his commands in Korea and Japan on the grounds of insubordination. It should be noted, however, that MacArthur did emphasize in his address to Congress, "No man in his right mind would advocate sending our ground forces into continental China;" and, therefore, MacArthur was also, like Truman, actually advocating a limited war, but with a victory over communism in Korea. The nation was surprised and shocked that Truman would fire one of the great American heroes of World War II. The President was widely attacked, and MacArthur accorded a hero's welcome when he returned to the United States.

After an address by the dismissed general before Congress, a Senate investigation exhaustively inquired into the removal. At the end of several weeks of hearings, during which the pitch of emotionalism gradually declined, the Senate committee agreed with General Omar Bradley when he said that MacArthur's policy would have extended the fighting to the mainland of Asia, which would "involve us in the wrong war, at the wrong place, at the wrong time, and with the wrong enemy." There was brief talk in Republican circles in 1952 of drafting MacArthur for a run at the Presidency, but Republican attention quickly shifted to another World War II general, Dwight Eisenhower.

THE EFFECTS OF THE KOREAN WAR

By demonstrating that aggression could be halted if the nations of the world were determined to do so, the Korean War stimulated the expansion of America's armed forces and put life into the recently created NATO. Domestically the Korean "police action," as Truman once called the war, forced the administration to institute economic controls, but not to the extent of World War II. Although both income and excise taxes went up in 1950 and a new excess profits tax became law in 1951, there was enough military production by the end of 1952 to permit the easing of many of the economic controls. Indeed, the war had pushed the nation into a new boom, quickly ending the recession of 1948–1949. Thus, conditions of life in the United States were such that many Americans, who had no relatives in Korea, hardly knew there was a war at all. That such was the case only made the war more unpopular among those who did have sons fighting overseas.

THE END OF THE KOREAN FIGHTING

Once the Chinese intervention demonstrated that the whole peninsula could not be united under Syngman Rhee, the Truman administration sought to end the fighting as soon as possible. By the end of 1952, strengthened UN forces had pushed the Chinese northward again to the region of the 38th parallel. Although the United States was prepared to strike a truce at that point, the Communists held off.

Although the American "kill ratio" against the Communists approximated 20–1, the war stalemated near the 38th parallel into a "you take this hill and I'll take that hill" war by mid-1951. Peace talks had begun between the United States and the communists in the summer of 1951, but went nowhere over the issue of repatriation of prisoners. The Communists demanded that all prisoners be returned, but the UN refused to repatriate those who did not want to go home. In a stinging indictment of the North Korean communist regime, some 80,000 of the UN's 170,000 North Korean prisoners opposed repatriation.

Dwight Eisenhower was elected President in 1952 and assumed office in 1953. Eisenhower opposed the repatriation of prisoners. The new President secretly offered the communists a cease-fire, but simultaneously threatened the use of nuclear weapons to win the war. The communists then agreed to an armistice that returned the border to the status quo ante bellum.

The cost, however, was great, with 54,000 American deaths and two million Korean and Chinese (one million on each side).

THE GREAT FEAR

Between 1949 and 1954, the nation was gripped by a pervasive fear that communism was about to subvert the Republic, and any program or any idea traceable to Communist ideology became suspect. Even an unproved accusation of having been a Communist was sometimes enough to condemn an individual to lose job or friends. A veritable witch-hunt for traitors and disloyal citizens was carried out by government and by private groups. Actually, throughout the whole period the number of disloyal persons discovered in positions of trust was insignificant, in proportion to the hysteria that had been engendered.

The Great Fear grew out of the deteriorating international situation of 1946 and 1947, when some Communists in the United States, Canada, and Britain showed that regardless of their formal citizenship, they owed first loyalty to the Soviet Union. In 1947 the federal government instituted a program to check on the loyalty of government employees, and many public educational institutions, like the University of California, demanded oaths of loyalty from their faculties. Congressional investigations in 1947 and 1948 revealed evidence of spying in government by Communists during the 1930s. During those investigative hearings of the House Un-American Activities Committee (HUAC), Elizabeth Bentley, a former courier for Soviet espionage, testified that Lauchlin Currie, a White House assistant during the Roosevelt Administration and former Lend-Lease Administrator for China, and Harry Dexter White, formerly Assistant Secretary of the Treasury and architect of the World Bank and IMF, had been involved in the transfer of government documents to Soviet agents. In the same hearings, Whittaker Chambers, editor of *Time* magazine and a former Communist, testified that he knew former State Department employee and President of the Carnegie Endowment for International Peace, Alger Hiss, to be a Communist. While in the State Department, Hiss had played a role in organizing the United Nations, was in attendance at Yalta, and was a friend of Secretary of State Dean Acheson, whom conservatives vilified for "losing

Whittaker Chambers *(AP Photo)*

China." In essence, Hiss perfectly fit the profile for the belief that communists, in some sort of grand plot against America, had infiltrated the United States government, especially the State Department.

In spite of these "discoveries" of Communist infiltration, Truman won the election of 1948, partially by beating his own anti-Communist drum. After the election was over, the anti-communist machinery set in place continued its onslaught against the imagined demons. In October 1949, the Department of Justice obtained the conviction of the leaders of the American Communist Party under the Smith Act of 1940 that had made teaching or advocating overthrow of the United States government illegal. In 1950, the Congress of Industrial Organizations expelled Communist-led unions from its organization. In essence, the Communist Party in the United States, which had never been a major force in American politics even during the worst years of the Great Depression, was at low ebb.

In 1949, however, Whittaker Chambers launched new fears by introducing new evidence to HUAC that Alger Hiss had actually passed State Department documents to him back in the 1930s. Chambers produced his so-called "pumpkin papers" (so named because he had supposedly kept them buried in his pumpkin patch), which included some State Department documents copied in Hiss' handwriting and some typed on Hiss' typewriter. Hiss could not be indicted for espionage due to the statute of limitations, but he was charged with perjury and, after one mistrial resulting from a hung jury, was convicted and given a five-year jail sentence in January 1950.

Hiss' trial and conviction, like other revelations about Communists in government, concerned espionage prior to 1945; but in 1950 the FBI revealed that American spies had transmitted secret A-bomb data to the Russians in 1945 and 1946. In February 1950, more "proof" emerged that the nation had been infiltrated by Communists when British physicist Klaus Fuchs, who had worked at Los Alamos, was arrested in Britain on charges of passing nuclear secrets to the Soviets. The apprehension of Fuchs then led to the arrest of Americans Harry Gold and Julius and Ethel Rosenberg on the charge of conspiracy to commit espionage. Although the information transferred to the Soviets was not the information that led to the Soviet development of the atomic bomb, the Rosenbergs, whose cause the Communists tried vainly to make into a new Sacco-Vanzetti case, were executed in 1953. For many, the discovery of espionage by nuclear scientists not only proved once again that there was Communist infiltration, but that it was also gravely dangerous.

To these and other sensational revelations of Communist activity in the United States, the Congress responded with the Internal Security (or McCarran) Act of 1951, passing it over Truman's veto. The new law required Communist and Communist-front organizations to register with the government and to identify as Communist all their mail and literature. It also forbade employment of Communists in defense work and barred anyone who had belonged to a Communist or fascist organization from entering the country. The most drastic of all provisions and the one that measured the extremity of congressional concern was the authorization for the government to place Communists, citizens and aliens alike, in concentration camps whenever a national emergency occurred. This provision was repealed only in 1970.

THE RISE AND FALL OF MCCARTHY

The person who more than any other intensified the Great Fear during these years was Joseph McCarthy, a Republican senator from Wisconsin. McCarthy first came into national prominence in February 1950 when he charged in a speech at

Senator Joseph McCarthy *(Library of Congress)*

Wheeling, West Virginia, that 57 or more Communists were then working in the State Department. "In my opinion," he said, "the State Department, which is one of the most important government departments, is thoroughly infested with Communists," and it was all the fault of Secretary of State Dean Acheson, that "pompous diplomat in striped pants, with a phony British accent." A Senate investigating committee later exonerated the department, but McCarthy continued to make similar unsubstantiated charges of Communists in government in his deep, bass Lone Ranger-type voice, occasionally naming a name but citing numbers by the score.

In the context of the Great Fear, his spectacular, headline-making accusations often gained credence. Occasionally he was courageously repudiated and criticized, but most government officials, including his fellow senators, feared to gainsay him. To do so laid his accusers open to charges of being "soft" on communism.

On February 20, McCarthy followed up his Wheeling performance with a speech in the Senate where he presented what he said were some 80 cases drawn from the loyalty files of the State Department compiled by Robert E. Lee, an investigator for HUAC. McCarthy ignored the fact that the FBI already had cleared 40 of the cases and not all of the "loyalty" files had anything to do with Communism in the first place. Republican minority leader Kenneth Wherry demanded a Senate investigation of McCarthy's charges, and a subcommittee of the Senate Foreign Relations Committee under Democratic Senator Millard Tydings of Maryland was given authority over the investigations. Tydings' lack of zeal for McCarthy's witch-hunt would give McCarthy reason to later target Tydings himself.

The anti-Communist right, however, rallied to McCarthy's aid. Reporters for the Hearst and McCormick media empires provided McCarthy with information and gave him favorable coverage. McCarthy did not bring forth any new information; instead he unearthed the names of 22,000 presumed communist sympathizers from a report that had been compiled by the Dies Committee staff in 1944, but then withdrawn by the full committee. McCarthy also used material from previous investigations by HUAC that had gone nowhere.

In March 1950, McCarthy recklessly named Owen Lattimore, a Johns Hopkins professor, as the "top Russian espionage agent" in the United States, and Louis Budenz, the former managing editor of *The Daily Worker* (the newspaper of the Communist Party), stepped forward to identify Lattimore as a Communist. Lattimore was anathema to Republicans because he was associated with the Institute of Pacific Relations, had been an adviser to Chiang Kai-shek, and had accompanied Henry Wallace on a trip to China in 1944. Unfortunately for McCarthy, Budenz' testimony directly contradicted statements he had given to the State Department in 1947—that he knew nothing to implicate Lattimore with the Communist Party.

The Tydings subcommittee also again investigated the Amerasia incident. Former Office of Strategic Services (OSS) employee Frank Bielaski testified that he had noticed a document in the Amerasia office that was marked "A-bomb;" but none of the other OSS officers who had accompanied him on the raid could remember such a document, and the term "A-bomb" had not come into use yet at the time of the OSS raid of the Amerasia offices. In the end, the Tydings subcommittee found McCarthy's charges to be groundless and, therefore, refused to conduct an independent investigation of the State Department as McCarthy wished. In July, the subcommittee issued a majority report, which described McCarthy's claims as "a fraud and a hoax."

During the election campaign of 1952, Senator McCarthy "invaded Maryland" and campaigned for John Marshall Butler against his nemesis Millard Tydings. The McCormick publishing empire that provided Butler with the *Chicago Times-Herald*'s printing services at cut-rate prices, thus aiding him. McCarthy's staff worked with *Times-Herald* employees to produce a faked photograph of Tydings conversing with Communist Party leader Earl Browder, with the result that Tydings was defeated in his Senate re-election bid. Tydings filed a complaint with the Senate's Subcommittee on Privileges and Elections, but the damage had been done and McCarthy had been vindicated.

McCarthy's attacks on government officials showed no limits other than his targets tended to be Democrats. McCarthy's allies even accused Truman's Secretary of Defense George Marshall of links to communism. Republican Senator William E. Jenner of Indiana exemplified the McCarthyist position when he referred to Marshall specifically as a "front man for traitors." Jenner denounced Marshall in apocalyptic language, arguing:

> "The day of reckoning had arrived concerning how the Democratic Party has been captured from within and used to hasten our destruction, both from within and without, during these tragic years."

Jenner then denounced and blamed Marshall for the Pearl Harbor defeat, for his role in helping FDR "trick America into a war," the extension of Lend-Lease to the Communist Soviet Union, the "selling out" of Eastern Europe at Yalta, the loss of China, and the inclusion of an offer of aid to the Soviet Union under the Marshall Plan

Joseph McCarthy emerged in June 1950 to also denounce Marshall on the floor of the Senate. McCarthy claimed that since World War II, the free world had been losing 100 million people per year to international communism. Though this might technically have been true since it had been only five years since World War II, and the Communist People's Republic of China had a population of 500 million, if China and Eastern Europe were removed from the picture, the "advance" of Communism appeared much less bleak.

Conservatives followed up McCarthy's tirade by accusing Acheson of "inviting" the North Korean invasion by excluding South Korea from the During the election campaign of 1952, defense perimeter. Conservatives further suggested that communist spies who had infiltrated the government under the direction of Moscow were manipulating the State Department. Senator Styles Bridges argued that there was a Soviet "Master Spy" in the State Department and demanded that Acheson be thoroughly questioned by the Tydings subcommittee. In December 1950, The Republicans passed a resolution at the Republican Conference in Congress demanding Acheson's resignation, but the Democrats blocked any such move.

Republican Dwight Eisenhower won the Presidential election of 1952, but McCarthy's attacks on the State Department and other agencies of the executive branch continued even under Eisenhower's Republican administration. Indeed, during the 1952 campaign Eisenhower hesitated to criticize the senator publicly even though it was widely known that Eisenhower deeply resented the scurrilous attacks that McCarthy had made upon General George C. Marshall, a man Eisenhower greatly admired. As late as January 1954, a Gallup public opinion poll showed that 50 percent of the American people favored McCarthy's activities and only 29 percent opposed him, although by then the senator had driven from the State Department almost all its experts on China on the grounds that they had "lost" China to the Communists. (For the story of another able American sacrificed on the altar of McCarthy's anti-communism, see *J Robert Oppenheimer: The Destroyer Destroyed.*")

Although President Eisenhower himself was not directly supportive of McCarthy's activities, he did not condemn them either; consequently, Eisenhower's inaction and silence on the matter had the impact of legitimizing McCarthy. Nevertheless, some Republicans were apprehensive about McCarthy, and Vice President-Elect Richard Nixon was dispatched from the White House to the McCarthyists to discuss the directions of McCarthy's attacks. At a meeting at Key Biscayne, Florida, on December 30, 1952, Nixon pressed McCarthy to agree that he would direct his venom only at the Democrats.

In spite of McCarthy's assurances to Nixon, McCarthy pressed forward in an effort to obtain the loyalty/security files of the United States Army. McCarthy's primary attack dog, Roy Cohn, however,

PEOPLE THAT MADE A DIFFERENCE

J. Robert Oppenheimer: The Destroyer Destroyed

Dr. J. Robert Oppenheimer *(AP Photo/Eddie Adams)*

To win the Second World War quickly, science and government became linked as they had never been before. The most awesome result was the invention of the nuclear bomb. Its detonation over Hiroshima and Nagasaki in August 1945 made the stakes of the later Cold War the highest imaginable: literally the destruction of the world. At the center of this new relation between science and government stood J. Robert Oppenheimer, often called the father of the atomic bomb. He was also one of the most illustrious victims of the Cold War.

Born in New York City in 1904, Oppenheimer, the son of a well-to-do businessman, was educated at the private Ethical Culture School in New York City and at Harvard. After graduating from college in three years, he spent almost four years more in Europe, earning a Ph.D. at Cambridge in England and studying theoretical physics in Germany, Holland, and Switzerland. Upon his return to the United States in 1929, he accepted posts at the University of California and the California Institute of Technology.

At Berkeley, Oppenheimer at first had only one graduate student, a young man no other professor would accept. Oppenheimer's exciting and lucid teaching, his mastery of the latest in theoretical physics, and his broad cultural interests soon changed that. Within four years the best young brains in physics were seeking him out. At that time, Oppenheimer had no interest in public affairs. Outside of physics, his greatest pleasure was studying Hindu scriptures in Sanskrit and reading English Renaissance poetry. He had no telephone or radio. Indeed, it was only in 1930, on a long walk with a fellow physicist, that he first learned of the stock market crash the year before!

This detachment from public affairs began to change in the middle 1930s. Through a love affair, he became caught up, as many idealistic young Americans of the time did, in the cause of the Spanish Republic, which was fighting for its life against a military coup headed by General Francisco Franco and aided by the troops of Hitler and Mussolini. In 1940 Oppenheimer married a young widow whose husband had been a Communist party official, killed in Spain. For a while his new wife was a party member and so were his brother and sister-in-law. These Communist associations, however, did not stand in the way of Oppenheimer becoming involved in the biggest secret undertaking ever initiated by any government.

The secret was the construction of the first nuclear weapon. Oppenheimer was made the director of the most important—and most secret—part of the Manhattan District Project: the design of the bomb at the isolated mesa in New Mexico called Los Alamos. Without the incentive of a war, the government probably would not have gambled on the project, and without Oppenheimer, there probably would not have been a bomb before the war ended. Oppenheimer brought the necessary scientists together in a totally isolated community of several thousand people and then kept them working amicably and productively to solve the myriad design problems. So intense was the secrecy that even the babies born at Los Alamos were given false birth certificates. During this period, Oppenheimer's weight fell from 130 to 116 pounds. His gangling frame, clothed in an unpressed suit, surmounted by his famous broad-brimmed porkpie hat, seemed never to be still. He was the heart as well as the brain of Los Alamos.

On that July dawn in 1945 when the bomb was tested at Alamagordo, in southern New Mexico, Oppenheimer was so nervous that the military commander had to take him outside for a walk in the desert to calm him. When the bomb exploded with a silent burst of light brighter than the sun itself, illuminating even distant mountains, a line from Hindu scriptures leaped into Oppenheimer's mind: "I am become Death, Destroyer of Worlds." Outwardly, though, he smiled with relief; his three-year mission was accomplished. This man who believed in "ahisma"—the Hindu principle of nonviolence—had built the most devastating weapon the world had ever known.

The success of the Los Alamos enterprise catapulted Oppenheimer into public as well as scientific prominence around the world. He acted as scientific adviser to several government agencies and to the President himself. But his great prestige was not enough to protect him against the fears spawned by the new weapon he had worked so hard to create.

In 1949, before any American political leader had thought possible, the Soviet Union exploded a nuclear device. With the United States no longer in possession of a nuclear monopoly and the Cold War in full swing, pressure mounted for new military weapons. For some, the answer was the thermonuclear or fusion bomb, many times more powerful than the nuclear bomb, but then little more than a theory. And for a while the practical difficulties seemed to rule it out.

By 1953, though, when Oppenheimer's term in government ended, work on a hydrogen bomb had been moving ahead for some time. Still, the new chairman of the Atomic Energy Commission, Lewis Strauss, was convinced the work was not proceeding fast enough. He persuaded President Eisenhower that Oppenheimer had delayed progress because of his Communist sympathies. Although by that time Oppenheimer no longer had any connection with the government, and even his advice had not been sought for months, Eisenhower in March 1954 ordered that "a blank wall be placed between Dr. Oppenheimer and any secret data," pending a hearing.

At the hearings all the old information about Oppenheimer's Communist associations in the 1930s was brought forward again. Especially damning, though, was the testimony of his old Los Alamos associate (and strong anti-Communist) Edward Teller, who pronounced Oppenheimer unreliable. No one ever accused Oppenheimer of giving away secrets. Nevertheless, the Atomic Energy Commission decided by a four-to-one vote to deny him security clearance. The sole dissenter, significantly, was the single scientist on the Commission.

Only with the moderating of the Cold War in the 1960s did Oppenheimer regain any of the recognition he had earned so laboriously during the war. In 1963 President Lyndon Johnson presented him with the Commission's prestigious Fermi Award for contributions to physics. At the White House ceremony an ill and emaciated Oppenheimer hobbled to the rostrum. In his brief, almost private words to the President, he succinctly described the special new relation between science and politics, which had lain at the root of his own public humiliation. Thomas Jefferson, he recalled, often wrote of " 'the brotherly spirit of science which unites into a family all of its votaries.' " But, Oppenheimer continued, "we have not always given evidence of that brotherly spirit in science. This is … because we are engaged in this great enterprise of our time, testing whether men can live without war as the great arbiter of history." Though Oppenheimer died in 1967, that testing continues. The figure of Oppenheimer continues to fascinate his fellow Americans. In 2006 a book on the father of atomic bomb, *American Prometheus* by Kai Bird and Martin Sherwin, won the Pulitzer Prize for biography.

had his own personal reasons for going after the army. The United States Army had drafted Cohn's assistant and homosexual lover, G. David Schine. Cohn pressed the army for special release privileges for Schine, but the Army refused to grant his requests. In retaliation, Cohn launched his ill-fated crusade against the United States Army. In taking on the Army, however, Cohn and McCarthy had taken on a formidable foe with near unlimited resources and legions of allies.

McCarthy's power to frighten came to an abrupt end in 1954 when he obliquely attacked President Eisenhower and directly assailed Secretary of the Army Robert Stevens as an "awful dupe" of the Communists. McCarthy's now-apparent demagoguery caused his popularity to plummet. McCarthy's hearings on the Army dragged on for two months and were televised to the nation, but there was little doubt as to who won the encounter. At the end of the hearings, McCarthy's approval rating had dropped to 35 percent. While Cohn ranted and raved, Army counsel Joseph Welch calmly revealed how McCarthy had introduced altered photographs as evidence in an attempt to smear Army personnel. Cohn resigned as McCarthy's chief counsel, and the Senate Select Committee recommended censure of McCarthy on two counts of contempt of the Senate. Specifically, the Select Committee cited McCarthy's refusal to appear before the Subcommittee on Privileges and Elections in 1952 and the abuse of Brigadier General Zwicker before the Permanent Investigations Subcommittee. The Democrats voted unanimously for Censure, 45-to-0, with only Senator John F. Kennedy of Massachusetts abstaining; and the Republicans were split evenly, 22 for and against, although a mere 12 months before only one senator had been willing to stand out against an appropriation for McCarthy's Committee on Government Operations. The senator's influence abruptly collapsed. Soon thereafter he went into a physical decline, dying in May 1957 of cirrhosis of the liver, thus ending the most reactionary wave that followed World War II. McCarthy's fall marked the end of the Great Fear. A product of that fear and not a cause of it, McCarthyism could last only so long as Americans believed that the internal menace of communism was greater than the external threat; and by 1954 they no longer thought so.

A REPUBLICAN INTERLUDE

THE ELECTION OF 1952

As early as 1950, leading Republicans, especially those of an internationalist persuasion, had been talking of Dwight D. Eisenhower as the ideal candidate for the party in 1952. Still incredibly popular because of his war record, Eisenhower also possessed political appeal because his rise from poor boy in Kansas to international renown seemed to epitomize the American dream. When his name was first suggested for the nomination, Eisenhower announced he was not interested; but in July 1952, after much public and private pressure, he resigned his command of the NATO forces and agreed to try for the nomination.

His most formidable opponent was Senator Robert A. Taft of Ohio, a conservative in domestic affairs and neo-isolationist. Twice Taft had been turned down in favor of Dewey. Now the senator's supporters, who were legion, felt Taft's chance had come; but the convention nominated Eisenhower on the first ballot with Senator Richard M. Nixon of California as his running mate. As a congressman a few years earlier, Nixon had gained national renown as a member of the House Un-American Activities Committee that unmasked Alger Hiss.

After Harry Truman took himself out of the race, the Democrats centered their attention upon new prospects, notably Adlai E. Stevenson, governor of Illinois. Although Stevenson was not sure he wanted to run, the July convention "drafted" him on the third ballot. In an effort to heal the wounds from the party split over civil rights in 1948, the convention nominated a Southerner, Senator John J. Sparkman of Alabama, for Vice-President.

From the outset Eisenhower was the favorite. While Stevenson was compelled to defend the Truman administration, the Republicans fiercely attacked it for alleged corruption, for coddling Communists in government, and, above all, for the Korean War. Late in the campaign Stevenson's manager, referring to the Republican barrage of criticism, remarked, "We are suffering from a new kind of KKK—Korea, Communism, and corruption."

Stevenson, however, proved to be an admirable candidate. His speeches were undoubtedly the most sophisticated addresses heard from a presidential candidate since the days of Woodrow Wilson. His ratings on the public opinion polls steadily rose during the campaign, but never to the level of Eisenhower's.

Toward the end of October Eisenhower capitalized on the pervasive discontent over Korea by promising that, if elected, he would personally make a trip to the battlefront in an effort to bring the fighting to an end. Even the prosperous times, which ordinarily would have worked to the advantage of the incumbent party, could not overcome the force of the Korean issue.

Eisenhower scored a sweeping personal victory with 442 electoral votes to Stevenson's 89 and almost 34 million popular votes to

Stevenson's 27 million. Eisenhower's popular vote ran 15 percent ahead of his party's vote for Congress, for the Republicans captured both houses by only slim majorities (and, in fact, lost that control to the Democrats in the mid-term elections two years later). Another measure of Eisenhower's victory was that he broke into the Democratic South, capturing not only border states like Maryland and Missouri, and Tennessee and Virginia, but Texas and Florida as well. Even in the traditionally isolationist Middle West Eisenhower won easily despite his record as an internationalist.

Blacks, rural Southerners, and the big city voters in the North remained loyal to the Democrats, but close post-election analyses showed that Eisenhower won support from all classes and income levels. A striking measure of his popularity was that perhaps as much as a quarter of his popular vote came from people who had voted for Truman.

THE FIRST EISENHOWER ADMINISTRATION

Many Americans, knowing Eisenhower's long record as a military man, anticipated a stern and exacting leader of Congress and the nation. In fact, Eisenhower turned out quite the opposite. Basically he conceived the President's functions to be quite distinct from those of Congress. He generally refused even to comment upon legislation while it was passing through the legislative mill.

The first administration was intended to be a businessman's government in the best sense of the phrase: It would not be subservient to business, but it would do its best to encourage business. Thus all economic controls left over from the Korean War were abolished early in February 1953. Similarly, government enterprises that competed with private business were dropped. A balanced budget became the guiding aim of the administration under the leadership of Secretary of the Treasury George C. Humphrey. When he took office, Eisenhower cut over a billion dollars from Truman's foreign aid budget; but in the main he would not let the drive for economy endanger the national security. When there was any choice, the administration generally gave preference to business over government; thus, it awarded an electric power contract to a private utility instead of to the Tennessee Valley Authority. Furthermore, and in 1956 the Atomic Energy Commission authorized the private development of electric power through nuclear energy.

In at least two respects the Republicans carried on New Deal-Fair Deal policies without question. One was in showing a willingness to use federal authority to counteract the recession of 1954, and the

Chief Justice Earl Warren administering the oath of office to Dwight Eisenhower (*Library of Congress*)

other was in expanding the coverage of the Social Security system in 1953. Eisenhower also tried to overcome the isolationism that still persisted among many Republicans. Indeed, it was to advance the cause of internationalism that he had run in the first place; but it required all of Eisenhower's prestige to prevent the passage in 1954 of the so-called Bricker Amendment, which would have limited the treaty-making power of the government and enlarged congressional control over foreign relations. Although advanced as a means of preventing the treaty-making power from being abused, this proposed amendment to the Constitution would have seriously handicapped the President's handling of foreign affairs.

THE ELECTION OF 1956

Normally, in view of Eisenhower's immense popularity, his renomination in 1956 would have been unquestioned, but in September 1955, however, the President suffered a severe heart attack that incapacitated him for two months. Although his steady recovery emboldened the party leaders to call once again for his nomination, the President himself withheld his consent until February 1956. That summer he was nominated, once again, along with Richard M. Nixon, and the Democrats also nominated Adlai Stevenson, who this time had eagerly sought the nomination.

Eisenhower would win again as the Republican campaign capitalized on "peace and prosperity," but the victory is better explained by the character of a man who could inspire millions of voters to display campaign buttons reading "I like Ike." Eisenhower's personal popularity won him 457 electoral votes to Stevenson's 73. That it was a personal victory was attested by the fact that Eisenhower failed to bring a Republican Congress into office with him, and the Democrats continued to control the Senate and the House. Ike ran 6.5 million votes ahead of Republican congressional candidates. Not since 1848 had a President failed to carry with him at least one house, and for a popular President such a failure was unprecedented.

WORKING WITH DEMOCRATS

Throughout his second term Eisenhower was confronted with Democratic majorities in both houses. (In the elections of 1958 these majorities reached numbers not seen since the mid-1930s.) Seeing his presidential role as one of resisting a "wasteful" Democratic Congress, Eisenhower regularly vetoed government salary increases and demands for tax cuts during the 1958 recession. Despite the Democratic majorities, all save one of Eisenhower's vetoes of antirecession measures held.

One of the three principal pieces of legislation of Eisenhower's second term was the Labor-Management Reporting and Disclosure Act (1959), growing out of Senate committee hearings on racketeering, corruption, and extortion in labor unions. (The others were the Civil Rights Act of 1957 and the National Defense Education Act of 1958, the latter discussed in the preceding chapter.) The labor act followed the thinking of the Taft-Hartley Act, assuming a divergence of interest between union members and leaders. Senator John L. McClellan, whose committee held the hearings, and Representative Philip M. Landrum, who sponsored the bill in the House, were Southern Democrats; so the bill also symbolized the Republican-Southern Democratic alliance that usually supported the President on labor and financial measures. The Landrum-Griffin Act, as it was also called, among other things set up a "bill of rights" to protect union members against assessments and coercion by labor leaders; required unions to make public, largely for the benefit of their members, all expenditures and all payments made to officers; and provided that unions must hold regular elections of officers.

THE SECOND RECONSTRUCTION

THE 1954 DECISION

On May 17, 1954, in handing down a decision in *Brown v. Board of Education of Topeka*, the Supreme Court of the United States unanimously concluded "that in the field of public education the doctrine of 'separate but equal' has no place." In the middle of the twentieth century, "separate education facilities are inherently unequal," the Court concluded. In thus overturning the decision in *Plessy v. Ferguson* (1896), on which all Southern states rested the validity of their segregated public facilities, the Court opened a new chapter in the history of African Americans in the United States.

For over a decade the Supreme Court had been invalidating state laws, which discriminated on grounds of race, but the school decision shocked the South. Although a few border-state communities like Baltimore and Washington, D.C., began desegregation of schools in 1954, in most of the South the decision met stiff and determined resistance. By the middle of 1956 only some 350 school districts out of 6,300 were desegregated in the South, and none of these desegregated districts was located in the middle or Deep South.

SOUTHERN RESISTANCE

In 1957 Southern opposition to school desegregation reached the point of clashes with federal military power. Under a plan of gradual desegregation worked out by the local school board and the federal district court, nine black students were scheduled to enter Central High School in Little Rock, Arkansas, in the fall of 1957; but Arkansas' Governor Orville Faubus used state troops to bar their entrance. Faced with state defiance of federal authority, President Eisenhower sent in United States paratroopers to enforce the orders of the federal court. For several weeks soldiers with fixed bayonets escorted the black students to classes. Later, federalized Arkansas troops remained to patrol the school grounds for the entire school year.

If the breakdown of orderly processes of law in Arkansas shocked the nation and the world, the use of federal troops temporarily stiffened resistance in the South. "Massive resistance" statutes, as they were called, were hastily enacted in a number of states, resulting in the closing of schools in Little Rock and in three communities in Virginia. By 1959, though, the more moderate people in Arkansas and Virginia accepted at least token desegregation in preference to no public schools at all, and in 1960 and 1961 token desegregation came to the Deep Southern states of Louisiana and Georgia, particularly in the big cities of New Orleans and Atlanta. It should be noted that white churchwomen in several cities organized to uphold the rule of law and the continuance of public education.

The determined opposition of segregationist leaders and White Citizens Councils in the Deep South was not to be broken so easily, however. In September and October 1962, a transfixed nation watched as the state of Mississippi, through its elected officials, defied a federal court order requiring the University of Mississippi to permit a black man, James Meredith, to enroll as a student. The federal authorities tried their best to avoid the use of armed force by working behind the scenes to secure compliance with the court, but Governor Ross Barnett's public statements of defiance encouraged thousands of segregationists, including many students, to attack physically the federal marshals assigned to protect Meredith upon his arrival at the university.

As a result of the vehemence of the attack, President John F. Kennedy (elected in 1960) dispatched thousands of federalized Mississippi national guardsmen and regular army troops to the university town of Oxford to restore peace and to ensure the execution of the court's orders. Meredith entered the university as its first known African American student.

Prior to the riots, desegregation at the state college and university level had been proceeding almost without incident in the Southern states, excepting Alabama and South Carolina. Thereafter, every state moved to integrate all levels of education, though primary and secondary schools had little more than token integration until 1968. The Elementary and Secondary Education Act of 1965, however, which for the first time authorized federal funds to aid school districts, allocated dollars based on the number of poor children whom districts educated and provided equipment and supplies to schools to be used for poor children. Many school districts, therefore, integrated to ensure that they could tap in to the federal funding by teaching poor black children. Between then and 1971 the proportion of black children doubled in Southern schools heretofore wholly white, reaching 39 percent. This was a greater increase and a larger proportion than that for the nation as a whole. As early as 1971 only 14 percent of black children in the South were still in schools that

New York City Mayor Robert Wagner greeting the teenagers who integrated Central High School. Pictured in the front row is Elizabeth Eckford. *(Library of Congress)*

were entirely black. In short, the movement toward integration in the South had proceeded further than it had elsewhere in the country.

Even so, resistance continued. The principal evidence was the growing number of private, all-white schools in the South. In 1971 it was estimated that about four percent of school age children attended such schools.

A NEW CIVIL RIGHTS MOVEMENT

The decline of segregation in the South during the 1950s and 1960s was hastened by a rising assertiveness among Southern African Americans in opposing segregation. One of the most influential efforts, as well as most successful, was the boycott of local buses in Montgomery, Alabama, by the 50,000 black residents. The boycott against segregation on the buses began in December 1955, when an African American seamstress named Rosa Parks refused to surrender her seat on a bus to a white person and was subsequently arrested. Parks had not intended to start a civil rights movement, but stated that she was merely tired and wanted to sit down. Although the subsequent bus boycott by Montgomery's black community brought hardship to the blacks that ordinarily depended upon public transportation to get to work, it was sustained for almost a year through working together in the black community and carpooling.

One of the leaders of this boycott was the Reverend Martin Luther King, Jr., a young African American clergyman who became

Segregated drinking fountains symbolized the separate worlds of the South until the 1960s. *(Library of Congress)*

nationally known for his remarkably effective oratory and his moral leadership, based upon the principle of nonviolence. His successes at Montgomery and later in other causes on behalf of equality and justice, in the North as well as in the South, brought him worldwide recognition and, in 1964, the Nobel Peace Prize. In the short term, the Supreme Court declared segregation of bus passengers unconstitutional in November 1956. In the long term, King went on to offer leadership in the battle for voting rights, in worker struggles, in the antiwar movement and, after his death, won recognition as one of the great Americans of the twentieth century. When Rosa Parks died in October 2005, her body lay in state in the Capitol rotunda in Washington, making her the first woman to be so honored.

In the late 1950s, the slow pace of desegregation, despite the efforts of the civil rights movement, provoked the federal government to take action against discrimination. In August 1957, Congress, after much debate, passed the first civil rights act since the days of Reconstruction. Its purpose was to protect the voting rights of blacks. Though the provisions were weaker than those originally advocated by the Eisenhower administration, they empowered federal judges to jail for contempt anyone—including state officials—who prevented a qualified person from voting. The law also created a temporary Civil Rights Commission to investigate violations of civil rights and to make recommendations for new legislation. (The Commission was continued into the 1970s.)

A second civil rights act, against which Southerners filibustered unsuccessfully, was passed in 1960 to further protect the voting rights of blacks. It was not until the Johnson administration, however, that a voting rights bill was passed that substantially increased voting by blacks in the South.

From 1960 on, African Americans themselves undertook new ways of attacking segregation in the South. There were "sit-ins" at segregated lunch counters and bus depots, "wade-ins" at segregated beaches, and even "pray-ins" at segregated churches—all aimed at nonviolent achievement of integration and equal rights. Out of the lunch counter sit-ins in Greensboro, North Carolina, in April 1960, where young black men sat down and waited to be served at lunch counters in whites-only establishments, came another of the major civil rights organizations, the Student Nonviolent Coordinating Committee or SNCC. Founded by one of the legendary civil rights leaders, Ella Baker, SNCC played an important role in the subsequent sit-ins, in Freedom Rides, where blacks rode whites-only buses, thus challenging segregated interstate bus travel, and many other campaigns. At first a bi-racial organization, SNCC evolved in the direction of Black Power by the late 1960s.

In August of 1963 occurred one of the most significant of the protests, the March on Washington. Some 250,000 Americans, black and white alike, converged on the nation's capital to call for more progress in achieving racial justice. The highlight of the event was Rev. King's "I Have a Dream" speech, one of the rhetorical high points in American history along with speeches, about which we've already learned, by Daniel Webster, Abraham Lincoln, and William Jennings Bryan.

Simultaneously with the anti-segregation movement in the South, Northern blacks in cities like New York and Chicago campaigned against segregated public schools. Northern segregation resulted from residential patterns rather than from laws, but the effects were often the same. Blacks demanded, with some success, that their children be accepted in white schools outside their local districts, where the schools were often crowded and run-down or underfinanced.

But when in the early 1970s the federal courts used compulsory busing to bring about racial mixture in Northern schools, as it had done in the South, strong white opposition exploded. In some Northern cities—like San Francisco, California, Pontiac, Michigan, and Brooklyn, New York—parents who opposed busing kept their children out of school for weeks. In Boston during 1974–1975, the resistance

Martin Luther King at the Civil Rights March in Washington, D.C. *(Library of Congress)*

to busing was as vehement—and violent—as resistance to integration had been at Little Rock in 1957. In 1971, a Gallup poll found that 76 percent of Americans opposed busing as a means of bringing about desegregation. Nevertheless, the courts continued to uphold busing as a constitutional means of breaking segregation. In 1979 the Supreme Court reaffirmed the principle, though by a divided vote.

By the close of the 1970s school segregation was clearly less pronounced in the once completely segregated South than in the North. Only 12 percent of Southern black children were in predominantly black schools as compared to 31 percent of Midwestern and Northeastern children. As recently as 1968 the proportion of black children in segregated schools throughout the nation had been 53 percent.

THE NEW ACTIVIST SUPREME COURT

In the 1930s the Supreme Court was the center of controversy because of its conservatism, but in the 1950s and 1960s it was the object of both criticism and praise because of its willingness to innovate. That willingness, as we shall see, was also the prime source of the strong desire on the part of the first Nixon administration to change its outlook by new, conservative appointments. In at least two different fields the Court exceeded even its customary importance as the final arbiter of American law.

RENEWED INTEREST IN INDIVIDUAL RIGHTS

One of these fields was civil rights and individual liberties. The most striking instance was the 1954 decision already mentioned, in which the Court struck down segregated education; but there were other examples, as well.

During the 1950s the Court spoke out clearly in defense of individual rights even when the accused were Communists. In the case of *Yates v. United States* (1957) the Court seriously modified the *Dennis v. United States* decision of 1951 that had upheld the conviction of 11 Communist leaders for conspiring to over-throw the government by force in violation of the Smith Act. Chief Justice Vinson had stated in his 1951 decision that government could act if "a highly organized conspiracy" to overthrow in the future were established. The *Yates* decision distinguished between "advocacy of forcible overthrow as mere abstract doctrine" (which is within the free speech protection of the First Amendment) and "advocacy that incites to illegal action" (proscribed by the Smith Act). Thus mere advocacy of a theoretical desirability of violence was now not sufficient for conviction. Moreover, "mere membership or the holding of office in the Communist party" was held not to be sufficient proof of specific intent to "incite" persons to overthrow the government.

Another landmark case of these years was *Griswold v. Connecticut* of 1965. In *Griswold* the Court struck down a Connecticut law that lim-

ited access to birth control devices, even for married people. By a 7–2 decision the Court established, in essence, a constitutional right to marital privacy that ensured access to birth-control information and devices. This decision was an important precedent for the following decade's *Roe v. Wade*.

The Supreme Court's most controversial assertion of individual rights since *Brown v. Board of Education* in 1954 was, in fact, the case of *Roe v. Wade*, decided in 1973 by a 7–2 division among the justices. In this decision the Court invalidated all state laws prohibiting

Norma McCorvey, left, who was the Roe in the 1973 *Roe v. Wade* case, with her attorney Gloria Allred (AP/Wide World Photos)

abortion in the first trimester on the ground that there was no compelling health/safety interest in the mother in the first trimester; more women were likely to die carrying the fetus to full term than through having first trimester abortions. Furthermore, there was no state health/safety interest in the fetus in the first trimester because it would be unable to live outside the womb and, therefore, was not yet "viable" life. During the second trimester, however, states could regulate abortions because there was at that time a state health/safety interest in the life of the mother since it was more dangerous to abort in the second trimester than to continue the pregnancy to full term. In the third trimester, the Court's decision struck down all abortions because the fetus was considered to be "viable" life and, therefore, received state health/safety protections.

The decision was welcomed by the women's movement, but opposed by many conservatives and by some religious groups, notably the Roman Catholic Church and its long-standing prohibition against any form of birth control. At the time, Protestant fundamentalists were essentially unconcerned with the abortion issue; and in 1971, the Southern Baptist convention voted in support of a resolution affirming a woman's right to have an abortion if the health of the mother were threatened. In fact, evangelist Jerry Falwell, who later became the leader of the Protestant fundamentalist political group, Moral Majority, did not preach his first sermon against abortion until 1978, five years after the *Roe v. Wade* decision.

In 1975, however, fundamentalist Protestant evangelists Billy Graham and Francis Schaeffer, along with *Christianity Today* editor Harold O. J. Brown and pediatrician C. Everett Koop, formed the Christian Action Council that lobbied Congress for measures to curb abortions. Koop and Schaeffer produced a five-segment film and companion book entitled *Whatever Happened to the Human Race?* These taught that abortion was both a cause and the result of the loss of appreciation for human life in American society and that acceptance of abortion would eventually lead to acceptance of infanticide and euthanasia. That same year Jerry Falwell, along with Paul Weyrich of the Heritage Foundation, started their conservative political organization known as the Moral Majority and made opposition to abortion a focus, with the goal of luring Catholic voters away from the Democratic Party.

In subsequent years, the question of abortion has become a highly charged political issue. Some anti-abortion organizations have sought to overturn the decision in *Roe v. Wade* by constitutional amendment. The necessary public support, however, has so far not been forthcoming. In 1980, though, the Republican Party platform called for such an amendment.

During the 1960s the Court also reached out to offer constitutional protection to citizens charged with crimes. In a series of cases beginning with *Gideon v. Wainwright* (1962) and culminating in *Miranda v. Arizona* (1966), the Court held that the police must not infringe in any way on an individual's right to be presumed innocent until proved guilty. The *Gideon* decision, overturning a 20-year rule, concluded that paupers had the right to a lawyer even if the court had to pay the lawyer's fee. In the *Miranda* decision the court ruled that police could not question an accused person unless his or her lawyer was present. Although many police officials contended that these decisions hindered the conviction of known criminals, defenders of civil liberties hailed the decisions as landmarks in the protection of the individual against arbitrary power.

A continuation of this line of reasoning in a case in 1972 was of particular significance because by then four members of the court were appointees of the Nixon administration, which had been among the prominent critics of the Court's liberal view of individual rights in criminal cases. In a 7–2 decision, the Court held that in all cases in which jail sentences resulted, including cases involving minor crimes (misdemeanors), a defendant must be provided with counsel if too poor to pay a lawyer. Only 40 years before, anyone convicted of a capital crime could be executed, even though deprived of legal defense because of lack of funds. Now a defendant could not be sent to jail for drunken driving except after a trial with adequate legal representation.

In 1972 the Court extended its protection of individual rights when it ruled in the *Furman* case that capital punishment violated the Fourteenth Amendment equal protection clause because black men were nine times more likely to be executed for premeditated murder than whites. In 1976, however, the Court modified that position somewhat by deciding that the death penalty was not unconstitutional so long as it was not arbitrarily or unreasonably applied. In *Coker v. Georgia*, the next year, however, a divided court held that exacting the death penalty for rape was unconstitutional because it was cruel and unusual punishment.

Despite the Court's concern for individual rights, some other government officials had been less than protective of them. In 1976 the head of the Federal Bureau of Investigation, Clarence Kelley, publicly apologized for the illegalities perpetrated by his agency while under the leadership of the best-known G-man of them all, J. Edgar Hoover. Among the violations were persecution and harassment of citizens and radical groups, and illegal tapping of telephone wires. Among those on whom the FBI had conducted illegal wiretaps was the Reverend Martin Luther King.

THE RIGHTS OF URBAN DWELLERS

The Court's decisions in *Baker v. Carr*, handed down in March 1962, and in *Reynolds v. Sims* two years later, were freighted with almost as much significance for the future as the *Brown* decision on segregation in 1954. The *Baker* case concerned the refusal of Tennessee to reapportion its legislative seats in accordance with changes in the distribution of population. The Court decreed that districts of markedly unequal populations constituted an inequity for which the courts could rightly be expected to provide a remedy.

For a number of years, as population flowed from the rural areas to the cities, urban dwellers had smarted under the failure of their growing numbers to be reflected in increased representation in the state legislatures. It was well known that rural-dominated legislatures simply refused, as in the case of Tennessee, to reapportion seats, for to do so might mean loss of rural control. Until the *Baker* decision the courts had always held that such inequity was a "political" question beyond their jurisdiction.

The *Reynolds* decision extended the reasoning of the *Baker* decision to include the upper as well as the lower houses of the state legislatures. These decisions opened up the possibility that with equitable apportionment of representation the cities would be able to get a better hearing in the state legislatures for their many and worsening problems.

The effects of the *Baker* decision were soon apparent. In a number of states where rural dominance in politics had long depended upon underweighting urban populations, the impact of the decisions was almost immediately evident in the new political strength of cities. Atlanta, for example, suddenly gained new strength in the Georgia legislature. In 1967 a reapportioned Tennessee legislature succeeded in repealing the anti-evolution statute passed in 1925, during the heyday of rural domination of the legislature. By 1971 more than half the states had reapportioned their legislatures although the courts had thrown out some of the new plans as inadequate.

SPUTNIK AND THE RACE TO CATCH UP

The Russians' successful launch of the first Sputnik into orbit around the earth on October 4, 1957, shook both the administration and the American people, used to thinking of themselves as second to none in science and technology. The effect of this shock on the educational system was discussed in the preceding chapter. Its effects on

American space capability and on our military hardware were far more dramatic.

AMERICA'S SPACE PROGRAM

After the launching of Sputnik I, it took four months for the United States to be ready to put a far smaller vehicle into space. By then the Russians had put into orbit a second satellite large enough to carry a dog. With the prestige of both countries now hinging upon successfully orbiting hardware, satellites were hurled into the skies in profusion during 1958 and in subsequent years. By 1961 the most obvious consequence of the first Sputnik was that the United States had mounted six separate series of rocket probes, each more ambitious and scientifically sophisticated than the preceding one.

In 1961 President John F. Kennedy announced the beginning of the most dramatic of all the rocket series, Project Apollo, which was designed to land a man on the moon by 1970. Despite some cutbacks in funds during the middle 1960s and the death of three astronauts, American successes in orbiting man-carrying satellites around the earth and in landing vehicles on the moon put the United States on a par with, if not ahead of, the U.S.S.R. On July 20, 1969, well ahead of the deadline President Kennedy had set, two American astronauts landed on the moon. Americans watched on television as Neil Armstrong, when he took the first human step onto the moon, called it "One small step for a man, one giant leap for mankind." Five other Apollo missions landed men on the moon over the next three years, with the last flight occurring in 1972.

THE MILITARY IMPACT OF SPUTNIK

A factor in most Americans' dismay over the initial Russian successes in space rocketry was the fear that the United States was vulnerable to a new kind of military attack. In 1949, the Soviets had shocked the Americans by developing their own atomic bomb, 20 years ahead of American expectations. Similarly, the United States developed the hydrogen bomb in 1952, only to find that the Soviets developed their own thermonuclear bomb in 1953.

Prior to the orbiting of Sputnik I, the Eisenhower administration had deprecated Russian boasts of being able to shoot off nuclear-tipped missiles that could reach the United States from bases in the Soviet Union. At that time American military missile capability was unable to reach more than 500 miles. With the orbiting of Sputnik I, the Russians proved their claim, and the immediate American response was a congressional and public clamor for a crash program to catch up with the Russians. In early 1958 Congress and the administration responded with a $1.27 billion program for accelerating missile development. In the budget of 1958–1959, President Eisenhower proposed the largest peacetime military expenditures in American history.

As a result of the new and feverish interest in military rocketry, the United States developed a whole new spectrum of weapons that included short- and medium-range rockets, which could be used against planes, troop formations, and ships, and giant intercontinental ballistic missiles (ICBM) that could span oceans at speeds in excess of 15,000 miles per hour and devastate cities with their nuclear warheads. Perhaps the closest to an invulnerable weapon was the 1,500-mile-range Polaris missile, designed to be fired from a submerged nuclear-powered submarine. Such a submarine could remain submerged for months at a time without refueling and would present an almost impossible target for an enemy to locate and destroy.

One measure of the character of the missile race between the two superpowers was that in the late 1960s the more powerful and longer-range Poseidon missile was replacing even the Polaris missile. By the early 70s the more sophisticated Trident, in turn, replacing the Poseidon.

Behind the missile race was the recognition that an all-out attack by nuclear-tipped missiles could devastate the whole country in a matter of an hour or so. The principal defense against nuclear attack became the threat of retaliation from secure bases, as invulnerable to surprise attack as engineers and scientists could make them. For once the first attack had been launched, there would be no time for mobilization. So in addition to the submarine missiles, the United States also placed ICBMs in great protective concrete emplacements in the ground in order to have them operational even after a direct enemy strike.

Meanwhile, military authorities on both sides developed an antiballistic missile (ABM)—a projectile to knock an enemy missile out of the sky before it could reach its target. By 1970 Moscow was ringed by ABMs and the United States had ABMs around some of its missile sites. Both sides were also beginning to arm their missiles with multiple warheads that could be independently targeted in order to complicate the work of the ABMs.

As weapons of nuclear power became ever more complicated—and more expensive—Congress and a sizable portion of the public began to have doubts that so much power was actually necessary to maintain the balance of terror. It was in the context of astronomical, escalating costs for the new missile systems that the disarmament agreements reached between the United States and the Soviet Union in 1972 and the discussions of further agreements in 1974 under Ford and in 1978 under Carter had such great importance. They will be discussed in the next chapter.

A NEW ERA IN FOREIGN AFFAIRS

THE DEATH OF STALIN

In January 1953 a Republican administration took office in Washington. On March 5 Joseph Stalin died in Moscow, and in July, the Korean War came to a halt. These events, coming so close together, marked a new era in the Cold War. Although no single Soviet leader emerged immediately to inherit Stalin's enormous personal power, the new Russian leaders demonstrated more flexibility and resourcefulness in foreign policy than Stalin had shown. Georgi Malenkov, who focused more on Soviet domestic problems than Cold War conflict, formally replaced Stalin. Malenkov resigned in 1955 and was replaced by Nikolai Bulgamin as Premier, but power gravitated to Nakita Khrushchev, the General Secretary of the Communist Party. Under Khrushchev, the Cold War began to soften a bit as the new Soviet regime approved visits by United States tourists and the United States in turn allowed visits by Soviet journalists and agriculturalists. Khrushchev stated at the Geneva Conference in 1955, however, that the Soviets would forget about Marx and Lenin "when shrimps learn to whistle."

In February 1956, Krushchev shocked the world by denouncing Stalin and calling for peaceful coexistence before the 20th Communist Party Congress in Moscow. Krushchev abandoned Lenin's thesis that war between capitalism and communism was inevitable and argued that communism could defeat capitalism by peaceful means. Stalin icons were destroyed all over the U.S.S.R., Stalin's body was removed from Red Square, and Russian history was rewritten to eliminate all of the false claims and self-aggrandizement by Stalin in the history books. In 1959 Khrushchev even visited the United States.

The Eisenhower administration also sought to alter foreign policy by taking a new approach. Despite his overall commitment to the major policies of the Truman administration, John Foster Dulles, the new Secretary of State, hoped to do more than merely contain communism. Toward the end of 1953, for example, he tried unsuccessfully to badger the European nations into a new defense community that would include a rearmed Germany. A looser grouping, agreed upon in 1954, did provide for a revived German army to be included in NATO.

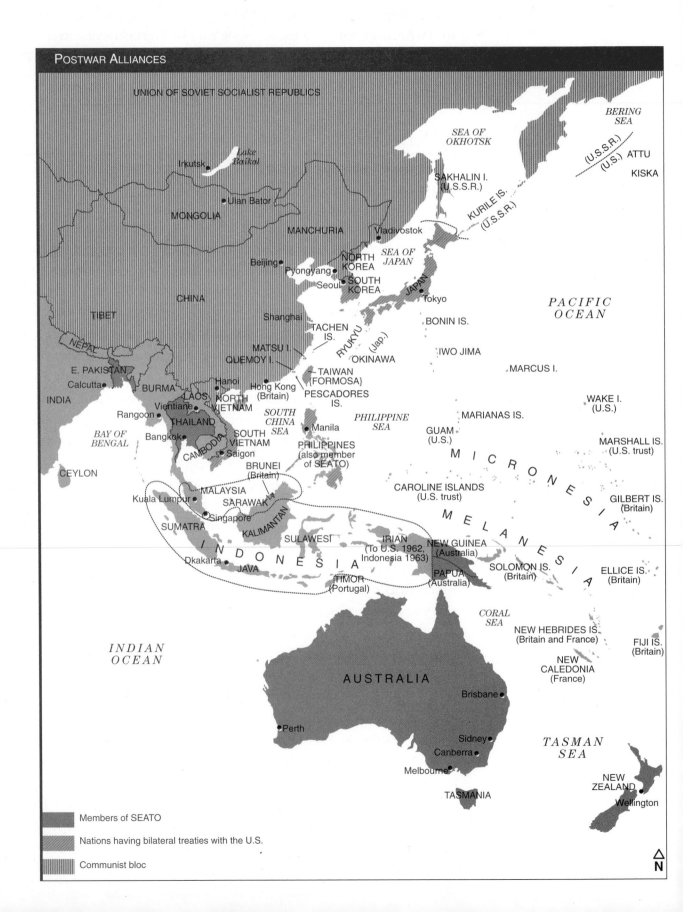

POSTWAR ALLIANCES

UNION OF SOVIET SOCIALIST REPUBLICS

BERING SEA

SEA OF OKHOTSK

(U.S.S.R.) (U.S.) ATTU

KISKA

Irkutsk

Lake Baikal

SAKHALIN I. (U.S.S.R.)

KURILE IS. (U.S.S.R.)

Ulan Bator

MONGOLIA

MANCHURIA

Vladivostok

SEA OF JAPAN

NORTH KOREA

Beijing

Pyongyang

SOUTH KOREA

Seoul

JAPAN

Tokyo

PACIFIC OCEAN

CHINA

TIBET

Shanghai

TACHEN IS.

RYUKYU (Jap.)

BONIN IS.

IWO JIMA

MARCUS I.

NEPAL

MATSU I.

QUEMOY I.

OKINAWA

TAIWAN (FORMOSA)

E. PAKISTAN

Calcutta

BURMA

Hanoi

Hong Kong (Britain)

PESCADORES IS.

WAKE I. (U.S.)

INDIA

LAOS

Vientiane

NORTH VIETNAM

SOUTH CHINA SEA

PHILIPPINE SEA

MARIANAS IS.

Rangoon

THAILAND

Bangkok

CAMBODIA

SOUTH VIETNAM

Saigon

Manila

GUAM (U.S.)

MARSHALL IS. (U.S. trust)

BAY OF BENGAL

PHILIPPINES (also member of SEATO)

M I C R O N E S I A

CEYLON

BRUNEI (Britain)

MALAYSIA

Kuala Lumpur

SARAWAK

Singapore

KALIMANTAN

SULAWESI

CAROLINE ISLANDS (U.S. trust)

GILBERT IS. (Britain)

SUMATRA

I N D O N E S I A

IRIAN (To U.S. 1962, Indonesia 1963)

NEW GUINEA (Australia)

M E L A N E S I A

Dkakarta

JAVA

TIMOR (Portugal)

PAPUA (Australia)

SOLOMON IS. (Britain)

ELLICE IS. (Britain)

CORAL SEA

NEW HEBRIDES IS. (Britain and France)

FIJI IS. (Britain)

INDIAN OCEAN

NEW CALEDONIA (France)

AUSTRALIA

Brisbane

Perth

TASMAN SEA

Sidney

Canberra

Melbourne

NEW ZEALAND

Wellington

TASMANIA

Members of SEATO

Nations having bilateral treaties with the U.S.

Communist bloc

N

On the other side of the world in Asia, soon after Communist-led Vietnamese guerrillas drove the French from Indochina in 1954, Secretary Dulles moved to counter further Communist expansion by the formation of the Southeast Asia Treaty Organization (SEATO). It was modeled after NATO but was conspicuously weaker on at least two counts. First the signatories were required only to consult, not to take action, in the event of attack. Second, the organization failed to include the chief powers of the region. Composed of Thailand, Australia, New Zealand, the Philippines, Pakistan, Britain, France, and the United States, SEATO did not include India, Indonesia, Ceylon, and Burma—all of which refused invitations to join.

Dulles also hoped to use the threat of American nuclear capability as a means of countering the superior manpower of the Communist bloc; but his threat of "massive retaliation" in the event of aggression was weakened by the fact that the Soviet Union also possessed the new weapons of war. The acquisition of nuclear weapons by the Soviet Union spurred arrangements for a meeting of the heads of government of the United States, Great Britain, France, and the Soviet Union. A meeting at the summit, as Winston Churchill called it, took place in the summer of 1955 at Geneva, Switzerland. There was little concrete achievement, but Eisenhower's suggestions that the United States and the U.S.S.R. exchange plans of their military establishments and permit aerial photography of each other's bases seemed, for a while, like promising ideas. Even though the Russians saw little merit in Eisenhower's "open skies" proposal, the suggestion made evident the American president's sincere and anxious search for a way out of the terrible nuclear impasse between the two giant powers.

MIDDLE EAST: ISRAEL

In 1948, there were some 250,000 Jewish refugees in Europe that had survived the Holocaust. Many of these refugees wanted to leave Europe, but major political factions in the United States and Britain opposed the immigration of large numbers of European Jews to Britain and the United States. The major Zionist movement that had been gathering strength since the late nineteenth century, however, suddenly found the political winds shifting in its direction. With support from Britain and the United States, United Nations partitioned Palestine into an Arab State (Lebanon) and a Jewish State (Israel). Both the United Nations and Zionists viewed this partition as the final solution to the Jewish refugee problem. American President Harry Truman recognized Israel 15 minutes after the new State of Israel was proclaimed by the United Nations.

Unfortunately, no one had asked the Palestinian Arab residents, who made up the majority of the population in Palestine, what they thought. Almost immediately, Egypt, Syria, Jordan, Lebanon, and Iraq attacked the new Jewish state of Israel. Israel's army, outnumbered 6-to-1, but armed with superior United States and British weapons along with arms purchased through communist Czechoslovakia, quickly routed their attackers. An estimated one million Arab Palestinians fled Israel with the retreating Arab armies, most to Jordan, the poorest country in the Middle East. Jordan and the other Arab countries were ill equipped to handle the flow of refugees, leading to widespread death, disease, and suffering. American support of the State of Israel produced widespread animosity toward the United States in the Arab Muslim world.

IRANIAN CRISIS

In 1950, Shah (King) Mohammed Reza Pahlavi was displaced by democratic and leftist forces within Iran and fled the country. The Iranians attempted to create a Parliamentary government, but the leftists within Parliament wanted a complete socialist revolution; the coalition government was in chaos. The British convinced the CIA that the only hope for stability in Iran was to return the deposed Shah. In 1953, the CIA aided the 22-year-old Shah of Iran in an overthrow of the Parliamentary government of Prime Minister Mohammed Mossadegh, who had nationalized the Iranian oil fields and seized millions in assets from United States oil companies.

Mossadegh was an eccentric who normally did not get dressed and walked around in his house in pink pajamas all day. Mossadegh was also a "crier" who would burst into emotional floods of tears at seemingly any occasion, and United States Secretary of State John Foster Dulles despised Mossadegh. Upon reviewing the CIA plan to oust Mossadegh in a coup, Dulles exclaimed, "Finally, a way to get rid of that madman!"

After the Shah's takeover, American oil companies regained control of their possessions. The United States government immediately provided massive aid to the Shah, including military aid to prop up his government, in spite of CIA intelligence that suggested that the Iranian people supported Mossadegh rather than the Shah. Given that he had little legitimacy with the Iranian people, the Shah ruled with an iron fist and used a secret police network, the SAVAK, which used torture, arbitrary imprisonment, and other repressive measures to ensure loyalty to the Shah.

CRISIS IN THE MIDDLE EAST; THE HUNGARIAN REVOLT

The foreign policies of both the United States and Russia were tested more severely in November 1956. Early that month Israeli, French, and British military forces invaded Egypt. All three countries had deep grievances against Colonel Gamal Nasser's nationalistic regime. Nasser had long been a champion of Arab opposition to Israel, refusing to recognize that new country and constantly threatening invasion. Nasser had desired to build a series of dams on the Nile River and had asked the United States for aid. When Eisenhower would not sell arms to Egypt and would not help build a dam, Nasser turned to the Soviet Union for assistance. The U.S.S.R. was willing to both build the Aswan Dam and supply military aid. When Nasser established relations with communist China in 1956, Secretary of State John Foster Dulles withdrew the offer of aid for the Aswan project and the building of the dam was left to the U.S.S.R. In retaliation, Nasser militarily seized and nationalized the British-controlled Suez Canal in July 1956 and then closed the canal to Israeli ships.

Without informing the United States, their ally, Britain and France dropped paratroopers on the Suez area 10 days after Israel invaded Egypt, quickly overwhelming the inefficient Egyptian army. Eisenhower was irate that he was not consulted and feared that the invasion would push Egypt into the Soviet Orbit. The United States then sponsored a United Nations resolution that condemned the invasion and cut off Middle East oil from France and England. Nakita Khrushchev threatened to send Soviet "volunteers" to Egypt and to launch nuclear missiles against France and England if they did not withdraw. Nasser then declared the canal open but, in actuality, closed the canal by sinking ships in it and blocking the passageway. Under such immense international pressure and without the support of the United States, on November 6, 1956, England and Israel announced a cease-fire and withdrawal from Egypt.

At almost the same time, the Soviet Union ruthlessly suppressed a widespread and heroic revolt of the Hungarians against Communist rule. The Hungarians had set up their own anti-Soviet government and asked the United States for aid. When the Soviets dispatched the Red Army to put down the rebellion, the Hungarian people staged a guerrilla war that became famous for civilian street participation and the "Molotov Cocktail" bomb; but it was quickly squelched by the Soviet forces. The Soviets executed the leaders of the revolt, and 30,000 Hungarians died in the repressive backlash. Once again, the United States denounced the Soviet action but did nothing else.

Both the Suez and Hungarian invasions took the United States by surprise. The administration opposed both, but its power over the Soviets was nil. The opposition of the United States to the Suez adventure was more successful, both because the United States was an ally of Britain and France and because world opinion and the United Nations vehemently condemned it.

The immediate consequence of the Suez crisis, however, was that Egypt drew closer to the Soviet Union, and Communist penetration of the Middle East seemed imminent. Reacting to this development and in response to a request from the President, Congress in March 1957 passed a resolution affirming America's intention to aid any country in the Middle East that seemed to be threatened by a Communist coup, internal or external. The first test of what came to be called the Eisenhower Doctrine occurred in July 1958, when American marines landed in Lebanon to forestall a possible invasion from neighboring Syria, then a satellite of Nasser's and judged to be overly friendly toward the Soviet Union. The pro-Western regime in Lebanon was not overthrown, and by the end of October 1958 all American troops had withdrawn.

The Middle East crisis of 1956–1958 brought the Eisenhower administration full circle. Once hopeful of avoiding "brush-fire wars," it found itself dispatching troops to trouble spots much as Truman had done in Korea. It was also evident after 1956 that Moscow was not the only source of instability in the world. Rising nationalism in Asia, Africa, and even the Americas presented new problems and dangers. Khrushchev was adept at winning friends in the new regions, and he consciously identified his country with the fierce opposition of the former colonial peoples to their old rulers. In part to offset Khrushchev's successful international salesmanship, the President in December 1959 and through the first half of 1960 embarked upon extensive good-will tours of the Middle East and Southeast Asia, Latin America, and eastern Asia. Although the first two tours were eminently successful, the last, to Asia, proved much less so. Anti-American riots in Japan prevented the President from visiting that country at all.

LATIN AMERICA

After World War II, the United States sought a mutual defense treaty against communism in the Western Hemisphere. In pursuit of that end, in September 1947, a Western Hemisphere defense alliance was signed at Rio De Janeiro between the United States and the Latin American states, and the Organization of American States or OAS came into being. Under the OAS Charter, the United States increased aid to Latin

America for economic purposes, but the primary United States purpose for economic aid was to prop up the Latin American political and economic systems against communism. At the International Conference of American States at Bogotá the next year, however, Latin Americans rioted and disrupted the conference, and over 1,000 people died in street violence. The Latin Americans were protesting the American offer of $500 million in aid, because it was only about three percent of what went to Europe under the Marshall Plan.

GUATEMALA AND THE OVERTHROW OF ARBENZ

In 1954 in Guatemala, the elected government of Jacobo Arbenz Guzman introduced Socialist reforms and imported Soviet weapons. American Secretary of State John Foster Dulles ordered the CIA to stage a coup—even though 54 of the 56 members in the Guatemalan Congress were not Communists and neither was Arbenz, although he did lean to the left. Dulles himself admitted that he could not prove a link between Arbenz and the Kremlin. Arbenz called for land redistribution in a country where two percent of the people owned 70 percent of the land and the largest landholder was the United Fruit Company of Boston. In furtherance of his goals of land reform, Arbenz expropriated 400,000 acres from United Fruit that were not at that time in use by United Fruit. Arbenz provided compensation, but not at the price demanded by United Fruit.

United Fruit pressured Dulles to intervene in Guatemala to regain for the company its assets. United States Ambassador John Peurifoy told his superiors in Washington, "Arbenz thought like a Communist and talked like a Communist and if not actually one, would do until one came along." The United States cut off aid to Guatemala, and then the CIA coordinated with a mercenary army led by exiled Guatemalan military officer Carlos Castillo Armas in Honduras to stage a coup. CIA pilots in United States planes provided air support for the rebels and bombed Guatemala City. The rebels under Armas overthrew the Arbenz government in 1954.

Armas installed a right-wing military dictatorship that ruled Guatemala for the next 30 years, and the repressive government killed over 100,000 people over the next three decades. The U.S. involvement was well known in Latin America, and the American actions engendered Latin American resentment of the United States. Eisenhower ignored the repression and hailed the demise of Arbenz as a "victory over communism." Four years later in 1958, Vice President Nixon toured Venezuela and was met with hostile crowds. Nixon's car was attacked by angry demonstrators with rocks and almost tipped over by the crowd before Nixon's driver abandoned the procession and sped away down back streets.

THE U-2 INCIDENT

Even before the Tokyo riots of June 1960, other events seriously tarnished the American image abroad and further impaired Soviet-American relations. Early in 1960 the President, still hopeful of being able to arrange some kind of disarmament agreement with Khrushchev, had agreed to another summit meeting in Paris; but just before the conference opened, the Russians announced the shooting down of a high-flying American espionage plane deep inside the Soviet Union. At first the American officials denied the accusation, claiming that the Russians had downed a weather plane; but after the Russians triumphantly produced the plane and its pilot, Francis Gary Powers, who was still alive, and published spy photos of Soviet military installations taken by the plane, the United States shamefacedly admitted undertaking this and other flights over the Soviet Union. Outraged, Khrushchev called off the summit meeting, deliberately insulting Eisenhower in the process. In their propaganda around the world the Russians made the most of the American admission. The incident of the U-2, as the special plane was called, dealt a heavy blow to American prestige and honor. Not only was the flight contrary to standard usages under international law, but also the United States had been caught in an official lie that undermined its credibility before the world. The capture of the plane and pilot also revealed that Soviet technology was more advanced than Americans had believed and gave the American people a sense of insecurity. President Eisenhower promised Khrushchev that there would be no more American U-2 flights over the Soviet Union during his Presidency.

TROUBLES WITH CASTRO

American relations with Cuba also deteriorated seriously in 1960. On January 1, 1959, a young revolutionary, Fidel Castro, aided by Argentine revolutionary Che Guevara, succeeded in overthrowing the corrupt dictatorship of General Fulgencio Batista. At first the new government enjoyed the support of the American people, who welcomed Castro when he visited the United States soon after assuming power. When it became evident that the social revolution Castro proclaimed also included the confiscation of American property and the wholesale execution of the "enemies of the revolution," the attitude of the American people and their government cooled noticeably.

By early 1960 over a billion dollars worth of American property had been confiscated without compensation, and a steady stream of refugees from Cuba entered Miami. Furthermore, in January 1960, Castro completed an agreement to sell sugar to the U.S.S.R., and Cuba resumed diplomatic re-

Fidel Castro *(Library of Congress)*

lations with the U.S.S.R. in May. Also in May, Castro demanded that American oil refineries in Cuba process crude oil purchased from the U.S.S.R. The American companies refused at the urging of the Eisenhower administration, and Castro expropriated the refineries. In retaliation, late in May 1960, the United States ended all economic aid to Cuba, and in July, at the recommendation of an angry Congress, the President cut imports of Cuban sugar by 95 percent. Since the United States was Cuba's principal customer and sugar the island's chief export, this action harmed the Cuban economy. Castro then retaliated by expropriating more American-owned properties. In October, Eisenhower banned all United States exports to Cuba, an embargo that remains through the present. The Castro regime, subsequently, became increasingly anti-American and looked to the Soviet Union for aid and assistance.

THE ELECTION OF 1960

Because the recently ratified Twenty-second Amendment limited Presidents to two terms, the Republicans in 1960 did not have to wait to learn whether Eisenhower would run for a third term. Vice-President Richard M. Nixon was the choice of most party leaders, including the President. Nixon was nominated on the first ballot, and Henry Cabot Lodge, the United States ambassador to the United Nations, was chosen as his running mate.

The front-runner at the Democratic Convention was Massachusetts Senator John F. Kennedy, who had shown strength in a

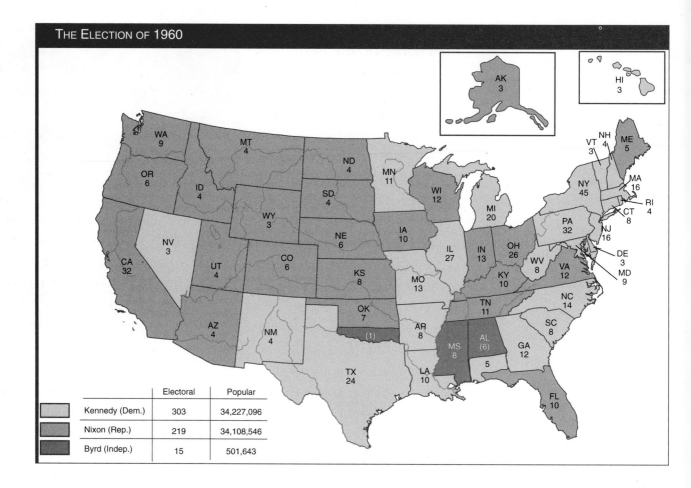

THE ELECTION OF 1960

	Electoral	Popular
Kennedy (Dem.)	303	34,227,096
Nixon (Rep.)	219	34,108,546
Byrd (Indep.)	15	501,643

number of state primaries. Thanks to a well-prepared campaign and a highly organized staff, Kennedy was nominated on the first ballot. Astutely, he urged the nomination of his erstwhile opponent, Senator Lyndon Johnson of Texas, for second place on the ticket because Kennedy, an Irish-Catholic from Massachusetts, lacked support in the South. Kennedy had expected Johnson, with whom he shared mutual animosity, to decline the offer and remain Majority leader in the Senate. Johnson, however, viewed the Vice Presidency as a good springboard to the Presidency itself and surprised Kennedy by accepting the nomination. The Democrats wrote a deliberately liberal platform, including support of the Supreme Court decision on desegregation.

Since both candidates were in their youthful forties, the campaigning was strenuous, despite extensive use of television and jet travel. Nixon personally visited all 50 states and Kennedy appeared in 44. The candidates also inaugurated a series of four joint appearances on television, which helped Kennedy since he had enjoyed less national recognition than Nixon and because he appeared to better able to take advantage of the new medium. Kennedy made the use of Hollywood makeup for his on-camera debates, while Nixon did not, with the result that the public witnessed a cool-looking Kennedy juxtaposed with a "sweating" Nixon with facial stubble. Though no one can say how much the television debates aided Kennedy, most historians argue that they did work to his advantage.

Kennedy also stole some of the conservatives' thunder by campaigning on a Cold War platform and arguing that the Eisenhower administration had allowed a "missile gap" to develop between the United States and the Soviet Union. Kennedy argued that the United States was behind the U.S.S.R. both in missile technology (as proven by Sputnik) and in numbers of missiles. The American "inferiority" in these areas that Kennedy spoke of was primarily fiction, but Sputnik provided all of the political ammunition Kennedy needed in order to make his point. After all, many conservatives had voiced the same criticisms of the Eisenhower administration for years; so the casting of America as "behind" the Soviet Union in missile technology was an easy sell.

Kennedy also ran under the handicap of being a Roman Catholic. Although the Republicans officially did not allude to his religion or use it against him, a number of private persons and organizations did question the fitness of a Catholic for the presidency. Kennedy met the prejudice head-on, candidly and without rancor. "I am not the Catholic candidate for President," he said at one point in the campaign. "I do not speak for the Catholic Church on issues of public policy, and none in that Church speaks for me. … Are we to say that a Jew can be elected Mayor of Dublin, a Protestant be named foreign minister of France … but a Catholic cannot be President of the United States?" Subsequent analyses showed that Kennedy's religion was the central issue for most voters.

The election turned out to be one of the closest in American history, with Kennedy winning by fewer than 113,000 votes out of a record 68.6 million votes cast. At least 4.5 million Protestants who had voted for Stevenson voted for Nixon, it has been estimated, but Kennedy's Catholicism brought out new Catholic voters, and he won support from some Eisenhower Protestants. Few Republican Catholics shifted. Lyndon Johnson was essential in helping to stem the Southern Protestant opposition to a Catholic President. Kennedy's election finally disproved the political platitude that a Catholic could not be elected President.

Although a shift of merely 12,000 votes in five states would have given Nixon an Electoral College majority, the congressional elections were one-sidedly Democratic. At that level, at least, it was clear that the country was still strongly Democratic.

THE KENNEDY ADMINISTRATION

LIMITED SUCCESS WITH CONGRESS

In keeping with the youthful, vigorous image he had projected during the campaign, John Fitzgerald Kennedy called his program "The New Frontier." More eloquent than any President since Woodrow Wilson, more concerned with elevating and educating the people than any President since Theodore Roosevelt, Kennedy entered office surrounded by driving intellectuals and men of high purpose; but he soon found that the conservative—albeit Democratic—Congress was decidedly cool, if not hostile, to his program. Twice during 1961 and 1962 Congress rejected his bills for medical care for the aged and federal aid to education. Congress also voted down his recommendation for a new cabinet post of urban affairs. In the first two years of his administration, Congress gave the President only a part of his requests for tax reforms. In 1963 it refused to act on his request for an income tax cut of $11 billion, which Kennedy had strongly urged as a necessary stimulus to the economy.

Like Roosevelt and Truman before him, Kennedy discovered that a heavily Democratic Congress was no guarantee that a Democratic President's program would be enacted. Most of the slowness or hostility of Congress centered in the House of Representatives, which was dominated by conservative Southern Democrats and Republicans, often working in coalition. In the congressional elections of 1962 the President vigorously campaigned for a Democratic Congress, and, contrary to the usual results of mid-term elections, the Democrats lost very few seats in the House and actually gained some in the Senate, yet the result for the President's program was largely negative. At the time of Kennedy's death by assassination on November 22, 1963, Congress had failed to pass a single major piece of the legislative program he had enunciated the previous January.

The administration's principal legislative success had come in the previous year. The Trade Expansion Act of 1962 was important because it marked an even more significant departure from protectionism than the Reciprocal Trade Act of 1934. It gave the President new and unprecedented wide powers to cut tariff rates although for decades Congress had jealously guarded its prerogatives in this field. The act also provided for federal aid to business firms and workers adversely affected by the resulting increased competition from abroad. Kennedy correctly hailed the act because it provided means for increasing the rate of American economic growth through the expansion of American exports. By permitting the importation of certain foreign goods, especially those from the booming European Common Market (composed of France, Italy, West Germany, and the Benelux countries) and from Japan, the administration hoped to secure important and wider markets for American goods abroad, while increasing, through competition, the efficiency of industry at home.

Several times Kennedy publicly denied that his administration harbored any of that hostility toward business usually associated with the Democratic regimes of Roosevelt and Truman; but the business community, however, clearly felt uneasy about Kennedy's leadership—particularly after he used threats of government intervention and harassment to force United States Steel to rescind its price increases in the spring of 1962.

LOSSES AND GAINS IN FOREIGN AFFAIRS

The Kennedy administration's foreign policy record was mixed. At his death, the long-term problems of the Cold War were still unresolved and some new ones had been added. Germany and Berlin were still divided, and the several thousand advisers and support troops that Kennedy had sent to South Vietnam to help its anti-Communist government fight Communist rebels constituted the beginning of a much larger involvement to come.

During the early days of his administration, Kennedy launched the Alliance for Progress in Latin America, a long-range economic aid program designed to combat the conditions of poverty that contributed to the spread of communism and denied a decent living to millions. Through technical advice, loans, and grants, theAlliance endeavored to help Latin Americans help themselves in effecting land reform, improving farming techniques, and accelerating industrial development.

Unfortunately, the Alliance's laudable aim of not permitting United States funds to be used to bolster undemocratic or unpopular regimes was not easily put into practice. Military juntas in Argentina, Brazil, and Peru in 1962 and in the Dominican Republic in 1963 interfered with or actually overthrew constitutional governments, thereby bringing into serious question the political stability and commitment to constitutional and democratic procedures of those nations. It could be said, though, that the Alliance at least ended the long neglect of Latin America, whose leaders and intellectuals had both resented United States indifference and feared its power and its intentions.

In 1965 President Johnson admitted that the program would have to continue for 20 years instead of the original 10 before it could be properly evaluated. By 1970 the rate of economic growth among members of the Alliance was higher than it had been in the early years of the program, but the average still fell below the planned-for 2.5 percent growth per year. An enduring problem was the unwillingness of governments in Catholic Latin America to encourage birth control, although birth rates in most of these countries were among the highest in the world. During the Kennedy administration the storm center of Latin American affairs proved to be Cuba. In April 1961, Kennedy ill advisedly lent token naval support to an invasion of Cuba by a small group of anti-Castro Cuban refugees at a place called Bay of Pigs; but the effort to overthrow Castro's avowedly Communist regime ended in fiasco when the 1,500-man invasion force was easily defeated and its members killed or captured. Kennedy had mistakenly believed that the people of Cuba would come to the aid of the invading exiles, but the Cuban peasants at that point sided with Castro. The Bay of Pigs invasion was easily thwarted. Kennedy had also promised American air support to the invasion, but then withdrew the support on the day of the invasion in an effort to mask American involvement in the entire affair. The United States suffered grievously in prestige because it had once again, as in the U-2 incident, contravened the normal procedures of international law and had broken its own agreements under the inter-American security system. The immediate result was the strengthening of the Castro regime and the tightening of Cuba's connection with the Soviet Union. One month after the Bay of Pigs, Castro announced the allegiance of the Cuban revolution to socialism. Two days prior to the invasion, United States Ambassador to the United Nations Adlai Stevenson had announced to the UN that the United States planned no such invasion; consequently, American prestige and credibility in the world was once again damaged.

OPERATION MONGOOSE

After the Bay of Pigs fiasco, President Kennedy remained committed to ousting Castro by any means possible and approved "Operation Mongoose," a CIA covert operation to bring down Castro. The CIA sponsored anti-Castro propaganda and violence in Cuba, including burning cane fields and blowing up factories, department stores, and oil storage tanks. The CIA even contaminated Cuban sugar headed for the U.S.S.R. Five times, the CIA attempted to work through the American Mafia to have Castro assassinated, essentially granting immunity to organized crime bosses in America in return for their cooperation in eliminating Castro, but all attempts failed. CIA plans to assassinate Castro included poisoning Castro's pens, pills, and cigars, implanting explosives in Castro's cigars, and placing a chemical in his shoes that would make his beard fall out. CIA propaganda specialist Edward Lansdale even launched a campaign to convince the Cuban peasants of the imminent return of Christ, by lighting up the Cuban night sky with incendiaries launched by submarines while driving home the allegation that the Lord was unhappy with Castro and wanted the people to overthrow him. In spite of all these efforts, Castro remained.

CUBAN MISSILE CRISIS

How close that Russo-Cuban tie actually was became painfully clear in the summer and fall of 1962, when the Soviet Union began supplying the island nation with large amounts of economic and military aid. Then, in early October, American reconnaissance planes photographed Soviet medium-range missile sites under construction on Cuban soil. Kennedy privately admitted to his brother, Attorney General Robert Kennedy, that he couldn't make heads or tails of the photos; but if the intelligence people were convinced they were missile sites, he found it unacceptable and would have to take action. In spite of the fact that some of Kennedy's advisors explained to him that the missiles did not actually alter the military equation since the Soviets had proven that they could hit the United States with nuclear missiles with the launch of Sputnik, Kennedy remained alarmed at what he termed the upsetting of the "nuclear status quo" in the world. Consequently, on

President John F. Kennedy discussing with his military staff the U-2 spy-plane flights over Cuba *(AP Photo/Richard Heyser private collection)*

October 22, 1962, Kennedy declared a naval quarantine of Cuba, broadcasting to the world, and particularly to the Soviet Union, the American intention to risk war rather than to permit a buildup of Soviet missile power in Cuba, only 90 miles from the United States. Adlai Stevenson presented the American case at the United Nations where the Soviets denied the presence of any missiles in Cuba. Stevenson then embarrassed Soviet Ambassador Valerian Zorin with pictures of the missile sites and declared he was prepared to wait until "hell freezes over" for the Soviet minister's response.

Soviet ships stopped dead in the water rather than attempt to run what amounted to an American naval blockade, thus avoiding a direct military confrontation. Though the crisis had brought the world to the very brink of nuclear war, but within three days the Russians agreed to withdraw their missiles in exchange for an American agreement not to support any future invasion of Cuba. Although Soviet technicians and support troops remained on the island, the extension of Soviet missiles to the Western Hemisphere had been stopped. The United States then withdrew its intermediate range missiles from Turkey.

Then and later Kennedy was criticized for risking a world holocaust in order to show the Russians how determined he was, but most observers in the United States and western Europe praised his coolness and his success in dealing with the crisis. In any event, he did not gloat over the Soviet retreat. Instead he continued to seek ways of breaking the circle of mutual suspicion that perpetuated the Cold War. His success in making some accommodations with the Russians suggests that the ordeal of the missile crisis of 1962 marked a significant shift in Soviet-American relations.

Kennedy's most concrete accommodation was the working out of a limited test-ban treaty with the Soviet Union during the summer of 1963. The treaty, which was ratified overwhelmingly by the Senate in October 1963, prohibited any testing of nuclear weapons in the atmosphere, in outer space, or under water. Although the stockpiles of nuclear weapons on both sides continued to grow, the test-ban treaty promised to reduce the contamination of the atmosphere and showed that careful and limited negotiations with the Russians could bear fruit.

The United States and the Soviet Union also agreed to establish a "hot line," or direct teletype circuit, between the Kremlin and the White House for instant communication between the two superpowers should an international emergency arise that made it crucial for them to know each other's intentions. The hot line proved valuable at the outbreak of the Arab-Israeli war of June 1967, and again in the war of 1973, when the leaders of the U.S.S.R. and the United States used it to assure each other of their intentions to refrain from direct intervention.

THE ASSASSINATION OF PRESIDENT KENNEDY

On November 22, 1963, in Dallas, Texas, to the horror of a stunned nation and a shocked world on both sides of the Iron Curtain, an assassin's bullet turned to ashes the shining but unfulfilled promise of John Fitzgerald Kennedy. Lee Harvey Oswald was arrested for the crime, and police concluded that he had fired the fatal shots, using a high-powered rifle, from the sixth floor of the Book Depository building. Two days later, Oswald was shot and killed by Dallas nightclub owner Jack Ruby. The new President Lyndon Johnson appointed a commission headed by Chief Justice Earl Warren to investigate the crime, and the Warren Commission concluded that both Oswald and Ruby acted alone. Unfortunately, the Warren Commission has been criticized in the years since for being less than thorough, and conspiracy theories persist.

In the short time that he had been before the world, his youthful vigor, self-deprecating wit, and incisive intellect had won favor among Americans of all political persuasions. Young adults, especially, were deeply affected by this novel political figure that spoke inimitably to and for their generation. Foreign nations, from leaders to ordinary citizens, responded to his image of the United States as a nation compassionate toward the weak, imaginative in confronting old problems, and firm in leadership. His eloquence and bright intelligence moved

Lee Harvey Oswald, center, was arrested for the assassination of President Kennedy. *(AP Photo)*

people in all walks of life, from affluent suburbanites to the inner-city poor. His death seemed horrifying even to an age hardened to violence and inured to irrationality.

In later years, the reputation of John F. Kennedy would tarnish somewhat as less admirable sides of his personality, most notably his sexual indiscretions with Hollywood starlets, but his assassination left unanswered forever the question of what John F. Kennedy might have been and done, given his potentialities and great popular appeal.

THE LEGACY OF THE KENNEDY ADMINISTRATION

In assessing the larger meaning of JFK's presidency, we can begin with his unusual wife, Jacqueline Bouvier Kennedy. Though a traditional woman in many respects—she did not enjoy a significant career before her marriage and she kept her silence about her husband's many infidelities—she was also a First Lady who foreshadowed a new and more accomplished type of American woman. Her beauty and her glamour gave her a position on the world stage that no other woman of the twentieth century would occupy, with the possible later exception of Princess Diana. Jackie Kennedy was more than a pretty face; she was a cultivated, multi-lingual woman as well as a devoted mother. For young women, she served as a role model. The preceding decade had featured blonde icons, Marilyn Monroe being the most famous, whose personae were often passive and unambitious, unlike the iconic female film stars of the 1930s, for example, Jackie suggested that being brainy did not rule out being attractive, a potent message to the young women of America.

Together the Kennedys seemed to embody a decisive break with the past and that included the realm of gender roles, despite what we now know about the president's womanizing. How much they had to do with inspiring later developments of the 60s is an open question; but there is no doubt that one of the most important steps in fostering women's rights was set in motion by President Kennedy—the Kennedy Commission on the Status of Women. In 1961, faced with a dilemma about what stance to take with respect to the controversial Equal Rights Amendment, Kennedy decided to form the first-ever presidential commission to study women's issues. The aging Eleanor Roosevelt—who had supported Adlai Stevenson for the presidential nomination in 1960—agreed to chair the commission, and with that a number of high-powered men and women accepted appointment to the commission, also. We cannot single out a particular piece of legislation that came out of this effort, but the group served as a catalyst for focusing attention on the shortfalls in women's access to educational and employment opportunities. Moreover, it inspired the creation of state commissions, also, and thereby created a network of activists for the legislative changes of the succeeding era.

Another important element in inspiring young people was the creation of the Peace Corps in 1961. Established by executive order, the Corps was later formalized by Congress as a means of sending American volunteers abroad to poor countries to help with educational and humanitarian projects. Critics have pointed out that the Peace Corps gave the United States the ability to go into Third World countries so as to combat Soviet influence "on the ground;" but the Peace Corps also called on the idealism of many thousands of those who wanted to help solve the world's problems in a direct way.

As for civil rights, critics have pointed out that JFK was very cautious—as had been Eisenhower—because he did not want to alienate Southern Democrats. Nonetheless, there were moments of great symbolic import in which the power of the presidency seemed to be ranged on the side of the movement. Perhaps most dramatic was an episode that occurred even before JFK occupied the White House. Martin Luther King had been arrested and sentenced to jail on a technicality in Georgia in October 1960. Mrs. King was pregnant, and she was distraught about the situation. Kennedy phoned her to express sympathy, and the following day his brother Robert (soon to be Attorney General in the new administration) called a local judge to try to help. Over the next few years, King and his followers would not always find the president to be so cooperative; but in the end events forced Kennedy's hand. He sent federal marshals to protect James Meredith in 1962, as already noted. The following year he addressed a national television audience to proclaim that the time had come for the nation to deal with civil rights.

One of the most consequential aspects of the JFK legacy, however, lay in the realm of culture. The Great Fear of the 1950s had tended to produce a somnolent and complacent popular culture. In the mid-1950s there began to be young, white male icons of rebellion such as James Dean and above all, Elvis Presley, but the rebellion they expressed was diffuse and apolitical. By the early 1960s, however, Bob Dylan was singing protest songs that were expressly political—including 1964's "The Times They Are A' Changing." Indeed they were.

THE PRICE OF POWER, PART II, 1963–1980

JOHNSON AND DOMESTIC REFORM

Within 90 minutes of Kennedy's assassination, Vice-President Johnson, who was also in Dallas that day, was sworn in as President; and immediately he flew back to Washington to evade any other possible attacks on high officials. The smell of conspiracy was strong in Dallas that November day.

The new President was quite a different man from the wealthy, Eastern-born Kennedy. Born in Texas in modest circumstances in 1908, Lyndon Johnson had spent almost all his adult years in the swirling politics of Texas and Washington, first as an aide to a Texas congressman, then as a member of the House of Representatives in the Roosevelt era, and finally as a senator and majority leader during the Eisenhower years.

"THE GREAT SOCIETY"

In his State of the Union message in January 1964, President Johnson called for "a war against poverty" as the central goal of his administration. The Economic Opportunity Act, passed in August 1964, was only the first of the legislative steps to be taken in that war. The act recognized that most of the poverty in the nation resulted from lack of education and training among the unemployed rather than from a dearth of jobs. The law appropriated almost $1 billion for agencies and programs designed to train or retrain the workless in order to fit them for the more highly skilled jobs available in an advanced society. The name the President gave to his program was the Great Society, which he defined as "a place where men are more concerned with the quality of their goals than the quantity of their goods."

Johnson's long and distinguished career in the legislative branch gave him an understanding of Congress that enabled him to push through legislation that had been stalled for half a year under Kennedy. Within Johnson's first year in office, Congress passed the first reduction in income taxes in 30 years, the Economic Opportunity Act already mentioned, the long-pending foreign-aid bill, the Higher Education Facilities Act, and the strongest and most far-reaching civil rights act ever put into law. Not all the measures that were put forward for the Great Society were enacted that first year, but the record made clear that in his dealings with Congress Johnson was highly successful, despite the handicap of following a martyred President. In fact, many historians have argued that Congress was willing to pass civil rights legislation as a tribute to the fallen Kennedy.

PRESIDENT IN HIS OWN RIGHT

Inasmuch as Johnson was advocating the same kind of a liberal program advanced by Democratic Presidents since Franklin Roosevelt, conservatives in the Republican party were convinced that, to win the presidency in 1964, the G.O.P. had to put forward a candidate with a political philosophy diverse from that of Eisenhower and Dewey—someone who did not represent the Eastern, liberal wing of the party. For too long, conservative Republicans contended, the party had been merely an echo of the Democrats. Victory would come, they believed, only if the voters were presented with a real choice.

The man the conservatives selected as their standard-bearer was Barry Goldwater, a senator from Arizona who ever since his election to the Senate in 1958, had been publicly opposing the liberal point of view and the liberal programs which had long dominated both parties. In 1963, for example, he said that social security should be voluntary and that the TVA should be sold. As a result of careful organization and arduous preconvention campaigning, the Goldwater forces won the Republican nomination for their candidate. The platform of the party reflected his philosophy. It called for an end to deficit spending, further tax reduction, and a more militant foreign policy, which it characterized as a "dynamic strategy aimed at victory," a reference to the increasingly frustrating war in Vietnam.

There was no doubt, of course, that Lyndon Johnson would be the Democratic candidate although his selection of Hubert Humphrey as his running mate came as something of a surprise. Humphrey had long been associated with the more liberal wing of the party, toward which Johnson was not thought to be favorably disposed. The platform was as liberal as Humphrey ever was, stressing civil rights for blacks, medical insurance for the aged, full employment, and aid to education. In addition, it denounced not only the Communist Party but also such supernationalistic organizations as the John Birch Society and the Ku Klux Klan. The contest between the Republican and Democratic parties, in short, was unusually ideological for an American presidential campaign, since it was devoid of the usual balancing of philosophies in candidates and platforms.

Johnson proved to be not only the more relaxed and experienced campaigner but also the more popular. His margin of votes was the largest in United States history, topping even Franklin Roosevelt's in 1936. He won 61 percent of the popular vote, carried 44 states and won 295 seats in the House of Representatives and 68 of 100 seats in the Senate. Goldwater's record as a believer in military solutions to problems of foreign policy, such as that in Vietnam, and his repudiation of the social gains of the New Deal lost him many votes among moderate Republicans, the poor, the aged, and ethnic minorities. Democrats successfully painted Goldwater as a reckless warmonger, helped in part by Goldwater's refusal to rule out the use of nuclear weapons in Vietnam. The Democrats countered with a highly controversial negative campaign ad, considered the first of its kind on television, where a young girl plucked petals off of a flower while a nuclear bomb detonated. Meanwhile, Johnson essentially campaigned against expanding the war in Vietnam, stating, "... We are not sending American boys 10,000 miles around the world to do what Asian boys ought to be doing." While Johnson's approach won big with the liberal "peaceniks," not surprisingly, Johnson's proportion of the black vote in the big cities of the North and in several Southern states reached as high as 90 and 95 percent due to his stance on civil rights.

Farmers, too, voted Democratic because they feared that Goldwater's laissez-faire views would jeopardize the government support program for agriculture. Four of the six states Goldwater carried were in the Deep South where it was believed that his position on the rights of black Americans (he had voted against the Civil Rights Act of 1964) was less dangerous to white supremacy than that of Johnson. While Goldwater was no bigot, he also endeared himself to the white South by his emphasis upon states' rights and his steady denunciations of centralization of power in Washington. The strategy of the Goldwater Republicans became known as the "Southern strategy, " whereby the Republicans would play on the racial fears of white conservatives in the South in order to lure them away from the Democratic Party. Northeastern Republicans led by Nelson Rockefeller, however, condemned the strategy as immoral, racist, and exclusive in character. In the words of Rockefeller:

> "Completely incredible as it is to me, it is now being seriously proposed to the Republican Party that as a strategy for victory in 1964, that it write off the Negro and other minority groups, that it deliberately write off the great industrial states of the North (representing nearly 50 percent of the country's population), that it write off the big cities, and that it direct its appeal primarily to the electoral votes of the South, plus the West and a scattering of other states. The transparent purpose behind this plan is to erect political power on the outlawed and immoral base of segregation and

to transform the Republican Party from a national party of all the people to a sectional party for some of the people."

What Rockefeller saw in the Goldwater supporters clearly contained elements of truth; but the white South, motivated by bigotry, would begin to abandon the Democratic Party in 1964 even though Goldwater himself was a landslide election loser. The landslide victory for Democratic candidate Lyndon Johnson over Goldwater owed more, perhaps, to the complex emotional reactions of the public to the Kennedy assassination than to any coherent grand strategy by the opposition. In essence, the groundwork for the future success of the conservative Republicans had been laid even if the immediate battle had ended in miserable failure. The debacle that the Republicans suffered in 1964 was somewhat repaired in the November elections of 1966, when the party was able to win 47 new seats in the House of Representatives and eight new governorships. That almost all the Republican winners had either opposed Goldwater's nomination in 1964 or simply ignored his conservative ideology in 1966 indicated once again how damaging the party's shift to the right two years before had been. Two years later Richard Nixon would be able to ride the "Southern strategy" to the White House.

CONSTRUCTING THE GREAT SOCIETY

Thanks to his overwhelming victory at the polls in 1964, Johnson found that the new Congress quickly passed the legislation he wanted. To continue the war against poverty, the legislators appropriated $1.1 billion to alleviate rural poverty in Appalachia and $3.3 billion for the economic development of depressed urban areas. By the end of 1968 some 162,000 new housing units had been constructed through federal aid, as compared with 34,000 five years before. A high of 400,000 units was reached in 1970.

At the President's urging, Congress in 1965 also authorized rent subsidies to the poor living in privately owned housing. The program was designed to help low-income people living outside public housing. Johnson called the act "the single most important breakthrough" in housing legislation. That same year Johnson secured the passage of the Medicare bill, which provided for medical aid for persons over 65 through the social security system, a measure that Kennedy had advocated earlier but had twice failed to get through Congress.

Johnson also redeemed Kennedy's 1960 pledge to revise the immigration laws in order to remove the discrimination against immigrants from eastern and southern Europe that had been a part of national policy since the 1920s. The Immigration Act of 1965 provided for the elimination by 1968 of quotas based on national origin but kept a ceiling on the total number of immigrants admitted each year and introduced the first ceiling on immigrants from the Western Hemisphere. No one at the time realized how profound an impact this law would have in transforming American society. With the refugees coming from Southeast Asia after decades of war in that part of the world and others coming owing to the poverty in their homelands, immigration rates would skyrocket. By 2000 the country would have more foreign-born than at any time since the 1930s.

THE EDUCATION PRESIDENT

One of Johnson's most dramatic and path-breaking contributions was in education. For years the role of the federal government in supporting education had been vehemently debated, without either side being able to prevail. Under Johnson the question was settled positively. From now on it would be a question only of how much support the federal government ought to provide. The National Defense Education Act of 1964, for example, offered federal support for the teaching of the humanities as well as the sciences in college. Federal support of education no longer needed to be confined to subjects useful in repelling foreign threats, as it had at the passage of the first NDEA under Eisenhower in 1958.

The Elementary and Secondary Education Act of 1965 was also a landmark measure. It provided for the expenditure of over $1 billion for improving education in schools below the college level and, also for the first time, permitted federal money to be granted to private church-supported schools. For 30 years the major stumbling block in the path of federal aid to education had been the demand of such schools—principally Roman Catholic—for funds and the refusal of many people to countenance such aid on the ground that it would violate the traditional separation of church and state. These obstacles were transcended in this act by confining the federal funds to nonreligious expenditures, while justifying such grants as aid to pupils rather than as aid to religious institutions.

In the Higher Education Act of 1965, the federal government for the first time provided scholarships for college students in an effort to realize President Johnson's goal of making it financially possible for any young American to attend college. The act also constituted a continuation of the long-term trend toward popularization of higher education that had begun in the 1920s and had been continued by measures such as the G.I. Bill, which had offered financial aid to World War II veterans wishing to attend college.

A SOUTHERN PRESIDENT AND BLACK AMERICA

John F. Kennedy's moving television appeal to all Americans in 1963 to accept the moral challenge of full equality for blacks justly earned him the distinction of being the first President in the twentieth century to attack the question of discrimination against black Americans in clearly moral terms, to Lyndon Johnson, however, must go the credit for the most sweeping attack on the unequal treatment of black people mounted by any President at any time. The Civil Rights Act of 1964 really originated under the Kennedy administration, but it remained for Johnson to push it through a three-month filibuster in the Senate. The Act prohibited racial discrimination in public places, in employment, and in labor unions. As a sanction of compliance, it provided for the withholding of federal funds from any state that practiced racial discrimination. Since much federal money went to support schools, hospitals, and other state services, this provision gave bite to the law.

This act also sought to get around the literacy requirements for voting, which were often used in the South as a means of disfranchising blacks. It provided that any adult with a sixth-grade education was presumed to be literate. The immediate effect was to open public accommodations in many cities of the South for the first time in the twentieth century—though not much was changed in the rural and small-town South—and to increase voting by blacks in many communities.

It is also worth noting that the Civil Rights Act of 1964 was the broadest statement of American belief in equality ever enacted. It outlawed not only racial discrimination but also discrimination in employment for reasons of sex, nationality, and religion, thus becoming fundamental to progress for the budding women's movement. The federal government was now committed to enforcing equality of treatment for two of the most visible groups in the United States—blacks and women. Within a very short time after its passage, women activists that had become acquainted through their work on various commissions on the status of women formed the National Organization for Women as an advocacy group to push for greater equality.

The Johnson administration also pushed through a new voting bill in 1965. Despite protections for black voters in the acts of 1957, 1960, and 1964, blacks were still being kept from the polls in the South by subterfuge, intimidation, or outright refusal by state officials.

The Voting Act of 1965 provided for federal officers to register black voters in any county in which the Justice Department found less than 50 percent of the eligible voters actually participating in presidential elections. State voter qualifications that discriminated against blacks, such as literacy tests and poll taxes, were struck down, and any new state electoral changes had to be approved by the United States Department of Justice. Federal examiners would oversee state elections to ensure compliance and federal marshals would provide enforcement if necessary. A striking measure of how far the country had come on the question of federal power as well as on the rights of blacks was that in 1890 a similar bill by Representative Henry Cabot Lodge had been denounced and killed in the Senate for being a "Force Bill." In 1965 such a bill seemed a mild and necessary measure to most Americans.

As a result of the protection and support provided by the law, registration drives over the subsequent years brought millions of black voters into the political process. By 1970 about two thirds of the eligible black adults in the South were registered, a proportion that had not been achieved since the days of Reconstruction. Black voter registration in the South doubled in the five years following passage of the Voting Rights Act of 1965. As a result, in that same year Alabama counted 105 black elected officials—the second highest number in the nation.

The new interest in black voting, in fact, led in the following years to the election of a large number of black elected officials throughout the country. In 1977, over 4,300 blacks held elective office, an increase of 150 percent since 1970, and by mid-decade black mayors headed scores of cities—including Los Angeles, New Orleans, Atlanta, Detroit, Gary, and Newark—Johnson also took pride in appointing the first black to the cabinet (Robert C. Weaver as Secretary of Housing and Urban Development) and the first to the Supreme Court (Thurgood Marshall).

The path-breaking legislation came about not only as a result of the president's leadership but also as a result of the pressure coming from grass-roots activism by African Americans, especially the non-violent protest then being met all too often by brutality, a spectacle that unfolded on national television and helped create popular support for the new policies. To summarize the events of those years is, in effect, to recite a litany of civil rights martyrs: civil rights leader Medger Evers gunned down the very night that President Kennedy made his television address to the nation in 1963, the four school girls killed in the bombing of a church in Birmingham that same year, and then the martyrs during Freedom Summer in 1964 when young people of both races went south to register voters and challenge the racial caste system. Those young men killed by a Klan mob in Mississippi were James Cheney, a local black activist, and two white volunteers, Michael Schwerner and Andrew Goodman. The following year, as a consequence of the protests to achieve the voting rights legislation, three people lost their lives: Jimmy Lee Jackson, a young black man; James Reeb, a white Unitarian

President John F. Kennedy *(AP Photo)*

minister; and Viola Liuzzo, a white Detroit housewife. In addition to the killings, civil rights workers were frequently beaten, jailed, and generally intimidated by those who opposed the coming changes.

TWO STEPS FORWARD, ONE BACKWARD

In 1966, Congress failed to pass an open housing bill—the first civil rights bill to fail in almost 10 years. Despite the administration's commitment to civil rights and the passage of four civil rights acts since 1954, resistance to acceptance of blacks as equals was persisting. White violence against black demonstrators in Alabama in the spring of 1965 had caused President Johnson to send federal troops into his native South to provide the protection that George C. Wallace, Alabama's segregationist governor, would not. In the elections of 1966, strong segregationists won the governorships in Alabama and Georgia.

Another factor in the changing racial equation was an upsurge in riots, an onset that began in Harlem in 1964 following an episode in which a white policeman shot a black teenager. The next summer there was a riot in Watts, a predominantly black area of Los Angeles, which lasted five days and cost 34 lives. In the spring and summer of 1967, riots in varying degrees of severity occurred in more than 30 cities. In Detroit and Newark alone, 68 persons lost their lives, about 1,400 others were injured, and almost 7,000 were arrested. Property damages from looting and burning were estimated in hundreds of millions of dollars.

President Johnson again asked Congress to enact a civil rights bill that would end discrimination in the sale and rental of housing, one of the bases for all-black schools in the North as well as a major handicap to blacks in achieving equal opportunity. Congress was slow to move on the measure until the assassination of Martin Luther King, Jr., on April 4, 1968, impelled it to action. King was undoubtedly the leading African American in the nation, uncompromising in his commitment to the achievement of equality through nonviolence. He was shot by a white racist, James Earl Ray, in Memphis where King had been participating in a protest movement on behalf of striking black garbage collectors.

Following King's death, there were outbursts of black rage in some 125 cities across the country. This time Washington, D.C., Baltimore, Chicago, and Kansas City were conspicuous for the level of damage and violence. All told, 46 persons were killed, more than 2,600 injured, and some 22,000 arrested in unrest throughout the country. Total property losses were put at $45 million. The civil rights bill that King's death hastened to the President's desk outlawed discrimination on racial grounds in the sale and rental of about 80 percent of the housing in the country.

During the late 1960s and early 1970s, however, there were many signs in various Northern cities that as the movement for racial equality sought to break down housing barriers and to desegregate schools with enrollments based on segregated housing patterns, white resistance would become stronger rather than weaker. The failure of the 1966 open housing bill was one sign. Another was the approval that greeted the Nixon administration's slowdown on implementing school integration in 1969 and afterward.

In spite of these setbacks, however, progress had been made. More blacks were voting in the South than had voted in almost a century. The whole legal basis of segregation in the South was gone, and by 1972 school integration throughout the region had moved far beyond mere tokenism. Although blacks still experienced a higher rate of unemployment than whites, that disparity in 1970, for the first time, was less than 100 percent. Between 1960 and 1970 the proportion of blacks that had purchasing power equivalent to $10,000 in 1969 dollars rose from 9 percent to 24 percent. That increase was considerably greater than the doubling that took place over the same period for whites; yet it was still true that blacks, constituting only 11 percent of the population, made up 30 percent of those who were below the official government poverty line.

Toward the end of the Johnson administration it was recognized that equality of opportunity would involve more than removing legal barriers. Instead, it would require efforts to eliminate a century of accumulated discrimination in housing, education, and jobs and the deep prejudices underlying it. Unfortunately, neither most white Americans nor the Nixon and Ford administrations, as would be shown by subsequent events, were prepared to do what was needed to achieve that goal.

"LET US CONTINUE"

With these words Lyndon Johnson announced his support of John F. Kennedy's policies after the assassination in Dallas. The same words might be used to sum up the deeper springs of Johnson's policies, for the new President was also following in the path of Franklin Roosevelt's New Deal during which he had first entered national politics. Indeed, Johnson's programs in education and civil rights went beyond anything done under the New Deal. The Housing and Urban Development Act of 1968, providing $5.3 billion over a three-year period for new housing, especially for low-income families, made New Deal housing expenditures seem paltry. Lyndon Johnson's Great Society, however, never went beyond the New Deal in concept; it simply moved forward in the direction the New Deal had pointed.

It was not, however, the limited imagination of the architects of the Great Society that diminished it in the eyes of the American people and brought it to an unexpected close. Instead, it was the inability of the President to end the Vietnam War. Dissatisfaction was already evident in the elections of 1966, when the Republicans picked up 47 seats in the House and three in the Senate. By the end of November 1967, according to a Gallup poll, only 38 percent of the American people were satisfied with the President's handling of his office, though three years before he had been elected in a historic landslide. To understand what one historian has called "the tragedy of Lyndon Johnson," we have to look at foreign affairs—an area of presidential activity where Johnson was neither expert nor happy.

JOHNSON AND VIETNAM

If Johnson was responsible for the enactment of much of the liberal legislation that Kennedy could not get through, he benefited, in turn, from his predecessor's superior handling of foreign affairs. Indeed, looking back on their administrations, it appears that Kennedy's successes lay principally in foreign affairs while Johnson's enduring monuments are probably found in his domestic programs. One advantage

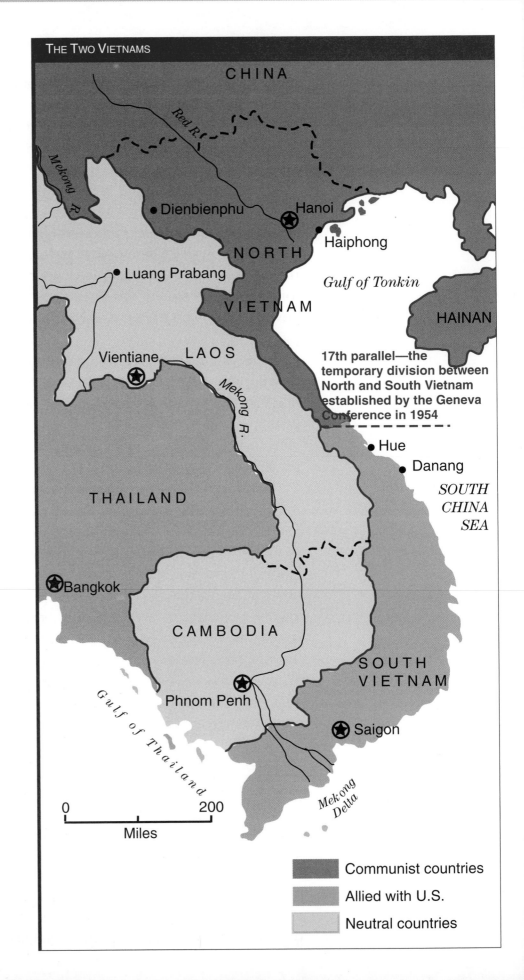

THE TWO VIETNAMS

CHINA

Red R.

Mekong R.

Dienbienphu

Hanoi

Haiphong

NORTH

Gulf of Tonkin

HAINAN

Luang Prabang

VIETNAM

LAOS

Vientiane

17th parallel—the
temporary division between
North and South Vietnam
established by the Geneva
Conference in 1954

Mekong R.

Hue

Danang

*SOUTH
CHINA
SEA*

THAILAND

Bangkok

CAMBODIA

SOUTH
VIETNAM

Gulf of Thailand

Phnom Penh

Saigon

*Mekong
Delta*

0   200

Miles

Communist countries

Allied with U.S.

Neutral countries

that Johnson inherited from Kennedy was a more relaxed and understanding relationship with the Soviet Union. The Cold War still remained, but it had obviously been moderated as a result of Kennedy's resistance to Russian pressures, as in Cuba. At the same time Kennedy had worked out accommodations to lessen tensions, like the test ban treaty, an agreement to sell wheat to Russia, and his conversations with the Russians to limit the spread of nuclear weapons.

It was in Southeast Asia that Kennedy's policies ill served his successor. After World War II, the Vietnamese people clamored for their independence and the end of French colonial rule, but President Truman desired French friendship in the Cold War against the Soviet Union and, thus, supported the return of Vietnam to France. As a consequence, the Viet Minh under Ho Chi Minh, who had fought on the American side in World War II against the Japanese, sought aid from the Soviet Union for a communist revolution in Vietnam; and the Soviets complied. The Viet Minh then launched an eight-year guerrilla war to oust the French colonialists. The French were eventually forced to surrender and withdraw, but not before asking the United States to intervene. President Eisenhower opposed intervention with ground troops due to expected high casualties and opposed intervention with air strikes as "against sound military judgment" and "just silly." Eisenhower believed that it would be impossible to defeat a guerrilla enemy dispersed in the jungle with air strikes.

Without American intervention, a French army of 20,000 was surrounded at Dienbienphu and surrendered on May 7, 1954. A conference was held in Geneva to decide the country's fate and the 19 countries in attendance decided that the country would be divided into two parts, North and South, divided temporarily along the 17th northern parallel as a demarcation line that was not intended to be a permanent border. The northern half of Vietnam was frankly Communist under Ho Chi Minh, while the southern half of the country, led by the Emperor Bao Dai, was strongly anti-Communist and supported by the United States. The Geneva agreement of 1954, which established the division, also called for unification of Vietnam within two years on the basis of free elections. Since it appeared that the elections would result in the triumph of Ho Chi Minh in both sections of the country, however, the Eisenhower administration encouraged the establishment of an independent republic in South Vietnam, as part of its global strategy to prevent the spread of communism. The United States installed Ngo Dinh Diem, a French-speaking Catholic in a country that was 98 percent Buddhist, as Premier. Diem was a fervent anti-communist who had lived in exile in the United States. Eisenhower increased aid to the

Diem government and, in 1954 sent 675 military advisors, who stayed throughout the decade.

The American policy of aid to Vietnam as part of the effort to contain communism would continue and expand under President Kennedy. After the Bay of Pigs fiasco, Kennedy decided to increase aid to Vietnam, both military and economic, and also increase the number of military advisors, which stood at 3,200 at the end of 1961. Expansion continued throughout Kennedy's Presidency so that the number of American advisors in Vietnam was at 16,000 by the time of Kennedy's assassination and 120 United States soldiers had been killed. These 16,000 people were only advisors, however, and Kennedy balked at sending combat troops. Kennedy once remarked, "Sending troops is like taking a drink. The effect wears off and you have to take another."

Kennedy's reasoning in escalating the American involvement was that the problems in Vietnam were part of the American strategy to contain the spread of communism on a global basis, an effort that Kennedy believed was vital to America's long-term security. In retrospect, however, the American commitment to resist the spread of Communist power everywhere was based upon an overly simple analysis and, in the case of Vietnam, misguided. Events would show that not all Communist governments were under the control or discipline of Moscow, as many United States officials in the 1950s and even into the 1960s insisted they were. Nor was it evident that a world order of peace depended, as Secretary of State Dean Rusk asserted during the Johnson years, upon resistance at any cost to any form of aggression by Communists. Nor was it accurate to see the war in Vietnam as simply a replay of the Korean conflict. The war in Vietnam began as a war of independence against the French and transformed into a civil war in the South—directed largely against the tyrannical rule of Ngo Dinh Diem, who lacked the support of the Vietnamese people.

One of Diem's problems was that his communist opposition was waging a guerrilla effort against his government; and it was impossible for Diem to know who among the population were the enemy since they gave the appearance of being law-abiding citizens and then covertly launched attacks on Diem's government. The United States, therefore, urged Diem to adopt a "strategic hamlet" program whereby peasants in problem areas, both communist and noncommunist since it was not known who among the populace were enemies, would be relocated to concentration camps—thus denying the Viet Cong (Vietnamese Communists or "VC") any recruits.

Unsurprisingly, the "strategic hamlet" strategy stirred up political unrest since innocents were concentrated into camps as well as

President Kennedy increased America's involvement in Vietnam in an attempt to contain the global spread of communism. *(Library of Congress)*

Buddhist monks *(AP Photo)*

insurgents; but the unrest became much more agitated in the spring of 1963, when the Catholic Diem prohibited Buddhists from flying their religious flags to commemorate Buddha's birth. Buddhists staged a protest in the city of Hue that was put down when government troops fired into the crowd and killed nine protesters.

A month later, an elderly Buddhist monk protested the government actions against Buddhists by dousing himself in gasoline and burning himself to death in the streets of Saigon. Diem's sister-in-law, Madame Nhu, enraged the public when she callously referred to the protest action as a "Buddhist Barbeque." Similarly, Madame Nhu's husband and Diem advisor, Ngo Dinh Nhu, stated that if any more wanted to do the same he would gladly furnish the gasoline and the matches. Troops working under the direction of Nhu then destroyed Buddhist shrines all over the country, and 1,400 Buddhists who tried to stop the attacks were arrested. Diem erroneously attributed the Buddhist unrest to the Communists.

By the end of 1963, it became clear to the United States that Diem would never have the support of the Vietnamese population. South Vietnamese military leaders led by General Duong Van Minh, encouraged by the CIA, then staged a coup on November 1, 1963, assassinated Diem and his top aid Nhu, and took over the government. The United States quickly extended recognition to the new government, thus giving the impression that it had backed the assassination. The North Vietnamese proposed negotiations with the new government for a cease-fire and free general elections to unify the country, but the United States rejected the offer fearing a communist electoral victory.

Johnson, in the campaign of 1964, promised to keep the United States free from a land war in Asia while continuing to support South Vietnam's resistance to the local guerrillas of the National Liberation Front—the "Viet Cong"—and the Communist troops sent from the North. The fall of General Minh's government in another military coup in January 1964, however, ushered in more political uncertainty in Vietnam and intensification of the civil war. President Johnson and his advisors believed that the unrest was caused by the communist threat from Hanoi and ignored the possibility that the revolt was merely a populist uprising against an illegitimate government by people who simply wanted to rule themselves.

GULF OF TONKIN

In early August, however, when North Vietnamese ships in the Gulf of Tonkin allegedly attacked two American warships, President Johnson seized the opportunity to broaden his powers. On August 2 and 4, 1964, North Vietnamese torpedo boats in the Gulf of Tonkin off the coast of North Vietnam attacked two American surveillance destroyers. The North Vietnamese torpedoes missed both boats. There is some speculation that there were never any torpedoes at all and the United States Navy was merely shooting at "flying fish." Johnson had been looking for a reason to justify escalation of the United States presence in the Vietnamese fracas, however; and the Gulf of Tonkin incident provided an opportunity. Johnson called the attacks "unprovoked" and "North Vietnamese aggression on the high seas;" but, in truth, the destroyers had been providing radar and reconnaissance for South Vietnamese raids against military installations on two North Vietnamese islands. Nevertheless, Johnson asked Congress to authorize him to take whatever measures might be necessary to resist aggression. On August 7, 1964, Congress passed the "Gulf of Tonkin Resolution," which authorized the President to "take all necessary measures to repel any armed attack against the forces of the United States and to prevent further aggression." The Gulf of Tonkin Resolution eventually became known as Johnson's "Blank Check" from Congress to do whatever he wanted in Vietnam. In Johnson's words, "It was like Grandma's nightshirt—it covered everything." The resolution passed almost without opposition, 416–0 in the House and 88–2 in the Senate, and asserted that peace and security in Southeast Asia were vital to the national security of the United States. The Gulf of Tonkin Resolution thus became the President's authority for an almost unlimited expansion of the American involvement.

After the Gulf of Tonkin Resolution, the North Vietnamese government in Hanoi offered negotiations; but Johnson refused, believing the communist threat could only be thwarted by force. Johnson also feared being viewed as "soft" on communism and subject to charges of "appeasement" in Vietnam. With negotiations failing, the North Vietnamese responded by sending 4,500 troops to South Vietnam.

ROLLING THUNDER

By early 1965, the likelihood of military and therefore political defeat in the South became so great that President Johnson sharply increased the American commitment to contain communism in Asia. On February 5, 1965, Viet Cong guerrillas killed eight and wounded 126 Americans in an attack on a United States base at Pleiku. Johnson responded with Operation "Rolling Thunder" which was a retaliatory bombing campaign of North Vietnam aimed at cutting off the supply lines to the communists in the South. Undersecretary of State George Ball warned that such action was likely to unite all of Vietnam against the fire from the sky, but his warnings went unheeded. Six months later, military intelligence concluded that the bombing had little effect on supply lines because supplies to the Viet Cong in the South had moved outside of Vietnam to what was known as the Ho Chi Minh Trail in Laos and Cambodia. Furthermore, the bombing destroyed no strategic targets, but killed innocents, thus alienating the United States from the population it was trying to support. Despite being informed of this information, Johnson continued the bombing campaign, believing that the United States military could handle any situation in any "piddly little piss-ant country." "Rolling Thunder" continued with a few interruptions until 1973. Four times the amount of bombs used in World War II were dropped on Vietnam, with the result that 1,000 Vietnamese civilians per week died in the bombings. After the bombing began, the North Vietnamese deployed another 6,500 troops to South Vietnam thus increasing, rather than decreasing, the number of armed communists in South Vietnam.

ESCALATION

Later that year Johnson not only increased the number of American military personnel in the South but also authorized for the first time the direct engagement of the enemy by American ground troops. This new turn in American involvement in the war had several consequences. For one thing, by 1966 the military presence of some 400,000 United States troops removed the possibility that the Communist-led guerrillas could take over the South as long as the Americans remained. It also meant that the war was now being fought largely by Americans, though some 500,000 South Vietnamese troops were also mobilized.

Rolling Thunder required American air bases in South Vietnam, so the Viet Cong quickly began launching sabotage raids on United States air bases. In March 1965, General William C. Westmoreland, as a result, requested more combat troops to defend the United States airfields. President Johnson responded by sending 3,500 troops to Danang on March 8, 1965, to protect United States air bases. Colin Powell described the circular reasoning that permeated the entire operation, stating, "When I arrived in Vietnam at an air field, I asked General Cho why the air field was there. He said that it was to service the supply depot. When I asked him why the supply depot was there, he said that it was to service the air field." Nevertheless, once Americans were "defending" the airfields, they quickly began roaming the countryside to ferret out saboteurs. Westmoreland called for more troops, and Johnson began to escalate the war rapidly. By the end of 1965, 184,000 American troops were in Vietnam, and by the end of 1968, the number was 538,000.

Despite this escalation, the United States had no plans for "winning the war" or destroying the enemy, as it was feared that an American invasion of North Vietnam might bring Chinese or Soviet involvement as the invasion of North Korea had done in 1950. The goal was simply to prevent communists from taking over South Vietnam, and this meant that the United States would maintain a military presence as long as the enemy retained the will to fight. Since the Vietnamese had been fighting for independence since the Japanese invasion in 1942, they had already proven their resolve. Fighting in their homeland, the Vietnamese people possessed a national will that the United States underestimated. Ho Chi Minh once stated, "You can kill ten of my men for every one I kill of yours, but even at those odds, you will lose and I will win." Ho proved to be prophetic since the American kill ratio was 10–1, but the communists would eventually win the war.

The Vietnamese, both North and South, generally viewed the United States as an unwanted invader in the "People's War." Essentially, the United States was primarily at war not only against the North Vietnamese Army, but also almost the entire population. Most of American casualties, including the wound to the foot of Colin Powell, for which he received a Purple Heart, were due to booby traps rather than engagement.

In general, American soldiers noted that children would spend the day picking up sticks and bamboo shoots. The children took their

Communist North Vietnam President Ho Chi Minh *(AP Photo)*

sticks home to the women, who would sharpen the sticks; and then the men would go out at night and dig pits with the sharpened sticks in the bottom. Fecal material or rotten food was often put on the shoots to cause infection. The pits would be covered with leaves and brush so that unsuspecting soldiers on patrol would fall in. The lucky ones would have their feet impaled and quickly be out of action, while the unlucky ones fell headfirst.

Because it was obvious that the villages and countryside were replete with Viet Cong, the United States Army began the policy of "Securing Sectors," which entailed removing the population of entire villages from their huts and then burning the villages so that they could not return. Those who resisted were removed by force. In such a situation, exactly who was the enemy became completely muddled. In the words of American serviceman Thomas Slate, "We were taught that our objective was to kill gooks. There was no distinction between a North gook and South gook; a gook is a gook and you shoot it."

In May of 1965, the United States called off bombings to encourage negotiations, but the North Vietnamese demanded a United States withdrawal before negotiations could begin and talks went nowhere. In June of 1965, South Vietnam became under the control of General Nguyen Cao Ky and General Nguyen Van Thieu. Nguyen Cao Ky imprisoned thousands of political enemies after another Buddhist upheaval, and South Vietnam became flooded with refugees.

In 1967, the head of the CIA in Vietnam, William Colby, created what was known as the "Phoenix Program," the goal of which was to promote "pacification" in South Vietnam through mass arrests and trials of civilians accused of helping the enemy. The Phoenix Program quickly became associated with assassinations where thousands of suspected Viet Cong (VC) and their sympathizers were "neutralized." The results of the bombings, pacification programs, etc. were that by 1968, four million people (25 percent of South Vietnam's population) were refugees.

MONKEYING WITH THE NUMBERS

United States military analysts argued that at least 3-to-1 strength was needed to win a guerrilla war. The British argued that their experience in the Boer War proved that 10-to-1 strength was necessary. In order to win the war then, military analysts needed to estimate the size of the enemy and then send at least triple that if the United States were to have any chance at victory. In 1964, the official "Order of Battle" set the number of the enemy forces at 270,000. Between 1964 and 1968, the United States military claimed to have killed 250,000 of the enemy. Based on these numbers, unless the enemy had gained many new recruits, the war was supposed to be winding down by 1968. Unfortunately, such was not to be the case.

CIA intelligence officer Sam Adams investigated the Order of Battle in 1968, expecting to find that the Viet Cong had been almost wiped out. Using captured Vietnamese documents, Adams instead estimated the total number of VC at 600,000. Adams informed his superiors and top military officials; but the military rejected Adams' numbers, and the official Order of Battle remained at 270,000, the exact figure from 1964. President Johnson did not want to send more troops, since already a half-million men were in Vietnam, nor did he want to increases taxes to pay for the war because such measures were likely to make the war unpopular. Consequently, the United States pretended that there were fewer enemy troops than there were so that they could justify limiting the troop strength to somewhere near 500,000, though Johnson never imposed an official cap on the number.

Nevertheless, within the United States, the Johnson policy of gradually but relentlessly escalating the war divided the American people. Few Americans wanted a full-scale war against China or the Soviet Union, yet it seemed that the policy might lead in that direction. Also many Americans had voted for Johnson in preference to Goldwater in 1964 on the ground that the war would not be expanded if Johnson were elected, and they now felt that he had misled them. Others found Johnson's policy faulty on moral grounds, contending that the regime the United States was keeping in power in South Vietnam was representative of neither its people nor their national aspirations. Still others opposed his policy on the more pragmatic level that the United States was overextended in commitments and power in Vietnam. Furthermore, others argued that the question of whether or not Vietnam fell to the communists did not impact national security

Advocates of American abandonment of the long involvement in Vietnam grew in number as the war dragged on. Most Americans, to be sure, supported the general policy of containing communism in Asia, just as they had supported it in Europe. As the cost of that containment mounted and the connection between the interests and safety of the United States and the interminable war became less and less clear, however, many Americans began to think that the price was too high. Even those who accepted the administration's claim that the war was primarily a defense against aggression from the North could not help but recognize that, even in 1968, with over a half million American troops in Vietnam, victory was still not in sight. Although President Johnson insisted that American withdrawal could mean national ignominy and national danger, the direct interest of the United States in the war was never spelled out. The administration relied more and more upon the argument that the war involved the prestige of the United States and the "credibility" of its word among its allies.

The effect of the war on American foreign relations elsewhere was evident when Johnson dispatched several thousand marines in 1965 to prevent an alleged Communist coup from overturning the government of the Dominican Republic in the Caribbean. Although the troops were withdrawn within a year, the United States had once again violated its pledge not to intervene in the affairs of Latin American nations.

The consensus was that Johnson had intervened out of fear of another Cuba near American shores. Though the evidence of Communist power in Santo Domingo was slight, the President was not willing to take the chance that the non-Communists could remain in control without help from the United States. In the context of the frustrating war in Vietnam and the continued existence of a Communist regime in Cuba, even the slightest threat of yet another Communist regime in the Western Hemisphere seemed too risky to contemplate.

On the other hand, when war between Egypt and Israel became imminent in May and June of 1967, the United States hesitated to get involved, despite moral and perhaps legal obligations to support Israel against a military threat to its survival. Undoubtedly the heavy involvement in Vietnam played an important part in the hesitation. The United States was unable to prevent the brief "Six Day War" in the Middle East, which began in early June 1967.

At home it was also evident that the rising cost of the war—at least $20 billion a year—was stiffening resistance in Congress and across the country to further expenditures on behalf of the Great Society. In November 1967, Senator Eugene McCarthy, a liberal Democratic senator from Minnesota, announced that he would run in the upcoming primaries against the President in order to provide an alternative on the question of the war. By this time the high cost of the war in both money and personnel, as well as its persistence, had aroused much public hostility, even within the President's own party. Yet few thought McCarthy's challenge would seriously affect the President or the continuance of the war.

TET OFFENSIVE

On January 29, 1968, at the beginning of Tet, the Vietnamese lunar New Year, the Viet Cong and the North Vietnamese launched a major offensive against 30 provincial capitals held by South Vietnamese forces. The power of the attack took the Americans and their Vietnamese allies by surprise. At one point fighting was going on within the American Embassy in Saigon itself. Although a shaken administration bravely called the Tet offensive a complete failure, few believed it.

A South Vietnamese soldier takes a position on a Saigon street (*AP Photo/Nick Ut*)

Two weeks prior to Tet, President Johnson had stated that South Vietnam was "nearly all secure" in his State of the Union address. The scope of the Tet offensive quickly proved otherwise, as perhaps 100,000 VC and VC sympathizers were involved in the offensive. Communist losses in the offensive were huge, and the United States claimed a 10-to-1 kill ratio; but Tet proved that the war was not near over, and the VC were not close to being wiped out as a fighting force. The American public turned against the war as a consequence. In February, NBC news showed footage of Saigon's police chief executing a handcuffed VC prisoner with a pistol shot to the head. In the provincial capital of Ben Tre, American and South Vietnamese troops killed 1,000 civilians while rooting out VC, further shocking the American conscience.

That March, Senator McCarthy received almost as many votes in the New Hampshire Democratic primary as the President of the United States. For months the President had been unable to appear in public without insulting harassment and even danger to his person from the opponents of the war, and this new measure of public repudiation put unendurable pressure upon him. He could either abandon the war—a policy he had resolutely refused to consider—or abandon the presidency. In a surprise television announcement at the end of March, Johnson removed himself from consideration for renomination, at the same time announcing a partial cessation of the bombing of North Vietnam.

Yet Johnson's withdrawal from political life was only the first of the shocks that preceded the election of 1968. Five days later, Martin Luther King, Jr. was assassinated in Memphis, Tennessee—an event that, as we have already noted, caused violence to erupt in over a hundred cities. Then two months after that, in the midst of the furious primary campaign for the Democratic nomination that Johnson's retirement had begun, Senator Robert Kennedy of New York, brother of the assassinated President, was shot and killed by a fanatical anti-Zionist, Sirhan Sirhan, after winning California's Democratic primary. With President Johnson's withdrawal from the race, the charismatic Robert Kennedy, almost as widely idolized as his brother, had been well on his way to being the Democratic presidential nominee, and the victory in California appeared to be only the first big step. The tragedy of his assassination in Los Angeles, however, robbed the nation of what might have been.

By the summer of 1968 antiwar protests had spread to many cities, and students—in particular the male students among them facing a possible draft—became increasingly vociferous in their demonstrations. A favorite chant was "Hey, hey, LBJ—How many kids did you kill today?" Mass graves uncovered at Hue after the Tet Offensive revealed over 3,000 bodies of civilians, many buried alive by the Viet Cong.

The most important event was the My Lai incident of 1968 that was made public in 1970. American troops at My Lai, a small Vietnamese village, killed over 200 people in cold blood under the direction of Lt. William L. Calley. The testimony of Paul Meadlo was particularly chilling:

> Calley's orders were "round everybody up and take care of them." "We huddled them up. We made them squat down. I poured about four clips into the group. The mothers was hugging their children ... well, we kept right on firing. They was waving their arms and begging."

Calley was court-martialed and sentenced to life in prison. The sentence was reduced to 10 years, and Calley was released in six months on parole.

THE NIXON YEARS

THE ELECTION OF 1968

Robert Kennedy's death assured the nomination of Hubert Humphrey, the Vice-President, as Democratic presidential candidate, but not until after the passions stirred up by Vietnam had disrupted the party convention in Chicago. Thousands of disenchanted young people—both moderates who had worked in Senator McCarthy's primary campaign and radicals out to "confront" the Establishment—demonstrated in the streets until they were brutally dispersed by the police in full view of television news cameras. The sight of the bloody clashes shocked the American people. Similarly, the video footage of Chicago's mayor Richard Daily pulling his hand across his neck horizontally in a "cut it" gesture that led to the silence of the microphones of several people at the Democratic Convention contributed to the image of cronyism and corruption by "the Establishment." Neither the Democratic platform, which offered no significant alternative to the Johnson war policies, nor the candidate, who was identified with those policies, provided a rallying point for opponents of the war.

Meanwhile, the Republican convention had nominated Richard Nixon, who had survived not only his defeat by John Kennedy in 1960, but also the subsequent loss of a race for the governorship of California, after which he briefly retired from politics, stating that the

THE ELECTION OF 1968

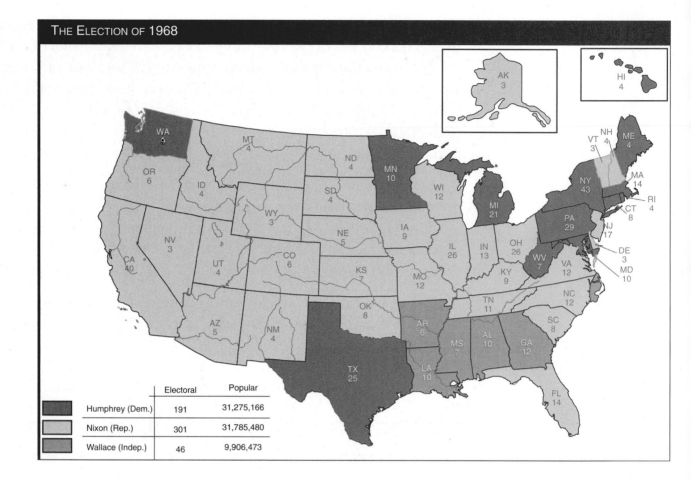

	Electoral	Popular
Humphrey (Dem.)	191	31,275,166
Nixon (Rep.)	301	31,785,480
Wallace (Indep.)	46	9,906,473

media would not have "Nixon to kick around any more." Since then he had worked hard at building support within the party and keeping in the public eye through meetings with world leaders. Recognizing that he must win a substantial number of Southern votes, Nixon chose Spiro Agnew, governor of the border state of Maryland, as his running mate.

The campaign was complicated by the candidacy of George Wallace of Alabama, who ran on the new American Independent Party ticket and its platform of a return to segregation and a premium on law and order. No one expected him to win, but he clearly threatened Humphrey in the traditionally Democratic South; and the enthusiasm he stirred in some Northern states reflected the opposition of many blue-collar workers to the Democratic stand on civil rights. There was a possibility that he could prevent either major candidate from winning a majority of the electoral vote and, thereby, throw the election into the House of Representatives.

The campaign revolved around the war overseas and the social problems at home. Nixon stressed the alarming increase of violence in the cities, which he attributed to the leniency of the Democratic administration toward demonstrators and rioters and of the Supreme

Richard M. Nixon, who appeared on nationwide television to resign his position. Nixon declared, "In all the decisions I have made in my public life, I have always tried to do what was best for the Nation." *(Library of Congress)*

Court toward criminals. Playing upon the public's fears, he promised to end the "permissiveness" that, he insisted, fostered lawlessness. Although he had supported the aims of the war against communism in Southeast Asia since his own vice-presidency, he promised to bring the conflict in Vietnam to an end—though he declined to say how. In the television appearances on which he chiefly relied, he shunned the issue of integration, which was unpopular among many whites, and concentrated on "law and order," about which there could be little controversy. Generally, he portrayed himself as a leader dedicated to national unity and peace.

Burdened with the Johnson record on Vietnam, Humphrey finally announced that, if elected, he would stop the bombing of the North. As Election Day approached, his popular support rose steadily, bolstered by the efforts of his powerful allies in organized labor to win working-class voters back from George Wallace. Just before the election, President Johnson announced the cessation of American bombing in North Vietnam.

Given the shambles at the Democratic convention, the election was remarkably close as George Wallace siphoned conservative segregationists in the South away from the Republican Party. Nixon won by only a half million votes out of 73 million cast. He carried 32 states, however, to Humphrey's 14. Nixon won seven Southern states, Wallace five, and Humphrey one—Texas. While the outcome indicated that the Democrats could no longer count on even a majority of Southern states in a presidential election, the vote for Congress showed that most Americans still voted Democratic. Both House and Senate remained comfortably in Democratic hands.

NIXON AND THE WAR

The political destruction of Lyndon Johnson and the mood of the country during the campaign made it clear to the new President that the public would no longer stand for the emotional and financial drain of an endless Asian war. Within six months after taking office, Nixon announced that he would withdraw 25,000 troops from Vietnam over the next 90 days. Thus began the policy of gradual withdrawal that was to continue for the next four years. Meanwhile, the South Vietnamese army was further trained and equipped to carry on the war by itself through an increase in American aid to the government of South Vietnam, most of it in the form of military hardware. This policy President Nixon called Vietnamization.

Nixon's willingness to use American power to ensure the success of his policy marked a new high in brinkmanship. In the spring of 1970, he ordered American forces to support a South Vietnamese invasion of neighboring Cambodia (and eventually of neighboring Laos) in order to destroy enemy supplies and troop buildups. This action, taken at a time when the war was supposedly "winding down," outraged Americans who saw it as expanding the conflict. That same week the killing of four students at Kent State University (two of whom were merely walking to class) in Ohio by national guardsmen during an antiwar demonstration, and of two students by police at Jackson State University in Mississippi, triggered student strikes at almost 300 colleges and universities. Furthermore, withdrawal of American troops from Cambodia and Laos did not end military action there, much to the chagrin of many.

As he continued to remove American ground troops from Vietnam, Nixon also continued the negotiations in Paris that President Johnson had agreed to in 1968; but neither side would accept the other's demands. In the early spring of 1972 North Vietnamese troops launched a powerful assault across the demilitarized zone in the North and the Cambodian border in the West. To support the reeling South Vietnamese forces, President Nixon widened the war once again. He ordered stepped-up bombing raids against North Vietnam, including the capital, Hanoi, and the major port, Haiphong, neither of which had been bombed since 1968, and the rail lines from China. He also ordered the navy, for the first time, to mine Haiphong harbor. His intention was to cut off the military supplies from the Soviet Union and China that made such offensives possible. China and Russia denounced the American "aggression" but took no other action.

The President was gambling for high stakes since in November he would be up for reelection. If the war was still going on then, his Democratic opponent would have an enormous advantage with an electorate that was clearly sick of the war. Yet if he withdrew all American power from Southeast Asia and the Saigon regime collapsed under Communist pressure, he would be held responsible for "losing" Vietnam to communism. Thus he needed to continue to withdraw the troops, but he also needed some assurance that Saigon could survive. As a consequence, Nixon increased the bombing of North Vietnam.

To critics of his policy, it seemed that Nixon was following the tactics of the Johnson administration and trying to bomb the North Vietnamese into an acceptable settlement. By 1970 more tons of bombs had been dropped on the small country of Vietnam than had been dropped on Germany and Japan in all of World War II, and the raids of 1972 were setting new records in sheer destructiveness. Yet after all the punishment, the Viet Cong and the North Vietnamese continued to fight and continued to score successes in the South. To make matters worse, in what was known as the "Christmas bombing" campaign of 1972, the United States was losing 10 percent of its B-52 bombers on each bombing mission, an untenable casualty rate.

DIPLOMATIC BREAKTHROUGHS

In the summer of 1971 the President made the dramatic announcement that he had accepted an invitation to visit the People's Republic of China. Henry Kissinger, a former Harvard professor of political science, had secretly arranged the visit. Kissinger was the President's trusted adviser on foreign policy, and his influence on the President clearly exceeded that of the Secretary of State, though Nixon at times exhibited jealousy of Kissinger's status with the media. The implications of the trip, which took place in February 1972, were far-reaching as it ended 20 years of frigid enmity between the two powers. Soon after the trip was announced, United

States opposition to seating Mao's China in the United Nations ended. Communist China took the place of Chiang Kai-shek's China on the United Nations Security Council and in the United Nations General Assembly in the fall of 1971. Nixon's visit ended China's long isolation (although it should be noted that Prime Minister Pierre Trudeau of Canada had visited the People's Republic of China prior to Nixon.) By 1973, following Nixon's visit, Japan too had established commercial and diplomatic relations with the People's Republic of China.

Nixon's visit did not convert China and the United States into instant allies. Diplomatic recognition did not immediately follow, and the United States pledged itself to maintain its treaty obligations to Chiang Kai-shek's regime on Taiwan, even though Communist China claimed the island. A new era in the relations between the United States and the Communist powers seemed to have begun, however. This was confirmed when the White House announced that, within two months after his visit to Beijing, President Nixon would visit Moscow as well. (He also became the first President to visit Communist Yugoslavia, Romania, and Poland.)

Behind this about-face by the long-time anti-Communist, Richard Nixon, and the leaders of the two largest Communist states was the hostility between the Russians and the Chinese. China, as the weaker of the two Communist giants, wanted a counterweight in the form of better relations with the United States. Russia, on the other hand, feared that the United States and China might combine against it. As a result, President Nixon was welcomed in both capitals, even as his bombers unloaded unprecedented tons of explosives on his hosts' ally, North Vietnam.

Nixon's primary goal in his diplomacy with China and the U.S.S.R. was to get them to agree to stop spreading communism abroad; and Nixon, evidently, believed that he had done that. If China and the Soviet Union were no longer going to spread communism abroad, then the United States no longer needed to contain it. Nixon could, then, pull the United States army out of the unpopular war in Vietnam. Furthermore, the new relationships with both China and the Soviet Union gave Nixon an opportunity to appeal privately to them both to put pressure on North Vietnam to conclude the war on terms the United States could accept. Since American troops were steadily being removed (the last ground combat forces were withdrawn in August 1972), Nixon's desire for an end to hostilities was clear. At the same time, the continued bombing of North Vietnam and the massing of naval power off the Vietnam coast and air power in neighboring Thailand made it equally clear that he intended to keep up the pressure until his minimum conditions were met.

Even after Kissinger had negotiated for months with the North Vietnamese in Paris for a cease-fire, however, the war had not been brought to a close. Just before Christmas 1972, Nixon increased the pressure further by massive bombings of the North, including Hanoi and Haiphong. Later he would contend (although not all historians agree) that it was these B-52 bombings that brought the cease-fire agreement, which was announced in January 1973. Soon thereafter, all remaining United States combat troops were withdrawn.

PARIS AGREEMENT

Under the Paris Agreement that ended American involvement in the Vietnam War, North Vietnam was allowed to keep troops in South Vietnam. The United States agreed to pull out, and its last troops left Vietnam on March 29, 1973. North Vietnam agreed to release United States POWs and released them March 29, though the United States contended that the North Vietnamese release of POWs was not complete. Henry Kissinger and Le Duc Tho of North Vietnam won the Nobel Peace Prize, but Le Duc Tho rejected the prize because he explained that the war was not over. The only change was that the United States went home.

For Americans the fighting was over, but for the Vietnamese it continued until April 30, 1975, when the South surrendered to Northern troops after the communists had launched a major offensive that spring and overwhelmed the South Vietnamese government. All of Vietnam was finally united, but under communism, and President Ford did not send the United States military to intervene. Earlier that same month rebels friendly to the Communists succeeded in defeating the pro-American government forces in Cambodia, which had gained power as a result of the American and South Vietnamese invasion in May 1970. Later, in 1975, Communist rebels also took over Laos. Thus, after more than 10 years of active American involvement in Southeast Asia to prevent Communist control, three of the four countries of the Indochinese peninsula were under rule friendly to communism.

On the other hand, for facing up to the changed international realities of the 1970s, the first Nixon administration was likely to go down in history as among the important influences in moderating the Cold War. After the Moscow meetings in the spring of 1972, the Soviet Union and the United States agreed to new limitations on missiles and submarines, as well as on joint explorations of space. By 1972 few Americans continued to look on China as the Great Red Menace a whole generation of Americans had been taught to fear. To have been instrumental in bringing about such an alteration in the world scene was no mean achievement.

A COSTLY WAR

Although fought far from American shores, the Vietnam struggle had been the longest in American history. Its cost in American lives (58,000) ranked behind only that of the Civil War and the First and Second World Wars. In 15 years the United States had spent $141 billion on behalf of South Vietnam, or $7,000 for each of the 20 million people in that country. Even those astronomical figures were dwarfed by the cost to the Vietnamese themselves. Between February 1965 and August 1972, the United States dropped three and one half times as many bombs and shells on Vietnam, both the North and South, as all the allies dumped on Germany and Japan during the Second World War. Perhaps as many as 10 million Vietnamese in the South alone became refugees, while civilian deaths there reached almost half a million. Moreover, 30 years of civil war and the corrupting intrusion of American money and power placed severe strains on the social and cultural fabric of the rural, traditional society of Vietnam.

NIXON IN DOMESTIC AFFAIRS

Nixon's flexibility in dealing with China and Russia was repeated in some aspects of domestic matters. As in foreign affairs, he surprised friend and foe alike with his ability to abandon or drastically modify attitudes and principles for which he had stood during a lifetime in public affairs.

When he took office, he proclaimed an end to federal deficits; and for two years he insisted that he would never impose economic controls. In 1969 Congress went along with his recommendations for a tax cut in an effort to stimulate the economy. In 1970, for the first time in nine years, inflation wiped out the gain in median income for a family of four, however; and since the economy was sluggish as well as inflationary, government tax receipts fell below expectations. (Unemployment was up from 3 million in 1968 to over 5 million in 1971.) In August 1971 the President ordered a freeze on prices, wages, and rents; and three months later he set up agencies to police observance of federal economic guidelines.

Thus, having for years pronounced himself an opponent of the "New Economics," he ended up embracing Keynesian theory and the familiar Democratic belief that government has a responsibility to regulate the economy. With the spiraling cost of the Vietnam War, his administration, by 1972, had run up not only the largest budgetary deficit since the Second World War but also two of the largest in American history.

Nixon also showed his flexibility by recommending that the federal government provide a minimum income of $1,600 for every family of four on welfare. Since liberals had advocated the idea years earlier, many Democrats could support it in principle; but liberal senators rejected the $1,600 figure as inadequate. No agreement was reached and no new welfare program was enacted then or later.

Another Democratic idea that Nixon sought to make a part of what he called his "New American Revolution" was that of sharing federal revenues with the states and cities. A revenue-sharing bill was finally passed in September 1972. Congress also accepted presidential proposals for making the Postal Service an independent agency, and for establishing the National Rail Passenger Corporation (Amtrak) to reorganize and run the nation's passenger rail service.

Congress, however, went far beyond Nixon's lukewarm recommendations on the improvement of the environment. At the end of the 1972 session, it passed a $24.6 billion sewage treatment bill that was vetoed by the President on the ground that such expenditure was inflationary. Nixon had recommended only $6 billion. Congress, in a rare exhibition of independence, quickly overrode the veto.

In June 1972 the President signed a landmark bill providing for the first time that nearly every college and university would receive some federal money. It also provided that, as a matter of policy, any student needing money to attend college could obtain a loan of up to $1,400 a year. Public colleges and graduate schools were prohibited from discriminating against women students on pain of loss of federal funds.

The bill also marked the first interference by Congress in the school desegregation issue because it prohibited any new court-ordered school busing for purposes of racial balance until June 1974. The President angrily denounced the provision for not prohibiting present as well as future court-ordered busing on any grounds and promised to carry the busing issue—merely a new form of the old segregated school issue—into the presidential campaign. In fact, busing became an issue in the 1972 campaign even when candidates avoided it.

Especially in some Northern cities, busing continued to be a hotly contested public issue long after Nixon was gone. At the end of the 1970s, despite its continued acceptance of busing, the Supreme Court was taking cognizance of the widely expressed complaint that the defense of minority rights was going too far. In the *Bakke* case in 1978 the Supreme Court struck down the quota system that a state of California medical school had set up to keep a certain number of places for minority applicants. A white student, Allan Bakke, who had been denied admission, contended that his civil rights had been violated because of the policy.

The opinion of the majority of the court, however, while rejecting the medical school's quota system, did not rule out some kind of preference for minority students in admission to state educational institutions. The intention was to provide some way of compensating minorities for damage done by past discrimination. In *U.S. Steelworkers v. Weber* (1979), the Court upheld a private company's policy of affirmative action, which gave some preference to blacks over whites in training programs. In short, the Court was not prepared to countenance rigid quotas for minorities but was willing to uphold the idea of opening preferential opportunities for minorities through special arrangements.

On balance, despite the liberal character of some of Nixon's policies, both foreign and domestic, his administration frankly repudiated the liberalism of the Kennedy and Johnson years in other areas, particularly civil rights. The conservatism was manifested most ideologically in the speeches of Vice-President Spiro Agnew, who went out of his way to castigate liberals—especially reporters and commentators critical of the administration—as dangerous to America and to condemn youthful protestors and demonstrators for their lack of discipline and lack of respect. The President himself spoke out against laws making abortion easier to obtain, and he vetoed a bill that would have provided federally supported child-care centers for working mothers, arguing that such measures weakened traditional family ties.

Nixon's first Attorney General, John Mitchell (who had been his campaign manager in 1968), considered the Supreme Court decisions protecting the rights of accused persons to be too lenient and sought to slow down school integration in the South. His efforts in this direction were rejected by the federal courts, as was his use of wiretapping without court orders in the name of national security.

Nixon appointed a new Chief Justice in 1969, but his next two nominees for the Supreme Court—Southern "strict constructionists," to use the President's description—were rejected by the Senate as inadequately qualified. Before his first term was completed, however, he appointed three more justices, all with records that revealed conservative legal philosophies. They soon began to make their views felt. In June 1972, for example, the Court for the first time in 18 years was unable to render a unanimous decision on school desegregation because two of the new justices voted against the majority.

THE AVALANCHE OF 1972

For a long time, Richard Nixon had made clear that he intended to run again for President. Before the Republican convention met in August he had also made evident that he wanted his Vice-President, Spiro Agnew, again as his running mate. The Democrats, however, could not settle as easily upon Nixon's opponent. Hubert Humphrey, who had been only narrowly defeated by Nixon in 1968, was eager to try again; but before the Democratic convention met in July, George McGovern, senator from South Dakota, Ph.D., and long an outspoken opponent of the war in Vietnam, showed that he was a favorite in the various state primaries where the Democratic base was making its voice heard. Those victories won him the nomination on the first ballot. The Democratic convention itself was unusual that year since a new process that guaranteed representation to ethnic minorities, women, and young people had selected its members. This new kind of party convention—more serious and dedicated to the question of political issues than any convention since the Progressives' in 1912—enthusiastically supported McGovern's liberal posture. The platform promised a quick end to the war, a deep reduction in military expenditures, tax revision, and increased expenditures on social services.

The vice-presidential candidate that the convention named, Thomas Eagleton, senator from Missouri, however, was soon compelled to resign because he admitted to having undergone psychological treatment in recent years. Sargent Shriver, a brother-in-law of John F. Kennedy, was named in Eagleton's place. This unexpected change gave a setback to the hitherto highly successful McGovern organization from which it never recovered.

As the weeks of the campaign passed, it became clear that McGovern was really the nominee of only a minority of his party and that his very liberal positions on tax reform and welfare and particularly on reductions in military spending were frightening many traditional Democrats into the Nixon camp. Roman Catholics, workingmen, Southerners, and ethnic groups were especially unhappy about McGovern. Rather than putting Nixon on the defensive for failing to end the war after four years in office, McGovern found himself on the defensive for being less than candid in his handling of the resignation of Eagleton and for being less than informed in proposing welfare and tax reform programs that he later had to withdraw. Although McGovern publicized what later became known as the Watergate break-in, the connection to the White House was not known and the country did not seem to think that McGovern's charges were worth taking seriously.

Moreover, when a gun-wielding assassin definitively removed George Wallace from the campaign in May because of permanent paralysis after an attempt upon his life, the Wallace supporters moved to Nixon, not McGovern. The President's stand against busing in school integration and a "hard line" on urban crime and on welfare won the support of many white Southerners and traditional Democrats in the cities of the North, who together made up what Nixon termed as the "silent majority"—in contrast to the very loud and violent Vietnam War protestors.

The enormous lead that the polls showed for Nixon over McGovern early in the campaign continued until Election Day. As a result the President left to Vice-President Agnew and other subordinates the actual campaigning. Nixon probably made fewer campaign speeches than Franklin Roosevelt did in 1944 in the midst of the Second World War. Although President Nixon and his foreign policy adviser Henry Kissinger worked hard to arrange an agreement with North Vietnam to end the war before the election, the foot-dragging of South Vietnam prevented that feather from being added to the President's cap.

The results of the election made clear that he did not need an end to the war in order to win one of the biggest victories in American history with Electoral College victories in 49 states and 61 percent of the popular vote. McGovern, by winning only Massachusetts and the District of Columbia, was as badly defeated as Alf Landon in 1936. Those who had contended that McGovern would be the "Democratic Goldwater"—too far out of the mainstream of either party to be able to win—proved to be right. Nixon completed the breakup of the Democratic solid South, which Harding had begun in 1920. He captured, with large majorities, every one of the former states of the Confederacy, a feat never before achieved by a Republican President. Significant for the future politics of the South was the election of three Republican congressmen from Mississippi and Louisiana for the first time since Reconstruction.

Yet it would be a mistake to see Nixon's victory as a Republican resurgence. Indeed, Nixon's campaign had concentrated on "reelecting the President," rather than on winning a Republican majority. In his few campaign speeches the President rarely mentioned his party and in some Southern states Nixon campaigners refused to help Republican candidates who were running against conservative Democrats. The result was that the Democrats continued to control both houses of Congress by substantial majorities, as they had done since 1957. Most Americans, it would seem, were still Democrats, but they apparently did not see George McGovern as their kind of Democratic President.

THE DEPARTURE OF RICHARD NIXON

The intention of the first Nixon administration had been to increase the power and autonomy of the President at the expense of Congress. Its overwhelming victory at the polls in 1972 encouraged the administration to reorganize the government so that the presidential office would be free from Congress on the one hand and from the federal bureaucracy on the other, By enormously increasing the White House staff it would be possible to bypass the permanent staff of the government. Since, as assistants to the President, none of the White House staff would have to be confirmed by the Senate, the office of the President would escape control or even influence from Congress and none of his staff would be a part of the permanent bureaucracy. In effect, the executive would now be accountable only to the voters once every four years.

This move toward plebiscitary government, which was to be put into operation through a reorganization of the executive branch in the first months of the second administration, was stopped in its tracks by the unraveling of the Watergate affair in early 1973. Watergate was a dramatic example of the great danger to constitutional government that could result when a few people whose first loyalty was to a person and not to the office he or she occupied were free to exercise power without accounting to anyone except themselves and the person they served.

WATERGATE

In the spring of 1969, the *New York Times* reported that the Nixon administration had secretly bombed communist sanctuaries in Cambodia, a neutral country in the Vietnam conflict that Nixon had no Congressional authorization to attack. The unauthorized bombings, therefore, exceeded Nixon's Constitutional powers as commander-in-chief since the President may only perform his commander-in-chief powers at the pleasure of Congress. The bombings also violated the President's Constitutional authority to keep Congress "fully and faithfully" informed. Nixon was infuriated at the "leaks" that led to the *New York Times* article and viewed the story as part of the liberal media conspiracy against his administration. Nixon also viewed the article as proof that there were those within his administration that were not only disloyal, but also co-conspirators bent on destroying his administration and undermining his authority. Consequently, Nixon fought back in a paranoid rage and asked the FBI for 17 wiretaps of newsmen and strategically placed White House staff, particularly members of Henry Kissinger's National Security Council staff. Nixon decided that power must be centralized in the White House so as to fend off those in the bureaucracy that were plotting against him. Displaying excessive vindictiveness and paranoia, Nixon demanded the resignation of all non-career officials the day after his reelection victory in 1972.

During the presidential election campaign of 1972, Nixon felt that he needed political intelligence on his opponents and, to that end, assigned G. Gordon Liddy the job of Director of Political Intelligence for the Committee to Re-elect the President. During spring and summer 1972, Liddy's political intelligence operatives made four attempts, only one successful, to burglarize the offices of the Democratic National Committee and install a wiretap. On their fourth attempt on June 17, 1972, five burglars were caught and arrested by Washington, D.C. police. Reflecting their own plot mentality and paranoia, Liddy and E. Howard Hunt had ordered their intelligence burglars to search for evidence of ties to Communist Cuba and other left-wing organizations within the United States.

Although the Democrats naturally tried to make political capital out of what the White House immediately dismissed as a "third-rate burglary," the Democrats' effort had no impact on the campaign. The trial and conviction of the five burglars, however, soon started newspapermen and then Senate investigators along a trail of evidence that quickly led to the White House.

Unbeknownst to Americans at the time of the Watergate break-in, but part of the revelations that came out in the course of various investigations, was the fact that the White House had set up an extra-legal unit known informally as the "plumbers" in the summer of 1971. The "plumbers" included David Young, an assistant to Henry Kissinger; Egil Krogh, an assistant to John Ehrlichman; Walter Minnick of the Cabinet Committee on International Narcotics Control; White House consultant E. Howard Hunt; and G. Gordon Liddy, Assistant to the Secretary of the Treasury. The plumbers' charge was to stop leaks to the media—whether by legal means or those that were dubious. The plumbers came up with plans to discredit Daniel Ellsberg, a defense intellectual, who had leaked the Pentagon Papers to the *New York Times* earlier that summer. In 1969 Ellsberg had prepared a detailed and top-secret study of United States decision-making in Vietnam, a study he came to believe the public had a right to know about; hence, Ellsberg leaked documents to the press. The Pentagon Papers revealed to the American public details of American involvement in Vietnam that were outside of that which Congress had been fully and faithfully informed about by the White House.

Though the study did not concern the Nixon administration per se, its disclosure horrified the White House, which went to court in an unsuccessful attempt to prevent its release. In addition to this open effort, it also set up the plumbers and began a process whereby the presidents' men justified illegal acts to themselves. Through discrediting Ellsberg, the plumbers hoped that they could also discredit other important members of the political opposition as well, including Lesli Gelb, Director of the Vietnam History Task Force that produced the Pentagon Papers; Paul Warnke, who had served as an Assistant Secretary of Defense; Morton Halperin, who had been Warnke's deputy; and Clark Clifford, the former Secretary of Defense in the Johnson Administration. Collectively, the men were viewed as the "doves" of the Johnson administration that opposed and undermined Nixon's Vietnam War strategy. Thus even before the Watergate break-in there had been discreditable episodes, most particularly a similar break-in to the office of Daniel Ellsberg's psychiatrist in an effort to discredit Ellsberg. The office of Ellsberg's psychiatrist was burglarized and vandalized by a group led personally by Liddy although the burglars were unable to find any evidence of value against Ellsberg in their raid.

In spite of this failure, the efforts of the plumbers continued unabated. The plumbers formulated a plan to disrupt the Democratic opposition—including a plan to harass and burglarize the Brookings Institution, a liberal-leaning Washington Think Tank. The plumbers also came up with a plan for "hush money" to prevent Nixon aides from providing evidence to federal investigators. A separate plan to discredit the liberal opposition was submitted to Attorney General John Mitchell by G. Gordon Liddy. The Liddy plan included infiltration of the Democratic Party leadership with spies and electronic surveillance, "demonstration squads" or "street-fighting teams" that could break up Vietnam war protests, "kidnapping teams" that could kidnap members of the demonstrating opposition, and prostitutes trained to extract information from the Democratic Party leadership via sexual relationships.

By spring 1973, Nixon's cover-up of the Watergate burglary began to unravel through a combination of the United States Senate investigation into the case and reporting by *Washington Post* correspondents

Bob Woodward and Carl Bernstein, based on their un-named source in the case, "deep throat." On March 19, 1973, a major break in the case occurred when convicted Watergate burglar and former CIA Agent James McCord handed a letter to Judge John J. Sirica asserting that there had been political pressure applied on the defendants to plead guilty and remain silent, and that perjury had occurred during the trial. Furthermore, McCord charged that there were others involved in the Watergate operation that had not been identified during the trial. Finally, McCord exclaimed that the Watergate burglary was not a CIA operation as had been alleged. Judge Sirica, hoping to elicit previously withheld information from the defendants, reacted by handing down harsh "provisional sentences" to the other defendants with the provision that they were to be reexamined in 90 days.

Throughout the spring and early summer of 1973, in the course of several weeks of public, televised hearings before a Select Committee of the Senate, presided over by Senator Sam Ervin of North Carolina, the public heard some of the evidence linking the illegal act at the Watergate to the President's office. It became clear not only that the men closest to the President, H. R. Haldeman and John D. Ehrlichman, had been instrumental in bringing about the break-in, but also that they had conspired with other White House and campaign officials to cover up the involvement of the President's staff in those activities. Eventually, three White House aides were convicted of crimes as a result of the break–in, and top Nixon aide John Ehrlichman was convicted of violating the civil rights of Ellsberg's psychiatrist, Lewis Fielding, and of lying to a grand jury. Ellsberg, however, had to defend himself against indictment for theft of government property and unauthorized possession of documents related to the national defense, as a result of his role in procuring the Pentagon Papers.

The President himself denied knowing anything about the matter, insisting, instead, that he sought only to uncover the extent and nature of the involvement. In seeking to maintain this claim, Nixon was forced eventually to ask for the resignations of Haldeman and Ehrlichman. Soon thereafter the Attorney General, Richard Kleindienst, and Nixon's former Attorney General, John Mitchell, were indicted and later convicted for their involvement in the cover-up and other incidents.

By 1975 some 33 former members of the White House staff or cabinet had been indicted or convicted or had pleaded guilty to various criminal acts. Moreover, the administration had used the FBI, the Internal Revenue Service, and the CIA for purposes that were illegal or unethical. (Still later investigations would show that previous Presidents had also misused these agencies in ways similar to those employed by Nixon, though not in cover-ups of criminal acts.)

In April, White House aide John Dean, seeing the writing on the wall, retained a lawyer and began negotiating with prosecutors for immunity. On April 30, Richard Nixon formally fired Dean, but the cover-up continued to unravel. Dean, who was a direct point of contact with the President himself, became the chief witness for the prosecution in implicating Nixon in the Watergate cover-up. Undoubtedly the most sensational revelation that came out of the Senate investigations and hearings was that in 1970 the President had had hidden microphones installed in his own office, thus preserving on tape every conversation in the Oval Office. On July 16, White House aide Alexander Butterfield revealed the existence of a tape recording system in the Oval Office that could verify the allegations of Watergate witnesses. Special Prosecutor Archibald Cox subpoenaed several of the tapes, thus making them evidence in the case; and their destruction then became illegal.

The news was earthshaking since it promised that the question of the President's involvement in the burglary could be answered, provided that the tape recordings could be obtained. The President, however, refused to permit the tapes to be examined by the Senate Committee or the Watergate trial court on the grounds of the constitutional separation of powers and executive privilege. Even when a Special Prosecutor was named to probe into the scandal, the President continued his adamant refusal, citing executive privilege. On October 19, 1973, when the Special Prosecutor, Archibald Cox, pressed too hard for the tapes, Nixon reacted by ordering his Attorney General, Elliot Richardson, to fire Special Prosecutor Cox. Richardson refused, and Nixon then accepted his resignation. Nixon then turned to Richardson's deputy, William Ruckleshaus and ordered him to fire Cox, but Ruckleshaus also refused and resigned. Finally, Nixon turned to Solicitor General Robert Bork, who dutifully fired Cox in what became known as the "Saturday Night Massacre".

This effort by the President to blunt the investigation backfired. On the following day the White House was deluged with letters and telegrams expressing the public's outrage over the self-serving dismissal. With public opinion beginning to turn against the President so did the Republicans in Congress. Republican Senator Howard Baker of Tennessee asked the famous question, "What did the President know and when did he know it?" For the first time Congress seriously considered impeachment of the President as the sole remedy still open for getting to the bottom of the matter. Nixon then retreated, agreeing to appoint a new prosecutor who would be free from presidential control or interference. The new prosecutor, however, found the President no more cooperative than before.

Meanwhile, Nixon continued to assert his innocence, announcing at one press conference, for example. "The people have to know whether their President is a crook. Well, I am not a crook. I have earned everything I've got." Up to that point no one had argued that the President had profited financially from the Watergate incident. Indeed, a sinister aspect of the whole affair was that Watergate was not a financial scandal along the lines of those of the Grant and Harding administrations, in which defrauding the government of money was the principal crime. Watergate, rather, was a scandal involving misuse of government power and authority, thus striking at the underlying assumptions of a democratic society. Even in his denial of financial gain, the President was not being completely honest. Later investigations would show that he had, in fact, padded his income-tax deductions while President, thus reducing his personal taxes by almost $450,000.

If the President misgauged what the public would stand for when he fired Cox in October, he repeated his misjudgment in April of 1974. By publishing selected excerpts from the tapes, Nixon sought to quiet the ceaseless public and investigatory clamor for free access to that invaluable evidence. His enemies discounted the usefulness or even the validity of these carefully culled documents; but when the verbatim transcripts were printed, they placed the inner councils of the Nixon administration in a devastatingly ugly light. The level of discourse was shockingly low, and was pushed several levels lower by frequent use of the phrase "expletive deleted." Instead of improving the image of the President, this device left entirely to imagination the degree of obscenity that had actually been used in the Oval Office.

More important was the petty, selfish, and often amoral content of the conversations—though they had been selected for the purpose of putting the best face on the evidence. Even hardened politicians were amazed. Some of the President's staunchest supporters now called for impeachment.

Thereafter, events moved swiftly. In July the Supreme Court ordered the President to turn over all the tapes to the Special Prosecutor, who had been seeking them for half a year. A few weeks later the Judiciary Committee of the House, which for months had been considering in closed session the evidence for impeachment, began to hold public, televised hearings. Not surprisingly, the Democratic majority on the Committee was unanimously in favor of impeachment. More threatening to the President were the seven out of 17 Republicans who also voted for two of the three charges and the two Republicans who went along with the Democrats on the third. The first charge cited Nixon for obstruction of justice, the second for abuse of power, and the third for contempt of Congress. Unlike the impeachment proceedings against Andrew Johnson over a hundred years before, these were carefully and fairly conducted. Not even Republican partisans could sustain allegations that procedures had been improper or that the President was being "railroaded."

Before the Committee's recommendations could be sent to the full House for a vote, the situation changed dramatically. When the President complied with the Supreme Court's order to deliver up the tapes, those long-sought-for pieces of evidence fully exposed Nixon's involvement in the Watergate cover-up. In June 1972, the FBI had begun investigating the source of funding for the Watergate burglary that had been routed through Mexico by the Committee to Re-elect the President. A week later on June 23, 1972, Nixon approved a plan to have the CIA intervene into the FBI Mexico investigation. The CIA was to provide the FBI with information that would throw them off-track so as to conceal the relationship of the Watergate burglars to the Committee to Re-elect the President. In furtherance of this plan, Deputy Director of the CIA Vernon Walters told FBI Director L. Patrick Gray that the FBI investigation into Mexico jeopardized CIA operations. Eventually, the taped recording of Nixon's involvement in this ploy to cover up the connection would become the "smoking gun" that the House of Representatives would use to construct an "Obstruction of Justice" case against the President. No

longer could there be any doubt that the President had lied from the beginning about his complicity in crime. Nixon's public approval rating dropped to 27 percent.

On August 9, 1973, before the House could respond to the recommendation of impeachment, Richard Nixon resigned his office, becoming the first President in history to do so. Characteristically, his emotion-filled farewell statement made no mention of his

Richard Nixon says goodbye with a victorious salute to his staff. *(AP Photo)*

complicity or guilt. It merely referred to his loss of "a strong enough political base in the Congress" to allow him to remain in office.

The President also argued that when national security is threatened, Presidents might operate above the law. The Supreme Court had visited that argument and rejected it after the Civil War in *Ex parte Milligan* (1866). If such emergency powers were rejected by the Court during the Civil War, obviously, it is a bit of a stretch to argue that "national security" had been so threatened by the Democratic National Committee that it justified emergency powers of the Executive Branch outside the powers granted in the Constitution or thus justified the President's aides in ordering a burglary of DNC headquarters. The fact that Nixon (and those that aided him in his attempts to thwart his political enemies) appears to have viewed it this way is a testimony to his personal paranoia. In the end, Nixon's downfall had, perhaps, more to do with his paranoia than anything else. Had Nixon not felt the need to illegally keep tabs on his political opposition due to his paranoia, there might not have been a Watergate break-in in the first place. Furthermore, if Nixon had trusted the entire sordid operation to his security apparatus, he would have been free to deny explicit authorization of the actions and, most likely, would not have had to resign. Nixon, however, was suspicious of both the FBI and CIA, believing that they had a globally liberal bias; therefore, he felt the need to create his own intelligence capabilities in the Committee to Re-elect the President.

The resignation brought into office Gerald R. Ford, the former Republican leader in the House, who had been appointed Vice-President under the Twenty-fifth Amendment only the previous year when Vice-President Spiro Agnew had been compelled to resign because of revelations of financial wrongdoing while governor of Maryland. Agnew had resigned after pleading no contest to tax evasion in a case in which he was accused of taking kickbacks from Maryland contractors. As Vice-President, Ford had been almost a last-ditch defender of the President's integrity. In assuming the presidency, however, he publicly emphasized the need to recognize that "truth is the glue that holds governments together." Nixon had chosen Ford, at least partially, because he believed that Ford offered an insurance policy against his own impeachment, given that Congress surely would not want to risk replacing Nixon with such an unproven commodity as Ford. Unfortunately for Nixon, Ford also had a reputation for honesty; consequently, the prospects of a Ford Presidency, regardless of any other shortcomings, appeared refreshing to many members of Congress, both Republican and Democrat, after the revelations of Watergate. Similarly, the American public was undoubtedly relieved to have a chance to restore some of the faith in government that the Nixon years had severely eroded.

In the White House, Ford proved to be straightforward, relaxed, and low-keyed where Nixon had been devious, tense, and pretentious. Ironically, one of the first acts of the new President was also his least popular. In September, within a month after taking office, Ford pardoned Nixon for any possible crimes he might have committed while President. A pardon implicitly acknowledges guilt, but Nixon, in accepting the pardon, neither alluded to nor admitted any wrongdoing. For some months he remained secluded in his mansion overlooking the Pacific Ocean in southern California, nursing his health, which had deteriorated seriously during the long ordeal of Watergate.

AN ABORTIVE ADMINISTRATION

Although Nixon tried to govern during 1973–1974 as if Watergate were not a major public issue, the forced and voluntary resignations of key administration officials because of the scandal weakened and distracted his government. At the same time the federal bureaucracy was increasingly alienated and presidential relations with Congress were blighted by the impeachment proceedings. As a consequence, little effective action could be taken against inflation. By June 1974 prices rose above an annual rate of 10 percent, a level not reached since World War I. A marked slowing down of the economy compounded the effects of inflation. This combination of economic burdens aroused more dissatisfaction with the administration and the Republican Party than even the revelations about Watergate.

The Nixon administration received further criticism for failing to anticipate the crisis in energy that the Arab-Israeli war of 1973 and then the rise in the price for oil imposed by the Arab oil-producing countries forcefully underlined. The President countered by committing the United States to a policy of self-sufficiency in energy by the end of the 1970s. Although the United States, as an industrialized nation, was second only to the Soviet Union in its ability to meet domestically a large share of its energy needs, the goal of self-sufficiency was unlikely to be achieved by a society as dependent on petroleum as the United States.

If domestically the Nixon administration seemed able only to mark time because of Watergate, in foreign policy there was not much more movement. Although not personally tainted by Watergate, Henry Kissinger, who had become Secretary of State in the fall of 1973, was not able to obtain congressional authorization for the

President to revise the tariff so that the Soviet Union could obtain the trade status of a "most favored nation." Kissinger sought this authority as part of his policy of détente with the Soviet Union. That the Russians, too, had doubts about the survival of the Nixon presidency was suggested by the rapidity with which they concluded agreements on strategic missiles and other military equipment with President Ford in November 1974, after months of dragging their feet during negotiations with the Nixon administration.

THE ELECTIONS OF 1974

The resignation of Nixon did not have the restorative effect upon Republicans in the congressional elections in the fall of 1974 that some members of the party had hoped. Ford's unpopular pardoning of Nixon, however compassionate the intention, probably lost votes for the Republicans. Clearly, the country still held the party responsible for Watergate and the cover-up. Democrats captured three quarters of the seats in the House—enough in theory, if not in fact, to make the body "veto-proof." They also won three fifths of the Senate seats and almost three quarters of the governors' chairs.

For the first time since the Johnson landslide of 1964, the suburbs voted heavily Democratic. Even Ford's old, sure seat in Michigan went to a Democrat. That Watergate had been an issue in the election was shown by the fact that four of the Republicans who had defended the President until his complicity was fully revealed went down to defeat. On the other hand, only one Republican who had supported impeachment before the final revelations failed to be reelected.

The election appeared to be a repudiation of Nixon's conservatism as well as his criminality. Many of the newly elected members of Congress were not only young but also known for their liberal views on public issues. Another measure of the voters' rejection of conservatism was the widespread success of black candidates, even in the South. Almost 100 state or national offices were now held by blacks, among them lieutenant governorships in Colorado and California.

Despite their numbers, however, the liberals did not run the new Congress, as the first year of the Ford administration would show. While Ford may not always have gotten his way, the liberals, despite their numbers, not only failed to get their way but showed themselves unable to agree on what their "way" was.

A further analysis of the election statistics provided a clue as to why the apparent liberal revival was less significant than it seemed. It was probably unrepresentative of the electorate. Only 38 percent of the eligible voters had bothered to go to the polls in 1974, as compared with 45 percent in the previous off-year election. The declining interest in voting undoubtedly stemmed from disenchantment with government, the cause of which extended back beyond Watergate and Nixon, at least to the Vietnam War.

THE FORD ADMINISTRATION

THE NEW PRESIDENT

Born in Nebraska in 1913 as Leslie King, Jr., but raised in Michigan after his parents were divorced and his mother remarried, Gerald Ford became a star football player in high school and college. Deciding against a promising career in pro football, he went to Yale Law School, then into legal practice, and finally into politics. In 1948 he was elected from Michigan to the House of Representatives, where he served for 25 years, eventually becoming Republican leader. Never known for anything but his conservative, rather combative Republicanism, Ford was a natural successor to Vice-President Agnew, who had also been known for his outspokenly conservative views.

As the first appointed Vice-President and President by the first resignation of a Chief Executive in history, Ford entered the White House with no popular mandate at all. His energetic personality and his willingness to laugh at himself and to recognize his limitations brought

President Gerald R. Ford addresses the audience after taking the oath of office. *(AP Photo)*

him instant appreciation. As he said at the time of his nomination for the vice-presidency, "I am a Ford, not a Lincoln."

In the White House, Ford removed many of the ceremonial, almost monarchical trappings of office that Nixon had insisted upon. Ford's relations with the press were friendly and open, a refreshing change after the secretiveness of Lyndon Johnson and the suspicious hostility of Richard Nixon.

The new First Lady, Betty Ford, was also in striking contrast to Pat Nixon and to most other Presidents' wives. Though a somewhat retiring person, Betty Ford was so open and liberal in her aspirations for women that she quickly became a public personality in her own right. Not since Eleanor Roosevelt had a First Lady cast herself so forthrightly in the role of a champion of policies. Betty Ford made no secret of her efforts to persuade her husband to appoint a woman cabinet officer (which he did in 1975) and a woman Supreme Court justice.

Unlike Nixon, Ford loved meeting people, and in his first two years in office he indulged himself to the fullest. In fact, he was frequently criticized in the press for traveling too much, not only to foreign countries but around the United States as well. Observers wondered how he could find time to think about large national and international issues while on such an incessantly active schedule. When he announced in early 1975 that he would indeed be a candidate to succeed himself, his travels and speechmaking acquired a political as well as a personal explanation. As *The New York Times* sternly noted at the end of 1975, President Ford "gives every appearance of having effectively abdicated the presidency today in favor of his candidacy for the nomination next year." Two attempts on his life in California in September 1975 brought the President's propensity for "pressing the flesh" under more serious criticism.

True to his conservative career in the House, Ford as President followed along the Nixon path in minimizing or deploring the government's intervention in the economy. "A government big enough to give you everything you want," he said several times in his first year in the White House, "is big enough to take from you everything you have." Not surprisingly, during his first year in office he kept almost all of the Nixon cabinet officers. Equating large government expenditures with "self-indulgence," the President vetoed several welfare measures on the ground that they were extravagant. In July of 1975, for example, he vetoed a $7.9 billion aid-to-education bill because he thought it inflationary. It was his 35th veto. The Democrats accused him of being niggardly with the poor in the name of cutting back on government costs while permitting increased expenditures for the military and higher prices for petroleum products in the campaign to reduce U.S. dependence on foreign oil. Ford denied that the country needed another Democratic New Deal. More to the point, he insisted, was "a fresh start." It is time, he said, "for us to declare our independence from governmental bureaucracies grown too large, too powerful, too costly, too remote, and yet too deeply involved in our day-to-day lives."

He sought, also, to reduce the regulatory activities of the federal government. Thus in late 1975 the administration submitted a bill removing some governmental controls over the bus and trucking industry in order to stimulate competition. Some of Ford's appointments to vacancies on the regulatory agencies were so favorable to business that in one month alone the Senate turned down four of them almost as soon as the names were submitted. Ford's conservatism, however, did not cause him to follow Nixon in trying to place a conservative Southerner and strict constructionist on the Supreme Court, however, when liberal Justice William O. Douglas resigned. The new appointee was John Paul Stevens, a moderately conservative federal judge from Chicago.

The administration's assessment of the economic problems of the country also reflected conservative Republican principles. Early in the Ford administration unemployment began to climb until in the spring of 1975 it reached its highest level (over 9 percent of the labor force) since the Great Depression. Simultaneously, inflation spurted to an annual rate of 12 percent. At first the administration concentrated its attention almost entirely on controlling inflation. The President warned Congress against excessive expenditures of any kind, including efforts to put people to work. To back up his warning, Ford vetoed a bill to spend $5.3 billion to create jobs for the unemployed, and another that would have raised farm prices. He also vetoed several environmental bills, notably a stiff anti-strip-mining measure in December 1974, because they would have increased the cost of business operation, thus adding to inflation and reducing the incentive to increase the sources of energy. As unemployment mounted and the economy remained sluggish, however, he came to recognize that inflation was not the only menace.

In March 1975 he signed the biggest tax cut in American history as a stimulus to the economy. Even after being pruned by Congress, the cut amounted to $22 billion. Again the President was careful to warn Congress against excessive expenditures that would increase the federal deficit beyond the current (more than $50 billion) figure. As it was, the Ford and Nixon administrations, for all their Republican character and emphasis on fiscal responsibility, had recorded the highest deficits in American history. By the end of 1975 Ford's efforts to deal with economic problems were showing mixed results at best. The rate of unemployment barely declined at all, going from slightly more than 9 percent in early 1975 to about 8 percent in early 1976. Inflation did slow down from a high of 12 percent a year to a low at the end of 1975 of six percent although the economy, as a whole, was still not working at capacity.

Having spent his political life in the House, the President showed himself adept in countering the lopsided Democratic majority in Congress. Although the Democrats promised to come up with energy and economic policies of their own, the administration's policies prevailed—if only because the legislature could not agree on what it wanted. In the contests with the White House, the legislators were no match for someone who had long known the ways of the House. Congress, even the allegedly liberal House with its extraordinary majority of Democrats, sustained all but seven of Ford's 41 vetoes in his first 16 months in office. Even Ford's veto of the jobs bill to combat unemployment could not be overturned.

At the beginning of his second year, in the fall of 1975, Ford demonstrated his political authority and self-confidence, if not his political shrewdness. He summarily fired James Schlesinger, the Secretary of Defense, and William Colby, the head of the CIA, because he had been too cooperative with congressional investigations of past undercover operations by the CIA. Schlesinger's removal stemmed from his long conflict with Henry Kissinger over the proper relation between the United States and Russia. Schlesinger thought Kissinger's policy of détente was too trusting of Soviet intentions and aspirations in the world.

A CHANGING WORLD SCENE

Ford, still depending upon Nixon's Secretary of State, Henry Kissinger, tried to implement the breakthrough that his predecessor had made in 1972 in visits of his own to Communist China (the People's Republic of China) and the Soviet Union. Ford met with Leonid Brezhnev in Vladivostok, Soviet Siberia, in November 1974 to discuss missile reduction and again in Helsinki in August 1975, along with some 30 other heads of government, to recognize formally Soviet and Western boundaries in Europe. Then in December 1975 he traveled to Beijing to show the Chinese, who were still fearful of Soviet military intentions, that he continued to be interested in expanding friendly relations with them.

One consequence of the détente with the Communist powers, as well as a measure of it, was a five-year agreement between the Soviet Union and the United States on the sale of American grain to Russia. This action assured a ready market for American farmers while avoiding a sudden, inflationary push on domestic American grain prices, as had occurred the year before when the Russians suddenly began to buy grain.

An effort to get the Russians to swap grain for oil and thus help the United States reduce its dependence on Arabian oil did not come off. Despite that failure, the Ford administration pressed toward the goal, also inherited from Nixon, that the United States be independent of outside sources of energy by the 1980s. Few observers thought the achievement of the goal was possible, and not many more thought it necessary. No one, however, was optimistic about the future since oil supplies were entangled in the always-smoldering conflict between Israel and the Arab states.

The elusiveness of a firm and enduring settlement in the Middle East threatened to produce a confrontation between the two nuclear superpowers, which were ranged on opposite sides in the controversy over Israel. Alone among the industrial nations of the world, the United States championed Israel. However much the other industrial nations might be mindful of the Nazi horror against the Jews, which had been the justification for the establishment of Israel in 1948, they could not ignore the central importance of Arab oil in their economies. Russia viewed Israel as an outpost of American imperialism and supported the Arab states in their hostility toward Israel.

It was this antagonism that threatened to shatter the peace that the ending of the Vietnam War had finally brought to the United States. For almost the first time since the end of World War II no large-scale war was being waged anywhere. Guerrilla fighters in the Philippines, Thailand, the Middle East, and Africa continued to operate, but no national army actively confronted a national enemy. In fact, the anti-colonialism that had lain at the root of most of the wars since 1945, including the Vietnam War, had come to a final close in 1975 when Portugal surrendered its last colony, Angola, to the contending independence forces in that African territory. The colonial dependencies now left in the world were mostly small islands or bits of territory, which neither desired nor seemed likely to profit from independence.

The Ford administration, then, coincided with the close of an era. The postwar world could now be said to have come to an end. Those social, economic, and political forces that the Second World War had set loose upon the world had run their course. Traditional colonialism had been ended. The relation between the two extra-European victors in the war, the Soviet Union and the United States, was not entirely amicable, but the Cold War as it had been known for a quarter of a century was over. Europe was not united, but it was entirely recovered from the war and once again carrying weight in the world. In Asia, Japan was not only the dominant economic power, but also the most stable democratic ally of the West. China was no longer hostile to either the West in general or the United States in particular, but was fearful of its Communist neighbor, the U.S.S.R. Economically, too, the world passed over a watershed in the middle 70s when it became clear that the price of energy, thanks to the cartel formed by the oil-producing countries of the Third World, was not only going to rise, but would also inevitably diminish that amazing prosperity that had dominated the economies of the industrial countries of the world for the preceding quarter of a century.

Domestically, 1976 was a dividing line because by then the social changes and upheavals associated with the 1960s and the early 1970s were clearly over. The Ford Administration had put the trauma of Watergate, like the nightmare of Vietnam, behind the nation, at least in part.

NEW ERA, NEW PRESIDENT

THE ARRIVAL OF JIMMY CARTER

Just about the time that Gerald Ford assumed office after the resignation of Richard M. Nixon, Governor James Earl Carter, Jr., of Georgia decided to run for the presidency. He was still in his first term as governor, not yet 50 years of age, and virtually unknown outside his own state. In fact, he had never tried for public office before 1962, and had been defeated then. Yet, in January 1977, Jimmy Carter was inaugurated President of the United States, just as he had said all along he would be.

Jimmy Carter, as he insisted upon being known officially as well as unofficially, was unusual in other ways. He was the first candidate from the Deep South since Zachary Taylor in 1848. He was a businessman-farmer rather than a lawyer, and he was the first graduate of the Naval Academy at Annapolis to be President. He actually served in the regular Navy for eight years before returning to his birthplace in the tiny village of Plains, Georgia, where he soon made himself a millionaire by raising peanuts. Carter was unusual for a white Southerner in that as governor he made explicit his belief in equality of opportunity for white and black people.

Nevertheless, Jimmy Carter was a Southern Baptist from a small town—the epitome of the conservative family values espoused by

Chief Justice Warren E. Burger administering the oath of office to Jimmy Carter on the east portico of the U.S. Capitol on January 20, 1977 *(Library of Congress)*

the emerging Christian right in the Republican Party. Carter, however, did not overstress his religious faith and believed in church-state separation as well; consequently, he was palatable to the secular left as well as the Christian right and quickly emerged as a serious challenger to now incumbent Republican Gerald Ford for the Presidency.

Carter also echoed a number of other conservative preferences on several important issues. For one, Carter expressed his disdain for the welfare system, always a conservative whipping post, and argued that the system needed to be reformed so that it "encourages work and encourages family life." In addition, Carter also promised to reform the tax system in a way that would help families stay together, encourage a program of family planning that would prevent the need for abortion, and require that federal programs all present "family impact statements" that show their impact on American families. Also, Carter favored federal aid to parochial schools, a position that both fundamentalist Protestants and Catholics embraced.

Thanks to a persistent and energetic campaign of almost two years, in the course of which he traveled around the country, often staying at private homes and talking to no more than handfuls of people, Carter captured most of the Democratic primaries in the spring of 1976. He was nominated on the first ballot at the Democratic convention that summer in New York.

Carter's choice of Senator Walter Mondale of Minnesota to be his running mate, however, suggested that he was also comfortable with a more liberal, activist Democrat in the Roosevelt and Kennedy mold. Indeed, Mondale's professional and effective campaigning helped Carter overcome some of his limitations as a campaigner, especially against the incumbent and more experienced Gerald Ford. On the other hand, Ford's selection of the strongly conservative and acerbic Robert Dole, senator from Kansas, as his candidate for Vice-President, weakened the President's appeal. Even so, the folksy and energetic Ford came from far behind in the public opinion polls in the late summer to almost win in November.

Ford had provided Jimmy Carter and the Democrats with a favor one month into his Presidency—when he pardoned Richard Nixon for any and all crimes connected with Watergate. Ford believed that losing the Presidency and the public disgrace associated with it were enough punishment for Nixon, and he also viewed the pardon as necessary for political healing. To a large segment of the American public, however, the pardon appeared to reflect a corrupt bargain between Ford and Nixon whereby Nixon appointed Ford Vice President (and later President) with the understanding that Ford would pardon Nixon of all crimes if and when the time came. Though there is no record of such a bargain between Ford and Nixon, Ford's approval rating, nevertheless, dropped from 71 percent to 50 percent inside of a week after the pardon; and his own Press Secretary, who had advised against the pardon, resigned in disgust. Ford would never regain the popularity he lost with the pardon, and voters would punish Ford at the polls two years later in the general election.

To make matters worse for Ford and the Republicans, the double-digit inflation and high unemployment that Ford had inherited from the Nixon administration continued unabated. Presidents Kennedy, Johnson, and Nixon, had spent a decade deficit spending to support the Vietnam War and Johnson's Great Society welfare programs, oil prices remained high, and the manufacturing sector experienced major problems due to international free market competition. The economic problems were decades in the making and simply too large for any President to solve in such a short period of time; but the electorate, both right and left, would not be so patient. Ford also alienated the right wing of the Republican Party with his nomination of their old nemesis, Nelson Rockefeller, for Vice President.

Finally, Ford had public relations problems that were related to his rather vanilla personality and an inaccurate public perception of his intellectual capabilities. Though a graduate of Yale law school, Ford was also an ex-collegiate football player from the University of

Michigan and not a dynamic speaker; consequently, Ford somehow became portrayed in the media as an ex-athlete who was a bit dull-minded. The fact that he stumbled to the ground on occasion in front of the TV cameras only contributed to this reputation, in spite of the fact that the link between sure-footedness and intellect is a dubious one at best. Ex-President Lyndon Johnson perhaps exemplified the inaccurate, general consensus with his assessment that Ford "can't fart and chew gum at the same time." Regardless of its fairness, Ford would be unable to ever completely shake the "dumb" label with which he became associated. To make matters even worse for Ford, he suffered through the traumatic experience of two assassination attempts, both by women in California. In Sacramento, a member of Charles Manson's Cult, Lynette "Squeaky" Fromme tried to shoot the President, and in San Francisco, Sara Jane Moore shot over the President's head outside the St. Francis Hotel.

Ironically, among those that thought Ford lacked the intellectual prowess to be President was Ronald Reagan. This is in spite of the fact that Reagan himself had been an average student at Eureka College, was not known to be an avid reader, had much less impressive governmental credentials than Ford, and was also not known as a deep thinker. Instead, Reagan was a Hollywood actor that previously had been a Democrat and had supported both Franklin Roosevelt and Hubert Humphrey in the 1940s.

Ford would win the Republican nomination, but only after a serious challenge from Reagan produced deep divisions within the Republican Party. In order to placate the conservative Reagan faction, Ford was compelled to dump Nelson Rockefeller as his running mate and replace him with the more conservative Kansas Senator, Bob Dole. Ford's victory was secured only after Ronald Reagan lost the Florida primary when senior citizens reacted negatively to his plan to invest the Social Security Trust Fund in the stock market. Ford was also forced to make major concessions to the right at the 1976 Republican convention, adding an anti-abortion plank and, essentially, abandoning Nixon's détente in foreign policy.

Nevertheless, the Reagan challenge in the primaries had weakened the Republican Party, and the economic malaise Ford had inherited from the Nixon administration continued. The Democrats gained mileage from the economic "misery index," that combined an inflation rate of over 6 percent with an unemployment rate of 8 percent. Ford then fumbled the second of his Presidential debates with Carter when he inexplicably asserted that the Soviet Union did not dominate Eastern Europe and stated, "I don't believe that the Poles consider themselves dominated by the Soviet Union." The episode

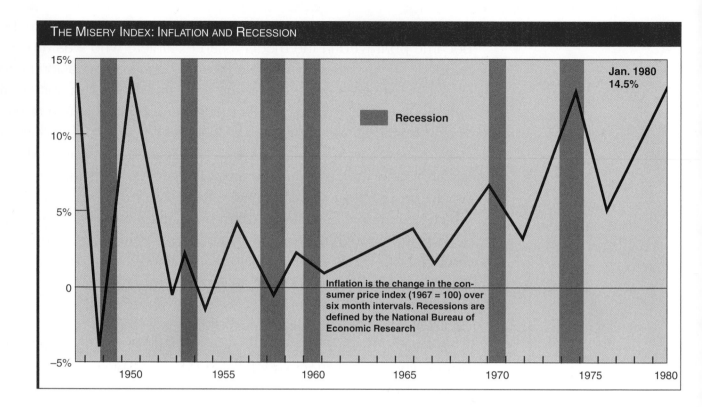

THE MISERY INDEX: INFLATION AND RECESSION

Recession

Inflation is the change in the consumer price index (1967 = 100) over six month intervals. Recessions are defined by the National Bureau of Economic Research

Jan. 1980 14.5%

reinforced for the American public that Ford was a bit slow-minded; and this—combined with the economic malaise, the bloodletting within the Republican party, and the inability of the public to disassociate Ford from his pardon of Richard Nixon—created the situation where the inexperienced Jimmy Carter could win.

On election day, Carter surpassed Ford by fewer than 2 million votes and the tally in the Electoral College was so close that a shift in 10,000 votes in two states would have given Ford the victory. Jimmy Carter had won the Presidency with the backing of Southern Christian fundamentalists due to his own Baptist religious beliefs and the moral outrage of Americans over the Watergate affair, coupled with Ford's pardon of Nixon. Carter also played the "regular guy" well to the American people, with his humble origins as a peanut farmer from the small town of Plains, Georgia. Carter held town meetings and call-in talk sessions and asked callers in good Southern fashion if they were kin to someone of the same name that he knew in Georgia. Carter wore a cardigan sweater while in front of the television cameras in the White House, mended his own clothes in front of reporters on an airplane, and carried his own luggage, thus proving to many Americans, conservative and liberal alike, that he was "just like them." Both houses of Congress, however, went overwhelmingly Democratic, as they had in 1972 and 1974. To this political inconsistency we will return later in this chapter.

A NEW ADMINISTRATION

In line with his promise during the campaign, Carter brought two women, one of whom was black, into his Cabinet, and named a black fellow Georgian, Andrew Young, to be the Ambassador to the United Nations. This was not as high a representation of minorities and women as had been anticipated, but it was greater than in any previous administration.

Carter's desire to signal the novelty of his administration was evident immediately after his inauguration when he eschewed the usual ride in a large black Cadillac down Pennsylvania Avenue. Instead he and his wife Rosalyn walked hand-in-hand down the avenue to the White House, waving and smiling broadly to the pleasantly surprised crowds along the way. Another novel act, within a month of taking office, was his pardoning of some 10,000 draft evaders from the days of the Vietnam War, something none of his immediate predecessors had wanted to do. (Even Carter, however, did not pardon the 69,000 military deserters.)

Carter tried, also early in his administration, to break new ground in foreign policy. He publicly encouraged Soviet dissidents who were seeking greater freedom within the Soviet Union, a gesture Henry Kissinger, the previous Secretary of State, had refused to make on the ground that it would interfere with impending agreements with the Soviet state on larger matters. The Carter administration, however, contended that international agreements were achieved because of self-interest on both sides, not because an American President refrained from criticizing the denials of free speech and press in the Soviet Union. Therefore, early in his administration, Carter dispatched his new Secretary of State, Cyrus Vance, to Moscow with a series of proposals to restrict the number and kinds of missiles that the two superpowers could maintain.

Contrary to his expectations, the Russians coolly turned down the proposals. One interpretation was that Carter had been too quick in his diplomacy. Some feared that Carter's insistence upon denouncing denial of human rights might revive the Cold War.

In subsequent months, as Carter continued to speak out in behalf of human rights, he seemed to be less than consistent in his denouncements. Violations of human rights among our allies were rarely noted. Yet there was no question that Carter's emphasis on human rights was consonant with America's long history of freedom and concern over the denial of freedom in other countries. Some highly placed cynics in some capitals around the world made fun of Carter's addition of human rights concerns to foreign policy, especially when the selectivity of application became evident; but the prominence the issue achieved thereafter at international conferences and at the United Nations suggested that Carter's initiative had made human rights a concern among nations such as it had not been since the 1930s.

RESTORING GOVERNMENT TO THE PEOPLE

During his campaign Carter had promised to bring government back to the people. Some politicians had complained that he had "campaigned against Washington while trying his best to get there." Early in his administration, Carter emphasized two policies that he thought would give Americans a sense of controlling their future.

One was his promise to balance the federal budget by 1980, though that had not been accomplished under Republican or Democratic Presidents since the beginning of American involvement in the Vietnam War. Only reducing government expenditures could do it. Although Congress is rarely happy about cutting expenditures, it did stay within the guidelines set by the administration during the first year, though not without the help of some presidential vetoes. A public works appropriation and a plan to build a nuclear carrier were both killed by the President for a saving of some $2 billion. The President demonstrated some willingness to cut down on military spending in his decision not to develop the B-1 superbomber, which many powerful Congressmen were supporting.

Carter's second effort to give Americans a sense of control over their future was his call in March 1977 for a "moral equivalent of war" on the energy shortage, particularly on the dependence of the United States on foreign oil. This was a subject that both Ford and Nixon had addressed, but oil imports had been continuing to rise. Essentially, Carter's program called for a reduction in consumption and provided for a series of incentives to industry and private citizens to use alternative sources of energy, such as coal, which was plentiful in the United States, and solar energy.

Despite the overwhelming majority his party held in both houses of Congress, Carter did not by any means obtain all that he asked for that first year. In fact, the energy program was bogged down for almost 18 months in Congress, as various groups debated the details of the program. All that the President received that year from Congress in regard to energy was agreement to create a new Cabinet of Energy. James Schlesinger, the former Secretary of Defense fired by Ford, was named the first Secretary of Energy. During the Vietnam War, Congress had been overawed by Johnson and Nixon and had followed their leads without much questioning. When the war was over, revelations about its conduct and about Watergate were evidence that Congress had been negligent. As a result, Congress under Carter became highly independent on both domestic and foreign affairs. Moreover, even Democrats became more conservative in their social outlook. As a result, even though the labor unions had supported Carter and the Democrats in the recent election, the unions' bill to revise the Labor Relations Act in order to control obstructionist employers was killed in the Senate after passing the House. Also, Carter's effort to get a new Department of Education, in order to bring the wide range of federal educational programs under one roof, died in committee.

Congress did agree to an extension of the time allowed for the ratification of the Equal Rights Amendment for women, as Carter recommended, though the ERA would eventually go down to defeat. The Equal Rights Amendment had been originally introduced in the 1960s with Republican support, and it passed both houses of Congress in 1972 under the Nixon administration. Conservatives, however, led by social conservative activist Phyllis Schlafly, would turn against ERA after its passage in Congress, and oppose its ratification by the states. Early on, it appeared that the Amendment would sail easily through the ratification process. ERA had been allotted seven years to achieve ratification by three fourths of the States and 22 States ratified the Amendment the very first year. Phyllis Schlafly, however, founded the Eagle Forum, a conservative women's organization opposed to the ratification of ERA. Schlafly and her followers depicted the ERA as leading to unisex toilets, homosexual marriages, women in combat, and the release of males from their responsibility to support their children. Schlafly and the Eagle Forum were also able to successfully confuse ERA with homosexuality and gay rights (never the intention of the amendment's sponsors), thus ensuring that the ERA would not be supported by the religious right and, therefore, ensuring that it would not be ratified in the Protestant fundamentalist-dominated Southern States or Mormon-influenced Utah and Idaho. Consequently, the window for ERA's ratification would expire, and the ERA would not be resurrected.

ABORTION AND THE MORAL MAJORITY

In 1973, the United States Supreme Court issued its decision in *Roe v. Wade* that essentially struck down state regulation of abortions in the first trimester. Falwell's Moral Majority would quickly catapult the religious right to a position of major importance in American politics in support of the Republican Party and ideologically conservative politics. Falwell himself characterized the Moral Majority as "pro-life, pro-family, pro-moral, pro-American, pro-Israel, and against abortion, divorce, and secular humanism." Falwell argued that the Moral Majority's goals would be to:

> "... exert a significant influence on the spiritual and moral direction of the nation by: (a) mobilizing the grassroots of moral Americans in one clear and effective voice; (b) informing the moral majority what is going on behind their backs in Washington and in state legislatures across the country; (c) lobbying intensively in Congress to defeat left-wing, social-welfare bills that will further erode our precious freedom; (d) pushing for positive legislation such as that to establish the Family Protection Agency, which will ensure a strong, enduring America; and (e) helping the moral majority in local communities to fight pornography, homosexuality, the advocacy of immorality in school textbooks, and other issues facing each and every one of us."

Falwell's exhortation to the religious right to become involved in politics was a reversal of his position in the 1960s when Falwell had urged Christians to stay out of the Civil Rights movement. By 1979, however, religious fundamentalists that had supported Jimmy Carter in 1976 due to Carter's religious faith were becoming disenchanted with President Carter due to his failure to adopt anything resembling the Moral Majority's platform. As Bill Godsey, a member of Jerry Falwell's Thomas Road Baptist Church put it, "Carter practiced a version of Christianity that, if you used the term 'liberal,' you would probably be close to what he was, and that was not popular with evangelicals and fundamentalists." Similarly, editorial columnist Bob Novak stated in 1979 that he knew that Carter was going to lose in 1980 because,

> "Minister after minister stood up and said, 'I was part of Carter's team in 1976. I delivered my congregation for Carter. I urged them all to vote for Carter because I thought he was a moral individual. I found out otherwise and I'm angry.'"

Falwell and his followers were drawn into politics due to what they viewed as attacks on the family and moral social issues, but they quickly adopted conservative positions on non-values issues as well. Both the Moral Majority and the Christian Voice (another Christian political organization) opposed, for example, American economic sanctions against Rhodesia for the human rights abuses by Idi Amin, abrogation of the United States military treaty with Taiwan, and the "giving away" of the Panama Canal.

CARTER'S RETRENCHMENT

Congress approved of Carter's plan to streamline the federal bureaucracy through new hiring and firing procedures and salary incentives. Carter suffered a deep wound officially as well as personally, however, when his trusted friend and adviser, Bert Lance, the Director of the government's Office of Management and Budget was compelled to resign in September 1977 for questionable banking practices in Georgia. Carter's reluctance during several weeks of public hearings to admit his friend's defects spoke well for his sense of personal loyalty but seemed to undercut the high moral claims of his campaign.

Carter entered office with the image of an activist, and during that first year many in Congress were heard to complain of being sent too many proposals from the White House in too short a time. By the second year, however, things had changed if only because so little had been achieved in the first year. The President's first State of the Union message reflected the change, and retrenchment and caution now seemed to be the watchwords. "Government cannot solve our problems," he warned. "Government cannot eliminate poverty, or provide a bountiful economy, or reduce inflation, or save our cities, or cure illiteracy, or provide energy, or mandate goodness." Only people cooperating with government can accomplish anything, he asserted.

In his budget message he did present his long-awaited proposal for tax reform and reduction, but it did not stir hearts or bring much that was new. The cuts were designed primarily to relieve the burdens on low- and middle-income Americans, who increasingly were feeling the effects of rising prices.

Although prices had been rising ominously throughout his first 18 months as President, Carter had hesitated to make a fight against inflation his first priority. He feared that slowing down the economy would produce unemployment. The most he ventured was to set guidelines on prices and wages, but they were only voluntary for business and labor. That half-hearted tactic did not work. By early 1979 the annual rate of inflation was over 10 percent and still rising. That fact probably explained why in early 1979 only 18 percent of Americans thought Carter's handling of the economy was satisfactory.

In the President's mind, a more crucial test of his leadership than the issue of inflation was the question of energy. He had begun his administration by calling for a "moral equivalent of war" on the energy problem, but the measure Congress finally passed was at best a compromise and at worst only an excuse for an energy policy. It cut in half the figure by which importations of oil were to be reduced in the next five years and offered only financial incentives for oil users to shift to coal or solar sources of energy. Obviously the question of energy would have to come before the administration and the nation again, for the nation had not yet faced up to the problem of American dependence on foreign oil and finite global oil reserves.

A PROMISING START IN FOREIGN AFFAIRS

Just as his personally democratic ways and high intelligence had won the President many admirers domestically, these qualities, at least at first, won him friends abroad. On an official visit to London in May 1977, to meet with the heads of government of the principal western European nations, Carter was an immediate hit with the British public and the leaders of government. At conferences his command of the issues was quickly evident.

On a two-week tour of Latin America, his wife Rosalyn also impressed governmental officials there with her solid preparation and skillful diplomacy as well as her clear authority to speak for the President. No other American President, including Franklin Roosevelt, had relied so heavily and drawn so much support from his wife as Carter. Rosalyn Carter frequently attended Cabinet meetings as well as accompanying him on virtually every trip abroad.

In fact, trips abroad were so successful for the Carters that in December the President embarked upon another one to Poland, Iran, India, Saudi Arabia, France, and Belgium, covering a distance of 18,500 miles in only nine days. Just when some observers were becoming concerned that travel might turn out to be the only diplomatic achievement of the new President, Carter managed to score two significant gains.

THE CANAL TREATY

The first significant gain was winning the Senate's acceptance of a new treaty with Panama regarding the Panama Canal. Ever since the early years of the Johnson administration, Panamanians had been demanding that they be given a more equal role in the management of the canal, but the Vietnam War and then the defeat of the United States in Asia made it difficult to bring the issue before the country. Finally, in August 1977, the American negotiators concluded a treaty that would turn the canal over to Panama by the year 2000.

Although leading foreign policy experts on the Republican side, like Henry Kissinger, supported the treaty, Republican opposition was vocal and adamant; and when conservative Democratic opponents joined it, the treaty seemed likely to be defeated in the Senate.

After lengthy hearings and the sometimes-acrimonious public debate, the Senate gave its approval in April 1978, but with only one vote to spare. To achieve even that narrow victory, certain reservations had to be added. Fortunately, Panama was prepared to accept them so that the treaty could be ratified without renegotiation.

Carter's close victory demonstrated that in foreign policy, as in domestic affairs, the President's influence over Congress was severely limited for a leader with a party majority in both houses. Thanks to the passage of the Canal Treaty, Carter's standing in the opinion polls rose from 37 percent to 42 percent of Americans approving his administration, but, significantly, those who approved were still less than a majority.

Carter and the two thirds of the Senators that ratified the Canal Treaty recognized that the Panama Canal no longer had the strategic or commercial importance that it once had. Commercially, the most important ships, the oil supertankers, could not use the canal because they were simply too large. Strategically, the canal had been reduced in importance since the largest and most important military surface ships, the latest aircraft carriers, were also too large for it. The canal was also useless to American nuclear submarines since use of the canal would reveal their positions (which were kept secret as much as possible as a check on the Soviet Union). Given these factors, Carter and the Senators calculated that the advantage in good will with Latin America gained by the Canal Treaty would outweigh any strategic or commercial negatives associated with the return of the canal to Panama. The opposition simply ignored such analysis and viewed the Canal Treaty as an agreement that sold out American interests and weakened America.

MIDDLE EAST ACCORD

That minority approval, however, swelled to a majority by the end of the summer, Carter had made the biggest gamble of his career by deliberately undertaking to bring about an agreement between Egypt and Israel in the Middle East.

The opportunity had been created by the surprise visit of President Anwar Sadat of Egypt to Israel in November 1977, just four years after the two countries had been at war. This melodramatic break in the long hostility between the two countries seemed pregnant with possibilities for an end to conflict in that war-torn region. Israel and Egypt had been at war with one another four times in the preceding 30 years. Prime Minister Menachem Begin of Israel and Sadat met several times again, their lieutenants met, and Secretary of

Egyptian President Anwar Sadat, left, and Israeli Prime Minister Menachem Begin embrace as U.S. President Jimmy Carter looks on. *(AP Photo)*

State Cyrus Vance met with both sides; but it seemed the differences between the two countries could not be ironed out. Suddenly it seemed that Sadat's courageous act of rapprochement would be wasted, and the opportunities he had opened up were about to be lost. At that juncture Carter acted.

Undoubtedly worried about his low standing in the polls and his inability to move Congress on energy and other domestic issues, and aware that Congressional elections would be coming up in the fall, Carter invited the two Middle Eastern leaders to come to Camp David, the private presidential retreat in the Maryland mountains, for a confidential conference. Obviously the risk was enormous. If nothing came of the meeting, Carter's prestige would sink still lower and he would be seen as acting impetuously and presumptuously. When before had a President presumed to act as a mediator in a situation so charged with animosity and bad history? Not even Theodore Roosevelt had been intimately involved in the actual negotiations at the Portsmouth Conference that ended the Russo-Japanese War in 1905. Besides, that conference had taken place after a war in which one side had been roundly defeated.

For over 10 days the three leaders were secluded at Camp David, a length of time none had expected, but Carter was insistent. The intransigence of Begin almost caused Sadat at one point to leave for Cairo. Then, on the ninth day, Carter convinced Begin to change his mind on one of the major obstacles to agreement. On September 17 a triumphant Carter presented the two leaders to a hastily assembled audience in the East Room of the White House to witness the signing of a framework for peace between the two longtime enemies.

Though the Camp David Accords were hailed as a major breakthrough in the progression toward peace in the Middle East, in fact, the delicacy and dangers surrounding the issues of the Mideast animosities were so great that even after the agreement at Camp David, Israel was slow to put into practice the principles that had been agreed upon. Ever fearful for its security after four wars, Israel could not easily give up territory it thought essential to its safety. Nevertheless, after months of further discussion in Cairo and Jerusalem and Washington, a treaty of peace was signed between Israel and Egypt at the White House on March 26, 1979. It not only ended the state of war between the two countries but, among other things, specified the withdrawal of Israel from the Sinai peninsula, which Israel had conquered in the 1967 war and had occupied ever since. The United States was to supply massive aid to both countries. The treaty was undoubtedly the most hopeful sign for future peace in the region since the creation of Israel 30 years before. That it should have been brought about by the twentieth-century President least informed or experienced in politics and foreign affairs was at once ironic and a tribute to the intelligence and educability of Jimmy Carter.

Thanks to his successful handling of the Middle East summit, Carter's standing in the polls shot up in September and his ability to convince Congress to go along with foreign policy recommendations improved. He managed, for example, to obtain Congressional approval to sell modern fighter aircraft to Egypt and Saudi Arabia as well as Israel, despite strong objections from pro-Israel members of Congress. Congress also approved his lifting of the arms embargo against Turkey, even though friends of Greece opposed it.

From a certain point of view, there ought not to have been any reason to emphasize his successes with Congress. After all, his own party dominated both houses as well as running all the committees of Congress, yet it was just that lack of party loyalty to the President and lack of party discipline that was one of the striking aspects of American politics increasingly evident in the middle 1970s. This situation was particularly noticeable in the results of the Congressional elections of 1978.

THE ELECTION OF 1978

One of the clichés of off-year elections is that the incumbent party usually loses seats in Congress, and the first off-year elections of

Carter's presidency were no exception. Republicans gained three seats in the Senate, 12 seats in the House of Representatives, and three gubernatorial chairs in the state capitals. The tally of state legislatures controlled by Republicans, however, revealed the lack of real significance for these gains. The number went from four to a mere 12! Even after adding the off-year gains, the Republicans still remained a decided minority in most of the states and in Congress.

This disparity between Republicans and Democrats was not new in 1978. Between 1960 and 1974 the proportion of seats in the House of Representatives held by Democrats had rarely gone below 60 percent. Though it went over that figure at times, it had never fallen as low as 55 percent; and except for four years (1966–1970) a majority of the governors of the states during that same span of years had also been Democrats. In 1977 only 32 percent of all state legislators were Republicans—as compared with 53 percent in 1948 and 44 percent in 1956.

It was figures like those that caused political commentators in the late 1970s to refer to the American polity as no longer a two-party system, but a "one-and-a-half" party system. When public opinion polls were examined in a similar light, it was evident that the Democrats were the "everyone party." The polls showed that virtually every social group was well represented in the party. Even wealthy people were Democrats, two to one.

At one time in American history it could have been assumed that college graduates would tend to be Republicans, but by the late 1970s, 42 percent of them were listing themselves as Democrats and only 31 percent identified themselves as Republicans. Since the poor, the blacks, and most of the middle class had been captured by the New Deal, if not before, and securely held ever since, no significant social groups were absent from the Democratic coalition. In the South where conservative ideology dominated the social structure, the Democrats still dominated politics due to the legacy of the Civil War, in which the Republican Party had been the Party of the Union.

A POLITICAL PARADOX

Despite this overwhelming preference of American voters for the Democrats, the party could never be sure of winning the White House. Between 1948 and 1976 the Democrats won only half of the presidential elections and even then the Republicans won 51 percent of the popular vote for the two parties! In short, a two-tier political system seemed to be emerging in the country: presidential and legislative levels. Voters apparently made little connection between their votes for Congress and their votes for President; changes occurring in the South provided some of the explanation for the development of the two-tiered politics.

One of the consequences of World War II was that the South finally began to catch up with the rest of the nation in industrial and urban development. As a result, its politics began to change, too. It was certainly significant that Republican Eisenhower had chalked up much of his unusually strong support for a Republican in the South between city and suburban dwellers, and in the 1960s Southern support for Republican presidents continued to be notable in the cities of the region. Moreover, the Second Reconstruction of the South during the 1960s was associated in the minds of many white Southerners with Democratic Presidents, an association that split off many old-line Southern Democrats from support of their party's presidential candidates. Segregationist whites could not support Democratic Presidential candidates that favored Civil Rights for blacks.

Beginning in 1960, the South began to give its votes to Republican presidential candidates, even when Jimmy Carter was elected, even though he was himself a son of the South. At the same time, white Southerners continued to support Democratic Congressional candidates, for they were local people, untainted by support for pro-black programs.

Outside the South the tendency for voters to split their party preferences between Congress and the President developed more slowly. As late as 1952 only a fifth of voters in the country cast ballots for congressional and presidential candidates from different parties. By 1968 the proportion was up to a third, and by 1972 it was over two fifths. (During the nineteenth century it has been estimated that probably less than 10 percent of voters split their tickets.)

Another phenomenon of these years was the rise in the independent or nonparty vote. At the end of the 1960s pollsters began to find a significant number of voters who said they had no allegiance to any party. By 1974 one third of Americans claimed to be independents; in the 1950s only a fifth had made that self-designation. Among college-educated people in 1973 the proportion that labeled themselves independent (38 percent) outnumbered those who designated themselves as either Republicans or Democrats.

A further measure of this decline in Americans' belief in their country's historical political system was underscored by the results of the 1978 elections when most Americans chose not to vote at all. The turnout in November 1978 was the lowest in recent history. Only 38 percent of eligible voters bothered to cast their ballots; 96 million people stayed away. As recently as 1962 some 48 percent of voters turned out even for an off-year election. Moreover, in presidential elections, Americans have one of the lowest turnouts of any modern democracy. In short, there was not only a disquieting turning away from political parties, but also a disturbing alienation from the whole political process as well.

Part of the explanation is quite properly sought in events of the 1960s and 1970s when government leaders of both parties, from the President on down, misused their authority to defend the Vietnam War and to cover up the Watergate crimes. During this period a deep sense of cynicism toward authority and its abuse of power spread among many Americans, particularly college-age people. By the end of the 1970s they were a large and influential part of the electorate. The shift can also be seen in a decline in trust of authority generally. In 1966, for example, 72 percent of Americans had said they had a "great deal of confidence" in the leadership of American medicine. By 1977 only 43 percent expressed that degree of confidence. For leaders of higher education the slide was from 61 percent to 37 percent. For the military, as one might expect, the decline was precipitous: from 62 percent in 1966 to 27 percent in 1977.

It was on a promise of restoring confidence in government that Carter campaigned in 1976, and presumably his victory was attributable, at least in part, to the voters' hope that he could do just that. In several ways Carter was in tune with the new mood. He was not authoritarian in his dealings with his family or his subordinates. He probably spent more time as a candidate and as President visiting the homes of ordinary citizens than any President in history. In fact, his thirst for the opinion of the average American was so strong that some observers thought it counterproductive. His effort to maintain an "open presidency" was clearly in response to the popular hostility to the Nixon administration's "bunker mentality," which had produced so many mistakes and abuses of power.

More was involved in the distrust of government, however, than particular evils committed by past Presidents and governments. Also at work were the profound social and cultural changes of the 1960s, among which was a new emphasis upon the dignity of all people—black, brown, and red, poor as well as rich, both female and male. The social order that emerged in America from the turbulent 60s and early 70s was less rigid and less deferential and more democratic than had been true before. As one commentator expressed it, "ordinary people in this country now have a higher estimation of their endowments and broader conceptions of their entitlements than ever before."

The upshot was that the country was probably more difficult to govern than at any time in American history. Americans in the era of

Jackson, for example, may have been more turbulent and even harder to discipline or guide, but they also expected less of government. Even with its social diversity, what the nation demanded was less dependence upon the federal government. It was these changes, long germinating, that the Carter administration had to contend with in the closing years of the 1970s. It was soon evident that the encounter and its resolution were not going to be easy. Without a strong sense of party loyalty in Congress and without a strong belief among the people in the virtues of parties, elections, and even the benevolence of government itself, solutions to the difficult problems of inflation, recession, and energy would be difficult for any President to carry out. That seemed to be the meaning of Carter's many problems as he entered upon the second half of his presidency in January 1979.

LOWERING EXPECTATIONS

In his State of the Union message in January 1979, President Carter stressed good management and efficiency in the federal government, rather than new programs. He talked about laying a "New Foundation," reminiscent of the New Deal and the New Frontier, but he was concerned primarily to steer a path between the continuing inflation and the threat of recession. As a result, established programs received no increases in his new budget and even the military received only a three percent increase. The national health insurance program he had promised the country at the beginning of his administration was clearly shaped by fears of fueling inflation. It was limited in scope to keep governmental spending down.

Worrisome and potentially dangerous as the long siege of mounting prices was, the sharpest crisis for the President came from a different though not unrelated source. In the spring of 1979 the enduring problem of what to do about American dependence upon foreign oil in the face of growing domestic demand leaped into dramatic prominence. The overthrow of the government of the Shah of Iran by internal revolutionaries abruptly reduced the world's supply of oil, causing new upward pressures on the cost of energy. Then, in May and June, motorists panicked—first in California and later on the east coast. Thinking gasoline would be impossible to obtain, they began to buy it in inordinate amounts that so strained the allocation system of the country that suddenly it was hard to find gas, and the price began to shoot up. Long lines of cars appeared outside gasoline stations, depressingly reminiscent of the days of the Arab oil embargo in 1973.

This time, however, when the lines finally disappeared, not only was the price of gasoline considerably higher, but the sense of urgency about the energy shortage remained. For the first time in their history, Americans paid a dollar a gallon for gasoline and the price promised to rise considerably more in short order. (Europeans had been paying a dollar a gallon or more for decades and in June 1979 they were paying twice what Americans were.) The day of cheap gasoline was now definitely over, but American adjustment to the new situation was only beginning.

The gasoline lines, which caught everyone by surprise, showed concretely the weakness of the President's grip on the problem and on the political process. Earlier that spring Carter had asked Congress to give him power to set up a standby gasoline rationing plan for just such an emergency as occurred in June. Congress refused, reflecting the reluctance of most Americans to admit that cheap energy was no longer a given. Once the gas lines materialized, however, the public clamor energized Congress. Within days, several bills setting up machinery for rationing gasoline in an emergency, along the lines advocated by the President only a few weeks before, went into the legislative mill. Congress suddenly became interested in the development of synthetic fuels, too. Meanwhile, the President's stand in the polls plummeted to a level similar to that of Nixon at the time of his forced resignation. Only 29 percent of the American people approved of his administration, while a whopping 56 percent said they disapproved. (In May 2006, according to some polls, President George W. Bush's approval ratings plunged to the same level).

A feeling that no one in Washington was in charge of the country reached the President himself in early July, soon after he returned from a meeting with European and Japanese heads of government convened to coordinate responses to the world energy shortage. Carter canceled a television address to the people scheduled for July 5 and went instead into seclusion at Camp David. Over the ensuing 10 days he invited scores of people from a wide range of professions to discuss the crisis of leadership he, as well as the country, now felt so deeply. In an unprecedented display of presidential self-criticism, Carter pleaded with his visitors and with the ordinary Americans he visited privately at their homes to advise him as to what he might do. At the conclusion of the extraordinary discussions and almost public self-examination, the President appeared on national television. The address he gave was almost devoid of policy statements. It called upon Americans to have faith and to use the energy crisis as a way of uniting the country and freeing the nation from dependence upon foreign sources of oil. In a second speech the next day he outlined a new program to reduce consumption of oil and to expand the production of energy. The new proposal was monumental in its conception and cost, dwarfing the giant Manhattan District Project during the Second World War that developed the atomic bomb. Carter's new moral equivalent of war was expected to cost $142 billion over the next 10 years and was to be financed largely by a tax on the so-called windfall profits of oil companies.

The immediate public response was positive. The President's standing in the polls improved considerably although those who approved his actions constituted still less than half of the voters. For all of the rhetoric of sacrifice in the President's speeches, however, little specific sacrifice was actually demanded. Some of his advisers had hoped that he would take the hard but necessary road of asking for a sharp increase in the price of gasoline in order to compel Americans to use less, but his plan to reduce consumption relied primarily on exhortations to be patriotic and to conserve.

Some hoped he would abandon reliance upon nuclear energy, which in the light of a serious and totally unanticipated accident at a nuclear reactor at Three Mile Island, Pennsylvania, shortly before, seemed increasingly dubious, if not dangerous. The President, however, apparently contemplated no changes in his past policy of including nuclear energy as a substantial part of the national solution to the shortage.

Later in July, presumably in an effort to strengthen his administration internally and to give an impression externally of being in direct control, Carter fired five of his cabinet officers. The replacements, however, did not suggest that there would be much change in policy.

The wholesale firing aroused a furor among many leaders of the Democratic Party and in Congress, and puzzled—even alarmed—many observers abroad who were already beginning to view Carter as indecisive or lacking in steadfastness. Nor did the summary dismissals encourage the Senate to act on the second SALT (Strategic Arms Limitation Talks) Treaty with the Soviet Union, which Carter had submitted just when the gas lines were capturing the attention of Americans in the spring of 1979. SALT had been in the works a long time, yet it constituted only a small step in the direction of limiting the largest nuclear weapons of the two superpowers. It placed ceilings on numbers of submarine- and land-based missiles, and on bombers capable of carrying nuclear bombs and limited each side to the development of one new weapon system. Many Republicans and some Democrats thought such acceptance of virtual nuclear equality with the Soviet Union was dangerous and so opposed the treaty, but even those who may have favored it soon were distracted by two significant events in the late fall of 1979.

One was the sudden capturing of the American Embassy in Teheran, Iran, with all its occupants, by a group of armed student supporters of the new religious and secular leader of the Iranian revolution, the Ayatollah Khomeini. They demanded the exchange of the American hostages for the former Shah, who, for a while, was in the United States seeking medical treatment for cancer. When the Administration refused to return the Shah, the militants continued to hold the hostages, threatening to put them on trial as spies. The Iranians would hold 52 Americans hostage in Iran for 444 days, releasing them only on the day of Ronald Reagan's inauguration in 1981. The anti-Americanism in Iran was not new, but had been virtually unknown to the American public who knew only the face of the friendly Shah. In fact, however, from 1953 onward there had been simmering anti-Americanism in Iran. That year the CIA had helped overthrow a political leader, Mohammed Mossadegh, who had wanted to nationalize foreign oil interests. Once the Shah was gone, the anti-American sentiment came to the surface—and was actively fomented by Iranian politicians loyal to the Ayatollah and Islamic Revolution.

The second event that virtually killed the SALT discussions in the Senate was the invasion of Afghanistan by Soviet troops in late December 1979, in order to shore up a faltering Communist regime on its southern border and prevent the takeover of Afghanistan by Islamic extremists. The President reacted strongly—even exaggeratedly—by calling the Soviet intrusion a most serious threat to peace and comity among nations. He sought to arouse other nations to condemn the Soviet action, though not with great success, as most European nations understood the security concerns of the Soviets who desired to avoid a hostile government on their border. At home, by contrast, the Senate and the country viewed the Soviet measures as inconsistent with SALT, and so the agreement did not even come before the Senate in 1980.

As the 1980 election primaries began, the President was hardly in good political shape. He was burdened with the problem of the American hostages in Teheran and with a rate of inflation that was close to 20 percent on an annual basis. Moreover, all indications were that unemployment, too, would increase as the economy slowed down in response to the high interest rates and other measures aimed at combating inflation. Despite these handicaps, however, the President emerged from most of his primaries as the favored Democratic candidate, easily winning over his once highly favored opponent, Senator Edward Kennedy. Many Democrats, leaders as well as rank and file, were not pleased with Carter, but Kennedy was apparently viewed as even less attractive due to the death of a woman in his company in an automobile accident at Chappaquiddick more than a decade earlier. Despite Kennedy's vigorous campaign and magical name, the Democrats again nominated Jimmy Carter. Meanwhile, Ronald Reagan, the aging former governor of California, an acknowledged conservative on both domestic and foreign policy issues, easily captured enough delegates in the Republican primaries to win the nomination on the first ballot at the Republican convention.

THE ELECTION OF 1980

Once the campaign began, it was apparent voters were unhappy about the options. Although Republican Congressman John Anderson offered himself as an alternative, his candidacy soon faded as Americans clung to their historic distrust of third party candidates. Carter and Reagan's campaigning was intensive and vigorous, but neither said much specific about how he would handle inflation—a concern of anxious voters—or any other problem. Neither was able to arouse voter enthusiasm; throughout the fall, polls showed a large proportion of voters stubbornly undecided.

For his running mate, after a brief flirtation with former President Gerald Ford, who indicated that he would decline any such invitation, Reagan chose George H. W. Bush, who had been his strongest challenger for the nomination in the Republican Primaries. In spite of Bush's resume as a Republican Congressional leader, Ambassador to China, Ambassador to the United Nations, and Director of the CIA, there were reservations in some Republican corners concerning Bush. In specific, Bush had vocally criticized the central feature of Reagan's "supply-side" economic plan as "voodoo economics," correctly arguing that the tax cuts and proposed defense spending increases espoused by candidate Reagan could only produce massive deficits. Furthermore, Bush had been a supporter of the Equal Rights Amendment and had a history of a pro-choice stance on abortion. In fact, Bush had been such an ardent supporter of population control in the 1960s that he had earned the nickname "Rubbers" in Congress.

Up until election day, the polls had been predicting a cliffhanger. The disappointing campaign, however, culminated in a stunning surprise when Reagan won by a landslide. Carter won only four states and the District of Columbia for 49 electoral votes. Surprising, too, was the Republican capture of the Senate for the first time in 25 years. Democrats lost in both the South and the North. The Democratic stronghold in the South crumbled with the victories of four new

Republican senators and 11 new Republican congressmen. In the North, Republicans defeated three liberal Democratic senators and two congressmen.

These victories seemed to assure Reagan's ability to reshape the judiciary along more conservative lines and to take a harder line in foreign policy. The Republican triumphs also forecast a strong turn to the right in domestic policy, in line with the Republican platform. Among other things, the platform opposed the Equal Rights Amendment and abortion, while favoring higher military spending and a substantial tax cut. Also promised was a greater role for the states in domestic matters and a cutback in Federal spending and social programs.

Yet, some old patterns persisted. Democrats still controlled the House, as they had done since 1930 with only two interruptions. More important, voter turnout continued to decline, as it had been doing for a third of a century. The election seemed more a criticism of the Carter administration's inadequacies in dealing with a weakening economy and declining prestige abroad than a sign of support for Reagan and the Republicans.

When Carter left office, he was a highly unpopular figure. Yet, it should be noted, he has restored his prestige as few other unpopular presidents have ever done. Writing some 20 books—including a novel—as of 2006, he has, in addition, dedicated his post-presidential years to furthering democracy and human rights around the world, as well as to Habitat for Humanity in the United States. In 2002 he won the Nobel Peace Prize.

REAGAN'S AMERICA

(Library of Congress)

THE FIRST COUPLE

When Ronald and Nancy Reagan moved into the White House in January 1981, they were a most unusual presidential couple: each had been a movie star, though Nancy on a lesser scale; each was more familiar with the halls of power in Hollywood than in Washington; and each had a personal style at odds with the usual expectations of the American people for White House occupants. Indeed, not since the Kennedys had so much glamour been injected into politics; and this would have consequences beyond the surface glitter because the president, in particular, deployed his celebrity status to excellent advantage in advancing his conservative political agenda. Another important piece of information about the couple is that their marriage was so close and trusting that it would give Mrs. Reagan the kind of clout that very few First Ladies have enjoyed. Finally, Ronald Reagan, born in February 1911 and thus nearly 70 when he took the oath of allegiance, was older than most American presidents have been upon inauguration; and when he completed his second term, he set a record, having become the oldest person to serve in the office.

Ronald Reagan was born in Tampico, Illinois, and spent the rest of his life celebrating the virtues of small-town America. In fact, his own childhood, which included the necessity of dealing with an alcoholic father, was not an easy or uncomplicated one. His ability to rise above such memories typified not only his approach to life in general, but also his approach to political life. Having graduated from Eureka College in Illinois, where he majored in economics, he went on to work as a sports broadcaster before being invited to Hollywood for a screen test. The screen test secured him employment in front of the cameras; and he enjoyed on screen success but not overwhelming success, which is to say that he was a leading man but not an icon, as were some of his contemporaries. In the 1940s he was the president of the Screen Actors Guild, where he became active in "ferreting out communists" during the McCarthy era. In the 1950s, he hosted a television series for General Electric and began to give motivational speeches for business groups, an activity that completed his conversion from New Deal Democrat to Republican. By the time of Barry Goldwater's nomination for the presidency in 1964, Reagan had become one of the most visible spokespeople for the

President Ronald Reagan delivering his inaugural address on the west front of the U.S. Capitol on January 20, 1981 *(Library of Congress)*

conservative cause, one whose geniality softened his sometimes harsh message.

His political rise coincided with a turbulent period of student activism on college campuses in California; and when he competed for governor of that state in 1966 against Pat Brown, an effective incumbent, he was able to run against "out-of-control activists" as well as his actual opponent, a strategy that served him well. Once in office, he governed more as a pragmatist than as an ideologue—contrary to what his rhetoric might have suggested—and served two terms. As we learned in the preceding chapter, he won the Republican nomination for president in 1980, going on to defeat an unpopular incumbent, Jimmy Carter.

His partner in life as well as in politics Nancy Reagan, was born in 1921, the child of a stage actress, who remarried a neurosurgeon, Dr. Loyal Davis, when Nancy was six. The girl had a fine education, eventually graduating from Smith College as a theater major and then pursuing her own acting dream. That dream carried her to Hollywood by the early 1950s, where she met Ronald

John Hinckley Jr., who tried to assassinate President Reagan, arrives at the U.S. District Court House. *(AP Photo/Evan Vucci)*

Reagan. The two were married in 1952, her first marriage and his second; hence, Ronald Reagan became America's first "divorced" President. As his political career advanced, Mrs. Reagan became known as a political wife of exemplary devotion, able to fix her husband with a rapt gaze, even when he was delivering a stump speech that she may well have heard many times before.

Just 69 days into Reagan's presidency, a deluded movie fan, shot Ronald Reagan in an assassination attempt that had many important repercussions, though the public did not know of the severity of the wounds at the time or, in fact, that it was nearly a successful attempt. What the public did know was that their president showed remarkable courage and gallantry, walking into the hospital unaided. Polls soon revealed how much more admiration he garnered after the episode, even from Democrats, and he became a far more formidable political figure, despite having to deal with a House of Representatives controlled by the opposition party. Thereafter, Mrs. Reagan became ever more anxious about her husband's well-being. It was at this point that she began to consult a San Francisco astrologer about his schedule, a practice that continued throughout the Reagan administration and that was revealed in a tell-all book by Mrs. Reagan's adversary (she worked to get him fired) former chief-of-staff, Donald Regan, and corroborated by her own daughter, Patti Davis.

DOMESTIC ISSUES

REAGANOMICS

Ronald Reagan signaled his intentions with respect to the economy by appointing a Cabinet filled with businessmen and conservatives, a move consonant with the pro-business speeches he had been giving for many years. The approach he favored, "supply-side economics," which was predicated on the belief that tax cuts would produce such a boost to the economy that the government would not run budget deficits, had been labeled "voodoo economics" by his adversary during the run-up to the 1980 nomination, George H. W. Bush, the man who then became his vice president.

In essence, supply side economics promised that it would be possible to cut taxes rigorously and thereby attract the productive investment of capital—all without damaging the fundamental soundness of the economy. Cutting taxes was dogma to conservatives, not merely to enhance their own pocketbooks but because they viewed it as an effective means of reducing big government, a highly desired goal in their eyes. Reagan went so far as to announce in his first inaugural that "In the present crisis, government is not the solution to our problem; government is the problem."

In fact, when Reagan took office, the economy was in bad shape. The late 1970s had featured an unprecedented—and unwelcome—phenomenon known as "stagflation" in which double-digit inflation was accompanied by double-digit unemployment. Johnson and Nixon had spent the previous decade spending on the Vietnam War unsupported by taxes, thus leading to deficits and eventually devaluation of the currency. The new president argued that an excess of regulation, taxation, and spending had created the problem—all of which had put a damper on business activity, had created the problem. Congress listened to him and passed the Economic Recovery Tax Act in 1981, reducing income tax rates by 25 percent over three years, in spite of the fact that the federal government was already operating at a deficit. The cuts were supposed to be linked to cuts in spending, but it proved easier to indulge in rhetoric about runaway spending than to find politically palatable ways to cut it. Furthermore, Reagan believed that the United States was behind the Soviet Union in the cold war arms race; and he, therefore, effectively doubled military spending. As a consequence, Reagan's legacy included a tripling of the national debt during the eight years of his administration and the worst economic recession since the Great Depression in 1982, but by 1983, the economy did improve. Many scholars would argue that this was because world oil prices declined (from $40 a barrel in 1981 to $9 in 1986), rather than because of his policies—but the improvement itself is unarguable. A second factor receiving credit in reviving the economy is the aggressive action of the Federal Reserve Board in tightening the money supply and thereby limiting inflation.

THE AIR TRAFFIC CONTROLLERS' STRIKE

Another episode of great historical significance involved one of the few unions to support Ronald Reagan in 1980, the Professional Air Traffic Controllers Organization or PATCO. PATCO'S president, Robert Poli, wanted wage increases of up to 40 percent for his members, as well as a reduction in their workweek. Reagan's Director of the Budget, David Stockman, who was trying to hold the line against inflationary pressures, opposed this step. In August 1981 PATCO's membership rejected a lesser offer from the government, and nearly 12,000 controllers went on strike, in so doing, violating a no-strike clause in their contract. Poli and his members were gambling on support from the public and perhaps from the president, a former labor leader. They made a fatal miscalculation.

The president's response was swift and decisive. He fired all the striking controllers, saying that they had broken the law by going on strike as public employees; and then he stipulated that they could never be rehired. He then ordered military personnel into the control towers. Except for those who were close to the labor movement, the public overwhelmingly approved of the president's action, and so, no doubt, did some union members. Most historians now agree that over the long haul Reagan's breaking the PATCO union did more to intimidate and weaken the labor movement than any other single episode since the 1940s. In concert with his pro-business appointments to the National Labor Relations Board, the PATCO debacle—for labor—intensified the hemorrhaging of union membership since the 1950s.

SHAPING THE SUPREME COURT

One of Ronald Reagan's most popular decisions was his appointment of the first woman to the Supreme Court, Sandra Day O'Connor, in 1981. Moreover, this is a decision that has only grown in stature over the years, inasmuch as Justice O'Connor garnered the reputation of being one of the truly outstanding justices in American history by reason of her ability to "count to five." This expression means that she was especially shrewd in staking out a centrist position and then shaping a majority to support it.

Reagan and his advisers felt that he needed to do something to reach out to women voters after a statistically significant "gender gap" in voting showed up for the first time in American history in the election of 1980, with women favoring Jimmy Carter disproportionately over the male vote for him. From the time that women had gotten the

Ronald Reagan making a speech *(Library of Congress)*

vote in 1920, activists had been waiting for a "women's bloc" to materialize, but they waited in vain—until 1980. Once aware of the phenomenon, Republican operatives were eager to counter it immediately. Hence the general concurrence that the time was right to put a woman on the nation's highest bench.

After a distinguished law school career, Sandra Day had graduated from Stanford Law School in 1952, being offered only secretarial jobs at first—in spite of her law degree from one of America's elite institutions. Marrying a law school classmate, John O'Connor, she returned to her native Arizona, began to practice law, and became involved in Republican politics. From 1965 to 1969 she served as the state's assistant attorney general. In 1969 she was appointed to the state senate, winning reelection twice. In 1973 she was chosen as the state's senate majority leader. Resigning from the legislature, she was elected to be a superior court judge in Phoenix in 1974 and then chosen to be a judge on the Arizona Court of Appeals in 1979; thus she had an unusual combination of legislative and judicial experience. What is more, during their interview, it was soon apparent that Reagan liked her. With all of these factors in her favor, the stage was set for her nomination, a selection confirmed by the Senate by a vote of 99 to 0.

Reagan also chose two other members of the Supreme Court, the very conservative Antonin Scalia and the more moderate Anthony Kennedy. Moreover, in 1986 he chose Associate Justice William Rehnquist to be Chief Justice. All told, his many appointments at various levels of the judiciary had a powerful impact, this despite the Senate's refusal to confirm his nomination of the ultra-conservative legal scholar Robert Bork to the Supreme Court in 1987.

ROBERT BORK APPOINTMENT

In June 1987, Justice Lewis Powell resigned his position on the Supreme Court, leaving President Reagan the task of appointing a successor. Reagan chose Yale law professor and United States Court of Appeals judge Robert Bork, a staunch conservative who had opposed the 1964 Civil Rights Act for "intruding on the rights of citizens." Bork also disagreed with the Supreme Court's "Judicial Activism" and the "creation of new rights," such as the Right to Privacy that had been the basis of the *Roe v. Wade* decision. Provoking further anger from the left, Bork had been the Solicitor General in the Watergate "Saturday Night Massacre" that had fired Special Prosecutor Archibald Cox at the behest of Richard Nixon. As a result, therefore, of what Democrats viewed as his extreme conservative views, coupled with his actions in the Watergate affair, Bork was voted down in the Senate by a vote of 58 to 42.

Reagan followed up the Bork appointment with the nomination of Douglas Ginsburg, a Harvard Law professor; but the Ginsburg nomination unraveled when it was revealed that Ginsburg had used marijuana while working as a professor at Harvard. Finally, Reagan appointed Appeals Court Justice Anthony Kennedy, who was confirmed unanimously by the Senate in 1988.

The Bork affair, however, had long-term consequences. Republicans charged that the Democrats had voted down Bork for his political views rather than for his legal qualifications. After the Bork affair, Senate confirmation of judicial appointees became highly politicized, and a series of similar affairs would rage on in cases of appointees to lower courts for the next decade and a half. Those who would fail to be confirmed were often said to be "Borked."

The reasons for the political firestorm over Bork were ideologically based and reflected the political realities of the new ideological bitterness that had developed in American politics in the late twentieth century. Members of the opposing political parties in Congress tended to socialize with each other less than they had in the past due to the increased emphasis on social, cultural, and moral issues that forced a premium on ideological consistency with parties and constituents. Demonization of the political opposition became more common and tended to produce more campaign contributions and political support for the "demonizers." Southern conservatives had largely exited the Democratic Party, leaving the Democrats more liberal by subtraction. The loss of their conservative faction rendered the Democratic Party more ideological and less flexible in dealing with their Republican counterparts. Simultaneously, religiosity in the United States had not become more intense, but the makeup of American religion had shifted away from the more liberal, old-line Protestant churches, and toward religious fundamentalist sects. Although members of religious fundamentalist Protestant churches were only approximately a fourth of the American population, fundamentalist Protestants had become a majority of the Republican Party. Both parties recognized the negatives of the development of ideological polarization; but religious conservatives that now had power in the Republican Party were not open to compromise, and neither party was able to make any headway in reducing the partisan and ideological strife that would continue into the twenty-first century.

THE GREAT CRASH

On October 19, 1987, known as "Black Monday," the New York Stock Exchange dropped 22.6 percent, almost double the record 12.8 percent drop of the 1929 crash that had signaled the dawning of the Great Depression of the 1930s. Although the market rallied to recoup 40 percent of its losses by the end of the week, economic prognosticators and the general public feared that another Great Depression might follow, thus causing a drop in consumer confidence and further depressing the economy. Many economic observers blamed the crash on the reckless deficit spending by the Reagan administration. Chrysler chairman Lee Iacocca summed up the views of many when he stated, "I don't know what they're on down in Washington. It's wacko time." The stock market would eventually recover, but the crash and fears that ensued suggested to many that "deregulation" of the financial markets might not be quite so wise after all, thus allowing a political opening for the Democrats in 1988.

ECONOMIC INEQUALITY

As perhaps could have been expected with the move toward a more free market-oriented economy during the Reagan years, economic inequality increased significantly during the 1980s. In 1979, the poorest 40 percent of Americans held 18 percent of the total income in America, and the wealthiest 5 percent held 15.6 percent of the total income. After eight years of Reaganomics, however, the wealthiest 5 percent of Americans produced 21 percent of all income and the poorest 40 percent of Americans earned only 14 percent of all income. Unfortunately for America's working class and poor, Adam Smith's "rising tide" did not lift all boats equally. Personal income for the wealthiest 20 percent of Americans increased, while it actually decreased 9.8 percent for the poorest 20 percent of Americans. No longer could all Americans expect, as they had in the previous decades following World War II, that their children would live better than they had. Similarly, between 1980 and 1988, the number of individuals living below the poverty line increased from 11.7 percent of the population to 13.5 percent, the highest poverty rate among industrialized democracies of the world.

DEREGULATION AND ITS CONSEQUENCES

In *Reckoning with Reagan*, Michael Schaller entitled one of his chapters "Prophets (Profits) of Deregulation." This play on words highlights the extent to which many of those who advocated the dismantling of the regulatory state, regulations put in place during the Progressive period and the New Deal years, managed to do well during the Reagan administration. In no area was this truer than that of the savings-and-loan (S & L) industry.

Deregulation had begun during the Carter years, but the pace greatly accelerated under Ronald Reagan. In some industries—telecommunications, for example—deregulation may have had a benign effect by encouraging competition to the ultimate benefit of the consumer. Between S & L's, however, the impact was to encourage high-risk investments because government oversight of investment practices was terminated. By the time the dust settled in the 1990's, some 1,300 financial institutions had failed; but no one lost money because the S & L's deposits were federally insured. On the other hand, American taxpayers were left with a bill of $160 billion to make up the losses.

The best-known instance of corruption in the thrift industry lay in the case of Charles Keating and the California-based Lincoln Federal

Savings and Loan. As an instance of illegal behavior, Lincoln's tellers sold "junk bonds"—not guaranteed like regular savings accounts—to thousands of gullible, mostly elderly customers, while misleading these customers into thinking that this was a safe investment. When Keating's shady practices came to light, it became known that he had contributed some $3 million dollars in campaign contributions to a bipartisan group of five United States Senators, one of whom was 2008 Republican Presidential nominee John McCain. In return the Keating Five had apparently tried to offer Keating help with his problems.

In a book about the Reagan years published in 1991, Haynes Johnson offered the following count: by that point 138 Reagan administration officials had been convicted, indicted, or officially investigated, including several cabinet officers up to Edwin Meese, the Attorney General, and Caspar Weinberger, the Secretary of Defense. Not personally corrupt, Reagan presided over an administration steeped in ethical problems. His desire to deregulate was based on an optimistic faith that business leaders and people in power would behave with integrity, all too often, it seems, a misplaced faith. Perhaps James Madison said it best, "If men were angels, no government would be necessary." Unfortunately, men are not; and the Reagan years demonstrated that at least some government regulation is an essential part of the mix, both to protect the public safety and to maintain the consumer confidence necessary to a vibrant economy.

FOREIGN POLICY

A NEW COLD WAR?

When he took office, Reagan arrived with as much baggage from prior speeches about the Soviet Union and the threat of international communism as he possessed owing to speeches about deregulating the economy. At a time that, to many, America seemed impotent in foreign policy (largely due to the Iranian hostage crisis and the Soviet invasion of Afghanistan), Ronald Reagan had campaigned against Jimmy Carter in 1980 promising to "make America strong again" and arguing for a foreign policy of "Peace through strength." Reagan talked of a "missile gap" between the United States and the Soviet Union; and he argued that the Soviet "Evil Empire" was the basis of all of the world's unrest and, therefore, had to be contained. Reagan also termed the Vietnam War as a "noble cause" to prevent the spread of communism. Reagan essentially reversed Nixon's détente by referring to the U.S.S.R. as the "focus of evil in the modern world." Reagan was not only anti-Soviet, but also determined to fight communism anywhere and everywhere in the world, through military means if necessary.

George Kennan, the original architect of the containment doctrine, was unimpressed with Reagan's new cold warrior attitude and termed the President's views as "intellectual primitivism;" but they played well with the American public, just as they had for Kennedy in 1960. In 1981, Reagan began a defense buildup that amounted to a 40 percent defense spending increase in the first three years of his Presidency. The defense spending increases were so immense that Reagan's defense budget exceeded Vietnam War spending as a percentage of the economy.

Adding to his massive buildup, in 1983, Reagan introduced the Strategic Defense Initiative (SDI) in his State of the Union Address. Without first consulting scientists, Reagan proposed to spend $24 billion on a space laser system designed to shoot down Soviet ICBMs. Despite almost unanimous proclamations from the scientific community that such a system was infeasible, Congress appropriated the funding for the program. By 2004, over $60 billion had been spent on the program with essentially no results. Reagan also installed new cruise missiles in Europe and doubled the size of the American nuclear arsenal in an attempt to gain "parity" with the Soviet Union. Reagan's claims, however, that the United States had fallen behind in the nuclear race, were true only if one merely counted land based missiles but ignored the fact that the United States had a 2-to-1 advantage over the Soviets in submarine launched missiles in 1982, which counterbalanced the disadvantage in land based systems.

Before the two countries reached comity, there were many rocky periods in the relationship, none more so than following the Soviet downing of Korean Air Lines flight #007 in September 1983. In a flight from Alaska to Seoul, the plane had wandered off course and had flown over Soviet territory. A Soviet fighter plane shot it down, killing all 269 people on board, a group that included a member of the United States Congress. The exact facts of this incident have never been fully determined, but Reagan denounced it as an "act of barbarism." For this and other reasons, there was a massive build-up in United States military might with the consequent impact on increasing the deficit spending by the administration of this avowed opponent of Keynesian economics.

Reagan also proclaimed the "Reagan Doctrine" whereby the United States would provide aid to "freedom fighters" resisting communism in Third World countries. As a practical matter, this often meant making dubious allies, as in Afghanistan, where Reagan continued Jimmy Carter's policy of aiding the mujahadeen who were fighting against the Soviets. Twenty years later many of these men comprised the Taliban forces, against which the United States would launch an invasion of Afghanistan following the terrorist attack of September 11, 2001.

THE MIDDLE EAST

President Reagan inherited an ongoing set of difficulties in this troubled region, difficulties that were compounded by the outbreak of a war between Iran and Iraq in 1980 that lasted till 1988 and claimed some two million lives. In addition to dealing with this, his administration faced the recurring tensions between Israel and the Palestinians and the outbreak of civil strife in Lebanon and Afghanistan.

In 1982, a civil war broke out in Lebanon between Maronite Christians, several groups of Lebanese Muslims, and the Palestinian Liberation Organization (PLO). In an attempt to remedy the chaos on their border due to the bloody Lebanese civil war, Syria invaded Lebanon with a "peacekeeping force." Israel retaliated against the Syrian invasion with an invasion of their own, and the Israeli "peacekeeping force" then pushed Syrian and PLO forces all the way to Beirut. Israel then shelled the city of Beirut, and the United States sent Ambassador Philip Habib to negotiate a cease-fire. The next year, the combatants signed an agreement to allow United States, French, and Italian troops to supervise the PLO withdrawal of Beirut, and the Syrian and Israeli withdrawals of Lebanon. Many Lebanese Muslims resented this intrusion, and on April 18, 1983, a suicide squad attacked the American Embassy in Beirut, with a death toll of 63 lives lost.

In response, the battleship *New Jersey*, off the Lebanese shore, shelled Muslim positions. American troops were deployed to Lebanon pursuant to the agreement; but on October 23, 1983, an Islamic suicide bomber, working for the Iranian terrorist organization Hizbollah, drove a truck full of explosives into the United States marine headquarters at the Beirut airport and killed 241 United States marines. Congress failed to pass a resolution authorizing the placement of American troops in a combat zone as required by the War Powers Act of 1973, so President Reagan was forced to redeploy the marines to ships offshore in the Mediterranean.

Liberals in the press criticized the Reagan administration for recklessly placing American troops in harm's way; but two days later, Reagan diverted attention from the Lebanon disaster by ordering a United States invasion of Grenada, a small island in the Caribbean that had been taken over by a Marxist group. Almost 6,000 American troops were involved in the operation, which quickly overwhelmed the Grenadan leftists and Cuban construction workers; however, 18 Americans were killed and 134 were wounded in the fighting. In addition, 396 Grenadans and Cubans were killed, but the invasion had the desired effect for the Reagan administration since the focus of the American media and the public shifted from the tragedy and defeat of Lebanon to the "victory" in Grenada. Furthermore, Reagan could boast that he had ended the "communist threat" on the tiny Caribbean Island. As for the Iran-Iraq war, it was destined to play a large role in the second Reagan administration, as we shall soon learn.

THE AMERICAS

Because Reagan was so concerned about the specter of international communism, he gave an enormous amount of attention to its possible spread in Central America, a region where poverty and social injustice were widespread. Cuba, where Fidel Castro had overthrown the dictator Fulgencio Batista in 1959, installed a Marxist state, and then engaged in what American policymakers perceived as anti-American activities was not a model that Reagan wanted to see emulated. The problem for him was that even he, referred to in the media as the Great Communicator, had a hard time convincing other world leaders, Congress, and the American people to take the threat as seriously as he did. Pierre Trudeau of Canada and Francois Mitterrand of France, for instance, considered Reagan's views to be an overreaction to a communist threat that was more imagined than real.

In his December 1985, State of the Union Address, Reagan announced what became known as the "Reagan Doctrine," proclaiming his administration's support for anti-communist "freedom fighters" as part of American "self-defense." The announcement was essentially a reversal of the policies of Nixon and Carter, where foreign countries would be held responsible for their own defense against communism. Instead, the Reagan Doctrine represented a return to the Cold War Truman and Eisenhower Doctrines that had been largely discredited since they had led to the disastrous war in Vietnam. Reagan's critics argued that the United States had been extracted from Vietnam for barely over a decade, but evidently the "lessons" of Vietnam already had been forgotten.

For Reagan, however, there were two countries in Latin America of particular concern. In one, El Salvador, a savage civil war was raging. Despite the presence of a nominally in charge civilian regime, in fact, the right-wing military held the actual power. Left-wing insurgents were fighting against this military, and in response the army waged a fierce campaign of repression. Reagan armed the government of the unpopular right-wing dictator, Jose Napoleon Duarte, against the leftist rebels. Aid to El Salvador was $6 million under Carter, and $82 million in Reagan's first budget. Critics charged that American aid to Duarte's government was partially to blame for the escalation of the Salvadoran conflict and for the fact that 53,000 El Salvadorans were killed in the civil war, along with a small number of American church workers. In advocating aid to the Salvadorean government, Reagan was tacitly accepting the price of supporting a bloodstained regime, hence the controversy attached to this policy.

Nicaragua presented a different set of issues. There the legitimate government was led by the Marxist Sandinistas, who had finally succeeded in defeating the dictatorial Somoza regime in 1979, after decades of struggle. The Sandinistas then confirmed their legitimacy by winning Nicaragua's first free election in 1984. Those opposed to the Sandinistas formed a guerrilla group known as the "Contras," and the latter were a natural focus for President Reagan, every fiber of whose being was clearly horrified by the presence of another Marxist regime, on good terms with both Cuba and the Soviet Union, so close to the United States. From time to time, Congress permitted American aid to go to the Contras, but at other times, it turned off the spigot. In fact, as Richard Reeves points out, the Sandinista government was often its own worst enemy, making it difficult for Congressional Democrats to oppose aid to the Contras by reason of the Sandinista leader, Daniel Ortega, showing up in Moscow around the time of a key vote. In furtherance of the Reagan Doctrine, Reagan armed the Contra rebels against the communist government of the Sandinistas in Nicaragua at a cost of $19 million. Reagan also mined the harbors of Nicaragua, an act of war under international law. In the end, the regime lasted until 1990, when it was defeated in an election.

AMERICA IN THE 80s

THE HIGH-TECH REVOLUTION

By the 1980s the power of a new and much smaller computer—and all that power would entail in the lives of ordinary Americans—was beginning to be manifest. Computers were not new—IBM was already a giant corporation—but personal computers only began to appear in the middle-class household in the mid-80s. Other types of consumer electronics, such as video games, fueled a strong growth in this arena as well. No region would have more to do with this revolution than California's Silicon Valley, as the Santa Clara Valley (about an hour's drive south of San Francisco) became known.

The growth of the high-tech industry in Silicon Valley in the post-war years was one of those remarkable regional spurts of creativity and economic dynamism that has periodically characterized the United States's economic development. In the early nineteenth century Yankee ingenuity in New England had spurred regional growth there, in the early twentieth century the big news was the development of the automotive industry in and around Detroit; and in the mid-twentieth century the action lay in a former agricultural and fruit-processing region in California, which happened to be adjacent to Stanford University.

As we have already learned, the military necessities created by World War II transformed California's economy, with a huge aircraft industry in southern California and a concentration of shipbuilding in the San Francisco Bay Area. Not too long after the war ended, the military necessities created by the Cold War ensured that the defense sector would continue to be a significant factor in the state's economic health. For example, Lockheed Aircraft created its Missiles and Space Division in the mid-1950s and located it in the former cannery town of Sunnyvale, about 12 miles south of Stanford. That, in turn, provided a market for the nascent electronics industry that was famously launched in a garage in Palo Alto (the town where Stanford is located) in 1938 when David Packard and William Hewlett started a firm, Hewlett Packard, that would become another one of the giants. Many scholars have pointed out that this juxtaposition of a great research university supplying the brainpower and a market for what their brainpower produced was a winning combination.

The next truly consequential development occurred when William Shockley, who had been in on the invention of that essential building block of the electronics revolution, the transistor, decided to forsake Bell Laboratories in New York and set up his own firm in his home town of Palo Alto. Shockley was an immensely difficult man, and before long a group of his most talented employees—"the traitorous eight" in his eyes—left to found their own firm, Fairchild. It was spin-offs from Fairchild that would create Silicon Valley, but first, research teams at Fairchild and at Texas Instruments independently developed the integrated circuit between 1959 and 1961. An integrated circuit contains several transistors (essentially tiny switches that "semi-conduct" electrons), plus resistors, capacitors, and diodes on one small portion of a silicon wafer, the portion being known as a "chip."

In 1968 defectors from Fairchild founded Intel in Santa Clara, which neighbors Sunnyvale, and the stage was set for the next breakthrough, the microprocessor, a more sophisticated cousin of the integrated circuit. What was so exciting about the microprocessor was that it permitted memory to be electronically embedded and thus was essential to the development of the personal computer. Having developed this, Intel would become yet another of the giants. In 1971 a journalist gave the Santa Clara Valley the nickname of Silicon Valley. Between 1959 and 1976, in fact, 45 semiconductor firms were established in the country, 40 of which were in the Santa Clara Valley; and with the invention of the microprocessor came a turn away from the military market to a burgeoning consumer market.

In 1977 Steve Jobs and Steve Wozniak founded another of the pioneering firms in the Silicon Valley, Apple Computers. Jobs and Wozniak were very young, and at that stage they looked like quintessential hackers. Though they may have resembled hippies, their firm's rise from zero to *FORTUNE 500* within five years was a phenomenon in American business history. Soon there were several manufacturers of personal computers, and Bill Gates and Microsoft in the Seattle region were on their way, also. Though Silicon Valley is no longer quite so dominant as it was at its height—and the dot.com bust of the early twenty-first century would take a terrible toll—it is noteworthy that as the Internet has developed in succeeding decades (to be discussed in the next chapter), Silicon Valley firms continue to be innovators in the early twenty-first century, with Google and eBay being two of the most famous.

THE NEW RIGHT

Though Barry Goldwater lost badly in 1964, from that campaign on there was a dedicated—and growing—group of conservative activists. Some lived in places like California's Orange County, where "suburban warriors," to use the title of Lisa McGirr's book about the rise of the New Right in Orange County, planned political strategies. Others were in the midwestern heartland, many were in the states that had once belonged to the Confederacy, and a sprinkling (but an influential sprinkling) were in such big cities as New York or Washington. They raised money, they created think tanks, they did grass roots organizing; and by the 1980s and Reagan's presidency, it was clear that all of the effort was paying off.

Taking nothing away from the remarkable energy and resources devoted to a restructuring of the American political landscape, it is also true that the rapid social change of the 1960s and early 1970s was bound to stir a backlash. In the space of two decades, racial mores in the South had been both challenged and changed, gender norms remade, abortion made legal by a decision of the United States Supreme Court, and there was the beginning of a new norm where sexual orientation was concerned. All of this change was clearly destined to be more popular on the coasts and in big cities than in regions that were still closely linked to the rural past.

To examine the career of one of the early activists, Phyllis Schlafly, is to gain insight into how the New Right could be so successful. Schlafly first came to public attention with the campaign biography she published about Goldwater, *A Choice Not an Echo*. She then began to write a monthly newsletter for her conservative constituency, the *Phyllis Schlafly Report*, in which she focused principally on the dangers of communism. Within a few years, she began to be alarmed about the changes set in motion by the birth of modern feminism, especially the looming possibility of ratification of the Equal Rights Amendment. (It will be recalled that Congress sent the ERA to the states in 1972). Rather than placing her faith in an amendment, Schlafly believed that women needed to be protected by the men in their lives. Hence she organized the single most effective organization opposed to ratification, STOP-ERA, and is widely credited with having been instrumental in the amendment's defeat, time running out in 1982. This defeat was all the more remarkable in that the ERA began its journey through the ratification process with widespread public support, according to polling data.

Schlafly's own life story both confirms and transcends her anti-feminist ideology. On the one hand, she was the stay-at-home mother of six children. On the other, she obtained a law degree from Washington University as a re-entry woman. Never practicing law, she used the legal training to help shape her testimony before various Congressional Committees.

In its earliest manifestation the New Right was held together more by fervent anti-communism than by the fundamentalist religion that is so important a factor in the constituency of President George W. Bush in the early twenty-first century. The New Right in the 1970s (as well as ever since) was decidedly anti-gay, and, as previously mentioned, the linkage of gay rights to ERA was most certainly a contributor to the demise of ERA; however, the religious right did not limit their opposition to homosexuality exclusively to the battle

San Francisco Supervisor Harvey Milk, left, and Mayor George Moscone in the mayor's office during the signing of the city's gay rights bill *(AP Photo/File)*

over ERA. According to Reverend Falwell, homosexuality was an evil sin in the same category with rape, adultery, and incest. Consequently, when San Francisco Mayor George Moscone and City Supervisor Harvey Milk, the city's first openly gay elected official, were assassinated, Falwell stated that the murders, which were committed by a fundamentalist Christian who admitted that his belief in God had prompted his action, were a judgment from God.

All conservatives were not comfortable with the positions of the New Right, including "Mr. Conservative," Barry Goldwater, who criticized it after 1981, stating, "... that Christian bunch is crazy." At the time of Reagan's administration, however, the religious right had begun increasingly to make its presence felt. Indeed, Jerry Falwell had founded the Moral Majority in 1979, and this date can be taken as among the first truly significant flexing of this set of muscles. In the ensuing decades, the growing clout of Southern white Protestants would make a profound impact on American politics.

AIDS

Early in Reagan's presidency there appeared a new scourge, Acquired Immune Deficiency Syndrome or AIDS. Because it is spread by the exchange of blood or bodily fluids, the disease has been linked in the public mind primarily with sexual intercourse, the likeliest mode of transmission, though it can also be transmitted by needle sharing among intravenous drug users, and in the early days, by the transfusion of infected blood.

AIDS was devastating, especially early on, when a diagnosis was an automatic death sentence; and because it has disproportionately (though by no means exclusively) affected male homosexuals and/or those who are sexually promiscuous, everything about it, from transmission to prevention to treatment, has been controversial. Certain fundamentalist clergymen, such as Jerry Falwell, have gone so far as to suggest that its toll on gay men has been God's punishment for the sin of their sexual orientation. Deferring to his New Right constituency, Ronald Reagan refused to even use the term AIDS in public until 1985, well into the epidemic. The Surgeon General of the United States is mandated by Congress to inform the American people about the prevention of disease and the promotion of health; but Surgeon General C. Everett Koop was instructed not to make any statements about AIDS because any federal AIDS education plan was likely to alienate Reagan's support from the religious right. Consequently, the media were told at Reagan's press conferences by Reagan officials that AIDS questions were not on the agenda.

With silence on the issue coming from the Reagan Administration, AIDS hysteria began to unravel in the media. Reverend Donald Wildmon of the American Family Association called for a quarantine of "all homosexual establishments." In Nevada, a newspaper ran a full page "AIDS Alert" advertisement posted by a fundamentalist minister who stated, "I think we should do what the Bible says and cut their throats." In 1988, a *Los Angeles Times* poll revealed that 57 percent of religious fundamentalists favored a quarantine of people with AIDS. *National Review* editor William F. Buckley added his contribution to the paranoia when he suggested that those afflicted with AIDS should be given an identifiable tattoo so that others could recognize them and thus avoid contact.

Congress, as the official representative of the people in the United States, was not immune to the hysteria. California Republican Congressman William Dannemeyer stated that if it were possible to identify every HIV positive person in the country, he would "wipe them off the face of the earth" if he were able to do so. The response of the Reagan administration reflected similar thinking. Dr. James O. Mason, Director of the Center for Disease Control, acknowledged that quarantine was being considered as an option as late as 1985.

With the AIDS hysteria in full swing, Surgeon General C. Everett Koop in July 1985, told his superiors that he could no longer remain silent about AIDS. Koop was then given the permission to say whatever he felt was necessary about AIDS, along with the authority to appoint a task force to study the problem. In February 1986, President Reagan asked Koop to prepare a special report on AIDS, and the report was finally released in October the same year. That year, Reagan's friend and fellow movie star Rock Hudson succumbed to the disease, a tragedy that began to change public attitudes. (Another important turning point in public attitudes came in 1991 when basketball star Earvin "Magic" Johnson announced that he was HIV-positive, the predecessor condition to full-blown AIDS. As of this writing, Magic Johnson is still alive and still vigorous although the condition did end his basketball career prematurely.) Reagan planned to mention AIDS in his 1986 State of the Union address, but plans changed owing to other developments. In 1987 he gave his first speech on the subject, telling the College of Physicians in Philadelphia that he considered AIDS to be "Public Health Enemy No. 1." By the end of his presidency, it should be noted, the federal government had begun to make a real commitment to a disease that would infect 65 million people worldwide by 2006.

The problem has been that to discuss effective prevention means to discuss "safe sex," anathema to conservatives. Prevention might also involve the wide dissemination of condoms, another controversial plan because it seemed to condone free-and-easy sex. Finally, as the past decade has shown, issues having to do with homosexuality have been a sure-fire way of engendering passion among members of the religious right.

THE ELECTION OF 1984

By 1984, the economy had made a comeback that would continue throughout the decade, largely due to the boom in the information-processing sector. In this election year, campaigning on the issue-less theme of "It's Morning in America," Ronald Reagan was decisively re-elected, his opponent being Walter Mondale, Jimmy Carter's vice president. The election was noteworthy for a reason other than Reagan's success, however; because Mondale chose a woman as his running mate, and for the first time in American history, that a woman had appeared on a national ticket for one of the major parties.

Geraldine Ferraro was a congresswoman from New York when she was tapped to be the vice presidential nominee. In general, she was an effective campaigner; but Reagan was a tough man to beat, especially when Mondale, the man at the top of the ticket, said that he would need to raise taxes, a bow to reality given the growing

A 1984 presidential campaign poster promoting the reelection of President Ronald Reagan and Vice President George H. W. Bush *(Library of Congress)*

deficit, but not popular with voters. Despite the fact that Reagan seemed confused during some of the debates—with people for the first time beginning to express public doubts about his failing cognitive ability—his optimism was still popular with voters. Reagan captured 58.8 percent of the popular vote, with Mondale winning 40.6 percent. In the Electoral College, the vote was 525 to 13. The Democrats were able to maintain control of the House, though, and would even go on to recapture the Senate in 1986. On election day, Reagan won every state except Mondale's home state of Minnesota and the District of Columbia. The Democrats even lost Geraldine Ferraro's home state of New York.

CHALLENGES OF THE SECOND TERM

THE IRAN-CONTRA SCANDAL

Shortly after Ronald Reagan's second inauguration, events began to unfold that would lead to the worst scandal of his presidency, the Iran-Contra affair. The background to the scandal, however, developed during the first term when a few American hostages were taken prisoner in Lebanon and when Reagan became frustrated with the limits Congress placed on his ability to supply as much help to the anti-Sandinista forces in Nicaragua as he would have liked. Reagan had termed the contra rebels in Nicaragua as "freedom fighters" without seriously investigating what kind of group they were. Since they were opposed to the communist Sandinista government of Nicaragua, that was all that the President needed to know; in Reagan's view, any group that was anti-communist was worthy of support. In 1984, however, Congress cut off Contra aid because the Sandinista government had been elected democratically in 1984; and many felt that it was questionable whether or not the contras, regardless of their anti-communism, were "good guys."

Between 1984 and 1986, however, Reagan's National Security Council kept aid to the Contras flowing secretly against the Congressional ban and, in doing so, violated a whole host of federal laws, as well as Reagan's Oath of Office where he pledged to "faithfully execute the laws of Congress," rather than circumvent them. The covert Contra aid was secretly funded through a scheme developed by Lt. Colonel Oliver North, who ran the operation out of the White House basement. According to the Congressional report that was eventually compiled about the operation, Lt. North was running his operation openly within the Reagan administration; and it would have been difficult for Reagan and his senior aides not to know what was going on.

In July 1985 an Israeli official suggested to National Security Advisor Robert McFarlane that providing arms to Iran (then engaged in hostilities with Iraq, which the United States was aiding in its war with Iran) could lead to the release of some of the American hostages. Despite maintaining a public profile of making no deals with terrorists to secure the release of any hostages—and Washington had labeled Iran as a terrorist regime—the administration decided to go along. The money provided by Iran to pay for the armaments was then channeled to a fund to aid the contras. It should be noted that at no point did the deal lead, unequivocally, to the release of all the hostages. Nor, for that matter, did the contras succeed in overthrowing the Sandinistas.

The arms sales to Iran violated a Congressional Embargo on Iran, which not only had held Americans hostage for 444 days during the Carter administration, but also was heavily engaged in an effort to spread Shiite Islamic revolution throughout the globe and was involved in the 1983 truck bombing of the United States marine compound in Lebanon. The Iran-Contra operation also made use of planes owned by South American drug lords, who flew cocaine into the United States with their planes under CIA protection and flew arms to the contras for the American government. South American cocaine trafficker George Morales admitted that he donated $3 million in cash and some aircraft, as well as his top pilots, at the request of the CIA. Also involved in aiding the arms-to-the-Contras scheme with planes was Panamanian President Manuel Noriega, who would later be indicted in Florida for drug trafficking during the same arms-to-Contras covert operation.

Mercenaries to help the contra operation were recruited in the United States, trained in Central America, and then sent to the contra camps to fight. Americans were involved in running two of the training camps and using Miami Cubans as contras, thus also violating the Neutrality Act.

Since Congress would not fund the Contra operation, the Reagan administration also solicited private funds to support the Contra rebels and was successful in gaining support from American right-wing groups and individuals. The largest single private donor among these was Pat Robertson's Christian Broadcast Network (CBN), which contributed between three and seven million dollars in contra aid.

Between November 21 and 25, 1987, Attorney General Ed Meese launched an inquiry into the Iran-Contra scandal at the request of the President. Meese then informed senior White House officials a day in advance of the impending document review, and immediately thereafter, Oliver North and his subordinates shredded most of the documents connected to the Iran-Contra affair. As a consequence of the headstart given by the Attorney General to those involved, the full scope of the scandal could never be completely known. North's actions (and Meese's) were essentially acts of Obstruction of Justice, one of the same charges that led to Richard Nixon's resignation in the previous decade.

Reagan first admitted on November 13, 1987, that he had ordered the covert Iran-Contra operation under John Poindexter and Lt. Colonel Oliver North, though he denied that the United States had sold arms to Iran in exchange for hostages. Furthermore, on May 15, 1988, Reagan stated that the arms-to-the-Contras covert scheme was "my idea to begin with." Reagan later changed his story, however, and said that he couldn't remember whether he had known about the operation or not. This was despite the possession by Congress of taped phone conversations of Reagan asking Poindexter if the arms did, in fact, get to the contras.

Upon reading the Congressional Report on the Iran-Contra scandal, CBS and National Public Radio correspondent Daniel Schorr stated:

> "What really emerges from this report is a picture of a President who doesn't want to know all the details of the things that he has ordered. He sits there and dreams. He dreams about freedom fighters. He dreams that in Nicaragua—and in Angola and in Afghanistan—there are these people, anti-communist freedom fighters. Boy, you could make a really great movie about these guerillas who selflessly fight for freedom against the Soviet horror. And he says, 'I think Congress is wrong to say we can't arm them. I want them kept alive.'"

In late 1986, the public began to learn some of the details of the scandal, and Reagan's immense popularity suffered a decline. Robert McFarlane unsuccessfully attempted suicide, and many of the other architects of the policy encountered serious legal problems; but the President—whose defense before a congressional committee of investigation substantially consisted of "I don't remember"—managed to regain his equilibrium. Indeed, it was during this troubled time in his presidency that the First Lady showed her mettle because she threw her influence behind a massive overhaul of the personnel in the administration—a move that most scholars credit for having helped him rescue the balance of his term.

The Congressional Committee that was constructed to investigate the Iran-Contra scandal included 26 persons, 17 of whom had favored Contra aid and were considered loyal to the President. As a consequence, the Committee essentially ignored the damning evidence against Reagan and chose to do nothing. By that time, Reagan was near the end of his term anyway, so the idea of impeachment and removal was, in a sense, pointless. President George H. W. Bush later pardoned Oliver North and John Poindexter, and a scandal that some view as a greater Constitutional breach than Watergate was essentially swept under the rug.

REAGAN AND GORBACHEV

Richard Nixon, who was an ardent cold warrior early in his career, was responsible for normalizing U.S. relations with Communist China. Another ardent cold warrior, Ronald Reagan, built a warm camaraderie with his Soviet counterpart, Mikhail Gorbachev, that led not only to improved relations between the United States and the U.S.S.R. while the Soviet leader implemented reforms that would lead to the collapse of the Soviet empire not long after Reagan left office.

In June 1987, President Reagan had given a speech in West Berlin—then a divided city in a divided country—in which he had memorably proclaimed, "Mr. Gorbachev, tear down this wall!" The wall in question was the Berlin Wall, which then separated east and west, preventing those living under communist rule from leaving. Six months later, Gorbachev made a trip to Washington on terms sufficiently friendly that at one point he plunged into a crowd of Washingtonians and greeted them in the style of an American politician. How did the change come about?

In the first place, Mikhail Gorbachev, chosen to lead his country in 1985, was a new-style Soviet leader, with a keen sense of urgency about repairing his country's economy. So eager was he to achieve that goal that he was willing to contemplate bold new initiatives, including a scaling-down of the arms race so that the Soviet Union could invest its resources in non-military ways. Although Gorbachev had intended to maintain some form of socialism and maintained that he remained a communist, he implemented the twin reforms of *perestroika*, which was essentially capitalist restructuring of the Soviet economy, and *glasnost*, which was a policy of openness and democratization. Toward the end of relieving cold war tensions, Gorbachev made numerous unilateral moves—putting a stop to nuclear testing and calling for on-site verification, and unilaterally halting the ongoing installation of Soviet intermediate-range missiles aimed at Europe. Gorbachev removed Andrei Gromyko, a cold war hardliner, from his position as foreign minister that Gromyko had held for almost three decades and replaced him with a more accommodating Eduard Shevardnadze. Gorbachev also reached out to the rest of the world, seeking technological assistance from Japan and West Germany.

Secondly, Mrs. Reagan, who had an ever-vigilant eye for burnishing her husband's image, believed that his legacy should be a peaceful one; and, by all accounts, she lobbied her husband to that end. Further, President Reagan himself had the imagination to meet Gorbachev halfway, though Gorbachev's changes were initially met with great skepticism in the United States. Fi-

Ronald Reagan and his chief-of-staff Donald Regan during the 1985 Geneva Summit with Soviet leader Mikhail Gorbachev *(Library of Congress)*

nally, given the political difficulties engendered by Iran-Contra, Reagan needed the good publicity brought about by the friendly meetings with a former foe.

The two leaders met for the first time in Geneva in November 1985, the first such meeting since 1979. On this occasion they concluded no agreements but came away with the dawning of a personal connection, though their wives found each other to be insufferable. Raisa Gorbachev was a highly educated woman with a doctorate in philosophy and a broad knowledge of global political issues while Nancy was an ex-actress with little in-depth political knowledge and consulted astrologers. The women could find little common ground. Similarly, Mikhail Gorbachev proved to have superior knowledge of global affairs and familiarity with details that caused President Reagan some embarrassment; however, the two experienced a remarkable absence of hostilities.

Their next encounter, a dramatic one, took place in Reykjavik, Iceland in 1986. They came very close to a major reduction in lethal weaponry. Here the sticking point was Reagan's devotion to "Star Wars," or the Strategic Defense Initiative (SDI), an extremely costly and ambitious missile defense program that, the Soviets argued, would destabilize the balance of power. Gorbachev offered what became known as the "grand compromise"—a halt in American research to-ward "Star Wars" in exchange for major Soviet reductions in nuclear weapons. Reagan, however, refused to consider any proposal that endangered the development of SDI since the entire idea had been his brainchild in 1983. In 1987, the breakthrough came, however ac-cording to Richard Reeves, because the Soviets had concluded that Star Wars was never going to work. The two former adversaries agreed to ban all land-based intermediate-range nuclear missiles in Europe in what became known as the Intermediate-Range Nuclear Forces Treaty (INF Treaty). Gorbachev also continued with more changes, agreeing to a United Nations mediation proposal calling for a Soviet troop withdrawal from Afghanistan. Gorbachev then visited the United States in December 1988, and he became the first Soviet Premier since Khrushchev in 1960 to speak before the United Nations General Assembly. Whereas Khrushchev's speech had included a cold war shoe-pounding tirade, Gorbachev's included an announce-ment of huge reductions in Soviet conventional military capabilities. The cold war was over; and Reagan and Gorbachev, whatever else might belong to their respective legacies, earned glowing mention in the media in this regard, though in retrospect it is clear that most of the movement came unilaterally from Gorbachev.

IMMIGRATION REFORM

As we have already learned, the Immigration Act of 1965 brought in many millions of newcomers, far more than Congress had antici-pated when it passed the law originally. By the mid-80s, there was growing concern about the influx of undocumented workers. In 1986 Congress passed the Immigration Reform and Control Act. Aimed at slowing down the flow of illegal immigrants, the act imposed sanc-tions on employers who knowingly hired those without documents. It also offered amnesty to millions of people who had arrived before 1982. What it did not do, however, was "fix" the problem, a problem that recurs in many parts of the world when desperately poor people seek access to a relatively well-off country.

REAGAN'S LEGACY

Even his most severe critics would concede that Ronald Reagan had a profound impact on the nation. Though he spoke warmly of Franklin Delano Roosevelt, his policies, in fact, did more to unravel the various safeguards created by the New Deal than did those of any president since 1945. Beyond the specifics of policy, Reagan used the bully pulpit of the presidency to convince a goodly proportion of his fellow Americans that "government is the problem"—though when it comes to tampering with Social Security and reducing the size of the federal government, neither he nor any of his successors to date has had much luck. Reagan introduced deregulation into the economy; but the results were mixed as the 1980s witnessed more bank failures than any decade since the Great Depression, and the taxpayers were stuck with a multi-billion dollar bailout of the failed Savings and Loan industry. Reagan also doubled American military spending, but he did so while cutting taxes and thus tripled the national debt from $700 billion in 1981 to over $2 trillion by the time he left office.

Tellingly, Reagan's personal hero among his predecessors was Calvin Coolidge, a choice made on the basis of Coolidge's laissez-faire, pro-business approach to governance. Coolidge, however, presided over balanced budgets in the 1920s due to a high tariff policy—in contrast to the free trading Ronald Reagan. Similar to Coolidge, Reagan's White House years followed a period of rapid social change, change alienating to conservative voters in what are now known as the "red states" owing to their seemingly reliable Republican voting habits. Much as the changes of the progressive era helped set the stage for the success of Republican conservatives in the 1920s, the rapid social changes of the 1960s and 1970s no doubt helped create the constituency for the Reagan Revolution.

Though slightly tainted by the Iran-Contra Scandal, President Reagan largely upheld his reputation as the "Teflon President" (nothing politically negative seemed to stick to him) and has perhaps become even more popular in the years after he left office. As President, Reagan typically charted a general course—whether it was tax cuts, less government, or a stronger military—and delegated authority to others to carry out the larger policy. President Reagan was America's oldest President, falling asleep in Cabinet meetings, taking regular afternoon naps, and, some say, showing the early signs of the Alzheimer's disease that would eventually take his life. Reagan spent more of his presidency on vacation than any previous President and generally did not arrive for work before 9:00 a.m, after which he first stopped to feed the squirrels before moving on to other business. Chief of Staff James Baker relays a story of how he once chastised the President for not reading a briefing book that Baker had given him the night before in preparation for an important meeting the next day. The President's response was, "Well Jim, the *Sound of Music* was on last night." If anything, Reagan proved that one could be considered a successful President without being involved in many of the details.

THE ELECTION OF 1988

Would Reaganism survive the end of Reagan's presidency? With President Reagan unable to run again in 1988 due to term limits, Vice President George H. W. Bush quickly emerged as the best candidate to continue the Reagan legacy, although he first had to withstand primary election challenges from Senator Bob Dole of Kansas and televangelist Pat Robertson. Bush was visibly irritated at his Republican challengers. There was a general sense in the Bush camp that it was simply "his turn," since he had waited patiently for eight years as a loyal vice president to Reagan during Reagan's Presidency. Nevertheless, the Bush camp would be forced to prove their mettle against more formidable Republican opponents than they had hoped. To make matters worse, Bush was not generally viewed as a dynamic personality type and was even referenced frequently in the media as a "wimp." For most Republicans, however, Bush was essentially viewed as "Reagan without the charm," and Bush was expected to continue the low tax, strong defense policies that Reagan had earlier initiated.

Polls, however, suggested that Bush lacked Reagan's popularity among women voters, however, so Bush chose Dan Quayle, a youthful Congressman from Indiana as his running mate in an attempt to appeal to women voters. For their part, the Democrats chose the well-respected governor of Massachusetts, Michael Dukakis, a political moderate and son of Greek immigrants and who personified the "self-made man" story that sells so well to the American electorate, as their nominee, with Lloyd Bentsen of Texas as the vice presidential nominee to balance the ticket geographically. Indeed, Bush, Dukakis, and Bentsen all had impressive resumes, and even Quayle had served in Congress for several terms. Bush, in particular had been a Congressman, Nixon's Ambassador to the United Nations, and the head of the CIA, among other things.

The Quayle selection, however, quickly turned against George Bush. Democrats criticized Quayle for ducking out of the Vietnam War by serving in the Indiana National Guard. Quayle further hurt Bush's campaign with repeated verbal gaffes that essentially became known as "Qualyespeak." Quayle quickly proved himself to be a less than adept public speaker, appearing nervous (even frightened) in front of television cameras, often fumbling his way through prepared speeches, and his extemporaneous comments frequently defied comprehension. For example, Quayle once exclaimed, "It isn't pollution that's harming the environment. It's the impurities in the air and water that are doing it." Quayle also stated in a manner most humorous to Democrats, "I am not part of the problem. I am a Republican." Finally, Quayle defended himself against the critics of his gaffes by stating, "I stand by all the misstatements that I've made."

Quayle and his gaffes soon became the butt of numerous jokes from late-night comedians, and the public and the media characterized Quayle as "stupid"—a label that would prove impossible for the Republicans to remove once it had been affixed.

The Democrats also painted the Republican candidate as the son of privilege, his father Prescott Bush having been both a partner in a top Wall Street firm and a United States Senator. At first, George Bush badly trailed Dukakis in the polls, with critics suggesting that he lacked the common touch required of a good campaigner. Then his staff decided to go negative, and through his negative propaganda, Bush was successfully able to tie Dukakis to most of the libertine social and cultural stances that conservatives had come to identify with "liberals." Given that Republicans expected their candidate to continue the Reagan legacy, Bush offered no real changes for the future, instead arguing, "We don't need radical new directions."

Without any new and exciting program to promote, Bush instead concentrated on attacking Michael Dukakis' record as governor of Massachusetts. In particular, the Republicans made mileage from their criticism of a furlough program for convicted felons in Massachusetts' state prison system. The Massachusetts furlough program that the Republicans so disparaged was actually initiated by Dukakis' Republican predecessor and simply inherited and continued by Dukakis, a fact that the Republicans neglected to mention. Furthermore, Ronald Reagan had favored a similar policy as governor of California in the 1960s. Nevertheless, the Republicans found and used the case of William Horton, an African-American, who had been serving a life sentence in Massachusetts for murder but was released on a weekend furlough—only to assault a couple in Maryland and rape the woman in the process. The Republicans referred to William Horton as "Willie Horton;" and pro-Bush groups, not directly affiliated with the Republican Party or the candidate, created commercials featuring Horton's unflattering mug shot that explained how Dukakis favored the furlough program that allowed convicted murderers to be released, only to commit crimes again. Dukakis then did the Republicans a favor with an ill-conceived publicity stunt where he donned a military helmet and rode around in a tank. Dukakis' tank episode backfired since he essentially looked, to many, like a *Saturday Night Live* parody of a military leader in a comedy sketch, and Dukakis dropped in the polls.

By November, the name of Willie Horton was as familiar to American voters as the names of the candidates themselves, owing to a television blitz linking Dukakis to Willie Horton and masterminded by campaign operative Lee Atwater—though Bush himself retained his distance from the attacks. The tactics worked, with Bush winning the popular vote by 53.4 percent to 45.6 percent for Dukakis and winning the Electoral College by 426 to 112. It should also be said that Dukakis himself must bear his share of responsibility for his loss because he proved to be a lackluster candidate. The Democrats did retain control of both houses of Congress. Interestingly, shortly before Lee Atwater died of a brain tumor in 1991, he expressed regret about the Willie Horton ads.

THE BUSH PRESIDENCY

FOREIGN POLICY

Within less than a year of Bush's moving into the White House, the world order had begun to change in profound ways, ways unimaginable just a few short years earlier. In June 1989, world attention was focused on China, when thousands of Chinese students held pro-democracy demonstrations in Tiananmen Square in Beijing. The visual images of the unarmed students standing up to the Communist

A lone man faces down a line of tanks in Beijing's Tiananmen Square. *(AP Photo/Jeff Widener)*

government roused feelings of patriotism and sympathy in the United States, but Chinese leader Deng Xiao Peng put down the demonstrations with the Chinese military on June 3 in brutal fashion. Bush responded with an embargo on military goods to China and announced that the United States would not consider reestablishment of good relations with China until the leadership acknowledged the "validity of the pro-democracy movement." On June 20, Bush then halted all contact with the Chinese government.

Bush's "get tough with China" stance, however, turned out to be little more than show and pandering to the anti-communist American right wing. One month later, Bush secretly directed National Security Adviser Brent Scowcroft to restore relations. Before the end of the year, Bush lifted the ban on weapons sales to China and approved loans to businesses dealing with China. In December, NSA Brent Scowcroft officially visited Beijing, thus restoring relations, and China retained its Most Favored Nation Trade status.

THE FALL OF COMMUNISM IN EASTERN EUROPE

In 1989, the Communist regimes that had dominated political life in Eastern Europe since 1945 all collapsed after Gorbachev, in July 1989, renounced the right of any nation to interfere with the sovereignty of another, thus essentially letting the Eastern European nations know that if they overthrew their Soviet-imposed communist governments, Gorbachev would not intervene. The Soviet Union was in dire financial straits from seven decades of their inefficient command economy, combined with the excessive Cold War military spending that had essentially bankrupted the country. Consequently, the Soviets no longer had the energy and resources to militarily control Eastern Europe. Without the Soviet tanks to prop up the illegitimate communist governments, the entire Soviet system in Eastern Europe collapsed like a house of cards.

In Poland, the Solidarity Union forced negotiations with the Communists through strikes and demonstrations. The Communists granted free elections, in which some seats were reserved for Communists. When the elections were held, Solidarity won an overwhelming majority. Further negotiations between Solidarity and the Communists led to the Communists peacefully giving up power in August 1989. The other governments of Eastern Europe would quickly follow the Polish footsteps in a series of bloodless revolutions (although the Romanian Revolution was not "bloodless" since the Romanian rebels assassinated Communist leader Nikolai Ceaucescu). Communists allowed the destruction of the Berlin Wall, one of the Cold War's most vivid symbols, on November 9, 1989; and free elections were held in East Germany in the spring of 1990, with the Democratic opposition winning easily.

In 1990 the two Germanys reunited. Another repressive government, the apartheid regime of South Africa changed its profile in February 1990 when the white leader, F. W. De Klerk, legalized all political parties—including the black-led African National Congress—and ordered the release of the revered black leader Nelson Mandela after a prison stay of 27 years. The pace of the change was breathtaking.

THE COLLAPSE OF THE U.S.S.R.

In the U.S.S.R. in 1990, new political organizations were forming everywhere, and nationalist groups emerged in all 14 Republics. Concurrently, street violence erupted all over the U.S.S.R. In the summer of 1990, Boris Yeltsin led radical reformers in a split with the Communist Party. Gorbachev reacted by increasingly turning to the communist hard-liners for support. In April 1991, Lithuania, Estonia, and Latvia all declared independence, and Gorbachev did not put down the revolts militarily. Realizing that the breakup of the U.S.S.R. was imminent, Soviet military leaders staged a coup against Gorbachev in August of 1991 and placed Gorbachev under arrest. Gorbachev and his wife were held hostage for four days until Boris Yeltsin led the people in the streets to overthrow the coup and free Gorbachev. The main arms of the Soviet Military turned from their military leaders and supported Yeltsin; communism in Russia was essentially finished.

On August 22, Gorbachev returned to power in Moscow, but by December 31, 1991, all 14 of the Soviet Republics had declared their independence. In December, the new leaders of each republic met and agreed to form a new Commonwealth of Independent States. Gorbachev then resigned as the President of the U.S.S.R., which ceased to exist on December 31, 1991. Given the new governments in Eastern Europe, there was no more Warsaw Pact, the formidable alliance formed in 1955 among eastern European nations, including and under the domination of the Soviet Union. Gorbachev was replaced by Boris Yeltsin, and the Russian Federation took the place of the Soviet Union in the United Nations.

As these monumental events of the twentieth century occurred across the waters, George Bush's approach was to adopt what he called a "status quo plus" approach to these developments. Bush used as his road map Secretary of Defense Dick Cheney's "Forward Defense Policy," where the now-defunct Soviet Union was still viewed as a threat that should be contained. Furthermore, Cheney's Forward Defense Policy called for the continuation of a forward American military presence throughout the globe. Bush himself essentially accepted the Cheney view that the Soviet Union should still be viewed as a threat. Instead of immediately assisting the Eastern Europeans in their transition to capitalist democracies, Bush was cautious and hesitant to alter the American approach to eastern Europe. Bush at first even opposed the reunification of Germany, fearing that a reunited Germany posed another "threat." Bush then only changed his position on German reunification after it became clear that reunification was inevitable. It also became clear very quickly that the old Soviet Union and communist threat were clearly gone, but Cheney's "Forward Defense Policy" premised on containing the Soviet Union would remain in place throughout the Bush Presidency.

Some scholars argue that such a forward defense policy was no longer necessary due to the end of the cold war; but many other scholars argue that the United States and the rest of the world have still not quite figured out what the new international system will look like because, for all of its terrors, the Cold War did create a kind of stability. What has, for the moment, replaced the bipolar world divided between the Soviet and the American superpowers—with a scattering of non-aligned states—has been the unquestioned hegemony of only one superpower, the United States, and this situation has caused misgivings, even among countries traditionally friendly to the United States.

Important treaties to reduce arms followed the collapse of the traditional adversary, but the U.S. continues to have an immense defense budget, now justified on the basis of the war on terror. Thus the hoped for "peace dividend" whereby domestic needs might benefit from the cooling-off of the decades-long competition with the Soviet Union has never materialized.

OPERATION JUST CAUSE

In Central America President Bush took a more hands-off approach than had Reagan. Indeed, Reagan's foreign policy there had been a notable failure, not having produced any concrete positive results. Despite the greater restraint, however, in December 1989 American troops invaded Panama so as to capture the Panamanian leader, Manuel Noriega, a long-time drug trafficker, for trial (and conviction) in Florida.

Noriega had been the head of the Panamanian military in 1983 and became the Head of State in Panama in 1984 with American CIA help. Noriega had also cooperated with the CIA against the Sandinistas in Nicaragua in the 1980s and was confident that the United States government was a friend who supported his regime, especially since Bush had been so heavily involved in the Iran-Contra affair. In 1988, however, Noriega was indicted by a grand jury in Miami and Tampa, Florida, for drug trafficking, gun running, and money laundering, some of it associated with his role in the Iran-Contra operation. Noriega's troubles were compounded in November 1989, when he lost the Panamanian election and then followed the defeat at the polls with a refusal to vacate office. Noriega then had his electoral opponents severely beaten, and their battered and bloody images were shown on international television. Given this gross violation of the democratic process and human rights, coupled with his status as a wanted fugitive in Florida, the Bush administration denounced the Noriega government and asked him to step down.

On December 15, 1989, Panama's National Assembly named Noriega head of government and proclaimed that Panama was in a "State of War" with the United States. The next day, Panamanian police beat four, off-duty United States servicemen, one of which was shot and killed. The Panamanian police also roughed up one of the officer's wives. That officer and his wife turned out to be personal friends of President George H. W. Bush, who was incensed that the Panamanians had put their hands all over his friend's wife. According to Colin Powell, the attack was very personal to the President, and he believed that retribution against Noriega would be a "just cause."

Bush responded with "Operation Just Cause," an American invasion of Panama on December 20, 1989. Twelve thousand troops landed and combined with the 12,000 United States troops already present in Panama for the invasion. Noriega attempted to flee from the invading force and hide in the Vatican Embassy, but then he surrendered to the United States on December 31. The invasion was considered a smashing success, but 23 United States soldiers were killed, as were 4,000 Panamanians, many who were civilians. Noriega was taken to Miami where he was imprisoned and convicted on drug charges stemming from his 1989 indictment.

PERSIAN GULF WAR

In 1990 came Bush's greatest foreign policy challenge when Iraq invaded the neighboring Kuwait, Iraq's leader, Saddam Hussein, having made the miscalculation that the United States would look the other way. Iraq had recently concluded its war with Iran, with a loss of some 400,000 lives. In the aftermath of the Iran-Iraq war, when

Saudi Arabia and Kuwait had flooded the world market with oil, Kuwait continued to produce oil at a rate of 40 percent over OPEC quotas and demanded payment of the $14 billion that Iraq owed to Kuwait. The continued production over the OPEC quotas angered Saddam Hussein of Iraq, who viewed the cheating on OPEC quotas as damaging to Iraq's economy and a hindrance to his ability to pay his international debts of $98 billion. Saddam Hussein was also un-enthusiastic about repaying the loans to Kuwait because he believed that his war with Iran had saved Kuwait from imminent takeover by Iranian Shiite revolutionaries. While Kuwait had supported the Iraqi war against Iran with billions in oil money, the Iraqis had paid with their lives; and Saddam Hussein viewed Kuwaiti aid as insufficient. Kuwait announced another increase in oil production one day after the Iran-Iraq truce—further angering Saddam Hussein. Saddam declared that he considered cheating on OPEC quotas to be "war on Iraq" and threatened retaliation. Saddam revealed that for every dollar that oil declined, Iraq would lose $1 billion annually. Saddam also, probably accurately, accused Kuwait of horizontal drilling near the Kuwait-Iraq border.

Facing war debts and a disgruntled population, Saddam hoped that access to Kuwaiti oil would shore up his rule. Because of ships sunk in the Shatt al-Arab Waterway during the Iran-Iraq war, Iraq had also lost the use of the waterway, its most important access waterway to the Persian Gulf. Kuwait possessed a fine port and coastline on the Gulf that Saddam Hussein coveted. Thus, Saddam Hussein had a number of motives for an invasion and takeover of Kuwait. A takeover of Kuwait would not only solve some of his debt problems, but also gain him better Gulf access and allow him to shut down Kuwaiti overproduction of oil, thus forcing an increase in oil prices.

On June 25, 1990, U.S. Ambassador to Iraq April Glaspie assured Saddam Hussein that the United States would not get involved in a dispute between two Arab neighbors. Glaspie testified before Congress, "I told him we would defend our vital interests, support our friends in the Gulf, and defend their sovereignty and integrity. My main mistake was that I did not realize he was stupid." With what he evidently believed was assurance from Glaspie, Saddam Hussein apparently believed that he could invade his neighbor and the United States would not intervene. August 2, 1990, Saddam Hussein's Iraqi army invaded Kuwait, and the conquest and occupation was completed in only eight hours. The United Nations Security Council reacted to the Iraqi aggression by condemning the invasion and voting 14 to 0 to demand withdrawal. The United States and the U.S.S.R. issued a Joint Statement of Condemnation, and the United Nations Security Council unanimously imposed trade sanctions. Saddam countered with an attempt to gain sympathy from his other Arab neighbors by announcing a peace proposal that involved the withdrawal of Israel from the occupied territories while Saddam withdrew from Kuwait.

In response to the invasion, President Bush and the members of his administration engaged in skillful diplomacy so as to convince not only traditional American allies but also most of the Arab and Islamic world to support his call for an economic boycott of Iraq. George Bush denounced Saddam Hussein's peace proposal, arguing that there could be no "linkage" between the Iraqi invasion of Kuwait and the Israeli/Palestinian issue. Meanwhile, Amnesty International published a report portraying widespread arrests, torture, and summary executions in Kuwait. Bush demanded that Iraq withdraw from Kuwait and, when Iraq did not do so, immediately began "Operation Desert Shield," building United States troop strength in Saudi Arabia to 580,000 in preparation for an invasion.

The war in the Persian Gulf, however, was a tough sell in Congress, even though the Iraqis had made an unprovoked attack on Kuwait. Memories of Vietnam were still quite fresh, and the vote revealed how divided Congress was. Bush's request for authorization of help for Kuwait passed the House by 250 to 183 and the Senate by 52 to 47. When war came, the assault on Iraq was of overwhelming force; and the hostilities only lasted until March 1. On January 16, 1991, the United States began a 42-day bombing operation in Iraq and Kuwait. On January 18, Saddam fired 12 SCUD missiles at Israel, and he fired three more on January 22, in an attempt to goad Israel into the war and, thereby, divide the Arab coalition that had joined the United States against him. Israel denounced the attacks, but realizing that any Israeli action against Iraq could unite all Arab nations against them, stayed out of the war so as not to divide the coalition that Bush had forged.

In an attempt to stave off the imminent destruction of his army, at 12:00 Greenwich mean time (GMT) on February 23, Iraq announced the acceptance of a Soviet peace plan that called for immediate and unconditional withdrawal from Kuwait. In spite of his knowledge of this development, at 18:00 GMT, George Bush ordered General Norman Schwarzkopf to expel the Iraqis from Kuwait. The ground war to expel the Iraqi military from Kuwait followed on February 24 and took 100 hours. At 10:00 GMT February 24, the United States launched its ground war. At 21:30 GMT February 24, Saddam ordered a withdrawal from Kuwait. Retreating Iraqis then set 640 Kuwaiti oil wells ablaze in one of the worst environmental disasters in human history. The black petroleum cloud that developed over Kuwait was clearly visible from satellites in outer space. By noon on February 26, the Iraqi troops had withdrawn from Kuwait City and its suburbs, and a long convoy of Iraqi vehicles was on its way to Basra along a six-lane highway. As it approached Mitla ridge, 20 miles north of Kuwait City, the Iraqi convoy was hit in a massive attack by U.S. ground-attack aircraft. U.S. planes would attack the convoy for the next 40 hours until the truce of 08:00 local time on February 28.

The end came all the more quickly because President Bush and his advisors decided to stop short of trying to topple Saddam Hussein. They felt, it seems, that they could not carry the coalition along with them, had they attempted regime change, and they also wondered who might replace Saddam. The toll of the war was disproportionate with some 40,000 Iraqis dying as opposed to 240 members of the allied troops. The Security Council of the United Nations then demanded that Iraq provide information about its various weapons systems, pursuant to Resolution 687. Most Iraqis died in the bombings (30,000 in the convoy alone), but some were buried in their bunkers by United States bulldozers when the Iraqis were given orders to surrender or suffocate. Americans generally approved of the attack on the retreating convoy, but many Arabs did not; and the event was reported in the Arab media as "the most terrible harassment of a retreating army from the air in the history of warfare."

Before the Iraqis fled Kuwait, Iraqi soldiers had looted virtually everything of value, even eating most of the animals at the Kuwaiti National Zoo and thus further justifying the war to the American people. Although many conservatives, such as future Undersecretary of State Paul Wolfowitz, argued that the United States military should go all the way into Iraq and remove Saddam Hussein from power, Bush would not do so because the United Nations Resolution did not call for ousting Hussein. For Bush to do so would surely destroy the international coalition. Bush also recognized that an impotent Iraq would make Iran the most powerful military nation in the region without a chief rival; hence, leaving Saddam Hussein in power made sense in the Persian Gulf balance of power. Ousting Hussein, as George W. Bush would discover in the next decade, would also mean a costly long-term occupation army with many more potential casualties and "another Vietnam" that the elder Bush was determined not to repeat. Finally, Bush had hoped that Saddam's own military officers would overthrow him, but after the war, Saddam carried out an internal purge on all of his political opposition within Iraq. A gruesome videotape was also circulated throughout Iraq and the Middle East that showed Saddam's executed military officers hanging on meat hooks, thus discouraging others from coup attempts.

Soldiers of the 2nd Brigade of the 3rd Infantry Division during exercise Desert Spring *(AP Photo/Ron Haviv/VII)*

Immediately after the war, Saddam Hussein also faced a Shiite uprising in the south that was aided by Iran. Iran sent not only supplies and weapons, but thousands of "volunteers" crossed the border into Iraq. On March 9, 1991, Saddam sent his Republican Guard into the South to put down the Shiite rebellion. The United States did not intervene because the Bush administration favored Saddam Hussein to Shiite revolutionaries. After all, the United States had aided Saddam Hussein in his war with Iran in the 1980s specifically to prevent a takeover by Shiite revolutionaries. Thirty thousand died in Saddam's crushing defeat of the Shiite rebellion, and 70,000 Shiites fled to Iran. The rebellion was over in a week. National Security adviser Brent Scowcroft told ABC News:

> "I frankly wish the uprising hadn't happened. I envisioned a post-war government being a military government ... It's the colonel with the brigade patrolling his palace that's going to get Saddam if someone gets him."

Similarly, Richard Haas, then director for Near East Affairs on the NSC stated, "Our policy is to get rid of Saddam, not his regime." Obviously, Democracy (or the lack of it) in Iraq was not the highest American priority in 1992.

Simultaneous with the Iraqi Shiite rebellion in 1991, Kurdish nationalists rebelled in northern Iraq as a 100,000-man Kurdish Auxiliary force in Saddam's army changed sides and turned on Saddam.

Turkey feared that an independent Kurdistan in Iraq might lead Kurds in Turkey to also revolt and demand that part of Turkey be united with a new Kurdistan. Consequently, Turkey urged President Bush not to intervene in the Iraqi Kurdish rebellion. Bush viewed the rebellion as an Iraqi civil war with potential as another Vietnam that should be avoided, so the United States again remained on the sidelines while Saddam's army quickly put down the rebellion, with the result that an estimated 1.5 million Kurds were forced to flee to Turkey.

In 1992, George Bush was voted out as President, and Iraq began challenging the no-fly zones imposed by the United States. The lame-duck President Bush, however, continued his resolve to keep Saddam subdued, and in December, the United States shot down an Iraqi MIG fighter. On January 10, 1993, Iraq refused to allow United Nations inspectors to use airspace south of the 32nd parallel as demanded by the United States. The United States responded on January 13 by bombing five Iraqi air bases, and on January 17, the United States hit an Iraqi factory with a cruise missile. The next day, United States' jets hit 75 Iraqi targets south of the 32nd parallel of southern Iraq. On January 21, Baghdad announced acceptance of United Naitons inspections so that the new American President could "study the no-fly zone," and thus was the status of the American-Iraqi situation upon the inauguration of Bill Clinton in January 1993.

DOMESTIC ISSUES

Early in George H. W. Bush's Presidency, the new Republican Executive quickly revealed that he was not genuinely the flag bearer for the Reagan legacy. Although Bush had well-played the part of the Vice Presidential loyalist during Reagan's tenure in office, Bush demonstrated his private disdain for his presidential predecessor when he quietly instituted a purge of Reagan loyalists from the federal executive branch. In the words of one close friend of Ronald Reagan, there was a "systematic purge ... of "anyone with any association with the Reagan-Nixon-Goldwater wing of the Party. Bush did not, however, favor a complete abandonment of the conservative "less government" mantra; and he used the veto 36 times during his tenure in office to block Congressional bills that would have lifted abortion restrictions, extended unemployment benefits, raised taxes, mandated family and medical leave for workers, and reformed campaign financing. The veto of such measures was not only consistent with Reaganism, but also was perhaps to be expected, given "divided government" with Democratic control of Congress and Republican control of the Presidency.

Bush, however, quickly embarked on a more activist approach to governing and implemented a much more hands-on management approach than Reagan. For example, billing himself as the "Environmental President," Bush signed the Clean Air Act of 1990, perhaps the strongest, most comprehensive environmental law in history. The Clean Air Act required power plants to cut sulfur dioxide emissions by more than 50 percent by the year 2000, and oil companies were required to develop cleaner-burning gasoline. Clearly, the Clean Air Act was hardly consistent with the deregulatory push of the Reagan administration and was instead the same type of federal government regulation of industry that conservatives had been fighting against for decades.

THE AMERICANS WITH DISABILITIES ACT

On July 26, 1990 President Bush signed into law the Americans with Disabilities Act, a law that drew upon and completed earlier civil rights activism by members of other disadvantaged groups. For decades the disabled had organized and protested; this law was the result of their years of effort. Not only did it prohibit discrimination against the handicapped in employment but also it mandated that many types of buildings and facilities contain provisions for disabled access. Americans have now become used to the sight of curb cuts, for example, which facilitate the movement of those in wheelchairs. It should be noted that the law, particularly as it relates to issues of employment, has generated litigation, as courts struggle to refine the meaning of terms such as "reasonable" accommodation or "essential" tasks of the job. Conservative opponents argued that ADA constituted a massive unfunded federal mandate to the states that forced states and local governments to spend billions in order to ensure that public accommodations were handicapped-accessible. The measure was, therefore, not only a violation of conservative laissez-faire ideology and a reversal of Reagan's "deregulation," but it also eroded state sovereignty by removing state discretion concerning the handicapped and thus violated the traditional conservative preference for the preservation of states' rights in juxtaposition with national power.

AN ERUPTION OF RAGE IN LOS ANGELES

In March 1991 police in a tough neighborhood in the San Fernando Valley section of Los Angeles gave chase to a speeding car. When

A Korean shopping mall burns in Los Angeles during the riots that followed the "not guilty" verdict of three policemen involved in the beating of Rodney King *(AP Photo/Nick Ut)*

they succeeded in stopping its African American occupant, Rodney King, he resisted arrest and appeared to be high. The police subdued him with great use of force, force that looked like a police beating as captured on video by a nearby resident. The video was widely aired, and as a result four policemen were charged with the beatings; but the trial was then moved to nearby Simi Valley in Ventura County, a largely white enclave. Testimony during the televised trial revealed many less than flattering facts about the LAPD. The department, for example, had historically been led by more than one white Chief of Police who had been insensitive about race, thus perpetuating a culture inappropriate to a multiethnic city. Moreover, police training was revealed to be woefully inadequate.

In April 1992, three of the four policemen were found not guilty, and the all-white jury deadlocked on the fourth. At that point the city's black neighborhoods, particularly South Central, erupted in several days of fighting, looting, and destruction. Such neighborhoods had long been breeding grounds for despair, it should be noted, with high unemployment and other indicators of social distress. Rodney King himself ultimately appeared on television to appeal for calm, saying, "Can we all get along?" When the rioting finally ended, 55 people had lost their lives; and 2,300 had been injured. With some 800 buildings destroyed, there had been an estimated $1 billion worth of property damage. During the fighting, the racial fissures of Los Angeles manifested themselves in ugly ways, blacks against the Korean Americans who owned small shops, for example.

On the third night of the riots President Bush addressed a national television audience and virtually promised that there would be subsequent federal prosecution based on civil rights issues, prosecution which did ensue. In April 1993 a trial on federal charges of civil rights violations ended with two of the four officers having been found guilty. The media were careful not to sensationalize this trial, and the city remained calm when the verdict was announced.

THE CLARENCE THOMAS NOMINATION

The well-respected civil rights lawyer, Thurgood Marshall, had been appointed to the United States Supreme Court by Lyndon Johnson in 1967, the first African American to serve on the nation's highest court. By 1991, at the age of 83, he was ready to step down. He would be difficult to replace, however, for many reasons. President Bush, whose choice of David Souter for the court in 1990 had sailed through, opted to nominate an African American conservative with little judicial experience, Clarence Thomas, to replace Marshall. Democrats on the Senate Judiciary Committee found themselves in a quandary during the hearings about Thomas's nomination. They did not want to appear racist in going after Thomas's relatively slim resume (he had only been a federal judge for 18 months), but, on the other hand, they were leery of Bush's choice because he had spoken out against affirmative action and was suspected of being opposed to *Roe v. Wade*. To make matters worse for Bush, the National Association for the Advancement of Colored People (NAACP), the leading organization for the championing of African-American causes, opposed Thomas' confirmation.

Just as the hearings appeared to be drawing to a close, a new witness came before the committee, Professor Anita Hill of the University of Oklahoma Law School, also African American. She testified that when she had worked for Thomas in the 1980s, first as his assistant in the U.S. Department of Education and then in the Equal Employment Opportunities Commission, he had repeatedly used crudely sexual language in speaking to her, language that had been unpleasant and unwelcome to her. Specifically, Hill alleged that Thomas asked her to view pornographic movies with him and once handed her a soft drink can with a pubic hair on the top. When testifying on his own behalf, Thomas alleged that he was the victim of a "high-tech lynching," thus bringing up the racial issue that Democrats had been so eager to avoid.

The country was riveted by the controversy, with both Hill and Thomas having their proponents. Certain Republicans went on the attack. "She's a little bit nutty, and a little bit slutty," said one. Polls at the time showed that Thomas had the majority of public opinion on his side. The Senate Judiciary Committee investigated the hearings, but dismissed Hill's charges after three days of nationally televised hearings in which other women who came forward with similar allegations were not allowed to testify. In the end, the Senate narrowly confirmed his nomination by a vote of 52 to 48.

University of Oklahoma professor Anita Hill testifies before Congress during the Clarence Thomas Supreme Court confirmation hearings (AP/Wide World Photos)

Though Hill appeared to have lost in the court of public opinion, in fact, the controversy galvanized the women who were on her side, many of whom had themselves been the victims of sexual harassment. What was particularly troubling to the women, by all accounts, was the fact that the Senate Judiciary Committee was all-male, not surprising given the breakdown in the Senate of 98 men and 2 women. In 1992, a number of women set out to rectify that imbalance.

"THE YEAR OF THE WOMAN"

If 1980 was the year in which a gender gap showed up in election returns for the first time, then 1992 was the year in which the promise of having a female voting bloc became fully manifest. An unprecedented number of women ran for office—chiefly as Democrats, though that has begun to change in the early twenty-first century—and an unprecedented number won.

In 1916 Republican Jeannette Rankin of Montana had been elected to the House of Representatives, the first woman in the world to be elected to a national legislature. In 1922 Georgia's Rebecca Latimer Felton served one day in the Senate, appointed to the position as a token by the governor of Georgia as a tricky maneuver to gain favor with newly enfranchised women en route to the accession of the "real" male senator. Progress for women office-holders was slow, both in achieving election and—in the unusual event that they did—in feeling free to articulate issues of concern to other women. Not only did women not vote as a bloc, but also a smaller percentage of them voted at all than did male voters, a pattern that did not change until the 1960s. In 1990 former Senator Margaret Chase Smith told an interviewer: "I never was a woman candidate," as she reflected on her congressional career of more than 30 years, a career that began in the 1940s. "Had I been a woman candidate I never would have been elected."

The birth of modern feminism would begin to induce more women to run than in the past, a few for major office. In 1974 Ella Grasso of Connecticut became the first woman to be elected as governor of a state in her own right, that is, not following the death of a husband or acting as a surrogate for a husband unable to run himself. In 1990 Ann Richards of Texas was elected as governor, a particularly noteworthy race because she had "run as a woman," even going so far as to pose with her hairdresser for campaign literature.

But 1992 was different. That year women raised money for women candidates in unprecedented amounts, drawing on a well of grass-roots anger about the treatment of Anita Hill. The election in November produced a tremendous amount of progress and many firsts. Women in the House had gone from 29 to 48. Women in the Senate had gone from 2 to 6. Carol Moseley-Braun of Illinois became the first African American woman to be elected to the Senate. California became the first state to be represented by two women in the Senate, Dianne Feinstein and Barbara Boxer. Nydia Velasquez of New York became the first Puerto Rican woman elected to the House and Lucille Roybal-Allard of California the first Mexican American woman. Women were also elected to state legislatures in unprecedented numbers, the state of Washington leading the pack with a legislature that was almost 40 percent female. When the new Congress convened in 1993, both Moseley-Braun and Feinstein were appointed to serve on the Senate Judiciary Committee.

Though the pace of change has slowed, women have continued to make progress. As of mid-2006 there are 14 women in the Senate and 67 in the House. Even more impressive is the fact that there are eight women governors, impressive because there have only been 26 women governors in all of American history.

ELEMENTS OF A ONE-TERM PRESIDENCY

During the short Gulf War President Bush was enormously popular, achieving a 91 percent approval rating then according to one poll. Despite effective leadership on several fronts, he seemed as unable to cope with the economy as had Jimmy Carter. With the nation entering a full-fledged recession following the war, with real estate prices and sales stagnating, with unemployment climbing to eight percent, with a growing deficit, Bush effected a compromise budget with congressional Democrats that called for tax increases. Because he had pledged in 1988, "Read my lips; no new taxes," his pragmatism once in office left him vulnerable to enemies in both parties; and the economy was the issue that Bill Clinton would ride to victory in 1992.

CHAPTER 17

AMERICA AT THE TURN OF THE MILLENNIUM

(AP Photo)

In his 1961 inaugural address, the youngest man ever elected president of the United States announced "that the torch has been passed to a new generation of Americans." When John F. Kennedy spoke those words, he meant that America was now led by those shaped in their young adult years by World War II and the early Cold War. In 1993, Kennedy's generation of leaders, embodied by World War II Navy flier George H. W. Bush, handed the torch of White House leadership to yet another generation, the postwar Baby Boomers in the person of William Jefferson Clinton. Eight years later, Bush's own son, George W. Bush, became the second Baby Boomer president.

The nation Bill Clinton and the younger George Bush led during the last decade of the twentieth century and the first decade of the twenty-first differed from that served by World War II veteran-presidents from John Kennedy through the first George Bush. Most crucially, of course, the Cold War was no more. Although many foreign policy challenges existed—from the security of the former Soviet Union's nuclear arsenal to environmental destruction and global warming—most Americans thought about domestic issues as they pulled the levers for Clinton in 1992 and 1996 and Bush in 2000. By 2004, needless to say, the domestic focus would have changed dramatically.

The first two Baby Boomer presidents had much in common. Both born in 1946, they attended prestigious eastern universities—Georgetown and Yale Law School in Clinton's case, Yale and Harvard Business School in Bush's. Neither served in Vietnam, their generation's war, although Bush flew for the Texas National Guard in the late 1960s and early 1970s. Through their thirties, both men lacked the discipline to control destructive impulses. Clinton's extramarital relationships and Bush's drinking caused them and their families great pain. Rumors of illegal drug use in their youth persisted about both. Indeed, Clinton had not entirely vanquished his demons before entering the White House, with unhappy results for his presidential legacy.

Despite their similarities, their routes through life to the White House greatly differed as Clinton came from very humble beginnings. His father died before he was born, and the future president spent his childhood either with his storekeeper-grandparents in the small town of Hope, Arkansas, or with his mother and abusive stepfather. Bright and fascinated by politics—as a delegate to a national youth conference in 1962, he met President Kennedy—Clinton received a Rhodes Scholarship to Oxford University. After law school at Yale, he went home to Arkansas to teach and enter politics. Just shy of 30, he became the state's attorney general and two years later was inaugurated as the nation's youngest governor. Serving as governor for 12 years, he established a reputation as a centrist who sought ways of using government to help people.

Bush was born into a prominent political family. His great grandfather, Sam Bush, was a Wall Street banker as was his grandfather, Prescott Bush, who served Connecticut in the U.S. Senate; and his father made a fortune in the Texas oil business before beginning a distinguished career that culminated in the presidency. Not known for academic excellence, the younger Bush was rejected by the University of Texas law school and scored in the 25th percentile on his Air National Guard exam, though he was accepted at Yale and received his MBA at Harvard. After his experience at Harvard, Bush worked for and had ownership in several oil companies in Midland, Texas and lost a congressional race in 1978 in a west Texas district. With assistance from his family's well-connected friends, Bush became co-owner of the Texas Rangers baseball team in 1986 with relatively little money down. Several years later, after convincing the city of Arlington to build the Rangers a showcase stadium, he sold his interest (for which he had paid slightly more than $600,000) for over $14 million. In 1994, Texans elected him governor, defeating popular moderate Democrat and long time veteran of Texas politics, Ann Richards, to hold his first public office. As the state's chief executive, he received good marks for his ability to work in a bipartisan way with conservative Democrats in the Texas Legislature to achieve his goals, which included reductions in the state's property taxes.

Both Clinton and Bush came to the White House with agendas to pursue, yet they found that changing events and surprising turns—the stuff of history—forced them to alter their plans.

THE CLINTON YEARS

THE ELECTION OF 1992

In the wake of the Gulf War in February 1991, 89 percent of Americans in a Gallup poll approved of President Bush's handling of his job; and his poll numbers remained elevated for some time, discouraging high-profile Democrats such as Governor Mario Cuomo of New York from entering the presidential race. Instead, a group of lesser-known Democrats, whom the press dubbed the "Seven Dwarves," competed for the right to take on Bush. The next year and a half, however, would see the country slide into a prolonged economic recession; and Bush's own ideological preference for laissez-faire would make him appear inattentive and uncaring about the plight of the average American. As unemployment rose to over seven percent in 1992, a large segment of the electorate began to call for bold action against the recession, but Bush would not deliver. Instead, Bush clung to his position that the economy was improving and that others should simply stop saying that it was not. In his contention that the economy was improving, Bush was actually correct because when the third quarter economic numbers were released that fall, they did indeed indicate that the economy was on the upswing. The economic recovery, however, would be too little and too late to save the Bush Presidency.

As Bush's popularity slid in the winter of 1991, Bush fired the unpopular White House Chief of Staff John Sununu, thus separating himself from one of his top advisers. To further complicate things for Bush, former Republican National Committee chief Lee Atwater had died of a brain tumor earlier in the year. Without these advisers, the Bush campaign was unable to articulate a message for his campaign. In the words of one Bush friend, "If you asked him why he wanted to be reelected, he'd have to look at his note cards. That's the fundamental problem at the core."

Arkansas Governor Bill Clinton emerged from the Democratic Party pack to claim his party's nomination, despite questions the press and opponents raised about his marital fidelity, his alleged countercultural past, and his participation in a failed real estate venture in the 1980s. Clinton succeeded largely because of his formidable skills as a campaigner and his moderate stance as a "pro-business" Democrat. A leader of the centrist Democratic Leadership Council, Clinton positioned himself as a "New Democrat" who abandoned the 60s liberalism of many of his primary opponents; and he sought to persuade white middle-class and working-class voters, including those known in the 1980s as Reagan Democrats, that he could be trusted on issues of importance to them. He supported new government spending—a traditional Democratic approach—to combat the recession that had wounded Bush's popularity by early 1992. (The recession made "It's the Economy, Stupid" the Clinton campaign's internal slogan.) At the same time Clinton signaled his support for more conservative social policies than those advocated by Democrats such as 1988 nominee Michael Dukakis. For instance, he favored the death penalty and distanced himself from black activist Jesse Jackson, who had run a strong, but ultimately unsuccessful campaign for the Democratic Presidential nomination in 1988. Clinton also chose a fellow southern moderate, U.S. Senator Albert Gore, Jr., of Tennessee, as his running mate.

Before he could take on Clinton, President Bush faced a primary challenge from Patrick Buchanan, a conservative television commentator and former aide to Presidents Nixon and Reagan. Buchanan ran a spirited but low budget campaign that appealed chiefly to blue-collar Republicans concerned about the recession, strongly pro-life social conservatives, gun advocates, libertarians, and isolationists uncomfortable with Bush's "new world order." Buchanan referred to the President as "King George" and denounced what he termed as the President's "moderate" policies that failed to put America first. Buchanan then embarrassed the President by gaining 37 percent of the vote in the New Hampshire Primary. Buchanan, however, never posed a serious threat to Bush; he won no primaries (his best showing was in New Hampshire where he lost to Bush, 53 percent to 37 percent) and only received 18 votes to Bush's 2,166 at the Republican convention. Still, he raised questions about the president's leadership. As a consequence, Bush was forced to move somewhat to the right so as to prevent alienation of the Buchanan voters, but a rightward move would hinder Bush in his effort to pick up Democratic middle voters in the November general election. Some argue, however, that Buchanan did the most damage to Bush with his performance at the party's Houston convention. There, while endorsing the president, Buchanan turned some centrist voters away from the GOP with a right-wing speech warning of "a religious war going on in our country for the soul of America."

As the Republican nominee, President Bush ran a lackluster campaign that reflected his inability to define his presidency. He had trouble with, as he put it, "the vision thing." Comfortable and generally successful with foreign policy, he seemed ill at ease dealing with domestic issues such as the fallout from the Los Angeles riots in the spring of 1992. In a series of presidential debates, he seemed detached and unable to connect with audiences as the empathetic Clinton did. During one debate, he glanced at his wristwatch as though wondering when his torment would end. In contrast to Bush's lackluster campaign, Democratic candidate and Arkansas governor Bill Clinton articulated a more dynamic campaign and better-defined message. Clinton stole some of the Republican thunder by denouncing welfare and calling for tax cuts to the middle class, as well as advocating the use of the powers of the federal government to combat the recession. The Bush camp mistakenly did not view Clinton as a serious threat in the spring of 1992, however, because of problems in Clinton's personal life that included marital infidelity. A Bush aide even wrote the President in April 1992, and told him, "The swing voters have dismissed Bill Clinton as a serious alternative to President Bush."

A third candidate, billionaire businessman Ross Perot, entered, then left, and then re-entered the presidential race as an independent during 1992. Perot popularized concern about the expansive federal budget deficits of the Reagan-Bush years and presented himself as a can-do, problem-solving executive. Although he appealed to many Americans weary of excessive partisan bickering, his behavior struck others as too mercurial—perhaps too unstable—for the White House. Many wondered about Perot's suitability for office when he alleged that the Bush administration had sought to disrupt his daughter's wedding.

In the end, Perot captured an impressive 18.9 percent of the popular vote, a higher percentage than any third-party candidate had received since Theodore Roosevelt ran as a Progressive in 1912. Polling of Perot supporters, however, revealed that one third would have supported Bush had Perot not been in the race, one third would have supported Clinton, and one third would not have voted at all; consequently, it is unclear whether or not Perot's candidacy impacted the election's outcome. Clinton would essentially defeat both Bush and Perot in the Presidential debates, thus harming Bush's popularity. The approval ratings of the President fell even further just five days before the election when it was revealed by Lawrence Walsh, the independent counsel investigating the Iran-Contra affair, that Bush had known as Vice President about the effort to exchange arms for hostages with Iran, an allegation that Bush had long denied. To make matters worse, former Secretary of Defense, Caspar Weinberger was indicted for his role in the affair, further suggesting that Bush was guilty by association. Compounding Bush's electoral problems, the economy was still in recession; and in spite of his tax hike, the debt situation inherited from the Reagan administration continued to spiral out of control, producing a crowding out of credit, rising interest rates, and sluggish economic growth. As a consequence, Bush would suffer the worst loss of any sitting President since William Howard Taft in 1912. Bush won only 37 percent of the popular vote as compared to 43 percent for Clinton and 18 percent for Ross Perot. The 12 years of Republican dominance of the White House that had been initiated by Ronald Reagan had come to an abrupt end.

CLINTON TAKES CHARGE

As he came into office, the youthful Clinton (the second youngest man ever elected president) brought a renewed vigor to the White House. He liked policy "bull sessions" that often lasted into the wee hours of the morning. A self-confessed "policy wonk," he impressed observers with his keen mind. He displayed a surprising lack of personal discipline, however, and allowed an inexperienced White House staff to behave in ways that bothered even Clinton boosters. Summing him up, historian Arthur Schlesinger, Jr., would once say Clinton was "a rare combination of talents and infirmities."

Stressing ethnic and gender diversity in government, Clinton promised "an administration that looks like America." His initial Cabinet included more African Americans (four) and women (four) than any other president's first Cabinet; the number of Hispanics (two) tied the number appointed by President Bush in 1989. In Clinton's second term, former Congressman Norman Mineta became the first Asian American in the Cabinet when he took over the Department of Commerce. In addition, an assistant secretary of housing and urban development, Roberta Achtenberg, was the first openly gay person appointed by a president and confirmed by the Senate. In putting together a Cabinet that drew on the talents of Americans from various backgrounds, Clinton hit a few snags in addition to criticism for playing into "identity politics." Two of his nominees for attorney general, both women, were forced to withdraw when it was revealed each had failed to pay Social Security taxes for her children's nannies. Finally, a third nominee, Janet Reno, a candidate favored by the President's political wife, Hillary, became the first woman to head the Justice Department.

Very early, Clinton realized that his lack of a strong electoral mandate—he had won only 43 percent of the popular vote—limited his policy options. In part to appeal to Perot voters, Clinton concentrated initially more on bringing down the deficit than on stimulating the economy with new spending programs. The president chafed at the prospect of supporting tax and spending policies that made him, as he fumed, such a good Eisenhower Republican. Still, his fiscal and spending proposals, which passed on party-line votes, helped insulate him from conservative charges that he was a "tax and spend" liberal. With the exception of a small increase in gasoline taxes and some higher taxes for the best-off Social Security recipients, the Clinton plan raised taxes only on the wealthiest 1.2 percent of Americans while reducing them for the working poor and small businesses. Moreover, the plan helped cut the deficit by $50 billion from 1993 to 1994 and another $40 billion the next year.

SETBACKS FOR THE CLINTON AGENDA

Clinton suffered political damage when he took on explosive issues at the outset of his administration. He stirred controversy when he sought to fulfill a campaign pledge to end the ban on homosexuals in the military. Congressional opposition, even from key Democrats, and a recalcitrant Joint Chiefs of Staff forced Clinton to accept a compromise policy. Under "don't ask, don't tell," military officials were not to seek out homosexuals for expulsion from the ranks, while gays were to be silent about their sexuality. The policy, which gay civil rights groups initially greeted with guarded optimism, actually led to increased numbers of discharges. "Don't ask, don't tell" ultimately satisfied few on either side of the issue, and this first major public policy battle weakened the new president.

Clinton's unsuccessful struggle to enact new national health care legislation damaged him even more. The 1992 Democratic platform pledged "universal access to quality, affordable health care" for Americans, and polls showed it a popular idea. Clinton appointed a task force, chaired by First Lady Hillary Rodham Clinton, in 1993 to devise a plan. The task force's proposals, submitted to Congress in 1994, envisioned a system of federally regulated private health insurance plans to cover all Americans. Some to Clinton's political left attacked this rather complex "managed competition" idea. They preferred to replace private insurance companies with the government as the "single payer" for health care costs.

Opponents on the political right proved more effective in stopping the Clinton plan. Many Republicans charged incorrectly that it amounted to "socialized medicine," complete with a new bureaucracy and lack of patient choice in the selection of physicians. They also criticized the leadership of the first lady, who enjoyed little popularity with conservatives, in drafting the plan. A trade association of private health insurance companies fueled opposition to the measure by spending millions on a television advertising campaign featuring a middle-class couple, known only as Harry and Louise, expressing theirs fears about the Clinton measure. These conservative attacks turned the public against the administration's plan; and, in the summer of 1994, the Senate let it die. This failure of the centerpiece of Clinton's domestic agenda represented a severe blow to the administration.

THE "GINGRICH REVOLUTION" AND CLINTON'S COMEBACK

In November 1994, Republicans capitalized on Clinton's perceived weakness and swept to power in both houses of Congress. Republicans gained an impressive 52 seats in the House and eight in the Senate (within months, two Democratic senators switched parties to add to the Republican margin). The 104th Congress, which took office in January 1995, was the first controlled by the GOP since the

83rd Congress of 1953–1955. The Republican victory extended to all levels of government; numerous well-known incumbent Democrats lost state races, including Governor Mario Cuomo of New York. Another prominent Democrat, Governor Ann Richards of Texas, lost her re-election bid to former President Bush's oldest son, baseball team co-owner George W. Bush.

Conservative talk radio hosts, led by Rush Limbaugh, contributed significantly to the Republican victory. Limbaugh spent three hours on the national airwaves each weekday blasting Bill and Hillary Clinton as radicals. New Republican members of the 104th Congress recognized Limbaugh's efforts by naming him an honorary member of their freshman class.

A brilliant, "nationalized" campaign also helped Republicans win Congress. GOP congressional candidates signed onto a set of 10 poll-tested items known as the Contract with America. Among other things, the Contract pledged Republicans to reform welfare, reduce crime, and pass constitutional amendments to balance the federal budget and limit the number of terms members of Congress could serve—all popular with the Republican public; but polls suggested that the majority of Americans actually disagreed with the majority of the specific items in the Republican Contract.

Republicans chose as the new Speaker of the House Georgia's Newton Leroy (Newt) Gingrich, an energetic and visionary leader who had spearheaded the Contract with America. Buoyed by his party's victory and his own high approval ratings, the colorful Gingrich quickly became the apparent center of power in Washington. As promised, he brought the 10 items of the Contract with America up for votes within the first 100 days of the new Congress. Few of the Contract items actually became law, and Congress failed to pass the balanced budget or term limits constitutional amendments. Moreover, in 1996, the Supreme Court struck down as unconstitutional one part of the Contract, the line item veto law. Still, Gingrich

Newton Leroy Gingrich *(AP Photo)*

and his Republican colleagues were setting the national agenda and certainly turning national policy in a more conservative direction.

Republican control of Congress and Gingrich's place in the media spotlight (*Time* magazine named the Speaker its 1995 "Man of the Year") appeared to diminish Clinton's importance. The president even found himself protesting his relevance to national politics in an April 1995 press conference. Smelling presidential blood in the water, numerous Republicans prepared to take on the hemorrhaging Clinton in 1996.

Then Clinton's excellent political survival instincts kicked in. Aided by sometime Republican political advisor, Dick Morris, and much to the dismay of liberal Democrats, the president responded to the Republicans by tacking to the right. "The era of big government is over," declared Clinton in his 1996 State of the Union Address, and later that year he signed welfare reform legislation formulated largely by Republicans. Under it, the number of welfare recipients dropped and the entitlement to welfare for impoverished children ended. Liberals complained that, for the first time since the Great Depression, children from poor families were not guaranteed financial assistance. Angering gay rights' supporters, the president also signed the Defense of Marriage Act, which permitted any state to refuse to recognize same-sex marriages contracted in another state. (No state actually allowed same-sex marriages in 1996, although Hawaii seemed on the verge of doing so. In 2000, Vermont became the first state to allow something like marriage—a "civil union"—for partners of the same sex.) On the economic front, Clinton also pushed to lower the budget deficit even more.

While agreeing to cuts in programs for the poor, Clinton shrewdly set himself up as the protector of popular middle-class entitlement programs such as Social Security and Medicare. When Republicans insisted on making cuts in Medicare, Clinton refused to go along. In resulting showdowns with Congress, Clinton even allowed all but the most important functions of the federal government to cease for a few days rather than agree to GOP budget demands. As national parks closed and Social Security checks stopped, the public overwhelmingly blamed congressional Republicans for the impasse. Gingrich and his allies caved to Clinton, whose approval ratings rose while those of congressional Republican leaders sank.

ELECTION OF 1996

No less than eight Republicans announced their candidacy for the Presidency in 1996, including Phil Gramm, Pat Buchanan, Bob Dole, publishing magnate Steve Forbes, California Governor Pete Wilson, and Lamar Alexander of Tennessee. Dole was the big money favorite, but his campaign essentially stumbled out of the gate in the 1996 primary season. Forbes stole some of Dole's thunder with a proposal to eliminate the graduated tax structure and replace it with a flat tax, and Pat Buchanan, a perpetual darling of the far right, defeated Dole in the New Hampshire primary. Dole regrouped, and in spite of the presence of Southerners Gramm and Alexander, did well in the Southern primaries and essentially locked up the Republican nomination prior to the convention. At the Republican Convention in July, Dole abandoned his history of support for fiscal responsibility and announced his support for tax cuts and reform of the tax code to produce a "fairer, flatter tax." Democrats charged that Dole's tax cuts would create massive deficits, but Dole, echoing Ronald Reagan, promised that he would offset the tax cuts with unnamed spending cuts. Dole then tabbed supply-side enthusiast Senator Jack Kemp of New York as his running mate.

Ross Perot once again ran as a third party candidate; but Perot met with much less success this time around since during his previous run, he had developed for himself a reputation as an eccentric, which he could not overcome. Furthermore, Perot offered little that voters could latch on to as a real difference between the conservative platform of Dole and Kemp. The Democrats, however, were able to paint Dole as a "mean spirited" man, and voters were generally turned off by Dole's age at 72. Clinton had helped himself by following a more moderate path since the failure of his health care proposal, and the Republicans had hurt themselves with the gridlock and shutdown of the government. Clinton led the race from beginning to end and won almost 50 percent of the popular vote to Dole's 41 percent. Clinton also won the largest gender gap in history, with 54 percent of American women casting votes for Clinton and only 38 percent for Bob Dole.

Clinton, however, failed again to capture a majority of the popular vote. This time, Perot, calling his the Reform Party, captured 8.4 percent of the popular vote, less than half his 1992 level, but still significant for a third party candidate. Republicans maintained control of both houses of Congress, though, and continued to cause Clinton trouble. For instance, despite calls by Chief Justice William Rehnquist and others to fill numerous vacant federal judgeships, Senate Republicans confirmed very few of Clinton's judicial appointments. In the last year of his presidency, the Republican-controlled Senate approved only 39 judges while a Democratic-controlled Senate had approved 66 in the final year of his Republican predecessor's term.

Clinton began his second term in the midst of a booming economy and soaring stock market that increased federal tax revenues.

The tax windfall from the economic good fortune allowed Clinton and the Republicans to compromise on a budget in 1997 that actually balanced for the first time in three decades. It was difficult to conclude anything other than the fact that Clinton's 1993 tax increase, which the Republicans had fought against, had produced long-term benefits for the fiscal health of the nation. Republican attempts to claim responsibility for the balanced budget success rang hollow after Bob Dole's presidential campaign based on tax cuts. Clinton's strong position was aided by Republican infighting in the House as a rebellious group of Republicans, unhappy with the Republican failures in the government shutdown and the 1996 election, attempted to oust Newt Gingrich as Speaker in the summer of 1997. Gingrich survived the attempted coup, but the Republicans were left in disarray.

CLINTON AND THE WORLD

Clinton came into office with very little interest in or knowledge of the complexities of international relations. By and large, he and his first secretary of state, experienced diplomat and lawyer Warren Christopher, continued Bush administration policies.

During the 1992 campaign, Clinton endorsed the North American Free Trade Agreement (NAFTA) negotiated by the Bush administration. Many traditionally Democratic groups strongly objected to the treaty, which lowered trade barriers with Canada and Mexico. Organized labor officials charged that NAFTA would accelerate the loss of jobs to Mexico while environmentalists pointed to dangers posed by heavily polluting Mexican factories. Although sensitive to these concerns, Clinton and "New Democrats" favored freer trade, so the President pressed ahead and achieved ratification of NAFTA, but with special side accords to allay the fears about the treaty's effect on labor and the environment. Economists differed as to whether NAFTA resulted in positive changes for the U.S. economy.

Even with the end of the Cold War, Russia remained a major focus of American foreign policy. Like Bush, Clinton supported the efforts of President Boris Yeltsin—who replaced Mikhail Gorbachev, to move his country towards democracy and a market economy. Clinton received praise from former Republican foreign policy specialists as well as Democrats when he stood by Yeltsin during the Russian president's 1993 power struggle with parliamentary opponents. Clinton and Yeltsin did not always see eye-to-eye, as for instance when the Russians used strong force against secessionists in Chechnya; but the American president had little choice but to back Yeltsin, given the alternatives of the right-wing Russian nationalism of Vladimir

Zhirinovsky or a resurgent Communist party. Elsewhere in Eastern Europe, Clinton pushed for the extension of NATO to include former Soviet bloc states. In 1998, the Czech Republic, Hungary, and Poland became the first of these to assume full membership in the western defense alliance. NATO softened this potential affront to Russia in its sphere of influence by including Moscow in some of its defense consultations.

Clinton also played the role of peacemaker in several international disputes, with mixed results. The president helped broker the 1995 Dayton Accords, which brought peace to Bosnia-Herzegovina, one of the former Yugoslavian republics wracked by civil war since 1991.

When the communist system collapsed all across Eastern Europe, individual "republics" within Yugoslavia quickly declared their independence; and the European Union quickly accorded official recognition to the new states. Minorities within the new states of Croatia and Bosnia, however, rose up against those who advocated independence from Yugoslavia. Croatia and Bosnia quickly devolved into civil war and "ethnic cleansing," complete with mass executions and the depopulation of entire areas, causing a massive refugee problem and over 250,000 deaths.

The government of Yugoslavia, located in the "republic" of Serbia and dominated by ethnic Serbs that wished to halt the disintegration of Yugoslavia, aided the minority rebels. In Croatia, the Serbian minority refused to recognize Croatian authority, and the Yugoslav army bombed the Croatian Capitol of Zagreb. In retaliation, the Croatians forcibly ousted thousands of Serbs from their country.

In Bosnia, which was 50 percent Muslim, 30 percent Serb, and 17 percent Croat, the Muslim-dominated government declared independence in 1992, resulting in a Serbian rebellion that was supported by neighboring Serbia. This civil war created over two million refugees over the next three years. The United States government under Bill Clinton held talks in Dayton, Ohio, in 1995, negotiating a truce that partitioned Bosnia into two sectors and was signed by all parties involved. The Dayton Accords required an international peacekeeping force to occupy Bosnia to enforce the cease-fire.

Under the Dayton Accords, the Serbs, who were 30 percent of the population, received 48 percent of the territory, while Muslims, who were 50 percent of the population, received only 27 percent of the territory with the rest allotted to the Croats. One narrow, three-mile-wide zone along the river port city of Brcko was not assigned under the Dayton Accords, but placed under joint jurisdiction. The area was under Muslim control before the civil war, but the Serbs also claimed the area as "vital".

As part of the peace package, Clinton committed American troops as peacekeepers there for a year, yet conditions required their continuing presence into the next administration. The president also took a great interest in Northern Ireland where Protestant and Roman Catholic factions had long been at loggerheads. Clinton's mediator, former Senate Majority Leader George Mitchell, brokered the Good Friday Agreement in 1998 that called for the disarming of sectarian paramilitary organizations and greater autonomy for Northern Ireland within Great Britain. Although snags lay ahead, the agreement brought a historic opportunity for peace.

The Israeli-Palestinian conflict, however, occupied much of Clinton's time and energy. In October 1993, he hosted Israeli Prime Minister Yitzhak Rabin and Palestinian leader Yasir Arafat at the White House for the signing of an historic agreement. The accord, made possible by years of secret negotiations in Oslo, Norway, transferred Gaza and Jericho from Israeli occupation to control by a new Palestinian Authority. It also urged more bilateral talks between Israel and its Arab neighbors. Soon, Jordan and Israel made an agreement; and during Clinton's terms in office, this Oslo peace process reached several crisis points, including just after the assassination of Rabin by a militant Israeli opponent of land cessions to the Palestinians. To break the impasses that developed, Clinton pursued personal diplomacy, not all of which resulted in progress, although the Wye River meetings of October 1998 did push the process along. There the Palestine Liberation Organization agreed to delete anti-Israel language from its founding charter, and Israel agreed to transfer more occupied territory to Palestinian control. Clinton's efforts in the fall of 2000 to seek a comprehensive settlement, including finalizing the status of Jerusalem, failed, however, largely because of Arafat's intransigence; and many loose ends remained as the Clinton administration came to a close. For a president famous for his opposition to the Vietnam War as a student—opponents delighted in calling him a draft-dodger, which he was not. (Clinton faced the draft along with other young American males, but his number did not come up). Clinton supported military intervention in a surprising number of global hotspots. He continued to enforce President Bush's no-fly zones in Iraq and authorized bombing of that country on several occasions.

CLINTON'S IRAQ POLICY

In April 1993, two years after the Persian Gulf War and three months after Bill Clinton's inauguration, Kuwaiti security services uncovered an Iraqi plot to kill former President George H. W. Bush with a car bomb during his visit to Kuwait. Kuwaiti officials arrested 11 Iraqis for the attempt on Bush's life, and four were executed. The next month President Clinton unveiled his policy of "dual containment" under which the United States was committed to containing not only Iran, but also Iraq. Clinton included in the policy a call for "regime change" in Iraq.

On June 26, 1993, the United States launched 23 Tomahawk cruise missiles at Baghdad, destroying the headquarters of Iraqi intelligence. It was the first time the Clinton administration used military force and the first such United States retaliation since the bombing of Moamar Qadafy in Libya in 1986. Of the 23 Tomahawks fired by the United States, three unfortunately went astray, hitting residential neighborhoods and killing eight people—including Leila Attar, a leading Iraqi painter. The Tomahawk missile attack by the United States technically violated the United Nations charter since Iraq had not launched an armed attack on the United States.

Clinton continued the American sanctions on Iraq, and in April 1994, Clinton's Secretary of State Warren Christopher stated, "The United States does not believe that Iraq's compliance with United Nations Resolutions is enough to justify lifting the embargo." In other words, whether Saddam complied with disarmament or not, Clinton was dead set on regime change. In doing so, the Clinton policy was unilateral in character and ignored the United Nations.

On September 3, 1996, Clinton fired 44 cruise missiles at Iraq's military command posts and air defense centers near the southern no-fly zone. In September 1997, the World Health Organization (WHO) published a report that claimed that over 500,000 Iraqi children under age five had died since 1991 as the result of malnutrition and lack of medicine caused by the United Nations embargo. By October 1997, the United Nations had dispatched 373 inspection teams to Iraq at a cost of $120 million—paid for from Iraq's frozen assets. On October 29, Iraq demanded the end of American "spies" on inspection teams, and six American inspectors were expelled the next month. Clinton responded to the expulsion of United nations inspectors by stating, "Saddam has ensured that the sanctions will be there until the end of time or as long as he lasts." Clinton then ordered a military buildup in the Persian Gulf. Arab states, however, unanimously opposed United States military action.

To educate the American public, Clinton had the National Security Council arrange a worldwide "town hall" meeting at Ohio State University with Secretary of State Madeleine Albright, National Security Advisor Sandy Berger, and Defense Secretary William Cohen to discuss Iraq's Weapons of Mass Destruction (WMDs). The audience of 6,000 in the town hall meeting was unconvinced that Saddam's

WMDs posed any real threat, and a February 22, 1998, *Newsweek* poll showed backing for military action against Iraq at only 18 percent. Clinton's options were further limited by the conclusions of the United States military as Chairman of the Joint Chiefs Henry Shelton argued that the United States would not be able to destroy Saddam's well-hidden weapons from the air.

In October 1998, Congress passed the Iraq Liberation Act that entitled the President to spend up to $97 million for military aid to train, equip, and finance an Iraqi opposition army and authorized the Department of Defense to train insurgents. General Anthony Zinni, commander of the United States Central Command, however, argued against the plan. Zinni argued, "I know of no viable opposition to Saddam in Iraq. Under such conditions any attempt to remove the Iraqi leader by force could dangerously fragment Iraq and destabilize the entire region. A weakened, fragmented, chaotic Iraq—which could happen if this isn't done carefully—is more dangerous in the long run than a contained Saddam now." This was perhaps especially true since the primary opposition group in Iraq at the time was the Supreme Assembly of Islamic Revolution in Iraq (SAIRI) that is funded by Iran.

Madeline Albright took a tour of the Persian Gulf states and was told by Middle-East rulers that change imposed on Iraq from outside would lead to rifts and civil war, and no Middle-Eastern leader stated that they would comply with a United States plan to oust Saddam. Instead, Middle-Eastern leaders warned Albright that United States support of insurgents undermined their credibility because it made them appear that they were American agents.

On October 31, 1998, Iraq ceased compliance with United Nations inspectors and demanded a review of its compliance linked to a timetable for ending sanctions. In response, President Clinton sent a fleet of B-52s armed with cruise missiles to bomb Iraq on November 14, 1998; but one hour before the planes released their missiles, Iraq announced that the inspectors could return. On November 18, 1998, the inspectors returned but found themselves obstructed by Iraqi officials. The next month, Clinton ordered the evacuation of United Nations' weapons inspectors so that he could launch a 100-hour bombing campaign aimed at ousting Saddam Hussein. On Wednesday, December 16, two days before the Impeachment hearings began in the House, Clinton ordered the bombing to begin. Four hundred fifteen cruise missiles (90 more than were fired during the Gulf War) and 600 laser-guided bombs were dropped on Iraq. Saddam survived, and weapons inspectors were no longer in Iraq. Essentially, it was Clinton, not Saddam, who ousted the inspectors.

In the months of January–August 1999, Clinton stepped up strikes against Iraq's air defenses in the no-fly zones. Over 1,100 missiles were fired at 359 targets in all. In August 1999, Clinton ordered the bombing of Iraqi air defense targets outside the United States-imposed no-fly zones. This would be the situation in Iraq that would be inherited by Clinton's successor, George W. Bush.

Aside from Iraq, but also from George H. W. Bush, Clinton inherited an obligation to provide military support to a U.N. humanitarian effort in war-torn Somalia. United States soldiers sought to create a secure environment for the delivery of food to famine victims, but this operation soon became hampered by armed struggles among various Somali factions. Forces loyal to warlord Mohammed Aideed killed some and captured others of the United States soldiers seeking those responsible for the deaths of a Pakistani U.N. contingent. In one instance in October 1993, which was recorded by television cameras, Aideed's men dragged the body of a Marine through the streets of the capital city, Mogadishu. Negotiations led to the release of captured Americans and the withdrawal of United States personnel. The operation saved thousands of Somalis from starvation, but it made Americans less willing to intervene for humanitarian reasons in unstable situations. In 1994, for instance, the Clinton administration did nothing to stop violence in Rwanda where members of one ethnic group, the Hutu, engaged in mass slaughter of another group, the Tutsi. During a four-month period in 1994, between 500,000 and 1,000,000 Rwandans died. After the killings, U.S. troops moved in to provide limited humanitarian assistance.

The Clinton administration did intervene militarily for humanitarian-linked missions in countries or regions where the United States traditionally had important interests. For instance, in 1994, the United States announced the dispatch of troops to Haiti to support the winner of a recent presidential election, Jean-Bertrand Aristide, against a dictator who refused to yield power. Just before troops were to go in, the dictator agreed to leave the country in a plan brokered by former President Carter with Clinton's blessing; and American troops entered Haiti as peacekeepers. Then, in 1999 Serbian troops began forcing the evacuation of—as well as slaughtering of—residents of Kosovo, a district within Serbia dominated by ethnic Albanians. Kosovo was a "republic" on the southwestern corner of Albania with a Muslim majority of two million people and a Serbian population of about 200,000. Kosovo had enjoyed local autonomy under Serbian rule since it was captured by the Serbs in 1912. Muslims had taken the area from the Serbs in 1389 and ruled it themselves for the next five centuries.

In 1989, Serbian President Slobodan Milosevic revoked Kosovo's local autonomy and began a campaign to suppress Kosovo's Muslim culture. Kosovars formed armed resistance groups that attacked the Serbian government officials and installations, as well as Serbian civilians in Kosovo. Milosevic responded with an armed invasion by Serbian troops aimed at expelling the Muslims from Kosovo. Thousands of Kosovars became refugees and 500,000 crossed the border into Albania. President Clinton attempted negotiations with the Serbs and Kosovars to reach an agreement that would return Kosovo to its autonomy and cease the ethnic cleansing. The Kosovars signed the agreement, but the Serbs refused.

Clinton and NATO responded with the first military action in Europe by NATO since its creation in 1949. In March 1999, the United States and NATO launched a massive bombing campaign that destroyed much of Serbia's infrastructure and military capability. Finally, Milosevic capitulated under NATO pressure, and U.N. peacekeeping forces were dispatched to prevent further bloodshed. Kosovo remained technically part of Serbia, but the Serbian population in Kosovo was less than half of what it had been prior to the unrest.

The next October (2000) elections were held in Serbia, and President Milosevic was defeated. Milosevic refused to abdicate his position, and Belgrade erupted in violent protests. Angry mobs stormed the Federal Parliament building in Belgrade and set fire to offices. Milosevic then announced that he would step down under both domestic and international pressure.

One of Clinton's great strengths as president lay in his ability to connect with people abroad as well as voters at home. During the course of his presidency he made a number of trips that must be accounted as successes, particularly the trips to several African countries and to the People's Republic of China. During the latter he even addressed the Chinese public directly on television. In short, his foreign policy decisions may be judged to have been only partially successful, but he made friends for the United States around the world when he traveled.

TERRORISM: AT HOME AND ABROAD

With the end of the Cold War, the United States no longer faced major security threats from another superpower. A new peril became apparent, though: terrorism. Carried out by individuals or small groups (sometimes associated with a foreign nation) attempting to make a political point, terrorism involves violence inflicted on civilian populations usually without warning. Until the 1990s, terrorist attacks had been rare in the twentieth century United States; yet during the Clinton years, Americans experienced several major attacks, both at home and abroad, and began to feel vulnerable as never before.

On April 19, 1995, 26-year-old Timothy McVeigh blew up a federal office building in Oklahoma City. The explosion killed 168 men, women, and children (one person died later of injuries sustained in the blast) and demolished the nine-story building. It was the worst act of domestic terrorism yet recorded in the United States.

McVeigh's terrorist actions brought to the forefront of the nation's consciousness the phenomenon of self-described "patriot" groups. Extremely right-wing in their politics and devoted to conspiracy theories, the members often formed paramilitary groups—militias—to defend American sovereignty against world government, of which they considered Bush's "new world order" the harbinger. They considered any gun control legislation, such as that Clinton advocated, an attempt to disarm Americans in preparation for a takeover of the country by a powerful United Nations. Primarily white (and often white supremacist and anti-Semitic) as well as lower middle class or blue collar, these "patriots" likely joined these groups to compensate for what they considered their loss of power and status in American society. They tended to live in relatively economically depressed areas, untouched by the expanding economy. Moreover, the white membership took umbrage at what they saw as preferential treatment for non-whites in the more multicultural America Bill Clinton celebrated.

McVeigh shared the ideology of these "patriots." A part-time gun dealer, he acted to strike back at the federal government for what he considered its anti-gun policies. In addition, he sought retribution for the deaths two years before of some 80 members of a millennialist religious group called the Branch Davidians. In that incident, federal agents had sought to serve an arrest warrant to the group's leader, David Koresh (born Vernon Howell), for the possession of illegal weapons. When Koresh and his followers rebuffed them by shooting to death four federal agents who were attempting to serve the Branch Davidians with a search warrant, a 51-day standoff ensued between the agents and the well-armed Branch Davidians barricaded inside their compound near Waco, Texas. Then, on April 19, 1993, agents moved in against Koresh. Shooting began, and reports differed as to who fired first. In the resulting struggle, most of the compound's residents—including some children—died in a fire. Although it is clear the blaze began within the compound—and conspicuously no Branch Davidians attempted to flee from the burning building, suggesting mass suicide—McVeigh and other conspiracy theorists asserted the federal government had purposely set the fire to massacre Koresh and his followers. In addition to domestic terrorists such as McVeigh, foreign terrorists also targeted the United States. In February 1993. Radical Islamic terrorists led by Sheik Omar Abdul Rahman set off a bomb in a parking garage at the World Trade Center in New York. Rahman's group also placed a barrel full of poisonous chemicals in the vicinity of the car bomb they detonated in the parking garage underneath the building. Fortunately, the heat from the bomb destroyed the chemicals before they could be dispersed or perhaps thousands could have died. As it was, the blast resulted in six deaths and nearly 1,000 injuries.

Because of United States support for Israel or U.S. military presence in Arab countries, other terrorist attacks by Islamic groups took place abroad. For instance, in June 1996, a militant group killed 19 United States soldiers in a bomb-blast at a military base in Saudi Arabia. This bombing eventually proved to be linked to several Islamic terrorist groups, most notably an international terrorist group known as al Qaeda (Arabic for "the base"), formed by Saudi millionaire and Islamic radical Osama bin Laden in the late 1980s. During the Soviet war in Afghanistan, al Qaeda organized Arabs to go to Afghanistan to fight what they viewed as a global jihad or holy war against the Russians, which put bin Laden on the same side as the United States in that struggle. The United States under Presidents Jimmy Carter and Ronald Reagan supplied massive aid to the Afghan resistance groups known collectively as the Mujahadeen. Famously, the American aid to the Mujahadeen included shoulder-fired missiles that were effective at bringing down Soviet attack helicopters. Much of the American money and aid was funneled to the Mujahadeen through Pakistani Intelligence, which was concerned not only with preventing a communist takeover of Afghanistan, but also with ensuring that Afghanistan would be dominated by Sunni Muslims rather than Shiites. As a consequence, Pakistani Intelligence funneled American aid to radical Sunni Muslim groups, including Al Qaeda. President Reagan praised the Mujahadeen as "freedom fighters," but American policy makers ignored the fact that the Mujahadeen were as anti-Western as they were anti-communist. Later, during the first Gulf War, bin Laden resented the reliance of Saudi Arabia on American troops for its defense. He preferred that a pan-Arab army, such as that he had deployed in Afghanistan, protect his home country, site of Islamic holy places. He also detested the United States because of its support for Israel. Consequently, bin Laden offered the services of his Mujahadeen, conquerors of the Soviet Red Army in Afghanistan, to the Kingdom of Saudi Arabia for the purpose of ousting Saddam Hussein's Iraqi army from Kuwait. In February 1998, bin Laden called for a jihad or holy war against Americans and issued a fatwa (religious ruling) that called for the killing of any American anywhere. Later that year, bin Laden associates killed at least 301 persons in attacks on United States embassies in Kenya and Tanzania. In the Nairobi bomb, at least 4,500 people, many of whom were Muslims, were also wounded. FBI task forces investigated the scene of both bombings, and in subsequent investigations two arrests were made and warrants were issued for the arrest of Osama bin Laden and other members of al Qaeda. President Clinton also ordered cruise missile attacks on selected al Qaeda targets in the Sudan and on six al Qaeda bases in Afghanistan. Numerous members of al Qaeda were killed in the attacks, but bin Laden escaped before the missiles hit their targets. The United States also linked al Qaeda to the October 2000 assault in Yemen that damaged the *U.S.S. Cole*, killed 17 sailors and injured 39 others.

Although American intelligence services and law enforcement officers headed off several potential terrorist attacks—including a plan to blow up the Los Angeles airport in early 2000—the government found it difficult to deal with all terrorist threats. American retaliation against al Qaeda following the attacks in Africa failed to damage the group significantly. Indeed, the Clinton administration suffered embarrassment when U.S. forces destroyed a suspected al Qaeda nerve gas production facility in the Sudan with approximately 13 Tomahawk cruise missiles. Evidence soon indicated that the facility was a legitimate pharmaceutical plant rather than an al Qaeda factory. Missile strikes against an al Qaeda training camp in Afghanistan also proved ineffective.

COMPUTERS AND THE INTERNET

As we learned in the last chapter, the high-tech industry began to achieve many breakthroughs in the 1960s, perhaps most significantly, the invention of the microprocessor. In the 1970s, new companies such as Apple began using microprocessors to manufacture early versions of microcomputers, and in the early 1980s industry giant IBM introduced its personal computer (PC). Macintoshes (Apple's microcomputers), IBM PCs, and PC clones produced by a variety of companies soon became common features in offices as well as in ordinary American homes.

In the 1980s, someone with a home computer might use it to write a letter, process financial records, or play a game, but in the 1990s, a computer owner's world expanded with the introduction of the Internet. The Internet's origins lie in the 1960s, when Pentagon-funded

Microsoft founder Bill Gates *(A/P Wide World)*

researchers developed a way to link networks of computers at various universities. They called this an "internetwork," or "internet" for short. A European computer scientist, Tim Berners-Lee, then developed a simple way to find information on the new Internet. Called the World Wide Web (www), Berners-Lee's system debuted to the public in 1991. After that, anyone with a computer and access to the Internet could tap into a truly global information system.

Americans enthusiastically took to the web not only for information, but also for entertainment, communication, and commerce. Universities, museums, and libraries created web sites for the dispersion of knowledge, as did enthusiasts of all sorts. Electronic mail (e-mail) and on-line "chatting" transformed the way many Americans interacted with one another. On-line businesses popped up to offer consumers everything from pet supplies to books to clothing. Anyone with Internet access and a credit card could shop late at night from home by the glow of a monitor.

The commercial potential of the Internet raised the interest of Wall Street as well as of eager entrepreneurs. The success of Microsoft, which developed the disk operating system (DOS) for IBM as well as other computer software, showed everyone the fortunes that could be made in computers. Indeed, the company's founders, Bill Gates and Paul Allen, were the first and third richest persons, respectively, in the world in the 1990s. With the introduction of the user-friendly

World Wide Web, pioneers in electronic commerce (e-commerce) rushed to spin their business ideas into Internet gold. Jerry Yang, co-founder of Web browser company Yahoo, and Jeff Bezos, who created Internet bookseller Amazon.com, provided the models of success as the value of their stock made them into millionaires if not billionaires practically overnight.

Investors willingly paid top dollar to get in on the ground floor of an Internet company. On the day in 1999 that Priceline.com—a seller of airline tickets—premiered on the stock market, the price of one of its shares rose from $16 to as high as $85 before closing at $68. The company's value as measured by its stock price reached nearly $10 billion that day—more than the net worth of several major airlines combined. Some questioned the rationality of such valuation in the new Internet economy. After all, Priceline had lost more than $114 million in 1998, the year before it went public. In early 2000, the skeptics were proven to be right. Too many new Internet startups simply found themselves losing too much money, investor confidence plummeted, and the "dot-com" bubble burst. To be sure, e-commerce was not dead; consumers apparently had taken to Internet shopping, and better-established companies lived on. Indeed, Amazon.com, founded in 1995, finally showed its first profit in the fourth quarter of 2001 and had expanded beyond books to include other merchandise. Similarly, eBay would become an enormous success and revolutionize the buying and selling of used goods.

THE "TRIAL OF THE CENTURY"

For over a year, from June 1994 to October 1995, the public attention was fixated on O. J. Simpson. Simpson had long been in the limelight, first as a football star, then as a television sports announcer, a commercial spokesman, and a movie actor. An African American, he enjoyed great popularity with audiences of all ethnic backgrounds. A poor boy who made good through hard work and talent, Simpson in 1994 lived the American Dream in the affluent Brentwood section of Los Angeles. In June of that year, the dream turned nightmarish, however. Authorities arrested Simpson for the brutal murder of his ex-wife, Nicole Brown Simpson, and her friend, Ronald Goldman.

The televised events of the Simpson case—from arrest through jury verdict—captivated viewers as the case seemed tailor-made for America's obsessions with celebrity and sensationalism. The trial helped the careers of various commentators, particularly on cable television outlets, who dispensed their analysis to a public with an apparently limitless fascination with the horrific details of the case.

Attorney Yale Galanter, left, with client O. J. Simpson as the judge reads the verdict *(AP Photo/Pool, Amy E. Conn)*

The seriousness of the crime often became lost in all the media attention, particularly in attempts at humor such as the *Tonight Show's* skits featuring dancers modeled on the trial judge.

Race also played a significant role in the trial. Simpson's attorneys sought to portray Simpson as a black man wronged by the system. (Ironically, many blacks before the trial thought Simpson culturally "too white"—which in their eyes his marriage to the white Nicole Brown had confirmed.) The lawyers wished to persuade the jury—nine African Americans, two whites, and one Hispanic—as well as the public that the police had planted evidence to frame Simpson. (Testimony did indicate that the detectives' work was sometimes shoddy.) During the trial, it became apparent that, in the aggregate, African Americans and whites thought differently about the trial based on their preexisting conceptions about the fairness of the justice system. When the verdict—not guilty—came down in October 1995, blacks and whites reacted in quite opposite ways. According to a Gallup poll, 89 percent of African Americans believed the jury made the right decision. Many blacks suspected the police had framed Simpson or that enough reasonable doubt existed. Others simply considered the verdict payback for all the times innocent blacks had been lynched by white mobs or treated unfairly by American courts. On the other hand, only 36 percent of whites endorsed the jury's verdict; indeed, a clear majority (53 percent) of whites deemed it wrong. Many noted that the jury only took three hours to deliberate following a trial lasting

133 days, hardly enough time to consider all the testimony thoroughly. Although a key piece of evidence, a "bloody glove" found on Simpson's property turned out to be beneficial to Simpson since it did not fit his hand, and one of the Los Angeles policemen, Mark Furman, was on tape making racial slurs against blacks, there was a lot of other evidence that many viewed as condemning of Simpson. Simpson had written a letter to his friend Al Cowlings that appeared to many to be a suicide note that while not admitting guilt, at least inferred it. Furthermore, Simpson and Al Cowlings led Los Angeles police down the freeway in a slow-speed chase toward Simpson's house in a white Ford Bronco before Simpson gave himself up to police. To many, this did not seem to be the action of an innocent man. The victims were killed with a knife, and Simpson had a cut on his hand and an instructional video in his house on the subject of how to kill someone with a knife. In addition, footprints at the scene matched Simpson's rare Bruno Mali shoes, samples of the victims' blood was found was found on Simpson's socks, and blood with DNA matching Simpson's was found at the scene. Television audiences also heard a frantic 911 call during a previous domestic disturbance at the Simpson home where Simpson appeared to be very threatening to his wife. Finally, Mark Furman had been the eighteenth policeman to arrive at the scene, so even if he did harbor ill will toward Simpson due to his racial attitudes, the idea that he could have rearranged the evidence at that point appeared to many to be suspect.

Later, in more conservative Orange County, California, the parents of Nicole Brown Simpson and of Ronald Goldman sued Simpson in a civil court, arguing that Simpson was responsible for the losses they had suffered as a result of the wrongful death of their loved ones. In February 1997, a heavily white jury found him responsible for the wrongful death and ordered him to pay $33.5 million in compensatory and punitive damages. Although O. J. was free, he had spent 15 months in jail, spent millions on legal fees, his celebrity career was over, and eventually he faded from the headlines.

Little serious discussion ensued about what the country might have learned from the Simpson trial about curbing police misconduct, bridging racial differences on the courts, or reforming the jury system. Instead, Americans looked for other scandals to fill their television viewing hours.

A WHITE HOUSE BESIEGED

Another American obsession, as measured by the number of stories in the news media, involved the scandals surrounding the first family.

During the 1992 presidential campaign, questions arose concerning an investment Bill and Hillary Clinton had made in an Arkansas real estate venture called Whitewater Development Corporation in the late 1970s. Whitewater was a reference to property in which the Clintons invested during the 1980s in a small, failed, Arkansas real estate venture. The Clintons' total investment in the Whitewater property in the Ozark Mountains together with their partner was only $200,000. If the deal had worked as well as they had anticipated, their total profit would have been $45,000. The Clintons' partner in the Whitewater venture, James McDougal, however, turned out to be less than honest in his business dealings and less than mentally stable in his personal life. McDougal was indicted in 1990 for fraud in a check-kiting scheme, but the FBI and the United States Attorney concluded that there was insufficient evidence to suggest that the Clintons had knowledge of McDougal's illegal activity. The venture lost money for the Clintons, but from that humble beginning came a major scandal that threatened Clinton's presidency. A year into his first term, the political pressure to look into the matter built to the point that Clinton authorized the appointment of a special prosecutor, Robert Fiske, to investigate. Later in 1994, after Congress passed a new independent counsel statute, a panel of federal judges selected Kenneth Starr, Solicitor General in the Bush Justice Department, to head up the investigation of Clinton.

When the Republicans gained control of Congress in 1995, House Speaker Newt Gingrich, who had stated during the 1994 election campaign that he would use "subpoena power" to wage political war with the White House, pressed forward anew with investigations of Whitewater, in particular, and the White House, in general. Gingrich referred to Clinton as "the enemy of normal Americans" and stated that he envisioned as many as "twenty Congressional committees simultaneously investigating the White House." Thus, the House Banking Committee under James Leach of Iowa and the Senate Banking Committee under new chairman Alfonse D'Amato revived the Whitewater probe with renewed vigor. Other probes were launched investigating the White House for firing of White House Travel Office employees, alleged misuse of FBI files, and, of course, the failed Madison Guaranty Savings and Loan in Arkansas that was connected to Whitewater.

Witnesses that could dispute accusations against the Clintons were not allowed to testify, and exculpatory evidence was repeatedly ignored. On June 26, 1995, the *Wall Street Journal* published details of a report prepared for the Resolution Trust Corporation (RTC) by the San Francisco Law firm of Pillsbury, Madison, and Sutro, concerning the Whitewater affair. The report showed that the Clintons were passive investors in Whitewater, weren't involved in its financial transactions until 1986, and, therefore, could not have played a role in the collapse of the Madison Guaranty Savings and Loan that transferred $43,000 to Whitewater prior to 1986. Furthermore, the report concluded that the Clinton's partner, James McDougal had, without their knowledge, taken money from their investment and transferred money between entities he owned (essentially a check kiting scheme)—including Whitewater.

After 10 weeks of hearings, some of it even occurring during the government shutdown, the Senate Banking Committee finally concluded without proving any of the Republicans' initial accusations. In spite of all of the allegations of perjury and obstruction of justice, not a single witness was ever charged with any offense. As Whitewater dragged on and on, even some of the most rabid Republicans began to give up on it. In February 1997, Independent Counsel Kenneth Starr, with essentially no more leads and all of his roads toward anything substantial exhausted, temporarily resigned his post as Independent Counsel in the Whitewater case in favor of a position as Dean of the Law School at Pepperdine University. In April 1997, even Republican Senator Alfonse D'Amato confessed that the entire affair needed to end.

During his brief tenure in 1994, Robert Fiske also examined the circumstances of the suicide of Clinton aide Vincent Foster, deputy White House counsel and close friend of the Clintons. Starr later re-investigated the Foster suicide—in both cases the conclusion was that Foster was suffering from depression and, in that state, decided to take his own life. Nevertheless, "rumors" that the Clintons had something to do with Foster's death persisted.

The investigation into these matters yielded the indictment and conviction of several persons, including Clinton's successor as governor, Jim Guy Tucker. Never did evidence of criminal wrongdoing by the president or first lady emerge. Starr's inquiry seemed to be at a standstill in late 1997 when suddenly it took a new direction because of a civil law suit originally filed against Clinton in 1994.

On May 27, 1997, the Republicans were handed a break in the case when the United States Supreme Court ruled that Paula Jones' sexual harassment civil suit against the President should go forward while he remained in office. Paula Jones had been a clerical employee of the Arkansas Industrial Development Commission in 1991, and had helped staff a state-sponsored "quality management" conference at Little Rock's Excelsior Hotel. Jones claimed that Clinton had invited her to a room at the hotel, made sexually aggressive advances, asked her for "a type of sex," and exposed himself to her in the hotel room. Jones' claims appeared dubious, however, since she claimed that she met Clinton on May 8, 1991, at 2:30 in the afternoon, but Clinton had given a breakfast speech at the hotel that morning and left the hotel not long afterward. That afternoon, a function at the governor's mansion precluded any secret return by Clinton to the Excelsior unless he could be in two places at once. Jones later changed her story and claimed that Clinton had ducked out of the reception at the governor's mansion and "walked three blocks" back to the Excelsior to meet with Jones. The governor's mansion and the Excelsior are at opposite ends of downtown Little Rock, however, over a mile apart and separated by a six-lane freeway. Seeking to establish a pattern of similar sexual advances, Jones's attorneys pursued information that Clinton had been involved with a young White House intern, Monica Lewinsky, for some time beginning in 1995. Fuel was added to the sex-scandal fire later that year when Kathleen Willey, a financially strapped widow and former White House worker, claimed that Clinton had groped her in the Oval Office in 1993. Ironically, Monica Lewinsky confidant Linda Tripp, who testified before a grand jury that there was "no harassment whatsoever" in the Willey case, unraveled Willey's story. Instead of Clinton chasing Willey, Willey had been chasing Clinton—because her husband had died and she was in dire financial straits. Nevertheless, in a deposition with the Jones attorneys, Clinton denied having had a sexual relationship with Lewinsky.

In January 1998, however, the Republicans received another break when Linda Tripp, a friend of former Presidential intern Monica Lewinsky, brought evidence of an extramarital affair between Lewinsky and Clinton to the attention of the Independent Counsel. Tripp had secretly taped conversations between herself and Lewinsky, in which Lewinsky discussed details of the affair, including her possession of a dress with stains left by the President's semen. Starr investigated the Lewinsky affair in conjunction with the Paula Jones case (a loose connection at best). The Jones case, of course, Starr had been investigating due to its purported connection to Whitewater. Then in early 1998 Starr received permission from Attorney General Reno to expand his investigation to include the Lewinsky matter. (Interestingly, before his appointment as independent counsel, Starr had provided legal advice to the Jones attorneys in their case against the president.) After some months, he struck a deal with Lewinsky under which she provided his office details about her sexual relationship with Clinton. The president agreed to testify before a grand jury, where a prosecutor questioned him at length about Lewinsky. The President, unaware that Lewinsky had kept the stained dress, would lie under oath to cover up his affair with Lewinsky and commit perjury, thus giving the Republicans the "crime" they needed to commence with impeachment, though Clinton and the prosecutors differed on the definition of "sexual relations." Based on Lewinsky's information and DNA evidence from the dress, the prosecutors now accused Clinton of lying to the grand jury.

In September 1998, Starr sent Congress a 445-page report on the Lewinsky matter outlining what he considered impeachable offenses. This impeachment referral went into graphic detail about Clinton's encounters with Lewinsky. This was necessary, Starr maintained, to demonstrate the falseness of Clinton's statements to the grand jury. Very soon, before members of Congress could review it, the House leadership authorized the report's posting on the internet so anyone could read about the president's alleged sexual indiscretions.

Despite widespread—often prurient—public interest in and overwhelming disapproval of the Clinton-Lewinsky relationship, most Americans opposed impeachment. Generally, they gave Clinton's job performance high marks (especially with the economy doing well) and considered his extramarital affairs a matter for him and his wife. Observers sympathetic to Clinton argued that his shading of the truth about the Lewinsky matter, even before a grand jury, did not constitute the "high crimes and misdemeanors" that the Constitution requires as a basis for impeachment.

Congressional Republicans pressed ahead toward impeachment nonetheless, even when the November 1998 congressional elections might have given them pause. Normally, the party that controls the White House loses a few seats in non-presidential election years. Amazingly, even with the Clinton scandal, his party picked up—and the Republicans lost—five seats in the House. In the Senate, where Republicans had believed they would gain several seats, there was no net change in party numbers. Still, two Republican senators who had emphasized the Clinton scandals—Alfonse D'Amato of New York and Lauch Faircloth of North Carolina—went down in defeat. The congressional defeats for his party shocked Newt Gingrich, who had expected to increase the GOP majority in the House by 20 seats or more. Many Republicans blamed Gingrich for the party's poor showing, and within days he announced that he would not seek re-election as Speaker and would, in fact, resign from Congress. That he himself had had widely publicized sexual improprieties in his life may have also been part of the equation.

After the election, the House Judiciary Committee moved forward and reported four articles of impeachment. Meanwhile Democrats— and some Republicans such as former President Gerald Ford—urged that Congress censure the president, a less severe punishment. At the same time, numerous Clinton opponents and newspaper editorial pages called for Clinton's resignation; but congressional Republicans, however, refused to pursue anything less than impeachment and removal from office, and the president steadfastly declined to step down. On December 19, 1998, the full House approved two of the articles largely on party line votes. One article alleged Clinton perjured himself before the federal grand jury in August 1998, while the other charged him with obstructing justice by seeking to influence potential witnesses in the case.

For only the second time in American history, the Senate conducted an impeachment trial for a president. The trial, which took five weeks beginning in early January 1999, ended with the president's acquittal on February 12. Forty-five senators supported and 55 opposed conviction on the perjury matter. On obstruction of justice, senators split 50-05. These results were not unexpected; it had been unlikely that enough Democrats would join the majority of Republicans to reach the constitutionally required two-thirds of senators needed to convict Clinton. Moreover, polls indicated that most Americans disapproved of conviction.

Although Clinton finished his term, the Lewinsky matter would certainly tarnish his legacy. Just before leaving office in 2001, Clinton agreed in a deal with the independent counsel to admit that he gave "misleading and evasive" testimony in the Jones case. The final report of the last Whitewater independent counsel appeared in March 2002, eight years and $70 million after the probe began. It cleared Bill and Hillary Clinton of any wrongdoing in the various matters pursued by the investigators.

HILLARY RODHAM CLINTON AS FIRST LADY

As the wife of a man whose infidelities were better documented than perhaps any other errant husband in history, Hillary Rodham Clinton had to endure considerable humiliation as an occupant of the White House. Painful though that experience must have been, it also seems to have garnered her more sympathy from the American people than she had enjoyed when she was seen primarily as the unsuccessful advocate of a failed health care reform package.

A brilliant woman and graduate of Wellesley College and Yale Law School, Mrs. Clinton had had her own legal career before moving into 1600 Pennsylvania Ave. Though she was the devoted mother of one child, she raised hackles among those for whom the social changes of the 60s had been experienced as a coup d'etat. Her enemies depicted her as a power-mad feminist who underval-

First lady Hillary Rodham Clinton, right, participates in the Million Mom March. *(AP Photo/Kamenko Pajic)*

ued the traditional female virtues and values. Not since Eleanor Roosevelt had a first lady been so polarizing; but after the Monica Lewinsky episode and the new public sympathy that affair engendered, she was able to win election to the United States Senate from New York with she and her family establishing residence there in time for the fall campaign in 2000.

Like her husband, Mrs. Clinton made a number of well-publicized trips abroad, especially to Third World countries, where she tried to call attention to women's issues and concerns. These trips constitute, perhaps, her most valuable legacy.

A SECOND BUSH PRESIDENCY

THE ELECTION OF 2000

In 2000, Republicans nominated Texas Governor George W. Bush, son of the 41st president, as their presidential candidate. Bush enjoyed the support of key insiders from the administrations of Reagan and his father. Moreover, financing proved crucial to his victory. Refusing to accept federal matching funds for his campaign so that he would be free from spending limits imposed by law, he overwhelmed his less well-financed competition in the primaries. On policy matters, Bush touted a program of "compassionate conservatism" that stressed cutting taxes, reforming education, and seeking non-governmental solutions to social ills. He selected the politically experienced Richard Cheney to run for vice president. A former Wyoming congressman, Cheney also served as chief of staff to President Ford and secretary of defense under President George H. W. Bush before taking over as chief executive officer of the world's largest oil field services company, Halliburton.

In the general election, Governor Bush faced Vice President Albert Gore, Jr., who had defeated former New Jersey Senator (and New York Knicks basketball star) Bill Bradley to win the Democratic nomination. He chose as his running mate Senator Joseph Lieberman of Connecticut, the first Jew ever nominated by a major party for vice president. Although most pundits considered Gore more conversant with public policy issues than Bush, voters seemed to find the Texas governor's folksier style more appealing. In a series of televised debates, Bush generally exceeded expectations and was deemed by pundits to have bested Gore.

Although not included in the debates, two other key candidates also sought the presidency in 2000. Ralph Nader, pioneering consumer advocate and environmentalist, ran on the Green Party ticket, while Patrick Buchanan served as the candidate of Ross Perot's Reform Party. In what was expected to be a close contest, many observers believed Nader might siphon voters from Gore and Buchanan from Bush.

Election night, November 7, 2000, proved to be one of the most exciting in a generation. Although early returns indicated Bush victories throughout most of the South and lower Midwest, they also pointed to wins for Gore in swing states rich in electoral votes such as Pennsylvania and Michigan. Just before 8:00 p.m. (EST), the networks predicted that Gore would win Florida, too, a sobering loss for Bush whose

President George W. Bush during the 2000 presidential campaign (A/P Wide World Photo)

Vice President Gore with his wife Tipper campaigning on the Larry King Show *(A/P Wide World Photo)*

brother, Jeb, served as that state's governor. Later in the evening, networks retracted their call and, after midnight, awarded Florida to Bush. Doubt remained, however, because of the extreme closeness of the vote there

As the sun rose on November 8, the electoral votes of three states—not only Florida but also New Mexico and Oregon—remained in question. Gore needed all three to win, whereas Florida alone would put Bush over the top. Oregon and New Mexico both shortly went to Gore, but uncertainty about Florida's returns persisted for five weeks. During this period, Americans received a national civics lesson about the meaning of voting in a democracy and the intricacies of the Electoral College system.

Bush led Gore by a narrow margin in Florida's popular vote; initial estimates ranged from around 350 to 1,000 votes out of nearly 6 million cast, and irregularities muddied the result. In liberal Palm Beach County, a confusing arrangement of names on the ballot almost certainly led some Gore supporters to cast votes inadvertently for the conservative Buchanan. Six thousand ballots in West Palm Beach County were double-punched for both Gore and Pat Buchanan and another 3,000 were double-punched for Gore and Socialist candidate David McReynolds. In all, Gore's name was included in 46,000 such "over-votes" while Bush's name was included in only 17,000. This unfortunate confusion, along with the 90,000 far-left votes in Florida that were siphoned from the Democrats by Ralph Nader, would essentially give Bush the Presidency; but there were other unsavory elements that surfaced as well.

In the summer of 1999, Florida Republican Secretary of State Katherine Harris arranged for the State of Florida to pay $4 million to a company called Database Technologies to go through Florida's voter rolls and remove any felons from the approved voter lists. Unfortunately, thousands of eligible voters with similar names to convicted felons, mostly minorities who typically vote Democrat, were also purged from the voter lists. Among the 181,000 citizens that were purged from the voter lists were 8,000 individuals on a list supplied by the State of Texas (where candidate Bush was governor at the time) of suspected felons from Texas that had moved to Florida. The Gore campaign also alleged that voting machine problems in several other counties affected the outcome, and it called for a recount of those ballots. In the first count, Bush was declared the winner by 537 votes, but Florida law called for a recount in an election so close. The Democrats asked for a hand recount this time since machine errors had left hundreds of votes unrecorded in several heavily Democratic counties. The Bush team then sued to stop the recount, in spite of the fact that Bush himself had signed a similar law in Texas in 1997 that required hand recounts in such cases and required that election officials accept various degrees of punching or indentation that "show a clearly ascertainable intent of the voter to vote." Partisan politics apparently intruded as Florida Republican Secretary of State Katherine Harris, the state's chief election official and the Bush campaign's Florida co-chair, supported Bush's position in several key procedural decisions, while the state's Democratic attorney general, Robert Butterworth, filed a friend of the court brief on behalf of Gore.

After a series of legal maneuvers by both campaigns and conflicting rulings by state and federal courts, the United States Supreme Court delivered its final opinion in the case of *Bush v. Gore* on December 12. By a five-to-four majority, the Republican-dominated Court barred any further recounts (which the Democratic majority on the Florida Supreme Court had previously authorized). The Court majority declared that recounting ballots in certain counties and not in others violated the voters' right to equal protection of the laws. With no recount possible and Bush slightly ahead in Florida's popular vote tally, Gore conceded the race on December 13. Nationwide, Gore received approximately 540,000 more votes than his Republican opponent, but with Florida's electoral vote secured, George W. Bush became the 43rd president of the United States. For only the second

Incoming President Bush with former President Clinton *(A/P Wide World Photo)*

time in American history, the son of a president took office as president. (John Quincy Adams was the other presidential offspring to be chief executive.) It should further be noted about the election of 2000 and the role played by the Florida outcome, that it was subsequently documented that Republicans in that state had attempted various means of suppressing the African American vote. Thus the Florida outcome has continued to trouble not only partisan Democrats but also scholars who study political processes because of all the irregularities there were during the election and its aftermath.

The election left Republicans with a slim majority in the U.S. House and the Senate split evenly between the two parties. Officially, Democrats held the Senate majority from the time Congress convened on January 3 until January 20 because until then Democratic Vice President Gore could cast tie-breaking votes as the Senate's presiding officer. After Bush's inauguration, Vice President Cheney took over from Gore so that the Senate became Republican again. In June, however, the control of the Senate shifted again when Republican James Jeffords of Vermont left his party to become an Independent. The departure of the moderate Jeffords, upset over the power of social conservatives within the GOP, meant Democrats now outnumbered Republicans, 50 to 49, and thus controlled the Senate.

THE BUSH DOMESTIC AGENDA

Some observers believed the new President Bush would be forced to seek consensus with Democrats and not stake out very conservative positions once he took office. After all, he had been elected in an unusual fashion and was the first president since Benjamin Harrison in 1888 to have received fewer popular votes than his major opponent; but it soon became apparent as he made his Cabinet nominations that Bush's administration would bear his stamp and no one else's. Some of his choices received wide bipartisan approval, most notably, Colin Powell for Secretary of State. Powell, former chairman of the Joint Chiefs of Staff, became the first African American to hold the top Cabinet post.

Other Bush Cabinet picks proved more controversial. He chose for attorney general the very conservative John Ashcroft (a man defeated the previous November in his Senate re-election bid by a dead candidate) and for interior secretary, Gale Norton, whom environmentalists disliked because of her work with former Reagan interior head, James Watt. Many of Bush's appointees came from big business, and several had worked in the petroleum industry—as had both he and the vice president had. The pro-business tilt of the new administration concerned labor, consumer, and environmental groups. Only one of his nominees, though, faced serious opposition. His labor secretary-designee, Linda Chavez, a prominent conservative commentator, withdrew her name when the press revealed she had employed an illegal alien to work in her home. Bush replaced Chavez with Elaine Chao, the first Asian American woman in the Cabinet. In the end, he selected only one Democrat for his Cabinet, Norman Mineta, Clinton's last commerce secretary whom Bush tapped for the transportation department.

In the first months of his administration, Bush moved ahead on his domestic agenda, including tax cuts, education, energy, and "faith-based" initiatives. True to his campaign pledge, Bush proposed and signed into law a significant income tax cut. The measure reduced tax revenues by an estimated $1.35 trillion over 10 years. It trimmed tax rates for all income groups, lowered the so-called "marriage penalty," and provided for doubling child credits over time. Supporters lauded the cut as necessary for stimulating economic growth and for giving Americans greater control over their paychecks. Opponents argued it would result in the return of deficit spending rather than providing continued surpluses to shore up the Social Security system. Indeed, by the next year, the federal budget again ran a deficit. Tax cut foes also noted that the law favored wealthier Americans. Those with incomes in the top 1 percent received better than 37 percent of the tax cut; by comparison, taxpayers in the bottom 20 percent pocketed just 0.9 percent of the cut. Moreover, the cuts raised the after-tax income for the top 1 percent by 6.3 percent, while no other group received more than a 2.8 percent income boost. The law also would eliminate the estate (or "death") tax by 2010. This provision also favored the wealthiest Americans, because they were the only ones subject to it.

Bush redeemed another campaign promise with the passage of new education reforms. The No Child Left Behind Act, signed into law in January 2002, tied increased federal funding for education to student scores on standardized tests. Ironically, this president who talked about reducing the role of the federal government signed this law that actually increased federal oversight of elementary and secondary education, traditionally a state responsibility.

On two issues, however, energy and faith-based initiatives, the administration experienced less success than on taxes and education reform. The fact that both Bush and Cheney were former oil industry executives primed Democrats and environmentalists to oppose the Bush energy plan unveiled in the summer of 2001. The plan's most controversial element involved its proposal to drill for oil in Alaska's environmentally sensitive Arctic National Wildlife Refuge (ANWR). Other controversy surrounded the plan. The task force that wrote the plan, chaired by Cheney, apparently included representatives of major energy firms, some of which had made large financial contributions to the Bush campaign. Cheney refused to divulge details about the composition or deliberations of his energy task force, so Congress's investigative arm, the General Accounting Office, sued the White House to obtain the information. The Republican-controlled House passed an energy bill very close to Bush's plan, while Democrats in the Senate insisted on eliminating drilling in ANWR. Because Bush demanded the ANWR provision, the plan stalled.

Faith-based initiatives formed a central pillar of Bush's campaign theme of "compassionate conservatism." Bush wanted to permit faith-based groups such as churches, synagogues, and other religious organizations to compete with secular groups to receive federal funding to administer social services. He established offices in the White House and five executive departments to promote the plan. Proponents argued that faith-based social programs had a higher degree of success than many secular ones while opponents suggested that the plan violated church-state separation. Even some conservative religious organizations that generally supported Bush feared that government regulations would inevitably accompany federal funds. Again, the administration made little progress on this plan in 2001, especially with the August resignation of the White House aide heading up the faith-based effort.

Despite some successes, Bush did not enjoy very strong job approval ratings in the first few months of his presidency. The Harris polling organization found that Bush's positive rating—49 percent in March 2001—was lower than that of all recent presidents (going back to Lyndon Johnson) at comparable points in their administrations. His positive ratings improved later that spring following the shooting down of an American spy plane in China—they stood at 62 percent in early May according to Gallup—but declined steadily to the low 50s by early September. One liberal opinion journal placed a picture of a diminutive Bush on its mid-August 2001 cover under the title, "The Incredible Shrinking Presidency." Shortly, however, as the United States faced a major new crisis, the country rallied behind George W. Bush.

9/11 AND THE AMERICAN RESPONSE

September 11, 2001, began as a beautiful late summer day in New York City. Then, at 8:45 a.m., a commercial airliner flew across the city's famed skyline and slammed into the 110-story north tower of the World Trade Center. Seventeen minutes later, a second plane crashed into the Center's south tower. The planes—each carrying about 60,000 pounds of jet fuel and traveling at 300 miles per hour—acted as enormous missiles. As stunned on-lookers below raced for cover from falling debris, balls of fire engulfed the upper floors. Shocked Americans realized that the crashes were no accidents, but that terrorists had attacked the United States. At 9:43 a.m., a third plane rammed into the Pentagon just across the Potomac River from Washington, D.C., while less than half an hour later in western Pennsylvania, a fourth plane heading from Newark to San Francisco came down in rural Somerset County. Later reports indicated that passengers on board that fourth flight, aware of the New York attacks, struggled with hijackers and foiled their plans to destroy another Washington-area building, possibly the Capitol or the White House.

The extent of the devastation was incomprehensible. More than 3,000 persons died in the attacks, including many New York City firefighters and police officers attempting to help victims in the burning buildings. The two World Trade Center towers collapsed, as did several surrounding buildings. Reports estimated the property damage from the attacks that day at $25 billion. September 11, 2001, replaced April 19, 1995, as the single worst day of domestic terrorism in American history. Unfortunately, more terror followed in the ensuing days and weeks as several news organizations and two Democratic United States senators received letters laced with the

The September 11, 2001, terrorist attacks on the World Trade Center (A/P Wide World Photo)

deadly anthrax virus. Investigators believed that a domestic terrorist, trying to piggyback on the airline crashes, most likely sent the letters. In any event, the attacks left many Americans feeling helpless.

U.S. authorities traced the 19 men responsible for hijacking the jets. They belonged to al Qaeda, the terrorist organization linked to the attacks on the United States embassies in Africa in 1998 and on the U.S.S. Cole in 2000. Headquartered since 1996 in Afghanistan where it enjoyed the protection of the fundamentalist Islamic Taliban regime, al Qaeda had cells in American and European cities. Several of the 19 men had lived for a number of years in the United States where they took flying lessons to prepare for their deadly mission.

"Make no mistake," President Bush declared on September 11, "the United States will hunt down and punish those responsible for these cowardly acts." In the days that followed the attacks, Bush called for a new war against terror. He demanded that Afghanistan hand over bin Laden and his key associates. After the Taliban leadership refused, the United States and allied forces initiated aerial bombing of suspected al Qaeda targets on October 7. They also joined anti-Taliban groups (the Northern Alliance) within Afghanistan to overthrow the regime militarily. The first United States commandoes parachuted in on October 19 and took over a key airfield. Within weeks, Taliban and al Qaeda forces began surrendering in droves, although many remained in fortified, remote mountain hideouts in eastern Afghanistan. After allied bombings and some cave-to-cave operations by American

President Bush with the First Lady attending a 9/11 memorial *(A/P Wide World Photo)*

and British forces, the United States in mid-December declared the Taliban defeated. Meanwhile, Afghani factional and tribal leaders opposed to the Taliban agreed on a new interim government headed by Hamid Karzai. In January 2002, the Taliban leaders officially gave up, although pockets of resistance remained in isolated spots. Polls indicated Americans overwhelmingly supported Bush and the war on terror. The president's job approval rating soared to 90 percent in the aftermath of September 11, and it remained above 70 percent well into the following year. Americans of all backgrounds—men and women, white and non-white, Republicans and Democrats—gave the president and his administration high marks.

Still, voices of dissent spoke out. A particularly vexing set of questions concerned the treatment of prisoners and detainees in the war on terror. The United States established a special detention center, Camp X-Ray, for Taliban and al Qaeda prisoners at the U.S. navy's base at Guantanamo Bay, Cuba, but refused to treat them as prisoners of war under international law. In addition, in the United States itself, the federal government rounded up and detained for months more than 1,100 persons of Middle Eastern or Islamic background suspected of violating immigration laws (and of potentially being terrorists) or because they could be material witnesses in terrorist investigations. Civil liberties groups objected to these detentions because the government denied detainees basic constitutional rights such as access to legal counsel. In addition, the government did not charge these alleged terrorists with any crime, a violation of the right to habeas corpus.

For its part, Congress gave strong approval to broader governmental powers to wage the war on terrorism at home by passing the USA PATRIOT Act in October 2001. This law weakened civil liberties guarantees by, among other things, expanding the government's ability to tap telephones, track e-mail, and conduct searches without warning. Supporters of privacy on both the political right and left raised concerns about how an open, democratic society based on individual liberties could permit such a law. In late 2001, however, security appeared more crucial than civil liberties to most members of Congress as they sought ways to prevent further terrorist attacks within the United States.

WAR IN IRAQ

Alarmed by the ongoing threat of terrorism that might be unleashed by Muslim fundamentalists in the aftermath of September 11, the American people and the Congress both overwhelmingly supported the American military action in Afghanistan—and much of the world concurred. Operation Enduring Freedom, to overthrow the extremist Taliban regime, was carried out in conjunction with NATO troops and in conjunction also, with the homegrown Afghan Northern Alliance, long opposed to the Taliban. The campaign, which began in October 2001, resulted by November of that year in the allies' capture of the capital, Kabul; but the elusive Osama bin Laden, however, remained at large.

By early 2002, it was becoming apparent that the Bush administration had its eyes on other foes besides the Taliban. Having already proclaimed a "war on terror," in his State of the Union speech in late January President Bush identified a so-called "axis of evil" consisting of the countries of North Korea, Iraq, and Iran. Using bellicose rhetoric, he made clear his administration's unwillingness to stand by while these states might be engaged in acquiring weapons of mass destruction or in sponsoring terror. During the course of 2002, it emerged that Iraq and its unsavory dictator, Saddam Hussein, were the chief targets of the administration's wrath, and President Bush foreshadowed his intentions by enunciating an American right to use preemptive force. Bush and others in the administration also began to issue stern warnings about the danger posed by the presence of alleged weapons of mass destruction in the hands of Saddam, the man whose invasion of Kuwait in 1990 had been responsible for the

In 2002 President Bush began to press for the invasion of Iraq on the grounds its leader, Saddam Hussein, was harboring weapons of mass destruction. *(AP/Wide World Photo)*

Persian Gulf War of 1991. In fact, it has subsequently emerged that certain members of the Bush team, above all, Vice President Cheney, had been eager to go after Saddam ever since the first President Bush had opted not to pursue this goal. The horror engendered by 9/11 then provided them with an excuse so to do because they were able to imply, if not outright assert, that Saddam was somehow connected with 9/11—an allegation since proven to have no substance. Cynics have suggested that the former oil man Cheney may have had oil-related motives that underlay his fixation with oil-rich Iraq.

While world opinion largely supported the action against the Taliban, the prospect of an American invasion of Iraq was another matter. America's French and German allies were strongly opposed; and while Prime Minister Tony Blair of the United Kingdom would send troops when the invasion took place, his government's action flew in the face of a British public opinion opposed to this stance. Trying to make its case, the Bush administration made ever-stronger claims about Saddam's weapons of mass destruction, culminating with a speech by the widely respected American Secretary of State, Colin Powell to the United Nations in February 2003. Secretary Powell provided detailed "evidence" of the weapons in question, evidence that has subsequently been proven to have been either flimsy or fallacious. The speech failed to persuade the U.N., but the administration's case did persuade the majority of the American public, many Democrats in Congress—and members of the President's own party—to authorize the use of force in Iraq in a vote taken in the fall of 2002. (It should be noted that some of the Democrats voting for the use of force might have been not so much persuaded by the administration's case as afraid to be painted as unpatriotic in the wake of 9/11 should they oppose the administration).

The invasion took place with a coalition consisting overwhelmingly of American troops with a smaller number of British troops, and a smattering of troops from Italy, Spain, Japan (those from Japan in Iraq only for humanitarian purposes), and a few other countries. The U.N., whose inspectors felt that their ongoing effort to determine the state of Iraqi weapons programs was working, refused to endorse the invasion, as did NATO. Within a few weeks of the opening salvos in March 2003, Saddam had fled, Baghdad had fallen, and the real work of subduing an unruly and divided populace had begun.

Before the invasion, many military officials had tried to convince Secretary of Defense Donald Rumsfeld that this war could not be fought on the cheap. Most prominent among those making this argument was General Eric Shinseki, Army Chief of Staff, who warned in February 2003 that the Iraq action would require several hundred thousand troops (the number used in the less ambitious Gulf War of 1991). When Rumsfeld refused to provide Shinseki with the troops Shineski believed he required, Shineski resigned shortly thereafter, his warning having been ignored. As events have unfolded, it has been clear that the 130,000 to 150,000 troops on the ground have had an extraordinarily tough assignment, especially as an Iraqi insurgency gathered steam. The troops' assignment has been rendered even more difficult because the military has found it challenging to maintain an adequate supply of the kind of armor necessary for the brutal conditions created by frequent roadside bombings (this according to widely-reported accounts). Indeed, reports of parents who have themselves sent armor to their sons and daughters have appeared in the press. The Bush administration had not anticipated that there would be an insurgency at all and, therefore, had not sent the American soldiers to Iraq with the appropriate protection.

There had been a certain amount of good news for the Bush administration coming out of Iraq. Saddam Hussein had been captured, brought to trial, and executed. Elections had been held, and an Iraqi government had come into power. As of mid-2008, however, the government was far from being able to maintain order on its own, and even the foreign troops had been unable to pacify the country fully. Not only are there still jihadis eager to kill Americans and those who cooperate with Americans, but there has also been strife between the two strands of Islam in Iraq, the majority Shia and the Sunnis, long in control under the Sunni, Saddam Hussein. Further, the Kurdish population also constitutes a significant element of the population, one often at odds with the Shia and the Sunnis. Experts differ on whether there is an actual civil war or merely the preamble to one, but polls have shown that most Americans have been growing increasingly uneasy about a war that has cost the lives of at least 4,000 Americans and tens of thousands of Iraqis—with no end in sight. Worst of all, no weapons of mass destruction have ever been discovered, and, belatedly, the administration has finally ceased to use this rationale for its Iraqi adventure.

Other unfortunate byproducts of the war have included a decline in the world's favorable opinion of the United States a phenomenon well documented by polling data collected by the Pew Research Center. Respect for the United States suffered an especially serious blow with revelations, in May 2004, about the widespread abuse of prisoners at Abu Ghraib, a facility built by Saddam Hussein but used by the Americans to house suspected troublemakers, The revelations were backed up by shocking pictures of American soldiers engaged in humiliating the inmates—or worse. At least one Iraqi inmate is known to have died from the abuse. To date, only low-level members of the military have been punished for the abuses at Abu Ghraib, in spite of the testimony of Private Lyndie England that she was only following "standard operating procedures."

Secondly, the war in Iraq has led to a diversion of attention and resources away from Afghanistan. Not only does bin Laden remain at large as of mid-2008, but also the Taliban has been resurgent, despite many hopeful signs of budding democracy in the beleaguered country. The respected Pakistani journalist, Ahmed Rashid, reported that as of late May 2006, "a revived Taliban movement has made one third of the country ungovernable." By late summer of 2008, more American soldiers were dying in Afghanistan on a monthly basis than in Iraq.

Thus five years after an exultant President Bush stood on the deck of an aircraft carrier near a sign proclaiming "Mission Accomplished" and three years after Vice President Cheney announced that the insurgency was in its last throes, the bloodshed was continuing. In fairness to the administration, it must be said that, as of mid-2008 there have been no new terrorist attacks on American soil since 9/11—though whether that owes to the Bush policies is an open question. After all, it was also eight years between the first bombing of the World Trade Center in 1993 and the second attack on 9/11. It must also be said that the administration has faced hitherto unknown challenges in trying to protect the American people from terrorism.

THE ELECTION OF 2004

With politics still revolving around 9/11 and its consequences, the Republicans found that pitching themselves as the party best-suited to wage the war on terror worked well for them. Indeed, in the mid-term Congressional elections of 2002 they were able to pick up two seats in the Senate and three in the House, contrary to the usual pattern of mid-term losses for the party occupying the White House. Most galling for the Democrats, perhaps, was the defeat of incumbent Democratic Senator Max Cleland of Georgia, a wheelchair-bound Vietnam veteran. His successful opponent, Saxby Chambliss, ran ads that questioned the patriotism of this profoundly disabled man, disabled because of having fought for his country.

President Bush also had to withstand a significant challenge in the primaries from Senator John McCain of Arizona, a decorated Vietnam Veteran who was famously shot down in Vietnam and spent the war in a North Vietnamese prison camp known as the Hanoi Hilton where he underwent torture and suffered from multiple injuries, such as broken bones, to which the North Vietnamese did not attend. Bush proved that it was his intention to win at all costs when Bush supporters conducted anonymous telephone polls in South Carolina in which voters were asked whether they would be more or less likely to vote for McCain knowing he had fathered an illegitimate black child. What McCain and his wife, Cindy, had actually done was adopt a girl from Bangladesh whom they had originally brought to the United States for medical care. When complaints about the "poll" were aired by the McCain campaign, Bush's campaign manager Karl Rove's response was that no one had ever produced evidence that he or anyone in the Bush campaign had sponsored a poll about an out-of-wedlock child. For his part, Bush did not disavow the underhanded tactics, which were evidently carried out by Bush supporters at Bob Jones University.

With the certain knowledge that Republicans would play up their strengths as the party best able to protect the country in the terrifying new post-9/11 world, the Democrats chose to nominate a war hero in 2004, Massachusetts Senator John Kerry, who had wrestled the nomination away from early leader Howard Dean after Dean had frightened voters with a speech where he intentionally threw a demonstrative emotional fit on stage to show his passion. The emotional tactic backfired, however; and Dean, who had grabbed the early lead due to his consistent opposition to the Iraq war and adept use of the Internet, quickly faded as Kerry emerged from the pack of Democratic challengers that had included at one time nine candidates, including Dick Gephart and Al Sharpton.

Kerry, however, was an unusual type of war hero. After being wounded in Vietnam, he came home and took a leadership role in the Vietnam Veterans Against the War, testifying before Congress on the alleged war crimes he had witnessed. In so doing, he made enemies that would haunt him more than 30 years later. In the short term, however, his outspoken opposition to the war in Vietnam gave him visibility and made him a public figure, a platform that led to a political career.

At the Democratic convention in 2004, however, Senator Kerry gave a speech that was long on his military credentials and short on his ultimate opposition to Vietnam, thus signaling his intention to position himself as a potentially effective commander-in-chief in the war on terror. If he thought that such credentials might afford him immunity from the type of attack suffered by Max Cleland (especially in the light of George W. Bush's own ambiguous military record), he would soon learn otherwise. A group of Vietnam veterans, long disgruntled about Kerry's critique of Vietnam, launched an initiative known as the Swift Boat Veterans for Truth. Obviously very well funded, these men disputed Kerry's valor, his account of his wounds, and much else. In just nine months in Vietnam, Kerry had earned a Bronze Star and a Silver Star for valor, and three purple hearts; but in the Swift Boat ads, he was portrayed as a coward who lacked leadership skills and was awarded medals he did not deserve. In spite of the fact that the ads were entirely bogus (the United States military does not hand out medals to those who do not earn them), in the view of most pundits, the Swift Boat campaign played a role in Kerry's defeat. President Bush was not directly responsible for the Swift Boat ad, and it is true that it was not directly funded by his campaign; but he did not denounce it either. Supporters of Kerry did not retaliate with a similar smear campaign of their own.

Most pundits further contended that the Republicans' adroit use of social issues also helped lead them to victory. Bush campaign strategist Matthew Dowd reviewed the 2000 election data and determined that the percentage of voters who could be persuaded to cross party lines had declined from 22 percent of the electorate in 1980 to just 7 percent in 2000. Conventional wisdom in presidential election strategy for decades had been that the party that wins the middle, wins the election. Dowd's analysis, however, suggested that the persuadable middle had become so small and politics so polarized that the party that would win would be not the one that won the swing voters but, rather, the one that did the best job at getting its own partisans to the polls. Consequently, their strategy was to do a superb job of turning out their conservative base by evoking the threat of gay marriage, for example. Whether the Republican success owed primarily to this strategy, to the Swift Boat campaign, to the lingering effects of 9/11, or to Kerry's own shortcomings as a candidate, in fact, Bush did better than he had in 2000, capturing 50.7 percent of the popular vote to Kerry's 48.3 percent, with voter turnout at 61 percent, the highest since the late nineteenth century. John Kerry actually received more votes than Al Gore had in winning the popular vote in 2000, but George W. Bush received more votes, over 59 million, than any candidate in history. The vote in the Electoral College stood at 286 for Bush and 251 for Kerry. The Republicans also did well in the Congressional races, picking up three seats in the House and four in the Senate. Bush only won Ohio by 118,000 votes, however; so if 60,000 of those voters had voted for John Kerry instead, Kerry would have won Ohio's 20 electoral votes and, thus, the election.

SECOND-TERM BLUES

Claiming that he had "won political capital" and intended to "spend it," George W. Bush announced at the beginning of his second term that he would seek to reform the Social Security system, in effect, privatizing it. He made many trips around the country to reach out to voters and convince them that this change would be in their interest, but his efforts were to no avail; and the projected change went nowhere as Bush's popularity diminished as the Iraq war dragged on. Unfortunately for Bush, the failure to mobilize public support for privatizing Social Security was only the beginning of the President's headaches as the year 2005 unfolded.

Bush's problems, and those of his party, deepened in 2005 when House Majority Leader Tom DeLay began to run into legal difficulties. Elected to the House in 1984 from a Houston district, DeLay had risen quickly through the ranks, becoming known as "the Hammer" because of his capacity to enforce party discipline. Within the halls of Congress, Delay's other nickname was "Hot Tub Tom" due to his proclivity for hot tubs and young women, while his supporters in Texas knew him as a Congressman who supported conservative Christian causes and referred to the occupied territories in Palestine as "Judea and Samaria." After the Republicans took control of the House in

1995, DeLay became Majority Whip. In 2002 he became House Majority Leader. Fiercely partisan, DeLay was known to be the driving force behind the impeachment of Bill Clinton. He also bore the credit—or blame, depending on one's point of view—for the K Street project, an initiative to reach out to lobbying firms (whose offices tended to be on K Street in Washington) and encourage them to hire only Republicans for leadership positions. What landed DeLay in trouble initially was his highly successful, from a partisan point of view, attempt to coordinate redistricting efforts in Texas so as to create more safe Republican seats in the House. In 2005, this attempt led to a Texas grand jury indicting him on criminal charges of conspiring to violate Texas campaign finance laws. DeLay fought back by asserting that the charges were partisan in nature—but he did step down as Majority Leader. Over the next year he gradually surrendered more of his power until he resigned altogether from the House in June 2006.

That DeLay was driven from office owed also to the legal problems of one Jack Abramoff, a Washington wheeler-dealer and lobbyist—as well as alleged DeLay crony—who ran into a legal buzz-saw of his own. In January 2006, Abramoff pleaded guilty to three felony counts of conspiracy, fraud, and tax evasion in conjunction with his dealings with certain clients. Soon thereafter, two former DeLay aides were convicted on charges related to the Abramoff scandal. Connections to Abramoff became so politically poisonous that the Bush administration classified the White House visitors' log, and critics charged that the motivation was to prevent the public from seeing that Abramoff had visited the White House.

Regardless, the reason why DeLay's fall was so problematic for his party and his president is that after his departure, there was no other Republican in the House with his ability to deliver the votes for the Bush legislative program. On the other hand, since Ronald Reagan took office in 1981, the GOP has proven itself to be more than adept at political strategy and political recovery. Hence even with this set of problems it will no doubt continue to be a match for the sometimes-hapless Democrats.

If Bush and his administration had shown themselves able to engage in successful combat with their political foes, they found Mother Nature to be a truly formidable foe when Hurricane Katrina hit the Gulf Coast in late August 2005. As Douglas Brinkley documents in *The Great Deluge*, the whole coast including its largest city, New Orleans, constituted a disaster waiting to happen. This was because of coastal erosion owing to natural causes and human alteration of the Mississippi River itself, with much of New Orleans, situated next to America's largest river, actually below sea level, and the situation

In 2005 Hurricane Katrina wreaked havoc on the Gulf Coast and left most of New Orleans under water for many days. *(iStock)*

was further compounded by engineering mistakes. Moreover, oil companies had installed miles of pipelines in fragile terrain, and shipping companies had pressured the government to install channels. For all of these reasons, the natural defenses that had prevented New Orleans at the mouth of the Mississippi River, and other coastal cities from being repeatedly swamped by big storms had been undermined. When added to the ineptitude of government at every level, the result was a human catastrophe of nearly unimaginable proportions.

Katrina first formed on August 23, and as it gathered strength it would become the third-strongest hurricane ever to reach land in the United States. It touched southern Florida as a category 1 storm; but by the time it made its second landfall along the Gulf Coast on August 29, it had morphed into a category 3. At first New Orleans itself seemed to have escaped truly major consequences, but before very long came word that the storm surge created by Katrina had breached the levees, leaving large sections of the city vulnerable to flooding—flooding that would eventually engulf some 500,000 homes. Thousands of New Orleans residents had either been unable or unwilling to evacuate the city; hence there arose an urgent need for rescue operations, operations that seemed to be feeble and ineffective. In the end, between the damage in New Orleans and in the rest of the devastated area, Katrina was estimated to have cost at least $75 billion in damages and nearly 2,000 lives.

As these events unfolded, a horrified nation watched television images of largely African American storm victims huddling in the New Orleans Superdome or the Convention Center and lacking basic sanitation—with the authorities seemingly dithering about how to alleviate their problems. Brinkley forcefully delineates the failure of leadership at many levels. In New Orleans itself, for example, Mayor Ray Nagin failed to use all of his powers to ensure the evacuation of as many people as humanly possible before it was too late. President Bush, on vacation in Crawford, Texas (where he had similarly been—and stayed—in August 2001 when then-National Security Adviser Condoleezza Rice had warned him about a possible al Qaeda attack) stayed put until the disaster was well underway. Michael D. Brown, head of the Federal Emergency Management Agency, received a briefing about the expected severity of the storm, but let a whole day go by before taking action. Finally, when Brown did mobilize for action, his e-mails reveal him to have been extremely preoccupied with how he would look on television.

At first President Bush praised Brown, saying to him publicly "Brownie, you're doing a heckuva job;" but within less than two weeks Brown had lost his job, a job for which he had no obvious qualifications—his most noteworthy previous job having been as head of a trade association for owners of Arabian horses. Trying to make amends, the President made a series of trips to the Gulf Coast to demonstrate his commitment to the region. As of mid-2006, however, there was still an overwhelming amount of work to be done, so overwhelming an amount that the *New York Times* reported an enormous surge in suicides and other mental health problems in New Orleans in the wake of Katrina.

Another casualty of Katrina had been President Bush's standing in the polls. Between the incompetent response to the hurricane and the increasingly unpopular war in Iraq, Bush's ratings plummeted, going as low as 27 percent approval at one point. That Vice President Cheney accidentally shot a friend in the face in February 2006, thereby becoming fodder for comics on late-night TV, did not help the administration's standing with the public. At this writing in the fall of 2008, any chance Bush may have to resurrect his standing in what most people view as a failed second term may rest on his administration's handling of the nation's worst financial crisis since the Great Depression. The situation in Iraq showed improvement in 2008, but it is still far too early to tell if the improvement is the beginning of a long term trend or merely false hope. Meanwhile, the summer of 2008 witnessed renewed intensity in the war in Afghanistan and American troops launched assaults across the border into Pakistan. After six years in Afghanistan and over five years in Iraq, neither war begun by the Bush administration had been effectively won.

ELECTION 2008

The election of 2008 was an election of historic proportions in a number of ways. Most notably, Barack Obama, the son of a black man from Kenya and a white woman from Kansas, became the first African-American to win the White House. In addition, Alaska governor Sarah Palin, a newcomer to the national political scene, became the first woman to be nominated for Vice President on the Republican Party ticket after receiving the nod from Republican presidential candidate Senator John McCain of Arizona, at age 72 the oldest Presidential nominee for either party.

In what should probably be considered the longest electoral campaign in history, Illinois Senator Barack Obama, who first burst on the scene with a dynamic speech at the 2004 Democratic National Convention, narrowly defeated the early favorite for the Democratic Party nomination, New York Senator and former First Lady Hillary Rodham Clinton, and the 2004 Democratic Vice Presidential Candidate John Edwards in the Democratic primaries. On the Republican side, Arizona Senator John McCain, who had run for the Republican nomination unsuccessfully in 2000, defeated a host of Republican candidates in the Republican primaries—including "America's Mayor" Rudy Giuliani of New York, who had become a national hero for his actions on 9/11; Hollywood actor and former Tennessee Senator Fred Thompson; former Massachusetts governor and successful businessman Mitt Romney, the first Mormon to be a serious candidate for President; and Arkansas Governor Mike Huckabee (a bass-guitar playing, former preacher, and favorite among social conservatives).

Senator McCain was legendary for his campaign energy and, even at 71 years of age, dedicated himself to "out-campaigning" his opponents. McCain had developed a reputation over the years as a political "maverick," sometimes reaching across the aisle and working with Democrats, most notably on the McCain-Feingold campaign finance reform bill that he sponsored with Democratic Senator Russ Feingold in 2002. Many viewed McCain as a Republican that could appeal to middle voters. McCain also had appeal due to his experience as a Vietnam veteran and former POW who spent five years imprisoned, suffering torture and broken bones at the hands of his communist captors while serving his country during the Viet Nam War. Given that McCain had opposed George W. Bush in the Republican primary in 2000, he could also appeal to anti-Bush voters. Even though most Americans in 2008 believed that the nation was headed in the wrong direction under the Bush administration, John McCain would be a formidable Republican candidate.

The Democratic nominee Barack Obama, however, proved to be an equally adept campaigner. Obama made extensive use of the internet in campaigning and fundraising and incorporated new tools, such as *Facebook* and *YouTube*, that had not even existed in 2004. As a graduate of both Columbia and Harvard Law School, Obama proved to be an excellent speaker, politically astute, and able to withstand the same kind of propaganda campaigns that had doomed Al Gore and John Kerry in 2000 and 2004, respectively. The Republican campaign machine found footage of Jeremiah Wright, preacher of the church Obama attended, proclaiming, "God damn America" for its history of racial segregation and discrimination. While Americans generally may have agreed with Reverend Wright that segregation and racial discrimination were regrettable, most Americans reacted negatively to Wright's audible expression of the words, "God damn America," regardless of context. That Obama had enjoyed a 20-year relationship with this man was unsettling to many. Simultaneously, right-wing talk show hosts questioned whether or not Obama was indeed a Muslim, rather than a Christian, and noted that "Obama" rhymes with "Osama" and his middle name is Hussein. Republicans also attempted to connect Obama with shady characters such as Chicago businessman Tony Rezko and former 1960s radical William Ayers, but the negative campaign efforts failed to produce a lead for John McCain. Republicans also lauded McCain's experience and argued that Obama was too young and inexperienced to be President. In response, Obama chose Senator Joseph Biden of Delaware, a 35-year veteran of the United States Senate and chair of the Senate Committee on Foreign Relations, as his running mate. Unfortunately for Obama, the choice of Biden angered many of the supporters of Hillary Clinton in the Democratic Party who believed that Hillary should have been his choice as a running mate.

After Obama had secured the Democratic nomination in a hard-fought battle with Hillary Clinton, the Republicans hoped to sway disgruntled Clinton supporters to John McCain. Some polls suggested that a significant number of Clinton supporters would not vote for Obama. In an effort both to reach out to women voters and young voters, as well as appeal to the social conservatives that were less comfortable with the "maverick" side of McCain, Senator McCain chose the relatively unknown 44-year-old governor of Alaska, Sarah Palin as his running mate. Palin then delivered perhaps the most effective speech ever by a Vice Presidential candidate at a party's national convention, and John McCain suddenly narrowed the gap in the polls between himself and Barack Obama. Palin connected with the Republican rank and file, describing herself as a "hockey mom" and stating that the only difference between a pit bull and a "hockey mom" was "lipstick." Palin was a pro-life Protestant fundamentalist Christian who had re-

President Barack Obama *(AP Photo)*

cently given birth to a child with Down syndrome rather than abort. Her husband raced snowmobiles, and one of her children was a veteran of the United States military—all things that energized the Republicans' social conservative base.

Just as quickly as things had come together for John McCain, however, they would rapidly fall apart. As Sarah Palin hit the campaign trail, potential voters were surprised to hear at her appearances the same speech they had heard at the Republican convention. Although the speech had been a great one, the repetition suggested that the candidate did not know anything else. Palin then botched a television interview with newswoman Katie Couric when Palin revealed that she did not know specifics of the Bush Doctrine. The Couric interview quickly became a sensation on *YouTube*, another technology phenomenon that did not exist in 2004. *Saturday Night Live* comedian Tina Fey then performed a television parody of Palin that became another *YouTube* sensation. Some voters were bothered by the fact that Palin was a social conservative, yet her teenage daughter was pregnant. Others were uneasy about the unconventional names for the Palin children—Trigg, Track, Willow, Bristol, and Piper. By the time of the November election, the supportive surge that Palin had provided to McCain at the Republican Convention had evaporated.

Obama won the Presidential election with 364 electoral votes to 174 for Republican John McCain. Obama won 52 percent of the popular vote to 46 percent for John McCain, making him the first Democrat to win more than 50 percent of the vote since Jimmy Carter

(Carter had won 50.1 percent) and giving him the highest vote percentage of any Democrat since Lyndon Johnson's win in 1964. Obama won handily in the Democratic strongholds of the Northeast and the Pacific coast; but he also fared well in the area surrounding the Great Lakes—even winning the normally Republican states of Indiana, Virginia, and North Carolina, and the key swing state of Ohio that John Kerry had narrowly lost for the Democrats in 2004. Obama also won in Florida where the election had hinged eight years before.

In 2000 and 2004, the Republicans won two close elections partially because they had built a better grass roots political machine and because the Democrats fielded candidates that lacked exciting personalities. In the election of 2008, however, it would be the Democrats with the better party organization, the better fundraising, and the more dynamic candidate.

Obama campaigned on the platforms of "hope" and "change" and benefited from John McCain's association with the same party of incumbent President George W. Bush, whose approval rating had fluctuated in the low thirties and high twenties for a year and a half prior to the 2008 election. With the nation in economic recession, the wars in Afghanistan and Iraq continuing, and a series of disasters in the Bush White House—including an inadequate response to Hurricane Katrina that flooded New Orleans in 2005, news of torture and human rights abuses at Guantanamo Bay, Abu Ghraib, and elsewhere, poor performances by Bush appointees such as Attorney General Alberto Gonzalez under Congressional inquiries, a scandal over illegal wiretaps, and Bush's incessant secrecy, Obama's messages of "hope" and "change" sounded refreshing to many Americans. Throughout the campaign, Republican John McCain was disadvantaged by the fact that approximately 75 percent of Americans thought that the country was on the "wrong track" and a solid two-thirds, on any given day, disapproved of the performance of the Republican President, George W. Bush. Of those that said that they expected John McCain to continue President Bush's policies, 90 percent voted for Barack Obama. By the time of the election, a full 93 percent of voters believed that the economy was headed in the wrong direction, a number that simply could not benefit the Party that had held the White House for eight years.

In September 2008, the announced bankruptcy of the large American brokerage firm, Lehman Brothers, triggered a financial collapse that may have been the worst since the Great Depression. Merrill Lynch, another brokerage firm, was forced to sell out to Bank of America, and Wells Fargo bought out Wachovia. Bank and financial stocks tumbled, some as much as 90 percent. Citicorp stock fell from a 12-month high of $38 to $2.80, and Bank of America stock fell from $47 to $5.10. Housing prices tumbled nationwide; mortgage lenders announced bankruptcies, and insurance giant AIG that provided insurance for many mortgage companies was also revealed to be insolvent. In addition, the American automakers announced that they, too, were also facing bankruptcy. Amid the economic calamity, Republican candidate John McCain publicly admitted that he knew little of economics and proclaimed, "the fundamentals of the American economy are strong." Although McCain had drawn essentially even in the polls with Obama after the Republican convention, he would fall behind after the mid-September economic collapse and never recover. Meanwhile, President Bush would ask Congress for a $700 billion emergency appropriation to bail out the sagging financial industry.

When election day finally came, unsurprisingly, Obama won 95 percent of the black vote; but the 47-year old candidate also appealed to young voters, winning 66 percent of those under 30 and 68 percent of first-time voters. He also appealed to other minorities, winning 66 percent of the Hispanic vote. In spite of his pro-choice position on abortion, Obama even won 54 percent of the Catholic vote, seven points better than that won by the Catholic Democratic candidate John Kerry in 2004. Where Obama did not do well, however, was among white voters without a college education, 59 percent of who voted for John McCain, and among voters 65 and over, 54 percent of who voted for John McCain.

Obama dedicated himself to a 50-state campaign strategy that stretched the less well-funded McCain campaign and helped the Democrats pick up seats to bolster their majorities in both houses of Congress, although they ended with 59 seats in the Senate—just short of the filibuster-proof number of 60. Obama then quickly began putting together his team that would take the helm in 2009 and formulating plans to address the nation's economic woes. On January 20, 2009, Barack Obama was sworn in as the first African-American President of the United States.

* * *

To take the long view of how far the nation had traveled by the first decade of the new millennium we have only to think about the first national census in 1790, which counted just fewer than 4,000,000 Americans, nearly 700,000 of them enslaved persons of African descent. They primarily lived in cities, towns, and farms hugging the Atlantic Coast; the mean center of population lay 23 miles east of Baltimore. In 2000, the census recorded 281,421,906

Americans—all legally free—spread out in states stretching from the Atlantic to the Pacific, and even in the Pacific. By 2000 the mean center of population lay in south central Missouri's Phelps County, reflecting the continuing westward and southward movement of the population. Moreover, the nearly 300 million United States citizens included persons who came (or whose ancestors came) from every country on earth. People have come to these shores because they have believed in their chances to better themselves, and many barriers based on race and gender have, indeed, crumbled. To cite just one example of positive change in breaking down barriers, leading Americans of Thomas Jefferson's day would have found it unimaginable that in 2006 an African American woman, Condoleezza Rice, would hold his old job as Secretary of State. Though the country is far from being a full embodiment of the American Dream of justice and opportunity for all, it is far closer to realizing the dream than it was 100 years earlier, let alone at the country's founding.

THE DECLARATION OF INDEPENDENCE

When in the course of human events, it becomes necessary for one people to dissolve the political bands which have connected them with another, and to assume among the Powers of the earth, the separate and equal station to which the Laws of Nature and of Nature's God entitle them, a decent respect to the opinions of mankind requires that they should declare the causes which impel them to the separation.

We hold these truths to be self-evident, that all men are created equal, that they are endowed by their Creator with certain unalienable Rights, that among these are Life, Liberty and the pursuit of Happiness. That to secure these rights, Governments are instituted among Men, deriving their just Powers from the consent of the governed, That whenever any Form of Government becomes destructive of these ends, it is the Right of the People to alter or to abolish it, and to institute new Government, laying its foundation on such principles and organizing its Powers in such form, as to them shall seem most likely to effect their Safety and Happiness. Prudence, indeed, will dictate that Governments long established should not be changed for light and transient causes; and accordingly all experience hath shewn, that mankind are more disposed to suffer, while evils are sufferable, than to right themselves by abolishing the forms to which they are accustomed. But when a long train of abuses and usurpations, pursuing invariably the same object evinces a design to reduce them under absolute Despotism, it is their right, it is their duty, to throw off such Government, and to provide new Guards for their future security. Such has been the patient sufferance of these Colonies:

and such is now the necessity which constrains them to alter their former Systems of Government. The history of the present King of Great Britain is a history of repeated injuries and usurpations, all having in direct object the Establishment of an absolute Tyranny over these States. To prove this, let Facts be submitted to a candid World:

He has refused his Assent to Laws, the most wholesome and necessary for the public good.

He has forbidden his Governors to pass Laws of immediate and pressing importance, unless suspended in their operation till his Assent should be obtained; and when so suspended, he has utterly neglected to attend to them.

He has refused to pass other Laws for the accommodation of large districts of people, unless those people would relinquish the right of Representation in the Legislature, a right inestimable to them and formidable to tyrants only.

He has called together legislative bodies at places unusual, uncomfortable, and distant from the depository of their Public Records, for the sole purpose of fatiguing them into compliance with his measures.

He has dissolved Representative Houses repeatedly, for opposing with manly firmness his invasions on the rights of the people.

He has refused for a long time, after such dissolutions, to cause others to be elected; whereby the Legislative Powers, incapable of the Annihilation, have returned to the People at large for their exercise; the State remaining in the mean time exposed to all the dangers of invasion from without, and the convulsions within.

He has endeavored to prevent the population of these States; for that purpose obstructing the Laws of Naturalization of Foreigners; refusing to pass others to encourage their migrations hither, and raising the conditions of new Appropriations of Lands.

He has obstructed the Administration of justice, by refusing his Assent to Laws for establishing Judiciary Powers.

He has made judges dependent on his Will alone, for the tenure of their offices, and the amount and payment of their salaries.

He has erected a multitude of New Offices, and sent hither swarms of Officers to harass our People, and eat out their substance.

He has kept among us, in times of peace, Standing Armies, without the consent of our legislature.

He has affected to render the Military independent of and superior to the Civil Power.

He has combined with others to subject us to a jurisdiction foreign to our constitution, and unacknowledged by our laws; giving his Assent to their acts of pretended legislation—

For quartering large bodies of armed troops among us;

For protecting them, by a mock Trial, from Punishment for any Murders which they should commit on the Inhabitants of these States;

For cutting off our Trade with all parts of the world;

For imposing Taxes on us without our Consent;

For depriving us in many cases, of the benefits of Trial by Jury;

For transporting us beyond Seas to be tried for pretended offences;

For abolishing the free System of English Laws in a neighboring Province, establishing therein an Arbitrary government, and enlarging its Boundaries so as to render it at once an example and fit instrument for introducing the same absolute rule into these Colonies;

For taking away our Charters, abolishing our most valuable Laws, and altering fundamentally the Forms of our Governments;

For suspending our own Legislatures, and declaring themselves invested with Power to legislate for us in all cases whatsoever.

He has abdicated Government here, by declaring us out of his Protection, and waging War against us.

He has plundered our seas, ravaged our Coasts, burnt our towns, and destroyed the lives of our people.

He is at this time transporting large armies of foreign mercenaries to compleat the works of death, desolation and tyranny, already begun with circumstances of Cruelty & perfidy, scarcely paralleled in the most barbarous ages, and totally unworthy the Head of a civilized nation.

He has constrained our fellow Citizens taken Captive on the high Seas to bear Arms against their Country, to become the executioners of their friends and Brethren, or to fall themselves by their Hands.

He has excited domestic insurrections amongst us, and has endeavoured to bring on the inhabitants of our frontiers, the merciless Indian Savages, whose known rule of warfare, is an undistinguished destruction of all ages, sexes and conditions.

In every stage of these Oppressions We have Petitioned for Redress in the most humble terms: Our repeated Petitions have been answered only by repeated injury. A Prince, whose character is thus marked by every act which may define a Tyrant, is unfit to be the ruler of a free People.

Nor have We been wanting in attentions to our British brethren. We have warned them from time to time of attempts by their legislature to extend an unwarrantable jurisdiction over us. We have reminded them of the circumstances of our emigration and settlement here. We have appealed to their native justice and magnanimity, and we have conjured them by the ties of our common kindred to disavow these usurpations, which, would inevitably interrupt our connections and correspondence. They too have been deaf to the voice of justice and of consanguinity. We must, therefore, acquiesce in the necessity, which denounces our Separation, and hold them, as we hold the rest of mankind, Enemies in War, in Peace, Friends.

We, therefore, the Representatives of the United States of America, in General Congress, Assembled, appealing to the Supreme Judge of the world for the rectitude of our intentions, do, in the Name, and by Authority of the good People of these Colonies, solemnly publish and declare, That these United Colonies are, and of Right ought to be Free and Independent States; that they are Absolved from all Allegiance to the British Crown, and that all political connection between them and the State of Great Britain, is and ought to be totally dissolved; and that, as Free and Independent States, they have full Power to levy War, conclude Peace, contract Alliances, establish Commerce, and to do all other Acts and Things which independent States may of right do. And for the support of this Declaration, with a firm reliance on the Protection of Divine Providence, we mutually pledge to each other our Lives, our Fortunes and our sacred Honor.

THE CONSTITUTION OF THE UNITED STATES

We the people of the United States, in Order to form a more perfect Union, establish justice, insure domestic Tranquility, provide for the common defense, promote the general Welfare, and secure the Blessings of Liberty to ourselves and our Posterity, do ordain and establish this Constitution for the United States of America.

ARTICLE I

SECTION 1. All legislative Powers herein granted shall be vested in a Congress of the United States, which shall consist of a Senate and House of Representatives.

SECTION 2. 1. The House of Representatives shall be composed of Members chosen every second Year by the People of the several States, and the Electors in each State shall have the Qualifications requisite for Electors of the most numerous Branch of the State Legislature.

2. No person shall be a Representative who shall not have attained to the Age of twenty-five Years, and been seven Years a Citizen of the United States, and who shall not, when elected, be an Inhabitant of that State in which he shall be chosen.

3. Representatives and direct Taxes[1] shall be apportioned among the several States which may be included within this Union, ac-

cording to their respective Numbers, which shall be determined by adding to the whole Number of free Persons, including those bound to Service for a Term of Years, and excluding Indians not taxed, three fifths of all other Persons.[2] The actual Enumeration shall be made within three Years after the first Meeting of the Congress of the United States, and within every subsequent Term of ten Years, in such Manner as they shall by Law direct. The Number of Representatives shall not exceed one for every thirty Thousand, but each State shall have at Least one Representative; and until such enumeration shall be made, the State of New Hampshire shall be entitled to chuse three, Massachusetts eight, Rhode Island and Providence Plantations one, Connecticut five, New York six, New Jersey four, Pennsylvania eight, Delaware one, Maryland six, Virginia ten, North Carolina five, South Carolina five, and Georgia three.

4. When vacancies happen in the Representation from any State, the Executive Authority thereof shall issue Writs of Election to fill such Vacancies.

5. The House of Representatives shall chuse their Speaker and other officers; and shall have the sole Power of Impeachment.

SECTION 3. 1. The Senate of the United States shall be composed of two Senators from each State, chosen by the Legislature thereof,[3] for six Years; and each Senator shall have one Vote.

2. Immediately after they shall be assembled in Consequence of the first Election, they shall be divided as equally as may be into three Classes. The Seats of the Senators of the first Class shall be vacated at the Expiration of the second Year, of the second Class at the Expiration of the fourth Year, and of the third Class at the Expiration of the sixth Year, so that one third may be chosen every second Year; and if Vacancies happen by Resignation, or otherwise, during the Recess of the Legislature of any State, the Executive thereof may make temporary Appointments until the next Meeting of the Legislature, which shall then fill such Vacancies.[4]

3. No Person shall be a Senator who shall not have attained to the Age of thirty Years, and been nine Years a Citizen of the United States, and who shall not, when elected, be an Inhabitant of that State for which he shall be chosen.

4. The Vice President of the United States shall be President of the Senate, but shall have no vote, unless they be equally divided.

5. The Senate shall chuse their other Officers, and also a President pro tempore, in the absence of the Vice President, or when he shall exercise the Office of President of the United States.

6. The Senate shall have the sole Power to try all Impeachments. When sitting for that purpose, they shall be on Oath or Affirmation. When the President of the United States is tried, the Chief justice shall preside: And no person shall be convicted without the Concurrence of two thirds of the Members present.

7. Judgment in Cases of impeachment shall not extend further than to removal from Office, and disqualification to hold and enjoy any Office of honor, Trust, or Profit under the United States: but the Party convicted shall nevertheless be liable and subject to Indictment, Trial, judgment and Punishment, according to Law.

SECTION 4. 1. The Times, Places and Manner of holding Elections for Senators and Representatives, shall be prescribed in each state by the Legislature thereof; but the Congress may at any

---

[1] See the Sixteenth Amendment.
[2] See the Fourteenth Amendment.
[3] See the Seventeenth Amendment.
[4] See the Seventeenth Amendment.

time by Law make or alter such Regulations, except as to the Places of Chusing Senators.

2. The Congress shall assemble at least once in every Year, and such Meeting shall be on the first Monday in December, unless they shall by Law appoint a different Day.

SECTION 5. 1. Each House shall be the judge of the Elections, Returns and Qualifications of its own Members, and a Majority of each shall constitute a Quorum to do Business; but a smaller number may adjourn from day to day, and may be authorized to compel the Attendance of absent Members, in such manner, and under such Penalties, as each House may provide.

2. Each House may determine the Rules of its Proceedings, punish its Members for disorderly Behavior, and, with the Concurrence of two thirds, expel a Member.

3. Each House shall keep a journal of its Proceedings, and from time to time publish the same, excepting such Parts as may in their judgment require Secrecy; and the Yeas and Nays of the Members of either House on any question shall, at the Desire of one fifth of those Present, be entered on the journal.

4. Neither House, during the Session of Congress, shall, without the Consent of the other, adjourn for more than three days, nor to any other Place than that in which the two Houses shall be sitting.

SECTION 6. 1. The Senators and Representatives shall receive a Compensation for their Services, to be ascertained by Law, and paid out of the Treasury of the United States. They shall in all Cases, except Treason, Felony, and Breach of the Peace, be privileged from arrest during their Attendance at the Session of their respective Houses, and in going to and returning from the same; and for any Speech or Debate in either House, they shall not be questioned in any other Place.

2. No Senator or Representative shall, during the Time for which he was elected, be appointed to any civil office under the Authority of the United States, which shall have been created, or the Emoluments whereof shall have been increased, during such time; and no Person holding any Office under the United States shall be a Member of either House during his continuance in Office.

SECTION 7. 1. All Bills for raising Revenue shall originate in the House of Representatives; but the Senate may propose or concur with Amendments as on other bills.

2. Every Bill which shall have passed the House of Representatives and the Senate, shall, before it become a Law, be presented to the President of the United States; If he approve he shall sign it, but if not he shall return it, with his Objections, to that House in which it shall have originated, who shall enter the Objections at large on their journal, and proceed to reconsider it. If after such Reconsideration two thirds of that House shall agree to pass the bill, it shall be sent, together with the objections, to the other House, by which it shall likewise be reconsidered, and if approved by two thirds of that House, it shall become a Law. But in all such Cases the Votes of both Houses shall be determined by Yeas and Nays, and the Names of the Persons voting for and against the Bill shall be entered on the journal of each House respectively. If any Bill shall not be returned by the President within ten Days (Sundays excepted) after it shall have been presented to him, the Same shall be a Law, in like Manner as if he had signed it, unless the Congress by their Adjournment prevent its Return, in which Case it shall not be a Law.

3. Every Order, Resolution, or Vote to which the Concurrence of the Senate and House of Representatives may be necessary (except on a question of Adjournment) shall be presented to the President of the United

States; and before the Same shall take Effect, shall be approved by him, or being disapproved by him, shall be repassed by two thirds of the Senate and House of Representatives, according to the Rules and Limitations prescribed in the Case of a Bill.

SECTION 8. The Congress shall have Power

1. To lay and collect Taxes, Duties, Imposts and Excises, to pay the Debts and provide for the common Defense and general Welfare of the United States; but all Duties, Imposts and Excises shall be uniform throughout the United States;

2. To borrow money on the credit of the United States;

3. To regulate Commerce with foreign Nations, and among the several States, and with the Indian Tribes;

4. To establish an uniform Rule of Naturalization, and uniform Laws on the subject of Bankruptcies throughout the United States;

5. To coin Money, regulate the Value thereof, and of foreign Coin, and fix the Standard of Weights and Measures;

6. To provide for the Punishment of counterfeiting the Securities and current Coin of the United States;

7. To establish Post offices and post Roads;

8. To promote the Progress of Science and useful Arts, by securing for limited Times to Authors and inventors the exclusive Right to their respective Writings and Discoveries;

9. To constitute Tribunals inferior to the Supreme Court;

10. To define and punish Piracies and Felonies committed on the high Seas, and Offences against the Law of Nations;

11. To declare War, grant Letters of Marque and Reprisal, and make Rules concerning Captures on Land and Water;

12. To raise and support Armies, but no Appropriation of Money to that Use shall be for a longer Term than two Years;

13. To provide and maintain a Navy;

14. To make Rules for the Government and Regulation of the land and naval forces;

15. To provide for calling forth the Militia to execute the Laws of the Union, suppress Insurrections and repel invasions;

16. To provide for organizing, arming, and disciplining the Militia, and for governing such Part of them as may be employed in the Service of the United States, reserving to the States respectively, the Appointment of the Officers, and the Authority of training the Militia according to the discipline prescribed by Congress;

17. To exercise exclusive Legislation in all Cases whatsoever, over such District (not exceeding ten Miles square) as may, by Cession of particular States, and the acceptance of Congress, become the Seat of Government of the United States, and to exercise like Authority over all Places purchased by the Consent of the Legislature of the State in which the Same shall be, for the Erection of Forts, Magazines, Arsenals, dock Yards, and other needful Buildings; And

18. To make all Laws which shall be necessary and proper for carrying into Execution the foregoing Powers, and all other Powers vested by this Constitution in the government of the United States, or in any Department or Officer thereof.

SECTION 9. 1. The Migration or Importation of such Persons as any of the States now existing shall think proper to admit, shall not be prohibited by the Congress prior to the Year one thousand eight hundred and eight, but a tax or duty may be imposed on such Importation, not exceeding ten dollars for each Person.

2. The Privilege of the Writ of Habeas Corpus shall not be suspended, unless when in Cases of Rebellion or Invasion the public Safety may require it.

3. No Bill of Attainder or ex post facto Law shall be passed.

4. No capitation, or other direct, Tax shall be laid unless in Proportion to the Census or Enumeration herein before directed to be taken.[5]

5. No Tax or Duty shall be laid on Articles exported from any State.

6. No Preference shall be given by any Regulation of commerce or Revenue to the Ports of one State over those of another: nor shall Vessels bound to, or from, one state, be obliged to enter, clear, or pay Duties in another.

7. No Money shall be drawn from the Treasury, but in Consequence of Appropriations made by Law; and a regular Statement and Account of the Receipts and Expenditures of all public Money shall be published from time to time.

8. No Title of Nobility shall be granted by the United States: And no Person holding any Office of Profit or Trust under them, shall, without the Consent of the Congress, accept of any present, Emolument, Office, or Title, of any kind whatever, from any King, Prince, or Foreign State.

Section 10. 1. No State shall enter into any Treaty, Alliance, or Confederation; grant Letters of Marque and Reprisal; coin Money; emit Bills of Credit; make any Thing but gold and silver Coin a Tender in Payment of Debts; pass any Bill of Attainder, ex post facto Law, or Law impairing the obligation of Contracts, or grant any Title of Nobility.

2. No State shall, without the Consent of the Congress, lay any Imposts or Duties on Imports or Exports, except what may be absolutely necessary for executing its inspection Laws: and the net Produce of all Duties and Imposts, laid by any State on Imports or Exports, shall be for the Use of the Treasury of the United States; and all such Laws shall be subject to the Revision and Control of the Congress.

3. No State shall, without the Consent of Congress, lay any duty of Tonnage, keep Troops, or Ships of War in time of peace, enter into any Agreement or Compact with another State, or with a foreign Power, or engage in War, unless actually invaded, or in such imminent Danger as will not admit of delay.

ARTICLE II

Section 1. 1. The executive Power shall be vested in a President of the United States of America. He shall hold his Office during the Term of four Years, and, together with the Vice President, chosen for the same Term, be elected, as follows:

2. Each State shall appoint, in such Manner as the Legislature thereof may direct, a Number of Electors, equal to the whole Number of Senators and Representatives to which the State may be entitled in the Congress; but no Senator or Representative, or Person holding an Office of Trust or Profit under the United States, shall be appointed an Elector.

The Electors shall meet in their respective States, and vote by Ballot for two persons, of whom one at least shall not be an Inhabitant of the same State with themselves. And they shall make a List of all the Persons voted for, and of the Number of Votes for each; which List they shall sign and certify, and transmit sealed to the Seat of the Government of the United States, directed to the President of the Senate. The President of the Senate shall, in the Presence of the Senate and House of Representatives, open all the Certificates, and the Votes shall then be counted. The Person having the greatest Number of Votes shall be the President, if such Number be a Majority of the whole Number of Electors appointed; and if there be more than one who have such Major-

---

[5] See the Sixteenth Amendment.

ity, and have an equal Number of Votes, then the House of Representatives shall immediately chuse by Ballot one of them for President; and if no Person have a Majority, then from the five highest on the List the said House shall in like Manner chuse the President. But in chusing the President, the votes shall be taken by States, the Representation from each State having one Vote; a quorum for this Purpose shall consist of a Member or Members from two thirds of the States, and a Majority of all the States shall be necessary to a Choice. In every Case, after the Choice of the President, the Person having the greatest Number of Votes of the Electors shall be the Vice President. But if there should remain two or more who have equal votes, the Senate shall chuse from them by Ballot the Vice President.[6]

3. The Congress may determine the time of chusing the Electors, and the Day on which they shall give their Votes; which Day shall be the same throughout the United States.

4. No person except a natural born Citizen, or a Citizen of the United States, at the time of the Adoption of this Constitution, shall be eligible to the Office of President; neither shall any Person be eligible to that office who shall not have attained to the Age of thirty-five Years, and been fourteen Years a Resident within the United States.

5. In Case of the Removal of the President from Office, or of his Death, Resignation, or Inability to discharge the Powers and Duties of the said Office, the same shall devolve on the Vice President, and the Congress may by Law provide for the Case of Removal, Death, Resignation, or Inability, both of the President and Vice President, declaring what Officer shall then act as President, and such Officer shall act accordingly, until the Disability be removed, or a President shall be elected.

6. The President shall, at stated Times, receive for his Services a Compensation, which shall neither be increased nor diminished during the Period for which he shall have been elected, and he shall not receive within that Period any other Emolument from the United States, or any of them.

7. Before he enter on the execution of his Office, he shall take the following Oath or Affirmation: "I do solemnly swear (or affirm) that I will faithfully execute the Office of President of the United States, and will, to the best of my Ability, preserve, protect, and defend the Constitution of the United States."

SECTION 2. 1. The President shall be Commander in Chief of the Army and Navy of the United States, and of the Militia of the several States, when called into the actual Service of the United States; he may require the Opinion, in writing, of the principal Officer in each of the executive Departments, upon any subject relating to the Duties of their respective Offices, and he shall have Power to Grant Reprieves and Pardons for Offences against the United States, except in Cases of Impeachment.

2. He shall have Power, by and with the Advice and Consent of the Senate, to make Treaties, provided two thirds of the Senators present concur; and he shall nominate, and by and with the Advice and Consent of the Senate, shall appoint Ambassadors, other public Ministers and Consuls, judges of the supreme Court, and all other Officers of the United States, whose Appointments are not herein otherwise provided for, and which shall be established by Law: but the Congress may by Law vest the Appointment of such inferior Officers, as they think proper, in the President alone, in the Courts of Law, or in the Heads of Departments.

3. The President shall have Power to fill up all Vacancies that may happen during the Recess

---

[6] Superseded by the Twelfth Amendment.

of the Senate, by granting Commissions which shall expire at the End of their next Session.

SECTION 3. He shall from time to time give to the Congress Information of the State of the Union, and recommend to their Consideration such Measures as he shall judge necessary and expedient; he may, on extraordinary occasions, convene both Houses, or either of them, and in Case of Disagreement between them, with respect to the Time of Adjournment, he may adjourn them to such Time as he shall think proper; he shall receive Ambassadors and other public Ministers; he shall take Care that the Laws be faithfully executed, and shall Commission all the officers of the United States.

SECTION 4. The President, Vice President and all civil Officers of the United States, shall be removed from Office on Impeachment for, and Conviction of, Treason, Bribery, or other high Crimes and Misdemeanors.

ARTICLE III

SECTION 1. The judicial Power of the United States, shall be vested in one supreme Court, and in such inferior Courts as the Congress may from time to time ordain and establish. The judges, both of the supreme and inferior Courts, shall hold their Offices during good Behaviour, and shall, at stated Times, receive for their Services, a Compensation, which shall not be diminished during their Continuance in Office.

SECTION 2. 1. The judicial Power shall extend to all Cases, in Law and Equity, arising under this Constitution, the Laws of the United States, and treaties made, or which shall be made, under their Authority;—to all Cases affecting Ambassadors, other public ministers and consuls; to all cases of admiralty and maritime jurisdiction;—to Controversies to which the United States shall be a party;[7]—to Controversies be-

tween two or more States; between a State and citizens of another States;—between Citizens of different States;—between Citizens of the same State claiming Lands under Grants of different States, and between a State, or the Citizens thereof, and foreign States, Citizens or Subjects.

2. In all Cases affecting Ambassadors, other public Ministers and Consuls, and those in which a State shall be Party, the supreme Court shall have original Jurisdiction. In all the other Cases before mentioned, the supreme Court shall have appellate jurisdiction, both as to Law and Fact, with such Exceptions, and under such Regulations as the Congress shall make.

3. The trial of all Crimes, except in Cases of Impeachment, shall be by jury; and such Trial shall be held in the State where the said Crimes shall have been committed; but when not committed within any State, the trial shall be at such Place or Places as the Congress may by Law have directed.

SECTION 3. 1. Treason against the United States, shall consist only in levying War against them, or in adhering to their Enemies, giving them Aid and Comfort. No Person shall be convicted of Treason unless on the testimony of two Witnesses to the same overt Act, or on Confession in open Court.

2. The Congress shall have power to declare the Punishment of Treason, but no Attainder of Treason shall work Corruption of Blood, or Forfeiture except during the Life of the Person attainted.

ARTICLE IV

SECTION 1. Full Faith and Credit shall be given in each State to the public Acts, Records, and judicial Proceedings of every other State. And the Congress may by general Laws prescribe

---

[7] See the Eleventh Amendment.

the Manner in which such Acts, Records and Proceedings shall be proved, and the Effect thereof.

SECTION 2. 1. The Citizens of each State shall be entitled to all Privileges and Immunities of Citizens in the several States.[8]

2. A Person charged in any State with Treason, Felony, or other Crime, who shall flee from justice, and be found in another State, shall on demand of the executive Authority of the State from which he fled, be delivered up, to be removed to the State having jurisdiction of the crime.

3. No Person held to Service or Labour in one State, under the Laws thereof, escaping into another, shall, in Consequence of any Law or Regulation therein, be discharged from such Service or Labour, but shall be delivered up on Claim of the Party to whom such Service or Labour may be due.[9]

SECTION 3. 1. New States may be admitted by the Congress into this Union; but no new State shall be formed or erected within the Jurisdiction of any other State, nor any State be formed by the junction of two or more States, or parts of States, without the Consent of the Legislatures of the States concerned as well as of the Congress.

2. The Congress shall have Power to dispose of and make all needful Rules and Regulations respecting the Territory or other Property belonging to the United States; and nothing in this Constitution shall be so construed as to Prejudice any Claims of the United States, or of any particular State.

SECTION 4. The United States shall guarantee to every State in this Union a Republican Form of Government, and shall protect each of them against Invasion; and on Application of the Legislature, or of the Executive (when the Legislature cannot be convened) against domestic Violence.

ARTICLE V

The Congress, whenever two-thirds of both Houses shall deem it necessary, shall propose Amendments to this Constitution, or, on the Application of the Legislatures of two-thirds of the several States, shall call a Convention for proposing Amendments, which, in either Case, shall be valid to all Intents and Purposes, as part of this Constitution, when ratified by the Legislatures of three-fourths of the several States, or by Conventions in three-fourths thereof, as the one or the other Mode of Ratification may be proposed by the Congress; Provided that no Amendment which may be made prior to the Year One thousand eight hundred and eight shall in any Manner affect the first and fourth Clauses in the Ninth Section of the first Article; and that no State, without its Consent, shall be deprived of its equal Suffrage in the Senate.

ARTICLE VI

1. All Debts contracted and Engagements entered into, before the Adoption of this Constitution, shall be as valid against the United States under this Constitution, as under the Confederation.[10]

2. This Constitution, and the Laws of the United States which shall be made in Pursuance thereof; and all Treaties made, or which shall be made, under the Authority of the United States, shall be the supreme Law of the Land; and the judges in every State shall be bound thereby, any Thing in the Constitution or Laws of any State to the Contrary notwithstanding.

---

[8] See the Fourteenth Amendment, Sec. 1.
[9] See the Thirteenth Amendment.

3. The Senators and Representatives before mentioned, and the Members of the several State Legislatures and all executive and judicial Officers, both of the United States and of the several States, shall be bound by Oath or Affirmation, to support this Constitution; but no religious Test shall ever be required as a qualification to any Office or public Trust under the United States.

ARTICLE VII

The Ratification of the Conventions of nine States, shall be sufficient for the Establishment of this Constitution between the States so ratifying the same.

Done in Convention by the Unanimous Consent of the States present the Seventeenth Day of September in the Year of our Lord one thousand seven hundred and Eighty seven, and of the independence of the United States of America the Twelfth. In Witness whereof We have hereunto subscribed our Names.

(Names omitted)

* * *

Articles in addition to, and amendment of, the Constitution of the United States of America, proposed by Congress, and ratified by the legislatures of the several States, pursuant to the fifth article of the original Constitution.

AMENDMENT I [DECEMBER 15, 1791]

Congress shall make no law respecting an establishment of religion, or prohibiting the free exercise thereof, or abridging the freedom of speech, or of the press; or the right of the people peaceably to assemble, and to petition the Government for a redress of grievances.

AMENDMENT II [DECEMBER 15, 1791]

A well regulated Militia, being necessary to the security of a free State, the right of the people to keep and bear Arms shall not be infringed.

AMENDMENT III [DECEMBER 15, 1791]

No Soldier shall, in time of peace, be quartered in any house, without the consent of the owner, nor in time of war, but in a manner to be prescribed by law.

AMENDMENT IV [DECEMBER 15, 1791]

The right of the people to be secure in their persons, houses, papers, and effects, against unreasonable searches and seizures, shall not be violated, and no Warrants shall issue, but upon probable cause, supported by Oath or affirmation, and particularly describing the place to be searched, and the persons or things to be seized.

AMENDMENT V [DECEMBER 15, 1791]

No person shall be held to answer for a capital or otherwise infamous crime, unless on a presentment or indictment of a Grand jury, except in cases arising in the land or naval forces, or in the Militia, when in actual service in time of War or public danger; nor shall any person be subject for the same offence to be twice put in jeopardy of life or limb; nor shall be compelled in any criminal case to be a witness against himself, nor be deprived of life, liberty, or property, without due

---

[10] See the Fourteenth Amendment, Section 4.

process of law; nor shall private property be taken for public use, without just compensation.

AMENDMENT VI [DECEMBER 15, 1791]

In all criminal prosecutions, the accused shall enjoy the right to a speedy and public trial, by an impartial jury of the State and district wherein the crime shall have been committed, which district shall have been previously ascertained by law, and to be informed of the nature and cause of the accusation; to be confronted with the witnesses against him; to have compulsory process for obtaining witnesses in his favor, and to have the Assistance of Counsel for his defense.

AMENDMENT VII [DECEMBER 15, 1791]

In suits at common law, where the value in controversy shall exceed twenty dollars, the right of trial by jury shall be preserved, and no fact tried by a jury, shall be otherwise reexamined in any Court of the United States, than according to the rules of the common law.

AMENDMENT VIII [DECEMBER 15, 1791]

Excessive bail shall not be required, nor excessive fines imposed, nor cruel and unusual punishments inflicted.

AMENDMENT IX [DECEMBER 15, 1791]

The enumeration in the Constitution, of certain rights, shall not be construed to deny or disparage others retained by the people.

AMENDMENT X [DECEMBER 15, 1791]

The powers not delegated to the United States by the Constitution, nor prohibited by it to the States, are reserved to the States respectively, or to the people.

AMENDMENT XI [JANUARY 8, 1798]

The judicial power of the United States shall not be construed to extend to any suit in law or equity, commenced or prosecuted against one of the United States by Citizens of another State, or by Citizens or Subjects of any Foreign State.

AMENDMENT XII [SEPTEMBER 25, 1804]

The Electors shall meet in their respective States and vote by ballot for President and Vice-President, one of whom, at least, shall not be an inhabitant of the same State with themselves; they shall name in their ballots the person voted for as President, and in distinct ballots the person voted for as Vice-President, and they shall make distinct lists of all persons voted for as President, and of all persons voted for as Vice-President, and of the number of votes for each, which lists they shall sign and certify, and transmit sealed to the seat of the government of the United States, directed to the President of the Senate; The President of the Senate shall, in the presence of the Senate and House of Representatives, open all the certificates and the votes shall then be counted; The person having the greatest number of votes for President, shall be the President, if such number be a majority of the whole number of Electors appointed; and if no person have such majority, then from the persons having the highest numbers not exceeding three on the list of those voted for as President, the House of Representatives shall choose immediately, by ballot, the President. But in choosing the President, the votes shall be taken by states, the representation from each state having one vote; a quorum for this purpose shall consist of a member or members from two-thirds of the states, and a majority of all the states shall be necessary to a choice. And if the House of Representatives shall not choose a President whenever the right of choice shall devolve upon them, before the fourth day of March next following, then the Vice-President shall act as President, as in the case of the death or other constitutional disability of the President. The person having the greatest number of votes as Vice President, shall be the Vice-President, if such number be a majority of the whole number of Electors appointed, and if no person have a majority, then from the two highest numbers on the list, the Senate shall choose the Vice-President; a quorum for the purpose shall consist of two-thirds of the whole number of Senators, and a majority of the whole number shall be necessary to a choice. But no person constitutionally ineligible to the office of President shall be eligible to that of Vice-President of the United States.

AMENDMENT XIII [DECEMBER 18, 1865]

SECTION 1. Neither slavery nor involuntary servitude, except as a punishment for crime whereof the party shall have been duly convicted, shall exist within the United States, or any place subject to their jurisdiction.

SECTION 2. Congress shall have power to enforce this article by appropriate legislation.

AMENDMENT XIV [JULY 28, 1868]

SECTION 1. All persons born or naturalized in the United States, and subject to the jurisdiction thereof, are citizens of the United States and of the State wherein they reside. No State shall make or enforce any law which shall abridge the privileges or immunities of citizens of the United States; nor shall any State deprive any person of life, liberty, or property, without due process of law; nor deny to any person within its jurisdiction the equal protection of the laws.

SECTION 2. Representatives shall be apportioned among the several States according to their respective numbers, counting the whole number of persons in each State, excluding Indians not taxed. But when the right to vote at any election for the choice of electors for President and Vice-President of the United States, Representatives in Congress, the Executive and Judicial officers of a State, or the members of the Legislature thereof, is denied to any of the male inhabitants of such State, being twenty-one years of age, and citizens of the United States, or in any way abridged, except for participation in rebellion, or other crime, the basis of representation therein shall be reduced in the proportion which the number of such male citizens shall bear to the whole number of male citizens twenty-one years of age in such State.

SECTION 3. No person shall be a Senator or Representative in Congress, or elector of President and Vice-President, or hold any office, civil or military, under the United States, or under any State, who, having previously taken an oath, as a member of Congress, or as an officer of the United States, or as a member of any State legislature, or as an executive or judicial officer of any State, to support the Constitution of the United States, shall have engaged in insurrection or rebellion against the same, or given aid or comfort to the enemies thereof. But Congress may by a vote of two-thirds of each House, remove such disability.

SECTION 4. The validity of the public debt of the United States, authorized by law, including debts incurred for payment of pensions and bounties for services in suppressing insurrection or rebellion, shall not be questioned. But neither the United States nor any State shall assume or pay any debt or obligation incurred in aid of insurrection or rebellion against the United States, or any claim for the loss or emancipation of any slave; but all such debts, obligations, and claims shall be held illegal and void.

SECTION 5. The Congress shall have the power to enforce, by appropriate legislation, the provisions of this article.

AMENDMENT XV [MARCH 30, 1870]

SECTION 1. The right of citizens of the United States to vote shall not be denied or abridged by the United States or by any State on account of race, color, or previous condition of servitude

SECTION 2. The Congress shall have power to enforce this article by appropriate legislation.

AMENDMENT XVI [FEBRUARY 25, 1913]

The Congress shall have power to lay and collect taxes on incomes, from whatever source derived, without apportionment among the several States, and without regard to any census or enumeration.

AMENDMENT XVII [MAY 31, 1913]

The Senate of the United States shall be composed of two Senators from each State, elected by the people thereof, for six years; and each Senator shall have one vote. The electors in each State shall have the qualifications requisite for electors of the most numerous branch of the State legislatures.

When vacancies happen in the representation of any State in the Senate, the executive authority of such State shall issue writs of election to fill such vacancies: Provided, That the legislature of any State may empower the executive thereof to make temporary appointments until the people fill the vacancies by election as the legislature may direct.

This amendment shall not be so construed as to affect the election or term of any Senator chosen before it becomes valid as part of the Constitution.

AMENDMENT XVIII [JANUARY 29, 1919]

SECTION 1. After one year from the ratification of this article the manufacture, sale, or transportation of intoxicating liquors within, the importation thereof into, or the exportation thereof from the United States and all territory subject to the jurisdiction thereof for beverage purposes is hereby prohibited.

SECTION 2. The Congress and the several States shall have concurrent power to enforce this article by appropriate legislation.

SECTION 3. This article shall be inoperative unless it shall have been ratified as an amendment to the Constitution by the legislatures of the several States, as provided in the Constitution, within seven years from the date of the submission hereof to the States by the Congress.

AMENDMENT XIX [AUGUST 26, 1920]

The right of citizens of the United States to vote shall not be denied or abridged by the United States or by any State on account of sex.

Congress shall have power to enforce this article by appropriate legislation.

AMENDMENT XX [JANUARY 23, 1933]

SECTION 1. The terms of the President and Vice-President shall end at noon on the 20th day of January, and the terms of Senators and Representatives at noon on the 3d day of January, of the years in which such terms would have ended if this article had not been ratified; and the terms of their successors shall then begin.

SECTION 2. The Congress shall assemble at least once in every year, and such meeting shall begin at noon on the 3d day of January, unless they shall by law appoint a different day.

SECTION 3. If, at the time fixed for the beginning of the term of the President, the President elect shall have died, the Vice-President elect shall become President. If a President shall not have been chosen before the time fixed for the beginning of his term, or if the President elect shall have failed to qualify, then the Vice-President elect shall act as President until a President shall have qualified; and the Congress may by law provide for the case wherein neither a President elect nor a Vice-President elect shall have qualified, declaring who shall then act as President, or the manner in which one who is to act shall be selected, and such person shall act accordingly until a President or Vice-President shall have qualified.

SECTION 4. The Congress may by law provide for the case of the death of any of the persons from whom the House of Representatives may choose a President whenever the right of choice shall have devolved upon them, and for the case of the death of any of the persons from whom the Senate may choose a Vice-President whenever the right of choice shall have devolved upon them.

SECTION 5. Sections 1 and 2 shall take effect on the 15th day of October following the ratification of this article.

SECTION 6. This article shall be inoperative unless it shall have been ratified as an amendment to the Constitution by the legislatures of three-fourths of the several States within seven years from the date of its submission.

AMENDMENT XXI [DECEMBER 5, 1933]

SECTION 1. The eighteenth article of amendment to the Constitution of the United States is hereby repealed.

SECTION 2. The transportation or importation into any State, Territory, or possession of the United States for delivery or use therein of intoxicating liquors, in violation of the laws thereof, is hereby prohibited.

SECTION 3. This article shall be inoperative unless it shall have been ratified as an amendment to the Constitution by conventions in the several States, as provided in the Constitution, within seven years from the date of the submission hereof to the States by the Congress.

AMENDMENT XXII [MARCH 1, 1951]

SECTION 1. No person shall be elected to the office of the President more than twice, and no person who has held the office of President, or acted as President, for more than two years of a term to which some other person was elected President shall be elected to the office of the President more than once.

But this Article shall not apply to any person holding the office of President when this Article was proposed by the Congress, and shall not prevent any person who may be holding the office of President or acting as President, during the term within which this Article becomes operative from holding the office of President or acting as President during the remainder of such term.

SECTION 2. This article shall be inoperative unless it shall have been ratified as an amendment to the Constitution by the legislatures of three-fourths of the several states within seven years from the date of its submission to the states by Congress.

AMENDMENT XXIII [MARCH 29, 1961]

SECTION 1. The District constituting the seat of Government of the United States shall appoint in such manner as the Congress may direct:

A number of electors of President and Vice President equal to the whole number of Senators and Representatives in Congress to which the District would be entitled if it were a State, but in no event more than the least populous State; they shall be in addition to those appointed by the States, but they shall be considered, for the purposes of the election of President and Vice President, to be electors appointed by a State; and they shall meet in the District and perform such duties as provided by the twelfth article of amendment.

SECTION 2. The Congress shall have power to enforce this article by appropriate legislation.

AMENDMENT XXIV [JANUARY 23, 1964]

SECTION 1. The right of citizens of the United States to vote in any primary or other election for President or Vice President, for electors for President or Vice President, or for Senator or Representative in Congress, shall not be denied or abridged by the United States or any State by reason of failure to pay any poll tax or other tax.

SECTION 2. The Congress shall have the power to enforce this article by appropriate legislation.

AMENDMENT XXV [FEBRUARY 10, 1967]

SECTION 1. In case of the removal of the President from office or of his death or resignation, the Vice President shall become President.

SECTION 2. Whenever there is a vacancy in the office of the Vice President, the President shall nominate a Vice President who shall take office upon confirmation by a majority vote of both houses of Congress.

SECTION 3. Whenever the President transmits to the President pro tempore of the Senate and the Speaker of the House of Representatives his written declaration that he is unable to discharge the powers and duties of his office, and until he transmits to them a written declaration to the contrary, such powers and duties shall be discharged by the Vice President as Acting President.

SECTION 4. Whenever the Vice President and a majority of either the principal officers of the executive departments, or of such other body as Congress may by law provide, transmit to the President pro tempore of the Senate and the Speaker of the House of Representatives their written declaration that the President is unable to discharge the powers and duties of his office, the Vice President shall immediately assume the powers and duties of the office as Acting President.

Thereafter, when the President transmits to the President pro tempore of the Senate and the Speaker of the House of Representatives his written declaration that no inability exists, he shall resume the powers and duties of his office unless the Vice President and a majority of either the principal officers of the executive departments, or of such other body as Congress may by law provide, transmit within four days to the President pro tempore of the Senate and the Speaker of the House of Representatives their written declaration that the President is unable to discharge the powers and duties of his office. Thereupon Congress shall decide the issue, assembling within forty-eight hours for that purpose if not in session. If the Congress, within twenty-one days after receipt of the latter written declaration, or, if Congress is not in session, within twenty-one days after Congress is required to assemble, determines by two-thirds vote of both houses that the President is unable to discharge the powers and duties of his office, the Vice President shall continue to discharge the same as Acting President; otherwise, the President shall resume the powers and duties of his office.

AMENDMENT XXVI [JUNE 30, 1971]

SECTION 1. The right of citizens of the United States, who are eighteen years of age or older, to vote shall not be denied or abridged by the United States or by any state on account of age.

SECTION 2. The Congress shall have power to enforce this article by appropriate legislation.

AMENDENT XXVII [MAY 7, 1992]

No law varying the compensation for the services of the Senators and Representatives shall take effect, until an election of Representatives shall have intervened.

PRESIDENTIAL ELECTIONS

YEAR	NUMBER OF STATES	CANDIDATES	PARTY	POPULAR VOTE*	ELECTORAL VOTE**	PERCENTAGE OF POPULAR VOTE
1789	11	GEORGE WASHINGTON	No party designations		69	
		John Adams			34	
		Other Candidates			35	
1792	15	GEORGE WASHINGTON	No party designations		132	
		John Adams			77	
		George Clinton			50	
		Other Candidates			5	
1796	16	JOHN ADAMS	Federalist		71	
		Thomas Jefferson	Democratic-Republican		68	
		Thomas Pinckney	Federalist		59	
		Aaron Burr	Democratic-Republican		30	
		Other Candidates			48	
1800	16	THOMAS JEFFERSON	Democratic-Republican		73	
		Aaron Burr	Democratic-Republican		73	
		John Adams	Federalist		65	
		Charles C. Pinckney	Federalist		64	
		John Jay	Federalist			
1804	17	THOMAS JEFFERSON	Democratic-Republican		162	
		Charles C. Pinckney	Federalist		14	
1808	17	JAMES MADISON	Democratic-Republican		122	
		Charles C. Pinckney	Federalist		47	
		George Clinton	Democratic-Republican		6	
1812	18	JAMES MADISON	Democratic-Republican		128	
		DeWitt Clinton	Federalist		89	
1816	19	JAMES MONROE	Democratic-Republican		183	
		Rufus King	Federalist		34	
1820	24	JAMES MONROE	Democratic-Republican		231	
		John Quincy Adams	Independent Republican		1	
1824	24	JOHN QUINCY ADAMS		108,740	84	30.5
		Andrew Jackson		153,544	99	43.1
		William H. Crawford		46,618	41	13.1
		Henry Clay		47,136	37	13.2
1828	24	ANDREW JACKSON	Democrat	647,286	178	56.0
		John Ouincy Adams	National Republican	508,064	83	44.0
1832	24	ANDREW JACKSON	Democrat	687,502	219	55.0
		Henry Clay	National Republican	530,189	49	42.4
		William Wirt	Anti-Masonic	33,108	7	2.6
		John Floyd	National Republican		11	
1836	26	MARTIN VAN BUREN	Democrat	765,483	170	50.9
		William H. Harrison	Whig		73	
		Hugh L. White	Whig	739,795	26	49.1
		Daniel Webster	Whig		14	
		W. P. Mangum	Whig		11	
1840	26	WILLIAM H. HARRISON	Whig	1,274,624	234	53.1
		Martin Van Buren	Democrat	1,127,781	60	46.9
1844	26	JAMES K. POLK	Democrat	1,338,464	170	49.6
		Henry Clay	Whig	1,300,097	105	48.1
		James G. Birney	Liberty	62,300		2.3
1848	30	ZACHARY TAYLOR	Whig	1,360,967	163	47.4
		Lewis Cass	Democrat	1,222,342	127	42.5
		Martin Van Buren	Free Soil	291,263		10.1

*Percentage of popular vote given for any election year may not total 100 percent because candidates receiving less than 1 percent of the popular vote have been omitted.

**Prior to the passage of the Twelfth Amendment in 1904, the electoral college voted for two presidential candidates; the runner-up became Vice President. Data from *Historical Statistics of the United States, Colonial Times to 1957* (1961), pp. 682–883, and *The World Almanac*.

PRESIDENTIAL ELECTIONS *(continued)*

YEAR	NUMBER OF STATES	CANDIDATES	PARTY	POPULAR VOTE	ELECTORAL VOTE	PERCENTAGE OF POPULAR VOTE
1852	31	FRANKLIN PIERCE	Democrat	1,601,117	254	50.9
		Winfield Scott	Whig	1,385,453	42	44.1
		John P. Hale	Free Soil	155,825		5.0
1856	31	JAMES BUCHANAN	Democrat	1,832,955	174	45.3
		John C. Frémont	Republican	1,339,932	114	33.1
		Millard Fillmore	American	871,731	8	21.6
1860	33	ABRAHAM LINCOLN	Republican	1,865,593	180	39.8
		Stephen A. Douglas	Democrat	1,382,713	12	29.5
		John C. Breckinridge	Democrat	848,356	72	18.1
		John Bell	Constitutional Union	592,906	39	12.6
1864	36	ABRAHAM LINCOLN	Republican	2,206,938	212	55.0
		George B. McClellan	Democrat	1,803,787	21	45.0
1868	37	ULYSSES S. GRANT	Republican	3,013,421	214	52.7
		Horatio Seymour	Democrat	2,706,829	80	47.3
1872	37	ULYSSES S. GRANT	Republican	3,596,745	286	55.6
		Horace Greeley	Democrat	2,843,446	*	43.9
1876	38	RUTHERFORD B. HAYES	Republican	4,036,572	185	48.0
		Samuel J. Tilden	Democrat	4,284,020	184	51.0
1880	38	JAMES A. GARFIELD	Republican	4,453,295	214	48.5
		Winfield S. Hancock	Democrat	4,414,082	155	48.1
		James B. Weaver	Greenback-Labor	308,578		3.4
1884	38	GROVER CLEVELAND	Democrat	4,879,507	219	48.5
		James G. Blaine	Republican	4,850,293	182	48.2
		Benjamin F. Butler	Greenback-Labor	175,370		1.8
		John P. St. John	Prohibition	150,369		1.5.
1888	38	BENJAMIN HARRISON	Republican	5,447,129	233	47.9
		Grover Cleveland	Democrat	5,537,857	168	48.6
		Clinton B. Fisk	Prohibition	249,506		2.2
		Anson J. Streeter	Union Labor	146,935		1.3
1892	44	GROVER CLEVELAND	Democrat	5,555,426	277	46.1
		Benjamin Harrison	Republican	5,182,690	145	43.0
		James B. Weaver	People's	1,029,846	22	8.5
		John Bidwell	Prohibition	264,133		2.2
1896	45	WILLIAM MCKINLEY	Republican	7,102,246	271	51.1
		William J. Bryan	Democrat	6,492,559	176	47.7
1900	45	WILLIAM MCKINLEY	Republican	7,218,491	292	51.7
		William J. Bryan	Democrat; Populist	6,356,734	155	45.5
		John C. Woolley	Prohibition	208,914		1.5
1904	45	THEODORE ROOSEVELT	Republican	7,628,461	336	57.4
		Alton B. Parker	Democrat	5,084,223	140	37.6
		Eugene V. Debs	Socialist	402,283		3.0
		Silas C. Swallow	Prohibition	258,536		1.9
1908	46	WILLIAM H. TAFT	Republican	7,675,320	321	51.6
		William J. Bryan	Democrat	6,412,294	162	43.1
		Eugene V. Debs	Socialist	420,793		2.8
		Eugene W. Chafin	Prohibition	253,840		1.7
1912	48	WOODROW WILSON	Democrat	6,296,547	435	41.9
		Theodore Roosevelt	Progressive	4,118,571	88	27.4
		William H. Taft	Republican	3,486,720	8	23.2
		Eugene V. Debs	Socialist	900,672		6.0
		Eugene W. Chafin	Prohibition	206,275		1.4

*Because of the death of Greeley, Democratic electors scattered their votes.

PRESIDENTIAL ELECTIONS (continued)

YEAR	NUMBER OF STATES	CANDIDATES	PARTY	POPULAR VOTE	ELECTORAL VOTE	PERCENTAGE OF POPULAR VOTE
1916	48	WOODROW WILSON	Democrat	9,127,695	277	49.4
		Charles E. Hughes	Republican	8,533,507	254	46.2
		A. L. Benson	Socialist	585,113		3.2
		J. Frank Hanly	Prohibition	220,506		1.2
1920	48	WARREN G. HARDING	Republican	16,143,407	404	60.4
		James M. Cox	Democrat	9,130,328	127	34.2
		Eugene V. Debs	Socialist	919,799		3.4
		P. P. Christensen	Farmer-Labor	265,411		1.0
1924	48	CALVIN COOLIDGE	Republican	15,718,211	382	54.0
		John W. Davis	Democrat	8,385,283	136	28.8
		Robert M. La Follette	Progressive	4,831,289	13	16.6
1928	48	HERBERT C. HOOVER	Republican	21,391,993	444	58.2
		Alfred E. Smith	Democrat	15,016,169	87	40.9
1932	48	FRANKLIN D. ROOSEVELT	Democrat	22,809,638	472	57.4
		Herbert C. Hoover	Republican	15,758,901	59	39.7
		Norman Thomas	Socialist	881,951		2.2
1936	48	FRANKLIN D. ROOSEVELT	Democrat	27,752,869	523	60.8
		Alfred M. Landon	Republican	16,674,665	8	36.5
		William Lemke	Union	882,479		1.9
1940	48	FRANKLIN D. ROOSEVELT	Democrat	27,307,819	449	54.8
		Wendell L. Wilkie	Republican	22,321,018	82	44.8
1944	48	FRANKLIN D. ROOSEVELT	Democrat	25,606,585	432	53.5
		Thomas E. Dewey	Republican	22,014,745	99	46.0
1948	48	HARRY S. TRUMAN	Democrat	24,105,812	303	49.5
		Thomas E. Dewey	Republican	21,970,065	189	45.1
		J. Strom Thurmond	States' Rights	1,169,063	39	2.4
		Henry A. Wallace	Progressive	1,157,172		2.4
1952	48	DWIGHT D. EISENHOWER	Republican	33,936,234	442	55.1
		Adlai E. Stevenson	Democrat	27,314,992	89	44.4
1956	48	DWIGHT D. EISENHOWER	Republican	35,590,472	457*	57.6
		Adlai E. Stevenson	Democrat	26,022,752	73	42.1
1960	50	JOHN F. KENNEDY	Democrat	34,227,096	303**	49.9
		Richard M. Nixon	Republican	34,108,546	219	49.6
1964	50	LYNDON B. JOHNSON	Democrat	42,676,220	486	61.3
		Barry M. Goldwater	Republican	26,860,314	52	38.5
1968	50	RICHARD M. NIXON	Republican	31,785,480	301	43.4
		Hubert H. Humphrey	Democrat	31,275,165	191	42.7
		George C. Wallace	American Independent	9,906,473	46	13.5
1972	50	RICHARD M. NIXON***	Republican	47,165,234	520	60.6
		George S. McGovern	Democrat	29,168,110	17	37.5
1976	50	JIMMY CARTER	Democrat	40,828,929	297	50.1
		Gerald R. Ford	Republican	39,148,940	240	47.9
		Eugene McCarthy	Independent	739,256		
1980	50	RONALD REAGAN	Republican	43,201,220	489	50.9
		Jimmy Carter	Democrat	34,913,332	49	41.2
		John B. Anderson	Independent	5,581,379		
1984	50	RONALD REAGAN	Republican	53,428,357	525	59.0
		Walter F. Mondale	Democrat	36,930,923	13	41.0
1988	50	GEORGE BUSH	Republican	48,901,046	426	53.4
		Michael Dukakis	Democrat	41,809,030	111	45.6

*Walter B. Jones received 1 electoral vote.
**Harry F. Byrd received 15 electoral votes.
***Resigned August 9,1974; Vice President Gerald R. Ford became President.

PRESIDENTIAL ELECTIONS *(continued)*

YEAR	NUMBER OF STATES	CANDIDATES	PARTY	POPULAR VOTE	ELECTORAL VOTE	PERCENTAGE OF POPULAR VOTE
1992	50	WILLIAM J. CLINTON	Democrat	44,909,806	370	43.0
		George Bush	Republican	39,104,550	168	37.5
		H. Ross Perot	Independent	19,742,240		18.9
		Andre Marrau	Libertarian	291,631		0.3
1996	50	WILLIAM J. CLINTON	Democrat	47,402,357	379	49.2
		Robert Dole	Republican	39,198,755	159	40.7
		H. Ross Perot	Reform	8,085,402		8.4
		Ralph Nader	Green	685,128		0.7
		Harry Browne	Libertarian	485,798		0.5
2000	50	GEORGE W. BUSH	Republican	50,459,624	271	47.9
		Albert Gore, Jr.	Democrat	51,003,238	266	48.4
		Ralph Nader	Green	2,882,985		2.7
		Patrick Buchanan	Reform	449,120		0.4
		Harry Browne	Libertarian	384,440		0.4
2004	50	GEORGE W. BUSH	Republican	62,040,610	286	58.9
		John F. Kerry	Democrat	59,028,111	251	56.1
		Ralph Nader	Independent/Reform	463,653		0.0
2008	50	BARACK OBAMA	Democrat	69,456,898	365	52.9
		John McCain	Republican	59,934,814	173	45.6
		Ralph Nader	Independent	738,771		0.6
		Bob Barr	Libertarian	523,686		0.4